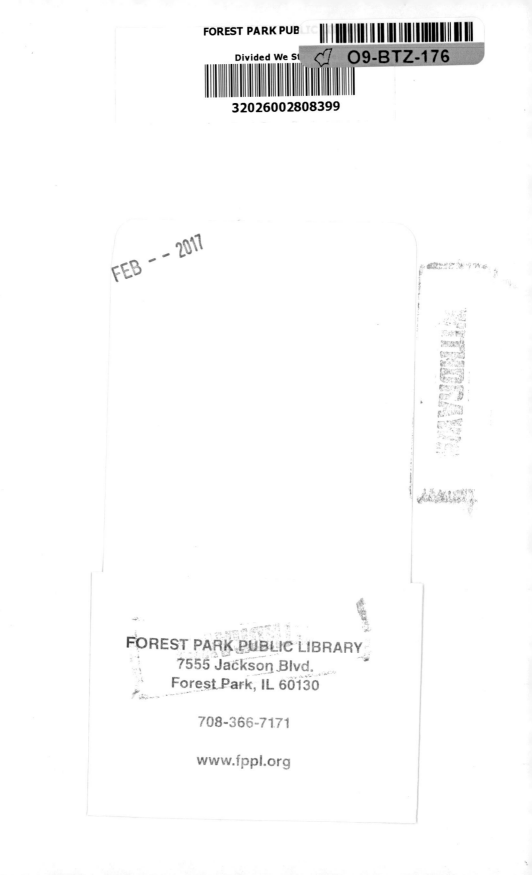

Divided We Stand

Also by Marjorie J. Spruill

New Women of the New South: The Leaders of the Woman Suffrage Movement in the Southern States, by Marjorie Spruill

One Woman, One Vote: Rediscovering the Woman Suffrage Movement, edited by Marjorie Spruill

Votes for Women: The Woman Suffrage Movement in Tennessee, the South, and the Nation, edited by Marjorie Spruill

The South in the History of the Nation: A Reader, Volumes 1 and 2, coedited by Marjorie Spruill and William Link

Mississippi Women: Their Histories, Their Lives, Volumes 1 and 2, coedited by Marjorie Spruill

South Carolina Women: Their Lives and Times, Volumes 1, 2, and 3, coedited by Marjorie Spruill

Divided We Stand

The Battle Over Women's Rights and Family Values
That Polarized American Politics

MARJORIE J. SPRUILL

BLOOMSBURY
NEW YORK · LONDON · OXFORD · NEW DELHI · SYDNEY

Bloomsbury USA
An imprint of Bloomsbury Publishing Plc

1385 Broadway	50 Bedford Square
New York	London
NY 10018	WC1B 3DP
USA	UK

www.bloomsbury.com

BLOOMSBURY and the Diana logo are trademarks of Bloomsbury Publishing Plc

First published 2017

Lyrics from "We Shall Go Forth" © Margie Adam, 1977. Performed by Adam
at the close of the National Women's Conference, November 21, 1977.
Used with permission.

ISBN: HB: 978-1-63286-314-0
        ePub: 978-1-63286-315-7

LIBRARY OF CONGRESS CATALOGING-IN-PUBLICATION DATA IS AVAILABLE.

2 4 6 8 10 9 7 5 3 1

Typeset by RefineCatch Limited, Bungay, Suffolk
Printed and bound in the U.S.A. by Berryville Graphics Inc., Berryville, Virginia

To find out more about our authors and books visit www.bloomsbury.com.
Here you will find extracts, author interviews, details of forthcoming events and
the option to sign up for our newsletters.

Bloomsbury books may be purchased for business or promotional use. For information
on bulk purchases please contact Macmillan Corporate and Premium Sales Department
at specialmarkets@macmillan.com.

To my husband,
Don H. Doyle

Contents

CHAPTER I

Four Days That Changed the World

For myself, Houston and all the events surrounding it have become a personal landmark in history; the sort of event one measures all other dates in life as being "before" or "after" . . . It raised hopes for a new openness and inclusiveness in national political events to come.

—GLORIA STEINEM, "AN INTRODUCTORY STATEMENT,"

WHAT WOMEN WANT, 1978

The weekend of November 18–21, 1977, in Houston was the decisive turning point in the war between Women's Lib and those who are Pro-Family. "Houston" was the "Midway" battle that determined which is the winning side.

—PHYLLIS SCHLAFLY, *PHYLLIS SCHLAFLY REPORT*,

DECEMBER 1977

There were two women's movements in the 1970s: a women's rights movement that enjoyed tremendous success, especially early in the decade, and a conservative women's movement that formed in opposition and grew stronger as the decade continued. Each played an essential role in the making of modern American political culture.

Tensions between feminists and their conservative critics exploded in 1977 during a series of state and national conferences culminating in a National Women's Conference held late in the year in Houston, Texas. Known as the International Women's Year (IWY) conferences, they were unique in American history as federally sponsored assemblies to which women were invited to tell Congress and the president what women wanted. After "Houston," the National Women's Conference that Gloria Steinem recently described as "the most important event nobody knows about," American politics would never be the same.[1]

The IWY conferences were inspired by a worldwide movement promoted by the United Nations that declared 1975–1985 as the Decade for Women. In 1975 the UN sponsored the first IWY conference, which took place in Mexico City and produced a World Plan of Action. President Gerald Ford appointed the National Commission on the Observance of International Women's Year to coordinate U.S. participation. He also directed the commission to devise recommendations for making the United States a "more perfect union" in regard to women's equality. Later in 1975, Congress mandated and funded IWY meetings to be held in every state and territory to vote on resolutions and delegates to send to a National Women's Conference. In November 1977, the delegates assembled in Houston to adopt a National Plan of Action that was to guide future policies relating to women.[2]

The Houston conference and the preliminary state meetings leading up to it proved to be thoroughly polarizing events. As women's rights supporters put aside their differences and united behind an expansive set of feminist goals, conservative women who opposed any of those goals joined forces to challenge them—with enduring consequences for the nation.

Divided We Stand draws the connection between the events that divided American women in the 1970s and the subsequent polarization of American politics at large as the two major parties chose sides between feminists and their conservative challengers. Whereas in the early 1970s both Republicans and Democrats supported the modern women's movement, by 1980 the GOP had sided with the other women's movement, the one that positioned family values in opposition to women's rights.

All too often this transformation in national politics is explained with little attention to the role of women and women's issues. They are at the center of the story told here. *Divided We Stand* provides insights into contemporary politics as it examines the growing power of feminism in the governing establishment, the growth of the conservative opposition, and the competition between them for influence in American politics—a battle that reached a crucial turning point in November 1977 in Houston.

On November 18, 1977, tens of thousands of people poured into Houston for a weekend *Ms.* magazine called "Four Days That Changed the World."[3]

Airports and hotels were jammed with travelers, mostly female. An estimated twenty thousand were there for the National Women's Conference, including the two thousand delegates elected at the preliminary meetings the past summer, members of the presidentially appointed IWY Commission that had organized the conference, one hundred observers from fifty-six countries, and thousands more eager to be a part of this historic event.

Over 1,500 reporters, photographers, and writers had requested press passes for what was turning out to be a media extravaganza. America's most prominent journalists and pundits, among them Tom Brokaw, Carole Simpson, Joe Klein, Sally Quinn, George Will, James J. Kilpatrick, Ellen Goodman, Vera Glaser, Anna Quindlen, Gail Sheehy, Garry Trudeau, and David Broder, came to Houston to cover the story. All three television networks and PBS sent cameras and crews. The *Today Show, Good Morning America, Face the Nation,* and *Meet the Press* broadcast live from Houston. When Egyptian president Anwar Sadat suddenly decided to make his historic journey to Israel, they had to send their B teams: the A teams were already in Houston.[4]

The National Women's Conference seemed to be the apogee of the modern women's rights movement, the crest of the "second wave" of American feminism. In many respects it resembled a national party convention. Delegates came from every state and territory, many arriving with hats to wear on the convention floor: cowboy hats from Wisconsin, tricornes labeled FREE D.C. from the District of Columbia, and *jibaros* (wide-brimmed sugarcane workers' hats) from Puerto Rico. Apart from the fact that all but six of the delegates were women, however, the conference was far more diverse than any political gathering in American history in terms of race, ethnicity, class, age, occupation, and level of political experience.[5]

Delegates ranged from students and homemakers attending their first women's conference to presidents of national women's groups. They included women from venerable organizations like the League of Women Voters, the American Association of University Women, and the National Federation of Business and Professional Women, as well as groups newly created to focus specifically on women's rights, such as the National Organization for Women, founded in 1966, and the National Women's Political Caucus, organized in 1971. In the 1970s all of these groups were working together for ratification of the proposed Equal Rights Amendment and involved in planning the IWY conferences.[6]

Not surprisingly, the conference attracted the nation's most famous feminists. Betty Friedan, author of the 1963 bestselling book *The Feminine Mystique*—which inspired the modern feminist movement—and the founder and first president of NOW, was among them. So was Gloria Steinem, the journalist, feminist activist, and founding editor of *Ms.* magazine, who had become increasingly prominent in the movement in the early 1970s and would play an important role in the conference. Eleanor Smeal, the new president of NOW and a relative newcomer among feminist leaders, was also in Houston. Steinem and Smeal served on the IWY Commission.[7]

Celebrities in every field, from academics to athletics, lent luster to the gathering, proud to be associated with this extraordinary event. World-famous anthropologist Margaret Mead, whose pioneering work on gender roles as "social constructions" varying from culture to culture laid the intellectual foundation for the academic field of women's studies and the modern women's movement itself, would give a plenary address. Tennis star and leading advocate for women in sports Billie Jean King, whose defeat of aging male tennis player and self-described male chauvinist pig Bobby Riggs four years earlier—in Houston—was watched by millions around the world, was also highly visible at the conference. King was one of the relay runners who carried a "Torch of Freedom" to Houston from Seneca Falls, New York, the site of the first woman's rights convention in 1848, symbolically linking the modern women's rights movement with its early history.[8]

Several of the celebrities were IWY Commission members, including poet, novelist, and actress Maya Angelou—familiar to television audiences for her then-recent appearance in Alex Haley's *Roots*. She had written a poem for the occasion. Commissioner Jean Stapleton, the actress who starred as Edith Bunker on the decade's most famous sitcom, *All in the Family*, drew crowds of autograph seekers. Then there was Commissioner Coretta Scott King, at least as famous as these other celebrities but in an entirely different way. Widow of the martyred Reverend Dr. Martin Luther King Jr., she was the "First Lady" of the civil rights movement and accorded a place of honor at the conference as well as special security protection. The *Atlanta Journal-Constitution* gushed that "the list of participants reads like a 'Who's Who' of famous American women."[9]

Bella Abzug—formerly a congresswoman from New York City and admired for her feisty, outspoken manner and amazing success in pushing feminist reforms through Congress—was the IWY Commission's presiding officer. Appointed by President Jimmy Carter, she was the star of the show, easy to spot in her trademark wide-brimmed hat. Sally Quinn, covering the weekend for the *Washington Post*, reported that in Houston women clustered around Abzug, eager for her attention: "Everywhere she went the women would come at her, pull at her, tug at her arm, her jacket, her skirt. Bella this and Bella that. It reminded one of the mother taking her brood to the circus and everybody wanting peanuts and popcorn at the same time."[10]

Abzug had been the primary advocate for the IWY conferences. A liberal and longtime supporter of the civil rights movement, Abzug was eager for underrepresented groups to enhance their political clout by joining forces. She saw the IWY as an opportunity to reach out to minorities and the poor, to develop grassroots support for the feminist movement, and to unite American women behind a feminist agenda that served them all.[11]

Women active in national politics in both parties were eager to be a part of this federally funded extravaganza. They came to Houston in droves. Famous Republicans included Jill Ruckelshaus, who had served as presiding officer of the IWY Commission under President Gerald Ford; Congresswoman Margaret Heckler of Massachusetts, who represented the House of Representatives on the IWY Commission; Mary Louise Smith of Iowa, former chair of the Republican National Committee; and Mary Crisp, the current RNC cochair. Elly Peterson, Republican cochair of ERAmerica, a new bipartisan organization created by the IWY Commission to coordinate ratification efforts, was in Houston along with Democratic cochair Liz Carpenter. The two would preside over a glittering preconference fund-raiser for the ERA.

Democrats included Congresswoman Elizabeth Holtzman of New York, who served on the IWY Commission. Congresswomen Pat Schroeder of Colorado and Lindy Boggs of Louisiana were also in Houston. Former congresswoman Martha Griffiths of Michigan, revered by feminists for the role she had played in adding protection against sex discrimination to the 1964 Civil Rights Act and steering the ERA through Congress, was also a commissioner. Texas's own Barbara Jordan, a congresswoman who electrified the 1976 Democratic National Convention, would lend oratorical brilliance to the conference as the keynote speaker.[12]

Dozens of high-ranking Carter appointees flew in from Washington, D.C., among them White House senior staffer Midge Costanza, who served as Carter's liaison to the women's movement; Eleanor Holmes Norton, the first woman to head the Equal Employment Opportunity Commission (EEOC); and Department of Agriculture lawyer Sarah Weddington, who as a young attorney had argued *Roe v. Wade* before the Supreme Court in 1973. These women were among the "distinguished women in government" scheduled to offer Briefings from the Top to the delegates and observers.[13]

First Lady Rosalynn Carter, together with former First Ladies Lady Bird Johnson and Betty Ford, would be addressing the conference, appearing together on the same stage for the first time. This underscored the high-level bipartisan support for the event.[14]

Over the four-day weekend, feminist leaders sought to unite these representatives of American womanhood behind an agenda reflecting their diverse interests but one they could all support. That was no small challenge. Amid pageantry, films, exhibits, self-defense workshops, women's history lessons, poetry readings, stand-up comedy, a Sweet Honey in the Rock concert, and occasional spontaneous outbursts of hugging, singing, and dancing in the aisles, the delegates labored in tension-filled caucuses to consider a proposed National Plan of Action drafted by the IWY Commission and to resolve their differences regarding what the final plan should look like.[15]

In the end, a remarkable spirit of compromise and expansiveness prevailed, leading the IWY Commission to title its report to Congress and the president *The Spirit of Houston*. The National Plan of Action adopted that weekend reflected the goals of the moderates who launched the movement and new issues raised by their younger, more radical associates. It represented a consensus that the federal government should direct its power and resources to resolving the problems faced by American women of many different circumstances as well as promoting equality.[16]

The twenty-six adopted recommendations or "planks," IWY leaders noted, "ran the gamut of issues that touch women's lives." The planks called for ending discrimination in education and employment and for opening up new opportunities to women in every field, including elective and appointive office. They urged greater participation and recognition of women in the media and an end to sex-role stereotyping both in the media and in schools. There were demands for equal access to credit and the extension of social security benefits to homemakers. They recommended programs to provide counseling and support for "displaced homemakers" needing to find employment. Other planks endorsed aid to "battered women," elderly women, disabled women, rural women, and women in prison, as well as action to prevent domestic violence, rape, and child abuse, and called for an end to the deportation of undocumented mothers of American-born children.

The National Plan of Action also included planks recommending comprehensive child care facilities, pregnancy disability benefits, jobs and training for poor women, and welfare system reform—in consultation with recipients. Reflecting the IWY's UN ties and American feminists' eagerness to help women elsewhere gain freedoms newly enjoyed in the United States, the Plan called for a greater role for women in formulating foreign policy and for international cooperation to advance women's rights worldwide and to promote peace.[17]

During the conference, representatives of African American, Asian, Hispanic, American Indian, and other minorities came together to form a Minority Caucus. It was a momentous convergence during which the term "women of color" was coined.[18] Rejecting as tame and inadequate the plank proposed by the IWY Commission, they drafted a new plank addressing their varied needs that the conference approved enthusiastically. Delegates were overcome with emotion when Coretta Scott King, speaking for the Minority Caucus, declared, "Let this message go forth from Houston and spread all over this land. There is a new force, a new understanding, a new sisterhood against all injustice that has been born here. We will not be divided and defeated again."[19]

Although most feminists regarded "reproductive rights"—including the right to legally terminate a pregnancy—as fundamental, others, including many Catholics, opposed abortion. A few IWY commissioners— among them National Council of Catholic Women leader Margaret Mealey and Congresswoman Margaret Heckler—opposed abortion. But the reproductive rights plank that was adopted called for widespread availability of birth control and abortion, with federal funding for women who could not afford to pay. The Plan recommended more attention to women's health care needs in general and the creation of a "national health system" that would better serve all Americans.[20]

The most controversial plank was one calling for equal rights for lesbians. Earlier in 1977, this issue—which had divided feminists since the early 1970s—suddenly became a hot political issue nationwide as conservatives led by Anita Bryant organized a movement to block or repeal antidiscrimination laws. In Houston some feminists argued that, since homosexuality was an issue involving both sexes, it was not one for them to take on. Many feared it would divert attention from reforms essential to all women, gay or straight.[21] Others argued that there was strength in unity and that the Plan should reflect the interests of all women.

In Houston it appeared that most delegates agreed with or came to accept the latter position. During the conference Betty Friedan was loudly cheered as she rose before a national television audience to second the proposed plank, putting aside her well-known opposition. "I have been known to be violently opposed to the lesbian issue in the women's movement," she said. "[But] this issue has been used to divide us too much . . . As someone who had grown up in middle America and has loved men too much I've had trouble with this issue . . . but we must help women who are lesbians in their own civil rights." When it passed with a comfortable margin, lesbians observing from the bleachers erupted with shouts of "Thank you, sisters." As the nation watched on television, they released balloons proclaiming, "We are everywhere!"[22]

On the Equal Rights Amendment, which in 1977 was facing stiff opposition and stood three states short of ratification, all feminists were in agreement. The largest floor demonstration, by far, came when the plank calling for ratification of the ERA was adopted. For many, it was the highlight of the conference. Delegates broke into long and enthusiastic chants of "Ratify the ERA!" and "Three more states," before singing "God Bless America" and "The ERA Was Passed Today" (to the tune of "The Yellow Rose of Texas"). Chains of women danced down the aisles and pandemonium reigned until nearly midnight. By then everyone was too tired to conduct further business. Presiding Officer Abzug dismissed the delegates with a "Good night, my loves," and adjourned for the day.[23]

Adoption of the 1977 National Plan of Action encapsulating the goals of the "pro-change" delegates filled feminist participants with a tremendous sense of accomplishment and unity. In her address, Margaret Mead, who urged American women to use their newfound solidarity to promote peace, declared, "This conference may well be the turning point, not only in the history of the women's movement, but in the history of the world itself." Jean Stapleton said Houston had been "a tremendous experience," and that she "felt so moved when the major resolutions were passed" that "the spirit of it just washed over me." Tanya Melich, a Republican feminist much inspired by the experience, recalled afterward: "Inside the cocoon of those four days of Houston, we women found sisterhood—that universal sense of being together honorably for a great cause."[24]

The National Plan of Action adopted in Houston was indeed a major accomplishment. It was a compendium of the goals of the American women's rights movement at its most expansive moment and a forward-looking agenda that would guide feminists for years to come.[25] It did not, however, represent a consensus among American women on what federal policy should be. Solidarity among feminists was not the same as solidarity among American women.

As the IWY conference got under way, a crowd variously estimated at fifteen to twenty thousand people gathered a few miles away at the Astro Arena for a massive Pro-Life, Pro-Family Rally. Denouncing the National

Women's Conference and its recommendations, they made it clear that the feminists did not speak for them.[26]

A few months earlier women who bitterly opposed the women's rights movement had turned out en masse for the preliminary IWY meetings in the states to challenge feminists and everything they stood for. Inflamed by the success of feminist leaders in gaining support for IWY from Congress and presidents Gerald Ford and Jimmy Carter, conservative groups came together in 1977 to face down the feminist threat. During the summer, in state after state, conservatives mobilized, hoping to gain control of the meetings and the recommendations and delegates to be sent to Houston. The challenge was coordinated by an organization called the IWY Citizens' Review Committee (CRC) headed by Illinois antifeminist leader Rosemary Thomson.[27]

The driving force behind the conservative women's challenge was Phyllis Schlafly, a gifted writer, speaker, debater, and political organizer, who had led Stop-ERA (Stop Taking Our Privileges) since 1972. A veteran politician from the Republican Party's right wing, Schlafly had taken up the antifeminist cause after years of fighting liberalism and communism. In 1975, she created the Eagle Forum to oppose feminism generally and promote conservative politics, advertising it as "an alternative to women's lib." Friends and foes alike believed that without her adroit leadership of the anti-ERA movement, the amendment would have been quickly ratified.[28]

Schlafly had been incensed at the creation of the National Commission on the Observance of International Women's Year and the fact that not one, but two presidents had appointed only feminists as members. As conservative on fiscal issues as on all others, she denounced Congress for appropriating five million of taxpayers' dollars for what she called "Federal Financing of a Foolish Festival for Frustrated Feminists." Critical of the United Nations and all its works, she accused feminists of using the UN-sponsored IWY program to force on Americans an unwanted constitutional amendment.[29]

As the IWY state meetings approached, Schlafly worked through the Eagle Forum and the ad hoc IWY Citizens' Review Committee to spread the word. Congressmen were soon swamped with letters calling on them to put the program to an end. IWY critics called it Bella's Boondoggle and Abzugate, demanding congressional investigation of alleged abuse of funds and authority.[30] Unable to stop the IWY conferences, Schlafly and other CRC leaders organized to challenge feminists for control of them and the right to speak for American women.

Between May and August of 1977, the IWY state meetings witnessed bitter battles between feminists and conservatives as both sides sought to turn out supporters. IWY Citizens' Review Committee leaders appealed to conservative Catholics, Mormons, and fundamentalist and evangelical Protestants. Though long hostile to one another, in the 1970s these groups were part of a loose coalition led by Schlafly to defeat the ERA, which they saw as a threat to traditional families.[31] CRC leaders also reached out to right-wing organizations such as the John Birch Society that opposed the ERA and feminism, big government, federal spending on social programs, and the United Nations. Opposition to IWY, in which African American women played a major role and that proposed more federal action to advance minority rights, also drew support from racial conservatives.[32]

One of the most important developments during the 1977 IWY fight was the close cooperation of anti-ERA and pro-life groups. Before 1977, they had overlapping but separate constituencies. But as feminists at the IWY state meetings endorsed the "right to choose" and federally funded abortion, pro-life groups increasingly saw ERA opponents as allies in the fight over the recommendations that would be sent to Congress.[33] Similarly, as feminists rallied behind their "lesbian sisters" who were under attack from the campaign led by Anita Bryant, the CRC found support from the rapidly developing movement opposing gay rights. These were prime examples of the polarizing effect of the IWY and of single-issue groups forging alliances with the enemies of their enemies.

Over the summer, as the clashes at IWY state meetings became increasingly heated and at times even physical, they attracted the attention of the media. Many reporters seemed to take particular delight in covering a story that involved women fighting other women. One of the few things feminists and conservatives agreed on was their resentment of reporters who trivialized their competition over serious policy issues as a giant "catfight."[34] Still, each side seized the opportunity provided by the media coverage to publicize its views and compete for the hearts and minds of the American people.

As the IWY state meetings ended in July 1977, the IWY Citizens' Review Committee had elected only 20 percent of the delegates. However, given the feminists' advantage, they hailed it as victory equivalent to that of David over Goliath.[35]

Aware that the badly outnumbered conservative delegates at the National Women's Conference could have little impact, CRC leaders focused their energies on making the Pro-Life, Pro-Family Rally competitive in size and spectacle with the National Women's Conference itself. However, according to the press, which also turned out en masse for the conservatives' gathering, there were obvious differences—including that the rally crowd was almost entirely white. It included large numbers of men and even children, which underscored the pro-family message.[36]

Both the National Women's Conference and the Pro-Life, Pro-Family Rally were loaded with American flags and other patriotic symbols, but the rally had strong religious overtones. The *New York Times* reported that there was a "revival-like atmosphere with cheering and 'amens.'" The arena was full to overflowing, thrilling the organizers who attributed their success to "the Lord." CRC leader Rosemary Thomson said God had "pulled off an undeniable miracle—with a little help from Christian women."[37]

After an invocation and a presentation of the flags from all fifty states, fifteen speakers, well known to their audience if not to the mainstream media or the feminists across town, addressed the crowd, each one receiving a rousing ovation. There was Lottie Beth Hobbs, founder of Women Who Want to Be Women, a predominantly southern organization that grew out of the movement to rescind the ERA in Texas and had spread through the region. In addition, there was Nellie Gray, founder and president of March for Life, which brought thousands of protesters to Washington, D.C., each year on the anniversary of *Roe v. Wade*. Dr. Mildred Jefferson, an African American physician from Boston and Harvard Medical School graduate, also addressed the crowd. Jefferson, president of the National Right to Life Committee, the oldest and largest of the organizations fighting abortion, was a pro-life movement superstar. Anita Bryant could not attend but cheered them on through a videotaped message, assuring them they were "truly the backbone of America" and that "in Houston and all over the nation the voice of motherhood will be heard."[38]

In contrast to the National Women's Conference, the protest rally featured several male speakers, most notably a newly elected, right-wing Republican from California, Congressman Robert K. Dornan, who was part of their small but growing group of allies in Congress. He offered a scathing denunciation of the IWY conference, especially its implicit endorsement by the First Ladies. "The greatest tragedy of all was to see these former First Ladies—excuse me, two former First Ladies and the current wife of the President of the United States—all sitting properly with their hands in their laps, all dressed according to White House protocol, and, by their very presence alongside of Abzug, approving of sexual perversion and the murder of young people in America. WHAT A DISGRACE!"[39]

For the rest of Dornan's speech, Sally Quinn reported in the *Washington Post*, "They were on their feet," wildly applauding such statements as "if George Washington could see those First Ladies nodding for abortion and perversion" and "let's tell the President that his wife was at the wrong rally." Dornan warned his listeners: "If you think the homosexuals, lesbians, abortionists are ready to give up you don't know about evil." The congressman then appealed to the press to be "fair" in covering the events of the weekend, and let the nation know how vehemently the IWY was being protested. As Dornan concluded his remarks, said Quinn, "he pointed to the assembled 'national media' and thanked them for being there. Then he told the audience to give them a standing ovation. They did."[40]

It was Phyllis Schlafly who most inspired the women and men who flocked to Houston. Schlafly began by thanking her husband, Fred, for "allowing" her to attend the rally: "I love to say that because it irritates the women's libbers more than anything," she added. Schlafly denounced the feminist movement for its radical aims, which now combined advocacy of the ERA with abortion and gay rights. The feminist movement, she charged, was out to "drive the homemaker out of the home" and to "forbid you to identify the traditional roles as wives and mothers." Babies did not need "two sex-neutral parents," she said, but "fathers and mothers." The crowd roared its approval as she declared, "The American women do not want ERA, abortion, lesbian rights, and they do not want child care in the hands of government!" She denounced the IWY as a costly mistake at taxpayers' expense.[41]

Along with other women leaders who had fought for control of IWY, Schlafly was thrilled that so many "God-fearing" Americans had come so far at their own expense to demonstrate their anger and determination to bring about change. If they held together, Schlafly insisted, they had the power to take control of the nation away from feminists and their allies in the government who threatened to destroy American families and undermine national strength. She assured her audience: "If you stick with us" in the fight for what was right, they would win.[42]

As the rally came to an end, conservative women leaders—astounded by their success in drawing such a large and passionate crowd to Houston to protest federally funded feminism—declared that this was just the beginning of a new "pro-family movement," one based on "family values" as opposed to "women's rights." Many participants said the fight against feminists during the IWY had been their "political baptism." The five million dollars Congress had spent on the IWY might have been worth it after all, one told reporters, if it awakened Christian women to the dangers facing the nation and the need to become politically active.[43]

The two Houston gatherings together constituted a major consciousness-raising session for participants, politicians, the press, and the American public. Press reports differed wildly, reflecting the political perspectives of reporters. But what was obvious, indeed unmistakable, was that women had become highly mobilized and politicized, but were sharply divided in their goals and at war with one another over what federal policy should be.[44]

Without knowing it, the nation had caught a glimpse of its political future. Only later would the full implications of the schism that had developed among American women become clear.

CHAPTER 2

The Rise of the Feminist Establishment

We are changing the nature of political power in America. The movement of women to full equality is the largest movement for basic social
and political change in this country . . . We are the best and the
bravest. And what we didn't know five years ago we're learning fast . . .
We have no right to fail our commitment to this moment, to ourselves,
to the women who come after us.

—BETTY FRIEDAN, REMARKS TO THE FIRST NATIONAL
WOMEN'S POLITICAL CAUCUS CONVENTION, FEBRUARY 1973

"You know the strange thing? About ten years ago we were busily
trying to persuade the world that there was a problem, that discrimination against women existed," Kathryn "Kay" Clarenbach, executive director of the National Commission on the Observance of International
Women's Year, told columnist Ellen Goodman in November 1977. "Now,
here we are, the establishment, being attacked by the radical right."[1] As they
gathered in Houston for the National Women's Conference, IWY leaders
also found it strange to be denounced so vehemently as part of the political
establishment when women were still severely underrepresented at all levels
of government. After all, the whole point of their massive effort to unite
women behind the National Plan of Action was to make women more of a
force in American politics.[2]

Nonetheless, by 1977, women's rights advocates knew they had come a
long way. In the early to mid-1970s, particularly, they made remarkable gains.
Between 1970 and 1975, the number of women in elective office doubled.

Women's rights enjoyed widespread support among Republicans and Democrats alike. As the decade began, a conservative backlash was under way, skillfully exploited by President Richard Nixon. But the central issue was race, not gender.[3] Even George Wallace was supportive, publicly endorsing the Equal Rights Amendment (ERA) in a letter to Alice Paul, the elderly former suffrage leader and feminist icon who had pressed for an equal rights amendment since 1923. Like most presidential aspirants, he sent Paul a letter declaring his support for "her amendment," which had become a central goal of the feminist movement.[4]

Public opinion polls showed widespread support for the women's movement and politicians felt compelled to at least appear to be on its side.[5] Government officials, especially at the national level, seemed to welcome not only the feminist message but the messengers into their midst. In 1975, Jill Ruckelshaus, the Republican feminist appointed by President Gerald Ford to lead the National Commission on International Women's Year, told the National Press Club: "When you write stories about the women's movement now, don't look for us in the streets. We have gone to the statehouse."[6]

The revolution in thinking by and about women that gave rise to the modern women's rights movement started more than a decade earlier, encouraged by commissions on the status of women that helped shape the agenda and establish the networks crucial to the rise of modern feminism. Kay Clarenbach, Catherine East, and other IWY leaders who had played essential roles on these commissions attributed the National Women's Conference and the National Plan of Action to a chain of events that began in 1961.[7]

Esther Peterson, then director of the Women's Bureau in the U.S. Department of Labor, persuaded President John F. Kennedy to establish a President's Commission on the Status of Women. Kennedy complied, some say to deflect criticism for having been the first president since Franklin Roosevelt not to appoint a woman to his cabinet. In addition, the president was honoring his substantial debt to Peterson—thirty-year veteran of the labor movement and advocate for working women—who played a major role in his election.[8]

Kennedy appointed former First Lady Eleanor Roosevelt, a champion of women's rights in the United States and around the world, as the commission's official chair, and she served until her death in 1962. However, this high-level commission consisting of fifteen women and eleven men was led by Esther Peterson. Four cabinet members plus Attorney General Robert

Kennedy and several members of Congress were members, along with private citizens prominent in business, labor, and education. Leaders of large national women's organizations—including the League of Women Voters, the National Federation of Business and Professional Women, the American Association of University Women, the National Council of Negro Women, the National Council of Catholic Women, and the National Council of Jewish Women—were commission members or served on one of its committees.[9]

The commission's report, *American Women*, issued in 1963, stimulated considerable interest. With sixty-four thousand sold, it was by U.S. Government Printing Office standards a bestseller. The report put the nation on notice that despite the post–World War II glorification of domesticity, the way American women lived their lives was changing. Though most American women were still homemakers, a role the commission applauded, the report and the massive amount of supporting data accompanying it showed that women were spending a smaller portion of their lives rearing children, living longer, and entering the workforce in growing numbers. Owing to divorce or simply outliving their husbands, women were increasingly self-supporting—or needed to be.[10]

Clarenbach and East recalled that the Kennedy Commission's work "raised some important issues, particularly with respect to inequities in public institutions, and the vulnerable situation of homemakers." The commission's report urged revision of public policy in accordance with changed circumstances and made numerous recommendations for reform, including government-supported child care centers and occupational training for women so they could move into jobs traditionally held by men. It also focused attention on the plight of low-income women and those who faced dual discrimination based on race and gender. The commission's optimistic conclusion was that "the quality of women's exercise of their capabilities and responsibilities will be higher as American institutions become more suitable to contemporary life." One of the earliest and most visible results of the report was the Equal Pay Act of 1963, which for the first time recognized the rights of women to fair and equal treatment as wage-earners. This was no small accomplishment in a nation where even most liberals believed that protecting and advancing the incomes of male breadwinners was the key to a healthy society.[11]

The Kennedy Commission raised expectations that the government would take an active role in fighting sexual inequalities. Following one of the recommendations in *American Women*, President Kennedy created by executive order a Citizens' Advisory Council on the Status of Women and an Interdepartmental Committee of cabinet members and agency heads, a practice followed by his successors Lyndon Johnson and Richard Nixon. The Kennedy Commission served as a model for and encouraged the formation of advisory commissions on the status of women that were established by governors and state legislatures across the nation, as well as many federal agencies.[12]

By 1967, there were commissions in every state. In most cases, in setting up the commissions, governors relied on women's organizations such as the National Federation of Business and Professional Women (almost always identified by its initials BPW) and the League of Women Voters, as well as church women's groups and other civic and professional groups. In some states they also relied on labor union women and minority women's organizations, though others were less progressive. In Mississippi, the governor appointed an all-white group who opposed both the civil rights movement and organized labor, but even there the commission's work led to changes including extension of jury service to women. After 1970, members of state commissions met annually at conferences of the National Association of State Commissions on Women, with Kay Clarenbach, a Ph.D. in political science who headed the Wisconsin commission, as chair.[13]

Betty Friedan, a veteran journalist and author, was a consultant for the Kennedy Commission, advising it on media portrayal of women and its impact. Her book, *The Feminine Mystique*, published in 1963, the same year as *American Women*, articulated the grievances of white, college-educated, middle-class women especially, let dissatisfied homemakers know that they were not alone in suffering from "the problem that has no name," and prescribed stimulating, paying jobs as a remedy.[14] Clarenbach and East recalled that it "penetrated the minds of its readers far more substantially than most bestsellers do" and led women to begin "thinking in a changed way."

The next year Congress adopted landmark legislation, the Civil Rights Act of 1964, including Title VII, which expanded the act to address sex as well as race discrimination. Ironically, a southern conservative who was adamantly opposed to the civil rights movement but somewhat supportive of women's rights, put Title VII forward as a poison pill, to the great amusement of many fellow congressmen. Yet, after Congresswoman Martha Griffiths, Senator Margaret Chase Smith, and others rallied in its support, it was adopted. Title VII proved to be one of the most important pieces of legislation in advancing gender equity, the basis for many subsequent feminist victories.[15]

Yet its complicated origins—the result of opponents' efforts to kill the bill and the efforts of women's rights supporters to have women share in the benefits of federal civil rights legislation—complicated implementation. At first the Equal Employment Opportunity Commission (EEOC) focused on race discrimination and disregarded complaints based on sex, despite the best efforts of two commission members, African American labor activist Aileen Hernandez, and Richard Graham, a white male sympathizer of women's rights.[16] One EEOC officer said Title VII was "a fluke . . . conceived out of wedlock." An article in the *New Republic* asked, "Why should a mischievous joke perpetrated on the floor of the House of Representatives be treated . . . with this kind of seriousness?"[17]

As the EEOC continued to ignore complaints based on gender, women began to sue. Among the first to come forward were airline stewardesses (as they were known at the time), who demanded an end to outlandish practices such as routine "measurement" checks and mandatory retirement at the age of thirty-two. When airlines executives, defending their policies before Congress, insisted such measures were essential to their business, Martha Griffiths famously asked them: "What are you running, an airline or a whorehouse?"[18]

EEOC inaction inspired feminist action. During the Third National Conference of State Commissions on the Status of Women in 1966, a small group of women gathered in Betty Friedan's hotel room and founded a new private grassroots organization, the National Organization for Women. Friedan later acknowledged that Catherine East, who served on the staff of the Kennedy Commission and as executive secretary of both the Citizens Advisory Council on the Status of Women and the Interdepartmental Commission on the Status of Women during Lyndon Johnson's administration, "cajoled" Friedan into taking the lead in creating NOW. East, Friedan recalled, was "the pivot of the feminist underground in Washington, spreading from government agencies to Capitol Hill." Given her position it would not do for her "pivotal" role in NOW's establishment to become public. But East was disturbed that Johnson and most politicians in Washington seemed to feel obliged to give lip service to women's issues but then failed to act.[19]

The idea was that NOW, operating from outside the government, could press for action in a way that politically appointed commission members could not. Richard Graham, for one, thought it essential that the women's movement have an organization somewhat like the National Association for the Advancement of Colored People (NAACP) to press forward its goals. Significantly, NOW's 1966 statement of purpose explained that the organization would not have a research division, but would seek action on the reforms recommended by the "excellent reports" of the state and national commissions on women.[20]

Like the Kennedy Commission's report, NOW's statement emphasized the need for reform as a result of major social, demographic, and economic developments and in bold language: "Enormous changes taking place in our society make it possible and urgently necessary to advance the unfinished revolution of women toward true equality, now." But it went beyond the reforms suggested by its predecessor, demanding change in every aspect of American life including marriage, which it insisted must become a partnership of equals. The movement aimed to reform the most private areas of life, a prime example of the personal becoming political. That was just a beginning.[21]

IWY leaders recalled that "NOW came into a world in which there were no women's centers, no rape crisis centers, no women's studies programs, in which few had ever heard of a 'displaced homemaker' or a 're-entry woman,' or a 'non-traditional' job or 'comparable worth.'" Ten years later: "All of these things and more had been created or identified, and we were beginning to realize that we really could change the world to make it a better place for women and children (and men too!)." Soon there were hundreds of new women's organizations and institutions, working for women's rights along with such groups as the BPW, the League of Women Voters, and the American Association of University Women that grew out of the first wave of feminism.[22]

By the early 1970s, most of these organizations were working along with NOW in a fight for the ERA. In the past, the amendment proposed by Alice Paul in 1923 had been a major source of friction between the National Woman's Party, "equal rights feminists" who believed any special legislation for women undermined their equality and injured their job prospects, and "labor feminists" such as Esther Peterson who believed that many women, especially those in poorly paid, arduous "women's work," needed the special protections (such as restrictions on night employment and the number of hours women could be required to work) that the ERA would make unconstitutional.[23]

The Kennedy Commission had urged piecemeal legal reforms rather than a constitutional amendment: some have charged that the commission was actually created as a means of sidestepping the ERA issue. However, during the 1960s, working together on the women's commissions, feminists were able to bridge this great divide. Even Esther Peterson dropped her opposition, saying: "Now I believe we should direct our efforts toward replacing discriminatory state laws with good labor standards that will protect both men and women." She added: "History is moving in this direction." Since the equal rights feminists who supported ERA tended to be Republicans and the labor feminists who opposed it were Democrats, this was a major step forward, facilitating the development of a bipartisan women's movement.[24]

In 1967, at its second national conference, NOW voted to make the ERA a top priority. NOW leader Marguerite Rawalt recalled that in the stormy meeting where the decision was made, there were "two rows of elderly dignified women . . . headed by Alice Paul . . . dear members of the National Woman's Party (NWP), whose sole purpose in life was the Equal Rights Amendment." They had joined NOW in order to vote yes. "They were tense," she said. "A few rows back of them sat the United Automobile Workers," active NOW supporters who had not yet gotten the UAW to support the ERA. NOW's endorsement of the ERA would require them to resign, only to return to the organization a year later when the UAW changed its position. As Betty Friedan remembered the meeting, when the elderly NWP women got up to speak on the ERA, very young women who had never heard of the amendment became excited about the idea "as they had not been by narrow job issues."[25]

At the same time, NOW also made the momentous decision to work for the legalization of abortion, another divisive issue. As a result, some of the organization's founding members departed and formed the Women's Equity Action League (WEAL) focusing on ending discrimination in education and jobs.[26]

In its earliest years, NOW was small. But its leaders—such as Kay Clarenbach, who was elected chair of the board, and Marguerite Rawalt, a lawyer who had been president of both the Federal Bar Association and the National Association of Women Lawyers who served on NOW's legal committee—were like a *Who's Who* of America's professional women. Well-known and respected, savvy and vocal, they were exceedingly effective. One of NOW's early victories was ending separate "Male Help Wanted" and "Female Help Wanted" ads in newspapers, after the EEOC banned separate ads for blacks and whites but continued to allow them for women and men. After NOW successfully pressured the EEOC to hold public hearings in 1967 regarding women's rights under Title VII, President Lyndon Johnson signed Executive Order 11375, prohibiting federal contractors from discriminating against women. Meanwhile, NOW's legal committee sponsored and won a number of landmark decisions challenging protective labor laws and sex bias in criminal law.[27]

In the late 1960s, as all of these groups, together with NOW and the government-supported commissions, labored away, the media was mesmerized by new converts to the movement. Many younger and more radical women had become feminists as a result of their experiences while part of civil rights or antiwar movements. In contrast to the pragmatic reformers then leading NOW who saw their organization's purpose as opening up the system to its constituency, these newcomers had more revolutionary goals, many of them challenging such basic institutions as capitalism, marriage, and heterosexuality. Disdaining traditional gender relationships and dependence on men—"a woman without a man is like a fish without a bicycle" was a favorite phrase—they embraced "women's liberation" as the goal as well as the name of their movement.[28]

Many of those who came into the women's movement from more radical social movements found large, formal organizations with chapters and elected leaders unattractive, preferring to work through smaller and less structured groups. Even more than their feminist predecessors in NOW, they embraced the idea that the most personal matters in life were political and, often through the popular "consciousness-raising" or "CR" sessions, they encouraged women to think deeply about how many of the challenges they faced were not individual but derived from systematic social injustice. Often CR groups turned from contemplation to social action, such as establishing cooperative child-care arrangements. One group in Chapel Hill launched a small company, Lollipop Power, Inc., to fill the need for nonsexist children's books. Another group that began in 1969 in Boston focused on liberating women from dependence on "condescending, paternalistic, judgmental, and uninformative" doctors, researched the answers to their own questions, and published the landmark feminist volume *Our Bodies, Ourselves*. Women's liberation groups also pioneered the establishment of rape crisis centers and shelters for victims of domestic abuse. This was a massive, creative, grassroots movement that mobilized hundreds of thousands of women.[29]

As women inspired by women's liberation flowed into the more traditional networks of professional women, they broadened the base of the women's rights movement. Many chose to join NOW, which pushed the organization further to the left—out of the control (and to the dismay) of its founders. Some were lesbians who challenged the feminists to take up their cause. When a group called the Radicalesbians disrupted a NOW-organized assembly of women's groups in order to challenge the homophobia within the women's movement, it alarmed feminist leaders—including Friedan— who feared that injecting sexual politics into the movement would alienate most American women. Friedan later recalled this issue "aroused the creeping horrors in me." At that time she thought, "For me, for every woman—or most women, surely—the women's movement, women's liberation, the equality we now demand, had nothing whatsoever to do with lesbianism. Or giving up, renouncing, denouncing the love of men." Friedan felt strongly that "introducing such an insistent sexual red herring in the women's movement" would "boomerang into an era of sexual McCarthyism that might really paralyze the women's movement."[30]

On this and other issues Friedan was at odds with new movement leaders such as Gloria Steinem, who in the early 1970s was becoming wildly popular, lending glamour as well as her journalistic skills to the movement.[31] Steinem believed feminists must stand together regardless of sexual preference and that lesbians within the movement deserved support. Moreover, as long as there was a stigma attached to women loving women, antifeminists would be able to use charges of lesbianism to divide feminists and discredit the movement. By 1971, this point of view became dominant in NOW, which passed a resolution affirming that lesbian rights are "a legitimate concern of feminism."[32]

By 1973, NOW had moved still further to the left, which was made clear in the twenty-one page booklet *Revolution: Tomorrow Is NOW*. This summary of NOW's positions suggested a departure from working within the political system. The point of view that guided Friedan and other NOW founders who were intent on enabling women to take a full and equal part in American society seemed to give way to the views of more radical feminists such as African American lawyer Flo Kennedy, writer Kate Millett, and socialist feminists who wanted to see a more radical restructuring of the nation.[33]

Thus, even as the "equal rights feminists" and "labor feminists" who had fought for decades over the ERA resolved their differences and united, other issues arose and divided the movement. With an increasingly ideologically diverse constituency, the women's rights movement entered another period of fractiousness and internal wrangling over goals and strategy. Late in the 1960s, as radical feminists began to engage in "street theater" and demonstrations to try to raise the consciousness of the public, moderate feminists were critical, fearing that such activities would undermine their hard-won progress.[34]

Few events in the long history of the American women's rights movement received as much media coverage or had as great an impact on public opinion as the 1968 demonstration in Atlantic City. Radical feminists, seeking to focus attention on societal overemphasis on beauty and conformity, staged a dramatic protest outside the Miss America pageant. They threw girdles, hair curlers, false eyelashes, *Playboy* magazines, and other "instruments of female torture" into a "freedom trash can." They intended to burn them, but were not so radical as to defy the ban on setting fires on the boardwalk. Though no bras were actually burned, the image of bra-burning radicals contemptuous of traditional womanhood was forever etched into the psyche and the vocabulary of the nation, much to the chagrin of more moderate feminists and even some organizers of the protest.[35]

Other demonstrations followed. Feminists wearing black veils crashed New York's annual bridal fair in Madison Square Garden. A hundred women conducted an eleven-hour sit-in in the office of the male *Ladies' Home Journal* editor, protesting the depiction of women in the magazine and demanding that it hire women as editors.[36] The demonstrations led some pundits to insist that the women's movement was outside the mainstream and appealed only to a radical fringe. But others recognized that the women's movement had now expanded to include a tremendous variety of women with wide-ranging points of view and it appealed to many men as well. Feminism was becoming hip. Everyone was talking about it.

Feminists were highly visible and vocal and there was no organized opposition. New conditions of life had already undermined many sexist practices and policies and when women pushed, many barriers went tumbling. The diversity of the movement that at times produced fractiousness also enabled it to appeal to a wider audience and have a greater impact on society.

As the new decade began, there was clearly a rising tide of support for women's equality. On August 26, 1970, the fiftieth anniversary of the victory for woman suffrage, women's rights supporters from across the ideological spectrum and across the nation took to the streets for the Women's Strike for Equality. After NOW put out the call, the response was overwhelming. Even women never formally involved in the women's rights movement were caught up in the spirit of the day, not only marching but also demonstrating their support through all kinds of ingenious activities.[37]

Women at one Louisiana newspaper placed men's pictures in engagement and marriage society news. Women in Massachusetts persuaded many churches to turn over the pulpit to women preachers, as suffragists had done fifty years earlier. A caravan of New York feminists visited graves of feminist foremothers across the state—ending at Seneca Falls where the governor of New York proclaimed August 26 a state holiday.

In New York City, women workers at city hall turned its grounds into a temporary day care center. Another group erected mock statues across the city of ignored women whose statues should have been there; others managed to drape a banner on the Statue of Liberty that said: WOMEN OF THE WORLD UNITE. On Wall Street, women workers protested the absence of women on the stock exchange by crashing White's, a men-only landmark, for lunch.

The largest and most spectacular march was along New York's Fifth Avenue. To the surprise of Betty Friedan and other organizers, an estimated fifty thousand marchers turned up, far exceeding even the largest suffrage marches the city had witnessed half a century earlier. As Friedan described it, there were all kinds of women: suburban housewives, women from Harlem, young women with their mothers and grandmothers, and many men—"some carrying kids on their shoulders or babies on their backs and walking with their wives." Even passersby who had known nothing about the march spontaneously joined in.

Friedan found herself marching between a judge in her eighties (a former suffragist who refused to ride in the special car they had provided for suffrage movement veterans), and a young radical in blue jeans. According to the parade permit, the marchers were restricted to one lane—all city officials thought necessary. However, as Friedan recalled, "I took their hands and said to the women on each side, 'Take hands and stretch out across the whole street.' And so we marched, in great swinging long lines, from sidewalk to sidewalk, and the police on their horses got out of our way. And people leaned out of office windows and waved and we said, 'Join us!'"

The press took a jab at Friedan for having stopped to have her hair done on the way to the march that morning, which for some reason they viewed as hypocritical, and some media sources trivialized the strike as a bunch of women just wanting to take a day off. But many journalists raved about the "proud and joyous crowd who marched down Fifth Avenue that day." Friedan concluded that after that day women had come to understand "the power of our sisterhood" and she predicted that "the politics of this nation will never be the same." The 1970 Women's Strike for Equality was a tremendous success, contributing to a 50 percent increase in NOW membership within months. The first feminist event to make the TV news and the front pages of newspapers across America, the strike put the nation on notice that women—at least lots of them—were ready for change.[38]

All of these developments contributed to feminists' optimism and clout. Congresswoman Martha Griffiths, speaking to the press in 1970, proclaimed that the revolution had "already occurred." "We're now in the mopping up operations."[39]

While some women's rights advocates had little interest in becoming part of the establishment, in the early 1970s there were plenty like Griffiths who were eager to work within the system. Building on the accomplishments of the past decade, they labored to put the power and resources of the government to work on behalf of gender equity and to expand women's opportunities and influence.[40] In Washington, a growing number of pragmatic women—intent on gaining for women the individual freedom and equal opportunity enjoyed by American men—became "Washington insiders," accepted as part of the political scene. In addition to the president's advisory committee, women's rights advocates were forming women's caucuses within federal agencies and think tanks to identify best policies on women's issues.[41]

Women's rights supporters were increasingly active and visible in both parties and worked together across party lines. Aware of the paucity of women in elected office (in 1971 men held 98 percent of the seats in Congress), they were intent on change. As the National Organization for Women was nonpartisan, established for lobbying rather than electoral politics, feminist leaders saw a need for a new organization focused on moving women and women's issues to the forefront of American politics.[42]

Betty Friedan—believing that the women's movement had gone about as far as it could go until it gained more political clout—shifted her focus away from NOW and began to reach out to prominent women about forming such an organization. In July 1971, together with fellow New Yorker and Democrat Bella Abzug, she brought together a diverse group of women for an initial planning meeting. Abzug, newly elected to Congress, hosted the event in her Capitol Hill office. By her side were two other congresswomen: Shirley Chisholm of New York, the first African American woman in Congress, and Patsy Matsu Takemoto Mink of Hawaii, the first Asian congresswoman.[43]

The group included women who were older and younger, moderate and radical, and from inside and outside government. Though Abzug's impulse was to limit the organization to liberal Democrats, she was persuaded by Friedan's vision of an all-encompassing organization, strengthened by its diversity and bipartisanship.

One key convert, Liz Carpenter, a seasoned veteran of Democratic politics who had worked as an aide to Lyndon Johnson and as Lady Bird Johnson's press secretary, was recruited by her old friend and fellow journalist Shana Alexander, on Friedan's behalf. Carpenter later recalled the gathering as a significant turning point in her life, the beginning of a major commitment to the feminist movement. It was a "kaleidoscope" of women, she said, with everyone rather excited about being together with such a diverse crowd. The room was "full of women I had seen on Capitol Hill through the years—wonderful women, who walked the halls for all the women's organizations that worked for better legislation, a scattered contingent of women from the peace groups, young women with their backpacks, fresh from the marches against the Vietnam War, black women, Hispanic women, and representatives from the new women's groups."[44]

As Liz Carpenter described the event, "Bella" began the meeting, passing out coffee and rolls, and asking everyone to stand and say why they were there. "Of course all eyes were on Gloria [Steinem] in blue aviator glasses and miniskirt, dramatic and cool with her soft voice and waist-long blond hair"—trademarks that were already making news and copied by young women everywhere. Carpenter recalled that "when Gloria spoke everyone was quiet. 'Looking around this room,' said Steinem, 'I see there is at least one thing we all have in common—a vagina.'" Carpenter remembered, "I jumped about two feet. I had never heard that word except in my gynecologist's office!"[45]

Shortly thereafter three hundred women gathered two blocks from the White House for a large, heavily covered meeting at the Statler Hilton Hotel, and announced the establishment of the National Women's Political Caucus (NWPC). Liz Carpenter was ecstatic: "That July weekend," she wrote, "we were born again, born this time to be heard." Establishment of the NWPC "shifted the fighting front of the women's movement to the political arena." Carpenter was bemused by the clash of personalities, especially Friedan and Abzug, but "exhilarated by these bright, determined women." Yet, as someone "experienced enough in politics and public images," she recalled, "I knew that we needed to stick together to show a united front, not discord which the press would label a 'catfight.'" The organization grew rapidly. Despite the fact there was no money for staff, there was tremendous enthusiasm. By December 1971, there were thirty state caucuses.[46] In February 1973, the organization held its first national convention in Houston, Texas, and elected Texas Democrat Frances Tarlton "Sissy" Farenthold—a state legislator who had won national attention attacking corruption in the Texas legislature—as its first chair.[47]

In addition to Friedan, Steinem, Congresswomen Abzug, Chisholm, and Mink, and Carpenter, Democrats in the NWPC included leaders from labor unions and minority communities and organizers of the poor.

There were many prominent African Americans, notably Dorothy Height, then president of the National Council of Negro Women, who had served on the Kennedy Commission; attorney Eleanor Holmes Norton; and civil rights icons Fannie Lou Hamer and Myrlie Evers, who brought the perspective of experienced civil rights activists to the NWPC. Other women's leaders involved in the early days of the NWPC included Beulah Sanders, vice president of the National Welfare Rights Organization; LaDonna Harris, Comanche leader and founder of Americans for Indian Opportunity; and Lupe Anguiano, Mexican American civil rights activist.[48]

Leading Republicans in the NWPC included Congresswoman Margaret Heckler of Massachusetts and Elly Peterson, a veteran Republican activist and former vice chair of the RNC. Peterson had worked with George Romney to build a moderate GOP in Michigan and pushed her party to reach out to African Americans and support racial justice, but by 1970 had quit her RNC post in disgust with Nixon's race-based southern strategy. Jill Ruckelshaus and Kay Clarenbach joined, as did Virginia Allan, a long-term BPW leader and deputy assistant secretary of state for public affairs. Bobbie Kilberg, an assistant to Nixon's domestic policy chief, John Ehrlichman, reported that GOP leaders George H. W. Bush and Robert Dole urged her to join and stay abreast of this important political development. Most of the Republicans in the NWPC were white women, but Audrey Rowe Colom, an African American welfare rights advocate politicized by her experiences in the voting rights campaigns in Mississippi, was a prominent Republican member who would rise to NWPC chair in 1975. One of the Republicans, Tanya Melich, recalled attending early NWPC meetings as a representative of the New York Republican Party and being "swept up like everyone else by the optimistic rhetoric and the exhilaration of starting a new political movement."[49]

The NWPC attracted the more liberal Republican feminists, but even so, within the NWPC, women from the two parties differed on economic issues and foreign policy. One Republican remarked that many Democrats angry about the Vietnam War turned hostile when they realized she "belonged to the party of Nixon" but were "glad to have experienced Republicans on hand." The differences extended beyond policy to the feminists' basic approaches to politics. While the Democrats in the NWPC were more "confrontational in style," the Republicans preferred to work behind the scenes, avoid controversial public stances, and preserve party harmony. Eventually, the NWPC recognized that while bipartisanship increased their clout, they ultimately had to fight battles within their two parties in their own ways—and they needed separate Democratic and Republican caucuses within the NWPC to do so. All agreed, however, that along with increasing women's political power they intended to work together—as the NWPC statement of purpose made clear—for action "against sexism, racism, institutional violence, and poverty."[50]

The NWPC promptly launched a Women's Education for Delegate Selection campaign to help women become delegates to the 1972 national conventions. Meeting with heads of both national parties, NWPC leaders gained pledges that they would work toward equal representation of women and men among national convention delegates—and in 1972 the results were striking. The number of women delegates at the Republican national convention doubled and the number at the Democratic national convention tripled.[51]

In both parties, feminists were allied with progressive elements seeking to make their parties more open and diverse. Democrats in the NWPC had been instrumental in the development of the McGovern-Frazier rules meant to steer the party from good ol' boy politics to a new politics of inclusion. The rules required that minorities, young people, and women be included in state delegations to national conventions according to their proportions in the state's population. When some states failed to comply, they were challenged. At the 1972 national convention, South Carolina feminists, encouraged by Abzug, Steinem, and actress/activist Shirley MacLaine, contested the seating of their state delegation that did not include the requisite numbers of women. In fact, an astonishing 40 percent of the delegates were challenged, most by feminists or minority groups.[52]

Shirley Chisholm's pathbreaking run for president in 1972 put feminist Democrats on the spot. On one hand, they were pleased and proud of her for running; on the other, feminists, just like many male African American politicians, knew that backing a winner in the primaries usually led to political clout they hesitated to sacrifice. Chisholm was more than a little disgusted by the lack of support from fellow feminists at the Democratic National Convention. When it was time to nominate candidates for vice president, they asked her if they could put her name forward. When she declined, believing McGovern should get to choose his own running mate, Gloria Steinem nominated Sissy Farenthold. As the balloting began, Farenthold rolled up so many votes it appeared she might win. After the McGovern camp realized what was happening and pulled their delegates into line, Farenthold lost, but in a field of four, she was second—behind McGovern's choice—the ill-fated Senator Thomas Eagleton.[53]

At the Republican National Convention, upbeat NWPC members heard addresses from former First Lady Lenore Romney of Michigan (who denounced Freud for not understanding women), current Michigan First Lady Helen Milliken (who praised Mary Wollstonecraft's 1792 arguments), and Jill Ruckelshaus, who cheerily declared that it was "the best possible time to be a Republican woman."[54] The GOP feminists encountered resistance from conservatives opposed to "McGovernizing" their party, but they successfully championed Rule 32, which said that state parties would "endeavor" to have equal representation of women and men at future conventions. Tanya Melich noted wryly that at the time, white male conservatives seemed less resistant to accepting more women than minorities and young people, presumably expecting women would be more compliant and conservative and less threatening.[55]

The burgeoning interest in politics led to more women candidates; in 1972 more women ran for Congress than ever before. Not all of them won, but there were dramatic successes. Barbara Jordan, a feminist Democrat from Texas, became the first African American woman to be elected to Congress from a southern state. Feminists were also thrilled—and surprised—by the upset victory of Democrat Elizabeth Holtzman, a thirty-two-year-old lawyer from New York who challenged one of the most powerful members of Congress, Emanuel Celler, and won. Celler, then eighty-four, was an ardent ERA opponent who liked to justify differential treatment of the sexes by rolling out such "old chestnuts" as there is just "as much difference between a male and a female as between a horse chestnut and a chestnut horse." Having been in Congress for half a century, Celler scoffed at Holtzman's effort to defeat him, likening it to trying to move the Washington monument with a toothpick.[56]

Decisions by Congress, the Supreme Court, and the executive branch suggested that Griffiths's comment about a "mopping up operation" being under way was right on target. During the Ninety-Second Congress, 1971–72, more women's rights bills were passed than in all previous legislative sessions combined. Among them was Title IX of the Education Amendments of 1972, prohibiting sex discrimination in educational institutions at all levels. In that same session of Congress, the ability of the EEOC to enforce Title VII of the Civil Rights Act of 1964 was strengthened. In addition, working parents received a tax break for child care expenses, and the status-free form of address "Ms." was added to federal forms. Bella Abzug recalled

1972 as a "watershed year," in which "we put sex discrimination provisions into everything. There was no opposition. Who'd be against equal rights for women? So we just kept passing women's rights legislation."[57]

Subsequent sessions brought more progress. In 1974, another major piece of legislation was adopted, the Equal Credit Opportunity Act, the result of extensive research by the newly formed Center for Women Policy Studies and massive lobbying by women's organizations. It was another highly visible symbol of strong bipartisan support for women's rights. Sponsored by Senator William Brock of Tennessee, a conservative Republican, it passed the Senate unanimously and the House with only one negative vote. The year 1974 also saw the adoption of the Women's Educational Equity Act to fund programs and books to counter "sex-role socialization and stereotyping."[58]

There were efforts to promote women's equality overseas at well as at home. In part, this was owed to Senator Charles Percy (R-Illinois), one of the strongest supporters of women's rights in the Senate, who served on the Foreign Relations committee. Congress adopted the Percy Amendment to the Foreign Assistance Act of 1973 requiring that all U.S. bilateral assistance programs "be administered so as to give particular attention to those programs, projects and activities which tend to integrate women into the national economies of foreign countries, thus improving their status." The act stipulated that no program that adversely affected women could be carried out.[59]

There was one major disappointment: the failure to gain a federally supported system of child care. Congress adopted an ambitious program, the Comprehensive Child Development Act of 1971, that would have created a national network of locally administered child care centers, with tuition subsidized depending on family income, providing meals, medical checkups, staff training—a program that would have helped a nation increasingly dependent on working mothers and families increasingly dependent on two incomes. It had strong backing in Congress from Republicans as well as Democrats. It passed the Senate 63 to 17. But when conservatives bombarded Congress and President Nixon with letters denouncing it as radical, social-istic, and antifamily, the president vetoed it. Its champions on the Hill, including Senator Walter Mondale (D-Minnesota), were unable to deliver the two thirds vote required for an override.[60]

Nothing so symbolized the tremendous support in Congress for the women's rights movement in the early 1970s as its approval of the Equal Rights

Amendment by overwhelming majorities. The amendment had languished in Congress for decades. In the 1940s, the Republican Party revitalized the amendment when it included it in the party platform, and the Democratic Party, despite labor union opposition, followed suit in 1944. But the amendment was never close to passing until 1950 and 1953 when the Senate approved it—but with the "Hayden Rider" providing that the amendment "shall not be construed to impair any rights, benefits, or exemptions now or hereinafter conferred by law upon persons of the female sex." ERA supporters saw special benefits as antithetical to the amendment's central purpose— equal rights—and did not support it, thus the House did not take up the measure. In the 1950s there was increased support for the ERA especially among Republicans, including President Dwight Eisenhower, but labor continued to fear loss of protective legislation for women and the Democrats remained opposed. Opposition declined after Title VII of the Civil Rights Act of 1964, which led to protective legislation being extended to men rather than removed for women.[61]

In 1971 and 1972, at the urging of Congresswoman Martha Griffiths and Birch Bayh, the leading champion of women's rights in the now all-male Senate, both houses approved the ERA in votes that were not even close. The House of Representatives acted first, endorsing the amendment on October 12, 1971, by a vote of 354 to 24. The Senate followed on March 22, 1972, with a vote of 84 to 8.[62]

Support came from every side, from Democrats and Republicans, the left and the right. Senator Ted Kennedy, Democrat from Massachusetts and a leading symbol of liberalism, voted in favor but so did Senator Strom Thurmond, conservative Republican from South Carolina. Thurmond issued a statement saying that the amendment "represents the just desire of many women in our pluralistic society to be allowed a full and free participation in the American way of life, without hindrance just because they are women." He added that he wanted his own daughter to grow up with the benefits that could come from the ERA.[63] In a memo to other Republican women leaders, Elly Peterson rejoiced that the "whopping victory" showed that members of Congress have "sensed that here too was a vast silent majority behind the militant organizations for equal status" and voted yes together with those who sincerely believed "that it was time women emerged from the status of second class citizens." Speaking for the NWPC, Bella Abzug told the press that the "overwhelming margin of passage of the ERA" affirmed "the significance of women as a new and powerful force" in national politics.[64]

The amendment proclaimed simply that "equality of rights under the law shall not be denied or abridged by the United States or by any State on account of sex" and gave Congress the power to enforce it. Such was the support for the idea of women's equality at the time that the ERA seemed, as bumper stickers proclaimed, "as American as apple pie." Senator Sam Ervin (D-North Carolina), a chivalrous defender of traditional sex roles and a long-term, passionate opponent of the civil rights movement, led the fight to block passage of the ERA, denouncing it in "florid, old style southern oratory." But in 1972 he found almost no support, even from other southern politicians.[65]

Unable to defeat the ERA, Ervin sought to amend it to preserve traditional "protections" women enjoyed, including requiring that husbands support their wives and exempting women from the draft. But, as in the 1950s, ERA advocates rejected the proposed modifications as contrary to the amendment's basic premise: that treating women as separate beings who required different treatment under the law buttressed outdated assumptions about woman's nature and social role. However, confident ERA supporters agreed to Ervin's suggestion of a seven-year limit for ratification. Apparently, they were oblivious to something Ervin understood well from decades of fighting integration, the ability of state legislators to stall progressive measures the federal government sought to impose.[66]

In 1972, there appeared to be little if any reason for ERA backers to worry. States scrambled to ratify, usually with little or no debate. Hawaii ratified within hours with no opposition and no debate. Nebraska ratified the next day, in such a hurry to be second they forgot to pass one section of the amendment and had to ratify again six days later. Delaware also had to ratify twice; the first time they jumped the gun and approved the amendment an hour and forty minutes before the Senate acted and sent the ERA to the states. Within the first week, New Hampshire, Kansas, and Iowa also ratified. Everywhere the vote was lopsided: Massachusetts approved the ERA with a vote of 205 to 7; West Virginia, 31 to 0; and Colorado, 61 to 0. Within a month, fourteen states ratified. Within three months, twenty states ratified. By one year, the ERA was ratified by thirty states. By 1975, only five more states were needed to have the three fourths required for the amendment to become part of the Constitution.[67]

The Supreme Court also issued several rulings celebrated by feminists—the result of hard work and careful planning by feminist lawyers, most notably

Ruth Bader Ginsburg. Building on a legal strategy first envisioned by Pauli Murray and Dorothy Kenyon of the American Civil Liberties Union (ACLU), Ginsburg worked to extend the Constitution's Equal Protection guarantee to women. Her first Supreme Court case was *Reed v. Reed* (1971), in which a wife, separated from her husband, contested his being designated administrator of their late son's estate. Siding with the wife, the court struck down an Idaho law favoring males as executors of estates, a historic first acknowledgment that women's rights were protected by the Fourteenth Amendment. After that Ginsburg convinced the ACLU to sponsor a Women's Rights Project that would, case by case, establish heightened scrutiny for sex classifications. In *Frontiero v. Richardson* (1973), the first case Ginsburg argued before the court herself, the Supreme Court ruled in favor of equality between the sexes as it declared that denying military benefits to husbands of females in the service was illegal. The case involved U.S. Air Force Lt. Sharron Frontiero's suit to allow her husband to receive benefits as her dependent. It was an example of Ginsburg's tactic of sometimes having male plaintiffs in equal protection cases, to make it clear that sex-based distinctions harm men as well as women. In another major ruling favoring women's equality, *Taylor v. Louisiana* (1975), the Supreme Court ruled that systematic exclusion of women from jury duty violated the Constitution.[68]

Court rulings relating to sex and reproduction also went the feminists' way. The 1972 decision *Eisenstadt v. Baird* legalized prescribing birth control for unmarried women. This step toward what feminists referred to as "reproductive freedom" built on *Griswold v. Connecticut* (1965) in which the court struck down laws in some states banning sale of contraceptives to married couples, thus assuring nationwide access for birth control.[69] To many Americans, these decisions seemed long overdue.

More surprising was the rapid progress on the issue of abortion. Since 1969, abortion rights advocates, working through groups like the National Association for the Repeal of Abortion Laws (NARAL), had urged states to lift long-standing bans on the procedure. By 1973, sixteen states and the District of Columbia had liberalized abortion laws and four—New York, Washington, Hawaii, and Alaska—allowed unrestricted abortion. Nonetheless many on both sides of this issue were surprised when on January 22, 1973, the Supreme Court issued its landmark decision *Roe v. Wade*, a case originating in Texas and argued before the court by twenty-six-year-old lawyer Sarah Weddington. In the 7–2 decision, announced the same day Lyndon Johnson died, the court declared that a woman is legally entitled to have an abortion until the end of the first trimester of pregnancy and that the state could not proscribe abortion until after the fetus became viable.[70]

The *Roe* decision prompted an immediate outcry among abortion foes, especially Catholics, who soon called for a constitutional amendment giving human rights to a fetus. The Roman Catholic Bishops' Committee for Pro-Life Affairs urged doctors and nurses in Catholic hospitals "to stand fast in refusing to provide abortion on request." A group of Catholic laymen in Virginia called for excommunication of William Brennan, then the court's only Catholic, who had voted with the majority.[71] Yet there seemed to be widespread support for *Roe*. In August 1973, a group of Protestant and Jewish leaders, seeing efforts to overturn *Roe* as a threat not only to women's constitutional rights but also to religious freedom, established the Religious Coalition for Abortion Rights, an organization to coordinate religious efforts to protect the legal option of abortion.[72] In addition, during the three years after *Roe*, poll after poll showed that most Americans supported the Supreme Court decision and believed that abortion should be legal in some circumstances.[73]

As for the executive branch, President Nixon was no fan of feminism. In the presumed privacy of the White House with the "president's men," the man Bella Abzug called "the nation's number one male chauvinist pig" bantered about women as "better halves" and "nags" or made crude jokes about them as sex objects while disparaging their abilities. He believed that women capable of great achievement were rare. Press secretary Ron Ziegler once spoke of a secretary as suffering from a "menopause problem." Vice President Spiro Agnew and Attorney General John Mitchell were hostile to feminism and to the ERA, as was Nixon's archconservative speechwriter, Patrick Buchanan, who said, "One prays the silly amendment will perish."[74]

Nixon knew that in his failed presidential campaign in 1960 he had greater support from women than from men, and in 1968, like the other presidential hopefuls, he had promised to appoint women and support the ERA. But during the campaign and as he began his first term, Nixon did little to honor those promises.[75] Instead, he courted social conservatives. Together with advisers Pat Buchanan and Kevin Phillips, Nixon envisioned making the GOP the majority party through his race-based "southern strategy" designed to attract disaffected white Democrats. He also pursued a "southern evangelical strategy" directed at religious conservatives, assisted by his friend, the Rev. Billy Graham.[76] Nixon's veto of the 1971 child care bill reflected his desire to woo those voters as well as his own traditional views.

Courting Catholics, another vital part of the New Deal coalition, Nixon publicly praised Terence Cardinal Cooke for opposition to legalization of abortion in New York and imposed limits on abortion in military hospitals. This seemed to be pure political expediency: he gave limited support to population control efforts at home and abroad and in later years disapproved of the GOP's extreme stance on abortion, saying: "That's people's own business."[77]

The growing popularity of the women's rights movement, however, pushed Nixon in a different direction. Public opinion polls, together with pressure from women's rights supporters—including women in his own party and own family—convinced Nixon that most women voters wanted him to support the women's movement. As a result, for the most part, he did.

At Nixon's second press conference in 1969, reporter Vera Glaser—the first female Washington Bureau chief—rose and asked what proved to be a highly consequential question: "Mr. President, in staffing your administration, you have so far made about 200 high-level Cabinet and other policy position appointments, and of these only three have gone to women. Can you tell us, sir, whether we can expect a more equitable recognition of women's abilities, or are we going to remain a lost sex?" After rolling his eyes upward in what one onlooker described as "a kind of sighing chagrin," he smiled at Glaser and quipped, "Would you be interested in coming into the Government?" Then he added, "Very seriously, I had not known that only three had gone to women, and I shall see that we correct that imbalance very promptly."[78]

It would take time and continued pressure before he made good on that promise. But the widely reported incident sparked immediate action on the part of feminists. Catherine East, still serving as executive secretary for both the advisory council and the interdepartmental commission on women and doing all in her power to promote feminist goals from within the government, fired off a note thanking Glaser and saying, "All women owe you a debt."[79]

As Glaser later recalled, East then telephoned her, saying her question indicated she could use some statistics on the status of women. A productive alliance ensued in which East sent the reporter information as well as questions to put to administration officials. Glaser produced a five-part series on the status of women in government, The Female Revolt, which was picked up by many newspapers across the nation. Forwarding the articles to Nixon's press secretary, Ron Ziegler, Glaser said she had no desire to become "the permanent floating expert on women's rights" but that she felt deeply on the subject as did women throughout the country. In fact, she insisted she had understated the "seething resentment" of women. Nonetheless, she said, Nixon had a "magnificent opportunity [to] mend fences with women" and to inspire the nation. Nixon began adding women appointees, usually announcing them in highly visible Rose Garden ceremonies, but needed constant prodding.[80]

Some of this came from within the White House. First Lady Pat Nixon quietly supported feminist goals including the ERA, a woman's right to choose abortion, and equal opportunity in education and jobs—including jobs in her husband's administration. But she usually avoided expressing such views publicly; her husband expected her to avoid controversial issues, not wanting "her to become like Eleanor Roosevelt." Soon after Glaser's question, however, she and the First Lady met at a White House reception, Pat Nixon requested a list of women who might qualify for a seat on the Supreme Court, and Glaser gladly complied. When Justices Hugo Black and John M. Harlan retired and Nixon had the opportunity to make not one but two appointments at once, the First Lady uncharacteristically told the press she wanted a woman nominated, adding "Don't you worry. I'm talking it up." Nixon went so far as to ask John Mitchell to recommend a woman (he suggested a Los Angeles judge, Mildred Lilley, that Chief Justice Warren Burger supported, but the American Bar Association declared her unqualified). When the First Lady learned he had appointed two men, she was hopping mad. According to daughter Julie Nixon Eisenhower, at dinner that night Pat Nixon barely spoke to her husband.[81]

Glaser and East kept up the pressure and at least some Nixon administration officials were listening. Invited to meet with presidential counselor Arthur Burns, the two women provided information on inequities to women in business, government, and professional education and on the political advantages to be gained by promoting fair policies. Throughout the summer, East sent analytical studies and relevant news articles to Burns, along with names to consider as appointees.[82]

Republican congresswomen were also pressing the administration for action. Soon after the Glaser question, Florence Dwyer (R-New Jersey) suggested Nixon create either a presidential commission or an Office of Women's Rights and Responsibilities under a special presidential assistant. Other Republican congresswomen and GOP feminists joined in, together with male allies, including Daniel Patrick Moynihan, counselor to the president for urban affairs. In a memo that caused quite a controversy among the White House staff, he predicted that "female equality will be a major cultural/political force of the 1970s" and warned that they had better wake up.[83]

Noting that America had "educated women for equality" but "not really given it to them," Moynihan said the inequality "is so great that the dominant group either doesn't notice it, or assumes the dominated group likes it that way." Such blindness would cause them problems, he predicted, yet the situation also provided an opportunity "for creative political leadership and initiative." Soon thereafter, Vera Glaser received a note from Arthur Burns's assistant stating that the president was setting up a task force on women and would like to know if she was willing to serve.[84]

By October 1, 1969, Nixon's Presidential Task Force on Women's Rights and Responsibilities was in operation. To lead it, he appointed Virginia Allan, well-respected leader of the National Federation of Business and Professional Women (BPW) and veteran of the state and national commissions on women. She promptly tapped Catherine East to serve on the staff. As Allan said, "Catherine East was the one who had the knowledge . . . She was the center." In less than two months the task force submitted its report, *A Matter of Simple Justice*, endorsing many of the goals widely shared by liberal feminists: the Equal Rights Amendment, affirmative action for women, federally funded child care, an end to gender discrimination in Social Security benefits, expansion of the Civil Rights Commission to include women's rights, expansion of the EEOC's power to enforce Title VII, naming more women to government offices, and creation of an Office of Women's Rights and Responsibilities headed by a special assistant to the president.[85]

Many hoped that endorsement of these goals from such well-respected women working within the establishment might give the women's movement much more clout. One task force member, Evelyn Cunningham, an assistant to New York governor Nelson Rockefeller, noted that in contrast to the "noisy" women's groups of the era who were pushing for change, this group had "a calmer, cooler kind of modus operandi" and had leaders who were "much respected." There was "something Republican about the technique, about the way it was done." *New York Daily News* columnist Ted Lewis offered a similar but rather sexist assessment: "Thanks to the Nixon task force report, the view of mature women—the establishment type—is now obtainable, and it basically agrees with what the aroused girls of the younger generation have been shouting and screaming about." Put forth by these "establishment types," however, the goals seemed different, he said. "What this task force has done has set a middle-of-the-road course for the equal rights movement," and men would be forced to pay attention. "For too long American males have underestimated the power of women . . . [but now] the danger of such thinking has been pointed out bluntly by a blue-ribbon presidential task force." He expected results.[86]

Still, John Ehrlichman and many of Nixon's senior advisers were opposed to the task force's recommendations, and the president dragged his feet on releasing the report. Finally pressure from Elizabeth "Libby" Koontz, director of the Women's Bureau in the Department of Labor—who wanted it out in time for a major conference on the anniversary of the Kennedy Commission's report—forced the issue. Meanwhile someone, most likely Glaser, leaked the report to the press. The botched release was a public relations nightmare. Nixon's political advisers including Charles Colson were dismayed, noting that the issue of women's rights was "beginning to build up a real head of steam."[87]

GOP leader Rogers Morton complained that such foot-dragging gave Democrats the opportunity to appear as the champions of women's rights instead of the Republicans. The highest-ranking woman in Nixon's administration, Patricia Hitt, assistant secretary of the Department of Health, Education, and Welfare, sent a strongly worded memo to Ehrlichman complaining about the late release and inaction on the ERA, which historically had enjoyed more support from the Republican side. "With the rising popularity of the women's 'liberation' groups and the increasing feminine interest in politics," she wrote, "it bothers me to see the Democrats taking the lead."[88]

From then on until the 1972 election, the Nixon administration was under growing pressure to act against gender discrimination in order to court women voters. Mostly notably, it took a strong stance on affirmative action for women. When the administration released Revised Order 4 directing firms with federal contracts to submit clear plans for recruiting women workers, some hailed it as "the Magna Carta of female employment."[89]

In addition, the administration launched an effort to identify and recruit women for leadership and policy-making positions in the executive branch on a scale never before attempted. Begun in 1971, it was carried out skillfully by Barbara Hackman Franklin, a young and talented Harvard M.B.A. who gave up a promising career at Citibank to take on the assignment. Glaser, seasoned observer of the ways of Washington, was at first skeptical, writing that this "pint-sized junior official from a New York bank" was "expected to succeed where others have failed." Breaking down "the 'women's place is in the home' philosophy of presidential advisers," which had "held down the number of female policy-level appointments," she knew, was no small challenge.[90]

The ham-fisted manner in which Barbara Franklin's appointment was made public did not improve perceptions. At a briefing restricted to women reporters, the White House unveiled this new initiative to recruit women and announced that Franklin would lead it as "staff assistant to the president for executive manpower." The reporters, including seasoned professionals such as Glaser and Helen Thomas, reacted with the appropriate level of shock and scorn, and the title was quickly stripped down to staff assistant to the president. But the skeptics were soon pleasantly surprised by the results. Franklin poured herself into the task, aided at the top by senior staffers Robert Finch and Fred Malek, a college friend who had chosen her for the post. She welcomed the aid of Virginia Allan and the BPW, which for a decade had been developing a talent bank with the aid of other women's organizations.[91]

Years later many people, especially Republicans, would celebrate this ambitious "women's program" as a tipping point in the history of women in government, one that launched the careers of women such as Elizabeth Hanford Dole, Kay Bailey Hutchison, and Franklin herself, who was appointed secretary of commerce by George H. W. Bush. Constance Berry Newman, an African American attorney tapped by Franklin to be director of VISTA (Volunteers in Service to America), would go on to have six more presidential appointments.[92]

The numbers of women in federal jobs expanded quickly and dramatically. Within a year the number of women in policy-making positions had tripled from 36 to 105. At the top level, more than half of the appointees were the first women to hold the positions. Nearly 1,100 more women were placed in midlevel positions and 339 appointed to boards and commissions.[93] Women even joined the Secret Service, which had never before hired women, and the military appointed its first women generals. Nixon also made efforts to increase the number of women in the armed forces (action that aided women but also helped the administration as it tried to shift to an all-volunteer army).[94]

By 1972, Tanya Melich and other Republican feminists were boasting that Nixon had "appointed more women to high government positions than in any time in U.S. history." In an August 1972 article "The Administration: Help Wanted (Female)," *Newsweek* agreed, declaring "the person in Washington who has done the most for the women's movement may be Richard Nixon."[95]

Still Nixon resisted pressure to go beyond his formal endorsement of the ERA. When the amendment was finally passed by the House and headed for the Senate, Gladys O'Donnell, president of the National Federation of

Republican Women, urged him to do more for the cause. Congresswomen Florence Dwyer, Margaret Heckler, and Charlotte Reid, plus several high-ranking women in the administration, sent Nixon a joint letter urging that he renew his 1968 election-year endorsement of the amendment. Pat Nixon also applied pressure, as did her daughter Julie Eisenhower, who wrote:

> Dear Daddy, The administration should support the Equal Rights Amendment. We have nothing to lose by supporting it more vigorously—and we lose support of many women by sitting back.

But Nixon did not act. Finally, after the ERA's resounding victory in Congress and with an eye to the upcoming election, he reaffirmed his support in a public statement: "Throughout twenty-one years I have not altered my belief that equal rights for women warrant a Constitutional guarantee."[96]

By the GOP national convention that summer, Nixon had ramped up his courtship of women's rights supporters, boasting in the printed convention program of his "unprecedented" record of support for women. Going further, Nixon supported the adoption of a 1972 Republican Party platform that espoused feminist goals—including federal child care programs.[97]

There was no mention of reproductive rights, however. Republican feminists believed they needed to pick their battles. Their priorities for the platform were the ERA endorsement and approval of Rule 30 calling for more equal representation at future conventions. Though the party's right wing was nowhere near as powerful as it would become later in the decade, there was considerable opposition to the reforms backed by GOP feminists and their progressive allies hoping to bring more minorities, young people, and women into the party. However, as Tanya Melich recalled, "most male Republican leaders in the northern states responded positively to our call to support our feminist goals."[98]

After his landslide victory, Nixon continued to appoint women. Anne Armstrong, cochair of the RNC with Bob Dole during the election campaign, was chosen to be a White House Counsel with cabinet rank. Barbara Franklin was appointed as a member of the newly established Consumer Product Safety Commission. Nixon also established the White House Office of Women's Programs (OWP) that his task force on women had recommended. It would fall under Armstrong's command. National Women's Political Caucus leader Jill Ruckelshaus became the OWP director, to the great disgust of Martha Mitchell, the far-right, outspoken media darling and wife of Attorney General John Mitchell who objected to Nixon's appointing such a "flaming women's libber" to a position in the White House. Ruckelshaus served until her husband, Deputy Attorney General William Ruckelshaus, famously resigned rather than carry out Nixon's order to fire the Watergate special investigator Archibald Cox, making both Ruckelshauses victims of the Saturday Night Massacre. Afterward, Jill was "much less effective doing what I cared about" and she too resigned.[99]

For the rest of Nixon's term, he continued to pay lip service to women's rights issues, but any advocacy issuing from the White House would come from the women of the OWP and them only. Nixon refused Armstrong's pleas to campaign for ERA ratification, influenced by other advisers wanting to please the newly organized movement to block ratification. After the 1972 election, Phyllis Schlafly had organized Stop-ERA and was now on the task. Among Nixon's staff members, Pat Buchanan especially opposed putting the president on the stump on behalf of the amendment. In a memo to Ehrlichman and Haldeman, Buchanan wrote: "Why we want to get the President back out front, when we don't have to on an issue whose hard chargers are the Women's Lib crowd is beyond me."[100]

Safely reelected, Nixon resumed courtship of social conservatives—and Republican feminists felt betrayed. Looking back, Tanya Melich regarded Nixon as "schizophrenic" when it came to women: "Admittedly Nixon's administration had been a mixed bag in terms of women's concerns—some of his actions had been supportive, while others suggested the new conservative agenda was making ominous inroads." Watergate had not been his only betrayal. While "flirting with us," she wrote, Nixon had been "in bed with the new conservatives."[101]

In August 1974, however, Nixon was forced to resign. Bella Abzug, the first member of Congress to insist that his abuses of power were grounds for impeachment, was vindicated. First-term congresswomen Barbara Jordan and Elizabeth Holtzman served on the House Judiciary Committee that impeached him, finding it a "somber and difficult" but necessary task.[102]

Fortune smiled on feminists when Nixon was replaced by Gerald R. Ford, a man inclined to support their movement and married to a woman, Betty Ford, who supported it openly and unequivocally. Under Ford, feminists would become even more a part of the establishment than before.

CHAPTER 3

To Form a More Perfect Union

Many of the legal, social, political, and economic rights women enjoy and accept so naturally today were won for them at great personal cost and always in the face of public resistance by our mothers and grand-mothers and great-grandmothers. We women of the 1970s have a legacy from those brave and determined women in our heritage. We have a responsibility to the young women who will come after us . . . We must encourage the growing recognition by women and men that equal rights is a matter of simple justice.

—JILL RUCKELSHAUS, NATIONAL COMMISSION ON THE
OBSERVANCE OF INTERNATIONAL WOMEN'S YEAR, IN
INTRODUCING ITS REPORT, "*. . . TO FORM A MORE PERFECT
UNION . . .*" *JUSTICE FOR AMERICAN WOMEN*, 1976

President Gerald R. Ford has not gone down in history as a major supporter of feminism. It is often implied that he tolerated it to support his wife—as Ford himself often suggested in a jocular fashion. Both Fords joked about her up-close-and-personal lobbying. At the start of his presidency, the new First Lady raised eyebrows by breaking with the White House tradition of separate bedrooms, ordering their king-size bed moved into "her" bedroom and their exercise bike into "his." Betty Ford told reporters with amusement that she could do only so much for politics and separate bedrooms was "just too far to go." She intended to sleep with her husband "as often as possible." She also made it clear she planned to take full advantage of "pillow talk" to promote feminist goals. This included the appointment of women to high-level positions in his administration and, if the opportunity arose, to the Supreme Court. The President once quipped that he was "married to one of the most powerful lobbyists in Washington . . . I say one wrong thing about women's rights and the next state dinner is at McDonald's."[1]

Going beyond the lighthearted banter, the new president moved quickly to express his sincere commitment to the advancement of women. Within weeks of taking office, Gerald Ford held meetings with top women appointees, women members of Congress, members of state commissions on the status of women, and representatives of major women's organizations. He reaffirmed his support for the ERA and invited them to help him place still more women in top positions. To one admiring audience he said he'd be grateful for their assistance, but he couldn't resist adding that appointing women was "the best way to keep . . . out of the doghouse with Betty!"[2]

The First Lady claimed credit for Ford's appointing Carla Hills as secretary of Housing and Urban Development (HUD), which made her the first woman on the cabinet since the Eisenhower administration and only the third in U.S. history. More high-level appointments followed. Anne Armstrong stayed on as a counsel in the White House—with Ford's blessing expanding the functions of the Office of Women's Affairs (OWA)—until the president named her U.S. ambassador to the United Kingdom, a plum assignment. Her assistant, Patricia Lindh, a Republican national committeewoman from Louisiana, took charge of the OWA until she too was promoted (to deputy assistant Secretary of State). To underscore his support for the OWA, Ford then brought into the White House the first female general in the U.S. military, General Jeanne Holm of the United States Air Force, as director. Holm was a forceful advocate for women and women's issues for the rest of Ford's presidency.[3]

Republican feminists had high hopes for Gerald Ford, who as minority leader of the House of Representatives had helped Martha Griffiths line up votes for the ERA. And as Tanya Melich recalled later, "We all agreed we had a strong ally in this remarkable and refreshing First Lady." From the outset of her husband's "accidental presidency," Betty Ford was besieged by a press corps eager to get to know this glamorous First Lady, a former New York fashion model and professional dancer, trained by the famous Martha Graham, who enjoyed dancing with her husband way into the night at the elaborate parties they held in the erstwhile somber White House.[4]

Betty Ford's life before and after moving into the White House was not all privilege and glamour, however, and her experiences shaped her views on women's issues. Her father, a conveyor belt salesman, died of carbon monoxide poisoning while working on a car when she was only sixteen. Her first marriage, to a childhood friend who turned out to be an alcoholic, ended in divorce. Her considerable experience in the job force included working as a food processor in a factory, a department store buyer, and a dance teacher to handicapped children.

After marrying Gerald Ford, she had struggled to cope with the pressures of rearing four rambunctious children virtually alone while her husband, as House minority leader, was on the road almost three hundred nights a year to assist fellow Republicans with reelection campaigns. One of her friends remarked bitterly: "She might as well have been a widow." Consequently, she suffered from depression and sought psychiatric help. An injury caused her to suffer intense neck and back pain, and her doctor prescribed Valium. During this dark period she became well acquainted with the housewife's malady that Betty Friedan described as the "problem that has no name."[5]

To the delight of the press, the First Lady spoke freely and with humor, as well as providing amazing photo ops. On one occasion she pulled off her shoes and danced on a conference room table; on another, she pushed her fully clothed husband into the pool at Camp David as cameras rolled. Soon after moving into the White House she announced her intention to hold frequent press conferences, which had not been done since the days of Eleanor Roosevelt. When her press secretary, Sheila Weidenfeld, sought advice from Democrat Liz Carpenter, the National Women's Political Caucus leader who had served as Lady Bird Johnson's press secretary, Carpenter recognized an opportunity. She urged that Mrs. Ford be herself, not let the West Wing dictate to her, and help supporters of the Equal Rights Amendment in the effort to secure its ratification.[6]

Betty Ford's famous openness about undergoing a mastectomy soon after becoming First Lady enhanced her reputation for candor and courage. It encouraged women to be unashamed and less secretive about breast cancer and to take preventive measures. The experience made her more aware of the opportunity provided by her time in the spotlight. She recalled later: "Lying in the hospital, thinking of all those women going for cancer checkups because of me, I'd come to recognize more clearly the power of the woman in the White House . . . a power which could be used to help."[7]

Betty Ford chose to use that power to promote the ERA, which in her view was a long-overdue extension of women's rights. As Gerald Ford took office in 1974, only five more states were needed, but efforts to block ratification had dramatically slowed the ERA bandwagon. To the delight of ERA proponents, the First Lady went right to work, phoning and writing notes to state legislators, and in early 1975 helped tip the scales in favor of ratification in North Dakota. She then called or sent messages to legislators in Missouri, Arizona, North Carolina, Indiana, Nevada, and Phyllis Schlafly's home state of Illinois, laying out the case for the ERA and politely asking for support.[8]

The First Lady's public advocacy brought waves of protest from ERA opponents. One outraged legislator claimed her lobbying was "demeaning" to her position and "sullied the integrity and respectability of the White House." Almost thirteen cubic feet of mail arrived at the White House, more than half of it opposing her efforts on behalf of the ERA. One critic stated, "What right do you have as a representative of all women to contact the legislators and put pressure on them to pass the hated ERA? You are no lady—first, second, or last. Keep your stupid views to yourself from now on." Another wrote: "Our recent history has seen this nation's First Ladies dedicating themselves to restoring the White House; beautifying America; and remaining silent. You, Mrs. Ford, should take an example from this latter group." Schlafly, of course, was livid. Outside the White House, protesters carried placards reading: BETTY FORD, GET OFF THE PHONE. In response, Betty joked that she was proud to be "the only First Lady to ever have a march organized against her."[9]

Schlafly's charges that Betty Ford's lobbying was illegal as well as inappropriate worried some in the West Wing of the White House. Ford's male advisers gingerly pointed out to the president that Mrs. Ford's activities were causing problems. White House counsel Philip Buchen wrote to the First Lady's staff, reminding them "if there were to be activities intended to influence the public" his office should be consulted. After 1975, Betty Ford continued to speak out for the ERA but stopped making phone calls.[10]

The calls seemed to be having little effect. Public opinion polls showed that a majority of Americans (58 percent) still favored the amendment, but legislators were rejecting ratification, and Nebraska and Tennessee had voted to rescind. Of the seventeen states that considered ratification in 1975, only North Dakota ratified. It was some comfort that the defeats were often by very narrow margins. But proponents were shocked and dismayed when state-level equal rights amendments went down in flames that year in two states— New York and New Jersey—that earlier had readily ratified the federal ERA. This was the first major sign that the amendment was in serious trouble.[11]

As Ford contemplated running for president in 1976, some of his advisers worried that the ideas and actions of the First Lady could be a liability. Even Betty Ford began to be concerned about this—particularly after she gave a sensational live interview with Morley Safer on *60 Minutes*. Her candid responses—that she might have tried marijuana had she been young in the 1970s, that she would not be shocked if her eighteen-year-old daughter, Susan, had "an affair"—shocked the nation. In addition, she called *Roe v. Wade* a "great, great decision." Gloria Steinem and other feminists sprang to her defense, but the White House was flooded with letters, most of them negative, expressing outrage about her "gutter type of mentality" that "disgraced" the nation and questioning how President Ford could run the country if he couldn't control his own wife. Director of March for Life Nellie Gray announced plans to picket the White House monthly until the 1976 election to protest the First Lady's comments on *Roe* and abortion.[12]

Betty Ford, however, believed that most Americans were with her. She told the *New York Times*: "It is those who are against [the ERA] who are doing the writing. Those who are for it sit back and say, 'Good for her—push on.'" Soon it appeared she was right. Within a few months of the *60 Minutes* interview, her approval rating had reached 76 percent—far exceeding her husband's—and again she was applauded for her honesty. A Harris Poll revealed she had become "one of the most popular wives of a president to occupy the White House." *Newsweek* named her Woman of the Year, not for embodying the traditional First Lady but for representing a new type of American woman that was coming into her own. Her "sixteen-month saga of courage, candor and exuberance," the *Newsweek* columnist observed rapturously, "is changing the way many Americans think of their First Ladies . . . For a nation schooled in bland, blameless public behavior from its Presidential consorts, the transformation is extraordinary."[13]

Gerald Ford's relatively brief presidency came at a time when the nation faced many challenges. There were rising levels of unemployment and inflation as the Vietnam War wound down to its anguished conclusion. Watergate had shaken American's confidence in the government and in politicians, especially Republicans. Still, the public responded to Ford with relief and genuine enthusiasm. As a congressman he had been popular with politicians on both sides of the aisle. That was one reason Nixon, fearing impeachment, picked him to replace Spiro Agnew as vice president when scandal compelled Agnew to resign.[14]

When he first took office, Ford was also phenomenally popular with the public. However, his pardoning of Nixon brought that popularity to a speedy halt, particularly with Democrats. And his clemency program for draft dodgers alienated many, especially Republicans. Ford's party took a shellacking in the November 1974 elections, giving Democrats huge majorities in Congress. As a result, the president was often at odds with Congress and vetoed a record number of bills.[15]

On women's rights issues, however, Ford and Congress were on the same page. His presidency proved to be a peak period of feminist influence, a golden age for the women's rights movement in which the president, Congress, and the Supreme Court all lent support. Ford appointed twice the number of women Nixon had appointed to positions in his administration. He did not, however, despite his wife's lobbying, appoint a woman to the Supreme Court. But as Congress adopted a stream of profeminist legislation, Ford signed the bills with gusto. There were a few interesting exceptions. In 1975, the Department of Health, Education, and Welfare (HEW) finalized the regulations to implement Title IX, the 1972 congressional action barring sex discrimination in higher education, and colleges were ordered to fund men's and women's athletics equitably. College football coaches protested fiercely, some taking the case to the Oval Office. These included Ford's old friend, Coach Bo Schembechler, a legendary coach at the University of Michigan, Ford's alma mater.[16] Ford, who had been the Wolverines' star center, signed that bill in the dead of night. More than once he thought HEW was going overboard in the quest to root out sex discrimination. When it announced a plan to ban single-sex activities in public schools, Ford intervened to preserve popular activities such as father/son, mother/daughter banquets, angering NOW and earning him rare praise from Phyllis Schlafly.[17]

However, Ford infuriated Schlafly and other right wingers within his party when he selected as his vice president liberal Republican Nelson Rockefeller, a staunch supporter of the women's movement who as governor of New York signed the bill making abortion legal and vetoed a bill to rescind. Richard Viguerie later recalled that Ford's choice of Rockefeller— "the very symbol of everything we conservatives had always opposed"— greatly shocked the right and exposed the "true colors of the so-called 'moderate' Republicans." It was one of the factors that led him and others in what became known as the New Right to begin strategizing, even to consider establishing a third party with Ronald Reagan and George Wallace running on its ticket in 1976—an idea both rejected. Ford later wrote in his autobiography that at the time he "was aware that the more conservative members of our party were pretty upset with me." But he "recognized that these right-wingers would always be on my back." Ford also believed he "had to call the shots as I saw them from the nation's point of view," and was convinced based on his own experience "that trying to satisfy these zealots would doom any general election hopes in 1976."[18]

On women's issues Ford assumed most Americans, including Republicans, shared his views. Conservative women had only recently begun to organize and to many Americans their ideas seemed anachronistic. Liberal and moderate Republicans regarded Phyllis Schlafly as a relic of right wing extremism. As the author of *A Choice Not an Echo*, she had played a crucial role in the GOP's decision to nominate Barry Goldwater, and after he lost to Lyndon Johnson in a landslide in 1964, they associated her and her way of thinking with the party's devastating loss. In the late 1960s, Rockefeller, George Romney, and other more progressive GOP leaders had gone to great lengths to diminish Schlafly's influence within the party, especially in the National Federation of Republican Women (NFRW), after Elly Peterson had sounded the alarm that Schlafly was in line to become its president and that the NFRW was about to be taken over by the "nut fringe" of the party.[19]

The president, the vice president, and the head of the Republican National Committee (RNC), George H. W. Bush, were all allies of Republican feminists in an effort to expand the base of the party by opening it up to increased participation from women, minorities, and youth.[20] At a 1975 GOP strategy summit convened to deal with the fact that the numbers of Americans identifying themselves as Republicans had declined to 18 percent, Gerald Ford famously urged the party to move in this direction. Ford declared: "We must discard the attitude of exclusiveness that has kept the Republican Party's door closed too often while we give speeches about keeping it open. It seems to me we must erect a tent that is big enough for all who care about this great country and believe in the Republican Party enough to work through it for common goals." In sharp contrast, Ronald Reagan insisted that the way to attract a wider following was not to seek diversity but to remain true to conservative principles, stating: "A political party cannot be all things to all people." It "cannot compromise its fundamental beliefs for political expediency . . . [and] by forsaking its basic beliefs, blurring its image so as to be indistinguishable from the opposing party."[21]

Right-wingers in the GOP were again angered when Ford, after naming George Bush to head the U.S. embassy in China, appointed Iowa feminist Mary Louise Smith to replace him as RNC chair—making her the first woman to hold that post in either party. Within the White House some grumbled, including an anonymous staffer who thought the RNC needed to "get back its manhood." William Rusher attacked Ford for his "recent cordial nods toward the black caucus and women's lib." Pat Buchanan—sacked by Ford from his job as speechwriter—proclaimed that the people "are unenthusiastic about militant women."[22] But even the male leaders of a nascent New Right—who would later ride the tide of outrage set in motion by Schlafly and other antifeminist women—were slow to recognize the potential of conservative women and the gender issues about which they were so passionate to mobilize conservatives. Paul Weyrich, who in 1975 founded the Heritage Foundation to promote a conservative agenda, at first saw Schlafly's crusade to defeat the ERA as a "fool's errand."[23]

Ford saw himself as a fiscal conservative, a staunch internationalist, and a moderate on domestic matters, including women's rights. As he took office he had joked that he would be the president "of women's liberationists and male chauvinists and all the rest of us in between." To him, advocacy of women's rights including the ERA and appointment of more women seemed in keeping with the wishes of most Americans as well as the ideals of the Republican Party, the party of Lincoln and freedom and equal opportunity. He presented his support for women's rights as consistent with his support for the civil rights movement.[24] Along with GOP feminists, Ford boasted that his party had been in the forefront for woman suffrage and had backed the ERA for decades while Democrats held back.

On abortion, the president at first said little, acknowledging there was a "wide division of opinion on this issue" and stating simply that "as President, I will abide by the Supreme Court's decision." He declined requests from several members of Congress to meet with abortion opponents, saying he was too busy but they could meet with his staff.[25] As March for Life and other pro-life groups launched ever larger protests in Washington and the press demanded a response, Ford was deliberately vague. He said he did "not believe in abortion on demand" but that women should be able to terminate a pregnancy legally to protect their health or in the case of rape or "any of the other unfortunate things that might happen." In addition, he stated, he personally believed abortion was an issue best left to the states. Ford characterized this as a "moderate position," and was mocked by pro-life leader Nellie Gray, who said, "That presumably translates into just a 'moderate' amount of killing preborn human beings."[26]

At that time, Ford's party had not aligned itself with the emerging pro-life movement. On the contrary, many prominent Republicans, including liberal senators, such as Lowell Weicker, and moderates including Robert Packwood and Howard Baker, were pro-choice, not to mention Barry Goldwater, the hero of the right. Aside from Senator Jesse Helms, pro-life advocates found scant support among GOP elected officials. Early opposition to the legalization of abortion came mostly from Catholics, a group that historically supported Democrats, and many Democratic leaders, even liberals such as Sargent Shriver, George McGovern's running mate in 1972, were anti-abortion. But there were quite a few Catholic conservatives in the GOP who were strongly pro-life and did not trust Ford, especially after he vetoed a bill banning federal funding for abortion—which was then overridden by Congress. After that Ford called for a constitutional amendment to allow the states to set abortion policy.[27]

Catholic leaders, aware that some Republicans hoped to exploit the abortion issue to attract Catholics, sought to persuade this first post-*Roe* president to take a firmer stance against abortion and support a constitutional amendment giving "the unborn" the right to life, a step he did not wish to take. After all, the First Lady, Vice President Rockefeller, and Ford's allies among Republican feminists supported a woman's right to choose abortion. Moreover, polls indicated that despite the growing visibility of pro-life advocates, in 1975 and 1976 a majority of Americans including Republicans saw the abortion issue as one that should be left to a woman and her doctor to decide.[28]

In the mid-1970s women's rights seemed to be ascendant worldwide, encouraged by the United Nations, which had promoted women's rights since Eleanor Roosevelt first insisted they be included in the UN's Universal Declaration of Human Rights. Thus external developments, as much as internal pressures, led President Ford to establish his own presidential commission related to women's rights.

In 1972, the UN announced that 1975 would be International Women's Year. The idea was not only to celebrate women but to improve their lives. Thus the UN called on all members to focus attention on the women of their nations and identify measures needed to enhance their status. The UN also planned a major UN-sponsored International Women's Year Conference held from June 19 to July 2, 1975, in Mexico City, through which to promote collective action on behalf of women around the world and empower them to be active in the cause of world peace. The IWY official symbol, a white dove intersecting with the biological symbol for female symbol on a field of UN blue, signified the goals of peace and equality.[29]

Women's rights advocates in the United States saw IWY 1975 as a great opportunity to advance their cause at home and abroad and to present their nation as in the forefront of this worldwide movement. Though President Nixon had earlier proclaimed that 1975 would be celebrated as International Women's Year in the United States, and the State Department had funded a nongovernment organization, the U.S. Center for IWY, to serve as a clearinghouse for programs within the nation, as Ford took office there was no official IWY Commission.[30]

State Department officials and members of Congress, notably Charles Percy, pressed for the creation of a commission to coordinate U.S. participation, insisting that women's groups were eager for strong American involvement, and that it was important for the image of the U.S. abroad. Ford agreed, and by executive order established the National Commission on the Observance of International Women's Year, the first presidential commission on women appointed since the Kennedy Commission fourteen years earlier. Ford chose Jill Ruckelshaus, who had served in Nixon's Office of Women's Affairs, as the IWY Commission's presiding officer. Mildred Marcy of the State Department served as executive director of the commission and coordinated the work of its staff, the "secretariat."[31]

Ford signed the executive order on January 9, 1975, joined by the vice president and First Lady and with cameras flashing. When he asked Betty if she had "any words of wisdom or encouragement," she responded: "I just want to congratulate you, Mr. President. I am glad to see that you have come a long, long way." Laughing, he said he didn't "know how to take that." The cheery crowd of women surrounding him in a famous photograph taken that day was delighted.[32]

As IWY 1975 got under way, there were hundreds of programs across the nation, sponsored by cities and states, universities and private clubs. Ruth Bacon, head of the U.S. Center for IWY, later boasted that the IWY programs had encouraged women to enter the professions, seek management positions, join the military, and stand up for their rights as homemakers, and also focused attention on problems "people had long avoided confronting" such as rape and domestic violence. Overall, she said, U.S. observance of IWY 1975 "increased public awareness of women's contributions and needs, and of the determination of women to do something about their situation."[33]

At one IWY program, a conference in Cincinnati, Ohio, First Lady Betty Ford urged women to continue to expand their activities while recognizing women's contributions as wives and mothers and "take that 'just' out of 'just a housewife.'" Defying her critics, and urging women to speak their minds, she said: "Why should my husband's job or yours prevent us from being ourselves." "Being ladylike does not require silence." Ford again spoke up for the embattled ERA, lamenting that a "cloud of fear and confusion" had developed that was impeding its progress. She defended change as necessary and positive. "Freedom for women to be what they want to be will help complete the circle of freedom America has been striving for during 200 years," Ford insisted. "As the barriers against freedom for Americans because of race or religion have fallen the freedom of all has expanded. The search for human freedom can never be complete without freedom for women."[34]

Meanwhile, state department officials prepared for IWY activities outside the U.S., particularly the Mexico City conference, eager to seize the opportunities it offered. IWY Commission executive director Mildred Marcy wrote, "if properly understood and responded to by the U.S. Government . . . [the UN's IWY program] can give our nation and the world something to think about as to whether this super-power, the United States, will be perceived both here and abroad as muscle-bound with hoary traditions of status-quo-ism, or, whether, on the eve of our nation's Bicentennial it demonstrates once again a profound responsiveness to a new current which is on the side of constructive change." In the context of the Cold War, the IWY provided the United States an opportunity to demonstrate to "the Third World, the non-aligned, the Communist and socialist countries, to all the so-called 'oppressed peoples'" as well as Western industrialized democracies and Japan, the nation's "willing responsiveness to changing aspirations." Marcy recommended that First Lady Betty Ford and Congresswoman Barbara Jordan, an African American, appear together on the dais, which "would say volumes about the United States in practice and its ideals."[35]

Yet Cold War politics, along with conflicts over racism and Zionism, and differences in goals between developed and developing nations created major problems and high drama before the UN's IWY conference even began. After the United States and its allies objected to proposals to hold the conference within the Soviet bloc, Mexico City emerged as a neutral alternative. When it appeared that the financial challenges of sponsoring the conference might make that impossible, Princess Ashraf Pahlavi, twin sister of the shah of Iran, stepped up with a large contribution to defray expenses.[36] In Washington, apprehensive officials in the White House ended Marcy's hopes of having the First Lady speak at—or even attend—the conference. When Israeli First Lady Leah Rabin stopped in Washington on her way to the conference and was reported to be eager for Betty Ford to go also, they worried she might press the issue.[37]

As the thirteen hundred delegates from 130 nations came together in June 1975, there were additional problems. Many countries had sent official delegations dominated by men, while seven thousand persons—mostly women—who had come to Mexico City to represent nongovernmental organizations were excluded from the proceedings. With Mildred Persinger, an American representing the World YWCA, in the lead, NGO representatives organized an unofficial parallel, the Tribune, that met independently at the same time five miles away.[38] American feminists including Betty Friedan and Bella Abzug played prominent roles at the Tribune where debates were often noisy and contentious. One of the most dramatic exchanges involved Friedan and a Bolivian tin miner's wife who accused North American women of overemphasizing political and economic equity, reproductive rights, and the subordinate position of women in the family when the focus should be on uneven distribution of wealth and the poverty of women in the developing world. Media coverage was another problem. Though serious issues were being discussed, many news outlets preferred to highlight the sporadic conflicts, suggesting women were incapable of running an orderly meeting and cooperating with one another.[39]

There were even problems among the Americans who had come to Mexico City for the conference. Many affiliated solely with non-governmental organizations were frustrated at their inability to participate in the official conference. Some challenged the validity of the official U.S. delegation, claiming it was not sufficiently diverse or representative of American women. But leaders of the U.S. Delegation, including co-chair Patricia Hutar and Jill Ruckelshaus, along with Senator Charles Percy and Representative Bella Abzug, the Congressional Advisers on the delegation, and Ruth Bacon, who acted as an intermediary between the official delegation and the NGOs, worked hard to build bridges. At a session at the American Embassy organized in hopes of dispelling tensions, there was a dramatic, three-hour confrontation between the two groups. According to Jill Ruckelshaus, after a loud, passionate, but honest exchange of ideas that she found exhilarating, the result was greater understanding and hopes for future cooperation.[40]

Despite all the problems, before the two-week meetings were over, much had been accomplished. The Tribune, participants insisted, led participating governments and UN officials to a better understanding of women's issues. The official conference produced a World Plan of Action, soon endorsed by the UN General Assembly, that women across the world could use to strengthen their positions and improve their conditions. The delegates also called upon the UN to declare 1975–1985 a Decade for Women, and to plan a second world conference to be held in Tehran, Iran, in 1980.[41]

The International Women's Year Conference in Mexico City would have a profound impact, enabling women who might never have met one another to exchange ideas and build networks, and inspiring the development of an international women's movement. Many American women, including Bella Abzug, would continue to participate enthusiastically in this budding movement. All of them, including Ruckelshaus—who praised the conference for focusing "the attention of the world on the prejudices and lack of opportunities that face women everywhere" and giving women of the world an opportunity to develop a "solidarity and sense of common interest [that] united women from every country"—went home inspired.[42]

Returning from Mexico City, Jill Ruckelshaus and others on the National Commission on the Observance of International Women's Year enthusiastically resumed the task assigned to them by President Ford: to identify remaining barriers to women's full and equal participation in American society and recommend steps the government should take toward that end.

In signing the executive order, President Ford stated, "I hope the Commission . . . together with leaders of the Congress, will infuse the Declaration of Independence with new meaning and promise for women here and around the world."[43]

Well supported and given considerable authority, the IWY Commission was very much a part of the political establishment.[44] At its first gathering, Vice President Rockefeller emphasized that it had a "unique mandate" from the president that gave it "unprecedented capacity to act," and assured members there was "no pre-arranged agenda" for them to follow. They were expected to set their own goals and move expeditiously to "enunciate a wide range of actions for the President, the Congress, and the Nation to implement."[45] The IWY Commission's charge did not include organizing the state and national conferences, an additional task assigned to the commission later as a result of a bill sponsored by Bella Abzug.

The work done by this important but largely forgotten body reveals much about the status of American women at that point in history and what this group, led by moderate Republican feminists, believed the government should do: retrofit laws and policies to make American society more equal and open to women. Their efforts to build public support for their recommendations by presenting them as reasonable and in keeping with American values and traditions is fascinating, as is their related quest to influence public opinion about feminism itself and correct "misunderstandings."

Like the man who appointed them, the feminists on the IWY Commission were moderates and centrists. They took for granted that there was a growing consensus that every American deserved equal rights without regard to gender or color. But they believed public perceptions of feminism created both by radical proponents and conservative critics needed revision and hoped to enhance the power and influence of the women's rights movement in the United States by re-branding it and making it appear more mainstream.

Confident that the president and the public were with them, as they pressed for further reform, they spoke constantly of the progress already made and emphasized that much of the task ahead had to do with increasing public awareness and stepping up enforcement of reforms already enacted. In that sense, this commission reflected the optimism of the feminists of the early 1970s who saw American women as "on the move."

Jill Ruckelshaus, Ford's carefully selected choice for chair of the commission, was an ideal candidate for the position. One of the most prominent women's rights supporters in his party, she was a founder and board member of the National Women's Political Caucus. A graduate of Indiana University, with an M.A. in English literature from Harvard, she had spent several years working in Europe before teaching English at a small Indiana college. She met and married William Ruckelshaus after his wife died giving birth to twins, then they had three more children. After he was elected to Congress and they moved from Indiana to Washington, Jill Ruckelshaus devoted herself to raising the children while at the same time becoming more involved in Republican politics. She had been a star among Republican women since 1968 when her husband was prevented at the last moment from addressing the Republican National Convention and turned the task over to Jill who, according to the press, "wowed them."[46]

This intelligent, attractive, well-connected mother of five, with extensive experience as an advocate for women and a moderate Republican, was the perfect person to head a commission that sought to advance feminist goals in a way that would strengthen—and not undercut—public support for women's rights and for the president who had given it this opportunity.

Jill Ruckelshaus was clearly a favorite with the press that never tired of pointing out how she differed from stereotypical feminists. "Lady of Liberty," a feature article on Ruckelshaus in the *Saturday Evening Post,* had emphasized her skills as a speaker, "by turns thoughtful, inspired, and forceful" with an "intellectual commitment to women's rights that is absolute," but "unhampered by the personal frustrations which—rightly or wrongly—seem to motivate so many of the more ardent women's libbers." In addition, with her "disarming sense of humor, a rarity among leaders of women's lib," she was the most "refreshing and perhaps the most effective figure" in the "increasingly significant movement for improving women's place in society." It did not hurt that her husband, one of the heroes of the Saturday Night Massacre, was regarded as the Mr. Clean of a party trying to shed the corrupt image left over from Watergate. Many also praised Jill Ruckelshaus for her looks. Some called her "the Gloria Steinem of the Republican Party"—including Phyllis Schlafly, though she did not intend it as a compliment.[47]

Like the IWY Commission chair, the thirty-one women and four men appointed by the president as members were well-known, much admired, and accomplished individuals from a variety of backgrounds, racial and ethnic groups, and religious persuasions. All of them, plus the two men and two women chosen by Congress as its representatives on the commission—Senators Charles Percy (R-Illinois) and Birch Bayh (D-Indiana) and Congresswomen Margaret Heckler (R-Massachusetts) and Bella Abzug (D-New York)—were women's rights supporters. Some of the Catholics on the commission, including Heckler, opposed abortion. Their minority viewpoint on that issue which most commission members regarded as satisfactorily settled was acknowledged respectfully later in the final report.[48] But there were no ERA opponents: since commission leaders saw women who opposed the ERA as misguided or misinformed they did not find it appropriate or necessary to include them.

Commission members were an all-star cast of Americans who lent their expertise and reputations to the cause.[49] The group included: Hanna Holborn Gray, a distinguished historian, then acting president of Yale University and later president of the University of Chicago; Barbara Bergmann, a professor of economics at the University of Maryland and an expert on discrimination against women and blacks; and Richard Cornuelle, author of books on social theory who argued that the women's movement was a primary example of unmanaged social change.

There were several distinguished journalists appointed, including Helen K. Copley, publisher of the *San Diego Union* and *Evening Tribune,* and director of the Inter-American Press Association; Lenore Hershey, the editor of the *Ladies' Home Journal*; and Patricia Carbine, formerly editor of *Look* and *McCall's* magazines and current editor in chief of *Ms.* There were also celebrities with the potential to broaden popular support, among them Alan

Alda, enormously popular for his role as Hawkeye Pierce in the popular television show *M*A*S*H* and an avid ERA supporter. Unlike some of the celebrity appointees, including Katharine Hepburn, he would play an active role. There were other lesser-known individuals from many parts of the nation including several corporate executives, and Winnfield Dunn, just finishing his term as governor of Tennessee.

Republican feminists Ford appointed to the commission were stars within their party including Patricia Hutar, cochair of the U.S. delegation to the Mexico City IWY, president of the National Federation of Republican Women, and U.S. representative to the UN Commission on the Status of Women; Anne Armstrong, former counselor to Nixon and Ford, and ambassador to Great Britain; Mary Louise Smith, chair of the Republican National Committee; Audrey Colom, president of the National Women's Political Caucus; and Ella Grasso, governor of Connecticut and the first woman in American history to be elected governor of a state in her own right. Ford also chose veteran feminist politician Martha Griffiths, a Democrat, who had retired from Congress in 1974, having served since 1955.

The IWY Commission also benefitted from the experience of women who had served on the previous presidential commissions on women. Virginia Allan, who had chaired Nixon's task force, was the State Department official most involved with the IWY program. As before, Allan was pleased to have the well-respected Catherine East serving as deputy to coordinator Mildred Marcy.[50]

By 1975, East, like Friedan, had long since lost influence with NOW, and most NOW members had probably never heard of East despite her crucial role in founding the organization. But in the 1970s as in the 1960s, she was the person to whom many feminists turned for information on Washington affairs from an insider's perspective. East and other members of the IWY's secretariat, on loan from other federal agencies, brought to the IWY Commission a wealth of expertise regarding federal programs. In the IWY they saw a great opportunity to forward the goals laid out for a dozen years by government commissions on women.[51]

As a centrist organization presenting feminism as mainstream, the IWY Commission drew criticism from women on the right and the left. Schlafly denounced it as a "tax-financed gimmick" through which feminists promoted "their special interests" under "the White House patronage of President and Mrs. Ford."[52] On the other hand, criticism came from leaders of the Women's Action Alliance (WAA), an umbrella organization created in 1971 by Gloria Steinem and others to coordinate the work of long-standing women's organizations and new feminist groups, including ones to advance the rights of minority women, welfare rights recipients, and lesbians. They held that that nongovernmental organizations, working together through the WAA, should formulate the U.S. agenda related to International Women's Year rather than a government-controlled entity appointed by a man and likely to be too conservative and cautious.[53]

When Ford first appointed the IWY Commission, the WAA moved quickly to prepare an agenda, the National Women's Agenda (NWA) they hoped the IWY Commission would adopt and present in Mexico City. They sought a meeting with President Ford to ask that he accept the NWA, but he declined, saying he had faith in the group he had appointed and would await its proposals. After the Mexico City conference, WAA head Ruth Abram spoke before the IWY Commission, continuing to promote their agenda and suggesting that the commission subcontract its work to the WAA. Ruckelshaus declined, though said she would welcome WAA input as the commission did its job.[54]

From the beginning the Ford IWY Commission solicited the input of nongovernmental organizations (NGOs) and all of its meetings were open to the public. One of the Ford IWY Commission's first steps was to hold a meeting where over two hundred invited NGOs discussed issues to be addressed by the commission. After the Mexico City conference, they also had the World Plan of Action that influenced their agenda; they considered it their mandate to implement its spirit and intent.[55]

The IWY Commission organized itself into thirteen committees including one on the Equal Rights Amendment cochaired by Congresswoman Heckler and Alan Alda and announced its determination to secure ratification of the ERA at the "earliest possible moment." Commission members viewed the proposed amendment as an important symbol as well as a means of realizing women's equality. Expecting attacks from ERA opponents, the commission requested—and received—a ruling from the comptroller general that working to educate the public on the advantages of the proposed amendment did not violate federal laws regarding government agencies.[56] The commission also aided the ERA effort by serving as a "convener and catalyst" for creation of a new bipartisan umbrella organization, "ERAmerica," a separate entity from the IWY Commission, to coordinate the activities of over a hundred groups working for ratification. They selected as cochairs two seasoned politicians much loved in their respective parties, Republican Elly Peterson of Michigan and Democrat Liz Carpenter of Texas, both active in the NWPC.[57]

Besides the one on the ERA, other committees paralleled many of the target areas outlined in the Mexico City plan: arts and humanities, child development, enforcement of the laws, government organization structure, the homemaker, international interdependence, media, reproductive freedom, special problems of women, UN conventions, women in employment, women in power. Committees were chaired by commission members, but included a number of "public members" with relevant expertise. All engaged in systematic research, including sponsoring open meetings where they heard testimony from expert witnesses and, in some cases, held hearings to solicit input from the public.[58]

As they worked, the committees benefitted from research conducted by the Interdepartmental Task Force, a parallel body to the commission and authorized in the same executive order. Consisting of two representatives from each of fifty major federal agencies and departments, its charge was to assess the impact on women of the U.S. government's ongoing policies and programs relevant to the World Plan of Action and develop plans for improvement.[59]

After concluding its research, on July 1, 1976, the IWY Commission presented the president with a 382-page report entitled *". . . To Form a More Perfect Union . . ." Justice for American Women*. Taking its title from the preamble to the Constitution, the report declared that securing equal rights for women was a "logical and overdue step toward our historical commitment stated in that preamble."[60]

Written for a general audience, the report presented social change as desirable and insisted that federal policy should be informed by solid research rather than emotional reaction or fear. The largest section of the report was called "Today's Realities," designed to "give readers a sense of some of the barriers that keep women from participating in American life as full partners," and to pave the way for the 115 recommendations and supporting data that followed.[61]

Rather than radical or impractical, commission members believed their proposals were all "of obvious benefit to women" and "reasonably realistic and capable of being achieved." Acknowledging that the United States was well ahead of other nations in the march toward justice for women, they emphasized "the enforcement and/or revision of laws already in existence" and "the modification of attitudes and policies that reinforce traditional stereotypes about women."[62]

The report addressed all aspects of women's lives and what government could do to improve them. Like earlier commissions on women, Ford's IWY Commission placed a heavy emphasis on ending sex bias in education and employment. On the latter, they insisted that the "now widely accepted" concept of "equal pay for equal work" be expanded to include "equal pay for work of comparable value."[63]

Other concerns addressed included the dearth of women among the nation's "power brokers." The commission suggested steps to get more women elected and appointed, including to the judiciary, and urged unions to take steps to bring women into decision-making positions. It also discussed ways of preventing violence against women and reforming laws and policies regarding rape, and addressed the problems of older women, rural women, and women who faced "double burdens" because of age or race as well as gender.

In its report, the commission also called for changes in the media portrayal of gender roles and rigorous enforcement by the Federal Communication Commission of nondiscrimination laws in TV and radio. The report criticized the media for giving equal credence to those who deliberately misrepresented the ERA—citing Phyllis Schlafly by name as an example. It recapped Jill Ruckelshaus's speech at the National Press Club intended to draw attention to "the imbalance of media coverage that gives the same weight to the opinions of the Stop ERA forces" as to the work of experts including the majority report of the Senate Judiciary Committee on the amendment. It also included excerpts from her article in *The Bulletin of the American Society of Newspaper Editors* criticizing papers "which have not done an in-depth new analysis of ERA and which, in ignorance or under a false assumption of fairness, have perpetuated inaccurate information spread by ERA opponents."[64]

Worried about discrimination holding back women's progress in the arts and humanities, the commission suggested blind competitions. It recommended that federal agencies such as the National Endowment for the Arts or the National Endowment for the Humanities be prohibited from discriminating against women.[65] In all cases the recommendations were calculated to appear reasonable to a public they believed supported equality for women and would respond to the recommendations if they were presented in a logical, nonthreatening way.

Toward that end, promotion of change was accompanied by affirmations of respect for homemakers and the importance of families. IWY commissioners and staff were aware that feminists were accused of disdaining homemakers and that ERA opponents insisted homemakers had all the protections they needed. Many also believed along with Catherine East that the women's movement would never be able to make further progress or retain its gains without convincing "a substantial number of homemakers that they too are discriminated against and have much to gain from it." At East's urging the IWY Commission hired women attorneys to produce reports on "The Legal Status of Homemakers" in their states, reports that would gradually become available to the public over the next few years and provided clear evidence that homemakers were not as protected as ERA opponents claimed.[66] The section of the report produced by the Homemaker Committee chaired by Martha Griffiths and written largely by East pointed out that homemakers made "invaluable contributions to the welfare and economic stability of our Nation," but received "no health, retirement, or unemployment benefits as a result of their labor, which left them vulnerable."[67]

To address this situation, the commission called for reform of state divorce laws, and pointed out the need for more equitable division of property, maintenance, child custody, and support and enforcement of support orders. Such laws, it insisted, should be based on the principle that a homemaker's contribution is equal in value to the contribution of the spouse who works outside the home. In addition, regarding social security, homemakers should be covered in their own right. The commission also recommended that taxation on transfers of property between husband and wife (inheritance) at death be eliminated. Finally, noting that increasing numbers of women became "displaced homemakers" in their "middle years" and left without any source of financial security after divorce or death of their husbands, they recommended programs to help them through a readjustment period and become self-sufficient.[68] The part of the report on "Today's Realities" included a section, "ERA—Let the Record Speak," showing that in the fifteen states already prohibiting sex discrimination in their constitutions, homemakers had been the chief beneficiaries.[69]

Eager to assist women who were mothers and men who were fathers, the commission recommended that federal policies be adjusted to correspond to new realities regarding child care. Government-supported child care, it emphasized, would serve the interests of women, children, families, and society. Insisting that "all working families, not only the poor and near-poor, should have quality child care services available," and emphasizing the national shortage of quality programs, the commission recommended that the federal government "assume the major role in directing and providing for universal voluntary child-development programs."

Such a step, the IWY Commission declared, would provide greater educational opportunities for children while the government would "avoid the cost of neglect." In addition, it would provide "real freedom of choice in life style for women." Implicit was the idea that the trend toward more mothers working outside the home was irreversible—and liberating for women. But the commission insisted that the impact on children need not be negative if the government stepped up to provide high-quality day care, which could be as good as or perhaps even better than care by mothers in the home.[70]

The commission strongly supported women's reproductive rights. This included access to legal abortion, which it presented as having widespread support from the public. It urged all branches of government to comply with the Supreme Court's decision. But it emphasized that the incidence of abortion could and should be lessened by preventive measures and endorsed family planning and sex education. It urged federal, state, and local governments to make available all methods of family planning to women who were unable to take advantage of private facilities. The commission was also concerned about women who were eager to have children and having problems and endorsed new research to aid women having difficulty conceiving. It also insisted on protection of women against involuntary sterilization.[71]

All members of the IWY Commission were strongly committed to the Equal Rights Amendment and, in the report, called for its ratification as a means of promoting and guaranteeing full equality for women in American life. The amendment was necessary, they believed, since—as currently interpreted by the Supreme Court—the U.S. Constitution did not provide women with full equality under the law. The report stated that while the women's movement, including the effort to ratify the ERA, had led to positive changes, this did not reduce the need for the amendment. Many of the new laws were state laws, not universal, and "all of the laws could be easily changed, and new threats to equality of rights under the law could be mounted under new guises if a guarantee is not enshrined in the Constitution."[72]

The commission insisted that ratification of the ERA would, with few exceptions, prevent federal and state governments from enacting laws or adopting official policies that made distinctions based on sex. It would provide leverage for further improvements in domestic relations and property law that would fulfill the commission's goal of making marriage "a full partnership." Noting that the amendment had already been approved by thirty-four states, the commission urged ratification in time for the bicentennial celebration in 1976.[73]

Finally, the committee on International Interdependence, referring to the goals enunciated in the World Plan of Action, offered recommendations intended to empower women to play a greater role in making and carrying out U.S. foreign policy. These included affirmative action to increase the numbers of women in agencies with international responsibilities, changes in the State Department and U.S. foreign policy structure (such as upgrading the Office of International Women's Programs to that of Special Advisor for International Women's Programs to the Assistant Secretary), and encouraging close cooperation between the government and NGOs dedicated to improving the status of women.[74]

President Ford received the report at a highly publicized ceremony at the White House on July 1, 1976.[75] This took place even as Ford was engaged in a heated battle with Ronald Reagan for the Republican nomination for president and was trying to appease social conservative critics whose rising strength within the GOP had now become clear. Ford had been forced to make concessions—even to dump Nelson Rockefeller as his running mate—in a vain attempt to prevent a challenge from the right.[76]

At the GOP national convention that summer, feminist Republicans managed to defeat an effort by Schlafly forces to get the party to drop its support for the ERA, but were appalled that their party would even consider reversing its long-standing position on the amendment. Audrey Rowe Colom, then president of the National Women's Political Caucus, was alarmed at the show of strength by women she saw as "to the right of Genghis Khan."[77]

For Elly Peterson, it was a painful reminder. "The right wing," she said, "was so unbending, so grim, and it was a reliving of the agony of 1964 as far as I was concerned." Peterson and other feminists were becoming increasingly frustrated and angry at Phyllis Schlafly though grudgingly recognizing the need to take her more seriously. Writing to Tanya Melich, Peterson said she was sick and tired of approaching Phyllis Schlafly and "her troops with reason and have them counteract us with lies—emotion, etc." Peterson thought "it would be the saddest mistake in the world to go backward [on the ERA] and just what this beaten up party does not need."[78]

In a statement Elly Peterson prepared for the platform committee, she said sarcastically (apparently in reference to Schlafly), "We do, of course, understand that sometimes people who cannot be elected to party or government positions need a platform for their views. Too, we understand the political significance of the opposition. But we find it discouraging and disheartening that these people, labeling themselves Republicans, contribute to the malaise affecting this nation by stationing themselves" against the president, governors, and members of Congress who supported the ERA. In the end, Peterson telephoned Ford and persuaded him to intercede on the feminists' behalf and the ERA remained in the GOP platform.[79]

On the abortion issue, however, Schlafly was gaining support from Republicans who saw an opportunity to bring Catholics into the GOP fold. In the summer of 1976, after Democratic feminists had gotten their party to include pro-choice statements in its platform and as Reagan appealed to pro-life delegates to help him upset Ford, strategists on the Ford team, including Senator Bob Dole, tried to counteract Reagan's strategy by accepting an anti-abortion plank in the platform. The plank, drafted by Reagan champion Senator Jesse Helms, called for a constitutional amendment to protect "unborn children." Twenty-eight GOP feminists signed a statement against the plank but the Republican Women's Task Force chose not to object, fearful that a fight over abortion would galvanize conservatives and they would lose the fight to keep the ERA in the platform. This strong pro-life plank was not what Ford wanted but he felt he was forced to accept it to gain the nomination.[80]

In the general election, both Carter and Ford ran as candidates personally opposed to abortion, but with the human life amendment in the GOP platform, pro-life leaders went for Ford. Three of them—including Mildred Jefferson, president of the National Right to Life Committee—issued a joint statement denouncing the Democratic platform and saying: "If the candidates of the Republican Party honor the plank in their platform that supports the enactment of a right-to-life amendment, the Republican Party will constitute the Party of Life."[81]

Yet, despite making these major concessions to the growing power of the right within his party, Gerald Ford never publicly criticized the National Commission on the Observance of IWY—or his wife—for embracing positions that were anathema to social conservatives. Nor did he try to disassociate himself from advocacy of women's rights.

During the primary Ford saw Reagan's increasingly conservative positions on women's issues, scorned by feminists, as a liability for his challenger. In the general election, he competed with Jimmy Carter to be perceived as the candidate most supportive of women and women's rights. Ford accused

Carter of being insincere in his stated commitment to women's rights: Ford's opposition research charged that Carter had appointed few women while governor of Georgia and two of the appointments went to his mother! When Carter criticized Ford for not getting the ERA ratified, Ford responded that Carter had not even been able to deliver Georgia—which remained an unratified state.[82]

As President Ford accepted the IWY Commission's report at the July 1, 1976, White House ceremony, he not only praised its work but took a bold step to show that his endorsement was not an empty one. In front of two hundred onlookers, he ordered a review of all federal laws to identify and eliminate those that unjustifiably discriminated on the basis of sex. Well aware that since the March 1975 victory in North Dakota, the ERA had won no new states despite the Fords' support, he declared: "Injustice cannot wait upon politics, nor upon the lengthy public discussion which has already delayed ratification of this constitutional amendment."[83]

After the GOP convention, Ford tapped Elly Peterson to head up People for Ford, a special program to rally women as well as minorities and young people behind his candidacy.[84] Republican feminists, including those disappointed by Ford's concessions to the pro-life forces, worked hard for his reelection, hoping to withstand the conservative surge within the party and to make even greater progress in a second Ford administration.[85]

Ford's staff prepared a *'76 Fact Book* boasting of his strong support "for greater opportunity for American women," including aiding the ERA effort, establishing the IWY Commission, directing the attorney general "to review the entire United States Code to determine the need for revising sex-based provisions," declaring his determination to "eliminate all vestiges of discrimination within the Federal government, appointing a Special Assistant for Women to maintain open liaison with over 300 women's organizations with a combined membership of over 100 million," and increasing the number of women in high-level positions in the federal government to a point "higher than all previous administrations."[86]

Republican feminists' support became all the more important as their Democratic counterparts rallied around Carter. Feminist Democrats were particularly critical of Ford for failing to appoint a woman to the Supreme Court (despite Betty's efforts). And they were eager to get someone in the White House more responsive to *them*. Working through the Women's Action Alliance (WAA), the feminist umbrella organization that had been disappointed by Ford's and Ruckelshaus's responses when they approached them in 1975 about their National Women's Agenda (NWA), Bella Abzug, Gloria Steinem, and other feminist Democrats gave Carter a boost.[87]

In early October 1976, only a month before the election, the WAA held a conference in Washington promoting the NWA and urging women's organizations to unite behind it. Candidate Jimmy Carter was invited and took the opportunity to deliver the major policy speech of his campaign on women's issues, endorsing many of their recommendations. WAA leader Ruth Abram stated that Carter's appearance marked "the first time that a presidential candidate has felt he had to respond to a women's agenda." In his thirty-minute address, Carter accused Ford and the GOP of neglecting women's issues, which he said was a "terrible indictment of the Ford and Nixon administrations." He expressed his "complete sympathy" with the National Women's Agenda, promising if elected, to take strong action on behalf of women in "politics, education, employment, health care, housing and justice," and to make more appointments of women to high office, along with vigorous efforts to ratify the ERA.[88]

As the election approached, Ford gained on Carter, but lost narrowly by the closest electoral college margin in sixty years. Later, some criticized Ford strategists for failing to put the First Lady on the stump during the general election campaign when she had proven to be wildly popular with audiences during the primary. Some analysts said it was perhaps the biggest mistake of the campaign. Elly Peterson was furious with the conservative men on Ford's campaign staff, especially the Reagan supporters who had come on board after the convention and had no interest in cultivating minorities or women's rights supporters and undermined her efforts at every turn. Indeed, Peterson and Melich suspected them of deliberately sabotaging the campaign in the hopes a defeat would position Reagan for a victory in 1980.[89]

Republican women's rights advocates were convinced that Ford's too-conservative platform hurt him. Melich pointed out that "the boost that an anti-choice stance was supposed to bring in Democratic states with large Catholic ethnic populations did not materialize." Carter won 57 percent of the Catholic vote and Ford 53 percent of Protestants. In addition, Carter, a southerner and a religious conservative, "destroyed the right's southern strategy, winning all of the border and southern states other than Virginia."[90]

Remarkably, considering his extremely unpopular pardoning of Nixon, and the damage done by the infighting within the GOP during the primary, Ford almost won. In this almost victory, women played a big role. A majority of women, 51 percent, supported Ford compared to 48 percent for Carter. In

1976, no one yet spoke of a "gender gap," but as Melich later pointed out, that election "showed the first glimmer of a women's voting consciousness separate from that of their male family members, which in pre-seventies voting studies had been a key indicator of how women would vote."[91]

Women's political activism was on the rise. More women were donating to campaigns and running themselves. Women remained appallingly under-represented in elected office, but there were small gains. The number of women state legislators rose to 9.1 percent from 8 percent in 1974, and two more Democratic women joined the sixteen women incumbents in Congress, five of whom were Republicans. Many women ran and lost, often in "no-win" districts, leading Melich and other NWPC feminists in both parties to be encouraged. In Massachusetts, feminists persuaded voters to adopt a state ERA. In Colorado, they defeated an attempt to repeal the state ERA adopted in 1972.[92]

As for the National Commission on the Observance of International Women's Year, after the election it continued to exist, indeed to begin planning the state and territorial IWY meetings, with the Ford feminists still at the helm. Back in July, Jill Ruckelshaus had resigned as presiding officer. Some later speculated it was because her husband was being considered as Ford's vice presidential running mate.[93] In addition, she had completed the task she was appointed to accomplish. Ruckelshaus was replaced with commission member Elizabeth Athanasakos, a former judge from Florida who had served on Nixon's task force. Mildred Marcy, Catherine East, and most of the staff stayed on, providing continuity.

The commission began the task of implementing Abzug's bill conscientiously but with a degree of trepidation.[94] Many of the Ford appointees as well as some IWY staff members had serious doubts about the wisdom of holding the IWY conferences which were mandated by an act of Congress in 1975. The conferences had not been their idea; they were the brainchild of Democratic congresswoman Bella Abzug, with whom they had not always seen eye to eye.

On the surface, Abzug and the Ford feminists got along swimmingly, but there were problems. Just as the last subcommittee, the Government Organization Structure Committee that Abzug chaired, was presenting its work and it was time to polish the recommendations for the final report, she suddenly introduced an additional recommendation. She proposed the creation of a cabinet-level position specifically to address women's issues, one that would encompass many existing federal programs from other agencies such as the Women's Bureau and the U.S. Commission on Civil Rights. Senator Percy put forward a different proposal, calling for an office for women's affairs beneath cabinet level—a plan many saw as more attainable.

The official records of the IWY Commission note only that there was lengthy debate, that the Abzug proposal narrowly passed, and that afterward some commission members requested that—given the controversy—the final report include a full explanation of the rationale for its adoption. However, a clipping from Vera Glaser's Offbeat Washington political gossip column revealed more.

The column, "Bella's Bellows Fan the Flames," disclosed that the debate over the Abzug proposal was not only lengthy but also heated. Unidentified individuals who had been present recalled—off the record—that Abzug had been rude and hostile to Percy. In fact, they said, they had never witnessed a member of Congress speaking so harshly to another, and that Abzug had spoken to Percy using the language of "a fishwife." In addition, Abzug had denounced the professional staff members of the commission as "Republican finks." Staff member Shelah Leader, who witnessed the incident, later recalled it as "shocking," adding that Percy "was too much of a gentleman to respond."[95] Glaser went on to criticize Abzug pointedly, saying that in her three terms in Congress "Abzug has shown she can get things moving in the molasses patch of Capitol Hill," but "she vents so much personal abuse in the process that she has alienated many—including feminists—who once considered her a hero."[96]

Abzug, one of the Democratic feminists critical of Ford, was a founder and leader in the Women's Action Alliance, the group that protested having the U.S. Plan of Action created by a government commission appointed by a man. Even as the IWY Commission was being established in January 1975, Abzug introduced a bill calling for state and national conferences to take place in 1976 so women outside the government could be involved in recommending future policy. In September 1975, after having been inspired by participation in the Mexico City IWY conference and the active role played there by nongovernmental organizations, Abzug again pressed for legislation calling for the conferences. Congresswoman Patsy Mink (D-Hawaii) introduced a similar bill, but she and several other women in the House of Representatives united behind Abzug's proposal. According to the bill, the government would continue to sponsor the gatherings, but they would be open to all, giving all women the opportunity to participate in developing the National Plan of Action. In addition, the bill called for extending the life of the commission in order for it to handle arrangements for the conferences that were to take place during the bicentennial year.[97]

At first Ford Commission leaders were less than enthusiastic in response. Though Abzug's proposed legislation would significantly alter and expand the duties of the IWY Commission, they had no input in drafting the bill. Abzug scheduled a hearing on the bill and, a week before the hearing, sent a letter to the IWY Commission asking for "prompt advice" on her testimony. She also invited Jill Ruckelshaus to testify. Ruckelshaus and the IWY staff were concerned that Abzug wanted to hold the conferences in 1976, which would give little time for preparation, especially since the commission would be hard at work researching and writing the recommendations as originally directed. In addition, since the purpose of the meetings would be to make recommendations for federal action, they duplicated the commission's efforts.[98]

And there were other concerns. State meetings open to the public would be difficult to control and might create political "cross currents" in an election year. Catherine East worried that the federal funding Abzug proposed in her bill would "stir up protests by Schlafly and ERA opponents." Though feminists had been holding smaller conferences without money for years, this massive allocation was likely to bring unaccustomed pressures and public attention. By this time East, who once found it hard to believe that people would take Schlafly with her "wild" views seriously, had developed a healthy respect for Schlafly's abilities after debating her on the ERA several times, and "realizing she was a brilliant woman." However Abzug persisted, fourteen congresswomen signed on as cosponsors, and the commission leaders fell into line, not wanting to present the president as opposed or feminists as divided.[99]

Through the fall, the proposed legislation many spoke of as "Bella's bill" encountered strong opposition in Congress. Congressman Henry Hyde (R-IL), Senator Jesse Helms (R-NC), and other social conservatives inside and outside of Congress predicted that conferences organized by the feminist-dominated IWY Commission would discriminate against conservative women. Not only conservatives but also representatives of southern states such as Congresswoman Lindy Boggs of Louisiana raised this issue, forcing Abzug to affirm that all women would have the opportunity to participate. Abzug also had to promise that the commission would not be involved in any lobbying for specific legislation, including the ERA. Abzug's bill, which failed on the first attempt, was eventually approved in late December 1975. In the spring, Congress voted on funding of the conferences in the midst of more pressure from conservatives. The $5 million allocated was half of what Abzug proposed.[100]

The Ford administration did, however, insist that the IWY conferences be put off until after the 1976 election. Thus, when Carter defeated Ford, he inherited the IWY program, which was clearly controversial long before the first conference began.

CHAPTER 4

What's Wrong with "Equal Rights" for Women?

The "women's lib" movement is *not* an honest effort to secure better jobs for women who want or need to work outside the home. This is just the superficial sweet-talk to win broad support for a radical "movement." Women's lib is a total assault on the role of the American woman as wife and mother, and on the family as the basic unit of society.

—PHYLLIS SCHLAFLY, *PHYLLIS SCHLAFLY REPORT*,
FEBRUARY 1972

The ascendance of the women's rights movement within the national governing establishment ignited a firestorm among women deeply invested in traditional women's roles. As feminists gained support and scored many victories, these women organized to make it clear that "women's libbers" did not speak for them.

In the 1960s, conservative women had watched the rise of the feminist movement with curiosity and concern. Like feminists, they were well aware of the rapid and far-reaching changes in American society that were affecting the lives of American women. But unlike feminists such as the members of the IWY National Commission, who viewed the changes as creating new opportunities and urged reform of laws and customs to fit "Today's Realities," conservative women perceived them—particularly the movement of women into the workforce—as losses for women, families, and society.[1]

The women's rights movement was more a result than a cause of these changes. Many women—whether they were working to augment husbands' incomes, self-supporting, or seeking career satisfaction—had grown frustrated by the rampant gender discrimination they faced in their jobs and the lack of opportunities for advancement. These frustrations, plus the growing dissatisfaction of more affluent women who remained in the home but were unhappy with their circumscribed existence, fueled the ascendant women's movement.[2] Yet conservatives blamed feminists for encouraging the mass movement of women into the workforce as well as dissatisfaction among homemakers and a whole host of other social problems from rising divorce rates to juvenile delinquency, which they attributed to women's abandonment of traditional responsibilities.

Rosemary Thomson, one of the primary leaders of the women who organized to oppose feminism in the 1970s, blamed "women's libbers" for leading women astray at great cost to themselves, their families, and the nation. In her book, *The Price of LIBerty*, written just after the 1977 battle to control the IWY conferences, she discussed the rise of the women's movement and why and how "traditionally minded" women worked so hard to defeat it. Thomson recalled that, in the 1960s, growing weary of the "popular assertion that women's roles are changing," she and others began to ask "the burning question, *who* is changing women's roles?" Thomson placed the blame on misguided feminists, who led women astray by promising "'liberation' from the plan God established for the family" with disastrous results. "The price of LIBerty," she wrote, "may be as costly as the one paid by our 'foremother' in the Garden of Eden."[3]

In the early 1970s, as all three branches of the federal government began to embrace the feminist message, critics of the women's rights movement were increasingly alarmed. Their alarm soon led to action. Conservative women mobilized to oppose continued concessions to feminists, to protest the growing influence of feminism and feminists within the government, and to offer an "alternative to 'women's lib.'"[4]

Thomson, a homemaker, mother of two sons, and former teacher from Morton, Illinois, expressed the frustrations of "traditionally minded" women. It was one thing, she said, to hear feminists trying to sell their message, but quite another thing to see so many women—and the government—buying it. For years "women's lib" had "fed American females this steady diet through education, women's magazines, television and movies:

women must work outside the home for pay, wives should be economically independent, divorce and 'living together' are acceptable. Children are burdensome so the Planned Parenthood Association teaches population control through contraceptives or abortion." Yet, Thomson recalled, in the 1960s few conservatives took the feminist movement seriously. "It was largely ignored by Christians, tolerantly joked about by average citizens."[5]

It was soon clear that "women's lib" was "not a laughing matter," Thomson stated. It "steamrolled into the '70s leaving in its wake burned bras, church veils, and sometimes husbands" as women fell victim to its false promises. "What young mother, wearied of diapers, toy-strewn floors, and lack of money did not read *The Feminine Mystique* in the 60s and exclaim, 'Betty Friedan understands me!'" "What middle-aged housewife, bored with an empty nest, did not theorize, 'Liberation must be the answer!'" To Thomson, a conservative Presbyterian, it seemed that everyone "not firmly grounded in Biblical principles" was accepting the notion "that women were oppressed by the facts of life, society and even the church." Intellectuals, educators, and even religious leaders were embracing the feminist message, along with "politicians who fancied expedient vote-getting."[6]

According to Thomson, Nixon's Task Force on Women's Rights and Responsibilities was the first clear signal that political leaders were "capitulating" to the demands of the feminist movement. The task force's report endorsed proposals that Thomson viewed as fundamental affronts to conservative beliefs. Afterward, conservative women began to pay more attention to the other federal and state commissions that had been established in the 1960s and were disturbed by what they found. In Thomson's words, "Without investigating the real motives of Women's Lib, Federal and state government dutifully doled out public funds to establish commissions on the status of women." To make matters worse, "instead of appointing ordinary homemakers and working women to assess their own concerns, female executives in government and politics were named." With the release of the task force's "little-heralded report," she wrote, it seemed clear that the "attack on family life and the traditional moral values of America's spiritual heritage had begun."[7]

To Thomson, the stream of congressional acts putting feminist proposals into practice offered additional proof that the American family was under assault from the federal government. In Thomson's estimation, passage of the Comprehensive Child Development Act of 1971 to establish publicly funded child care, was particularly sobering.[8] While feminists hailed it as the first major effort since World War II to respond to the nation's child care needs, she and other conservatives saw it as a horrifying first step on the slippery slope toward a godless government invasion of the family like that in the U.S.S.R. Opponents flooded President Nixon with letters of protest, pressuring Nixon—wavering on whether or not to sign the bill—to veto it. In his message justifying the veto, Nixon echoed their rhetoric, saying the bill threatened family stability by encouraging women to work outside the home and by committing "the vast moral authority of the National Government to the side of communal modes of child-rearing against the family-centered approach"—a "long leap into the dark." The veto message, written by speechwriter Patrick Buchanan, who hoped to bury permanently the idea of a national child-care entitlement, was deliberately crafted to make supporting expanded child care politically dangerous.[9]

Few knew that a young woman, Connaught "Connie" Marshner, a conservative Catholic with firm convictions but little political experience, was behind the letter-writing campaign. Marshner would soon become a key figure and the highest ranking woman at the New Right think tank the Heritage Foundation, founded in 1973. But in 1971 she was a recent graduate of the University of South Carolina and an active member of the staunchly conservative Young Americans for Freedom (YAF), founded by William F. Buckley in 1960.

Marshner had just arrived in Washington, D.C. As she later recalled, unable to get a teaching position she accepted a job as secretary to the editor of the YAF magazine, the *New Guard*. Marshner learned of the Child Development Act when her boss gave it to her to type. Instead, she took it home and "wrote the fact sheet on it," the "definitive analysis of what was wrong with it." Through the YAF she had access to the addresses and technology newly assembled by Richard Viguerie, a pioneer in the use of direct mail for political fund-raising, and her critique was circulated widely. Marshner and her coworkers were astonished by its success.[10]

It took years, Connie Marshner later recalled, to figure out that "all over the country there were little clusters of evangelical and fundamentalist Moms' groups" who were "unstructured" but "in touch with each other" and just beginning to be aware of the danger posed by feminism. The response to her call for action against the Child Development Act was a pathbreaking demonstration of the power direct public appeals could have on legislation. It foreshadowed the direct mail campaigns by Viguerie and others seeking to harness the latent power of social conservatives who were beneath the radar of national politicians and the press, and felt that no one cared about their views. It also foreshadowed the awakening of a second women's movement whose aim would be to protect "family values" rather than to push for women's rights.[11]

Conservatives were comforted by the defeat of the Child Development Act. Yet as the 1972 election approached, Nixon again took action to appeal to feminists, one of the many feints to the left and center that outraged the far right in his party. What finally moved conservative women from anger to action was congressional approval of the Equal Rights Amendment, the proposed constitutional amendment that had languished in Congress for half a century and in 1972 appeared to be sweeping toward victory. These women were astounded and outraged that Congress had approved the amendment by overwhelming margins while rejecting the modifications proposed by conservative congressmen and senators to preserve traditional protections and exemptions for women, particularly requiring husbands to support their wives and excluding women from the draft.[12]

Thomson and other like-minded women concluded that the real goal of ERA proponents was a "radical restructuring of women's responsibilities."[13] Instead of simply extending women's rights, feminists seemed intent on taking rights and privileges away. Clearly, defenders of traditional womanhood were going to have to organize, to compete with the highly visible and vocal feminists, and to "tell the truth to American men and women and legislators in fifty states" that the ERA was a colossal error made by politicians eager to satisfy a vocal minority by approving an amendment, the dangers of which they did not comprehend.[14]

In 1972, with states rushing to ratify, it appeared that the Equal Rights Amendment was unstoppable. The women's movement was powerful and entrenched. The ERA had the backing of most women's groups from the League of Women Voters to the Girl Scouts of America, not to mention professional organizations and labor unions. Many mainline religious denominations as well as the National Council of Churches had endorsed it. Polls showed strong support from men as well as women, and it was favored by the press.[15]

As conservative women organized to stop ERA ratification, however, they had several major advantages unknown or underappreciated by those who thought their quest impossible. In Phyllis Schlafly they had an experienced leader with uncommon organizing skills and a large network of admirers who were political activists and ready to respond to her call. In addition, large numbers of women not previously engaged in politics were ripe for recruitment—and would enlist, armed with the conviction that they were on the right side of a religious crusade and had God on their side. The anti-ERA coalition would also have automatic advantages as opponents of a constitutional amendment, as amendments are, by design, difficult to win. To succeed, ERA supporters had to convince the majority of Americans of the amendment's merits and persuade three fourths of the states (thirty-eight) to ratify. However, ERA opponents, like defense attorneys, needed only to create reasonable doubt and defeat the amendment in one fourth of the states.

Exasperated ERA proponents dismissed Schlafly as just "a housewife from Illinois," a defender of yesteryear, presuming to speak for American womanhood with whom she was completely out of step. Senator Birch Bayh, one of the ERA's main champions in Congress, once complained that his television debate with this woman "who had absolutely no legal training, had had no legislative experience" but was "trying to tell women of the country what the ERA actually meant," made him want "to commit mayhem, live and in full color."[16] Such comments would inspire Schlafly to enroll in law school at Washington University in 1975 in the midst of the ERA battle and graduate in 1978.

Phyllis Schlafly proudly personified the ideal traditional woman. The mother of six children, she was married to a wealthy, Harvard-trained lawyer who was proud of his smart and beautiful wife and supported her in every sense of the word. She played up her attractive, feminine image, boasting that she breast-fed the children, taught them to read before they started school, and could still fit into her wedding dress. Schlafly was always perfectly groomed with her blond hair done up in "a French twist," and wore dresses in pastel colors—never pants. Her critics considered her to be prim and old-fashioned; her admirers saw her as the embodiment of a lady.[17]

Schlafly had overcome tough circumstances in her early life in St. Louis. As a result of the Great Depression, her father, an engineer, lost his job and her mother worked as a librarian in an elite Catholic girls' school in order for her daughters to get a good education. During World War II, Phyllis paid for college by working at night as a gunner, test firing rifles in a munitions plant so she could attend classes at Washington University by day. Nonetheless she graduated Phi Beta Kappa after only three years and went on to earn a master's degree in political science from Radcliffe. After a brief stint in Washington working as an aide to a congressman, she returned to St. Louis and began writing a conservative newsletter for a local bank—work that impressed local attorney Fred Schlafly, who became her husband in

1949. Before long they settled into a beautiful mansion in Alton, Illinois, a suburb across the river from St. Louis that eventually became command center for the conservative women's movement.[18]

For both Schlaflys, religion and politics went hand in hand. They were devout Catholics and fervent anticommunists, prominent within the Old Right in the politics of Cold War America. Fred was for years the president of the World Anti-Communist League. The Schlafly family established the Cardinal Mindszenty Foundation in honor of a Hungarian cardinal imprisoned for opposition to communism. Its purpose was to organize Catholics to resist the communist threat. Phyllis worked with her husband on these projects, including writing newsletters for the foundation.[19]

Both Fred and Phyllis spoke at Fred Schwarz's Anti-Communism Crusade programs and at the John Birch Society's God and Country rallies. Robert Welch, founder of the archconservative and secretive John Birch Society—widely denounced after Welch accused Dwight Eisenhower of being a communist—once described Phyllis as a loyal member of his organization. She always denied it, saying the JBS—which saw subversion from within the nation as the main way communism threatened the United States—did not share her commitment to a strong national defense. However, she shared many of its positions, including its opposition to the United Nations as a threat to American sovereignty and its opposition to New Deal programs and strong federal government in general.[20]

In 1955, Phyllis Schlafly ran unsuccessfully for Congress. She ran and lost a second time in 1970, employing a slogan (ironically, also used by Bella Abzug): "A Woman's Place is in the House."[21] Her active engagement in electoral politics while bearing and rearing six children seemed at odds with her emphasis on women devoting themselves to home and family and led some critics to call her a hypocrite.[22] However, in her view, devotion to home and family and active participation in politics were not at all contradictory: she insisted that from the earliest days of the republic, women had carried tremendous responsibility for preservation of morality in government. Her admirers praised her for sacrificing precious family time for Christ's sake to promote righteousness in society and government and "preserve America for future generations." As Thomson stated in *The Price of LIBerty*, Schlafly's "untiring dedication to God, home and country" inspired thousands of other God-fearing women "to defend our faiths and our families."[23]

In the 1950s, Schlafly was active in the Daughters of the American Revolution (DAR) and enjoyed working with these women who shared her Christian, patriotic, anti-communist, and anti-internationalist views. She became an officer at the state level and then served five terms at the national level as the DAR's Chairman of National Defense. In the 1960s, she had her first experience as a media personality through her fifteen-minute DAR-sponsored radio program *Wake Up America*. Schlafly also served as president of the Illinois chapter of the National Federation of Republican Women and became one of the NFRW's most popular speakers, traveling all over the state and nation and developing a large following among conservatives, particularly in the West and South. In 1964, she became First Vice President of the NFRW, in line for the presidency.[24]

Like many Republicans from the Midwest, Phyllis Schlafly resented the dominant position of the Eastern establishment "kingmakers." She despised Nelson Rockefeller. Her book, *A Choice Not an Echo*, played a key role in getting the GOP to choose Barry Goldwater over Rockefeller as the party's nominee for president in 1964. Three years after Goldwater was defeated in a landslide election, Rockefeller and many other liberal and moderate Republicans including Elly Peterson, George Romney, and NRC chairman Ray Bliss, eager to rein in her influence, blocked her ascension to the NFRW presidency.[25]

In 1967, Schlafly lost to their handpicked candidate, Gladys O'Donnell, after a vicious, six-month-long contest that reflected the bitter struggle between GOP moderates and rightists in the late 1960s and rocked the party. The normally decorous NFRW conference—holding the first contested election in its long history—was packed with several times the usual number of delegates plus observers and the press, which described "riotous scenes of booing, weeping, and teeth gnashing." When the winner was declared, Schlafly—with three thousand livid supporters, some sobbing, some shaking their fists—walked out of the federation convention to a rump session in the hotel basement and started their own conservative movement outside the GOP—complete with a newspaper: the *Phyllis Schlafly Report*, and an Eagle Trust Fund to finance their work.[26]

Ultimately, Schlafly's 1967 defeat paved the way for her political resurrection and a level of influence within her party and the nation beyond anything anyone could then have imagined. It left her with an embittered and impassioned following with enormous potential for expansion. The women who had backed her candidacy were furious that, as Schlafly put it, the "liberals are not even willing for our side to have anything at all—not even the crumb of a non-paid woman's position with practically no power." Many withdrew from the NFRW. Ronald Reagan's daughter Maureen Reagan Sills, who had supported Schlafly in this race but was friendly with women in O'Donnell's camp, talked Schlafly and her followers out of starting a rival Republican women's club, insisting it would damage the party.[27]

Instead, working through the *Phyllis Schlafly Report* and her extensive mailing list, Schlafly established an informal empire run from an office in her home. Her goal was to create what she called "an army of dedicated women wearing eagles as the symbol of American freedom," women with "a strong pro-American viewpoint," ready to fight for "morality in government, constitutional government, a strong national defense, and free enterprise."[28] That her growing network of conservatives was officially nonpartisan would put her in an excellent position to attract additional support among women who were increasingly disaffected with the policies of the national Democratic Party.

In the early 1970s, as the last congressional debates on the ERA took place, Schlafly showed little interest. Her passion was national defense. An isolationist to the point that she opposed the Vietnam War as a communist diversionary tactic to induce the United States to spend on conventional weapons and neglect its nuclear arsenal, she devoted herself to writing books denouncing Nixon and Kissinger for capitulating to the Soviets and "Red China." But she said nothing about politicians pandering to the women's rights movement. Looking back, she said, "I figured ERA was something between innocuous and mildly helpful."[29]

When it seemed that Congress was likely to endorse the Equal Rights Amendment without modifications to permit traditional protections and exemptions, other conservative women asked Schlafly to examine the issue. In December 1971, friends in Connecticut invited her to participate in a debate about the ERA. Schlafly demurred, saying she did not even know which side she was on, and suggested a focus on national defense. Her hosts, however, insisted on the ERA and sent materials for her to study.[30] Meanwhile a friend in Florida, Shirley Spellerberg, was urging Schlafly to come out against the ERA and finally managed to convince her. Rosemary Thomson saw it as an act of God. "When the Lord intervened," she wrote, "he acted not through a great statesman or famous writer or VIP" but instead chose Spellerberg, a "godly Christian woman in Miami, Florida, who had researched the legislative history of ERA" to persuade Schlafly of the ERA's "inherent dangers."[31] Later, Spellerberg, the host of a conservative talk radio program called *Speak Out Miami*, lamented she had not been able to recruit Schlafly earlier. "Phyllis and I could have stopped ERA while it was still in Congress," but "I just couldn't get her to move."[32]

Once persuaded of the evils of the ERA, Schlafly took up the fight with a vengeance. In the February 1972 issue of the *Phyllis Schlafly Report* entitled "What's Wrong with 'Equal Rights' for Women?" she excoriated the ERA and its supporters. Schlafly's powerful polemic reflected the values that pervaded all issues of the *Phyllis Schlafly Report* including her religious and patriotic fervor, her nationalist and anti-communist convictions, and her admiration for the free enterprise system. It also reflected her own privileged existence and assumption that the life she lived was typical for American women.[33]

Schlafly's opening statement and main point was this: "Of all the classes of people who ever lived, the American woman is the most privileged. We have the most rights and rewards, and the fewest duties." American women, she insisted, had "the immense good fortune to live in a civilization which respects the family as the basic unit of society." They were "the beneficiaries of a tradition of special respect for women which dates back from the Christian Age of Chivalry" when the "honor and respect paid to Mary, the Mother of Christ, resulted in all women, in effect, being put on a pedestal." Later, Schlafly's attacks on the ERA often featured statistics and opinions from constitutional experts. But this document was essentially a passionate defense of the ideal feminine role in the post–World War II United States.

The "great heroes of women's liberation" Schlafly insisted, were not "the straggly-haired women on television talk shows and picket lines" but men like Elias Howe, creator of the sewing machine; Clarence Birdseye, inventor of frozen food; Henry Ford, who mass-produced the automobile "to put it within the price-range of every American"; and Thomas Edison, "who brought the miracle of electricity to our homes . . . the equivalent, perhaps, of a half-dozen household servants for every middle-class American women." As a result, she said, "household duties have been reduced to only a few hours a day, leaving the American woman with plenty of time to moonlight." She could take a full- or part-time job, or "indulge to her heart's content in a tremendous selection of interesting educational or cultural or homemaking activities."

Life for American women, Schlafly insisted, contrasted sharply with that of women in the U.S.S.R. There a woman was guaranteed "equal rights," but that meant being forced "to put her baby in a state-operated nursery or kindergarten so she can join the labor force" and "do the heavy, dirty work American women do not do," including mining coal, working in heavy construction, and laboring in the fields while the "men are still the bosses."

Schlafly decried the plethora of "aggressive females on television talk shows yapping about how mistreated American women are, suggesting that marriage has put us in some kind of 'slavery,' that housework is menial and degrading, and perish the thought—that women are discriminated against." Everywhere new women's liberation organizations were "popping up, agitating and demonstrating, serving demands on public officials, getting wide press coverage always, and purporting to speak for some 100,000,000 American women." In Schlafly's view, they had obtained the endorsement of so many women's organization by deliberate deception, claiming falsely that it would bring better jobs and pay without stating what women would sacrifice.

She singled out for special criticism the National Federation of Republican Women that under the leadership of her nemesis, Gladys O'Donnell, endorsed the ERA in 1971. That "tight little clique running things from the top," wrote Schlafly, presented speaker after speaker to promote the Equal Rights Amendment, but refused to give "equal rights" to "delegates who wished to speak against it." Then NFRW officers "published intemperate attacks" on Republican congressmen who wanted to exempt women from the draft or allow adoption of "reasonable" laws based on sex differences.[34]

Schlafly's scornful, often sarcastic denunciation of ERA advocates in this edition of the *Phyllis Schlafly Report* set the tone for the campaign against the ERA that followed. *Ms.* magazine, "the most pretentious of the women's liberation magazines," she wrote, was full of "sharp-tongued, high-pitched whining complaints by unmarried women" who "view the home as a prison, and the wife and mother as a slave." In one article after another, she stated, *Ms.* praised women who refused to do dishes and laundry and proclaimed "how satisfying it is to be a lesbian."

Yet, when speaking to the public, Schlafly wrote, feminists sugarcoated their message in order to seem mainstream. Worst of all, they had convinced Congress they spoke for American womanhood and "that American women are downtrodden and unfairly treated"—a claim Schlafly denounced as "the fraud of the century." It was high time "to set the record straight." When "What's Wrong with 'Equal Rights' for Women?" went out to the five thousand *Phyllis Schlafly Report* subscribers, the effect was almost immediate.[35]

On March 22, 1972, the Senate approved the ERA, states rushed to ratify, and ERA supporters were jubilant. Within seven days, seven states had ratified. However, within that week, Schlafly supporters in Oklahoma who had read the February *Phyllis Schlafly Report* dealt the amendment its first defeat.[36]

The Oklahoma senate had approved the ERA by a voice vote one day after it was sent to the states. When *Phyllis Schlafly Report* readers learned that the House was about to follow suit and ratify the ERA, they went into action. Armed with Schlafly's arguments, her supporters persuaded a friendly Republican legislator to keep the amendment in committee while they organized in opposition, liberally distributing copies of the February *Phyllis Schlafly Report*. At hastily organized hearings they made it clear large numbers of women in the state were opposed. Suggesting the amendment might have dangerous unintended consequences, they insisted it at least warranted careful study and that there was no rush to ratify as they could always approve it later if they chose. The House then rejected the ratification proposal by a margin of 52–36.[37]

Ann Patterson, the leader of the Oklahoma ERA opponents, promptly contacted Schlafly, volunteering to call conservative women elsewhere using the *Phyllis Schlafly Report* contacts list and urge them to follow her state's example. Patterson then phoned women in twenty-eight states who leapt into action, and in each case managed to stop or slow down the ERA bandwagon. Schlafly quickly assumed command of this emerging grassroots effort, coordinating the efforts of the organizations opposing ratification, and creating new ones.[38]

This was the beginning of the national effort by conservative women to block ERA ratification. The swift response to her call to arms and the success in Oklahoma convinced Schlafly she had an issue that would rally conservatives across the nation. What happened in Oklahoma suggested that in many states simply dispelling the illusion of consensus among women would be sufficient to delay ERA ratification as conservative women mounted a campaign to convince the public of its dangers.[39]

Working with key lieutenants, Schlafly moved quickly to put together an effective fighting force of experienced activists with similar political and religious convictions and already connected through the *Phyllis Schlafly Report*. They were well trained. In the four years since the NFRW debacle, Schlafly had held annual "political-action leadership conferences" in St. Louis that attracted three to four hundred women from across the nation, most of them veterans of the NFRW battle. The conferences were meant to empower these women who were, as Schlafly told the press, no longer content to do the menial work in the party while "being told they have to accept the candidate presented to them." The training was designed to help them fight liberal "Rockefeller Republicans" at the local level and keep them from controlling party meetings.[40]

In July 1972, Schlafly assembled a small group of Illinois supporters at the O'Hare Airport to define their mission—a single-issue campaign to block ratification. They also chose a name—the National Committee to Stop ERA—and a symbol—a red stop sign. "Stop" was an acronym for "Stop Taking Our Privileges," which would be a main theme. Some proposed linking the ERA to other issues, such as fighting the UN or socialism, perhaps working through the American Conservative Union, an organization created by Goldwater supporters that has worked since his defeat to keep the conservative movement alive.[41]

Schlafly believed, however, that by focusing tightly on the social and legal implications of the ERA they could create a much broader coalition that included establishment Republicans and disgruntled Democrats.[42] Men were allowed to join and were welcome—and would provide valuable assistance. But this would be primarily a fight led by women for women, an effort to convince male politicians that feminists did not speak for American women and that the ERA would hurt not help their sex.

In September 1972, Schlafly brought together in St. Louis a larger group of women to launch Stop-ERA and discuss strategy. From then on the annual fall training sessions focused on honing ERA opponents into an effective fighting force. Given packets of information on the ERA's history and its dangers to the family and the nation, participants prepared three-minute talks to use back home. By that time, five states—Oklahoma, Ohio, Illinois, Nevada, and Louisiana—had rejected ratification. Ann Patterson plus four other women who had led the successful anti-ERA battles testified about tactics that had worked for them.[43]

By early 1973, Schlafly could proudly inform the *New York Times* that anti-ERA chapters had been organized in twenty-six states. Focused on the unratified states, Stop-ERA was best developed in the Midwest and the South. It was particularly strong in Arizona, Florida, Illinois, Louisiana, Missouri, Ohio, Oklahoma, and Virginia. With the exception of Ohio, none of them would ever ratify the ERA. The other states that did not ratify were Alabama, Georgia, North and South Carolina, Mississippi, Utah, and Nevada.[44]

Schlafly personally selected women to be the "chairmen" of Stop-ERA chapters. In addition to her National Federation of Republican Women allies, she drew on contacts developed through the National Council of Catholic Women, the DAR, the Goldwater campaign, and right-wing politics. Ann

Patterson, a Republican, would head the anti-ERA effort in Oklahoma throughout the ten-year fight. Rosemary Thomson, a Republican and DAR member, became the Stop-ERA leader in Illinois. Schlafly's friend Shirley Spellerberg, also a Republican, became chairman of the Florida chapter of Stop-ERA. Kathryn Dunaway, who assumed leadership of Stop-ERA in Georgia, had worked with Schlafly since the Goldwater campaign and had been an ardent supporter during the NFRW fight. Dunaway was a DAR member, a fervent anti-communist, and bitter critic of the civil rights movement. Kathleen Teague, a YAF veteran active in the American Conservative Union and the anti-communist United States Council for World Freedom, led the Virginia Stop-ERA organization. Dorothy "Dot" Malone Slade of North Carolina, who knew Schlafly through the NFRW, became the indefatigable leader of Stop-ERA in her state.[45]

Many prominent Stop-ERA leaders were members of right-wing groups, including the John Birch Society, which actively opposed the amendment and feminism. In the February 1973 JBS *Bulletin*, Robert Welch, the society's chairman and founder, urged members to "lunge in and help to relegate this subversive proposal to early and complete oblivion." As noted, Schlafly always denied membership and the JBS did not disclose members' names, but many of her followers acknowledged being current or former members and using JBS connections to recruit supporters.[46] North Carolina's Stop-ERA chairman, Dot Slade, was in the JBS and invited fellow Birchers to help her fight the ERA.[47] Beverly Findley who joined Ann Patterson in opposing the ERA in Oklahoma was a former member; she and Patterson worked with John Birch Society members in planning the anti-ERA hearings and enlisted members from JBS ranks.[48] JBS women in Utah had begun working against the ERA in December 1972 through a group they called HOTDOG, the acronym for Humanitarians Opposed to Degrading Our Girls, and were instant allies of Stop-ERA.[49] In many states, including Mississippi and Oklahoma, anti-ERA forces recruited through the state Farm Bureau, an organization that had a long-standing affinity with the John Birch Society at the national level.[50] Later, JBS publications featured anti-ERA articles by Schlafly and JBS leaders boasted of playing a major role in the ERA's defeat.[51] In 1977, a spokesman for the society, John F. McManus, told the press that Birchers had been "in leadership positions in every state where the ERA was scotched."[52]

Stop-ERA also attracted experienced activists from another far-right group, Women for Constitutional Government (WCG), whose membership overlapped with the John Birch Society. Founded in Mississippi during the

1962 crisis in which federal troops forced the University of Mississippi to admit African American James Meredith, the WCG quickly spread to other states. Believing it was a white woman's responsibility to "preserve the good life for her children," members pledged to work for "constitutional government, free enterprise, the Christian faith, racial self-respect, and national sovereignty." In the 1970s, the WCG was a national organization but strongest in the southern states.[53] WCG members played a key role in opposing the ERA in Mississippi, South Carolina, Georgia, and Texas. Carolyn Morgan, the Stop-ERA chairman in Mississippi, was a member, and Mary Cain, one of the WCG's founders and editor and publisher of its official newsletter, *The Woman Constitutionalist*, heaped praise on WCG members for helping suppress the ERA in the state. South Carolina's George Ann Pennebaker was at one time the national WCG president. The South Carolina chapter of WCG funded state legislator Norma Russell's participation in Schlafly's annual training camps in St. Louis.[54]

Whether Schlafly knew about these Stop-ERA leaders' involvement in Women for Constitutional Government or knew anything about the organization is unclear. One biographer who had full access to her papers insisted that she and her associates in the anti-ERA movement "never had contact with the "segregationist Right." She and her supporters claimed with pride that the anti-ERA movement drew support from African Americans including religious leaders in Chicago.[55]

Schlafly did not shy away from reaching out to the former Alabama governor and defender of segregation, George Wallace, concerned that his 1968 endorsement of the ERA was undermining her efforts. At the urging of supporters in Alabama, she requested a meeting so she could personally convince him to retract, saying that his endorsement "made our task difficult." In a letter to his aide, she stated, "I KNOW he would NOT be for ERA in its PRESENT form after he hears the arguments." Shortly thereafter, Wallace appeared on *The Dick Cavett Show* and made it clear he no longer supported the amendment, and she withdrew her request.[56] The American Party, created to support his campaign for president in 1968, was part of the anti-ERA movement. Its 1972 platform stated: "Women of the American Party say 'NO' to this insidious socialistic plan to destroy the home, make women slaves of the government, and their children wards of the state."[57]

The movement to stop ERA ratification could not have developed so quickly without this cadre of experienced activists—Schlafly's lieutenants—but it also required foot soldiers. They were soon forthcoming as large numbers of women with conservative religious beliefs joined the fight. Many were younger women and most had little or no political experience. Some were fundamentalists whose religious beliefs—which included not only biblical literalism but separation from the corrupting influence of others outside their group—had kept them away from politics altogether.[58]

This was particularly true in the South, a stronghold of evangelical and fundamentalist Protestantism. There, large numbers of religious conservatives mobilized against ratification, many of them through an organization called Women Who Want to Be Women (WWWW), which became a sister organization to Stop-ERA. Its founder, Lottie Beth Hobbs, a Church of Christ leader from Fort Worth, was crucial to the development of the conservative women's movement. Together with other Church of Christ women, particularly Shirley Curry and Tottie Ellis, both ministers' wives from Tennessee, and Beverly Findley of Oklahoma, Hobbs mobilized women from outside the orbit of Schlafly, a Catholic from the Midwest, and joined forces with Stop-ERA in 1975.[59]

The WWWW began as an effort to get Texas to rescind its ratification of the ERA and quickly spread to other states, mostly within the region. Owing to years of work by the National Federation of Business and Professional Women (BPW), Texas had adopted a state equal rights amendment even before the ERA was sent to the states and was one of the earliest states to ratify. Despite strenuous efforts by the WWWW in 1975 and 1977, it remained the only state in the South that ratified but never rescinded. With a state ERA already in place, claims about the proposed national amendment's potential destructiveness seemed less credible. The WWWW played a major role in anti-ERA and rescission efforts in other states, however, including Tennessee, which voted to rescind in April 1974.[60]

Through these campaigns Lottie Beth Hobbs and the WWWW mobilized thousands of previously apolitical women from evangelical and fundamentalist churches. As a Church of Christ member, Hobbs was herself new to politics: separation from politics was part of its creed. The daughter of a rancher and a teacher, she grew up in Abilene, Texas, attended Abilene Christian College, and after working in defense plants during World War II, supported herself by writing and distributing books for use in Bible classes. Hobbs was well-known and admired in Church of Christ circles, having published eight popular books. Though women in her denomination were not allowed to address mixed (male and female) Bible classes, she was much sought after as a speaker for women's Bible classes and conferences all over the South. At one of these conferences, she saw a flyer on the ERA, read it as a direct attack on the way of life decreed by God, and put her career on hold to devote herself to the fight against ERA ratification.[61]

By many methods, but notably through a highly influential flyer "Ladies Have You Heard?" that became famous among conservative Christian women, Hobbs warned that the ERA would wreck their lives and ruin family life. The flyer, known as "The Pink Sheet" for the color of the paper, was distributed through church newsletters, printed in small-town papers, left in mailboxes and beauty shops. It spread like wildfire across Texas, Oklahoma, and other southern states.[62]

The WWWW mobilized women from other conservative denominations as well. Some were Baptists, Methodists, and Presbyterians, but in the South there were many varieties of these churches—some much more conservative on women's issues than others—and women from these denominations could be found on both sides of the ERA question. For instance, Keller Bumgardner (later Barron), a League of Women Voters national officer from South Carolina who served as the LWV's representative on the board of ERAmerica as well as the cochair of a coalition supporting ratification in her state, was a Baptist. The largest group of Baptists, the massive Southern Baptist Convention, which later became a vital part of the burgeoning Religious Right, was in the early 1970s neutral on ratification. The WWWW especially targeted members of fundamentalist churches that emphasized Biblical literalism, such as Assemblies of God, Bible Churches, Missionary Alliance, that "generally believe that women should not be ministers and that the man is Divinely ordained to be head of the family."[63]

The Church of Christ was unequivocal in its position on women's roles, which was based on its interpretation of the Bible. Women were to be subordinate within the home and the church though they were not prohibited from holding positions of authority outside the church. Ultimately that single denomination furnished 43 percent of anti-ERA activists in Oklahoma, 45.1 percent in North Carolina, and 59.7 percent in Texas. In comparison, the same study showed that Baptists made up 9.2 percent of the "antis" in Texas, 36.4 percent in North Carolina, and 17 percent in Oklahoma, and that Methodists were 9.2 percent of antis in Texas, 9.1 percent in North Carolina, and 5 percent in Oklahoma. Church of Christ members also played a major role in Tennessee, Arkansas, and Florida.[64]

The fact that Hobbs and the WWWW, as well as other religious conservatives in the South, were willing to work with Schlafly against the ERA was crucial to the success of the anti-ERA movement. Though

Stop-ERA had no formal connection to the Catholic Church, her Catholicism was well-known, and could have limited her effectiveness in a region with large numbers of conservative Protestants long hostile to Catholics. Schlafly understood this and assiduously cultivated these connections, drawing Hobbs and other WWWW leaders into her network, emphasizing the commonalities in their Judeo-Christian beliefs about the roles of women and men in the family and society, and the need to work together against the feminist threat. Schlafly later recalled that, when they started out in 1972, her group was largely Catholic with some orthodox Jews, especially rabbis in Chicago who in those early years were very helpful. But "little by little we were bringing in the Protestant groups and by 1976 we just had a tremendous array of the different Protestant groups, all of them."[65]

Schlafly also found support from another group with conservative views about gender roles and family life: the Church of Jesus Christ of Latter-Day Saints (LDS), or Mormons. Interestingly, it was not a foregone conclusion that Mormons would become a key part of the coalition fighting ratification of the ERA or the battle against feminist control of the IWY.[66]

Mormon lawmakers supported the ERA in Congress and, when the amendment was sent to the states, contributed to ratification in Idaho, Colorado, California, and Hawaii. Even in Utah, the LDS stronghold, a 1972 poll of candidates running for the legislature showed that regardless of party a majority supported the ERA. The next year ratification failed by only eighteen votes and its sponsors included devout Mormons. In 1974, the church president declined to make a statement on the ERA because the church did not take stands on political issues. It was a point of pride for many in the state that Utah enfranchised women in the 1870s, one of only four states to do so in the nineteenth century. In the early 1970s, many in Utah, as in the rest of the nation, saw the ERA as a general statement of women's equality before the law. There were Mormon feminists just as there were Mormon liberals. Historically, unless the church took a position on an issue, individual Mormons were free to act on their own convictions.[67]

ERA prospects in Utah changed dramatically, however, after Schlafly secured a meeting with Mormon leaders through one of her allies, Utah House of Representatives member Georgia Peterson. Schlafly convinced them the ERA threatened traditional gender roles and the patriarchal family. Later she recalled it had not been hard to do.[68] The male leadership of the LDS had recently shown signs of wanting to strengthen the political influence of church presidents as well as to rein in the Mormon women's organization the Relief Society, which had carried out charitable work with considerable independence since its origins in the nineteenth century.[69] In addition, some top-ranking Mormon leaders, most notably Ezra Taft Benson, were staunchly antifeminist. Benson—secretary of Agriculture under Dwight Eisenhower and an early and influential member of the John Birch Society—believed the ERA would "weaken men."[70]

Prominent Mormon leaders met with Barbara Smith, the head of the Relief Society, and urged her to speak out against ratification. About the same time a *Church News* editorial denounced the amendment as "unnecessary," "uncertain," and "undesirable" and condemned it as a "unisex" law that failed to acknowledge that "men and women are different, made so by a Divine Creator." After several church leaders issued statements opposing ratification, polls showed that support dropped rapidly. Several Mormon legislators withdrew their support and in 1974 the ratification bill was easily defeated.[71]

In 1976, the LDS officially declared the ERA to be "a moral issue," stating that the amendment failed to recognize inherent emotional and biological differences between males and females, and might "stifle many God-given feminine instincts." It was also a great threat to the "humankind's basic institution." The formal statement of the church declared: "WE RECOGNIZE men and women as equally important before the Lord, but with differences biologically, emotionally and in other ways. ERA, we believe, does not recognize these differences. There are better means for giving women, and men, the rights they deserve."[72]

This declaration was tremendously important. It meant full institutional involvement: all church members—not just legislators—were expected not only to oppose the ERA but also to do all in their power to secure its defeat. The LDS First Presidency instructed church members to "join actively with other citizens who share our concerns and who are engaged in working to reject this measure on the basis of its threat to the moral climate of the future." The church also created and directed groups of Mormons who lobbied vigorously against the ERA in many states while following church instructions, to conceal any LDS connection. After 1976, Mormons would play a key role in the battles over the ERA not only in heavily Mormon Utah, Nevada, and Arizona, but throughout the United States, in most cases having an impact sharply disproportionate to their percentage within their state's population. In Virginia, for instance, Mormons were less than 1 percent of the population but produced 85 percent of the letters received by state legislators. In retrospect, the ERA seems to have been a test case as church leaders tested their ability to mobilize and direct church members toward a political objective.[73]

Catholic women were divided on the ERA and could be found playing active roles on both sides. The church hierarchy took no official position. Catholic ERA supporters founded the ad hoc group Catholic Women for the ERA in 1974, and there were even nuns' organizations actively supporting ratification. However, some bishops spoke out against it and most of the major Catholic lay organizations including the massive National Council of Catholic Women, in which Schlafly had long been active, were firmly opposed and were influential in the defeat of the ERA in Illinois, Missouri, and Florida.[74]

These religious conservatives—evangelical and fundamentalist Protestants, conservative Catholics, and to a lesser extent Orthodox Jews who insisted on sharp divisions in the roles of men and women and feared government intervention—were the main force behind the battle against the ERA.[75]

Religion was at the core of the anti-ERA movement. Though it was not as clear to observers in the 1970s as it was later to scholars, active participation in churches was the greatest common denominator among ERA opponents and a far greater indicator than class or levels of education. The majority of women on both sides were white and middle class. Support for the ERA was strongest among women who were highly educated, but many ERA opponents had college educations. The ERA had strong support from women who were married but working outside the home, divorced women, and young single women. Most anti-ERA activists were married women, but many of them had jobs. But when it came to church membership, the differences were striking: 98 percent of anti-ERA activists claimed membership in churches in contrast to 31–48 percent of pro-ERA activists.[76] Moreover, in terms of statistics, it appeared that the religious left was in decline while the Religious Right was on the rise. Whereas the 1960s had seen active involvement of liberal religious groups in movements seeking political reforms, throughout the 1970s religious groups with moderate or liberal positions on gender equality were losing support, while Catholics, Mormons, and evangelical and fundamentalist Protestant groups were rapidly increasing in numbers.[77]

Women from these conservative Protestant denominations and the LDS, though often new to politics, were especially valuable allies as they were already organized and could be readily mobilized. For example, when Beverly Findley, the main WWWW leader in Oklahoma, was asked how she got the organization off to such a successful start, she said it was "really very simple. I just notified the people I worshipped with. They are the people that think the way I do, and I knew they would be likely to feel the same as I did."[78] Because of her church's tradition of separation of church and state, many churches in her denomination would not even announce a meeting at services, but Findley and others commonly circulated church newsletters that spread the word about the anti-ERA effort quite effectively.

Some of these women faced opposition to their political involvement from their pastors, fellow church members, and husbands, but they won support by arguing that the threat to church and family was sufficiently high to justify at least a short-term commitment to political activism—a regrettable but necessary sacrifice. Thomson's *Price of LIBerty* contained many such stories, notably Shirley Curry's account of how her minister husband, despite their belief in "God's plan for wives submitting to their husbands," urged her to take action rather than just "wring her hands" and complain about "terrible effects of ERA." "Shirley," he suggested, "why don't you do something? Perhaps, like Queen Esther, you have been called to the kingdom for such a time as this." Sharing her concern, he "respected her unselfishness" and not only tolerated but encouraged her "outside the home" activity. Defense of traditional women's roles seemed to require deviation from them, at least temporarily.[79]

As for Mormons, they were organized hierarchically and geographically into "stakes" and "wards" through which messages from church leaders were communicated. All women eighteen and older were automatically enrolled in the Relief Society, which in addition to its charitable work was supposed to organize and teach women to prepare for eternal life. Unique features of Mormon theology related to the afterlife meant that Mormons, particularly the women who did most of the work in opposing the ERA, would have seen their efforts as enhancing prospects for reaching "exaltation," the highest sphere of a multitiered kingdom of heaven, as well as demonstrating to other church members that they were headed for that eternal reward.[80]

The sense of working for a righteous cause was empowering. Ironically, so was political inexperience. Unlike seasoned political activists who knew how difficult it was to change the direction of government policy, these newcomers were not easily discouraged. Besides, they were convinced that God was on their side. As Findley put it, "They're not just fighting us, they're fighting God!"[81]

Yet long-standing mutual antagonism between these groups of religious conservatives made it challenging for them to work together. Fundamentalists in the anti-ERA coalition had a deep-seated antipathy toward Catholics, did not recognize Mormons as Christians, and were deeply hostile to Jews. Each group saw itself as the true religion. In many cases, religious beliefs required that members save others by converting them. In the past such beliefs had worked against interfaith cooperation (risky, among other reasons, as it created opportunities for "poaching") and most of these groups had scorned the ecumenical movement that in previous decades had swept through many mainstream religious denominations.[82]

However, one of Schlafly's key strengths as an organizer—crucial to the success of the anti-ERA movement—was an extraordinary ability to unite in a coalition religious conservatives from groups hostile to one another. She accomplished this by emphasizing their common belief in the primacy of divinely created gender roles and familial structure while respecting denominational differences. For instance, at her annual training sessions in St. Louis, one of the few times representatives of the disparate parts of the coalition came together, she arranged separate religious services to meet the needs of women whose creed forbade worshipping together with people from other faiths. Schlafly later explained how she managed to get Protestants of all denominations and Catholics, Mormons, and Orthodox Jews to work together: "At our meetings, I taught them that, although they might be sitting next to someone who might not be saved, we could nevertheless work together on behalf of a political/social goal we all shared." They needed to "be nice to each other and work together." It was "the policy of my organization, and it was very successful."[83]

For the most part, the various groups worked in a coordinated fashion rather than by blending. Being part of the coalition meant coordinating attacks on the enemy rather than joining forces and, under Schlafly's leadership, they were well coordinated indeed. It helped greatly that for the first time in American history, leaders from these previously hostile religious groups seemed to fear encroaching secularism and the threat posed by feminism more than they feared one another.[84]

CHAPTER 5

An Alternative to "Women's Lib"

We were certainly a little flock pitted against a formidable array of forces supporting the Women's Lib Amendment—the President, the Congress, the Federal bureaucracy, the mushrooming feminist organizations, the nationally respected League of Women Voters, Business and Professional Women and major religious denominations. Yet, we believed the Lord's admonition: "Know ye the truth, and the truth (not Women's Lib) shall make you free" (John 8:32).
—ROSEMARY THOMSON, *THE PRICE OF LIBERTY*, 1978

As they organized, women fighting ratification of the Equal Rights Amendment worked through their churches, civil and political organizations, speaking to any group that would give them a hearing. "Across the nation," Rosemary Thomson recalled, "Christian women took the message to Bible classes, Altar and Rosary societies, garden clubs, Republican and Democratic women, mother/daughter banquets, Wednesday night church meetings, Rotary, Kiwanis, college campuses, radio and television. Concerned citizens were asked to write their state legislators. Rallies were organized in our state capitols."[1]

Phyllis Schlafly was their indispensable leader, communicating with her troops through the *Phyllis Schlafly Report*. She continued to write on favorite themes relating to foreign policy, limited government, and fiscal conservatism. But she also devoted considerable attention to social issues of concern to conservative women, such as the "textbook wars" in which women in West Virginia fought against materials they thought obscene, shelters for battered women that she denounced as feminist training camps contributing to the breakdown of families, and of course the Equal Rights Amendment. From 1973 on, almost every issue of the *Phyllis Schlafly Report* contained a special supplement dispensing ideas and information to be used in the battle against ratification. This included not only the results of Schlafly's own research and arguments but also descriptions of tactics developed by anti-ERA groups across the country that readers could apply in their own states. Schlafly did not just repeat the same information. As Shirley Spellerberg said, "You can't just keep talking about the same thing over and over and over and Phyllis keeps coming up with new ammunition."[2]

A shrewd tactician, Schlafly sought to make her troops seem as numerous as possible. In addition to Stop-ERA, she created a number of apparently separate organizations with different names such as AWARE (American Women Already Richly Endowed) to coordinate letter-writing efforts directed at legislators in unratified states. There was also Scratch Women's Lib, organized by Stop-ERA's legal adviser, Evelyn Pitschke, for disgruntled members of groups such as the League of Women Voters or the National Federation of Republican Women that had endorsed the ERA.[3]

In some states Stop-ERA affiliates went by other names, such as Spellerberg's Miami-based Women for Responsible Legislation and Dot Slade's North Carolinians against ERA—which made it appear that the anti-ERA movement was a varied, grassroots movement springing up irrepressibly across the nation. After the Mormon Church joined the battle, and created and funded anti-ERA organizations with names purposefully chosen to hide the LDS connection—such as the Arizona Home and Family Committee, Virginia Citizens Coalition, Illinois Citizens for Family Life, Families Are Concerned Today (FACT) of Florida, and Save Our Families Today (SOFT) of Tennessee —it added to the impression of a massive, spontaneous grassroots insurrection.[4]

Shirley Curry was proud that, after "only six weeks of work and prayer," she and Tottie Ellis and their followers convinced the Tennessee legislature to rescind its ERA ratification. "When we descended on the Capitol, the legislators thought there were thousands of us. We wore Stop-ERA buttons and lined up along the hallways and in front of the chamber doors to the House and Senate. Everywhere they went, there we were!" Kathryn Dunaway boasted in an essay entitled "How Nine Convinced 22,680" about how a small group of ERA opponents at a Georgia Southern Baptist Convention managed to make themselves appear far larger, and to convince the meeting to denounce the amendment.[5]

At the same time, a key part of the anti-ERA movement's strategy was presenting itself as an underdog. By so doing, they turned their chief disadvantage—that the feminists had nearly all the politicians, national women's groups, a vast array of religious organizations, and the media—into an advantage. To sympathizers outside their group, they were populist heroines struggling against a powerful profeminist establishment that included even the president and the First Lady. To themselves, they were courageous crusaders strengthened by a divine hand. The words "David and Goliath" came up frequently.[6]

Schlafly was also good at making strategic alliances, most notably when she reached across party lines to Democratic senator Sam Ervin of North Carolina. Having tried to stop the ERA in Congress, the senator was eager to do all he could to prevent ratification. He had persuaded ERA supporters to accept a seven-year deadline, and now counted on conservative legislators to delay ratification while he and others worked to raise doubts about the amendment. Schlafly supplied the senator with addresses of key state legislators to contact and, at her suggestion, Ervin allowed Schlafly to use his congressional franking privilege (allowing members of Congress to post mail to constituents without payment) to send anti-ERA literature at public expense. This included his own essay denouncing the amendment—which Schlafly edited to make it more "readable." By the end of 1973, Ervin's speeches had been distributed to Stop-ERA activists in twenty-four states and legislators in twenty-five states and a jubilant Ervin told allies: "We are holding in more states than we need."[7]

Schlafly also hit the road, speaking against ratification. She seemed to pop up everywhere, frequently brought in by her followers to take on the local feminists' strongest debaters. By the end of 1975, she had testified against the ERA at forty-one state hearings.[8] She became a constant presence on news shows. Borrowing a page from her feminist adversaries who had invoked the FCC's fairness doctrine to demand time on air to present their views, she demanded time to present hers. With husband Fred's assistance, she backed up her demands with lawsuits. Her strategy worked. Feminists were outraged that, after 1972, newscasters seemed to feel obligated to invite Schlafly to present the "other side" every time they had an ERA supporter as a guest.[9] To feminists it was like inviting a Klansman to present the "other side" in a debate about civil rights.

The media liked that the anti-ERA side had a clearly identified, easily accessible leader they could turn to who answered her own phone and was always ready with a pithy quotation. Newscasters with little appetite for the ideas of the feminists they'd featured over the years were all too willing to welcome a woman with an opposing point of view. Journalists not at all sympathetic to Schlafly's views, especially women reporters, could barely conceal their hostility toward her.[10]

Lisa Wohl wrote in *Ms.* magazine: "In some ways she [Schlafly] might be called an artificial creation of the fairness doctrine. Wherever pro-ERA views of the vast majority of Americans are presented, Schlafly—the only nationally known spokeswoman against it—is brought out in the name of objectivity." Grace Kaminkowitz, chairwoman of public information for ERA-Illinois, published a column in the *Chicago Sun-Times* with the head-line: PRESS SHOULD NOT BE SO DARN FAIR, saying, "As a result of sincere good intentions, the media have provided a forum for the lies and distortion of ERA opponents, frequently without providing an opportunity for rebuttal." Kaminkowitz added that they seemed to "forage for these unfavor-able comments just so no one can accuse their news columns of being biased in behalf of the amendment."[11]

Feminists' critics claimed that by singling her out as their particular enemy, Schlafly's opponents had inadvertently contributed to her rise as a media star. Their frustrations often boiled over as they encountered a glib and icily poised Schlafly. At a May 1973 debate with Betty Friedan at Illinois State University, Schlafly stated that having only 18 women out of 535 members of Congress "does not prove discrimination at all." It just showed that "most women do not want to do all the things that must be done to win elections." She added that most women would prefer "to devote their energy to other things, like having babies." Friedan completely lost control, shouting at Schlafly: "I consider you a traitor to your sex, an Aunt Tom" and "I'd like to burn you at the stake!" At that point Schlafly replied calmly, "I'm glad you said that because it just shows the intemperate nature of proponents of ERA."[12]

On national television, the ERA opposition was nearly always repre-sented by Schlafly. Few Americans, then or now, know the names of any other anti-ERA leader.[13] That Schlafly did not delegate more of these media appearances to other ERA opponents suggests elevated levels of pride or perfectionism. Yet clearly, one of her primary goals and satisfactions was preparing her supporters to interact with the press, and she went to great lengths to train them, especially the political novices, to be more skilled, confident, and effective. In the process she won their devotion.

Ann McGraw, the Stop-ERA leader in Missouri, greatly resented the media's focus on Schlafly, saying: "When they say there are no leaders on the Stop-ERA side" other than Schlafly, "it makes my blood boil." But she blamed the media, not Schlafly, for these slights. "Even in St. Louis, reporters always call Phyllis because they know their readers are more interested in Phyllis Schlafly's opinion of an ERA vote in the Missouri legislature than in Ann McGraw's," she said.[14] McGraw effusively praised Schlafly for encouraging her and others "to jump in where 'angels fear to tread' and accomplish what needed to be done" and for giving them the tools and confidence to handle it. Phyllis, she recalled, "inspired and motivated so many 'thirtyish' year olds in the 1960's and 70's, by giving us responsibilities far beyond our own expectations." She instilled in them the confidence that they "could go on television and debate the opposition, doing television editorial rebuttals at the drop of a hat, driving around to radio stations across the state to present our point of view because she had given us the tools and information to accomplish great things."[15]

Another Schlafly devotee, Dianne Edmondson of Oklahoma, said that "by watching Phyllis on TV whenever I could, and reading her Reports, I got plenty of well-documented information and I soon began speaking to individuals and then groups . . . I learned how to turn a hostile question into one you want to answer, how to get your message across in a radio or TV interview in sound bite sections."[16] Elaine Donnelly, a young Schlafly protégé from Michigan, became an expert on handling the press and won the job of Stop-ERA media chairman.[17]

Schlafly schooled her followers on the art of lobbying, dividing them into "combat teams" with particular lawmakers as their targets, and teaching them how to utilize publicity stunts and symbolism. She later recalled that many of them had much to learn. "When we had our rally [in Illinois], most of them, they didn't know where Springfield was. They had never been to the capital . . . And they came, a lot of them carrying their babies. They didn't understand— for example, the feminists would announce 'we're gonna pass the ERA today' and we'd come up and we'd have our big rally and be there and all standing around. And then the sponsors realized they didn't have the votes so they didn't call it up. And our people, a lot of them who were new to politics just didn't understand, I mean 'what happened?' You know, they didn't vote. And they didn't understand that's a victory. We hope they never vote!"[18]

When lobbying legislators, the anti-ERA forces employed tactics that underscored their support for traditional gender roles. Rosemary Thomson recalled how, in Illinois, they "took loaves of bread to 'the bread-winners' from American bread bakers" and "once baked nearly 400 pies for our lawmakers!" In South Carolina, ERA opponents placed home-baked cakes on the desks of each legislator. Similar tactics were used in Georgia—though

Kathryn Dunaway's files contain a copy of a thank-you note written to "Mom's Bakery" thanking them for donating the "homemade pies."[19]

ERA opponents approached legislators with a carefully concocted combination of carrots and sticks. In Texas they supplied legislators with a hefty package laying out "the facts" about ERA, lavishing praise on those who had committed to supporting rescission and gently warning the rest. The cover letter stated: "We are a sincere, rapidly-growing League of Ladies, and will remember our friends – and foes – at the polls. Think about this: the 'silent majority,' housewives, etc., have the time to vote and convince others!"[20] Generally speaking, ERA opponents relied more heavily on promising to support men who stepped up to save them from the ERA rather than on threatening to defeat those who did not. Most took it for granted that men were as eager to retain traditional gender roles as they were. Beverly Findley composed a poem for WWWW members in Oklahoma to deliver to legislators along with the homemade bread:

> Women Who Want to Be Women
> Have made this bread for you
> Because they love being homemakers
> All the year through . . .
> So enjoy your bread,
> Appreciate it too,
> Cause unless the ERA is stopped,
> The Homemaker may be YOU!

Everywhere, ERA opponents took care to present themselves as feminine rather than feminist—leveraging the quintessentially feminine color pink as their trademark. Lottie Beth Hobbs printed her famous flyer in pink. And when women of the WWWW in Texas went to Austin to demand rescission of the Equal Rights Amendment, they dressed in pink, which led the Texas press to dub them the Pink Ladies. Hobbs's "Pink Sheet" and other WWWW literature was openly distributed by the Texas-based Mary Kay cosmetics firm (famous for awarding top saleswomen pink Cadillacs) until the company was threatened by a national boycott. (Its major competitor, Avon, supported the ERA ratification campaign.)[21]

For all of their hostility to their feminist rivals and their professed anxiety about the imminent threat to all they held dear, women who were part of this conservative movement often seemed to be enjoying themselves. They relished their camaraderie, making up silly songs and corny poems, and swapping recipes and stories about their children as they exchanged ideas for lobbying and fund-raising. It was fun besting their opponents and they never seemed to doubt they were on the winning team. They called each other "honey" and "dear," referred to themselves as "girls" or "gals," and took pride in one another's accomplishments.[22]

Women in the movement to stop the ERA were especially proud of the leading role women elected officials such as Arizona's Donna Carlson, Utah's Georgia Peterson, Virginia's Eva Scott, and other "First Ladies of the Legislatures" that Schlafly celebrated in the *Phyllis Schlafly Report* played in the amendment's defeat.[23] Ann McGraw later described the way the women of the anti-ERA movement felt about one another: "We established a nation-wide network of women who knew one another and we fed on each other, talking on the phone, reassuring one another, and meeting once a year . . . reviving our minds and hearts for the tasks to come." Ironically, for those who may have felt bored or isolated, the campaign to stop the ERA provided excitement and companionship, as well as an acceptable reason to escape temporarily the homes from which they did not wish to be driven.[24]

Through their political activism many discovered unknown talents and new purpose in their lives that they attributed not only to Schlafly but also to God. Dianne Edmondson said she gradually realized that her "normal inability to remember dates and names was miraculously transformed as the good Lord knew that when I spoke, I'd have to be able to quote those court decisions and legal authorities!" Another follower, Barbara Dolan Atherton, thanking Schlafly, said, "Shy by nature, I became bolder and more effective because of God's Word, and your example."[25]

As Illinois chairman of Stop-ERA, Rosemary Thomson found a new calling as a writer as well as a speaker. She was surprised to find herself "a humble homemaker," called by the Lord "to be an ambassador for him in the political arena." An article she had written for an evangelical family maga-zine became so popular that thousands of requests for it flooded in, leading her to get it copyrighted as "A Christian View of ERA." Along with Schlafly's "What's Wrong with 'Equal Rights' for Women?" and Hobbs's "Pink Sheet," it was one of the best known statements of the arguments against the amend-ment. According to Thomson, it was used in nearly every state, with a total "perhaps in the hundreds of thousands." In her view, she and others were simply telling the truth to their fellow Americans, confident they would reject the ERA if only they understood what was at stake.[26]

*   *   *

The "truth" they set out to tell was that the ERA, though presented as helping American women by expanding their rights, would take rights and protections away. As Thomson put it in her widely circulated pamphlet, the fact that the ERA made "no exemptions or exclusions whatsoever" was its "fatal flaw."[27] Frequently quoting their hero Senator Ervin, who had tried and failed to modify the amendment to preserve a woman's "right" to be supported by her husband, Hobbs called the ERA "the most drastic measure in Senate history," one that "strikes at the very foundation of family life, and the home as the foundation of our nation."[28]

To Christian conservatives, upholding traditional gender roles was to uphold the divine hierarchical plan in which God was the head of man and man the head of woman. In "A Christian View of ERA," Thomson proclaimed that "obedience to this plan was essential for the preservation of the family, the basic unit of society." While God created men and women equal, he created them with different talents, abilities, and roles: "The husband was to be the provider and the wife his helpmate and mother of his children—both equal but each with a special position."[29]

ERA supporters contended that many traits and behaviors assumed to be "natural" in women and men were the results of socialization and insisted that laws assigning different roles and responsibilities to the sexes were relics of a bygone era. Conversely, opponents of the ERA argued that immutable, divinely created differences between the sexes required different treatment under the law. Schlafly condemned federal laws banning gender stereotyping in education and textbooks as "child abuse," foolhardy and destructive efforts to train children in unisex behavior that if successful would deprive them of their natural identities as women and men. In the February 1972 *Phyllis Schlafly Report*, she posited that traditional American laws and customs were "based on the fact of life—which no legislation or agitation can erase—that women have babies and men don't," and added that if you didn't like it "you [could] take up your complaint with God because He created us this way."[30]

ERA advocates claimed their opponents were engaging in fear-mongering. Thomson, Schlafly, Hobbs, and other leaders of the movement to block ratification believed that fear was in order. Their goal was to alert women committed to traditional family and gender roles that if the ERA was ratified they would not be able to live their lives as God intended. This was the main point of Hobbs's "Pink Sheet," which began: "God created you and gave you a beautiful and exalted place to fill." Echoing Schlafly's first salvo against the ERA, Hobbs maintained that women in history had never enjoyed such privileges, luxuries, and freedom as American women. "Yet a tiny minority of dissatisfied, highly vocal, militant women insist that you are being exploited as a 'domestic drudge' and 'a pretty toy.' And they are determined to 'liberate' you—whether you want it or not!"[31]

ERA opponents argued that establishing equal rights could cost women dearly. Thomson warned her readers, alarmed by soaring divorce rates, that feminists had already cost women privileges as they persuaded lawmakers to establish equal rights regarding property and custody in divorce.[32] Such changes, Schlafly claimed, threatened a woman's "most precious and important right of all," the "right to keep her own baby and to be supported and protected in the enjoyment of watching her baby grow and develop." And what about older women who had married decades earlier and devoted themselves exclusively to home and family, women with no jobs skills or experience, who in the case of divorce badly needed alimony? Schlafly liked to point out that the ERA "does not even include a 'grandmother clause.'"[33]

Anti-ERA literature also conjured fearful images of "liberated women"— ones that affirmative action laws forced employers to hire—potential home wreckers who would be working alongside *other women's husbands*. What's more, Hobbs reminded readers, "if your husband is in the armed forces, or a fireman, what can you expect under ERA? . . . Your husband will be sharing sleeping quarters, restrooms, showers, and/or foxholes with women."[34]

In the "Pink Sheet," Hobbs also warned that if the ERA were ratified "there could be no segregation of the sexes in prison, reform schools, public restrooms, and other public facilities" including all public schools, college dormitories, and hospital rooms."[35] The idea that women would lose the privacy and protection of designated separate areas in public spaces seemed to feminists—who called it "the potty argument"—trivial. But it played to women's fears about physical violence. In the South many whites had feared mixing blacks and whites in public accommodations: now they feared that the ERA would force everyone—white and black, male and female—into what they perceived as unwanted and dangerous proximity.

The issue of homosexuality was much less prominent in anti-ERA literature in the early years of the battle than it would become after 1977. But it did play a role. Schlafly relied on the views of her favorite legal expert, Harvard professor Paul Freund, who claimed that if the law had to be as undiscriminating toward gender as it was toward race, it would follow that laws outlawing marriage between two members of the same sex would be as illegal as laws forbidding miscegenation.[36] Hobbs also addressed this unthinkable threat to traditional marriage, emphasizing that "according to leading law counsels, the ERA will permit homosexuals to 'marry' and adopt children."[37]

The military draft issue loomed large in anti-ERA literature from the outset. The argument that the ERA would require women to be included in any future conscription was one of the most effective as well as irrefutable arguments offered against the ERA. Schlafly claimed that large numbers of young women joined the anti-ERA effort because of this issue. When pressed, feminists acknowledged they supported this change because to have equal rights women must have equal responsibilities. Schlafly found it "amusing" to watch the "semantic chicanery" of ERA advocates as they had to "admit" this fact.[38] This was a real liability in a nation experiencing the final, painful throes of the Vietnam War which had produced such dreadful carnage.

Hobbs raised another issue clearly intended not only to horrify members of conservative churches and the men that led them but also to countermand any reluctance toward supporting women in the anti-ERA campaign or hesitation about supporting it themselves. The National Organization for Women, she announced, had demanded that "women be ordained in religious bodies where that right is still denied" and to refuse to do this would be illegal under the ERA.[39]

Hobbs warned that feminists were determined that churches "conform to their idea of non-sexist equality or lose their tax-exempt status . . . a total perversion of the right to freedom of worship!"[40] Schlafly claimed the ERA would force the Catholic Church to ordain women and abandon its single-sex schools. Such arguments were also alarming to Orthodox Jews fearful that the federal government would require them to ordain women as rabbis, integrate Hebrew school classes, and allow women to sit next to men to whom they were not married as well as conscript their women into the military.[41] The dispute then taking place in Israel between Orthodox Jews and the government over compulsory service for women made this threat seem credible as well as terrifying.

Even as they emphasized the ERA's many dangers, Schlafly, Thomson, and Hobbs insisted that if the ERA was really about equal opportunities for women in education and employment, appointing more women to high positions, and "other desirable objectives which all women favor," they would be all for it. "We all support these purposes, as well as any necessary legislation which would bring them about," Schlafly stated. However, "All this is only a sweet syrup which covers the deadly poison masquerading as 'women's lib,'" put out by "radicals who are waging a total assault on the family, on marriage, and on children" as their own literature made clear.[42] To make her point, Schlafly republished at her own expense the National Organization for Women's twenty-one-page 1973 manifesto *Revolution: Tomorrow Is NOW,* and distributed it to her followers, politicians, and the public, even reprinting it in full in her book *The Power of the Positive Woman.* Ironically, such was the demand for *Revolution: Tomorrow Is NOW* among conservatives that Stop-ERA began publishing it as a fund-raiser.[43]

In another well-known treatise against the ERA, Schlafly's 1972 "The Right to Be a Woman," she again denounced the "women's liberationists" as radicals who "hate men, marriage, and children" and out to destroy the family. In a rare departure, Schlafly did express some understanding and empathy toward "another type of woman supporting the ERA from sincere motives": the "business and professional women" who had "felt the keen edge of discrimination in their employment, and been in a situation where the woman does most of the work, and some man gets the bigger salary and the credit." To them she said, "We support you in your efforts to eliminate all injustices," but "we believe this can be done through the Civil Rights Act and the Equal Opportunity Act." She also insisted that "if the Hayden modification had remained in the Equal Rights Amendment, we would have supported it."[44]

Driving home her point Schlafly stated, "You have every right to lobby for the extension of *your* rights—but not at the expense of the rights of *other* women." She was speaking primarily of homemakers, but Schlafly also presented herself and her movement as the champions of working-class women—who stood to lose workplace "protections"—against elitists who did not understand or care about their needs. "It comes with exceedingly poor grace," she wrote in the July 1973 *Phyllis Schlafly Report,* "for a woman who sits at a comfortable desk to demand legislation which will deprive a woman who stands on her feet all day of the right to have a chair."[45]

Ironically, Schlafly, Thomson, Hobbs, and others cited the feminists' own recent congressional victories as well as Supreme Court decisions to make their case against the ERA. Pointing to *Reed v. Reed* particularly, they insisted that even without an ERA "the Supreme Court increasingly uses the Fourteenth Amendment to repeal laws which unfairly discriminate against women."[46] To them, this "proved" that truly beneficial reforms could be made piecemeal, without resorting to a constitutional amendment with all its risks.

Anti-ERA literature emphasized that there was no way to know how the vaguely worded Equal Rights Amendment would be interpreted. Section 1 stated: "Equality of rights under the law shall not be denied or abridged by the United States or by any State on account of sex," which proponents saw as establishing for laws relating to gender the same high level of scrutiny that was applied to race. However, Thomson reminded readers that the Supreme Court had in recent years handed down decisions that went against the "previous consensus of centuries, as well as past law" and that a court that "takes away prayer in public schools will be free to interpret ERA any way it desires."[47]

Section 2 of the amendment: "The Congress shall have the power to enforce, by appropriate legislation, the provisions of this article" became increasingly important in Schlafly's attack on the ERA. "If you like ERA," she warned, "you'd better like congressmen and Washington bureaucrats and federal judges relieving you of what little power you have left over your own life."[48] In southern states where the issue of federal "imposition" of unwanted social change was still sensitive in the extreme, conservatives such as the anti-ERA leaders in Women for Constitutional Government saw in ERA opposition an opportunity for a new form of massive resistance.

Religious conservatives, of course, were also disturbed over Supreme Court decisions on matters relating to sex and reproduction, such as legalizing contraception for unmarried women. In their view, the so-called sexual revolution had undermined religious authority and conventional mores, and these Supreme Court decisions further contributed to the nation's growing problems with promiscuity and illegitimacy.

The campaign against the ERA that was launched in 1972 gained strength in 1973 when staunch opponents to abortion mobilized in the wake of *Roe*. Many ERA proponents denied any connection between the ERA and abortion, but Schlafly, Thomson, and many other anti-ERA leaders disagreed and linked them effectively. And while the pro-life movement had not yet caught fire among most Protestants—even Protestant conservatives—*Roe* undercut the appeal of the ERA, especially for Catholics to whom opposition to abortion was a moral absolute.[49] Thomson, a Presbyterian, was as convinced as any Catholic that the "murder of innocents" was not only a terrible sin but also a step toward the erosion of belief in the sanctity of all human life and would lead to infanticide for the deformed and euthanasia for the old.[50]

Invoking legal authorities—including archconservative Clarence Manion, former dean of Notre Dame Law School, and Charles E. Rice, a constitutional lawyer advising the Right to Life movement—Schlafly insisted the ERA would make it even more difficult to get *Roe* overturned or to limit its impact.

Moreover, she claimed that ERA supporters were in league with the U.S. Commission on Population Growth and the American Future—headed by John D. Rockefeller III—that not only strongly supported legal abortion, but also believed it should be covered by health insurance companies in order to reduce fertility and birthrates. Schlafly quoted Congresswoman Patsy Mink, an ERA supporter, as saying: "Keeping women in the home may be the major contributor to excess population growth."[51]

The ERA was not just a foolish error by misguided futurists and feminists, they claimed. Thomson and Schlafly and others who were steeped in anti-communist ideology viewed the ERA and feminism as part of a larger conspiracy to undermine America by undermining its moral power and paving the way for collectivism and internationalism. Asking, "How had a whole generation been conditioned to reject Judeo-Christian standards?" they concluded "it did not happen overnight and it did not happen by accident." As the 1970s went on, increasingly they blamed the changes on "secular humanists" with base designs. By 1978, Thomson, like many other Christian conservatives, was arguing that decades of public education based on the philosophy of John Dewey had "schooled" American children to question traditional values. Secular humanists—working through the National Education Association (NEA) and fully supported by feminists like Betty Friedan—had used public schools to promote moral relativism and tolerance of religious beliefs outside the Judeo-Christian heritage. This and the Supreme Court victories of atheists had paved the way for the radical visions purveyed by feminists that threatened the strength of America, the leader of the free world, and left it vulnerable to communists' incursions.[52]

The implication was that the nation was in danger from enemies within as well as without. Population control, secular humanism, and feminism all seemed to be part of a communist plot. Encouraging women to enter the workforce and eschew traditional duties, particularly childbearing, would in time weaken the national economy and stem crucial population growth. Legalization of abortion was but the most heinous part of the plot. Schlafly and her followers also found it suspicious that feminists were so eager to install women in positions equal to and alongside men in the military, making the nation unable to defend itself. In fact, conservative rhetoric against feminism closely resembled the anti-communist rhetoric with which many ERA opponents had long been familiar.[53]

*   *   *

Feminists were fond of conspiracy theories of another sort, about who was really behind the anti-ERA movement and how their opponents were funded. They frequently disparaged anti-ERA women as pawns of big corporations and wealthy corporate donors with right-wing views that bankrolled them and made their victories possible. Anti-ERA activists found this amusing. They viewed themselves as God's agents paying their own way. One Texas ERA opponent insisted their work was "financed strictly by individual donations. There's no tax money, no foundation grants for us. I'm amazed to read of 'well-financed' opposition to ERA. I know of none; everywhere it's a matter of scrounging for every penny. I give up a beauty shop appointment occasionally to pay the printing costs of literature . . . two-dollar, five-dollar, ten-dollar donations, that's all."[54]

For the foot soldiers like this woman, it is probably true that their low-budget operations were self-funded. Even Schlafly claimed that her expenses were underwritten by her husband and small contributions, and that when she had speaking engagements, her hosts paid her plane fare. Grassroots activists who distributed her literature, including the *Phyllis Schlafly Report*, she said, "buy extras for eight dollars a hundred to send out."[55] Schlafly also solicited donations from her subscribers. When she began publishing the *Eagle Forum Newsletter*, a brief usually two-page sheet tucked into the *Phyllis Schlafly Report* filled with updates and advice, she included personal appeals for contributions for specific purposes. One such appeal, to fund anti-ERA campaigns in four upcoming state battles, netted thirty thousand dollars. She frequently offered anti-ERA buttons, bumper stickers, and literature for purchase as well as her books and the WWWW's "Pink Sheet." Readers also wrote in with ideas for local fund-raising activities—in one case suggesting breeding poodles for sale.[56]

In contrast to ERA leaders who publicized their fund-raising efforts and boasted when they received good results, Schlafly was relatively silent on the subject of finances. This—and her success—fueled the conspiracy rumors. Feminist critics charged that rich and powerful right-wingers were using the anti-ERA movement to stimulate a conservative political resurgence while trying to make it look like an unorganized movement of "frightened housewives."[57] However, reporters and scholars as well as feminists who tried to run down these rumors to prove right-wing ownership of Stop-ERA said they came up empty.

Elly Peterson, Schlafly's bitter antagonist in the GOP, said she was always suspicious about where Schlafly was getting financial support, and was often asked about it. "I've had more reporters calling saying they're investigating where Phyllis gets her money. But that's the last I hear of it. They're not finding a thing and, as much as I hate to admit it, neither am I." After Betty Friedan held a press conference to announce she and several news organizations were investigating charges that Stop-ERA received funds from the John Birch Society and the Ku Klux Klan, Schlafly denied she ever "received a dime" from either, and said she hoped Friedan spent lots of time investigating her. "She won't find anything and it might keep her out of other mischief."[58]

Many conservative political groups and individuals who were Schlafly's allies spent heavily to defeat the ERA. But they had alternative methods of influencing legislators that didn't necessitate going through Schlafly. In addition, Schlafly liked to be the captain of her own ship. Even as New Right organizations such as the Conservative Caucus —founded in 1974—began to cooperate with Schlafly and fund mass-mailing drives directed at legislators in battleground states, she kept Eagle Forum activities separate, refusing to turn over her mailing list to these allies. In any case, contributions from sympathizers did not detract from the authenticity of the movement of conservative women who did not consider themselves anyone's pawns and who funded their own participation in the movement. Thus it made them particularly angry that they—and other taxpayers—were funding their feminist foes.

As they worked against ERA ratification, Schlafly and her supporters also targeted government-sponsored commissions on the status of women— which Schlafly disparaged as SOWs (Status of Women groups). Though the media tended to focus on public demonstrations by more radical feminists and failed to grasp the importance of these hard-working commissions, the newly activated conservative women did not.[59]

Schlafly was incensed that many state commissions, including in her home state of Illinois, openly supported the ERA. In the May 1973 issue of the *Phyllis Schlafly Report*, she accused ERA proponents of having a "secret scheme" to fund ERA lobbyists at state capitols through the professionals hired by the nonsalaried commissioners. The activities of these "tax-funded lobbyists' vary from state to state," she wrote, but they included "testifying at hearings, coordinating pro-ERA efforts, and sometimes directly confronting State Legislators and threatening them with defeat if they vote no." It was high time, she declared, "to put a stop to the shocking way that our State Legislators are being lobbied and our citizens are being politically propagandized at the taxpayers' expense."[60]

In the same issue, Schlafly held up for imitation a lawsuit filed in February 1973 by Theresa Hicks and other South Carolina conservatives to "halt the improper and illegal lobbying for ERA by a tax-funded professional hired by the State Commission on the Status of Women." The petitioners stated that the commission—charged "with making objective reports and acting for the good of all"—had instead "taken up a cause commonly known as 'women's lib' and in so doing totally ignored the needs and rights of those like Petitioners who see the overall situation in a different constitutional, legal and historical perspective." The commission, they claimed, was determined "to destroy the traditional mores, customs and laws, all of which pose a serious and present threat to break down the social fabric of our State and nation and destroy the family as the cornerstone of society."[61]

Later in 1973, ERA opponents in Arkansas—having just defeated ratification and angry that the Governor's Commission on the Status of Women joined a coalition to resume the fight at the next legislative session in 1975—launched an attack on the commission, claiming that as a "tax-supported institution, it was too liberal and therefore unrepresentative." They accused one prominent commission member of being "a self-identified member of the Marxist Progressive Labor Party" and "comrade" to a University of Arkansas professor who "favors violent overthrow of the U.S. Government." The ERA opponents demanded a meeting with the governor, who at first denied even knowing who was on the commission and then promised to reform it. The "self-identified Marxist" soon resigned.[62]

In the February 1974 *Phyllis Schlafly Report* article "Are You Financing Women's Lib and ERA?" Schlafly reported that the Missouri legislature "that 'trounced' the ERA in 1973" had now cut the "SOW's" budget by 75 percent after its leader "flung down the gauntlet at the Legislature," declaring the commission was right to bring the ERA and abortion reform to the attention of the public. In the April 1974 *Phyllis Schlafly Report*, she "exposed" the fact that the Rockefeller Foundation, "which pours money into the anti-life movement," had awarded a $288,000 grant to the California Commission on the Status of Women for a two-year study of women's rights that would be used to promote the ERA.[63]

In 1975, Schlafly and another Illinois Stop-ERA leader were appointed to the Illinois Commission on the Status of Women. Announcing the appointments to her followers in the September 1975 *Phyllis Schlafly Report*, Schlafly wrote: "The ERA lobby in Illinois, which has used the Illinois SOW Commission as a means of spending taxpayers' money for ratification of ERA, has been making feline shrieks in the press about these appointments.

But it is about time that this state Commission has some representatives of women who want to be women."[64]

By 1975, the efforts of Schlafly and her supporters had clearly produced results. They had slowed if not stopped the ERA bandwagon. Thirty-four of the necessary thirty-eight states had ratified, though all but one of those had done so between 1972 and the end of 1974—and two of them (Nebraska and Idaho) had voted to rescind. During 1975, only one state, North Dakota, ratified in a close vote (after Betty Ford's phone calls) while sixteen rejected ratification bills. Most alarming to feminists was the defeat of state equal rights amendments in two states that had easily ratified—New York and New Jersey—defeats that reverberated throughout the nation and suggested the seemingly inevitable victory for the ERA was in question.[65]

In the December 1975 *Eagle Forum Newsletter*, Schlafly congratulated her readers, urging them to "rejoice in our many successes during 1975," but to "humbly remember that the forces arrayed against us were so formidable that there is simply no way we could have accomplished what we did without help from God." Not so humbly, she gloated that Bella Abzug had been heard "complaining in the corridors of the Capitol that the N.Y. vote has set the women's movement back 100 years!"[66]

Actually, feminists still expected to win. They viewed the problem as the need to soothe women's anxieties about change that were instilled or encouraged by ERA opponents. In November 1975, columnist Ellen Goodman observed that the ERA battle was no longer about the facts but about fear: "The ERA has become the villain of a fearful social fantasy, not a legal controversy. It's a drama in which many women fear trading in child care for waitressing, being thrown out in the cold, being forced into 'liberation.' We are in the fallout zone of change. It takes time to pass through it without casualties." To Goodman, the defeat of the ERA in New York and New Jersey did not "signal the return of the Feminine Mystique." It showed that "many women remain unconvinced that a legal amendment will resolve social conflicts rather than produce them. The problem right now seems to be that one woman's independence is another woman's insecurity."[67]

Feminists' federal allies were doubling down on their efforts to support ERA ratification and women's rights generally and were dismissive of Schlafly and the movement to stop the ERA. When Ford took office in August 1974 and promptly met with heads of national women's organizations, Schlafly and others in ad hoc anti-ERA organizations were excluded.

Repeatedly she wrote to ask that Ford attend the Stop-ERA national board meeting coming up in St. Louis and give ERA opponents a chance to present their views. Anne Armstrong, counselor to the president, replied for Ford, stating that the president was quite familiar with Schlafly's point of view, which had been amply conveyed at the meeting by representatives from the DAR and the National Council of Catholic Women: "It is the sincere belief of the Administration, as well as both major political parties and a broadly based list of both women's and men's organizations, that the Equal Rights Amendment will ensure equal rights for both sexes, that it will not abridge any personal liberties presently guaranteed under the law, and that it will strengthen, rather than weaken, the family structure."[68]

In January 1975, when Ford announced the creation of a National Commission on the Observance of International Women's Year consisting solely of feminists, Schlafly again protested strenuously: "The militant women who are determined to erase all differences of treatment between the sexes in order to force us to conform to a 'gender-free' society, are not willing to compete fairly in the marketplace of ideas" and thus work "tirelessly to acquire public monies in order to cram their programs down our throats whether we like them or not." This commission, created as the ERA was going down in defeat in state after state, was just their newest "tax-financed gimmick to promote their special interests," she said, blaming it on the work of the feminists' "lobbyist in the White House who boasted in the press about how she gets her way by 'pillow talk.'"[69]

Schlafly was indignant that not a single leader of an anti-ERA or pro-life organization was represented and that Jill Ruckelshaus, "a pro-abortionist and pro-ERAer known to many as the 'Gloria Steinem of the Republican Party'" was in charge. She complained that Catherine East, a woman Betty Friedan called the "pivot of the feminist underground" in Washington, D.C., and the "midwife to the birth of the women's movement," headed the staff. Worse still, the commission's committee on homemakers was chaired by former congresswoman Martha Griffiths, "the principal ERA sponsor in Congress."[70] If it had not been clear before, she insisted, in creating the IWY program and appointing feminists to lead it, the federal government left no doubt that it was taking one side in a national debate.

Schlafly and other ERA opponents were livid when the IWY Commission announced that one of its priorities would be getting the amendment ratified at the "earliest possible moment." That the ERA subcommittee requested and received a ruling from the General Accounting Office (GAO), stating that . . . "the Subcommittee's planned activities are within the scope of the Executive order, both in letter and spirit" made no difference to ERA critics. To them it was yet another sign of the bias toward feminism permeating the federal government and the difficulties they faced in fighting an entrenched feminist establishment.[71]

In August 1975, Schlafly sent an invitation to subscribers to the *Phyllis Schlafly Report* asking them to join her in a new organization, the Women's Forum, which she offered as the "alternative to women's lib." The goal was to "confront the anti-family forces across the full range of their attack." In October, at the first national organizational meeting, they selected a permanent name, the Eagle Forum. In a brochure signed by Phyllis Schlafly, president, and Shirley Curry, vice president, they explained why "another organization" was needed: "There are many destructive forces in our country today—organized forces that are anti-family, anti-religious, anti-morality, anti-children, anti-life, and anti-self-defense. We need a spiritually-motivated group of women and men who can cooperate to oppose such forces—in the legislatures, in the media, in the schools, and in the courts."[72]

As to why it was a "woman's organization" the brochure stated, "Men are welcome as members. But Liberty is a woman, Justice is a woman, Victory is a woman, and Mother is a woman. Western civilization cannot endure without women of virtue and courage who provide leadership on the moral issues." By joining the new organization, women would "become part of a national organization of women and men who believe in God, Home, and Country, and are determined to defend the values that have made America the greatest nation in the world."

In the August invitation, Schlafly explained that "the chief women's lib organization [the National Organization for Women (NOW)] has only about 40,000 members," and that as impossible as it seemed, she believed "we can have a larger membership than that by Christmas." By December they reached their goal, signing up 42,000 members "with God's help, and the beautifully cooperative spirit of our Eagles." Shirley Curry, her title changed from vice president to director, challenged them to set goals. "Short-term and long-term goals are necessary" if they were to defeat the ERA and "achieve our long-term objective of keeping American great by keeping America good."[73]

The fight was no longer only about the ERA, or about the ERA and abortion: Schlafly was mobilizing conservative women in an all-out offensive against the full range of feminist goals, to roll back the movement's gains, and to end collusion between the federal government and feminism.

Such collusion seemed at an all-time high when in December 1975 Congress approved Abzug's bill extending the life of the feminist-dominated IWY Commission to organize the conferences that would identify "what women want"—with "Uncle Sam" picking up the $5 million tab. Again, Schlafly was livid. This was another unfortunate result of the UN's International Women's Year conference in Mexico City, an "international consciousness-raising" session, which "disintegrated into disorderly wrangles among the delegates." Now, she reported, Congress had approved a bill mandating a national IWY conference, and despite the efforts of her allies— Congressmen Sam Steiger of Arizona, Robert Bauman of Maryland, Henry Hyde and Robert Michel of Illinois, and John Ashbrook of Ohio—it had passed. Badly outnumbered, all they gained was Abzug's promise that women from all points of view would be allowed to participate and that the conferences would not be used to lobby for the ERA. In the subsequent vote on funding, they managed to cut the allocation for the conferences to half of the ten million requested.[74]

The new year brought more bad news. When in 1976 the IWY Commission created ERAmerica, cochaired by Schlafly's old nemesis Elly Peterson and Liz Carpenter, it added insult to injury. When the commission released its 1976 report "*. . . To Form a More Perfect Union . . ." Justice for American Women*, chock full of recommendations feminists favored from the ERA to abortion to federally supported child care, Schlafly and her conservative allies were all the more determined to go to war against federally funded feminism.[75]

By 1976, the ad hoc campaign that began as an effort to stop the ERA was becoming a full-blown social movement. As a political movement, however, the conservative women's movement was still unfocused. In 1976, conservative women remained divided in terms of political party affiliation. Schlafly and the other conservative women who were Republicans supported Reagan's challenge, and when it failed, did little to support Ford's reelection. Elaine Donnelly, the Eagle Forum leader from Ford's home state of Michigan, warned the president that the feminists he and his wife supported were likely to vote Democratic and that conservative Republican women like her had long memories. "You and Mrs. Ford will have to answer to history for your part in 'The Selling of the ERA.' You can be sure that women will not forget what you have done as the devastating effects of the ERA become more apparent during 1976, the Bicentennial and an election year."[76]

In the South, most social conservatives were still Democrats. When Georgia governor Jimmy Carter—a Baptist and "born-again Christian" who announced his personal opposition to abortion early in his campaign— became the Democratic nominee, they contributed to his victory. Carter himself attributed his win in part to the conservative response to Betty Ford, who had applauded *Roe v. Wade*.[77]

During his campaign, Carter succeeded in selling himself to both feminists and social conservatives. Later he would find that a moderate course would satisfy neither, indeed that the national political culture was shifting and that moderation—along with compromise—was increasingly unacceptable in a polarized society. But in 1976 Carter's partial concessions and overtures to both sides helped him win. It took a few more years and some dramatic developments—including the IWY conferences of 1977—before social conservatives would come to the conclusion that the Republican Party was the best mechanism through which to get the federal government back on course.

After the election, Schlafly and other social conservatives continued to demand abolition of the IWY program. But when it seemed clear that the 1977 IWY conferences were going forward, they determined to mobilize conservative women to attend the open meetings in the states and territories and compete with feminists for the right to speak for American women. By then they were ready for the fight.

CHAPTER 6

The Gathering Storm

International Women's Year, and its World Plan of Action, have focused attention on the problems of women throughout the world, and have pointed to the need for an evaluation of the discrimination which American women face because of their sex . . . [It is time] to recognize the contributions of women to the development of our country, to assess the progress that has been made toward insuring equality for all women, to set goals for the elimination of all barriers to the full and equal participation of women in all aspects of American life, and to recognize the importance of women to . . . world peace.

—UNITED STATES CONGRESS, PUBLIC LAW 94–167

In the spring of 1977, feminists and conservative women prepared—separately—for the tumultuous IWY conferences set to take place by year's end. At the same time, hard-fought contests over the ERA, abortion, and an explosive new political issue—gay rights—heightened the animosity between the two sides, raised the stakes, and made each of them more determined to control the state meetings and the blueprint for federal action to be produced.

As the year began, no one seemed to realize that a storm of such intensity was brewing. The new president, Jimmy Carter, had campaigned as a friend of the women's rights movement, and feminists were optimistic. Feminist Democrats were especially excited, expecting Carter to be even friendlier to their cause and to *them* than Ford had been. At the 1976 Democratic National Convention in New York, Carter had promised that if elected he would appoint more women to office than any president in history and use the power of his office to get the ERA ratified. Afterward, Betty Friedan told a reporter: "This is so different . . . I was moved to tears by Carter. He made a commitment to us in such a substantive way that unless he's an absolute liar, he'll do something for women."[1]

Even Bella Abzug—characterized by one reporter as "the first to take almost anyone to task"—emerged from the convention "elated." Abzug told reporters: "I think women can expect a real commitment from this nominee . . . He took the opportunity to take stands on key issues such as ERA . . . He strongly believes in an active involvement of women in his administration." Abzug added that Carter had made "a very important commitment we have never had from any president, candidate or nominee. He said LBJ eliminated many of the legal barriers against blacks, and as president he would want to eliminate legal barriers against women." That phrase, generally stated as "Carter promised to do for women what President Johnson had done for blacks," was one that really stuck with feminists. It was repeated often, cited in pro-ERA literature, and accepted as a firm commitment by women who believed that at last they had found their champion.[2]

Even on the issue of abortion, feminists felt confident that the new president was on their side—or at least not against them. When meeting with them at the convention, he had been honest and direct about his personal abhorrence for abortion. But the feminists were equally direct and it seemed they had reached a compromise position everyone could live with. "I'm so pleased we held firm on abortion," Friedan said. "He included language in the platform that said he would not support an amendment to do away with the Supreme Court decision."[3]

Upon taking office, President Carter appointed two women to his cabinet: Patricia Harris, secretary of Housing and Urban Development (HUD), and Juanita Kreps, secretary of Commerce. There were also other high-level appointments, including Eleanor Holmes Norton, an African American, as chair of the Equal Employment Opportunity Commission (EEOC). Ironically, it was the EEOC's failure to enforce the ban on gender discrimination a decade earlier that had led to the founding of the National Organization for Women. So the appointment of an African American woman to head the commission was viewed as a real sign of progress. Esther Peterson, who had led the Women's Bureau in the U.S. Department of Labor and the Kennedy Commission on women, was appointed to direct Carter's newly created Office of Consumer Affairs.[4] Like each of his two predecessors,

Carter boasted that he had appointed more women to high office than all previous president combined. All of these appointees were firmly associated with the women's movement.[5]

Feminists in both parties had high hopes for the new First Lady, Rosalynn Carter. She was a shrewd and able businesswoman who had kept the books in the family peanut business and had been an activist First Lady of Georgia. She had played a crucial role as a strategist and tireless campaigner in her husband's campaign. The press quickly discovered that the soft-spoken woman with a southern drawl was strong and determined. They began calling her a "steel magnolia," a term coined by Judy Klemesrud of the *New York Times*. To feminists, it was quite encouraging that Rosalynn Carter supported women's rights and seemed to have great influence with her husband. She was said to have tipped the scales in favor of the selection of Walter Mondale as Carter's running mate. In a lengthy and glowing feature story in *New York* magazine, Gail Sheehy wrote: "The candidate himself gave us the name of the key figure in his projected inner circle. The name is Rosalynn Carter."[6]

There was a little of the joking that was characteristic of the Fords: When asked if he would object if Rosalynn were "as outspoken as Betty Ford?" Jimmy Carter answered, "No, I wouldn't object." Then, laughing, he added, "If I did, it wouldn't do any good!" But he emphasized that they had been partners in life, business, and politics, and boasted that Rosalynn would be like Eleanor Roosevelt: "She'll be active in both her domestic and foreign programs, and she'll help me to carry out mine, both in this country and abroad." Rosalynn Carter would be the first First Lady to sit in on cabinet meetings and travel abroad to address matters of substance with foreign leaders on behalf of her husband.[7]

From the outset of Carter's presidency, both Carters—plus daughter-in-law Judy Carter—worked for ERA ratification. Even before the January 20, 1977, inauguration, they used the power of the presidency to further the cause. In Indiana, when it appeared that ratification was going to come down to one vote, Senator Birch Bayh tried to reach candidate-elect Jimmy Carter, but when he could not he called Rosalynn. She made the telephone call, the wavering legislator voted yea, and the ERA gained the first new state ratification in two years.[8]

Rosalynn kept it up, telephoning legislators in the battleground states where ERA supporters hoped to gain the remaining three states. She also aided the opposition to rescission efforts in other states that had already ratified. This was all very bad news to Phyllis Schlafly, who protested outside the

White House.[9] Later, looking back, President Carter recalled, "I personally made hundreds of phone calls, Rosalynn made even more. We called individual members of the Houses and the Senate of all the delegate states in the nation and we sometimes spent two or three hours every night calling them, begging them to please support the Equal Rights Amendment."[10]

Feminists across America were thrilled. "GOD BLESS THE CARTERS!" one previously skeptical Connecticut feminist wrote. "They've got more spunk and more guts than any First Family we've had in Washington. FROM NOW ON, I'M FOR THEM!"[11] Feminists were not happy, however, that the new First Lady (like her husband) was "personally opposed" to abortion. And unlike Betty Ford, Rosalynn Carter made it clear that whatever her own ideas, she would not publicly oppose her husband.

Jimmy Carter had won the election with feminist support, but he also received backing from social conservatives, including large numbers of white southerners who had not voted for a Democrat since before Goldwater. But Carter's appeal was more than geographical. A Southern Baptist, he had tried to appeal to fellow southern Protestants as well as a Watergate-weary nation hungry for a dose of morality in politics by emphasizing his born-again Christianity. He had lost some Christian conservatives with his notorious *Playboy* interview in which he talked about "lusting after women in his heart," but most stayed with him.[12] Carter hoped that declaring personal opposition to abortion but opposing a constitutional ban on it would allow him to keep the support of both feminists and conservatives. The IWY conferences looming on the horizon were going to make that even harder, indeed impossible, to do.

As he began his presidency, Jimmy Carter seemed oblivious to the importance of the IWY to either side—or to his presidency. One of the first acts of his transition team was to bump the National Commission on the Observance of IWY secretariat from its prime location in the State Department and commandeer the space for its own headquarters.[13] Though Carter started earlier and put more thought into choosing leaders of his administration than any previous president, he was slow to make his appointments to the commission. When he did, he handled it in a way that worried many feminists and infuriated conservatives.

By law, the state and national IWY conferences needed to take place by the end of 1977, yet he announced his choices only in late March of that year. Most of the preliminary planning for the IWY—including setting up state IWY coordinating committees and selecting Houston as the site of the national conference—had already been completed by the Ford-appointed team, guided at first by Jill Ruckelshaus and then by her replacement, Elizabeth Athanasakos and staff members Mildred Marcy, Catherine East, and Kay Clarenbach.[14] One state, Vermont, had already held its IWY meeting in February while elsewhere state organizers were at work planning the rest of the meetings to take place in May, June, and July.

Though Carter consulted with the men on his West Wing team—a tight group of loyalists who had run his campaign—on other issues, when making these decisions on women's issues he relied mainly on Midge Costanza, the first woman to ever serve on a president's senior staff. A liberal feminist from New York, Costanza was a close friend and ally of Bella Abzug and Gloria Steinem. Carter first met Costanza when, as governor of Georgia, he was seeking northern support for a presidential bid. At the time, she was the vice mayor of Rochester and running for Congress. To her astonishment, Carter offered to come up and campaign for her. Later, when Governor Carter launched his presidential campaign she was more than willing to return the favor. A veteran Democratic politician and daughter of Sicilian-born sausage makers, she rendered valuable access to northern ethnic and working-class voters as well as women's groups. In addition, Costanza helped convince progressives inclined to support Mo Udall, a liberal politician also vying for the presidential nomination, to support Carter instead. At the 1976 Democratic National Convention, she gave one of Carter's seconding speeches. When he took office, Carter appointed Costanza to his senior staff with an office down the hall from his—a highly publicized gesture meant to reassure feminists who had backed him.[15]

In the West Wing, Midge Costanza was a definite contrast to Hamilton Jordan and Jody Powell and other members of the so-called Georgia Mafia. By her own description, Costanza was a "loud-mouthed, pushy little broad," passionate about her feminism. In contrast, as one political scientist has noted, "at a time when it was fashionable for hip men to pretend enthusiasm for feminism, Carter's Georgians rarely did." During the campaign, women reporters, even veteran White House correspondent Helen Thomas, complained that most of Carter's aides would not give them the time of day. Carter's chief of staff—the thirty-two-year-old and chauvinistic—Jordan, was known to be more than a little interested in the female sex. Stories of his proclivities would soon become legendary in Washington, including an incident in which he allegedly leered at the chest of the Egyptian ambassador's wife, saying he had "always wanted to see the pyramids." Neither he nor other male members of Carter's inner circle, including Press Secretary Powell, shared their boss's interest in feminism.[16]

Costanza served as Carter's Assistant for Public Liaison. Unlike the Nixon and Ford administrations, the Carter White House did not have a separate Office for Women's Affairs and Costanza's duties included handling relations with interest groups of all kinds including women's organizations. In the more open presidency Carter had promised, Costanza was supposed to be his "window to the nation." Carter joked to the cabinet that she was there "to keep him honest."

Midge Costanza saw herself as Carter's "progressive conscience" and always believed he was more progressive on social issues than he was willing to acknowledge publicly. She was very popular with the press, and liked to tell stories of "plopping" down in a chair in his office to discuss their days. Costanza's description of their banter was revealing: "Carter said, 'Midge, have you been busy this week?' And I said, 'Yes.' And he said, 'Then maybe you can tell me what I'm supporting that I don't know I'm supporting.' . . . I'd start laughing and say, 'Ah, don't worry. These are things you'll love.' So he'd say, 'Why don't you just tell me what they are in the event I'm asked, as the President of the United States.'" Carter was clearly very fond of the woman he called Midgie—as well as grateful to her.[17]

Following Costanza's advice, Carter reappointed several members of the Ford-appointed IWY National Commission.[18] The former presiding officer, Elizabeth Athanasakos, stayed on, as did Lenore Hershey, editor of *Ladies' Home Journal.* Two of the four African Americans on the commission—Ersa Poston, former deputy presiding officer who had previously been part of the U.S. delegation to the UN, and Audrey Rowe Colom, president of the National Women's Political Caucus—remained on the commission. Gerridee Wheeler, a Native American and former president of the National Association for Mental Health, remained as well.

Carter also reappointed the four commissioners Ford had tapped during the summer of 1976, including Liz Carpenter; Jean Stapleton; Gloria Scott, national president of Girl Scouts of the U.S.A. and National Urban League board member; and John Mack Carter, editor of *Good Housekeeping.* Ironically, Carter had been editor of the magazine in 1970 during the feminists' famous sit-in to challenge its sexist treatment of women's issues. Three of the representatives appointed by Congress, Charles Percy and Birch Bayh from the Senate and Margaret Heckler from the House, remained on the commission, joined by Elizabeth Holtzman, who was selected to replace Bella Abzug who was no longer in Congress. In 1977 Abzug had given up her safe seat in the House of Representatives to run for the senate—then all male—but was narrowly defeated in the Democratic primary by Daniel Patrick Moynihan. At Catherine East's insistence, former congresswoman Martha Griffiths, who had served on the Ford commission, was also invited to continue and agreed.

Carter graciously appointed Betty Ford. But most of his new appointees were from his own party, including Koryne Horbal, chair of the Women's Caucus of the Democratic National Committee (DNC); Mary Ann Krupsak, lieutenant governor of New York; Connie Plunkett, deputy director of the Carter-Mondale campaign; Jeffalyn Johnson, a member of Carter's campaign and transition staff; and Betty Blanton, First Lady of Tennessee.

The president also added representatives of key Democratic constituencies including unions and minority groups, such as Mildred Jeffrey of Detroit, founder of the Coalition of Labor Union Women and chair of the Democratic Task Force within the NWPC, and Addie Wyatt, director of women's affairs for the Amalgamated Meat Cutters Union. African American appointees included poet Maya Angelou and Coretta Scott King. Among the Hispanic appointees were Rhea Mojica Hammer, publisher of *El Clarin*, and Carmen Delgado Votaw, president of the National Conference of Puerto Rican Women and U.S. delegate to the Inter-American Commission of Women of the Organization of American States (OAS). Carter also selected LaDonna Harris, president of Americans for Indian Opportunity; March K. Fong Eu, secretary of state for California; and Rita Elway, founder of the Asian and Pacific Women's Caucus and a board member of the Japanese American Citizens League.

Several appointees brought particular expertise in areas that would be of great use to the commission. Harry T. Edwards was a University of Michigan law school professor. Sey Chassler was editor of *Redbook* magazine and vice president of the American Society of Magazine Editors. Alice Rossi was a professor of sociology at the University of Massachusetts and a pioneer in women's studies. Claire Randall was general secretary of the National Council of Churches in Christ in the U.S.A. and former associate executive of Church Women United. Other appointees represented large national women's organizations including Ruth Clusen, League of Women Voters; Jane Culbreth, the Federation of Business and Professional Women; Margaret Mealey, the National Council of Catholic Women; and Mildred Persinger, a YWCA leader who had been the organizing chair of the Tribune (conference of NGOs) at the UN's Mexico City Conference.[19]

Some of the new commissioners brought with them more liberal perspectives and more controversial agendas. Given her closeness with fellow New Yorkers Gloria Steinem and Bella Abzug, it is not surprising that Costanza recommended them for the IWY Commission; in fact they sat down with her to consider who else would be appointed. Costanza also suggested the president choose Eleanor Smeal, the new leader of NOW, and Jean O'Leary, a former nun and co-executive director of the National Gay Task Force who had supported Carter in his effort to win the gay vote.[20] In addition, Costanza recommended Ruth Abram, executive director of the Women's Action Alliance (WAA), the NGO that in 1975 had tried to get the Ford-appointed IWY Commission to accept its more liberal National Women's Agenda instead of devising its own recommendations. Steinem had been a key WAA founder and Abzug had served on its board.[21]

Most of the seasoned professionals on the IWY staff stayed on, including Catherine East and Kay Clarenbach. Clarenbach, who had served previously in a part-time position, took a leave from her job as a political science professor at the University of Wisconsin to become the IWY staff's executive director when Mildred Marcy was appointed deputy assistant secretary of state for cultural affairs. Veteran staff members Shelah Leader and Patricia Hyatt, who also continued on the IWY staff, had tremendous admiration for both East and for Clarenbach, whom they described as "a laconic, quiet spoken Midwesterner who never sought the limelight at the IWY." East and Clarenbach, they recalled, "were old comrades in the women's movement and shared similar ideas about how to achieve legal and economic gains 'within the system.'" Unofficially, Clarenbach also took on the role of "peace-making intermediary" between the sometimes difficult-to-work-with presiding officer, Abzug, and the IWY staff. Yet, while many staff members had been apprehensive about "Bella's bill" and the multiple challenges of organizing these conferences for which there were no precedents—"we were just flying by the seat of our pants," as East put it—by this time they had come to relish the challenges, found the work fascinating, and enjoyed working together to plan this event that was clearly to be an event of such importance to American women.[22]

Like Ford, Carter showed little concern about appeasing social conservatives as he made his appointments. Even if he were concerned, the 1975 congressional act that established the IWY conferences specifically mandated that the appointed leaders and elected delegates have records of involvement in "groups which work to advance the rights of women" as well as reflect the full racial and ethnic diversity of their states.[23] In selecting members of the state coordinating committees, the IWY Commission and staff were guided by the same criteria. Many women chosen as state IWY leaders had served on the state commissions on the status of women. In choosing leaders for southern states in which governors had appointed white conservatives to women's commissions, the IWY Commission looked instead to women who had served in progressive organizations including civil rights groups. Many appointees were well-known civil rights movement veterans.[24]

Within the White House, the only real controversy over Carter's IWY Commission involved the choice of its leader. Costanza was adamant that he name Bella Abzug as presiding officer. There was never any doubt she would be appointed as a commission member. In addition to being the IWY's chief sponsor, she had represented the House of Representatives on the Ford commission. For Abzug, no longer in Congress, serving as presiding officer of the IWY Commission would be very attractive. In spring 1977, she had been meeting with Carter about possible posts within his administration and they had not come to satisfactory terms. Abzug was considering running for mayor of New York, and if she ran it would be an advantage to be serving in this high-profile but part-time position.[25]

Yet for Carter it was a bold move to appoint as the new presiding officer the outspoken former congresswoman, the living symbol of liberalism as well as feminism who was despised by conservatives. Born Bella Savitsky, she was the daughter of Russian immigrants and grew up in the Bronx. In the 1950s, Abzug had become well-known as a defender of civil liberties and civil rights, fearlessly representing victims of McCarthyism before the House Un-American Activities Committee. In an era when women lawyers were few and many male lawyers as well as clients didn't take them seriously, Abzug began her famous habit of wearing a hat, part of her efforts to gain their respect. As a young and pregnant lawyer, she defied death threats to defend Willie McGee—a black man facing execution in Mississippi for allegedly raping a white woman—when no white lawyer in the state would represent him. She spent five years on that ultimately unsuccessful case, which became an internationally renowned cause célèbre. The *Jackson Daily News* editorialized that they should fry Willie McGee's white woman lawyer along with him in the electric chair.[26]

In 1970, at age fifty, Bella Abzug was elected to the House of Representatives from New York's Greenwich Village, becoming the first Jewish congresswoman. On her first day in Congress, Abzug introduced a bill to end the Vietnam War. She had a well-established antiwar record and was one of the founders of the organization Women Strike for Peace, which promoted disarmament—a stark contrast to Phyllis Schlafly's campaign to strengthen America's nuclear arsenal.[27]

Bella Abzug was also a stark contrast to the stereotypical man-hating, antifamily "women's libber." She was happily married to Martin Abzug, a stockbroker and novelist with a great sense of humor, who always spoke of her as "my beautiful Bella." Their friend Marlo Thomas described the two as "lovers and pals and teammates," and said Martin always encouraged Bella with her political career.[28] Martin Abzug was constantly being asked what it was like to be married to the flamboyant feminist icon. On a talk show featuring Phyllis and Fred Schlafly and Bella and Martin Abzug—couples with two powerful, controversial wives and lesser-known husbands—they were asked how their marriages survived. As Gloria Steinem recalled, "Martin looked straight at the camera and said, 'Great sex.'"[29]

Bella was the proud mother of two daughters and understood well the challenges of combining family life and trying to "repair the world." She trained her daughters to fight injustice and stand up for their beliefs. Her daughter Liz recalled being hauled into the principal's office frequently for such things as refusing to hide under her desk in the 1950s "duck and cover" drills and confronting a coach who kept black girls on her team on the bench. Bella and Martin Abzug lived their values. When they decided to move into the city, they sold their Westchester County home to Malcolm X's widow, Betty Shabazz.[30]

As a congresswoman from 1971 through 1976, Bella Abzug fought for underdogs of all sorts with motherly ferociousness and humor. Irrepressibly positive, she believed in the power of the state to solve problems if the people would rise up and demand it. As she took office, she vowed to "help organize a new political coalition of the women, the minorities and the young people, along with the poor, the elderly, the workers and the unemployed, which is going to turn this country upside down and inside out." It would be a movement of and for the "millions of people in this country whose needs, because of the callousness of the men who've been running out government, have taken a low priority to the cost of killing people in Indochina." The job of the government, she insisted, was to create programs that met the needs of the people, and she worked to make that happen. The December 1975 *Ms.* magazine cover featured a picture of Abzug in a Santa Claus suit, with the caption: "What Santa Won't Bring, Bella Will." Completely unintimidated by her male colleagues on Capitol Hill (though many of them professed to being intimidated by her), Abzug was for three terms one of the most visible and influential members of Congress.[31]

The darling of liberal New Yorkers, socialites, and Hollywood celebrities, Abzug was close friends with Diane von Furstenberg, Barbra Streisand, and Shirley MacLaine. Andy Warhol created a portrait of her, featured on the cover of *Rolling Stone* magazine.[32] To her admirers, "Bella's" brashness was endearing, but to critics it was jarring. Norman Mailer, no fan of Abzug or feminism, famously said of her that she had a voice that "could boil the fat off a taxicab driver's neck."[33] Abzug found such comments hurtful and was sensitive when criticized about her weight. But she seemed to enjoy being at the center of controversy as long as she could be effective.

In her 1972 book *Bella! Ms. Abzug Goes to Washington*, she boasted about her first year shaking up a Congress full of timid, infighting liberals and scheming conservatives: "I've been described as a tough and noisy woman, a prizefighter, a man-hater, you name it. They call me Battling Bella, Mother Courage and a Jewish mother with more complaints than Portnoy. There are those who say I'm impatient, impetuous, uppity, rude, profane, brash and overbearing. Whether I'm any of these things, or all of them, you can decide for yourself. But whatever I am . . . I am a very serious woman."[34]

In Congress, Abzug had demanded that equal rights for women be acknowledged as a national priority and championed many of the feminist reforms approved by Congress in the early 1970s. Supporters of the women's rights movement in all parts of the nation—even, perhaps especially, women far more moderate and circumspect themselves—admired Abzug for her outspokenness and fearless advocacy of their cause. At a time when there were pitifully few women in Congress, as one woman said, "Bella was like the congresswoman for every woman in the world!"[35]

Still, even strong supporters of feminism had concerns about Abzug's appointment as the presiding officer of the National Commission on the Observance of International Women's Year, most significantly Rosalynn Carter, who told her husband: "No way!" According to Costanza, both Carters liked Bella, but the First Lady understood that feminists needed to develop grassroots support through IWY and get the ERA ratified, including in her beloved Georgia and the South. The First Lady was "from a southern state where women were different than those of us in New York," Costanza recalled, and she feared Abzug would attract only political activists and liberal feminists instead of broadening the appeal to moderate women outside the Northeast. Rosalynn later acknowledged her frustration with feminists like Abzug who "didn't know what they were doing to upset the women at home and make them draw together in opposition rather than helping."[36]

Republican feminists who had high hopes for the IWY were also concerned. When she heard rumors about Carter's pending appointments, Elly Peterson worried that with the immoderate and staunchly partisan Abzug at the helm, the IWY would lose its valuable bipartisan image, never mind the bipartisan image of the ERA. "Turning that into a Democratic women's caucus with Bella at the head can just murder us." She could not "believe they are so dumb" as to do this. If the rumors proved to be true, Peterson thought "Republican women should just say, 'Well, it is an all Democratic women's rally so count us out' but I am sure there will be those who will cling by their teeth—ye Gods."[37]

Costanza, however, persuaded the president that Abzug was the right choice. "Right now," she argued, "what we need is the strongest woman we can find. You have no idea the egos involved—not just individual women, but women's organizations. No one will be able to control this group, to bring about the good and right as Bella Abzug." Even Hamilton Jordan and Jody Powell agreed that Bella should be the chair. She was the most prominent feminist Democrat and she had been a big help to Carter at the 1976 convention and in the election. When Carter finally approved the appointment, Jordan insisted on being the one to call her.[38]

Even with Abzug at the helm, at first it did not appear that the Carter-appointed IWY Commission would introduce controversial changes. The newcomers definitely raised new questions that produced lively debates. Reviewing plans for the Houston conference, for instance, some of the newly appointed Democrats protested that one of the convention hotels was nonunion.

Much of the discussion focused on a list of sixteen "core recommendations" the IWY Commission had prepared to send out to state coordinators for consideration at the state meetings. WAA leader Ruth Abram insisted the core recommendations the Ford commission had chosen were far too narrow in scope, nowhere near as comprehensive as the National Women's Agenda the WAA had proposed. Other new members, including Claire Randall of the National Council of Churches, protested the exclusion of religion from the topics deemed appropriate for discussion at the state meetings. Ford-appointed commissioners and veteran staff members explained that religion was excluded to avoid major eruptions that would inevitably occur if feminists sought to prohibit gender discrimination in the ordination of clergy or confront Mormons about their opposition to the ERA—ironic given that conservatives would later castigate the commission for inattention to religion at IWY conferences.[39]

All knew that for the IWY to succeed, women from all parts of the feminist movement would need to put aside differences and rally behind an agenda they could all support. Further, it would have to be an agenda that *most* American women, including the newcomers they hoped to attract, could accept. Thus, as Abzug and the IWY Commission prepared to send out the list of core recommendations, they made few changes in the plans formulated previously by the moderate, Ford-appointed commission and its staff.[40]

The sixteen recommendations, based on the 115 detailed recommendations in the Ford IWY Commission's 1976 report, related to child care; equity in education and employment; representation of women in government, business, the arts, and the media; health care; older women; women in prisons; rape prevention; and the legal status of homemakers including access to credit. In addition, owing to the IWY's UN connection, there was a recommendation concerning international interdependence and women's influence in foreign policy. Gloria Steinem regarded the "core" as rather tame, familiar to the public, and noncontroversial. "Most of these," she told the press, "have been in existence for twenty years on presidential commission reports." Though well aware of organized opposition to the ERA and abortion, polls in 1977 showed that the majority of Americans backed the ERA and thought abortion should be legal, and the IWY Commission did not anticipate major battles over these issues at the upcoming meetings in the states.[41]

As IWY organizers laid out the plans for the conferences, however, gender-related issues—old and new—lit up the political landscape. Suddenly it appeared there was little concerning women's issues that was "noncontroversial." Events that spring, particularly regarding what became known as the "hot-button" issues of ERA, abortion, and gay rights, created a highly charged political climate in which women attending IWY meetings would be developing recommendations to send to the president and Congress—and rendered those recommendations far more important.

The January 1977 ERA ratification by Indiana that inspired feminists and infuriated Schlafly was only the beginning of the fierce battle that spring over the ERA. With only three more states needed for ratification, both sides pulled out all the stops, especially in key battleground states. For women on both sides of the issue, those months were an emotional roller coaster. One week after the Indiana victory, the Virginia Senate came within a single vote of ratifying—a heartbreaker for feminists, and a tremendous relief for Schlafly and anti-ERA supporters who were alarmed that the ERA bandwagon might regain steam.[42]

Feminist hopes soared again in early February as the Nevada Senate approved the amendment with a tie-breaking vote cast by the lieutenant governor, but were dashed three days later when the Nevada Assembly rejected the ERA by a 24–15 vote. Almost half of the no votes came from legislators who earlier pledged to support ratification, a change of heart that NOW leaders attributed to pressure from Mormon bishops.[43]

In North Carolina, ERA advocates, buoyed by support from the Carters and funds from ERAmerica, invested a tremendous amount of effort and resources in the battle over ratification. But so did the anti-ERA forces, aided by former senator Sam Ervin, Senator Jesse Helms, and the Conservative Caucus. Their well-financed campaign called on the expertise of mass-mailing guru Richard Viguerie, who generated a deluge of anti-ERA cards and letters. The Conservative Caucus director, Howard Phillips, later boasted that they had spent nineteen thousand dollars for postage alone, causing significant erosion of support in the state. Schlafly warned Ervin that if North Carolina followed Indiana, proponents would develop a "momentum we cannot match." On the other hand, she said, if they saved North Carolina from the ERA, "I promise we can hold the other fifteen unratified states."[44]

When the North Carolina House of Representatives voted to ratify the ERA on February 9, 1977, ERA supporters rejoiced. But four days later, Ervin and Schlafly addressed a crowd of fifteen hundred women and men in Raleigh's Dorton Arena, where Schlafly had them raise their right hands and solemnly vow to defeat every state legislator who dared vote for the ERA. The state senate then defeated the ERA by two votes.[45]

In Florida, another key battleground state, there was a heated and dramatic fight that produced a narrow victory for the conservatives. Pro- and anti-ERA forces flocked to the state. Phyllis Schlafly worked with her old friend Shirley Spellerberg while Betty Friedan lent support to the Florida legislators working for ratification. These included Gwen Cherry, a NWPC leader and the first African American woman in the state legislature, and Lori Wilson, a forceful state senator and media magnet, another glamorous blond often likened to Gloria Steinem and married to Gannett founder Al Neuharth. Numerous polls showed a majority in the state favored ratification. In early April, however, the state senate voted against ratification 21–19 after two longtime supporters switched their votes.[46]

Before the vote, a consistent theme of ERA advocates was that Florida, considered by many as part of a more progressive "New South," would embrace equality. After the vote, an exasperated Senator Wilson excoriated her colleagues for clinging to traditional Southern ideas that had impeded the struggles for civil rights for African Americans and for women. "Good Ole Boys in Southern politics," she insisted, had refused to approve the Nineteenth Amendment in 1920 and "fought the 1964 Civil Rights Act down to their last axe handles" but had been overcome in both instances. Now, with ten southern states holding out against ERA ratification, it appeared they were trying desperately to hold on to their "weakening power, for one last hurrah."[47]

That spring, Arkansas and Oklahoma also rejected ratification. In Mississippi, a woman state legislator who had asked the infamous Mississippi Sovereignty Commission to investigate Michael Schwerner before he and fellow civil rights workers Andrew Goodman and James Chaney were murdered in 1964, continued to keep the ERA locked up in committee. Georgia defeated ratification despite the pleas of ERA backers in the legislature for it to ratify as a tribute to native daughter Rosalynn Carter. Outside the South, Missouri, Illinois, and Arizona also defeated ratification campaigns and Idaho voted to rescind. The spring battle at an end, a jubilant Schlafly thanked the "wonderful women and courageous legislators who defeated ERA in 1977" and "the Lord who guided our way to victory."[48]

Convinced that pleading was not enough, NOW decided to play hardball or "pull off the velvet gloves," and launched a boycott of states that had not ratified the ERA. National organizations that had endorsed the ERA—religious, educational, scientific, labor—began to cancel upcoming conventions. New Orleans, Chicago, St. Louis, Miami, and Las Vegas were all hit hard. The boycott was highly controversial especially in tourist-dependent states such as Florida. It angered many Florida legislators and may have damaged ERA prospects. Schlafly accused NOW of having a "public tantrum" and ridiculed NOW president Ellie Smeal for refusing to take her daughter to Disney World. Schlafly ally John Ashcroft, then the attorney general of Missouri, and his counterpart in Nevada filed suits charging NOW with violation of federal antitrust laws.[49]

That same spring other gender issues roiled the public as the IWY state meetings approached. Congress was virtually paralyzed over the issue of federal funding of abortion. After *Roe*, feminists had regarded the abortion issue as settled, but a fast-developing pro-life movement was intent on limiting the effects of the Supreme Court decision and hoped eventually to have it overturned. The Hyde Amendment, introduced by Illinois congressman Henry Hyde, was its first major success against *Roe*. Adopted in fall 1976 and up for renewal in spring 1977, the measure prohibited the use of Medicaid funds for abortions except in the case of rape or incest. For months, appropriations bills for HEW and the Labor Department were stalled while Congress fought out this issue.[50]

Feminists were hopeful that the restriction on federal funding would be voted down in Congress or ruled unconstitutional as a result of a case that was argued before the Supreme Court in January 1977. But on June 20, in *Maher v. Roe*, the court ruled that the federal government was not required to fund abortion.[51]

This huge setback for the abortion rights movement precipitated a major setback in relations between President Carter and feminists, including those within his administration. When asked at a press conference for his reaction to the ruling, Carter issued a statement that enraged them: "Well, as you know, there are many things in life that are not fair, that wealthy people can afford and poor people can't. But I don't believe that the federal government should take action to try to make those opportunities exactly equal, particularly when there is a moral factor involved." It became instantly notorious among feminists as Carter's "life is unfair" statement.[52]

Carter's assistant for public liaison, Midge Costanza, at the center of the abortion imbroglio, called a meeting of women in the administration who were eager to discuss the ruling and the president's reaction. She intended the meeting to be strictly confidential, but *Washington Post* reporter Myra MacPherson found out about it even before Costanza returned to her office. When Carter learned of the meeting, he was "furious" with Costanza, which was also leaked to the press. At the next cabinet meeting he reiterated his position on abortion and put out the word to his senior staff that he would not tolerate such disloyalty.[53]

Meanwhile, pro-life leaders, though pleased about the Hyde Amendment and the *Maher* decision, were strategizing about ways to reverse *Roe* altogether. Contemplating the difficulties of winning the two thirds of Congress and three fourths of the states needed to gain an amendment to protect the life of a fetus from the point of conception, they sought ways to broaden the base of their movement. Success would require reaching beyond their Catholic base to attract more Protestants and cultivating more support in the historically anti-Catholic South. Thus in 1977 they started a major drive to convince religious conservatives in the region to join them in the campaign against abortion.[54]

If all this wasn't enough to inflame tensions around gender issues as the summer of IWY state meetings approached, that spring gay rights emerged as a new political issue, one even more volatile than the ERA or abortion. In January, after Dade County, Florida, adopted an antidiscrimination ordinance, pop singer and Christian conservative Anita Bryant started a repeal effort. When polls revealed that most women voters in the county were sympathetic to gay rights, the campaign developed a strategy targeting mothers—denouncing gays as child molesters. Bryant's Save Our Children campaign launched a national antigay rights movement. It quickly caught national attention and drew support from Phyllis Schlafly, Jesse Helms, and Ronald Reagan, who sent Anita Bryant messages of support. On June 7, 1977, 70 percent of Dade County voters voted to repeal the ordinance, a huge victory for Bryant that was celebrated by social conservatives across the nation.[55]

Bryant's campaign against gay rights also galvanized gay rights supporters, and underscored their need for allies and political power. Jean O'Leary, the co-executive director of the National Gay Task Force (NGTF) appointed to the IWY Commission, saw the IWY as a means toward that end. Since 1972 when the UN conference in Mexico City totally ignored the issue of gay rights, O'Leary, Charlotte Bunch, Barbara Love, and other lesbian rights activists on the board of the NGTF Women's Caucus had tried without success to get the Ford-appointed IWY Committee to consider it, working through the National Women's Alliance. In 1976, gay leaders, including O'Leary, had also tried to cultivate support within the Democratic Party with little success. In the process of lobbying the DNC, however, O'Leary discovered a key ally soon to join Carter's inner circle: Midge Costanza.[56]

In March 1977, without Carter's advance knowledge and while he was away at Camp David, Costanza organized a historic meeting in the White House at which fourteen gay rights leaders made appeals for reforms in federal policy. Gay rights supporters hailed this meeting as a major break-through. Predictably, it ignited furious protests from conservatives and even some moderates and liberals who were outraged. Carter never criticized Costanza for the meeting, but his aides certainly did.[57]

Shortly thereafter, at the IWY Commission's first meeting in April, O'Leary tried to persuade other commissioners to make protection of lesbian and gay rights one of the core recommendations to be sent to the states. After discussion of this issue, along with others not addressed by the Ford commission, the commissioners declined O'Leary's request. According to NOW leader Eleanor Smeal, one of the new commission members, most feared the issue was too divisive and would ignite controversy at the IWY state meetings that were intended to cultivate grassroots support and broaden the appeal of the feminist agenda. According to O'Leary, only Smeal, whose organization had formally endorsed inclusion of protection of the rights of lesbians as a legitimate issue of the women's movement back in 1971, backed her effort.[58]

Even Abzug, who had in 1975 sponsored the first bill in Congress to protect the rights of homosexuals, had reservations. In Congress she had represented one of the most liberal districts in the nation, which included Manhattan's West Side and a large constituency of gay voters. But she had been of little help to O'Leary and other gay rights leaders when they sought to gain power within the Democratic Party in 1976. O'Leary later claimed that Abzug had physically held the door shut when she tried to enter a New York Democratic Party meeting about delegate selection. According to Costanza, Abzug was not at all happy about O'Leary pressing this issue on the IWY Commission. "Let me tell you," Costanza later remarked. "Bella had a hard time with Jean O'Leary on that commission" and "Jean O'Leary felt personally betrayed by Bella Abzug."[59]

The IWY Commission did agree to draw up "guidelines" on "Sexual Preference" similar to the ones designed to guide discussion of the core issues at preliminary workshops at the meetings. It also approved a resolution encouraging state coordinating committees who so chose to deal with topics not addressed by the Ford Commission report, including "sexual or affectional preference," as well as poverty, prostitution, disarmament, domestic violence, health, housing, and the "special problems of girls and young women."[60]

Martha Griffiths, who had been unable to attend the commission meeting, was appalled. In a letter she asked Abzug to forward to IWY Commission members and state leaders, she insisted that expanding the topics to be addressed—and especially taking on the highly controversial issue of sexual preference—would undermine feminists' efforts to make further progress in ending discrimination in jobs and education which she deemed most essential to women's advancement. The distinction between the core recommendations and issues recommended for discussion workshops would be overlooked, or deliberately ignored, by appalled conservative leaders seeking material that would appall others.[61]

O'Leary and other lesbian activists immediately went to work to assure that their issue would be taken up at IWY state meetings and that a recommendation to protect their rights would be on the list of planks to be voted on in Houston in November. This required gaining resolutions of support at a large number of state meetings, which would then compel the IWY Commission to add it.[62]

According to Charlotte Bunch, who worked closely with Jean O'Leary in this effort, after the IWY Commission approved the resolution, the National Gay Task Force sent out mailings and press releases announcing that "lesbian rights was now considered a 'legitimate' women's issue" and "urging lesbians to get involved in all phases of the state conferences." In one mailing O'Leary emphasized that "in order to get any pro-gay resolutions passed at the National Conference, we need a groundswell of support coming out of the earlier [state] meetings." Their goal was to gain resolutions addressing four issues: "Passage of gay civil rights laws prohibiting discrimination in employment, house, etc.; Repeal of all laws governing private sexual behavior between consenting adults; Passage of laws making sexual preference irrelevant in determining child custody and visitation rights; and Inclusion of more and better lesbian visibility in the media."[63]

Much of the effort to build support for lesbian rights proposals involved turning out large numbers of lesbians. But by the summer, having witnessed the homophobic campaign led by Bryant, many more feminists—gay or straight—who would be attending the state meetings were inclined to support these proposals.

Each of these developments—Carter's controversial appointments, the heated battles over ERA, abortion, and gay rights—portended trouble for the coming IWY state meetings, even as they magnified the meetings' importance. Both sides recognized that whoever controlled the meetings had the power to control the recommendations for future policy that would be adopted and therefore validate their claims to represent American women.

Carter's appointment of prominent feminists to the IWY Commission—particularly Bella Abzug, Gloria Steinem, Ellie Smeal, and Jean O'Leary—produced an instant and entirely predictable reaction from conservatives already outraged over congressional funding of the IWY. Focusing on the four relatively radical appointees, they said little or nothing about the other commission members: the national leaders of the League of Women Voters and the Girl Scouts; the Tennessee First Lady; the male editors of *Good Housekeeping* and *Redbook*; or Jean Stapleton, the famous actress then wildly popular for her role as the beloved homemaker, Edith Bunker, on the hit comedy *All in the Family*. Above all they denounced the appointment of Abzug as the IWY presiding officer. A Georgia-based right-wing newsletter *The Voice of Liberty* decried Abzug's "95% liberal voting record" and her introduction of the nation's first gay rights bill, "which, if it had passed, would have meant that sex deviates could teach our children, etc." And it did so under the caption "Communist-Fronter Heads IWY."[64]

Carter was deluged with letters of protest. One writer asked why he felt "constrained to seek out women like Mrs. Abzug for important government posts" and denounced her as "an irresponsible, rather loud-mouthed leftist." Another called her a "washed up politician who leaned" too far to the left and would be a detriment to the Democratic Party as head of the IWY. One protested Abzug's appointment to this "high post" because "Bella does not support family values, she has consistently voted a pro-abortion platform," and said, "I do not want my husband's hard earned tax dollar to be funding such a cause as Bella will lead." Abzug's critics seemed to delight in her recent defeat in the 1976 New York senatorial primary. A Missouri man wrote: "If the people of New York don't want her you can be assured that we out here in the hinterland don't want her in even greater degree," adding, "Wishing you every success in your administration."[65]

Nationally syndicated columnist and television pundit James J. Kilpatrick, who for years as editor of the *Richmond News Leader* in Richmond, Virginia, had lent the power of his pen to southern "massive resistance" to desegregation and once described himself as "ten miles to the right of Ivan the Terrible," was one of the most vociferous critics. He immediately pounced on the news, denouncing Carter's choices and the whole IWY program, which he called "Bella's Boondoggle." "The gentlewoman from New York," he said, "whose views are as predictable as the vernal equinox," has been "handed a $5 million kitty to stroke." The money would fund "stacked and rigged" state meetings plus a big "national whoop-te-doo" at which feminist leaders, representatives of every minority group, appointed "according to demographic rules as immutable as the law of physics," a "smattering of Republicans" and "a celebrity or two" would put together recommendations meant to stand for the wishes of all American women.[66]

The "ulterior purpose," Kilpatrick assured his readers, was to promote the ERA. "Unless I am vastly mistaken," he wrote, this commission will be spending money "taken from the people under the compulsions of taxation" for the "unpardonable" and "probably unlawful" purpose of "making a last ditch effort to get the ERA ratified." Kilpatrick urged conservatives to mount a counteroffensive. "Bella tends to overwhelm opposition," he wrote, "but the gentlewoman is not invincible." Through "vigorous effort . . . conferences can be unstacked, rigged schedules of witnesses unrigged."[67]

Phyllis Schlafly and other conservative women, of course, were already on the job. As she reminded readers of the *Phyllis Schlafly Report*, she had opposed the National Commission on Observance of IWY since Ford first established it in 1975 and stacked its membership with feminists. She had filed lawsuits to prevent the commission from lobbying the government, which she claimed violated federal law.[68] She had petitioned Congress and the courts to end the IWY program before wasting more taxpayers' money, and when these efforts failed, had instructed her followers to prepare to turn out in force and challenge feminists for control of the state meetings and the recommendations to be produced. "If you do your job right," she told them, "you can make the 'libbers' sorry they ever held the IWY conferences."[69]

The March 1977 announcement of Carter's appointments to the commission, however, put Schlafly through the roof. Carter, she reported, had appointed commission members who were forty-one pro-ERA and one con-ERA, including "many of the most militant women's libbers in the country" and the "co-executive director of the National Gay Task Force."[70]

Rosemary Thomson, then Illinois Eagle Forum director, sent a blistering letter to Carter denouncing him for "refusing to name any [commission members] from Eagle Forum—'the alternative to women's lib'" which "represents the traditional Judeo-Christian women's viewpoint, a position you claim to espouse as a 'born-again' Christian." She warned that women from evangelical churches would be outraged at his "elevating homosexuals, lesbians, and women who reject Biblical principles to a prestigious national position on the IWY."[71]

Schlafly and other leading conservative women watched to see what would happen as feminists laid plans for the IWY and planned their counterattack. Again she filed a lawsuit to stop the IWY Commission from using its funds to lobby for the ERA as she also mounted a fund drive to counter the millions feminists would be getting from Uncle Sam. Listing the amounts the IWY had allocated to the states for their meetings, she asked Stop-ERA members "to help raise just 3% of the amount the IWY Commission has allocated to each state" to be used in the battle ahead.[72]

Keeping a close eye on IWY activities, Nellie Gray traveled to Vermont to observe its February 1977 IWY meeting, the only one that would take place before May. Gray, president of March for Life, was a Washington, D.C., Labor Department attorney and a devout Catholic who, after *Roe v. Wade*, gave up her legal career to devote herself to overturning the decision.[73]

In 1976, she had testified before the U.S. House Appropriations Committee against funding of the IWY, arguing that the meetings were likely to promote "abortion-on-demand" and the "deceptive ERA." Returning home from the Vermont meeting, Gray raised the alarm, reporting that things were even worse than they thought. After the organizers had made a "calculated attempt" to exclude all but liberal feminists from the meetings and endorsed the ERA and abortion—as expected—Vermont feminists had added what Gray described as "an additional anti-Christian category: gay rights!"[74]

Another Schlafly lieutenant, Stop-ERA leader Kathryn Dunaway, a self-described conservative "token" on the Georgia IWY coordinating committee, also had appalling news to report. As one of the few conservatives appointed to a state IWY committee, she received a packet of information from the IWY Commission containing the core recommendations and the workshop guidelines. Reviewing the material, she concluded that the commission planned to push through these recommendations. In addition—although ERA advocates had long denied any connection between the proposed amendment and abortion—the material she received showed that IWY leaders planned to promote both, which, she claimed, exposed their "true intentions" and "anti-family" values.[75] Dunaway immediately notified Schlafly and other anti-IWY leaders. As Rosemary Thomson recalled, Dunaway telephoned her, saying: "We've got to warn Christians in other states that IWY plans to 'railroad' these Women's Lib resolutions through all the meetings then tell Congress and the President that the majority of women want these laws!"[76]

This small group of well-organized conservative leaders then sprang into action, launching a new antifeminist campaign in which they presented themselves as righteous warriors battling the feminist establishment on behalf of God, country, and family. Together with these trusted lieutenants from Stop-ERA and the Eagle Forum, Schlafly founded a new ad hoc organization, the IWY Citizens' Review Committee (CRC).[77]

Schlafly appointed Rosemary Thomson as CRC chairman and Kathryn Dunaway as coordinator of the organization's state campaigns. Elaine Donnelly, Michigan Stop-ERA chairman and Eagle Forum media chairman, became media chairman for the CRC as well.[78] Lottie Beth Hobbs—Women Who Want to Be Women (WWWW) founder and now serving on the board of the Eagle Forum—was also a key figure in the CRC along with Nellie Gray.[79] The CRC advisory board included other long-term Schlafly allies—state representative Donna Carson of Arizona and two Virginians, Eva Scott of the Virginia House of Delegates and Kathleen Teague, director of the American Legislative Exchange Council (ALEC), a corporate-sponsored organization that worked closely with conservative state legislators to gain business-friendly laws.[80]

Schlafly announced the formation of the CRC under Thomson's leadership and invited women interested in becoming state leaders of the organization to apply. As in the anti-ERA campaign, they worked through several key and overlapping organizations, those they referred to as "our groups," Eagle Forum, Stop-ERA, HOW (Happiness of Womanhood), and WWWW, and adding Nellie Gray's organization, March for Life. On May 1, 1977, Thomson sent a letter to CRC heads in each state warning that IWY leaders were using the $5 million federal grant to promote feminist goals and excluding conservatives. Describing how "pro-feminist, pro-abortion, anti-free enterprise views" had dominated the Vermont conference, how federal regulations to nominating and electing delegates were "openly violated," and how immorality and lesbianism were advocated, she said, "We can easily predict what will happen in your state." Thomson instructed them to immediately contact state IWY committees demanding they put "our groups" on their mailing lists and supplying names of conservative women to serve as speakers.[81]

To the press, IWY Citizens' Review Committee leaders presented their organization as "an educational coalition" formed to urge like-minded women to participate in IWY meetings and to "assist non-feminist women, many of whom have never been to a convention as large as an IWY conference, in preparing for the State and National Conference." Their other goal was to gather information about what transpired at the conferences and bring violations of federal statutes to the attention of Congress and the public.[82]

Citizens' Review Committee leaders used the May issues of the *Phyllis Schlafly Report* and *Eagle Forum Newsletter* to carry out those goals. To inform conservative women what to expect and how to vote, they supplied a list of the sixteen core recommendations alongside their own interpretations of them. For example, the IWY recommendation calling for "vigorous and expeditious enforcement of all laws, executive orders, and regulations prohibiting discrimination in employment" and extension of "protections and privileges afforded minority business owners . . . to women business owners," was translated as meaning "the full power of the Federal Government should be used against private employers to enforce preferential treatment of women" and employers "compelled to reach affirmative action quotas . . . even when this means hiring less qualified women with no dependents instead of more qualified men with many dependents." The *Phyllis Schlafly Report* also supplied the names of senators and congressmen who had voted for and against authorization of the IWY conferences and the cowards who "ducked out"—instructing readers to keep reminding these men that "you know how they voted" and expressing "continued indignation" against "federal financing of the radical women's libbers."[83]

The *Eagle Forum Newsletter* gave specific instructions on what to do once the conferences began: send teams to monitor the IWY meetings; take notes about "misuse of taxpayers' money to promote women's lib goals"; and document instances of "biased program, agenda, speakers, workshops, and printed materials" and "crooked" voting—all of which they assumed in advance would take place. After the meetings, they were to hold press conferences to publicize this malpractice and send "indignant" letters to lawmakers to protest their funding only one side of this battle over public policy.[84]

IWY Citizens' Review leaders also reached out to old allies, encouraging them to become involved in the battles set to take place in their states.[85] Religious groups and political organizations that had been involved in the anti-ERA effort would again support an effort launched by a small cadre of extremely conservative women—a development that would have major consequences for national politics.

The forthcoming summer meetings would provide an opportunity to mobilize conservatives like never before. This would be a nationwide fight. Whereas the ERA battle was confined to the "unratified states" plus a few where rescission seemed possible, the IWY would be fought in every state and territory and in the space of a few months. In states where the ERA had been ratified quickly and with little discussion, the IWY would produce the debate that had never taken place.

In addition, the battle between feminists and conservatives for control of the IWY would involve more conservatives than the ERA fight and focus their anger all at once against ungodly, government-sponsored feminism. It would include, but not be limited to, the ERA issue. Other hot-button issues that over the spring were being debated with a new ferocity were also on the table. CRC leaders—women who had launched the fight against the ERA—now called on leaders of another single-issue movement, the fight against abortion, to join them against a common foe. During the battle for control of the IWY, the enemies of their enemies would become their friends.[86]

CRC leaders warned religious conservatives that the stakes had never been higher, that these government-sponsored conferences led by "the most notorious women's libbers in the country" were a grave threat to the traditional family and to the United States as a moral, Christian nation. They urged their followers to turn out their congregations to defend their way of life at these upcoming state meetings. Many of these women, including Pentecostals, were still largely untouched by politics and knew almost nothing about the women's movement, but the same ministers who had insisted they stay away from politics would, in the coming months, literally bus them to the IWY meetings.

CRC leaders never failed to point out that the upcoming IWY meetings were inspired by the United Nations, an institution they opposed as a threat to national sovereignty. This was particularly disturbing to groups such as the John Birch Society, which saw creation of the IWY as a UN maneuver to promote "one-world government." Most had heard about the World Plan of Action adopted at the UN's IWY Conference in Mexico City in 1975, which they believed had been a chaotic event at which the United States and Israel were unfairly criticized by radical and demanding Third World countries as women fought among themselves. Martha Andrews, editor of an archconservative Georgia newsletter, reported that besides "howling and hair pulling," participants had adopted a plan of action that "in addition to endorsing so-called women's issues, delved into other domestic and foreign matters, including 'equitable distribution of income' (socialism) and world disarmament." Yet, she said, the U.S. delegation unanimously endorsed the World Plan of Action and "pledged to strive to IMPLEMENT IT INTO U.S. LAW." That, she said, was "what IWY meetings are about."[87]

CRC leaders also fanned flames of resentment about big government, high taxes, and federal spending on social programs, pointing out the millions being spent on IWY. In 1977, Americans suffered from the combined effects of inflation and economic stagnation dubbed "stagflation." There were already signs of the looming "tax-payer revolt" that would soon shock the nation as Californians approved the tax-slashing Proposition 13.

Many IWY critics were outraged at the degree of authority and respect bestowed on black women by national IWY leaders, many of whom were themselves African American. Some white conservative women viewed it as profoundly insulting for the IWY Commission to insist on racial, ethnic, and economic diversity among the commission members, state organizers, and delegates elected to Houston, and to court participation by civil rights veterans and welfare mothers, while snubbing their leaders, including Phyllis

Schlafly, a woman they revered for her "Christ-like" sacrifices for country, family, and faith.[88]

Occasionally, during the weeks of preparation prior to the state meetings, feminists caught glimpses of the conservatives' intentions. In Oklahoma, feminists in charge of the state coordinating committee discovered a notebook left behind by a state Eagle Forum leader who had attended one of their meetings as a guest. It contained notes of a December 20, 1976, phone conversation with Phyllis Schlafly in which she instructed the leader to conduct a fake poll of state coordinating committee members to ascertain their positions on the ERA, abortion, federally funded child care, and a few other issues. All spring, Eagle Forum members attended the committee meetings (which by law were open to the public), asking questions, delaying the meetings, and always bringing tape recorders.[89]

In South Carolina, according to NOW leader and attorney Malissa Burnette, in mid-May "anti-ERA forces" had "virtually ransacked" the IWY office in Columbia. She told the press: "Approximately twenty persons entered the office en masse, opened drawers, searched through files and disturbed the operation of the office" and "apparently" stole lists of organizations and letters. State CRC leader Zilla Hinton denounced the charges as "slanderous" and "completely false," saying she had come to the office requesting IWY materials and had picked up material that was on the floor.[90]

Most women involved in planning the upcoming IWY meetings, however, had no hint that the conservatives were even organizing, much less the extent of it. Much of the CRC's mobilization effort took place through church newsletters, telephone trees, and mailing lists of conservative political organizations—all off the radar of the liberal feminists. And not wanting to tip off feminists about their plans, conservatives generally ignored IWY organizers' requests that participants preregister for the state meetings. For all of their planning, the feminists were virtually unaware of the gathering storm soon to engulf them.

CHAPTER 7

Armageddon State by State

Whether you receive food stamps or bank dividends, whether you compete in beauty contests or bowling tournaments, whether you give the boss coffee or ulcers or you ARE the boss, whether you are deaf or deafening ... IF YOU ARE A WOMAN ... You are needed at the Oklahoma Women's Conference.

—OKLAHOMA IWY COORDINATING COMMITTEE, 1977

From May through July 1977, approximately 130,000 women and several hundred men would participate in the state and territorial IWY meetings. Intended to celebrate women's achievements and chart a path toward a better future, they quickly became contested battlegrounds in a new kind of cultural warfare. As the meetings went on, feminists with high hopes of bringing women together to find common ground were surprised to find themselves challenged by growing numbers of angry conservatives who turned out to defend God, country, and family—from *them*.[1]

The organizers—groups of women appointed to serve on state IWY coordinating committees—were for the most part moderate feminists who had high hopes that these federally funded conferences would produce good results for women in their states and nation. Selected primarily by the Ford-appointed IWY Commission from names suggested by members of Congress, state women's commissions, and hundreds of national and state organizations, they were respected members of their communities. Many were officers in voluntary organizations or elected or appointed officials. Many were wives and mothers and churchgoers in mainline denominations that supported ERA.[2]

Since by law appointees had to be "members of diverse racial, ethnic, and religious groups, unions, publications, women of all incomes and women of all ages," few coordinating committee members had worked together previously and they were hard-pressed to get the state meetings organized in such a short time. Looking back, one Mississippi IWY organizer remarked it was "a wonder the conference ever got off the ground." Given the "initial shock of having to work with virtual strangers in such close contact," the "wide-spread distances over which they were scattered," and the fact that many of the members were employed full time and gave their time "at a great financial sacrifice," only their "tremendous commitment to the goals of the conference" enabled them to accomplish their task.[3]

State IWY coordinating committees were given their shares of the $5 million allocation, the amounts—like the numbers of delegates they could elect—determined according to state population. Much of the money was reserved to pay delegates' travel expenses to the national conference. To ensure that low-income women could participate, all delegates would be fully funded.[4]

There were ground rules for registration (any state resident female or male over sixteen who signed up was eligible) and procedures for voting on delegates and resolutions—all carefully designed by the Ford IWY Commission to prevent fraud and maintain order. State coordinating committees were instructed to prepare slates of nominees—again carefully configured to achieve the requisite diversity—to present to participants who could also nominate additional candidates.[5]

State leaders were expected to present the sixteen core recommendations for consideration. The IWY Commission supplied them with material for workshops on the core issues and the additional topics added by the Carter Commission. Charlotte Bunch of the National Gay Task Force Women's Caucus believed, however, that because of "subtle" or "blatant" resistance in the national IWY office, the booklet *Sexual Preference: Why Is Lesbianism a Woman's Issue?* that she and Jean O'Leary prepared "never received the circulation and attention that other such educational materials were given." For the most part, each state coordinating committee was free to set its own agenda and choose its own plenary speeches, workshops, entertainment, and complementary events so each meeting might "reflect the character and particular concerns of its state or territory."[6]

State organizers were keen on making these conferences address state as well as national issues of concern to local women. In places where antifeminists were particularly active, state coordinators tried to ward off controversy by downplaying hot-button issues, including reproductive rights, homosexuality, and even the ERA. They hoped to focus instead on matters such as improving women's legal status, aiding displaced homemakers, preventing violence against women and children, and meeting the needs of the poor and elderly—issues on which they assumed most women would agree. Linda Hayes, an IWY organizer in Alabama, said her committee had been careful to put aside the ERA and abortion issues because "the problems of women are so much broader." In Georgia, the state coordinating committee headed by Georgia State University vice president Kathleen Crouch stipulated that candidates for delegate slots could not reveal their positions on ERA and refused to allow ERA debate in the plenary session, "bending over backwards to be fair," according to one reporter.[7]

Of course, once the conferences began, participants could—and did—bring up any topics they wished, and the meetings produced thousands of resolutions beyond the sixteen suggested by the IWY Commission. In many cases coordinating committees invited conservatives to participate in workshops and included them on the slates of nominees—though never to the extent that feminist control was at risk.[8] As women who were more radical or conservative mobilized and engaged in battle state by state, however, best laid plans often went awry.

Coordinating committees went to work with energy and imagination, planning weekend conferences to take place at university campuses, hotels, and civic centers with themes such as "Missouri Women, a Strong Past, a Confident Future"; "South Carolina Women, from Heritage to Horizons"; "Colorado Women: Moving Mountains Together," and "Mississippi Women: Awake and Aware." They recruited keynote speakers including IWY Presiding Officer Bella Abzug; former Presiding Officer Jill Ruckelshaus; IWY Commissioner Gloria Steinem; Congresswomen Shirley Chisholm, Barbara Mikulski, and Lindy Boggs; women prominent in the Carter administration; celebrities; and many state elected officials—who were fairly responsive before the conferences and the conflicts began.[9]

Organizers planned many forms of "entertainment" designed to highlight the accomplishments of the women of their states such as the "Indian Women's Cultural Pageant" in New Mexico. Athletic exhibitions, including a women's crew team race sponsored by the University of Wisconsin, reflected the feminist movement's emphasis on women and sports. Many programs focused on women's history. Missouri planned to open its meeting with an appearance by six elderly suffragists who had taken part in the "Walkless,

Talkless Parade" outside the Democratic National Convention in St. Louis in 1916. South Carolina planned to honor women who had been trailblazers in the state. Each would wear a badge saying: "I broke a barrier. Talk with me." All of it was, as one Mississippi organizer put it, "to help women realize their potential."[10]

For weeks before the meetings, state organizers went all out to attract participants, taking seriously the mandate to reach women who had not previously attended women's meetings. They blanketed the airwaves with public announcements and seized every opportunity to appear on TV and radio talk shows. All too often, however, they had to rely on paid advertising. At that point press interest was limited; after more than a decade of feminist activity, a women's conference, even federally sponsored, did not seem like breaking news.

National IWY leaders were pleased and impressed with the creative and unconventional methods of reaching newcomers that state organizers devised such as posting signs in beauty parlors and stuffing rural mailboxes. In West Virginia, there was "excellent outreach by widows of coal miners who went door-to-door to spread the word about the meeting." In many states they distributed literature written in foreign languages. Rhode Island circulated materials in Portuguese, while in Maine they printed pamphlets in French. In California, bilingual teams went into the fields to reach Spanish-speaking agricultural workers. Working through advocacy groups such as the National Welfare Rights Organization, organizers reached out to the poor, inviting them to apply for special assistance to pay for travel and registration expenses and offered child care at no cost. The wording of the "calls" the state organizers put out varied, but everywhere the message was the same: "Drop those dishes . . . cover up your typewriter . . . stop doing the same old thing . . . Join in an extraordinary weekend meeting . . . the first Federally-sponsored women's meeting ever held. Here's your chance to discuss and act on issues of concern to all women—in the family and home, employment, health, education, public life, and in this International Decade of Women . . . Make yourself part of the action."[11]

Outreach committees in many states sponsored preliminary rallies and "speak outs," seeking to build excitement and enhance turnout for the upcoming meetings. Utah sponsored fifty simultaneous pre-meetings, each one cochaired by a local woman and a high school student. Some states promoted the meetings by publicizing the reports on *The Legal Status of Homemakers* in each state, prepared by local lawyers—usually women—sponsored by the IWY Commission. In Puerto Rico they held preliminary meetings at which there was some rather important "consciousness raising" taking place: one speaker asked if anyone had to ask her husband's permission to come and nearly every hand went up. During the meeting many women took advantage of the free health screening offered. Alabama sent a "Voices and Faces of Alabama Women" program on tour that featured theatrical performances and photographs of women prominent in the state's history. Supportive mayors proclaimed it IWY Day in their towns. One textile mill donated a hundred T-shirts to teenagers who helped distribute posters advertising the program. In Arkansas, the coordinating committee even rented a Goodyear Blimp to fly over the meeting site. Later, state IWY organizers pointed to these elaborate promotional schemes when conservatives accused them of withholding information about the upcoming conferences.[12]

Given the years of battling conservatives over the ERA and abortion, feminists were surprisingly confident that the meetings would attract more friends than foes, but national polls indicated that only a small minority of women held strong antifeminist views. IWY commissioner Eleanor Smeal later recalled that before the summer conflicts began, "Bella thought you would just advertise the state conventions and people would come, and they would be representative of women in the United States."[13] They had no idea that their critics were as organized and determined as they were—or that IWY would make them more so.

Actually, IWY organizers *hoped* that the newcomers they worked hard to attract would include conservative women—presumably alienated by fear, misinformation, and/or pressure from men—whose minds would be opened by the experience. Confident in their cause, buoyed by previous victories, IWY leaders expected that when exposed to real feminists and feminist ideas rather than media-created stereotypes, most American women would support them.

In the past, conservatives had given feminist gatherings a wide berth, but this was something different. Precisely because the IWY meetings were official government-sponsored gatherings intended to guide Congress and the president, conservative women were not about to concede the field. Unknown to feminists, and guided by the IWY Citizens' Review Committee (CRC), they too were working hard to stimulate participation in the upcoming state meetings, spreading the word about the appalling changes radical feminists hoped to impose on the nation through the IWY.

*　*　*

The first skirmish between the opposing forces took place May 6–7, 1977, at the Georgia IWY meeting held in Atlanta's Sheraton-Biltmore Hotel. More than twelve hundred people turned out for the meeting, promoted throughout the state as an "unprecedented opportunity for Georgians at the grass-roots level to examine women's lives and experiences, to build an appreciation of the contributions women have made and will continue to make to all aspects of national life, and to work towards common goals." Participants were asked to register in advance and select from a list of workshops: Athletics and Women, Education and Training, Female Offenders, Health Care and Services, Homemaking, Housing, International Interdependence, Legislation and Legal Status, Media and the Arts, Minority Women, Older Women, Unions and the Working Woman, Women in Public Life, Working Women, Younger Women. There would be exhibits and "speakers of national prominence." Brochures promised it would be "EXCITING AND CHALLENGING." It was.[14]

The Georgia IWY meeting was much anticipated as the first to take place since Bella Abzug and the Carter-appointed IWY Commission took charge and was held in Jimmy and Rosalynn Carter's home state. Presiding Officer Bella Abzug opened the gathering in person. After reading a telegram of welcome from the First Lady, she delivered a keynote address denounced by Schlafly as "a rousing appeal for ERA and other lib goals."[15]

Georgia was also a stronghold of the IWY Citizens' Review Committee. It was home to Kathryn Dunaway, the CRC officer tasked with coordinating its state challenges, described by Rosemary Thomson as the "70-year-old dynamo who heads Georgia's Stop-ERA." One of the few conservatives serving on a state coordinating committee, Dunaway had full access to IWY plans. From her perspective, it was a happy coincidence that national IWY leaders chose to have the first meeting in her territory.[16]

A month before the meeting, Dunaway sent out a letter from Stop-ERA and Eagle Forum of Georgia summoning the troops: "We urgently need 1,500 women to attend this two-day meeting and represent the viewpoint of responsible, freedom-loving, Christian women. We realize that to many this may seem something of a sacrifice in time and effort, but we believe it is of such great and far reaching importance that we ask you to make this sacrifice gladly." This idea—that taking time from home, family, and church to attend these meetings was a great sacrifice—was a persistent theme in the conservatives' calls to arms. But this meeting—that feminists had scheduled for Mother's Day weekend—demanded more sacrifice than most.[17]

Dunaway, assisted by other IWY Citizens' Review Committee officers, prepared her troops with great thoroughness. CRC chairman Rosemary Thomson came from Illinois and media chairman Elaine Donnelly arrived from Michigan. Schlafly herself flew in weeks before the meeting to conduct an April 20, 1977, training workshop at Atlanta's First Baptist Church. The plan was to have at least one representative of their group at each workshop to present the conservative view on the matter at hand. They handed out workshop observation forms and devised a buddy system so no "non-IWY woman" would find herself alone among the "women's libbers."[18]

It was imperative, CRC leaders told their forces, to document all offenses, especially violations of the congressional legislation mandating IWY, including discrimination against conservatives. When possible they were to record the proceedings for later use in filing affidavits. While it was not possible to anticipate everything their enemies would propose, they were to oppose "anything calling for more government control" or taking away rights from people "under the guise of 'doing good.'" Support for resolutions advocating job training or health care would increase government spending and "add support to the IWY program." Finally, CRC leaders counseled: "Do not be intimidated" and "maintain your dignity at all times—even if you are treated rudely. A soft voice and a smile work miracles."[19]

IWY Citizens' Review Committee leaders also issued instructions for voting on delegates. In their hospitality suite—accessible only to those escorted by someone known to CRC leaders or able to give a secret sign— they distributed a list of conservative candidates to compete with the slate proposed by the state coordinating committee.[20]

In the end, Georgia elected what organizers described with pride as a "racially and ideologically mixed delegation" to go to Houston with far more feminists than conservatives. As for the core recommendations, Georgia "adopted some, defeated some, and failed to act on some" and passed many additional recommendations proposed by workshops. Carole Ashkinaze, a reporter for the *Atlanta Journal-Constitution*, declared the meeting a success, as participants reached a consensus on several important recommendations including recognition of the homemaker's contributions in the home.[21]

Rosemary Thomson saw it differently. It was only because of the CRC's strenuous organizing efforts that Georgia would be sending "three Christian delegates and one alternate to represent women of traditional moral values" in Houston. Later, in her book *The Price of LIBerty*, she said that Christian women had been deeply offended by what they witnessed at the IWY meeting, which was financed by the U.S. government, yet had "no invocation, no pledge to the flag, [and] no American flag in sight!" There was "a somewhat dubious prayer offered by a female clergyperson" at the evening banquet that began: "Our Creator who nurtures us like a mother." Moreover, lesbian participation in the meeting had been shocking. Thomson described an incident in which two "Christian ladies," curious to see what the "Sexual Orientation Workshop" was about, "made a prompt retreat upon entering a roomful of lesbians who were patting each other's bodies and calling out dirty names." Others were distraught at the defeat of a resolution offered by the conservative coalition asking that public school textbooks "reflect the moral and religious values of parents." Thomson described dozens of women walking out in tears, with one "visibly shaken mother" sobbing: "The IWY just used our own tax money to cast a vote against God."[22]

Too few in number to control the meeting, Kathryn Dunaway and her companions sought to disrupt it. *Atlanta Journal-Constitution* reporter Carole Ashkinaze described them sitting together in a bloc and keeping up "a running commentary, speaking loud enough to keep those around them from hearing what was being said from the platform" and making motions to adjourn. After three such motions were voted down, Dunaway "and 30 or 40 of her companions finally rose instead and left the meeting, permitting the hundreds who remained to complete their discussions without further interruption."[23]

By Ashkinaze's account, IWY organizers had gone to great lengths to be fair to the conservatives, even extending the registration deadline to accommodate "review committee" members who could not arrive until the second day. Yet "the latecomers then expressed their 'gratitude' by demanding that workshops on such 'controversial' topics as sex stereotyping in elementary textbooks be halted, and by using 'point of information' and other parliamentary procedures, such as repeated motions for adjournment during the plenary session, to delay, disrupt and sabotage the business at hand."[24]

Ashkinaze was amazed at the behavior of some of the "antis" who definitely failed to follow CRC instructions about maintaining dignity and a smile. "Many of us came away with the enduring image of a red-faced, mannishly built woman in red, white and blue permanent press polyester, screaming at the moderator of one workshop that 'boys should be boys and girls should be girls,' and that to say they should have equal educational and career opportunities is 'against God.'" Ashkinaze concluded that "if there is one conclusion to be drawn by an observer who sat through the whole fretful process, it's that the strident, unladylike, intolerant behavior so often attributed to 'feminists' is out of date. The only stridency, intolerance and militancy in evidence throughout the two-day event was that exhibited by the hot-headed minority who tried to throw a monkey wrench into the otherwise commendable proceedings, and failed."[25]

When the meeting ended, IWY Citizens' Review Committee officers held what Kathryn Dunaway described as a "blistering press release" at which she accused the IWY organizers of suppressing ideas that ran counter to those suggested by the IWY Commission and blasted both Abzug and the Carters for using IWY to promote ERA. In the May *Phyllis Schlafly Report,* "Federal Financing of a Foolish Festival for Frustrated Feminists," Schlafly charged that in Georgia feminists had rigged the election by bringing in "boxes of pre-voted ballots" and "re-marking ballots." This first state IWY meeting, she declared, "proved what a fraud the whole process is."[26]

The Georgia meeting concluded, Kathryn Dunaway dispatched a memo to CRC leaders in other states, listing "things we learned that can help you." She reported with pride how upset the "libbers" were that "we had spoiled their conference" by watching them "like eagles" and "protesting all the illegal operations." According to Dunaway, three members of the IWY Commission had asked her to sit down and discuss with them "how we could cooperate in the remaining state meetings."[27]

Soon thereafter, at the May meeting of the IWY Commission, commissioner Connie Plunkett of Georgia warned the rest of the group that the IWY Citizens' Review Committee was "a national group, and they'll show up at other meetings." Abzug waved a copy of the May *Eagle Forum Newsletter* in which Schlafly had told readers it was "urgent that we send more women [to the state IWY meetings] than the women's libbers do, so we can outvote them." The commission discussed possible defensive action, such as training parliamentarians to deal with the challengers, but they did not appear very concerned. Harry Edwards, commission member and law professor who advised the group about parliamentary procedure, insisted they should not "waste a lot of time being defensive about the anti-ERA people. This commission shouldn't spend more than a half a second worrying about it." Abzug agreed, suggesting optimistically that some Schlafly supporters might be converted by attending an IWY meeting.[28]

The IWY Commission was far more interested in all the good news that was coming in from the state meetings. At the end of the month, in one of its regular *Updates* to IWY organizers across the nation, it celebrated the conferences in Georgia, Alaska, and Idaho as great successes. In reference to

Georgia, it praised Abzug's speech, the First Lady's telegram, and the sixty-four workshops conducted by local experts that had produced over thirty recommendations. Commissioners were pleased that groups as varied as the League of Women Voters and residents of a halfway house for women prisoners had helped with the conference and that the elections produced a "well-balanced" delegation to go on to Houston.[29]

Update 5 congratulated Alaska organizers for their "successful attempt to reach out to all women," as reflected in the election as delegates of "four Caucasians, three Tlingit, two Eskimos, one Athabascan, one Black, and one Japanese."[30] It also praised the May 21–22 state meeting in Idaho for reaching out to homemakers. Actress Valerie Harper, who starred as Rhoda on the popular television series *Mary Tyler Moore*, emphasized the problems of homemakers in her keynote address. Her listeners responded by adopting a resolution asking the federal government to better protect homemakers' rights by developing a "uniform code of equitable child support laws, property laws, divorce laws and inheritance laws as a guide for states to adopt." The resolution was based on the concept that "the value of the homemaker's role is equal to that of the spouse employed outside the home."[31]

IWY organizers were also pleased that Idaho adopted all of the core resolutions, including the one supporting the ERA, especially since the state had just voted to rescind its ratification. In news reports it appeared that the leader of the rescission movement, Susan Hill, was caught off guard and failed to mobilize her troops for the meeting. Hill blamed Idaho IWY leaders for inadequate publicity, while Hope Kading, chair of the state coordinating committee, insisted they had "tried every single thing anyone could dream up to be all-inclusive," including providing free bus transportation from all parts of the state. Kading also said the meeting coordinators kept the controversial ERA off the agenda, but others had brought it up from the floor. Hill claimed the results did not represent the views of most Idaho women, and, signing on to work with the Citizens' Review Committee, she demanded another meeting. Hill's congressman, George Hansen, a Mormon and ERA opponent, came to her assistance, demanding an investigation of the IWY.[32]

Hill and her objections, however, were not discussed in *Update 5*. The only mention of conservatives was a calm, brief statement entitled "Not to Be Confused With," advising state organizers that a group calling itself the Citizens' Review Committee for the IWY had formed, and that, despite its name, it had "no official relationship to the State meetings." The article went on to say that the Citizens' Review Committee "opposes any changes in the role of women in society" and was "seeking contacts to distribute flyers in all states." As the group's name had "caused some confusion among reporters," state coordinators "may need to clarify for press and others."[33]

Otherwise, *Update* 5 ignored the CRC and its activities. As Patricia Hyatt, the IWY Public Information Officer responsible for the *Updates*, recalled later, the *Updates* "were composed as tools to let organizers know what outreach, publicity, and procedures were succeeding in other states." The feeling at the time was that the media would surely report the news about the CRC's attempts to disrupt the conferences and that "excessive 'scare-mongering' would have been a disservice to hard-working volunteers still trying to pull together their state meetings."[34]

The next weekend, June 2–5, there were eight state meetings, most of which went smoothly from the IWY Commission's perspective: seven adopted all of the core recommendations. IWY organizers were pleased that the New Mexico meeting drew large numbers of Native American women who traveled long distances from their reservations to get there. At the Oregon meeting, Governor Robert Straub made a firm promise to appoint a woman to the bench. In North Dakota, IWY commissioner Koryne Horbal entertained the gathering with comical tales of experiences as a woman in politics that made her into a feminist. In Madison, Wisconsin, Karen Grassle, who played Caroline Ingalls on the popular television series *Little House on the Prairie*, described her feminist conversion, which was followed by the university women's crew race on Lake Mendota.[35]

The IWY Commission praised Colorado's "Moving Mountains Together" meeting, which drew far more than earlier meetings with over three thousand participants—a big success. It produced a "Colorado Plan of Action" and adopted all of the core recommendations. Congresswoman Patricia Schroeder, commending the organizers, reminded them how some members of Congress had opposed the IWY meetings on the grounds that "women could not organize such a project."[36]

The conservatives saw the meeting quite differently. Drawing on their reports, Schlafly accused IWY organizers of rudeness to "non-IWY groups" who were "denied hospitality rooms, table space for literature, and invitations to speak." In the *Phyllis Schlafly Report*, she also denounced them for having twelve workshops "devoted to sexual matters" including on lesbian mothers and lesbian rights. She claimed the meeting was overrun by lesbians with the "voting strength to carry any issue of concern to them." As for

Schroeder's story, Schlafly ridiculed the feminists for criticizing the "old boy network" and those "turkeys on Capitol Hill," when these were the men who had funded the IWY conferences. She also denounced keynote speaker IWY commissioner Mildred Persinger, who "exultantly exclaimed," "This is the only revolution in history financed by the Federal Government!"— handing Schlafly a juicy quotation she would put to good use.[37]

The Minnesota meeting held in St. Cloud June 2–5, 1977, drew an even larger crowd. In this case the IWY Commission acknowledged there had been a confrontation between anti-abortion and pro-choice groups but that the majority not only "supported all IWY goals" but also went further: calling for wages for housework and self-defense courses for girls.[38] After some minority women complained about lack of attention to their problems, conservatives invited them to join in a "walkout." Declining, one African American woman told the assembly she had waited far too long for such an opportunity to discuss the concerns of women and minorities, and was not about to walk out. Several participants, eager to keep the peace, then drafted a resolution that was approved by an overwhelming majority, stating: "Recognizing that we will never all agree on every issue, we pledge to bind ourselves together in love, to continue to work on the concerns of universal importance—the need for our personal dignity, the relief of our suffering, the achievement of our aspirations—so that we can go on to that great victory: equality for all women, not only in Minnesota, but around the world."[39] After all was said and done, feminists in Minnesota, as in most previous state meetings, remained in control.[40]

The June 3–5 state meeting in St. Louis, Missouri, however, was a different story. Conservatives showed up in large numbers, were well organized, and scored their first significant victory—though an incomplete one. Since Missouri was one of Schlafly's two home states, and she was then finishing law school at St. Louis's Washington University, there was speculation that she might show up. While Schlafly did not appear at this or any other IWY meetings Missouri conservatives had another able leader in Ann O'Donnell. Like Kathryn Dunaway of Georgia, O'Donnell served on her state's IWY coordinating committee.[41]

President of the Missouri chapter of the National Right to Life Committee (NRLC), O'Donnell was drawn into the IWY controversy as a result of the IWY Commission's proposed recommendation on reproductive rights which endorsed legal abortion. O'Donnell considered herself to be a feminist and much resented women's rights supporters who insisted that supporting "choice" was de rigueur. Before 1977, there were many pro-life women who were women's rights supporters. Like the Stop-ERA movement, the pro-life movement was a single issue movement intent on attracting as many supporters as possible regardless of their beliefs on other issues. In 1972, women opposed to abortion who found themselves uncomfortable or unwelcome in women's rights organizations had founded a group they called Feminists for Life. In 1975, as many ERA opponents insisted the amendment would make it impossible to prohibit abortion, NRLC leaders voted on a proposal calling for pro-lifers to take a stand against the ERA until "such a time as this ambiguity is removed." But they resoundingly defeated the motion.[42]

In 1977, however, feminists' embrace of abortion rights along with the other core IWY recommendations pushed O'Donnell and many others into the conservative camp. That summer, NRLC voted again on the proposal on ERA they had earlier defeated and this time it passed easily.[43]

On the first day of the two-day conference, a coalition of pro-life and anti-ERA groups brought in more than five hundred women and some men by chartered buses. In a move meant to suggest they were the true advocates for women, O'Donnell and other conservative challengers called themselves the "New Suffragists" and wore yellow sashes in emulation of the six suffragists honored at the meeting. With little or no interaction with other participants, they voted on the delegates, swept the election, and returned home in time to attend church the next morning. Some Missouri IWY organizers complained that the protest was orchestrated by Catholic officials in St. Louis, a church stronghold.[44]

On Sunday, the remaining participants met again and endorsed feminist resolutions including one calling for reproductive rights, and attempted to bind the conservative delegation to support the resolutions at the national conference in Houston. In response, the elected delegates—who chose O'Donnell as delegation chair—filed suit, and a bitter legal battle ensued. Over the next few months, the Missouri IWY coordinating committee would refuse to release the federal funds meant to pay the travel costs of delegates from their state, return the money to the IWY Commission, and organize an unofficial caucus committed to abortion rights and the ERA to represent the state in Houston.[45]

In Arizona, there was a flap when many participants refused to eat the lettuce cultivated by nonunion labor—the only controversy noted in a summary prepared by IWY staff. In actuality it was a dramatic meeting in which feminists, despite a fierce conservative challenge, managed to elect an ethnically diverse delegation—"six Chicanas, four American Indians, one Black, one Japanese, one Chinese, and five Caucasians"—and adopt all core recommendations as well as 104 other recommendations in an "Arizona Plan of Action."[46]

Arizona was a conservative state in which the ERA had been defeated several times, in part owing to the leadership of state legislator and IWY Citizens' Review Committee board member Donna Carlson. As in Georgia, Schlafly came two weeks in advance to help prepare for the state meeting. But in Arizona, National Women's Political Caucus members, tipped off by friends in Missouri and Ohio about the conservatives' plans, rallied their forces to defeat them—implementing a strategy even some women on their own side thought unfair and gave conservative critics "proof" of feminist railroading. Senator Jesse Helms, now in communication with CRC leaders, and sensing an opportunity to exploit the IWY issue, had a copy of the NWPC plan, dubbed by feminists the Monitoring and Mobile Operation Partnership Program (MMOPP), entered into the *Congressional Record* within three weeks.[47]

As Mary Peace Douglas, one of the NWPC conspirators, described MMOPP:

A core group of women wore a bright strip on their shoulders—visible front and back—one was assigned to monitor each work-shop. If the conservatives packed any workshop that woman quietly left, went to a central location—word was quickly passed and quietly people moved into the packed workshop—thus when a resolution came to a vote, we had the majority. It was simple, effective and it worked beautifully.

"We" consisted of women from the Arizona Women's Political Caucus, NOW, the Republican Women's Caucus, Lesbian Caucus, Minority Caucus, and "interested friends." "It was an exciting bring together of feminists working for a common goal!!!!" Douglas wrote. But Elly Anderson, the MMOPP coordinator, admitted it had created some unease within feminist ranks as some "thought our tactics were too blunt and maybe even unfair." Her view, however, was that "Congress functions on this 'call in the vote' system all the time" and, secondly, she was "tired of being a 'good sport' and losing. Never give your enemy an even break. This philosophy still has difficulties for many good-hearted women."[48]

Meanwhile conservatives were also scheming to gain control of the meetings. (At a later point, Thomson would speak of having "our own MMOPP.") On June 5, 1977, Rosemary Thomson sent CRC chairmen a letter boasting about the work "our girls" are doing and insisting, "We ARE making an impact." She enclosed a set of instructions Elaine Donnelly had prepared explaining how to mobilize "our groups" for greater effectiveness in workshops and elections and for handling the media. Donnelly, too, suggested a scheme for recognizing their people by marking the backs of their badges, and reminded them to keep their methods secret and adopt security measures. She urged them to challenge anyone trying to enter their hospitality suites "who seems doubtful" and to require that they "show their Citizens' Review sign." "Husbands can be helpful here, and in the monitoring or voting procedures."[49]

At these meetings much rested on knowledge of parliamentary procedure and Donnelly "strongly advised" the CRC leaders to employ professional parliamentarians as the "U.S. IWY . . . will certainly try to outwit us." Alternatively, they should rely on one of their own people who not only had experience with *Robert's Rules of Order* and was well versed on the issues, but who also was "courageous" enough to challenge the chairs when necessary. Donnelly said that Donna Carlson was drafting alternative recommendations for conservatives in other states to promote should they get a chance, but in the meantime suggested CRC leaders just "insert the word NOT into each of the national IWY recommendations."[50]

Again Thomson reminded them of their goals and the reasons "for going to all this trouble." They must: "1) get delegates elected to go to Houston, and 2) compile information from eyewitness observers that will totally discredit the Conferences and everything coming out of them." "I know," she said, "that some people would rather boycott the whole thing, but that would leave the ERA proponents to themselves to drum up all sorts of propaganda about how 'everyone' at the Conference was in support of their goals, which are really to implement ERA without the Amendment itself."[51]

The IWY provided a great opportunity for the conservative women's movement to grow, Thomson pointed out. The CRC "can be a useful vehicle to build our organizational strength, and to avoid a demoralizing effect," which "is especially important in the unratified states." That was all, she said, "except that every hospitality headquarters should be equipped with a large bottle of aspirin, and each day should be opened with a prayer."[52]

*   *   *

The next weekend, June 10–13, 1977, was critical with sixteen—nearly twice as many as usual—state meetings taking place. IWY Citizens' Review Committee national leaders Rosemary Thomson of Illinois and Elaine Donnelly of Michigan were leading the challenge to feminists at the IWY meetings in their home states. Though they had spent months advising other CRC members on how to mobilize conservatives, in both cases their forces were badly outnumbered.

Tensions were high as twenty-five hundred participants gathered at the Normal, Illinois, State University campus for the IWY meeting. The previous week, the Illinois legislature shot down the ERA—as it did annually—but this time by only six votes. Just before the meeting, attorney Fred Schlafly filed a suit on behalf of six legislators and Stop-ERA contending that conference organizers were not balanced in terms of points of view and that the meeting would be used as a rally point for ERA forces. With Presiding Officer Bella Abzug scheduled to give the keynote address in Phyllis Schlafly's home state, and with rumors circulating that Schlafly might appear (she didn't), the press speculated that "the scene is being set for a national battle between two opposing titans of the women's movement."[53]

Abzug flew in from New York, according to the Rockford *Morning Star*, "travel worn" and "sleepless." Having decided to run for mayor of New York, she was burning the candle at both ends. In her speech, she dismissed conservative women's concerns as based on fear and misconception, comparing women who opposed the ERA to those who had been afraid of the vote and had called it a sin that "would destroy the home, the family— and even religion." Yet even now, "we find women so afraid of change they oppose the ERA on the same grounds." According to one reporter, she then "propelled . . . bits of feminist history, employment and childcare statistics into the audience like a bazooka, in a voice that could have held its own in a back-room Brooklyn political caucus," stopping several times for "both cheers and shouts of protest." Abzug was totally nonplussed by the "large bloc of unfriendly faces in the audience" and their hostile comments. She responded, "We are listening to women expressing their feelings here. And how!" Then she hurried back to New York, saying only to the local IWY organizers, "Good luck."[54]

IWY commissioner and senator Charles Percy—who for years had endured attacks from fellow Illinois Republicans Schlafly and Thomson for his support of feminism—also spoke, delivering an address on "Women of the '70s." Illinois governor Jim Thompson, however, declined to attend. This was becoming a trend, as increasingly politicians hesitated to become involved. CRC leaders bitterly denounced those who were: It was "horrible," said Thomson, to discover "state and federal legislators such as Senator Charles Percy, participating in promotion of these IWY goals to restructure society!"[55]

When the majority of participants at the Illinois meeting voted to recommend passage of the ERA, about five hundred ERA opponents—singing "God Bless America"—marched out. Once outside, surrounded by television cameras, Thomson denounced the meeting as "a phony festival for frustrated females" and urged conservatives to send protest telegrams to President Carter.[56]

The Illinois IWY meeting also approved most of the core recommendations. And as Schlafly reported in the *Phyllis Schlafly Report,* they added new resolutions calling for prohibition of discrimination on the basis of sexual preference and repeal of all statutes prohibiting any sexual conduct among consenting adults in private. Still, Schlafly was pleased that conservatives managed to elect 40 percent of the delegates—including Rosemary Thomson. They would have "done better but our women didn't want to leave their families for an entire weekend and spend it with a group of lesbians," Schlafly claimed. "They're very offensive to all of us."[57]

Despite their success, Illinois IWY organizers worried that the IWY meetings were producing such bitter confrontations between intransigent groups. Luellen Laurenti, executive director for the Illinois coordinating committee, said, "We had hoped to find some common ground, but there was so much emotional feeling that people immediately broke up into pro and anti." She also expressed concern about men, experts in parliamentary procedure, "moving around on the floor, engineering the opposition." And she was distressed that there was actual physical struggle that began, according to the press, when "opposition women tried to control the microphones on the floor." Said Laurenti, "We have to pay $210 in damages for four broken mikes. I think the Houston meeting will be a real showdown."[58]

In Michigan, CRC media chairman Elaine Donnelly led conservative forces in a state where many prominent politicians, including Republicans, supported the women's rights movement. Governor William Milliken, for example, whose wife, Helen, was a staunch ERA and IWY supporter, welcomed the participants. A former IWY presiding officer, Judge Elizabeth Athanasakos, also a Republican, gave the keynote address, asking, "How long can we wait to tell the Congress and the President how we want our specific problems solved? And by God, solve them, not talk about them."[59]

With the three hundred conservatives in a distinct minority among the twenty-one hundred participants, the national recommendations were approved—but not before an explosive debate. According to the press, the CRC forces "interrupted the nominating proceedings repeatedly, claiming their right to present their slate of delegates had been denied." They were opposed by a hastily formed Unity Caucus, a coalition of nineteen groups organized to combat disruption and keep the meeting on task. A well-publicized clash developed when a "microphone monitor" covered the mike with her hand to shut off Elaine Donnelly when she interrupted Michigan First Lady Helen Milliken. The feminist majority won all forty-eight delegate positions while the four alternate slots went to conservatives.[60]

Afterward, there was a verbal battle in the press as feminists and conservatives each characterized what happened. "The 300-or-so in the minority who voted against most of the resolutions that were passed didn't understand parliamentary procedure and they tried to interrupt, hassle and bog down the meetings and workshops," said Mary Aikey, who chaired the meeting. "If the opposition has so many followers, why didn't they all attend the meeting and vote the other side down?" Elaine Donnelly countered, "We had more than enough to elect some delegates. But the women were cut off before we could nominate our people. It was all outrageous. International Women's Year is nothing more than a yearlong joke and an insult to the intelligence of women."[61]

In Ohio, participants endorsed the core recommendations and approved the ERA by a 2–1 margin, but anti-ERA and pro-life forces worked together to elect a delegation that was 80 percent conservative. Schlafly considered it "a spectacular victory." Once again, conservatives showed up just for the elections and went home. It seemed they were not willing to make the sacrifice of spending a whole weekend debating feminists about recommendations. Their primary concern was who was going to represent American women in Houston when the votes would matter most.[62]

At the other meetings that weekend and throughout June, feminists continued to win far more often than they lost on both recommendations and delegates. However, conservatives continued to challenge them, and the meetings were heated. An overwhelming majority of IWY meetings supported the core proposals—including ERA and abortion—and many added additional feminist recommendations, which included protection of gay and lesbian rights.

Conservatives were growing more angry and belligerent, especially in states that had defeated the ERA. In ultraconservative South Carolina, the moderate feminists on the state coordinating committee—preferring to focus on reforms that were possible—had announced in advance that the ERA was not on the agenda. At the meeting, however, other feminists raised the issue in workshops and on the floor. When the session chair, Dr. Marianna Davis—a distinguished African American scholar from nearby Benedict College who chaired the state's IWY coordinating committee—announced that the ERA resolution was adopted, a white man in the audience jumped up and shouted: "You can shove that up your ass!"[63]

More than at any meeting to date, conservative men participated actively, not just as advisers but also registering, attending workshops, and voting. Of the 130 men in the antifeminist forces, feminists estimated that at least 40 were John Birch Society members. Local NOW leader Eunice "Tootsie" Holland told the press: "In this state, Birchers don't mind admitting they are members." Oliver "Runt" Willis was the most active of the male participants, working closely with the CRC, even seeking election as a delegate. Willis reported back to state senator Marion Gressette, the most powerful man in South Carolina politics. Gressette had used his chairmanship of the state legislature's judicial committee to block the ERA, just as he had blocked civil rights bills for decades.[64]

Norma Russell, a member of the South Carolina House of Representatives—one of the "Lady Legislators" who had received Schlafly's Eagle Award for helping defeat the ERA—was proposed as a delegate by both the IWY nominating committee and the conservative forces. She was the only conservative elected, though Oliver Willis, George Ann Pennebaker, and several CRC women won as alternates. Pennebaker was the current national president of Women for Constitutional Government. Russell, whose participation in Schlafly's annual training conference was regularly bankrolled by Women for Constitutional Government, was such a Schlafly admirer that the Columbia newspaper the *State* ran a political cartoon with Russell coifed like Schlafly with "Phyllis" and "Anita" posters and singing, "I Enjoy Being a Girl."[65]

Some said the South Carolina IWY meeting, which was billed as "Heritage and Horizons," represented a fight between the state's past and future. In addition to Dr. Marianna Davis, a specialist in the Gullah language—the creole language spoken by Gullah people, African Americans in coastal South Carolina, Georgia, and northeast Florida—there were many black women among the organizers. One of the women honored for having "broken barriers" to women's full equality was Modjeska Simkins, an iconic figure in the state's civil rights movement. Simkins was an NAACP leader who had hosted Thurgood Marshall in her home while conferring with him on a Clarendon County, South Carolina, case that when combined with several other individual cases resulted in *Brown v. Board of Education* in 1954. In the election for delegates, she received the second-highest number of votes.[66] There were a good number of women white and black who were elected or appointed officials who participated in the conference including Lucille Whipper, a descendant of an African American state legislator who served during Reconstruction. Most male politicians stayed away from the state IWY meeting, including Governor James B. Edwards who had promised to give opening remarks, but James Clyburn, an African American politician serving as the state's human affairs commissioner and later chairman of the Democratic Caucus in the U.S. House of Representatives, attended.[67]

Conservatives protested the disproportionate emphasis state IWY organizers had placed on African Americans as well as their efforts to get them to attend. State representative Norma Russell held a press conference at which she complained that the "well-heeled leaders of the conference" were exploiting the poor and minorities, bussing them in, sometimes using University of South Carolina buses paid for by taxpayers, in order to get their votes, and offering them a "'sugar daddy' from the cradle to the grave." Russell insisted that the feminist claim that the resolutions approved at the IWY state meeting came from the grassroots, when they had actually come from the 1976 "... *To Form a More Perfect Union* ..." was "a travesty of the lowest sort." She and other conservatives then went to work preparing formal complaints for CRC use in which they denounced the state meeting as a fraud and a waste.[68]

Conservative activity was picking up all over the country. That weekend, June 10–11, 1977, there were also clashes between feminists and conservatives in states with more progressive reputations, including New Jersey and Rhode Island. Three thousand participants, mostly women but including some men, gathered at Princeton University for the New Jersey state meeting, where conservatives were again too few in number to gain control of the meeting but still determined to make their objections known. In well-attended morning workshops, participants engaged in discussions on a wide range of topics, from "the problems of the displaced homemaker" to "anger, 'the forbidden feeling.'" Nonetheless tempers flared.[69]

According to the feminists, noisy, well-organized women and men from the "so-called Pro-Lifers and anti-ERA forces" raised havoc at many of the workshops. Shelah Leader, the IWY Commission staffer serving as the "federal officer" at the meeting, reported that the protesters "disrupted" the plenary session by continually blowing whistles. That summer such disruption of meetings when conservatives lacked the numbers to control them would become a familiar pattern.[70]

At the Princeton meeting, feminists won both the election of delegates and the vote on recommendations. An ERA-Reproductive Freedom slate headed by conference coordinator Clara Allen competed against a forty-member, pro-life, anti-ERA slate and 138 independent nominees and won easily. Press reports stated that "all but a handful of the large body voted for resolutions supporting ratification of the ERA and guarantees of reproductive freedom . . . with unequivocal enthusiasm." In addition, the New Jersey meeting adopted resolutions advocating social security for home-makers, laws to aid battered women, legislation protecting pregnant women from job discrimination, extension of programs to aid minority business owners to include female business owners, "affirmation of the needs of black, Hispanic, Asian-American and native American women," and prohibition of discrimination on the basis of sexual or "affectional" preference. Feminist organizers were pleased that so many women encountering the women's movement for the first time were responding as the feminists had hoped. As one reported, "Women came to the conferences and learned they were feminists."[71]

As word spread about what was going on at the meetings, both conservatives and feminists ramped up their mobilization efforts. Some who earlier had no intention of showing up changed their minds: radical feminists, who had been uninterested in what they assumed would be tame, government-sponsored conferences pushing the same old reforms, reconsidered when they learned about the conservatives' attempts to take them over. The competition for influence at the state meetings spurred mobilization efforts and instilled passion and paranoia on both sides.[72]

At the June 11–12 Rhode Island IWY meeting held at Brown University, feminists triumphed after a last-minute telephone campaign to boost their numbers. The entire core was adopted as well as a gay rights resolution. This victory came despite strenuous efforts on the part of the IWY Citizens' Review Committee, Catholics for Life, and the Interfaith Family Advocates—the latter described by the press as a "council of 14 Rhode Island churches opposed to the entire concept of International Women's Year and the ERA" that began organizing a month earlier. According to the *Providence Journal*, the feminist victory represented "a defeat for the vocal, well-organized army of fundamentalist Christians who arrived by the busload to oppose what they described as an immoral and un-American proceeding." Barbara Bartlett of the Apponaug Pentecostal Church told the reporter that "a Satan-like spirit is behind the ERA. It is the pit of hell trying to destroy everything the Lord stands for." Another woman stated that services at her church had been canceled so that members could go to the conference and vote.[73]

Press reports emphasized that workshops were tense as participants debated topics from employment and health to aging and child care. One workshop that was planned as a constructive dialogue between homosexual and heterosexual women was abruptly adjourned when a crowd of Christian fundamentalists stormed the room and monopolized the discussion by quoting Scripture. According to the reporter, "By the time the workshop was closed, women on both sides of the issue were in tears."[74]

Fear and frustration prompted misconceptions and accusations. Conservatives claimed that a bus with New York plates was bringing in male homosexuals to pack the convention. The astonished driver, however, explained to the press that he was transporting swimmers to compete in a meet at the Brown University pool. Meanwhile a gay rights advocate charged that the conservatives had "brought in mentally retarded adults from local group homes to vote for their side."[75]

Voting on the nearly 115 proposed resolutions dragged on for hours. Participants endorsed the ERA by a standing vote of 439–337, and defeated a recommendation for an anti-abortion amendment to the Constitution 385–359. Voting on delegates was also complicated and drawn out. To prevent nonresidents from participating, IWY guidelines required that voting for delegates be conducted by paper ballot and that all voters must be credentialed. This meant that the eighteen hundred voters had to stand in lines that spilled outside the auditorium—a scene that became common at IWY state meetings throughout the nation. The League of Women Voters, charged with handling the election, was unable to count the ballots before the meeting adjourned. When the results were announced afterward, conservatives protested. They also insisted that had they been given more notice and information about the meetings they would have been better organized, and the results would have given "a real indication of what women think."[76]

The rest of the state meetings that weekend—in Connecticut, New Hampshire, Wyoming, Iowa, Kentucky, Maryland, and the District of Columbia—adopted all or most of the core resolutions.[77] In Virginia, feminists outnumbered and outvoted conservatives, despite the efforts of CRC board member and state legislator Eva Scott. IWY Commission reports noted that participants "voted to boycott Virginia products until ERA is ratified" and that a comic opera about a pregnant male was a big hit. Arkansas organizers were pleased with themselves for shutting off registration as soon as they heard about conservatives' plans to turn out in big numbers.[78]

Feminists were increasingly concerned about conservative attempts to take over or disrupt the IWY meetings, and fear of conservative victories prompted a new unity among them. A group of feminists from eleven states with no official connection to the IWY Commission formed a Pro-Plan Caucus to turn out supporters of the core recommendations and prepare and promote slates of feminist candidates. Key support came from the Women's Action Alliance, the group founded in the early 1970s to coordinate the efforts of feminist groups. Though once highly critical of the IWY, after Carter appointed more left-leaning women such as Abzug, Steinem, and WAA executive director Ruth Abram, things had changed, and they threw their support behind the IWY.[79]

In some states, feminists adopted versions of the plan developed by Arizona members of the National Women's Political Caucus. In mid-June, the NWPC's national membership director forwarded the Arizona plan for "organizing feminists to prevent Anti-ERA, Anti-abortion take-over" to state chairs with upcoming IWY conferences.[80] Both sides were developing strategies to maximize their voting power while criticizing the other for doing so.

NOW played a prominent role in feminists' efforts to counter conservative forces and retain control of the meetings. According to Eleanor Smeal, after it became clear that the conservatives were organizing, feminists had "an emergency meeting and said, that's enough of this. If they're organizing, we've got to counter-organize." NOW members began presenting slates of their own that were 100 percent feminist as opposed to the slates carefully prepared by state coordinating committees that had included some conservatives. At this point, electing conservatives—*any* conservatives—seemed risky as well as distasteful. They were determined not to allow "anti-change women" they saw as wanting to remain in chains rather than break down barriers, women they believed represented a small but vocal and well-organized group of ultraconservatives, to gain control of the IWY.[81]

While feminists worked to line up supporters, those with strong interest in particular aspects of the feminist agenda began horse trading. Like conservatives, they were developing new skill in coalition building. Lesbian rights advocates, among others, saw an opportunity to bargain. At the June 10–12, 1977, IWY meeting in the District of Columbia, for example, they sought support for an antidiscrimination plank from African American women who constituted a majority of those attending. Charlotte Bunch, who worked with O'Leary in the effort to gain the state endorsements needed for their plank to be considered in Houston, recalled that she and others pleaded for solidarity, saying: "The conservatives are against you and against us. We'll support you if you'll support us." She recalled that they also "made common cause with abortion rights activists."[82]

Success of this strategy depended on getting a large turnout of lesbians or lesbian-rights supporters to the meetings, which they did. Bunch remembered working the phones to make this happen. "We were mobilizing women to come and we basically were saying to the other women's groups, we have a bloc and this is what we want and our bloc will . . . support the planks that you want, but we are not going to vote for and support those planks if we don't get support back."[83]

This effort to seek the support of other feminists represented an attitude adjustment for lesbians as well as straight feminists. According to Bunch, once a lesbian separatist, there was a "shift from a more separatist identity mode to really understanding that we need each other." After the bitter fights of the early 1970s in which many straight women opposed inclusion of lesbian rights as part of the feminist agenda, many lesbians were fed up. But by 1977 Bunch had reached the same position as O'Leary, that it was important for gays and lesbians to become a political movement seeking equal rights legislation, and the IWY represented an opportunity to gain mainstream feminist support. Just as the feminists hoped to unite with the newly triumphant civil rights movement through the IWY, lesbian rights leaders hoped for inclusion of gay rights in an expanding movement for equal rights for all.[84]

Convincing other feminists that the IWY should endorse a goal that at that time most Americans opposed—and many opposed passionately—was a real challenge. It required convincing straight women that antidiscrimination legislation was not only just, but expedient: beneficial for the equal rights movement as a whole. In this shift, the anti-gay movement emerging in early 1977 played a key role.

As Bunch recalled, "Because of the way in which they were attacking us and the viciousness of the Anita Bryant kind of campaign . . . all of a sudden people who might have said, 'Well this is a secondary issue,' began to change their minds." She recalled that women like Gloria Steinem, who had previously been quite supportive, as a member of the IWY Commission had not backed O'Leary's proposal to include gay rights in the core recommendations. However, said Bunch, as the year progressed they began "even more strongly to see that you have to stand firm against this kind of [right-wing] strategy."[85]

At the California IWY meeting the next weekend, June 17–19, 1977, feminist attendance soared in response to rumors that Phyllis Schlafly or Anita Bryant might appear in person and that conservatives planned to turn out in force.[86] An estimated sixty-five hundred participants showed up for the meeting, which was held on the campus of the University of Southern California at Los Angeles, and opened with a welcome from Mayor Tom Bradley. An IWY report described the meeting as reflecting the spirit of the women's movement in California, which "is big, highly organized, diverse, socially advanced, politically sophisticated, and boisterous."[87]

In this case gay men did turn out in large numbers to show support for lesbians. Another group perhaps equally offensive to the conservatives turned out as well, members of a San Francisco–based group called COYOTE (Call Off Your Old Tired Ethics) that promoted decriminalization of prostitution. This was not lost on Schlafly, who proclaimed that IWY meetings around the country were supporting repeal of "all statutes prohibiting sexual conduct among consenting adults in private," which meant "legalizing homosexuals and prostitutes." The Los Angeles meeting adopted all of the core recommendations and elected a solidly feminist delegation of ninety-six, the largest number from any state.[88]

This dramatic showdown between coalitions involving Christian conservatives on the one hand and lesbians and prostitutes on the other—taking place in a major media market—electrified the press. CALIFORNIA FEMINISTS BEAT BACK RIGHT WING one headline screamed. Reporters had already begun to pay attention but the stories coming out of California in mid-June seemed to ignite new interest across the nation. The IWY meetings, now almost half over, had at last become a huge story. From then on they would receive tremendous attention from reporters who, of course, covered them quite differently according to their own points of view.

According to the "independent socialist paper" *In These Times*: "Conservative forces came organized and prepared with typed-up resolutions" but "were met by a well-organized feminist coalition that significantly defused their efforts." "Workshops were often heated as the outnumbered Schlafly forces struggled for a foothold." Only two of the "Schlafly/Bryant resolutions" made it to the closing session, where all resolutions had to pass a two-thirds vote before becoming a part of the official California program.[89]

One of the conservatives' resolutions opposed government-supported day care "on the basis that it weakens the family unit; is not the kind of care preferred by most families; is not needed and will have negative effects upon children involved at greater cost to the American taxpayer." Another condemned the idea of wages for housework, saying that "we as women feel that the present compensation in love and economic support that we receive is satisfactory." According to the reporter, "Both resolutions brought laughter and disbelief from the audience."[90]

Schlafly saw it differently. Reporting on the California IWY meeting in the *Phyllis Schlafly Report*, she blasted the meeting for the high level of participation by homosexuals and claimed they were not only shocking but abusive to "non-IWY women." "There were about 2,000 lesbians in attendance, wearing all kinds of lesbian T-shirts and signs such as: 'How dare you presume I am heterosexual?' 'Lesbians fight for our friends.' 'Anita sucks organs.' 'Warm Fuzzy Dykes.' 'Let she who is without sin cast the first orange.' 'Boycott Florida.' And 'Hitler, McCarthy, Bryant, Schlafly.'" She claimed that people with "non-IWY views were in fear for their personal safety" and that "one man taking pictures was attacked by 75 lesbians." In addition, Schlafly alleged that "a lesbian group targeted and monitored five leading conservative women, followed them from workshop to workshop, surrounded them and cut them off from the rest of the group, and threatened them with violence."[91]

Most of the other meetings that weekend were less dramatic. According to IWY reports, participants in the Louisiana, South Dakota, Delaware, Maine, Nevada, and North Carolina meetings held June 16–18, 1977, passed all or most core recommendations. In Nevada, IWY officials noted, "A luncheon address by Gloria Steinem attracted more persons than the number who had registered for the meeting." IWY meetings the weekend of June 24–25 in Pennsylvania, Tennessee, Massachusetts, Texas, and the Virgin Islands also endorsed the core.[92]

However, in those two weekends, conservatives suddenly broke through, reaching a level of strength that allowed them to gain control of three meetings, a sign of things to come.

CHAPTER 8

Out of the Kitchen and into the Counterrevolution

What is happening is a kind of counterrevolution within the women's revolution. For the past ten years, the Gloria Steinems have had things pretty much their own way. Now the Phyllis Schlaflys are venturing out of their kitchens. For the first time, militancy on the left is encountering militancy on the right.

—JAMES J. KILPATRICK, "CHRISTIANS 1,000;
LIONS 200," JULY 9, 1977

From early May through mid-June 1977, as feminists and conservatives battled one another at IWY state meetings, feminists nearly always came out ahead. In most states, "the non-IWY women" (borrowing Phyllis Schlafly's term) put up a good fight. In three states they scored partial victories and managed to elect a substantial number of delegates: Missouri, where they swept the elections; Illinois, where they won 40 percent; and Ohio, where they won 80 percent. However, even these IWY meetings adopted feminist resolutions—including most of the sixteen core recommendations proposed by the IWY Commission. In most states, except for a few token conservatives included on slates of nominees put forward by state coordinating committees, conservatives went away empty-handed. As Rosemary Thomson, leader of the IWY Citizens' Review Committee challenging feminists for control of the meetings put it: "Ours was not an impressive record."[1]

Feminists were shocked by the acrimony and disappointed that in many states it made meaningful exchange of ideas impossible. Their main concern, however, was that feminist delegates and a feminist message went forth to Houston. Thus they were pleased that the unexpectedly strong challenge from conservatives was countered effectively by high turnouts from those "committed to equality for women." Conservative forces had been able to do little more than cause "disruptions" and delay the inevitable. Then came Oklahoma.

The Oklahoma state meeting would astonish IWY organizers and feminists, hearten Citizens' Review Committee leaders and their troops, and change the momentum of the summer battles. For Oklahoma feminists, it was a completely unanticipated disaster.[2]

As they prepared for the June 16, 1977, start of the Oklahoma IWY meeting, state coordinating committee chair Ann Mulloy Ashmore, state legislator Cleta Deatherage, ERA leader Jan Dreiling, and other feminists on the committee knew the Eagle Forum was carefully monitoring their activities. Ann Patterson, leader of the Oklahoma conservatives who dealt the ERA its first defeat and who worked with Phyllis Schlafly to launch Stop-ERA, along with Ann Bowker, another Schlafly ally, were members of the state IWY coordinating committee. Ashmore had heard reports that conservatives were turning up at IWY meetings in other states but had no idea they had mounted a coordinated national campaign and were planning to take over the meeting in her state.[3] However conservatives led by Bowker and by Dianne Edmondson, who had volunteered to lead the IWY Citizens' Review Committee in Oklahoma, intended to do just that.

The conference was held at Oklahoma State University in Stillwater. It began on Friday with workshops attended by two hundred women's rights supporters who had preregistered. However, early Saturday morning more than a thousand conservative men, women, and children arrived on buses from all over the state and seized control of the conference. While the organizing committee and other astounded conference participants retreated to the student union to figure out how to respond, the conservatives, guided by "vote leaders" wearing red gloves, defeated all of the resolutions presented by the state coordinating committee. They then proceeded to adopt resolutions of their own, including one stating that homemaking was "the most vital and rewarding of careers for women."[4]

After the meeting, Dianne Edmondson savored the victory, telling the press how they pulled it off. "We started organizing about six weeks before the conference was held in Stillwater. We relied heavily on the fundamentalist church groups here to tell their members to attend and vote against the feminist slate. They helped us because about 1,000 of the 1,200 attending were anti-feminists."[5]

Edmondson, a Church of Christ member and native Texan, was active in Women Who Want to Be Women (WWWW), Stop-ERA, the Eagle Forum, and the pro-life movement. A Republican, a John Birch Society member, and an ardent Phyllis Schlafly admirer, she had been one of the first to respond to the call for volunteers to challenge feminists at the IWY meetings. As Rosemary Thomson recalled, when the announcement appeared in the *Phyllis Schlafly Report*, Edmondson phoned her immediately. "Because Mrs. Edmondson did not know it couldn't be done," Thomson wrote, she pulled off this "major miracle" for the conservatives' cause, a crucial turning point in the story.[6]

Edmondson's particular genius was in producing a cassette tape for distribution to conservative audiences, especially churches, carefully designed to appall them. In it she denounced the IWY as a "great evil" and called on Christians to "do good as the Lord commands" by opposing it. The cassette was widely distributed to persons "recommended as one who can influence others"; they were urged to use it to instill in listeners a solid commitment to attend the state meeting. The tape, which would become famous among conservatives, painted a portrait of a demonic and powerful feminist enemy.[7]

The cassette, which featured quotations from the most radical feminists of the modern era, gave no hint that there was such a thing as moderate feminism. It depicted the women's rights movement as a movement of radical feminists and lesbians who "want your child taught that there is no right or wrong, nor normal or ideal circumstances for sexual intercourse," and intent on undermining conservative parents' efforts to teach their children that the ideal place for sex is within marriage. IWY, she informed her listeners, was the tool of radicals led by Bella Abzug, who had sponsored the first gay rights bill in Congress. "If this bill had passed that Bella introduced," she stated, "it would mean that homosexuals could teach our children in schools [and] could be counselors in city, state, or federally supported camps."[8]

With the aid of archconservative columnist James J. Kilpatrick—who had earlier urged conservatives to stand up against Bella and her IWY "boondoggle"—word of the dramatic Oklahoma takeover caught the attention of the nation. His gleeful description of what happened in Oklahoma appeared in his syndicated column, which was carried in newspapers across the country. It was cited or reprinted in political journals from the moderate Republican *Ripon Forum* to the ultra-rightist *Human Events*. Out in "Indian territory," he announced, the "troops of Bella Abzug got scalped."[9] It was just what he had hoped for.

"In a fair fight at the Oklahoma Conference of Women," boasted Kilpatrick, "the women's libbers were out-maneuvered, out-thought, and out-hustled." Up to this point, most of the conferences had gone according to script, and "unwelcome dissenters, like so many flies at a formal dinner" had been "swatted into silent submissions." But, thanks to the "skill and energy of two determined women," Oklahoma was a different story. As Kilpatrick told it, the conservative women, far more clever than the feminists, had tricked them into altering their procedures to the conservatives' advantage.

> They went to work early in May, just as soon as the Stillwater confer-
> ence was scheduled. They saw that the registration rules had been
> rigged. The idea was to fix a deadline of noon on Friday. Anyone
> who registered after that hour could observe, but could not vote at
> Saturday's plenary session. Mrs. Bowker and Mrs. Edmondson
> complained to the national office in Washington that the rule
> would discriminate against working women and housewives who
> could attend only on Saturday. Behold: The unsuspecting national
> office cordially went along with a revised rule that would permit
> Saturday morning registrants to participate fully.[10]

Then the buses started to roll. "The libbers were aghast." There were "reports of hysteria" and of language "more suited to stevedores and to hockey players than to gentle ladies."

In the end, Kilpatrick rejoiced, the "200 libbers rumped off" to another location and the "thousand anti-libbers took over the ballroom." "[When] the dust settled that Saturday night in Stillwater," he wrote, "little remained but a scene of dreadful carnage. The surviving libbers had fled in disarray. The victorious anti-libbers had boarded buses to take them home to church." The final score was "Christians 1,000; Lions 200."[11]

In Kilpatrick's opinion this slaying of the feminist lions was long overdue and foreshadowed big changes ahead. For years an intellectual leader and strategist for white southern conservatives in their "massive resistance" to integration, he was supremely contemptuous of liberals and the federal government for forcing unwanted change on American citizens. That fight was now over and Kilpatrick—seeking to continue his career as a pundit—had reluctantly adjusted to the new reality: overt racism was beyond the pale in American politics and journalism.[12] But there was no such ban on anti-feminism, and Kilpatrick embraced it with gusto. The IWY offered a new opportunity to stick it to the liberals and the feds.

* * *

One week later conservatives scored another great victory at the largest state IWY meeting of all. This time the Mormons rather than Protestant fundamentalists were in the lead. On June 24, 1977, fourteen thousand women and men jammed into the Salt Palace in Salt Lake City, Utah, summoned by the vast Mormon women's organization, the Relief Society, to stand up for "correct principles." According to the national IWY report, the Utah meeting "reversed the intent of all the workshops designed by the pro-IWY State coordinating committee."

The press reported that although only three thousand women had preregistered, "the Mormon Church provided buses for 10,000 more who were instrumental in the passage of resolutions against the ERA, against abortion under any circumstances, against the wider availability of contraceptives, and against sex education in schools." When it was announced that the ERA had been voted down by a huge margin, the crowd in the Salt Palace erupted in cheers. A resolution to dissolve the IWY altogether also passed. To the astonishment of feminists, a resolution calling for the repeal of women's right to vote actually reached the floor. That would be surprising anywhere in 1977, but quite a surprise in a state that had boasted for a hundred years of its precociousness in adopting woman suffrage as a territory back in 1870.[13]

Utah state coordinating committee members expected and welcomed Mormon participation. Esther Landa, the head of the National Council of Jewish Women who presided at the conference, said this was a big part of their outreach efforts. Committee members, themselves divided between LDS and non-LDS women, insisted that "diversity doesn't have to divide people." The coordinating committee chair, Jan L. Tyler, a thirty-four-year-old former professor at Brigham Young University, was both an active member of the LDS and an ardent supporter of the ERA. Having "a foot in both camps," she had hoped to be a bridge between women with different views on feminism. Another IWY organizer, Margaret S. "Maggy" Pendleton, described by friends as "the closest thing to a radical feminist as one can find in this fundamentally conservative state," likewise told the press they had hoped IWY would open up a dialogue "that might begin to reverse the polarization that has existed in Utah between churchwomen and feminists for some time."[14]

Toward that end, Utah organizers had written to Rosalynn Carter in April, imploring her to be their keynote speaker: "Instead of dividing these women we hope to work together toward the goal of full participation for all individuals. Because you are a strong woman with a keen family and religious orientation, yet still willing to take strong stands of your own . . . you would have the greatest appeal for Utah women. The balance you provide would be non-threatening to our women . . . You are perfect for us."[15] When the First Lady declined, they invited Belle Spafford, a prominent Mormon. She accepted the invitation, but in her address echoed the church's position: that liberation is "a choice and wonderful blessing" but one that could sometimes lead the overzealous to faulty attitudes and extreme actions.[16]

After the meeting, IWY coordinating committee members protested that the Relief Society had "packed" the conference. Maggy Pendleton told the press that Mormon women who outnumbered non-Mormons by about ten to one "could vote down anything they wanted to. They ran the whole thing." Worse still, "the acrimony that prevailed at the convention overrode nearly every attempt at a thoughtful discussion of women's issues." She said she had "never been so rudely treated in my life." Jan Tyler acknowledged gloomily that the convention had produced a number of "unfortunate things that gave me personal pain," among them that many of the women "professing a tremendous concern for life" were "very abusive in their actions towards others" with different views.[17]

IWY organizers blamed Schlafly and "her organizations" for the Mormon Church's decision to influence the outcome of IWY meetings in Utah and elsewhere. Perhaps hesitant to accuse the church itself, they suggested that some Mormon leaders had acted in complicity with Stop-ERA and Right to Life, and that groups they had just begun to hear of, such as the Conservative Caucus, had improperly used church authority in meetings prior to the conference at which they instructed Mormon women on voting procedures.[18] Schlafly's old ally, state legislator Georgia Peterson, took the lead in preparing a slate of antifeminist nominees for delegate positions that had been circulated on the floor of the Salt Palace under the auspices of the Eagle Forum, and most were elected. All but one of the fourteen delegates and five alternates elected were Mormons, including Peterson, who was chosen as head of the delegation. In contrast to the carefully balanced, diverse list of nominees prepared by the state IWY coordinating committee, all were "Caucasian" (one was a Chicana), all were middle-class, all but one were over the age of forty, and all but one were Republican.[19]

Relief Society president Barbara Smith also suggested that conservative groups had borrowed church authority in urging women to attend and vote in certain ways. She acknowledged that a letter had gone out over LDS leader Ezra Benson's signature suggesting that each ward send at least ten women. But Smith denied that the society had given out instructions on voting.

Rather, she insisted that the fact it had *not* given specific directions had "created a vacuum into which various conservatives stepped to advise on voting and strategy." She did not apologize for urging women to participate, however, reminding critics that the IWY Commission had asked women's organizations to do just that.[20]

Don LeFevre, a spokesman for the Mormon Church, also defended the LDS, including in a rather dramatic conference call when Abzug and other members of the IWY Commission questioned the church's role in the Utah meeting. He acknowledged that the Relief Society had encouraged its membership to take part "and vote for correct principles" and had distributed reminders of the church's positions on relevant issues. He insisted that the church had "always been concerned with threats to the stability of the family and the home." "We don't make any excuses for our women's participation," he added. "We're proud of them. Other women's groups could probably take a note from their book.[21]

LeFevre noted that the LDS placed a heavy emphasis on early marriage and large families, that birth control was frowned upon, and abortion was viewed as "one of the most revolting and sinful practices of this day." Indeed, he said the church's opposition to the Equal Rights Amendment was "founded more on physiology than theology."[22]

Leading Mormons similarly defended their decision to send letters urging mobilization of Mormon women to Relief Society leaders in Alabama, Florida, Hawaii, Indiana, Kansas, Montana, New York, Washington State, West Virginia, and Mississippi—the states that had not yet held their state meetings. For the rest of the summer, Mormons would play a huge part in the IWY story.[23]

Nearly all of the other IWY meetings taking place that weekend in Pennsylvania, Tennessee, Texas, Massachusetts, and the U.S. Virgin Islands adopted all or most core recommendations. However, with women from the pro-life organization, National Right to Life, in the lead, conservatives scored another big victory at the meeting in Lincoln, Nebraska, widely celebrated by the Nebraska press.

In an article entitled "Homemakers Take Over," a sympathetic reporter praised "the God-fearing homemakers of this corn and cattle rich state" who came "from every corner of the state to take over the Nebraska women's meeting, which appeared all set to send a delegation of liberal, 'liberated' women to Houston as representative of this conservative Cornhusker state," as "had been the trend in most Eastern states." The Nebraska homemakers had "made it a family project." According to the reporter, "all week-end golf and fishing plans and harvest work was set aside [as] mom, pop, and the kids took off for a week-end here" at the IWY conference. After a stormy nine-hour marathon session dominated by conservatives, "those representing the 'traditional values' and pro-life forces had elected a full slate of 21 delegates to the national convention" and "the women 'libbers' were left without a single delegate and a ripped up and changed platform."[24]

The victory was particularly satisfying, he said, as the "the so-called 'liberated' women groups" that organized the Idaho IWY meeting had tried to pack the conference with ERA and abortion advocates by spending the state's $25,000 allocation to provide free transportation, housing, meals, and child care.[25] But the Nebraska coordinating committee, in the view of this reporter, had not counted on "the growing political awareness of the pro-life and pro-American forces in the state" led by Ann Bowen, a pro-life leader from Omaha.[26] Church buses brought in an estimated 1,200 people. The feminist serving as conference organizer, Donna Polk, told the press it "was a well-orchestrated effort prompted by the Catholic and Lutheran Churches" with nuns and priests much in evidence.[27]

At this point in the summer, the media was fully engaged in covering the IWY meetings. Journalists including Vera Glaser, Peggy Simpson, Gail Sheehy, and Kay Mills were among those supportive of the women's rights movement, and their description of events reflected that. Other members of the press, particularly conservative men, were clearly delighted to see "their women" step up and deal blows to the feminists.[28] Some seemed to be delighted to see women fighting women. And there was quite a show to cover as feminists and conservatives maneuvered for advantage through behind-the-scenes organizing and convention floor struggles, exchanging charges and countercharges, insults and innuendo. By the end of the summer the conflict would get physical.

The late June victories gave a tremendous boost to conservatives' spirits. On July 5, 1977, Rosemary Thomson sent out another missive to IWY Citizens' Review Committee chairmen and Eagle Forum presidents congratulating them on their hard work and success. IWY coordinating committee leaders, she reported, had been phoning her to learn if the CRC had a review committee operating in their state. "One Chairman told me she would not have *her* conference disrupted by anyone speaking against abortion, and that people who do not agree with IWY goals should stay home. I have not heard from her since we won all the delegates there!"[29]

Thomson expressed outrage at all the "horribles" they had witnessed: the "mass infusion of lesbians at many conferences, pornographic literature on display, withholding registration blanks from our people to prevent them from attending, strong-arm control of floor microphones by IWY, flaunting improper parliamentary procedure, and even worse, discovering political party leaders, state & Federal legislators such as Sen. Charles Percy, participating in promotion of these IWY goals to restructure society!" Yet, despite the feminists' advantage and dirty tricks, they had won the bulk of the national delegations in Missouri, Nebraska, Ohio, and Utah.[30]

Still, Thomson reminded them, they had much to do to prepare for the remaining conferences. If they had "any friends or relatives in these states," Thomson urged that they "please alert them or pass along any helpful hints." They might consider using Dianne Edmondson's "motivation tapes," pointing out that the Oklahoman's cassettes "have had wide distribution and success in informing church groups."[31]

Thomson also urged them to reach out more to men in civic, fraternal, and church groups in their areas "explaining what really happened at your IWY conference and what the goals of the libs are." It was important, she said, to "zero in on businessmen (not just women's organizations) so they will be aware of proposed legislation which will increase their taxes and Federal regulation and intrusion into private enterprise." Also important, when holding "speakers' seminars" to train new people as speakers, "don't neglect inviting the men!"[32]

Despite the fact that conservative women were trying to get men to stand up and join them in defending traditional womanhood and the family, there was no doubt that the anti-IWY movement was a women's crusade. Signing off, Thomson thanked these women serving as Citizens' Review Committee and Eagle Forum leaders "for your dedication, your prayers and cooperation." And, she added, "while the libs may call each other 'sisters,' it is evident that our bond is the real way of sisterhood as the Lord intended! Love to you all, Rosemary."[33]

July belonged to the conservative sisterhood, now well organized, fully mobilized, and building a sense of momentum as they succeeded in state after state. The coordinating committee leaders unfortunate enough to have their state IWY meetings that month scrambled to retain control. But the tables had turned. Ten states held IWY meetings in July, but—with the exception of West Virginia and Bella Abzug's home state of New York—conservatives emerged victorious in every one.

At the Washington IWY meeting held in Ellensburg, Mormons again played a key role, in league with Catholic leaders. There was a particularly intense battle, and both feminists and conservatives turned out in force. Earlier in the year, ERA opponents in Washington had been engaged in a campaign to rescind the state's ratification. For months they had labored to get the requisite number of signatures on a petition that would have put the rescission issue before the voters in a November 1977 referendum. By coincidence, about the same time as the state IWY meeting, rescission leaders learned that their effort would fall short. Frustration over this issue—together with Dianne Edmondson's cassette tape widely circulated among Christian conservatives in the state—contributed to a huge conservative turnout.

The day before the conference, as the coordinating committee held its final meeting, 2,500 had pre-registered. But as they were about to adjourn, Susan Roylance, a Mormon, knocked on the door, and firmly but politely notified them that she represented about two thousand "Christian women" who were not pre-registered but planned to attend. She understood, Roylance said, that this might cause logistical difficulties, but they had made their own housing arrangements and would bring their own food, as well as pay the required surcharge for late registration. Alice Yee, chair of the arrangements committee, later recalled that receiving this news at that moment after months of planning was "traumatic."[34]

As the word spread, feminists in a broad coalition known as "Friends of Equal Rights" who had worked together against rescission, realized it was urgent that they attend. Radical feminists in the state who had shown little interest in what they expected to be a staid, government-sponsored event changed their plans and headed for Ellensburg.[35]

Some of them organized a Friday evening session to plan strategy for the Saturday voting and put together their own slate of candidates. In their view the slate prepared by the organizers—who had chosen to provide some degree of ideological diversity, along with diversity of other kinds—was not sufficiently feminist. Some declared they had not worked so hard to come this far only to see their state IWY meeting dominated by women opposing the ERA and abortion.[36]

During the weekend, the conservatives, known as the "Blue and White Coalition," wore ribbons with those colors (selected by Catholic leaders in honor of the Virgin Mary) so that coalition members were known to one another. The ribbons were hardly necessary, one of their Mormon allies said, since they all wore dresses and the feminists all wore pants—"the emblem" of their movement.

Between these warring coalitions were many women, not affiliated with either side, who had no idea they were stepping into a war zone. As one said, "I planned to go to some workshops, maybe get to know some interesting women, sit in the sun with my friends." Many resented the organized coalitions—which were, as one said, "directing me around like they were God and I was a mindless robot"—and left Ellensburg in disgust in the middle of the conference.

Feminists charged that Mormon men were on the convention floor directing the women's votes. Mormon women indignantly denied that accusation, particularly Susan Roylance, an experienced Republican activist with considerable knowledge of parliamentary procedure, who did in fact coordinate the conservatives' challenge. She insisted the men were there only because they had driven the women to the meetings. To avoid misimpressions, Roylance said, she commanded them to sit in seats high in the rafters and away from the convention floor.

At the plenary session where the state's recommendations for Houston were adopted, the conservatives scored an almost complete victory. One of the most dramatic and widely reported incidents was the defeat of a joint statement supporting the ERA and minority rights. According to the Associated Press, "Mormon representatives joined with conservative Christian women to dump it." However, Washington conservatives indignantly protested these accusations of racism. They insisted that the feminists who controlled procedures during the meeting would not allow amendments to separate the ERA and the minority rights issues. But since defeating the ERA was among their main reasons for coming, they said, they had little choice but to vote against the resolution.[37]

The results of the voting on delegates were not announced until after the meeting, and conservative women left Ellensburg believing that they prevailed in that election as well as in the vote on resolutions. Therefore they were shocked and angry when informed that a totally feminist slate had been elected, with conservative women as alternates. As in the case of Missouri, the divided verdict led to legal action.[38]

In Montana, conservatives dominated in a particularly acrimonious gathering at which all core recommendations went down in flames. Mormons were again influential but objected to charges that they "railroaded" their views through the conference. Some accused feminists of being poor losers. Yet, according to press reports, even conservatives were upset at the manner by which the "takeover" was achieved. One Montana woman, a former head of the Montana Right to Life Association who supported women's rights, told the press, "The deliberate sabotage of the state International Women's Year Conference in Helena is an occurrence that future generations will review with shame and disbelief. It will be like the feelings today's blacks must have when they encounter historical revelations that many of their ancestors actually opposed their own emancipation."[39]

The biggest surprise that weekend was the news that the Hawaii IWY meeting had elected a conservative slate. Observers across the nation were shocked. Five years earlier Hawaii had won the competition to be the first to ratify ERA.[40] Hawaii voters repeatedly elected Patsy Mink, a prominent feminist as well as the first Asian-American woman in Congress, a major figure in the National Women's Political Caucus, and other than Abzug the strongest supporter of the bill mandating the IWY.[41]

Distraught Hawaii feminists, tried to make sense of what happened. They had been totally unprepared for the arrival of a large group of women with radically different and staunchly conservative views on women's issues. This was evident in their choice of "entertainment," a performance by a dance troupe, the Common Woman's Theatre, in which young women dressed in black leotards performed a series of dances and skits with lesbian themes—which shocked and appalled the conservative women. However, as Hawaii feminists reported later, the dancers were also upset. Having never performed for "so large and varied an audience," they were "surprised and taken aback" by the hostile response.[42]

The Hawaii coordinating committee soon learned that many of the women in this large and unexpected group of conservative women were non-citizen women bused in from a LDS-owned Polynesian cultural center. In fact, the election produced a 63 percent Mormon group of delegates despite the fact that Mormons constituted only 3.2 percent of the state's population. Beverly Creamer, reporting for the Honolulu *Advertiser*, wrote, "Direction for Mormon women to get 'involved' in the International Women's Year convention here last weekend came directly from the church's national head-quarters in Salt Lake City."[43]

Creamer interviewed Relief Society president Barbara Smith, who said it was just coincidence that she was in Hawaii at the time of the meeting; she had come to attend an insurance convention with her husband. But she acknowledged stopping by the IWY conference and meeting with the four-teen Hawaii delegates elected to go to Houston, adding she was impressed by their eagerness to represent the women of the state. Smith was convinced that the positions adopted by the conservatives at the state meeting were truly representative of Hawaii women and women across the nation. Smith also acknowledged that the summer had heightened Mormon women's political activism. Although Mormons "try not to get involved politically as a church," the way the issues were presented at the IWY, requiring people to have to vote for or against proposals they had no chance to modify, she said, had made the IWY a polarizing experience for women and made the conservatives feel a greater need to engage politically.[44]

The New York IWY meeting held that same weekend of July 8–10 in Albany—the last feminist victory that summer—was high on attendance and drama. It was a massive showdown between feminists and conservatives that one conservative described as "a war between God and the devil." Conservatives were determined to mount a powerful offensive and defeat feminists in their stronghold, the home state of Abzug and Steinem. Feminists were determined not to let them.[45]

A conservative coalition consisting of the Eagle Forum; Right-to-Life; Birthright, Inc.; Wake Up America; and the New York State Conservative Party—groups that had worked together in 1975 to defeat the state ERA—advised conference organizers that they would be bringing busloads of their members to the conference, which produced a scramble to find a larger meeting hall that would hold 5,000—2,000 more than they had been expecting. Yet 11,000 people showed up. Again the Mormons played a big role; according to the press "in New York they were bussed in by the hundreds to vote for the anti-change slate."[46]

News that conservatives were planning a surge sent feminists scrambling for reinforcements. Pulling out all the stops, conference organizers worked to encourage turnout with the support of the rich and famous. The IWY meeting would open with a "privately funded, professionally mounted, three-hour show, 'Celebrating Women' . . . featuring actresses Helen Hayes, Diane Keaton, Celeste Holm, Ruby Dee, Kim Hunter, Kitty Carlisle Hart, Hattie Winston, an Hispanic dance troupe, and a black rock group." Ellen Cohn, writing for the *Village Voice*, stated that "in the last few days, women who were headed anyplace but have decided to go to Albany instead this weekend."[47]

Just before the conference got under way, six representatives of the IWY Citizens' Review Committee held an afternoon press conference at which they accused the feminist organizers of discrimination during advance planning. Virginia Lavan of Schenectady stated: "Right-to-life forces were barred deliberately from important women's meeting planning sessions and were left off the nominated slate of New York delegates to the National Women's Conference. We're bringing our people here in droves to vote in our own slate of delegates." Lavan also announced that the committee had hired a certified parliamentarian to "make sure the microphones are not turned off when we get up to speak."[48]

Feminists also worked hard to prepare proposals and a slate of delegates. Joanne Edgar of *Ms.* magazine recalled going up to Albany to help staff the event after hearing rumors that right-wing women were sending busloads to try and stack the state delegation. As Edgar recalled, "We stayed up all night in this huge government building, making hundreds of copies of the feminist plan and collating lists of delegates." Not only the staff volunteers but Steinem, Abzug, and Mary Anne Krupsak, New York's lieutenant governor, were there, "all of us running the collating assembly line and planning for the next day's vote. Bella kept us laughing all night long." In the end, she said, "our teamwork paid off. We distributed our platform and list of delegates to everyone at the meeting the next day, and the group that went to Houston from New York State was solidly feminist."[49]

To ward off charges of voter fraud, New York IWY leaders had engaged the American Arbitration Association, a neutral agency, to count the ballots. Participants elected eighty-eight delegates to send to Houston and adopted all of the core recommendations and more. As the Associated Press reported, of all the state IWY meetings that weekend, "only New York seems to have been concluded with a pro-ERA and pro-abortion note."[50]

With the exception of the West Virginia meeting on July 22–23, 1977, where they won the day, the remaining conferences were either headaches or nightmares for the feminists. All took place in the Midwest and the South, where conservative forces were the strongest.

In Indiana on the weekend of July 15–17, a coalition of conservatives and religious fundamentalists defeated the entire core and won 31 of the state's 32 seats. Conservatives were still furious over losing the January 1977 fight over the ERA in which Rosalynn Carter persuaded a wavering legislator to vote yes and ERA forces gained their first victory in two years. Conservatives had felt robbed and were eager to "redeem the reputation" of their state.[51]

Since May, Indiana Stop-ERA leaders had worked with leaders of other conservative organizations to establish an Indiana Citizens' Review Committee. Rolena Jackson, Indiana Stop-ERA chairman, was among the leaders, as were two staunch Schlafly allies, Evelyn Pitschke, an Indianapolis attorney who served as Stop-ERA's legal adviser, and Joan Gubbins, a three-term state senator. Jean Harvey, president of Indiana Pro America, a conservative women's organization, worked with them. These experienced activists recruited Kathryn Nikou, a senior at Indiana University – Indianapolis, a skilled public speaker and former "Miss Indianapolis," to serve as the state IWY Citizens' Review chair and spokesperson. For Nikou and many other newcomers to politics the anti-IWY campaign amounted to a "crash course" in political organizing. The Indiana CRC had the whole summer to organize and turn out their people.[52]

Although Indiana was represented in the Senate by liberal senator Birch Bayh, a staunch supporter of feminism, there was a strong conservative presence—and history. The Ku Klux Klan, which held sway over Indiana politics in the 1920s, was still alive in the state, as was the John Birch Society, which had been founded there in 1958. It was also the national headquarters for the American Legion. Not only religion and antifeminism but a long history of anticommunist activism also contributed to the outcome of the Indiana IWY meeting. Right-wing Hoosiers saw the ERA and the IWY as a multifaceted political menace that was connected to but not limited to feminism. Referring to the plan adopted at the 1975 Mexico City IWY conference, CRC literature proclaimed that the "World Plan of Action is actually a blueprint for the United Nations to institute its One World Government." Feminists, in their view, were either dupes of subversives working for a one-world government, or traitors willingly participating in an internationalist conspiracy to undermine America's national sovereignty and strength. Their sharp anti-internationalism prompted them to understand the UN-backed IWY as "the coalescent event of a conspiracy decades in the making."[53]

Feminists did little to plan for the IWY meeting until it was too late. After their January victory, the Indiana ERAmerica chapter, the only state-wide coalition of feminist groups, disbanded. Ironically, the ERA victory had made them complacent and ill prepared even as it galvanized the conservatives. A month before the Indiana IWY meeting, Sharon Boothby, Indiana NOW coordinator, intercepted some of the conservatives' mailing and learned of their "mind-boggling" degree of organization, including a clear plan for poll watchers, floor leaders, and more. Springing into action, NOW created the Unity Coalition, which hastily sought to mobilize women's rights supporters, but the conservatives were way ahead of them.[54]

Even the CRC leaders who had worked hard to produce a large turnout were surprised at the results. While only 1,600 people had registered, 4,000 showed up, enough that they could control the conference. But while they dominated the election, they had not come prepared with alternative resolutions to pass, and the Indiana meeting produced no resolutions.[55] According to Carol Sutton, editor of the Louisville *Courier-Journal,* the conservatives distorted the issues, and "real problems [were] pushed aside in favor of imagined ones, and reason overwhelmed by emotion." Indiana, she charged, defeated a motion demanding that more women be appointed in state and federal governments and struck down a demand for better enforcement of the Equal Credit Opportunity Act, while a resolution urging American women to join in the crusade against world hunger "was twisted into a call to abolish the United Nations because it allegedly promotes world government."[56]

Feminists were dismayed by the right-wing victory in Indiana and the manner in which it was achieved. Two evangelical ministers from the Terre Haute Temples wandered the halls urging participants to reject the wickedness proposed by state IWY organizers, calling them "whores, prostitutes, and lesbians." IWY leaders were disturbed that conservative women chose men to marshal the anti-IWY forces. The men included Greg Dixon, pastor of Indianapolis Baptist Temple (later a co-founder of the Moral Majority), and Daniel Manion, a lawyer and son of Clarence Manion, founder of the conservative Manion foundation. They roamed the convention, using walkie-talkies to tell participants what to do. Molly Rucker, a member of the Indiana IWY coordinating committee, later recalled, "No one can completely describe the intensity of the emotions that were felt . . . and certainly the mere recollection of those two days is extraordinarily painful."[57]

After the meeting, Louisville *Courier-Journal* editor Carol Sutton expressed alarm at what had happened in Indiana and at many other IWY conferences that summer. Although the goals of the IWY sponsors were worthy, she wrote, "the women's meetings are turning out to be a sterile battle-ground between those who want to see inequities redressed and those who want to turn the clock back to a world that never was." It was truly disturbing, she said, that "the kind of people who encouraged the McCarthyite smears of the 1950s and defended segregation in the 1960s are now permeating the ranks of those who fear guaranteed equal rights for women." She also noted the increased cooperation between anti-ERA and pro-life forces and noted that "this extreme right-wing influence is also beginning to creep into some anti-abortion literature."[58]

In Kansas, there was more acrimony and accusations of fraud after conservatives won twelve of the twenty delegate slots even as feminists dominated the vote on recommendations. Despite the efforts of a "pro-family" coalition supported by Stop-ERA, Right to Life, and religious groups including Baptist, Catholic, and Mormon women, the assembly still approved most of the core. Schlafly insisted that the feminists did so well in the vote on resolutions only because of trickery. She claimed that IWY leaders announced that a fire marshal set a limit of 2,500 for the auditorium, meaning that many of the 4,600 registered for the conference must be kept out. Then doorkeepers went ahead and admitted ERA proponents who "were secretly identified by a little dot on their badges." After the conference, Schlafly charged, the anti-IWY forces learned that the official capacity of the hall was 5,200. "If all the registered delegates had been admitted, the IWY resolutions would have been defeated because the pro-family participants were clearly the majority (as proved by the fact that pro-family women elected most of the delegates to Houston)." Afterward, however, angry conservatives established a Wichita chapter of the Eagle Forum to carry on the fight.[59]

Well-organized conservatives also presented a major challenge to feminists at state IWY meetings in the Deep South, where the conflict got even uglier. In Alabama more than 2,000 crowded into the Montgomery Civic Center on Saturday, July 9, for the daylong meeting. The large turnout resulted from statewide registration drives by forces supporting and opposing the Equal Rights Amendment. Despite everything that had happened at previous meetings in other states, Alabama coordinating committee leaders were still "surprised at the organization and power of the Eagles" led by state Eagle Forum vice president Eunice Smith of Birmingham. They came "by the busloads," in church buses from various denominations, wearing red, white, and blue and "with blue badges of an Eagle and the American flag." One reporter noted that a surprising number of men attended, apparently assisting the Eagle Forum efforts.[60]

Conservatives narrowly lost a fight over rules early in the day, which prevented an outright takeover of the conference. Eagle Forum and NOW strategists (who wanted a purely feminist delegation) each objected to some of the proposed delegates on the list devised by the state IWY coordinating committee, which included a few, but only a few, conservative nominees. The conservatives managed to nominate and elect their entire slate, and then employed stalling techniques to prevent Alabama from sending any resolutions to the National Women's Conference.[61]

During a workshop on the problems of rural and minority women, a young African American college student, Mary Carstarphen, standing at the microphone to speak in favor of the right to abortion, was slapped across the face by a white Eagle Forum member shouting, "God is going to punish you."[62] Eunice Smith was booed by NOW members when she spoke about how the Eagle Forum opposed ERA "as Christians" but was "handicapped" because it was not given the $53,000 the federal government allocated to the Alabama conference.[63] Members of the Alabama coordinating committee struggled to maintain order in the face of conservative tactics designed to create disorder, such as paying the two-dollar registration fee with two hundred pennies or twenty-dollar bills.[64]

Alabama IWY leaders reported woefully that, despite their hopes and careful preparations, "the entire proceedings at the conference were marred with conflict." Like feminists in other southern states where leading social indicators suggested that women faced deep-seated problems, including poverty and lack of opportunities in education and employment, they saw the state IWY meetings as a much-needed opportunity to address and confront these problems, and were dismayed that these opportunities were lost.

The Alabama meeting's keynote speaker, Patricia Derian, a Mississippi native serving as State Department Coordinator for Human Rights—a key figure in Carter's human rights campaign—addressed this theme specifically. In 1977, she said, women remained "second-class citizens" in many places despite the fact that they represent "half of all humanity." But the plight of southern women, black and white, was particularly bad, as most were undereducated, and those who did manage to finish college were "paid as if they had not gone at all."[65]

Derian told reporters she was "very troubled" by the "reactionary backlash" she was witnessing at the IWY meetings that summer and that progressive-minded people were going to have to mobilize against it. There would have to be some "on the ground" political action to confront it if the nation was going to be able to continue to achieve reforms, she said. "That needs to happen; it needs to happen soon; and it needs to happen decisively. And we ought to get going on it."[66] One Alabama leader said that if this clash with conservatives at the IWY meeting had to happen, perhaps it served as a useful wake-up call. Feminists were going to have to organize and combat the growing threat from the right.

Meanwhile, Alabama journalists were having a field day. Many seemed to find it amusing to see women fighting with women at an "all-girl" political gathering. The *Montgomery Independent* contained a column entitled "In Perfumed Combat," stating:

Not since the old days when the State Democratic Executive Committee met here—squawling, cussing and hurling scurrilities at each other—has Montgomery seen such fury as that engendered by Alabama's International Women's Year conference. It was a veritable cat fight between those favoring abortion and the equal rights amendment and those opposed. In the end, the agginers won but not before they startled even some battle-wise male politicians who were watching . . . Not to be cute, but the women unarguably demonstrated that in political combat, they are, indeed, the equal if not the superior of men. The Civic Center is still smoking.[67]

Another local newspaper, the *Montgomery Advertiser*, published an editorial, "The Powder Puff Duel," expressing admiration for the "selfless dedication" of anti-ERA women who sacrificed their time to register this protest, especially those who had been elected as delegates and would now have to attend the national conference dominated by feminists, where they would be "looked upon as oddballs from a benighted land."[68]

At the Florida meeting, a three-day conference held at the Orlando Sheraton–Twin Towers hotel on July 15–17, there was more conflict. Feminists were still reeling from the narrow defeat of the ERA in this key battleground state. Many wore black armbands in honor of Alice Paul, who had first proposed the ERA back in 1923 and had died that summer with ERA still stalled.[69] Florida ERA opponents were furious about the NOW-sponsored boycott of unratified states, which spelled trouble for their tourist-dependent state. Both sides were roiling over Anita Bryant's "Save the Children" campaign, which had resulted in Dade County's antidiscrimination ordinance being rescinded one month earlier.

IWY Commission members and IWY Citizens' Review Committee leaders were both on hand, working with local women. Representative Gwen Cherry, leader of the pro-ERA forces in the state legislature active at the national level in the National Women's Political Caucus, had been appointed head of the Florida IWY coordinating committee and chaired the meeting, assisted by Florida judge Elizabeth Athanasakos, former IWY presiding officer. Florida CRC leader Rani Davidson, of Clearwater, coordinated the opposition, guided by CRC state coordinator Kathryn Dunaway of Georgia. Of course Shirley Spellerberg, president of the Florida Federation of

Women for Responsible Legislation—the woman Thomson said had been chosen by God to get Schlafly to lead the fight against the ERA—was also on hand, helping coordinate the conservative challenge. Ann O'Donnell, leader of the conservatives at the Missouri IWY meeting, was also there, representing National Right to Life and assisting Jean Doyle, the Florida NRLC leader. O'Donnell told the press it was her fifth IWY conference.[70]

Conservative religious leaders also prepared their forces for the battle. Freeman Baggett, Stake President of the Central Florida area of the Mormon Church, acknowledged being part of the "loose-knit organization" (presumably the CRC) that had been created of "people who are concerned and interested in the same basic philosophy of protecting the family." He insisted this anti-IWY effort was not just by Mormons but other faiths, including Catholics, Baptists, Presbyterians, and Episcopalians, but said he was expecting several hundred Mormon women from throughout the state. Church of Christ members, women and men, also attended, including a minister who roamed the aisles denouncing the proceedings as "an autocratic, dictatorial façade."[71]

The most bitter debate centered on the nomination and election of candidates for the forty delegate slots. As the conference began, Chair Gwen Cherry accepted nominations from the floor for an hour—as announced—then cut off the process as dozens of women, including Spellerberg, crowded around the five microphones, demanding the floor, some pushing and shoving one another. Conservative women were angry that they had only been able to nominate thirteen candidates before nominations were closed. The next day participants stood in line for over four hours as they waited to vote. Throughout the weekend there were fifty "workshops" with heated discussions that produced large numbers of resolutions in addition to the IWY Commission–recommended "core."[72]

As the meeting was about to vote on resolutions, conservative leaders withdrew enough of their forces to prevent a quorum and demanded adjournment. Cherry was forced to conclude the meeting without a vote—two hours early and before all ballots were counted and the official delegates had been announced. In the end Florida elected the thirteen conservatives and twenty-seven women's rights supporters; the fiery state senator and ERA champion Lori Wilson was chosen to serve as delegation chair. Both sides declared victory. But as one delegate, who stared at the singing, chanting women at the conclusion of the meeting, told the press: "We are all losers. We didn't get anything done."[73]

Both sides hurled charges of bad behavior and official misconduct.

Carmen Delgado Votaw, representing the IWY Commission at the Florida meeting, said that "little old ladies in tennis shoes" tried to keep them from voting on several issues, including the ERA and the gay rights plank. "They would put out their feet and trip people, trying to obstruct them from getting out of the pew to vote." They had "people stationed at every elevator to make sure it only went up, not down to the voting place. They would stand in the voting line and then get in line again—the idea was to make people stand in line to vote for two hours." Votaw had gone forward with her speech despite rumors that "Anita Bryant's people" were going to "pelt us with oranges," but the threats led Mary Anne Krupsak, the New York lieutenant governor, to cancel her address.[74]

There were allegations that the conservatives were aided by the Ku Klux Klan, a rumor confirmed by a reporter for the *Wall Street Journal*. In an article entitled "Klan Cardholder Wanted to Help," he wrote that Mississippi Klan leader George Higgins Jr. had served as the bouncer outside the CRC hospitality room in the Sheraton Hotel's penthouse suite. However, the conservative women expressed shock when learning from the press about his identity. And Higgins acknowledged that he had not told them of his Klan affiliation—even as he boasted to the press about influencing the outcome of the meeting.[75]

Conservatives again protested that the IWY was a taxpayer-funded effort of the federal government to force the ERA on the nation along with other unwanted changes. One of the signs on the convention floor stated, "If you like what the Supreme Court did with forced bussing, you'll love what they do with ERA." Some loudly expressed their disapproval at seeing Gwen Cherry, an African American, banging the gavel and shouting, "This is a federal conference and federal rules are supreme," as she cut off nominations."[76]

When it was all over, Shirley Spellerberg announced that conservatives planned to challenge the elections on the grounds that there was a lack of a quorum on key votes and that they intended to call for a congressional investigation "of this whole nonsense."[77]

The conservative takeover of the Mississippi IWY meeting held July 8–9 was the most notorious of the conservative victories as well as the most complete. A well-organized and secretive group of conservatives working with the CRC and calling themselves "Mississippians for God, Country and Family" shocked feminist organizers by flooding the meeting at the last minute, outnumbering and outvoting them. According to one of the leaders,

Carolyn Morgan of Hattiesburg, who identified herself as head of the state organization, their group was a "loose coalition" representing Stop-ERA, Eagle Forum, Right to Life, the John Birch Society, the American Party of Mississippi, and Women for Constitutional Government. Other conservatives were affiliated with the Southern Conservative Lobby and the Farm Bureau. They came from several different denominations but many were Baptists, Presbyterians, and Pentecostals.[78]

Men were prominent among the leaders. Dr. Shelton Hand, a specialist in constitutional and family law at the Baptist-affiliated Mississippi College School of Law, was one of the most influential. Richard Barrett, a Jackson attorney well known as a white rights advocate, was one of the most vocal. As in several other states, feminists reported that male "controllers" were using walkie-talkies and handheld radios to instruct women how to vote.[79] Linda Williams of the *South Mississippi Sun* reported that the "group that wielded the most power . . . was a group of Pentecostal ministers who bused in entire congregations and controlled their every move." AP correspondent Peggy Simpson quoted two of the women on their reasons for coming: "We were told in our church that ERA meant the end of marriage, that schoolbooks would show pictures of people having sex with animals, and we've got to protect our children." Another woman, attending with her husband, told a reporter that "the only way for women to be equal with men is to step down from the pedestal where men have us. I wouldn't want to be thrown away from what 2,000 years of Christianity has done for us."[80]

Tensions were high as supporters and opponents of the various resolutions stood outside the room where the voting would take place and sang hymns before the final session of the two-day meeting began. Then, according to one reporter, as "Mississippians for God, Country, and Family" broke into a chorus of "God Bless America," the "liberal forces" responded with a ringing rendition of "We Shall Overcome." As the session began, conservative men swept toward the podium carrying American flags. Dr. Jessie Mosley, an African American veteran of the civil rights movement who chaired the Mississippi IWY coordinating committee, stood at the podium and calmly requested that everyone stand and join in singing the national anthem.[81]

Throughout the meeting, Mosley and other committee members—most of them married women with children, from strong religious backgrounds, and with extensive records of service to their state, nation, and churches— were shocked and dismayed to be called "godless communists" as well as "anti-family," "immoral," and "perverse," especially by people who knew them and knew better.[82]

After using parliamentary maneuvers to take over the Mississippi meeting, the conservatives rejected all the core recommendations and adopted recommendations of their own, including denunciations of day care, abortion, homosexuality, ERA, and "sin and immorality" generally. They adopted other resolutions urging privatization of Social Security and opposing Social Security benefits for homemakers, which, they claimed, would lead to higher taxes. They opposed affirmative action (which they called "reverse discrimination") and programs, including Title IX, that required equal opportunities for women in educational institutions. They also opposed proposals for gender equality in the military and international cooperation to promote women's rights and world peace. Richard Barrett introduced several successful resolutions, including one extending "moral support to our anti-communist allies and friends of the Free World," specifying not only the Republic of China (Taiwan) but also Rhodesia (now Zimbabwe) and South Africa, then fighting to preserve white supremacy.[83]

The conservative majority then proceeded to elect a delegation that included Dr. Shelton Hand and five other men. They would be the only men elected as delegates to the Houston conference. Some of them had not even attended the conference. Eddie Myrtle Moore, a self-described "farmwife from Pelahatchie" and the IWY Citizens' Review Committee state leader, was elected as delegation chair. The delegation included John Birch Society members, members of the white supremacist group Women for Constitutional Government, and Dallas Higgins, the wife of the state KKK leader. Her husband boasted to the press that the Klan had controlled the conference.

The Mississippians for God, Country, and Family also elected Willie Lee Latham, a member of the state coordinating committee, not knowing she was black. She promptly resigned rather than serve in this delegation. Mississippi would be represented in Houston by an all-white group. Even in a summer marked by sensational clashes, the Mississippi takeover sent shock waves through the nation.[84]

CHAPTER 9

Mama Said There'd Be Days Like This

Something totally unexpected and disturbing has happened in recent weeks. The [IWY] conferences, instead of providing a forum for some sort of feminism, however diluted, have become a vehicle for anti-ERA and anti-abortion forces around the country . . . The backlash can be fought . . . [but] "feminists can no longer make the bland assumption that their voices will dominate any women's conference."

—ELLEN COHN, JULY II, 1977, *VILLAGE VOICE*

As the summer battles ended, feminists were reeling, stung by what had happened to the conferences for which they had such high hopes. In their final report to the IWY National Commission, Mississippi coordinating committee leaders stated, "It was not at all as we had envisioned, a chance for Mississippi women to come together to discuss their problems, their dreams, and plans." It may have been "naïve," they wrote, "but we never dreamed for a moment that such an innocent goal could be construed by observers as a meeting meant to tear down those institutions that all of us on the Committee hold dear: our families, our churches, and our country."[1] In her column in the *Village Voice,* "Mama Said There'd Be Days like This," Ellen Cohn sympathized, recognizing the conservatives' strong showing as a major wake-up call for feminists.[2]

Not that the state IWY meetings had been a complete disaster for feminists. There was in fact much for them to celebrate. Most who showed up at the state meetings, and 80 percent of the delegates elected to go on to Houston, were supporters of the women's rights movement. Thousands of women who had never been active in politics had come to the meetings and learned from the workshops and speakers and from one another. They forged lasting friendships and alliances across divisions of class and race and sexual preference. According to the feminists, many women said that it was only through their participation in the IWY that they recognized that they were feminists.[3]

IWY leaders regretted that so many conservative women had been bused in and bused out with very little contact with other participants. Organizers of the Mississippi conference were full of compassion for some of their "adversaries," women from rural churches who had arrived on the buses, in many cases shabbily dressed and looking tired and bewildered. Looking back, feminists continued to hope that such women had benefitted from the experience and left with a raised consciousness about women's issues. Keynote speaker Velma Strode, director of equal employment opportunity for the U.S. Department of Labor and the keynote speaker in Mississippi, insisted that the meeting had been "an educational experience for women of diverse backgrounds, economically and culturally," who had "been exposed to information that they've probably never heard." "Believe me," she said, "a lot more will stay with them than their male leaders think."[4]

Even the "wake-up call" Cohn warned of could be counted as a gain. Kathryn Compton Smart, a church-going, married mother of two young children who said she had been a fence-sitter on women's issues before the IWY, was transformed into a feminist activist by exposure to "the rabid, angry women of the Eagle Forum" she encountered at the Oklahoma IWY meeting. In a letter to her local newspaper she claimed that, before the meeting, she "didn't really consider myself an activist. But those days are over now. Being nice and hoping equality will somehow happen because it's just and right hasn't worked." Elynor Tryson thought the defeat in Mississippi had galvanized feminists to face the antifeminist threat: "Even if we lost this time, this meeting will serve as a rallying point. We have identified the enemy."[5]

As for "the enemy," conservative women also claimed that their participation in the IWY meetings over the summer of 1977 had "awakened" them to the need for political activism and strengthened their convictions and resolve. The state meetings clearly cemented the alliance between anti-ERA and pro-life forces. The *National Right to Life News* reported that pro-life women who showed up for the IWY meetings (seeking to join "the establishment" and finding out all was "pre-established") were turned off by the domination of abortion-on-demand advocates as well as proponents of lesbian rights and the ERA. The "rigging" of the conferences "turned them off and turned them out," with the result that they have "coalesced into pro-life, pro-family" alliances. The newsletter quoted one women who said that attending the Pennsylvania IWY meeting had been a life-changing experience and that she now intended "to work harder than ever to educate people to the anti-life, anti-family philosophy of the women's liberation movement."[6]

Phyllis Schlafly boasted that the political battles generated by the IWY conferences had bolstered membership in conservative organizations, including the Eagle Forum, which, she claimed, had surged to over 50,000. IWY had "speeded the demise of the women's movement by showing the nation what the movement is about," Schlafly proclaimed. "It is completely apparent now that the women's lib movement means government-financed abortions, government-sponsored day care and lesbians teaching in our schools. When they pass a resolution saying lesbians ought to be able to teach in schools, you think that's going to enhance the women's movement? I think that's going to kill it."[7]

In the August 1977 *Phyllis Schlafly Report* story on the conferences, "IWY: A Front for Radicals and Lesbians," she stated: "Our friends who attended the International Women's Year State Conferences have realized that, *if family-oriented Americans don't stand up and fight for their values and their legal rights now*, it may soon be too late to save the next generation from those who are trying to destroy our family structure. The libs will replace it with a society that does not respect gender differences, moral values, church, or family." She added, "Now is the time to join EAGLE FORUM so you can be part of an effective national organization of God-fearing, highly-motivated, well-informed men and women."[8]

Schlafly seemed convinced that feminists had utterly discredited themselves and their movement. "The biggest joke about the IWY Conferences is the picture they paint of the pro-ERA and women's lib movement. Pro-ERA women have been bragging that women can do any job just as well as men. The IWY State Conferences show that the women libbers can't even run a fair and orderly meeting." Even their demands proved, she said, that feminists were not as independent and self-reliant as they claimed. "Their IWY resolutions reveal that they are asking the Federal Government to solve all their personal problems. They want Big Brother to take care of their children, pay their bills, find them jobs, and give them a center to cry in when things go wrong." Yet, she charged, "they are the most 'sexist' of human beings. They even objected to men attending the IWY Conferences or being elected as delegates."[9]

IWY leaders did not object to the presence of men but were outraged that antifeminist men had claimed such an extensive and negative role in the summer meetings. It disgusted them that men in the John Birch Society and the Ku Klux Klan boasted about their role in the conservative challenge to the IWY, and that male ministers seemed to be signaling or even coercing their congregants on how to vote on the convention floor, leading them to oppose measures that would improve their lives and those of all women.

They were particularly upset about the powerful role played by the Mormons, not only in Utah or western states but across the country. As journalist Kay Mills observed, feminists were accustomed to conflicts with Catholic conservatives, but during the summer "the women's movement had discovered a new enemy—the Mormon Church."[10]

ERAmerica leader Liz Carpenter provided distressed feminists with some much-needed comic relief as she addressed the summer conference of the National Women's Political Caucus: "I do not think we should allow Salt Lake City, where the church leaders historically over-married, or Rome, where the head of the church never marries, to delineate what the American Family is!" On another occasion she emphasized the seriousness of this church—with its powerful influence over its members—becoming politically active in opposition to feminist goals. "We have a right to know," she said, addressing an ERA workshop, "whether a tax-exempt church is using its two years of servitude"—young Mormon men spend two years in missionary work—"to go out to preach on a political issue."[11]

Gloria Steinem later recalled that the summer of 1977 was her introduction to the political power of the Mormon Church. Nikki Van Hightower of Houston, the city's liaison to the IWY Commission as they planned for the November meeting, said that no one involved with the IWY anticipated such involvement from the LDS "but it has grown and grown." Fortunately, she said, the church did not become active in the anti-IWY effort until most of the summer conferences had ended, but "if they had gone on much longer . . ."[12] For feminists, the potential impact was disturbing to contemplate.

Political analysts, including Dick Behn of the moderate Republican organization the Ripon Society, also took note of the events of the summer and pondered what they might portend for the future of American politics. In a *Ripon Forum* article entitled "Antifeminism: New Conservative Force," Behn noted that a "serious . . . conservative movement emerged at state conferences for the International Women's Year."[13]

Although "the state gatherings began uneventfully enough in late winter of this year," Behn observed, "the conferences held in June and July turned into fiercely fought conflicts between 'change' and 'anti-change' groups. The significance of these battles extends beyond the International Women's Year (IWY) because they presage a new coalition of 'social conservative' groups. The groups range from Catholic right-to-lifers to Protestant fundamentalists to members of the Mormon Relief Society." Behn predicted that these groups, which "often hated one another before," would "in the future vote similarly." This development, together with the fact that "they have demonstrated considerable skill in both coalition politics and convention plotting," meant they could be "a powerful force" if teamed up with anti-gay as well as "anti-abortion, anti-gun control, [and] anti-busing groups that have proliferated along with Richard Viguerie's mailing lists." The IWY, he said, "seems to have been granted a dubious honor. It's the newest conservative rallying cry."[14]

Abzug and other IWY leaders accused Schlafly and her allies of using the IWY to promote a resurgence of the political right. They turned for help to the president who had appointed them. But within the Carter White House, some had already concluded that "this whole thing" (the IWY program) appeared to be "going sour." They thought the president should leave all contact with IWY to Midge Costanza and try to maintain "the lowest possible profile."[15]

Several times in the spring and summer of 1977, Abzug and IWY Commission staff members had written to President Carter entreating him to attend the National Women's Conference in Houston. They urged him to take the occasion to give a major televised address on women's rights as central to human rights. On August 12, 1977, as the commission met in Washington, D.C., they tried again. In an earnest and impassioned letter crafted by the commission's most talented writers and editors, Liz Carpenter, Gloria Steinem, and Sey Chassler, they stressed the meeting's importance, noting that this "first-time, historic, federally-funded representative meeting of American women is likely to receive more immediate attention and have more lasting impact than any other in the past, and than any other for years to come." It would be "the largest representative meeting of women ever gathered together in this country; women of diverse views as well as racial, ethnic and religious groups and women of all ages," and thus a great opportunity for the president.[16]

Such an address, they told Carter, would "demonstrate nationally and internationally that your commitment to human rights includes the rights of women." The address could "become a page in the history of the national and international struggle for women's equality." On the other hand, his absence might "be perceived by many women—already disillusioned by lack of attention to their concerns for many many years—as an indication that this lack of concern continues." His absence would "give heart to the ultra-right forces that have sought to disrupt the State Meetings, to stop the National Conference altogether, and to prevent further progress in the area of women's rights." Should he accept the commission's invitation, Carter's "presence in Houston will be taken as a signal that reinforces the seriousness with which the elected delegates are now approaching their task of voting on a plan of action for instruction of the Congress and the Executive."[17]

At the end they emphasized that the letter of invitation was signed individually by all of the IWY commissioners in order to indicate to the president "how strongly they feel about the importance of your participation in the Houston Meeting." The letter ended optimistically: "We look forward to welcoming you with respect and appreciation in Houston."[18]

However, as early as late July the West Wing had already concluded the president should give the conference a wide berth. One staffer wrote that, although it was too early to announce that the president would not address the National Convention in Houston, it would be "suicidal" to do so, adding, "This may be a repeat of the '68 Democratic Convention."[19]

Carter advisers were hearing things about the IWY that clearly worried them, some of it coming from "National Commission members threatening to resign." There were rumblings that preparation for Houston was "proceeding poorly," and that some blamed Bella Abzug, who was "actively running for Mayor of New York City." They heard rumors that "extreme right-wing women who are non-delegates [would be] coming to disrupt the convention." Far more worrisome, the administration was hearing eyewitness accounts of the state IWY meetings that characterized them as anything but the open forums they were supposed to be. Instead, they were "controlled by whatever faction was able to bus in the greatest number of supporters," with "Right-to-Lifers, Gay Liberation, Mormon Church, and anti-gay rights groups" doing the most busing.[20] It was troubling to see conservatives, already angry about federal support for ERA and abortion, becoming further inflamed as the issue of lesbian and gay rights became so important at the IWY meetings taking place under Carter's watch. It now appeared likely that this volatile issue would be front and center at the National Women's Conference in Houston, ratcheting up the level of controversy.

Back in March the IWY Commission had denied Jean O'Leary's request that protection of the rights of lesbians and gays be added to the list of recommendations state meetings were asked to consider. Abzug, as the newly appointed presiding officer of the IWY Commission, seeking to put together a platform that a majority of women would support, had hesitated to include it. Charlotte Bunch recalled that as she and others pressed for a gay rights recommendation, "Bella was nervous about it on the platform," adding, "I think that she was a supporter of gay and lesbian rights but she was also trying to make a production work and I think Bella was very realistic."[21]

After Anita Bryant's homophobic "Save Our Children" campaign in the spring, however, more feminists, straight as well as gay, supported lesbian activists' pleas. Bunch believed that when their campaign to gain state endorsements succeeded, Bella "was glad we'd done it." But "I don't think she would have made it happen."[22]

Abzug may have been influenced also by an event that took place in early June as the state IWY meetings were getting under way. On June 7, 1977, the night that Bryant forces won their fight for repeal of the Dade County, Florida, ordinance protecting gay rights, Abzug was awakened at two in the morning by hundreds of lesbians and gay men chanting her name on the street outside her second-floor apartment in Greenwich Village, turning for comfort to the former congresswoman who two years earlier had introduced a gay rights bill. According to press reports, she threw on a robe and went downstairs, grabbing hands, consoling people, and in her "booming voice" assured the crowd that this defeat would create more determination and a mature political movement.[23] After that, it would have been very difficult for the IWY leader not to stand up for lesbian and gay rights. Later, some feminists would praise her courage. But others would criticize Abzug for "caving in" to lesbian demands and saddling feminists across the nation with this issue, and accuse her of making the wrong call out of a desire to get the gay vote in her quest to win the September 8, 1977, Democratic mayoral primary.[24]

In any case, by the end of the summer, the fact that more than thirty state meetings had endorsed gay rights resolutions virtually ensured that the IWY Commission would include the issue on the list to be voted upon in Houston. During the summer, as the state meetings were in progress, feminist endorsement of antidiscrimination resolutions and lesbians' active engagement and visibility at the state meetings, however, inflamed conservative resentment and gave IWY critics a potent weapon in their mobilization effort.

For many feminists this was an ominous development. Catherine East, who feared that demanding lesbians' rights would scuttle progress the movement had made over many years, was among them. In September 1977, dismay over the way the IWY program was going and Abzug's handling of it would lead her to resign from the commission staff—despite the fact she had been on the staffs of all presidential commissions on women since 1961. In Houston she would publicly oppose the sexual preference plank.[25]

While the Carter administration was concerned that criticism of the IWY program was coming from some members of the IWY Commission and its staff, far more was coming from the public.[26] The president's fellow Georgian, Kathryn Dunaway, was a bearer of bad news about the growing rage in the conservative Christian community. Soon after attending the IWY state meetings in Florida and Mississippi, she sent a letter informing Carter that the Southern Methodist Church was adopting protest resolutions to be sent to the president, members of Congress, and the governors of their states. In the resolutions, the church reaffirmed its "Biblical position" upholding "Godliness, the family and home, the sanctity of life and the support of sound government." As a result, it declared, the church strongly opposed passage of the Equal Rights Amendment and the National Commission on the Observance of the International Women's Year, which had declared ERA ratification to be its "highest priority" and promoted "Unilateral Disarmament under strict International control."[27]

Dunaway noted that the Southern Methodists also voted to "highly commend the successful efforts and sacrifices of Anita Bryant and those supporting her in preserving the integrity of the family from the abominable influence in Dade County, Florida," and to "thank her for awakening the Nation to this widespread insidious evil and destructive influence." They urged defeat of H.R. 2998 (Abzug's bill protecting gay rights), "defeat of the objectives of the National Commission on the Observance of International Women's Year," and defeat of the ERA, declaring, "Sin should not be blessed with civil rights." Dunaway concluded, "I pray for you and your decisions, Sincerely in Christ, Kathryn F. Dunaway, Mrs. John A. Dunaway. Atlanta GA."[28]

With such a cloud of controversy enveloping the IWY, Carter tried to keep his distance. However, as requested by the feminists, he did agree to issue a strong statement on August 26, 1977, the anniversary of the adoption of the Nineteenth Amendment. At the signing ceremony, he declared that adoption of the woman suffrage amendment "was only the first step in achieving full equality for women" and needed to be followed by ratification of the ERA. Lamenting the death of Alice Paul in June of that summer, he declared that the sacrifices she and others had made for the ERA must not be in vain, and he pledged to do all he could to gain the necessary last state. It was a strong statement in which he declared that equal rights for women are an inseparable part of human rights for all—exactly the kind of statement the IWY Commission was so eager for him to make in Houston. In addition, like Gerald Ford one year earlier, Carter requested further action from the attorney general and heads of all federal agencies to eliminate sex discrimination from the laws and policies of the United States.[29]

Still, feminists were alarmed by the progress conservative women were making in convincing politicians that *they*—not the feminists—were the constituency most important to please. In the opinion of Republican feminist Tanya Melich, the IWY program and its image had declined. It presented a much more radical image and was far more vulnerable to attack from the right. The bipartisan IWY Commission appointed by Ford and headed by Republican feminists, she claimed, "gave the women's movement a centrist cachet and a mainstream legitimacy that was needed, for most Americans knew little about the movement beyond the more radical headlines it had attracted in the early seventies."[30]

While there were from the beginning those who charged the IWY was radical, Melich wrote, "given the support of Ford—by no stretch a radical—these attacks had little credibility." When responsibility for the IWY shifted to the Democrats, however, and Carter appointed "liberal New Yorker Bella Abzug to replace Ruckelshaus," it was, in Melich's opinion, "an unfortunate change." The image of IWY "respectability" that was so "reassuring to those for whom the women's movement was a new concept was blurred." Abzug was "outspoken and intense and moderation was not her style." Attacks on the IWY increased, reached new heights during the summer meetings, and were clearly having an effect.[31]

Melich believed the attacks had particular impact on "the polite but valuable backing IWY had been receiving from Republican officeholders" like Charles Percy. By the fall of 1977, the relentless pressure Schlafly and others in Illinois applied to the senator was taking a toll. There were press reports that the New Right planned to target him for defeat in 1978 and that Schlafly would be the challenger. Percy's support for the women's movement declined precipitously and he, too, planned to skip the Houston conference.[32]

In August, Abzug wrote to the IWY Coordinating Committee chairs in the states indicating that the national office was being flooded with mail criticizing the IWY conferences and demanding a congressional investigation. She asked that they make sure that the politicians heard from them and their supporters as well. There were more problems. The commission's lawyer, Linda Dorian, reported that 133 separate challenges from 36 states had been received, officially challenging the results of state IWY conferences. In addition, columnist James Kilpatrick had visited the IWY Commission office and submitted a Freedom of Information Act request demanding all minutes of commission meetings since Abzug took office.[33] Worse still for the feminists, Senator Jesse Helms announced plans for ad hoc hearings where the legality of the IWY program would be challenged.[34]

This was part of a new strategy developed earlier in the summer by the IWY Citizens' Review Committee and the politicians who came to their aid—most notably Helms. In late June 1977, Helms—or rather Sarah Simms, the female staffer he assigned to the task—corresponded with CRC leaders Thomson and Dunaway. Informing them of the senator's plans to launch an investigation of IWY, Simms asked them to "to compile as much information as possible" to show the IWY's violation of federal law requiring appointed commissions to be fairly balanced in terms of viewpoints and not be inappropriately influenced by any special interest.[35]

In early July, Thomson informed state Citizens' Review Committee leaders that, while they still intended to take over as many conferences as possible, because of the "illegal and unethical voting procedures" of IWY leaders, the CRC would probably end up "with around 200 delegates to 1000 libs." Therefore their new goal would be to work with allies in Congress to stop the IWY national conference scheduled to take place in Houston in November from happening. The plan called for the House Appropriations Committee chairman, George H. Mahon of Texas, to get Congressman Tom Steed of Oklahoma, who chaired a committee appropriate for investigating their allegations of improper conduct, to investigate improper expenditures by the IWY Commission. Thomson urged them, if they had evidence that lobbying had taken place directly or indirectly, to contact Steed immediately and send her a copy. She also urged them to "keep the biased actions of IWY before the public" through letters to the editor, press conferences, radio and TV talk shows, or call-in programs and keep up the flood of protest letters going in to state and Federal legislators.[36]

However, when Congressman Steed refused the request to hold House Appropriations Committee hearings, Helms decided to hold ad hoc hearings himself before whatever members of Congress wished to attend. Helms put together a panel of sixteen senators and congressmen and announced that forty women from across the nation would come at their own expense and testify about discrimination at the state meetings.[37]

The hearing took place on September 14 and 15, 1977, in a caucus room in the Russell Senate Office Building and was chaired by Kathryn Dunaway's ally Congressman Larry McDonald (D-Georgia). McDonald had campaigned openly as a John Birch Society member and was a member of the organization's National Council.[38] During the hearings Henry Hyde (R-Illinois) and freshman Congressman Robert Dornan (R-California)—two men Schlafly later praised as her most courageous allies—gave remarks. According to Rosemary Thomson, the room "was astir with new reporters, a CBS-TV crew, and more than 200 women from 42 states, some with infants in strollers." Over two days, the bipartisan panel of sixteen senators and congressmen heard testimony from seventy witnesses.[39]

The witnesses, including Thomson and IWY Citizens' Review Committee leaders Kathryn Dunaway, Elaine Donnelly, and Nellie Gray, denounced IWY as an attempt to foist UN goals on American women—never an attempt to really find out "what women want." They accused Presiding Officer Abzug of violating her promise to Congress that all women would have the opportunity to participate, claiming that state IWY coordinating committees had failed to publicize the meetings among "non-radical women" and were "hostile" to those who came. Jacquelyn Sumner of Iowa charged that "time and time again anyone who stated an opposing viewpoint was met with a common tactic: they were demeaned by name calling, sneering, laughter, and labelled as 'idiots,' 'racists,' 'uninformed,' 'unintelligent,' 'imbeciles,' or 'deranged.'" They testified about "rigged elections" and "railroaded resolutions" as well as "voting irregularities" and the "inability to challenge election results." IWY leaders, they insisted, had also violated federal laws against lobbying by promoting ERA ratification and "abortion on demand."[40]

More surprising to those present and those who later read abstracts from their testimony in the press or the *Congressional Record* were their accusations of "anti-religious expressions," political extremism, and "aggressive lesbianism" they had witnessed at the state meetings—including material rarely seen in the *CR* and words considered inappropriate to be printed in full. Sindy Miller of Colorado testified that, despite the official prohibition of topics pertaining to religion, the Colorado coordinator of American Atheists "was allowed to conduct an anti-religious workshop on removing the tax exempt status of churches," and feminist bookstores "were allowed to exhibit and sell . . . materials such as, 'The Feminist Bible,' 'A Call for the Castration of Sexist Religion,' and 'Beyond God the Father.'" Eloise Becker of Minnesota charged that "in several lesbian workshops the Catholic Church was ridiculed." Jo Ann Gasper of Virginia stated that "there was a workshop entitled 'Women and Spirituality'—run by witches."[41]

Helen Manwaring of Illinois protested the showing of a film "produced by the Socialist Party" that "presented their solutions to the problems of society, especially the feminist issue." She objected to the film's emphasis on "revolutionary tactics and spirit" and its overall effect, which was to "discredit free enterprise and shame the diversity and flexibility of democracy." Jacquelyn Sumner of Iowa made similar complaints, declaring, "I never thought I would live in America and hear a guest speaker at a convention paid for by tax dollars, openly make the statement that 'Capitalism must be replaced by the only effective and proven method of government—Socialism.'"[42]

Witnesses highlighted the significant levels of participation by lesbians during the summer meetings. There were numerous accusations of "gutter" entertainment with lesbian themes. The most lurid and lengthy came from Helen Priester of Hawaii, who described in great detail the "shocking" entertainment she had witnessed at the Hawaii IWY meeting and demanded that they bring action against the persons who used her tax money for the "showing of a porno stage show featuring the sex acts of deviates." One dance, she testified to the assembled Congressmen, involved a girl "standing in front of a mirror, and examining her body in great detail, including between her legs." In another, a dancer portraying a man "pinned a paper _ _ _ _ _ on the front of her leotard" and a dancer playing a doctor "operated and cut some off." Priester then described the most shocking segment, the dance simulating two lesbians making love in a public toilet. Priester insisted she would surely have walked out had she not been trying to retain a seat for the subsequent voting session in a hall that could hold only a small portion of those attending.[43]

Mary Schmitz of California charged that at her state meeting "lesbians had display tables of their unique equipment such as female masturbating wands, clitoral vibrators, vaginal speculums for self-examination, suction devices for extraction of the menstrual discharge or for performing a self abortion." A pregnant woman, she said, was "offered instruction on how to perform an abortion on herself."[44]

Terry Todd of Minnesota drove home the message: "I would like to leave you with this picture, of hundreds of purple-banded lesbians . . . with their gestures of clenched fist defiance, with the posters and tables of lesbian, social and militant Marxist literature; with all the workshops on revolutions and sex, including an explicit 'how to' course on oral sodomy by a counselor in the Sexual Attitudes Reassessment program at the University of Minnesota . . . a horrifying picture traditional family women will never forget." They concluded by demanding that Congress bring the program to an end.[45]

After the hearings, the conservatives were extremely heartened. Besides Jesse Helms, Larry McDonald, Henry Hyde, and Robert Dornan, several other members of Congress who were already or would soon become their allies had attended and were clearly paying attention. Among them were Congressman Gene Taylor (R-Missouri), Senator Carl Curtis (R-Nebraska), and several newcomers to Congress, including Senator Orrin Hatch and Representative Dan Marriott, Mormon Republicans from Utah. There were also Congressmen Billy Lee Evans (D-Georgia); Robert Badham (R-California), a freshman and close friend and ally of Ronald Reagan; and Mickey Edwards (R-Oklahoma), one of the three founding trustees of the Heritage Foundation, later national chairman of the American Conservative Union and chairman of the annual Conservative Political Action Conference. Afterward, Congressman McDonald issued a press release stating: "I find it inexcusable that the federal government is spending $5 million of taxpayers' money for the advancement of issues that are not in accordance with the majority of American women, such as passage of the Equal Rights Amendment, federally subsidized and supervised child care, legalization of prostitution, lesbianism and other radical feminist goals. This is a flagrant misuse of federal money for lobbying purposes."[46]

Writing to state Citizens' Review Committee leaders, Rosemary Thomson described the Helms hearings as "the high point of our eight months of CRC activities." It was "an exciting two days of spiritual unity for several hundred women and a few men dedicated to traditional moral values." While media coverage was "minimal," "the effect on Capitol Hill was electrifying." The women who testified also visited or phoned all congressional offices as well as the IWY headquarters at the State Department. Three CRC members obtained an audience with Midge Costanza at the White House. She boasted, "No one could miss the fact that, for the first time, traditional women had invaded Washington and launched a persistent lobbying effort!"[47]

Thomson also passed along words of thanks from their approving leader, Phyllis Schlafly, who had kept a discreet distance during the hearings. "I deeply appreciate the dedication and efforts of all those who traveled to Washington to present evidence of wrongdoing at their IWY State Conferences. I know you came at great personal sacrifice. With best wishes and love, Phyllis."[48]

Feminist leaders were being placed on the defensive before a national audience that was becoming increasingly negative. In response, they went on the offensive to "expose the disruptive tactics of the right." The IWY Commission, which declined to attend the Helms hearings, issued a press release protesting the hearings and insisting that Helms had no authority to call them. It complained that the witnesses "were hand-picked by Senator Helms to parrot groundless accusations which have been refuted by this Commission in the courts and elsewhere." It denounced the hearings as "a showcase for bigotry and deceit" and an "abuse of congressional office," since Helms served on none of the committees connected to the IWY.[49]

An irate Congresswoman Pat Schroeder (D-Colorado) presided at a press conference at which she denounced the Helms hearings as a "dog and pony show." She then announced the formation of a new coalition of feminists and civil rights activists created under the leadership of the American Association of University Women (AAUW) to defend the IWY. Called the "Women's Conference Network," its goal was to counter the efforts of a conservative coalition including Stop-ERA, the Eagle Forum, the John Birch Society, the Ku Klux Klan, and the White Citizens' Councils that threatened to sabotage the November IWY Conference in Houston. Schroeder insisted that the IWY program, "the most democratic, grassroots conference that ha[d] ever been held," must not be distracted by the "emotional hysteria and side-show circus we see on the other side."[50]

In the wake of the Helms hearings the IWY Commission members felt considerable heat from other congressmen who continued to be flooded with letters demanding that they stop the National Women's Conference from taking place. Abzug, on the defensive, decided to make a formal statement to her "Dear Friends and Former Colleagues" in Congress, introduced into the *Congressional Record* by Senator and IWY commissioner Birch Bayh. Her statement, she said, was an effort to remind former colleagues of the specific purposes and goals of the IWY program according to its congressional mandate and to "assist them in understanding . . . some of the events which have occurred at the state meetings."

Addressing charges that conservative women had been excluded, Abzug emphasized that organizers had succeeded in attracting participants from every conceivable background and "from every possible point of view." She denied charges that the IWY Commission had stacked the coordinating committees with pro-ERA supporters and persons who "favored choice in the matter of abortion," saying that no one being considered was asked her views on these or any other issues. In addition she stated that, during the state meetings, the commission had representatives on hand who enforced its own regulations requiring that there be nominations from the floor and new recommendations considered to the extent possible given time constraints.

Abzug denied that she or other IWY leaders violated laws against using federally appropriated monies for lobbying activities. The lawsuits filed against the commission members and staff, she insisted, represented an "attempt to parlay a lobbying restriction in a federal law into a mechanism for muzzling people and inhibiting their freedom of speech under the First Amendment." Rather, there had been, on the part of "a militant and well-organized group," a deliberate attempt "to disrupt, to spread misinformation to infuse the state meeting process with distrust and to polarize the partici-pants."[51]

Abzug insisted that it was conservatives who were preventing women from freely participating in the meetings. She called attention to the active participation of men who at state meetings tried to control conservative women, calling this a clear violation of congressional intent. She also accused conservatives of "monolithic anti-change voting." While claiming to be defenders of women and "pro-family," they had opposed not only abortion and ERA but many resolutions that should not have been controversial and were clearly designed to aid women, children, and families.[52]

At the same time, in the House of Representatives, Congresswoman Pat Schroeder introduced into the *Congressional Record* a statement from Marjorie Bell Chambers, AAUW president and head of the Women's Conference Network created to support the IWY conference. Chambers urged Congress "on behalf of the undersigned organizations, comprised of millions of members representing the widest cross section of American women," to "support the National Women's Conference and the concerns which will emerge from it." She declared that members of these groups "believe that women's rights as human rights are a priority issue for the nation and deserve the consideration and support of everyone including members of Congress."

The National Women's Conference, Chambers declared, was of tremendous importance: "For the first time in the 201-year history of the United States, women will come together and discuss issues which have an impact upon their lives and the lives of their daughters." The IWY conferences "are indicative of positive emerging cooperative spirit among women today." Providing a list of organizations that made up the Women's Conference Network that ranged from AAUW, BPW, and WEAL to the Girl Scouts, the National Education Association, and the National Women's Democratic Club, as well as the Religious Coalition for Abortion Rights and the National Gay Rights Task Force—together representing "millions of members"—she concluded: "The support of the conference from a group with as broad a membership as the Women's Conference Network illustrates that spirit."[53]

Demands for a full congressional investigation or an end to IWY—which conservatives were now calling "Abzugate" in hopes the term would catch on—failed. The National Women's Conference would go on as scheduled. As summer turned to fall, both sides turned to preparations for the Houston showdown that was now certain to take place in November and in the glare of national publicity.

CHAPTER 10

Crest of the Second Wave

What we are doing here in Houston is part of an irreversible world-wide movement in which women are speaking out for our needs and trying to create a better world . . . There can be no turning back to a time when women were segregated in auxiliaries, prevented from using their skills and abilities, barred from places of power. We can no longer accept a condition in which men rule the Nation and the world, excluding half the human race from effective economic and political power.

—BELLA ABZUG, ADDRESS TO FIRST PLENARY SESSION, NATIONAL WOMEN'S CONFERENCE, NOVEMBER 19, 1977

"Hardly anybody was paying attention when the United Nations declared 1975 to be International Women's Year and President Gerald Ford established a national IWY Commission to draw up recommendations 'to promote equality between men and women,'" wrote Charles B. Gordon of the *Jackson (MS) Daily News*, but after the fierce battles at the state meetings, things had changed. Gordon admitted the obvious—that, from the media's perspective, "the more emphatic, even vociferous, the news gets, the better"—and stated: "I believe this affair in Houston, and the inevitable byblows such as the anti-feminist rallies Saturday in Houston . . . constitute the most important distaff side story to come along since the inception of today's feminist movement . . . fifteen years or more past."[1]

IWY organizers planned feverishly. For feminists, the National Women's Conference was an extraordinary opportunity, their long-awaited moment in the national spotlight. They aimed to present the women's move-ment at its best, showing the nation what it was really about. Houston, they hoped, would raise the nation's consciousness and vastly expand the reach of feminism in America. Already the federally funded IWY program had focused attention on the women's movement and made people think. Scoffing at Schlafly's "rather naïve" comment that the Houston conference would kill the women's movement, Bella Abzug predicted that Houston was going to make the women's movement even stronger.[2]

IWY leaders were delighted that despite the surprisingly strong conser-vative challenge over the summer, the state meetings had, as planned, produced a highly diverse group of delegates, most of whom supported the women's movement and would be heading to Houston to adopt a National Plan of Action. They were determined not to let conservatives "disrupt" their plans or undermine their message that, more than ever, American women supported the women's rights movement and were a force to be reckoned with in American politics.

IWY leaders' pre-Houston strategy was to control the message distrib-uted by the media. According to the *Washington Post*, organizers were rather explicit in their view that the conference was largely "a media event," its success contingent on the way the press covered the story. In "casual conver-sation, organizers frequently told reporters, 'It all depends on you.'"[3] Across the nation, "Truth Squads" from the Women's Conference Network, the coalition of women's groups created in August 1977 to defend the IWY, were hard at work. Holding press conferences in major cities, they sought to educate the public about the importance of IWY, the recommendations of the state meetings, and the tactics used by opponents. Everywhere, they urged women's rights advocates, whether elected delegates or not, to go to Houston and take advantage of the exciting activities being planned and show their support. Thousands of women did just that, holding bake sales and car washes and selling T-shirts to raise money for their journey to Houston to be part of this historic event.

Likewise, IWY Commission members crisscrossed the nation to promote a positive image of the upcoming National Women's Conference, clearly eager to defuse critics' claims about the radical nature of IWY and feminism. Commissioner Jean Stapleton lent her celebrity and image to this effort to win the hearts and minds of Middle America. She appeared on numerous talk shows and videotaped public service announcements distrib-uted by the IWY Commission, and otherwise associated the IWY with the beloved housewife who championed tolerance against bigotry every Saturday night on TV. At one news conference, Stapleton told the story of a Vermont woman who was forbidden by her husband to attend the state IWY meeting but got up at 4:00 a.m. and snuck out of the house, then added, "Boy, if that isn't Edith Bunker!" Edith, she said, would have been "thrilled" to go to Houston and, "as the soul of justice," would have favored the proposals that would be considered there.[4]

One of the three male IWY Commission members, *Redbook* editor Sey Chassler, enthusiastically applied his journalistic and public relations skills to the effort, with great results. He persuaded the editors of twenty-three women's magazines to run stories promoting the upcoming IWY conference in their November issues and spread the word that Houston was the place to be.[5] Chassler helped implement the brilliant public relations scheme—the Torch Relay—which had been his idea. The relay, carried out by the National Association of Girls and Women in Sports, the Road Runners Club of America, and the President's Council on Physical Fitness and Sports, with funding from corporate sponsors Colgate-Palmolive and *womenSports* magazine, began with torch-lighting ceremonies at Seneca Falls, New York, on September 29, 1977. For the next six weeks, relay runners would carry the torch across the country to Houston. Intended to connect the IWY with the iconic Seneca Falls Convention that had given birth to the American women's movement and to emphasize women's athleticism and determination, the Torch Relay was also intended to demonstrate that the IWY and its goals had widespread support from all types of people.[6]

The two thousand runners included celebrities: Kathy Switzer—the first woman to compete in the Boston marathon, who famously defied efforts to physically push her off the course—was the torch bearer as the relay began, but most runners were "ordinary" people. The relay coordinator, Pat Kery, enlisted mayors and business leaders, high school and college track teams, elementary school students and their teachers, and expectant mothers to carry the torch. To the delight of small-town papers and national news outlets, the runners wound through cities and towns, highlighting popular support for the cause. Wearing bright blue T-shirts emblazoned with the IWY emblem and the slogan "Women on the Move," and accompanied by a matching bright blue Lincoln (custom-made by the Ford Motor Company), runners brought the torch 2,600 miles through New England, the Mid-Atlantic states, and across the South, offering up fabulous "photo ops" and personal stories seized upon eagerly by the press.

In New York, schoolchildren ran with the torch through Central Park, then handed it off to Olympic medalist Cheryl Toussaint, who delivered

it to a midday press conference at the Cooper Union conducted by Bella
Abzug and UN assistant secretary Helvi Sipilä. Passing through Washington,
D.C., runners handed the torch to Midge Costanza, who joined them in
a lap around Lafayette Park, making a spectacular front-page story in the
Washington Post. A photo of runners along the route from Selma to
Montgomery, scene of Martin Luther King Jr.'s 1965 march, appeared in the
New York Times. The *Chicago Tribune* covered the scene as the relay runner
crossed the state line into Texas, welcomed by a sheriff's posse of men and
women on horseback and a band playing "The Eyes of Texas."[7]

The message feminists hoped to convey was that IWY was patriotic and
wholesome and anything *but* radical. The radicals, they insisted, were the
conservatives who opposed this thoroughly democratic, all-American project.
In numerous speeches and press releases Abzug boldly tarred "extremist
groups" with trying to sabotage the conference. The anti-IWY coalition, she
told America, included not only the Eagle Forum and Stop-ERA but also
the LDS, the John Birch Society, and the Ku Klux Klan, who "still want to
keep their women home washing their sheets." The media pounced upon the
story and repeated it endlessly. As IWY leaders continued to lump the LDS
together with the Klan, it infuriated the Mormons and caused a huge stir in
Washington, leading many politicians to denounce this tactic. But the IWY
fight had become a contest over message control and both sides were playing
hardball.[8]

When KKK leaders boasted to the press that "their people" had "infiltrated" IWY meetings in "most states," announced plans to send Klansmen
to Houston to "protect our women from all the militant lesbians who will
be there," and denounced "women's libbers" for trying to "destroy all the
principles and heritage" that they cherished, Abzug and other IWY organizers made sure that their statements received all the attention possible.[9] As
members of the press received their credentials in Houston, each was given a
"National Women's Conference Briefing Book," which, along with explana-
tions of the proposed planks, contained reprints of news stories about the
IWY meetings, including accounts of Klan involvement.[10] Abzug also
announced plans to hire a security force of 150 off-duty policewomen, saying
what a shame that more than $40,000 of taxpayers' money would have to be
spent to maintain order and protect participants![11]

It was a public relations bonanza when intimidation efforts by antifeminists (some said the Klan, others the "Eagles") caused the torch relay runners
in Birmingham to cancel their run at the last minute. The stalwart Catherine
East, who had been following along in the blue Lincoln, was one of those

who took up the torch and walked or ran with it until officials flew in a replacement. Peggy Kokernot, a young physical education teacher and marathon runner from Houston, ran nineteen miles and became a celebrity, her photo appearing on the cover of *Time* magazine.[12]

Opposition from extremists also made great copy. After the displaced Mississippi IWY coordinating committee challenged the seating of the delegation from their state, charging that it violated IWY diversity requirements, the IWY Commission dealt with their challenge and several others by appointing additional "at-large delegates" to achieve balance.[13] They were not about to relinquish the public relations advantage presented by the all-white, partly male, all-conservative delegation from Mississippi containing alleged Klansmen and one confirmed Klansman's wife. It was a public relations windfall not to be squandered, a gift that would keep on giving.[14]

Feminists scored a major public relations coup when the current and two former First Ladies from both parties agreed to attend the IWY in Houston, a signal of bipartisan support that roundly refuted charges of feminist radicalism.[15] Although President Carter determinedly kept his distance from Houston, in October he gave feminists a big boost by publicly endorsing a three-year extension of the deadline for ERA ratification. After that, critics stepped up accusations that the whole IWY effort was just an effort to get the amendment ratified, and roundly condemned the president for supporting it. To the dismay of some men on Carter's staff eager to avoid controversy, not only Rosalynn and Judy Carter but Midge Costanza, Jane Frank, Mary King, and Margaret McKenna on the White House staff, plus large numbers of women from the Carter administration enthusiastic about the upcoming National Women's Conference, signed on to speak or offer workshops in Houston. Forty-seven of them participated in the highly publicized "Briefings from the Top" series in which high-ranking "Carter women" shared insights about what went on inside the federal government.[16]

In preconference public relations efforts, feminists continued to insist that opinion polls backed the feminist movement and its key goals, including ERA ratification and the right to choose abortion. According to a new Roper poll aired on PBS during the conference, only 19 percent of American women identified with Schlafly and her stand against the ERA.[17]

No one claimed, however, that the majority of American women supported gay rights. Yet, as the IWY Commission met in October to consider which among the 4,500 proposals from the state meetings would be presented and voted upon in Houston, it had to make a final decision about the thorny issue of lesbian and gay rights about which feminist delegates were likely to be divided.[18] IWY commissioner and National Gay Rights Task Force cochair Jean O'Leary insisted a gay rights plank must be included despite being controversial because it was *right*. In any case, since she and other lesbian activists had succeeded in getting thirty state meetings to adopt resolutions calling for protection of lesbians' rights, the commission had little choice but to add a "Sexual Preference" plank to the list of recommendations to be voted on in Houston.[19]

On November 11, 1977, a week before the conference, O'Leary sent a letter to all elected delegates asking that they come to the conference with open minds and seek to understand the "pain and discrimination lesbians face and why protective legislation is so necessary." Lesbian delegates, O'Leary insisted, intended to support *all* of the twenty-six recommendations that "will affect each of our lives for many years to come." But they, in turn, deserved support. O'Leary then took a page from history, invoking the analogy of Elizabeth Cady Stanton and Frederick Douglass, who persuaded delegates to the 1848 Seneca Falls Convention to include woman suffrage in the Declaration of Sentiments—despite the fact that it would bring ridicule and condemnation.[20]

Many supporters of the women's movement, the ERA, *Roe v. Wade*, and the IWY were quite concerned about the impact of the lesbian rights issue and the high visibility of lesbians during the summer of the IWY meetings, and worried about the potential impact on the Houston conference and the future of feminism. Georgie Anne Geyer, a distinguished journalist and women's rights supporter, predicted that unless "the irrepressible Abzug repressed herself" or Jean Stapleton "stifled somebody," there could be big problems. Geyer recalled an earlier NOW meeting in 1975 attended by "Bella's ideological group, with its stocky lesbians standing like storm troopers, arms crossed and legs apart, before the stage, shouting obscenities and intimidating anybody who did not agree with them." She added ominously: "If, despite the best efforts of the good IWY staff here, this happens November 18 to 21 in Houston, it could well be one mass female clawing match that will have the men howling for years—and responsible, rational women disavowing everything feminist for many more years."[21]

Some IWY leaders dealt with this delicate situation by downplaying the gay rights issue to the extent possible while Jean O'Leary fought to keep it alive and in the public eye. When the IWY Commission decided to take up each of the twenty-six planks in alphabetical order, O'Leary requested that the plank be retitled "Affectional Preference" or "Alternative Lifestyle" and thus be the first plank considered. Again she had scant support from other commissioners, and the plank continued to be labeled "Sexual Preference." O'Leary believed this was a deliberate decision made in the hope that time would run out and the controversial plank would never come up for a vote. Press reports cited several IWY leaders predicting anonymously that if the plank came up, it would be defeated.[22]

While IWY organizers labored to counter an image of radicalism, their worst nightmare was that the conference would dissolve into factiousness and infighting among women as the world watched. They recalled that press coverage of the UN's Mexico City IWY Conference of 1975 had emphasized fighting between women to discredit it, and worried that the same thing would happen in Houston. Among the 1,500 press representatives slated to attend, many were already predicting and some were clearly *hoping* for "catfights." James Kilpatrick, naturally, was one of them, predicting that "November's International Women's Convention in Houston already is shaping up as the liveliest brawl since John L. Sullivan licked Jake Kilrain in 75 bare-knuckled rounds." *Newsweek* predicted Houston would pit "women against women." The *Washington Post* editorialized that the conference "was a poor idea," as it might "create a public impression of even more discord than actually exists." And if that occurred, Americans watching on TV would witness a brawl that would "confirm the most harmful stereotypes of women in politics."[23]

Betty Friedan—whose venomous attacks on Abzug and Steinem were well-known by 1977, and who had been bypassed by not one but two presidents as they appointed members of the IWY Commission—also offered up dire predictions. Although Friedan had accepted the commission's invitation to participate in the Houston conference as a delegate-at-large, she told the *New York Times* she saw "potential for a 'female Nuremberg fire'" if conservative groups such as Stop-ERA, the Eagle Forum, the John Birch Society, and the KKK disrupted the conference. Her worry was that it would create an "inflamed hysteria" that would "encourage legislators from the 15 unratified states to vote against the Equal Rights Amendment."[24]

It was all taking a toll on conference organizers. Associated Press reporter Peggy Simpson, a distinguished journalist and feminist who wished the best for the conference, noted that, after the stormy meetings of the previous summer, some feminists were so "fearful of Houston" that they "gladly would have done without the conference at all."[25] The unquestionably sympathetic columnist Ellen Goodman expressed such fears of her own in an early November column: "My worst scenario is that it will end in total chaos and disaster, with nothing accomplished except the performance the national media is expecting." She worried that the conservatives "may divert all the media attention, and turn the conference into a fight-and-folly show for the evening news. At worst, they could accomplish their current goals: To halt the proceedings entirely."[26]

Such was the concern about potential warfare between women at the upcoming IWY conference that one well-meaning group tried to convene a peace parley. Members of the Martha Movement, a national organization seeking to improve the status of homemakers and did not take stands on abortion or the ERA, invited representatives of the "pro-change" and "anti-change" groups to come together at the home of Eleanor McGovern, a member of the organization's board and wife of Senator George McGovern. To their astonishment, IWY Citizens' Review Committee leaders Nellie Gray and Kathy Teague showed up, but the feminists all declined. Kay Clarenbach, executive director of the IWY Commission, said that when she saw the invitation she was "appalled at the naïveté of the Martha Movement people" regarding "how fundamental the differences are between the extreme right wing and those of us working to make this conference a success."[27]

Another well-intentioned group devised a scheme to prevent mayhem at the upcoming conference. Twenty women from several different religious groups had come up the idea of having a "Kum Baya Room" in the Albert Thomas Convention Center, the site of the National Women's Conference, where "trained volunteer listeners" along with "several social workers, psychologists and other professionals with backgrounds in counseling" would be on hand to allow participants to express their frustrations and "to assist in solving more serious problems that might arise."[28]

Yet feminists seemed to worry less about conflicts with conservatives than about dissension within their own ranks. Gloria Steinem told a San Diego reporter that in some state delegations "there are signs that coalitions between whites and minorities, gays and non-gays have become strained," yet feminists desperately needed a strong show of unity behind the National Plan.[29] Later she recalled that, although she continued to work hard on the preparations for the conference, at that time she "would have given almost anything to be able to avoid the possible conflict, to stop worrying, to stay home, to delay this event that I cared about too much." In addition, after Houston, Steinem confided to her good friend Jacquelyn Kennedy Onassis the suspicion that her own pre-conference jitters—that kept Steinem from urging Onassis to attend—were based not only on the "strength of the ultra right forces" but a fear "somewhere inside that women couldn't pull off such a big populist event."[30]

Bella Abzug also worried about discord in feminist ranks more than conservatives' participation, which she and other I WY leaders saw as a plus—if handled properly. The challengers would be too few in number to seize control in Houston as they had at most I WY state meetings at the end of the summer. Visible conservative participation, even dissent, could redound to the I WY leaders' advantage by refuting charges of unfairness and exclusion, encouraging unity among feminists, and alienating the public. Yet the "anti-change forces" had proven their skills at parliamentary maneuvers and other forms of disruption during the state meetings and must not be allowed to stall or stop the proceedings.

I WY leaders planned carefully to maintain control once the conference began. Even if all went smoothly, it would be a challenge to consider and vote upon—in four days—all twenty-six "planks" now proposed for the National Plan of Action. With I WY commissioner and law professor Harry Edwards taking the lead, they developed a method, a combination of *Robert's Rules of Order* and congressional procedures, designed to enable a large body to get a lot done in a short time. They appointed experienced leaders such as Ruth Clusen, the League of Women Voters national president who had moderated the Carter-Ford debates in 1976, to chair the plenary sessions, especially those in which the voting would take place. According to the rules, "speeches were limited to two minutes. Debate could be closed by majority vote. The chair could decide whether voting was to be by voice, by standing, or by the count of tellers, depending on the closeness." Roll call votes were ruled out. With two thousand delegates, one roll call could tie up proceedings for hours.[31]

I WY organizers wanted the conference to be not just efficient but truly impressive. Everything possible was done to demonstrate that women could manage such a huge political undertaking—indeed, show that a conference planned by women would be fairer and better organized than the male-dominated political meetings of the past. They hired women contractors and women security officers, provided for the needs of the disabled (in full compliance with new 1977 federal guidelines opposed by conservatives), and offered "non-racist, non-sexist, multicultural" child care throughout the conference "as a reminder that all public meetings should provide it as a matter of course."[32] A team of twenty-seven oral historians recruited by Dr. Constance Ashton Myers of the University of South Carolina and funded by the National Endowment for the Humanities made plans to roam the conference soliciting interviews. Before the weekend was over they would have produced hundreds of interviews with individuals they encountered randomly, including author Kate Millett, lawyer Ruth Bader Ginsburg, and black activist and author Eldridge Cleaver, who came to Houston planning to write a book about it.[33]

For the thousands of non-delegates who flocked to Houston they set up an expansive exhibit area dubbed "Seneca Falls South" in the convention center across the street. It offered a place to relax on 1970s-esque beanbag chairs and shag carpets, and a full range of workshops, lectures, and entertainment. The "Seneca Falls Stage" would feature famous women performers including Cryer & Ford, the Deadly Nightshade, Maxine Feldman, and the comic Robin Tyler. They planned programs ranging from a reading of the grim report of 1976 Brussels Tribunal on Crimes Against Women (that would leave some in tears) to performances by female comedians and musicians (that would have them in stitches). Visitors from abroad gave briefings on women's rights in their countries, and—to the consternation of isolationist critics—there were "World Peace Hearings" chaired by Congresswoman Pat Schroeder.[34]

Ultimately the massive exhibit area would have more than two hundred exhibit booths run by states and territories and federal agencies, nonprofit organizations, small businesses, and unions. In the spirit of tolerance, all types of organizations were allowed to exhibit, and groups from the political left, right, and in between signed up. After Houston, conservatives would exploit the fact that socialist, lesbian, and pro-choice groups had booths, as well as the prostitutes' rights group, COYOTE, that had turned out in force at the California IWY meeting. But Eagle Forum, Stop-ERA, and pro-life organizations also had booths.[35]

IWY organizers sought to make the federal money go as far as possible; feminist leaders would later boast about doing so much with so little. They pointed out that the $5 million was only half what they asked for, and that "as usual" a women's event was underfunded and had to rely heavily on ingenuity, penny-pinching, and volunteers. Around one hundred women from the media volunteered to pitch in and help a local monthly newspaper, the *Houston Breakthrough*, produce daily special editions that provided some of the most in-depth and insightful coverage of the conference.[36] Much of the groundwork was done by the famous "Houston Committee" of local women, a volunteer group headed by Mary Keegan that deserved even more credit than they got; at the end of the conference they presented Abzug with roses but it should have been the other way around, given that Abzug did not send staff to Houston to assist until the last minute.[37]

Plenary sessions were carefully designed to impress the vast television audience that would be watching and to pump up the enthusiasm of the participants. Every effort was made to showcase the talents of leading feminists, celebrate the achievements of women and their contributions to the nation, and remind the nation that this was a movement with which the best and brightest women of America wished to be associated. The women invited to address the conference were some of the nation's most powerful orators, including leading women politicians both Democratic and Republican.

IWY leaders were determined to promote compromise and consensus, to keep internal disputes out of sight, and to present a united front. Before and during the conference, Abzug drew upon the full force of her personality to gain cooperation from women's rights advocates of all persuasions and bring them together in a strong show of feminist solidarity before the American public.

At last the long-awaited weekend arrived amid great excitement. At the Albert Thomas Convention Center, where the conference would take place, an all-woman crew from California set up a stage with "WOMAN" spelled out in letters a dozen feet high while camera crews from PBS and all three commercial networks prepared to keep the nation fully informed about this much-anticipated event.[38]

Yet, as delegates and observers poured into Houston, the best-laid plans for an orderly conference immediately went awry, at least in terms of lodging. Excited travelers arrived only to confront a logistical nightmare involving hotels that were massively overbooked: hotel managers were not accustomed to everyone showing up! At the main convention hotel, the Hyatt Regency (soon dubbed "the Riot Hegency"), women stood all day in lines winding throughout the lobbies amid a sea of luggage. Rumors that the snafu was part of a conservative plan to disrupt the conference proved to be untrue.[39]

According to the press and to IWY leaders (who were determined to turn this and any other problem to advantage), the women took it well. The *Washington Post*'s Sally Quinn compared it to opening day at a women's college, "with people lugging their suitcases, waiting for room assignments, singing songs, and making new friends. It was nice."[40] Women were used to coping, some stated.

The arriving delegates showed real interest in each other, appearing to revel in their diversity. Lindsy Van Gelder, reporting for *Ms.*, described black women "sporting Jewish Women's Caucus buttons" and "Irish faces seen above buttons proclaiming 'Viva La Mujer.'" Women took advantage of their hours standing in line to learn about and from one another. Van Gelder described two muumuu-clad Samoans who had never before been to the mainland, having a frank chat with activist prostitutes from COYOTE, the Samoans asking, "How often do you do it? What's it like? What does it pay?"[41]

On that Friday, after checking in, feminist delegates began hearing rumors that Phyllis Schlafly would be holding a counter-rally across town at the Houston Astro Arena. The word was that she had set up a media center and was denouncing the feminist delegates to the press as "sick," "immoral," "unGodly," "unpatriotic," and "antifamily."[42] Conservative women's embrace of the term "pro-family" and their claim to be the defenders of "family values" was a new development that feminists very much resented.

Presiding Officer Abzug, joined by her predecessor Jill Ruckelshaus, held a press conference in which, among other things, she challenged their terminology. Insisting that feminist goals including the ERA would enhance the rights of homemakers and benefit women, men, and children, Abzug declared, "No one has a monopoly on the family." Former congress-woman Martha Griffiths was vehement on this point, saying that, in all of her years in legislative bodies, she had "never seen any one of these people testifying on anything for the family." Betty Friedan declared that feminists did not intend "to let Phyllis Schlafly take over family, love, and God."[43]

The Torch arrived right on time, a thrilling spectacle. NBC's *Today Show* with Tom Brokaw launched coverage of "the largest gathering of American women ever held" that Friday morning with images of the Torch Relay. NBC began taping as runners started their last lap from Dayton, Texas, thirty-nine miles northeast of Houston. Three young women, Michele Cearcy, African American, a local high school student; Sylvia Ortiz, Hispanic, a University of Houston student; and Peggy Kokernot, white, the Houston teacher and marathon runner who had saved the relay back in Alabama, were the official torch bearers for the last mile. As a thousand women, including feminist celebrities, star athletes, and many IWY commis-sioners—Bella Abzug herself among them—joined the runners that after-noon for the ceremonial last mile, it was dramatic and inspiring, a great beginning to the weekend.[44]

President Richard Nixon welcomes Barbara Franklin to the White House in April 1971. Franklin was brought on board specifically to recruit women for high-ranking positions in the administration. USED WITH PERMISSION FROM THE EBERLY FAMILY SPECIAL COLLECTIONS LIBRARY, PENN STATE UNIVERSITY LIBRARIES

Gloria Steinem and Jill Ruckelshaus on NBC's *Meet the Press* in September 1972, representing the National Women's Political Caucus. Ruckelshaus was often called "the Gloria Steinem of the Republican Party." AP PHOTO/HENRY BURROUGHS

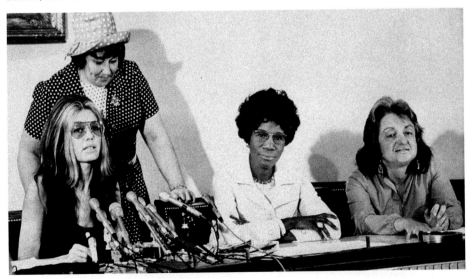

Several of the key leaders of the National Women's Political Caucus hold a press conference in July 1971 to announce the creation of the organization and its goals. Seated, from the left, are Gloria Steinem, Rep. Shirley Chisholm (D-N.Y.), and Betty Friedan; standing behind them is Rep. Bella Abzug (D-N.Y.). AP/CHARLES GORRY

TOP: First Lady Betty Ford congratulates President Gerald Ford on signing the executive order establishing a National Commission on the Observance of International Women's Year on January 9, 1975. GERALD R. FORD LIBRARY

CENTER: Betty Ford with Liz Carpenter, former press secretary to Lady Bird Johnson, and Elly Peterson, veteran Republican National Committee leader. Carpenter and Peterson became co-directors of ERAmerica in 1976, coordinating the efforts of groups working for ratification of the Equal Rights Amendment. ERAMERICA RECORDS, LIBRARY OF CONGRESS, MANUSCRIPT DIVISION

BOTTOM: Left to right: Jill Ruckelshaus, President Gerald Ford, Senator Charles Percy, Major General Jeanne Holm (head of the White House Office of Women's Affairs), and Elizabeth Athanasakos in the Oval Office on July 1, 1976, the day that the Ford-appointed National Commission on the Observation of International Women's Year presented its report, *". . . To Form a More Perfect Union . . ."* USED WITH PERMISSION FROM THE EBERLY FAMILY SPECIAL COLLECTIONS LIBRARY, PENN STATE UNIVERSITY LIBRARIES

Stop-ERA leader Phyllis Schlafly in her home office in Alton, Illinois, February 28, 1975. Her home was the center of operations for the conservative women's movement. PHOTO BY MICHAEL MAUNEY/THE LIFE IMAGES COLLECTION GETTY IMAGES

Phyllis Schlafly and National Organization for Women (NOW) president Eleanor Smeal debate each other on *The Phil Donahue Show* in the summer of 1979. COURTESY OF THE EAGLE FORUM ARCHIVES

President Jimmy Carter and Margaret (Midge) Costanza, Assistant to the President for Public Liaison. Costanza was the first woman to hold the title of assistant to the president. JIMMY CARTER LIBRARY AND MUSEUM

At a White House meeting in March 1977, Midge Costanza meets with leaders of the National Gay and Lesbian Task Force (NGLTF) to discuss critical policy issues affecting their community. The event was attended by Jean O'Leary, NGLTF co-executive director and an IWY Commission member, and by Charlotte Bunch, who worked with O'Leary to get the issue of lesbian and gay rights on the agenda of the National Women's Conference in 1977. JIMMY CARTER LIBRARY AND MUSEUM

Two hundred opponents of the Equal Rights Amendment, led by Phyllis Schlafly, march in front of the White House on February 5, 1977, to protest Rosalynn Carter's advocacy of ERA ratification. LIBRARY OF CONGRESS

Gloria Steinem holds a mock-up of *Ms.* magazine's January 1978 cover with a photo of a pregnant Jimmy Carter. It quotes his "Life is Unfair" statement in reaction to a June 1977 Supreme Court ruling that the federal government was not required to fund abortion. AP PHOTO

This cartoon by Jeff MacNelly of the *Richmond News Leader* (Va.) reflects the controversy over the November 1977 National Women's Conference in Houston, which Phyllis Schlafly denounced as a "Federal Financing of a Foolish Festival for Frustrated Feminists." © 1978 MACNELLY INC. DISTRIBUTED BY KING FEATURES SYNDICATE, INC.

Betty Friedan, Liz Carpenter, First Lady Rosalynn Carter, former First Lady Betty Ford, Elly Peterson, Jill Ruckelshaus, and Bella Abzug join hands in unity at an event designed to raise funds and inspire activists for a final push to get the ERA ratified. The star-studded event, which demonstrated strong bipartisan support for the amendment, took place November 18, 1977, the night before the National Women's Conference got underway. PHOTO BY STEVE NORTHUP/THE LIFE IMAGES COLLECTION/GETTY IMAGES

The National Women's Conference in session at the Albert Thomas Convention Center in Houston, Texas. BETTYE LANE PHOTOS, SCHLESINGER LIBRARY, RADCLIFFE INSTITUTE, HARVARD UNIVERSITY

At the opening ceremonies of the National Women's Conference, former First Ladies Lady Bird Johnson and Betty Ford, with the current First Lady Rosalynn Carter between them, and IWY presiding officer Bella Abzug receive the Torch of Freedom from relay runners after it was carried to Houston from Seneca Falls, New York, the scene of the first national women's rights conference in 1848. PHOTO BY DIANA MARA HENRY

Congresswoman Barbara Jordan of Texas, a rising star in the Democratic Party whose oratory had thrilled the audience at the 1976 Democratic National Convention, gives a stirring keynote address at the National Women's Conference. PHOTO BY DIANA MARA HENRY

Mary Crisp, a delegate from Arizona and co-chair of the Republican National Committee, knits as she listens to speeches at the National Women's Conference. Within two years Crisp would protest her party's decisions to end support for the ERA and to take a pro-life stance. PHOTO BY DIANA MARA HENRY

Jill Ruckelshaus, a leading Republican feminist who had served as presiding officer of the National Commission on the Observance of International Women's Year under President Gerald Ford, follows the proceeding as delegates consider and vote on a National Plan of Action. PHOTO BY DIANA MARA HENRY

Actress Jean Stapleton greets fans at the National Women's Conference. Stapleton, best known for playing Edith Bunker on *All in the Family*, was appointed by Ford as an IWY commission member. BETTYE LANE PHOTOS, DAVID M. RUBENSTEIN RARE BOOK & MANUSCRIPT LIBRARY, DUKE UNIVERSITY

Surrounded by other members of the Minority Caucus at the Houston Civic Center, Coretta Scott King reads the resolution on minority women's rights that won the support of the National Women's Conference. Many participants remembered the November 21, 1977, adoption of the resolution—followed by the singing of "We Shall Overcome"—as the emotional highlight of the conference. Left to right: Rita Elway, Carmela Lacayo, Gloria Scott, Ethel Allen, Mariko Tse, Coretta Scott King, Angela Cabrera, and Maxine Waters. GETTY IMAGES

Betty Friedan, known for her opposition to adding the defense of lesbian rights to the women's rights movement agenda, surprises the audience at the National Women's Conference by speaking in support of the sexual preference plank. BETTYE LANE PHOTOGRAPHS, DAVID M. RUBENSTEIN RARE BOOK & MANUSCRIPT LIBRARY, DUKE UNIVERSITY

Pro-family delegates, dismayed by the adoption of planks on reproductive rights and gay rights, turn their backs to the podium and bow their heads in prayer. Their ribbons reflected their claim that the majority of American women shared their views. PHOTO BY JO FREEMAN

The Stop-ERA booth, one of more than two hundred booths in the massive exhibit area at the conference. A wide variety of groups, including state and federal agencies and organizations as diverse as the Girl Scouts of America and COYOTE, a prostitutes' rights group, were represented. NATIONAL ARCHIVES

Members of the all-white delegation from Mississippi, the only delegation that included men, stand to vote against a proposed plank at the National Women's Conference. In the front row (left to right) are Dr. Shelton Hand, Eddie Myrtle Moore (delegation chair, holding notebook), and Carolyn and Homer Morgan. PHOTO BY JO FREEMAN

Rosemary Thomson, a leader of the pro-family delegates at the conference, speaks to the press. She chaired the IWY Citizens' Review Committee, a group that challenged feminists for control of the IWY meetings. PHOTO BY BILL JOHNSON/THE DENVER POST VIA GETTY IMAGES

Lottie Beth Hobbs, a Church of Christ leader and founder of Women Who Want to Be Women (WWWW), played a crucial role in mobilizing evangelical and fundamentalist women to fight the ERA. The Pro-Life, Pro-Family Rally that took place November 19, 1977, to protest the National Women's Conference was her idea. PHOTO BY PERMISSION OF HARVEST PUBLICATIONS

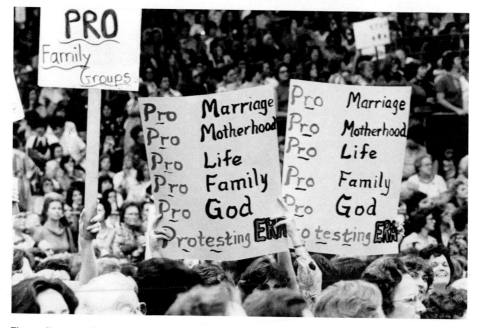

The audience at the Pro-Life, Pro-Family Rally held in Houston's Astrodome. An estimated fifteen to twenty thousand women, men, and children came from across the nation to protest the IWY and the National Plan of Action. BETTYE LANE PHOTOGRAPHS, SCHLESINGER LIBRARY, RADCLIFFE INSTITUTE, HARVARD UNIVERSITY

Phyllis Schlafly speaking at the Pro-Life, Pro-Family Rally. A star lineup of conservative leaders addressed the audience that afternoon. COURTESY OF THE EAGLE FORUM ARCHIVES

Nellie Gray, a lawyer from Washington, D.C., founded March for Life, the organization that sponsors massive demonstrations each January on the anniversary of *Roe v. Wade*. Gray was a leader of the IWY Citizens' Review Committee and helped plan the Pro-Life, Pro-Family Rally.

Dr. Mildred Jefferson, a Boston physician who had been the first African American woman to graduate from Harvard Medical School and who in 1977 was president of the National Right to Life Committee, also addressed the rally. PHOTO FROM JEFFERSON'S PAPERS AT THE SCHLESINGER LIBRARY, RADCLIFFE INSTITUTE, HARVARD UNIVERSITY

The March 22, 1978, White House ceremony at which IWY presiding officer Bella Abzug presented President Jimmy Carter with the National Commission on the Observance of International Women's Year's report, *The Spirit of Houston*, with Rosalynn Carter and Midge Costanza (at the left) looking on. PHOTO BY DIANA MARA HENRY

NOW president Eleanor Smeal, wearing white and a purple-and-gold sash like the suffragists, addresses the crowd at a massive June 1978 rally for the Equal Rights Amendment. At the rally, held on the one-year anniversary of the death of suffrage leader Alice Paul, who first proposed the ERA in 1923, feminists demanded an extension of the ERA deadline. LIBRARY OF CONGRESS

A tearful Bella Abzug speaks at a press conference after President Carter fired her from her post as presiding officer of the National Advisory Committee for Women in January 1979. Her co-chair, Carmen Delgado Votaw, and most of the committee members resigned in protest. PHOTO BY DIANA MARA HENRY

Senator Jesse Helms (R-N.C.), Phyllis Schlafly, and Senator Orrin G. Hatch (R-Utah) at a March 22, 1979, "gala" to celebrate the date of what would have been the expiration of the seven-year ratification period for the Equal Rights Amendment had it not been extended by Congress. AP PHOTO/CHARLES TASNADI

Phyllis Schlafly and the Reverend Jerry Falwell holding a news conference in San Francisco to outline the pro-family movement's program opposing abortion and gay rights. Falwell founded the Moral Majority in 1979. AP PHOTO/PETER MORGAN

Eagle Forum leader Elaine Donnelly (center) along with Dorothy Sheldon (left) and Anne Polcha (right) celebrate victory in the Stop-ERA office at the Republican National Convention in Detroit in July 1980. Conservative women played a key role in getting the GOP to endorse Reagan and not endorse the ERA—ending the GOP's forty-year record of support for the amendment. PHOTOGRAPH FROM THE ELAINE DONNELLY PAPERS, BENTLEY HISTORICAL LIBRARY, UNIVERSITY OF MICHIGAN; PHOTO BY WILLIAM ARCHIE OF THE DETROIT FREE PRESS

TOP TO BOTTOM: Gloria Steinem is presented the Presidential Medal of Freedom by President Barack Obama in the East Room of the White House on November 20, 2013. PHOTO BY LEIGH VOGEL, GETTY IMAGES

Democratic presidential candidate Hillary Clinton addresses supporters at a March 15, 2016, rally in West Palm Beach, Florida. After defeating Senator Bernie Sanders, the former First Lady and secretary of state made history as the first woman to be nominated for president by a major political party. PHOTO BY JOE RAEDLE/GETTY IMAGES

In this photo taken on March 11, 2016, ninety-one-year-old Phyllis Schlafly, a conservative icon, announced her endorsement of Republican presidential candidate Donald Trump. Her endorsement played a major role in Trump's nomination and election. AP PHOTO/SETH PERLMAN, FILE

Excited spectators huddled under coats and umbrellas, cheerful despite the rain, while photographers went wild taking pictures of Abzug jogging in heels, a skirt, and her trademark hat "arm-in-arm with the young torch-bearers in gym shorts and bright blue T-shirts." Abzug quipped to reporters, with her characteristic humor and bravado, "Some of us run for office. Some of us run for equality—but none of us runs for cover!"[45] Sally Quinn described Abzug as "different at this convention . . . not the strident, loud, tough, politician" but "softer, warmer, easier, more mellow, funnier. Somehow she sensed that success or failure lay on her shoulders."[46]

Commissioner Maya Angelou delivered a dramatic reading of a poem, ". . . *To Form a More Perfect Union* . . ." which she had composed for the occasion. It was written on a scroll that had been carried along with the torch and signed by thousands of supporters along the way. The crowd roared as the torch was handed to Florida delegate Susan B. Anthony, namesake of the famous suffrage leader, who repeated the phrase famously associated with her great-aunt: "Failure is Impossible!"[47]

That evening there was a huge "gala" in the Hyatt's Imperial Ballroom on behalf of the ERA organized by the presidents of ten national women's organizations. It was a spirited affair in which people dressed up in whatever passed as dress-up for them, from boots and embroidered jeans to pearls and fur stoles. The goal was to raise funds and reenergize supporters for an all-out effort to gain the states still needed for ratification. In both respects it exceeded expectations. Four thousand excited people packed the room to hear leading congresswomen, feminist celebrities, plus the three First Ladies and Coretta Scott King give inspiring speeches about achieving a final victory. "If I should die," Liz Carpenter quipped, "don't send flowers. Just send me three more states!" At the end everyone at the rally joined upraised hands, and wire service captured a triumphant photo of First Lady Rosalynn Carter, former First Lady Betty Ford, Elly Peterson, Carpenter, Bella Abzug, Jill Ruckelshaus, and Betty Friedan in front of an ERA banner.[48]

On Saturday morning, November 19, the National Women's Conference finally got under way. The opening session, loaded with symbolism and carefully staged to impress the vast television audience, went off splendidly, beginning with the presentation of the colors by the San Jacinto Girl Scouts and the singing of the national anthem by Shirley Baines of the Houston Opera Company. Gloria Scott, national president of the Girl Scouts of America, opened the conference with a gavel presented to Susan B. Anthony by the National American Woman Suffrage Association in 1896, loaned by the Smithsonian for the occasion.[49]

After a welcome from Houston mayor Fred Hofheinz, Bella Abzug introduced the three First Ladies, whose "sheer physical presence was more moving than many women expected."[50] According to Sally Quinn, the sight of these women sitting on the platform "with their legs neatly crossed, in their conservative, brightly colored dresses, with their sprayed hair, their smiling faces . . . made everyone feel it was okay to be a woman, okay to be in Houston, okay to think about yourself." As the young women carrying the torch ran into the hall and up to the platform, presenting it to Abzug and to the First Ladies, "tears streamed down the faces of the women and even the least emotional woman had to catch her breath."[51]

Addressing the vast audience, Rosalynn Carter stated that the joint appearance of the current First Lady and her two predecessors "affirmed the continuity of our government's efforts to improve life for all." She brought greetings from the president and spoke of his support for the women's movement, including appointing so many women—many of whom were on the program. She declared that although "Jimmy asked me to be his personal emissary today and to talk to you briefly about his concerns and his goals . . . I am here for myself, too." Lady Bird Johnson, accompanied by her feminist daughter, Lynda Bird Johnson Robb, admitted she had once thought the feminist movement was more for her daughters than herself, but "I have come to know that it belongs to women of all ages." After that, there was a tremendous response as the three young women runners—white, black, and Latina—delivered the torch and Maya Angelou's poem to the three First Ladies as an all-female bugle corps dressed in golden Amazon helmets saluted them.[52]

Presiding Officer Abzug was in fine form and gave an inspirational address in which she emphasized the conference's historical significance: "The torch we see here today is a symbol of our past victories and our hopes for future ones." She emphasized that this was the first time that Congress and the president had "mandated American women to identify and help remove the barriers that stand between us and full equality with men," and the question was no longer *if* women should have equality but *how* it was to be achieved. Now, after years of planning, they had come to Houston to prepare for a "future in which women will be free to live and work as individuals, as members of families, as members of society without the constraints of narrow customs and prejudices that demean our self-worth or laws that treat us as inferiors or weaklings." But their intention was not to "tell women how to live or what to do" but to say simply "that women must be free to choose what they do." Again she emphasized the diversity of the movement as represented by the assembled delegates. After Houston, Abzug declared, "the whole Nation will know that the women's movement is not any one organization or set of ideas or particular lifestyle. It is millions of women deciding individually and together that we are determined to move history forward."

In her address the presiding officer returned to an idea that had guided women's commissions ever since the report of the Kennedy Commission: new conditions of life for women in American society required changes in policies. They had come together in Houston to help determine what those changes should be. Their gathering, Abzug reminded them, was "part of an irreversible worldwide movement in which women are speaking out for our needs and trying to create a better world in which men and women do not victimize each other, but work together for a decent life for all people."

Abzug concluded by repeating the words of a southern suffragist when the Nineteenth Amendment was finally ratified: "The pedestal has crashed." She then stated: "There are many even now who would patch the idol together. It was only an image after all . . . In its place is a woman of flesh and blood, not a queen, or a saint, nor a symbol, but a human being with human faults and human virtues, a woman still only slowly rising to full stature, but with the sun of freedom on her face . . . Let the sun shine on our deliberations, and let us celebrate womanhood and woman power."

As she left the podium, Abzug urged them, "Let us agree to disagree, if we must. It would be a dull weekend if we didn't feel free to state our beliefs. But I hope all of us here will remember our common interests as women who have for too long been treated as merely auxiliary human beings."[53]

Liz Carpenter then welcomed the delegates to her home state and, according to New York delegate Tanya Melich, "brought everyone to their feet when she described the spirit of Houston: 'So here we are, the faces and voices ignored and silenced too often by the decision makers . . . Unafraid, uninhibited, let us speak to the future well-being of America.'" To the member of the Carter family who was absent she said, "Until the women of the United States are full equal operating citizens, your cry for human rights around this globe will have a very hollow ring." The crowd roared when she cried, "We mothered this nation. Are we to be penalized for it forever? We have no intention of abandoning our role as nurturer or wife, mother, responsible sisters, loving daughters, tax-paying citizens" but "are we to be forever shackled by the unending audacity of elected men? . . . America, look at us. Listen to us. Have faith in us. Help us. Love us as we loved you."[54]

Carpenter likewise seized the occasion to highlight the diversity in the women's movement by introducing selected delegates: a sixteen-year-old Girl Scout from Louisiana, an eighty-five-year-old retired government worker who had pushed for an end to child labor; a nun from Kansas who returned 60 percent of her salary to the college where she taught; a UAW worker supporting an invalid husband and five children on a small paycheck; a farm wife putting her children through college by raising chickens; and a welfare activist from New York. In each case she had them stand and then asked, "Would you deny this woman her rights?" Melich said that, by the time Carpenter finished, the delegates and observers were applauding, cheering, hugging. "We were one with the women of Seneca Falls . . . the suffragists." Carpenter, she recalled, had "touched our sense of each other, our linkage and necessary dependence on other women," feelings that sustained them through the conference.[55]

Then Barbara Jordan brought down the house with a stirring address that emphasized the historic importance of the conference in the overall struggle "for total recognition and total inclusion." She reminded them of the tremendous responsibility that rested upon the delegates there assembled. "The success or failure of this Conference is our responsibility and we should not waste one moment trying to find scapegoats," she said sternly. "If this Conference succeeds, there will be ample accolades for everybody. And, if it fails, all of you may look into your mirror and identify a contributing culprit."

They must not allow themselves, Jordan declared, "to be brainwashed by people who predict chaos and failure for us. Tell them they lie and move on." Of course they would disagree on these matters of great seriousness and importance. Yet, she insisted, they must remember Isaiah's invocation: "Come now, let us reason together." Invoking fellow Texan Lyndon Johnson, she emphasized the importance of compromise as they voted on the planks in the National Plan of Action. Each one would "have a better chance of passage if support for that recommendation is widespread."

Jordan, who was not on the IWY Commission, may or may not have known how IWY leaders had pleaded with President Carter to come to Houston and make a major address, to seize the moment to link women's rights to his campaign to improve human rights worldwide. But in his absence Jordan made that connection herself, comparing the goals of the conference to President Carter's goals regarding human rights in America's foreign policy:

If Americans were asked to differentiate or distinguish between what characterized other countries and what characterizes us, we would say our high regard for the individual. That's the thing which makes us different. We endorse personal and political freedom as a national right of human pride. Human rights are more than abstractions, particularly when they are limited or non-existent. Human rights apply equally to Soviet dissidents, Chilean peasants and American women.

As the crowd roared she drove home her point: "Women are human. We know our rights are limited. We know our rights are violated. We need a domestic human rights program!"

In closing, Jordan again reminded them of the seriousness of their task. Congress had given them an opportunity to provide guidance. If they did nothing "productive, constructive or healing, we will have wasted much more than money," she said, "we will have wasted, lost, negated an opportunity to do something for ourselves and for generations which are not here. Not making a difference is a cost we cannot afford." She concluded: "The cause of equal and human rights will reap what is sown November 18th through November 21st, 1977. What will you reap? What will you sow?"[56]

After the stirring oratory, the feminist majority was fired up, and at countless caucus meetings and sessions redoubled their efforts to work together. Behind the scenes, however, there were tensions.

After the high of the ERA rally Friday evening, many delegates had spent a long night of strategizing in preparation for the voting ahead. Leaders of the "Pro-Plan Caucus" sought agreement to approve the proposed plan without amendment to avoid the appearance of squabbling or delays that would prevent consideration of all twenty-six planks. Carol Bellamy, newly elected president of the city council of New York and chair of the state IWY delegation, chaired the meeting. The spirit of unity was tested when several groups complained that, as drafted by the IWY Commission, the suggested planks did not fully address their concerns. Minority women were offended by the brief and incomplete statement on their issues. Disabled women and welfare rights activists also demanded changes in the planks relating to them.[57]

The Pro-Plan Caucus agreed to support revisions of these three planks. In devising the new minority rights plank, a young black California assemblywoman, Maxine Waters, played a leading role, as did IWY commissioner Carmen Delgado Votaw, a leader among Hispanic women. Professional writers

Gail Sheehy and Gloria Steinem lent their talents. In addition, Steinem's diplomatic skills were put to good use. Well known, admired, and trusted, she played an important role as a go-between during a dramatic, all-night session, in which Asian, Hispanic, Native American, and African American groups—unaccustomed to working together and none wanting their special concerns overlooked—produced a statement as comprehensive as it was eloquent. It received resounding support when put to a vote.[58]

Lesbian rights activists complained that neither lesbians nor gay rights issues were highlighted in the three plenary sessions. "Lesbians are seemingly being squeezed out of the conference," one told an interviewer. "I was suspicious the minute the major speeches were being made. I didn't like the fact that Barbara Jordan, who should have mentioned us, didn't mention us. And I didn't like the fact that Liz Carpenter seemed to include everybody of every color and every conceivable background and not include lesbians."[59]

Lesbians worried that the resolution they had fought so hard for was set to be considered so near the end of the conference. Fearing stalling techniques from other feminists as well as from conservatives, supporters of the gay rights plank distributed buttons saying "Keep the Agenda Moving." When the plank came before the conference, some feminists, including Catherine East, spoke against it. On the convention floor, she and others insisted that endorsing gay rights in the National Plan of Action would be a great mistake. Commissioner and former Presiding Officer Elizabeth Athanasakos was also opposed, believing that the issue had hurt them in the ERA fight in Florida and would be used against them again. A feminist leader from Georgia insisted it would become "an albatross" to the women's movement and undermine the ERA effort. Another Georgia delegate, Jo Cross, voted in favor of the resolution, saying, "You can't come here and talk about human rights and put a limit on your ideology." But she agreed "that this is one of the issues that hurts the ERA."[60]

Most delegates lent their support. Many, like Cora Norman, one of the moderate feminist coordinators of the disastrous Mississippi meeting, had learned a great deal from the IWY experience. Speaking to one of the roaming oral historians she said: "I know since the IWY conference in Mississippi, that even I, a married woman of thirty-one years to the same man, a mother of two children, a grandmother, I have been labeled a lesbian . . . I can't name one lesbian that I know. I don't know if I know one or not." However, having "worn this label that was given to me by ultraconservative groups," and having been "in a position of having to defend the lesbian, merely because to defend the lesbian is defending my own rights as a woman," she had learned that protection of their rights was a protection of her rights. "Lesbian or no, we're all children of God, we're all made by God, and it seems to me that what we're asking for in the Equal Rights Amendment is that we be treated as citizens, whatever our sexual attraction might be." When the plank was adopted, the much-publicized demonstration in which lesbians displayed signs saying "Thank You, Sisters" was a demonstration of relief as well as joy.[61]

Other issues and ideological and generational conflicts also threatened the show of unity the organizers hoped to produce. More radical participants denounced the IWY Commission for paying undue homage to the First Ladies. The wrong women were being honored at the conference, one complained. Why laud these women, famous as wives of presidents, instead of the first feminists who in the 1960s had created and supported the movement at great risk and sacrifice? Some thought the recommendations were much too mild—that all they were doing was "tinkering within a structure that itself needs to be changed"—and viewed IWY leaders as too much a part of the system.[62] One lamented that the women's movement had been co-opted. "It's no longer radical; it's no longer a movement. It's now a part of the establishment."[63] As Kay Clarenbach noted, the women's movement was now denounced as part of the establishment by both the left and the right.

There were hiccups rooted in old divisions and jealousies, displayed most notably by Betty Friedan—one of the "egos" Midge Costanza had predicted would be hard to "manage." Though passed over twice for the IWY Commission and, in her view, upstaged by Abzug and Steinem, she accepted their invitation to serve as a delegate-at-large, offered in recognition of her contributions to the movement and to promote harmony. She was invited to share the limelight with Abzug and others at key, highly photographed moments, such as the arrival of the Torch. At the conference she was in a feisty mood, however, telling an oral historian interviewing her that she intended to cause trouble. Fear of the right was being used to frighten feminists to fall in line, she charged. They were losing the freedom to disagree. The IWY, she claimed, was all a big effort by "politicos" and those who had appointed them to control the women's movement—to give them Houston instead of the ERA.[64]

Friedan surprised many by supporting an amendment proposed by Oklahoma IWY Citizens' Review Committee leader Dianne Edmondson— the feminists' bitter enemy—to limit the time states had to ratify the ERA to the original seven-year time frame. Most IWY leaders were now pushing for the three-year extension; later many would boast that the extension came about in part because of Houston. Friedan insisted, however, that the president and Congress must be compelled to act before the 1979 deadline and not defer the issue. At the microphone Friedan declared: "If the ERA is not ratified in the next year and three months it will be the signal to take away all that women have gained. If the President and his politicians do not pit their own power against the Far Right in the 15 Democratic States that have not ratified it, women will have been 'had' by the Government's $5 million."[65]

Later, Friedan shocked the audience with her dramatic speech in support of the sexual preference plank—despite her well-known opposition to making lesbian and gay rights a feminist issue. It is generally interpreted as a spontaneous as well as gracious gesture, a "change of heart" according to *Time* magazine. Friedan herself described it as such. But whether or not it represented a genuine shift in her views, the speech was definitely not spontaneous. During the conference, Barbara Love, active in the lesbian caucus, approached Jean O'Leary and Charlotte Bunch with the news that Friedan was willing to make this public endorsement. After much discussion among caucus leaders, they accepted her offer, recognizing the huge symbolic value. However, some lesbians not in on their plan were outraged that their old enemy had the honor of seconding the sexual preference plank.[66] Possibly Friedan was not averse to irritating some of the "politicos" in charge of the Houston conference who were apprehensive about inclusion of the plank; this may have been the mischief she hinted at to the interviewer. In any case, it would not be long before she returned to her old theme of blaming overemphasis on sexuality for hurting the movement and contributing to the growing power of the political right.[67]

At the end of the Houston conference, Friedan surprised Abzug by holding her own separate press conference to criticize National Women's Conference leaders and cast doubt on the whole project. Sally Quinn reported that Abzug was "stunned." Abzug had appointed Friedan as a delegate-at-large, invited her to share the spotlight at key moments, and even lent Friedan her own room when the "Riot Hegency" debacle left Friedan with no place to stay. Friedan told the press, "I had made a resolution to be sweet. But it's been too easy for them to tell us not to express our differences because of the fear of the right wing. It's the same as fear of communism in the McCarthy era." Again she charged that women were in danger of being co-opted. "If words and rhetoric are not translated into political power then the enemy is the Democratic administration and President Carter."[68]

*   *   *

In most respects, however, the conference went smoothly and achieved most of the IWY planners' goals. Just barely, they managed to get through the entire agenda. "The women knew that their political skills were on trial," *Time* observed, "and they passed the test with flying colors . . . Order was achieved by the kind of discipline any male politician would give his eyeteeth to attain." Even James Kilpatrick was impressed. Presumably he thought it high praise when he described Anne Saunier, who presided during several key votes, as "a long-legged militant, man-hating tiger" and "the best presiding officer I ever watched in action." There was, of course, none of the violence he had hoped for. Joe Klein, covering the conference for *Rolling Stone*, noted tongue in cheek that, despite strong feelings, "there was a remarkable absence of aggression." "There was real anger," he said, "but not even the slightest intimation of violence, not a push or a shove. There was intolerance, but not all that much yelling . . . Try as they might, women had never been trained to be aggressive, and therefore weren't too good at it, which made for a more civilized gathering."[69]

All the planks were considered. In each case IWY organizers strategically selected the woman who would present and speak for the plank. For instance, Commissioner Gerridee Wheeler, a Republican National Committeewoman with eight children, was chosen to present the plank on "Reproductive Freedom." She was followed by Sarah Weddington, the Texas lawyer who had argued *Roe v. Wade* before the Supreme Court, who spoke on its behalf—thus highlighting feminist support for childbearing and the right to abortion.[70] Commissioner Lenore Hershey, editor of the *Ladies' Home Journal*, presented the plank on "Homemakers," which called for legal reforms based "on the principle that marriage is a partnership in which the contribution of each spouse is of equal importance and value."[71]

Ann Richards, then a young county commissioner, was selected to speak for the ERA; Abzug personally selected her for the task, impressed both with Richards's ability and the fact that she was from Texas, the only southern state to ratify and refuse to rescind the ERA. Richards later recalled being in awe when invited to meet with Abzug in her suite, saying it was like a Catholic being summoned to the pope. Introducing the ERA plank, she spoke on behalf of "the divorced who may not get credit, the widows who are incapable of making a living . . . my own daughter [Cecile Richards, later president of Planned Parenthood], who cannot find women in the history texts of this country in the elementary schools," as well as the "men of America in thirty-five states, who had the guts to stand up and ratify the Equal Rights Amendment."[72]

Conservative women were allowed to speak, though sometimes ruled out of order or cut off. At one point Abzug intervened to make certain their objections to the abortion plank were aired on live television. According to the feminists, "when the microphone monitor made a mistake and raised a white card calling for the close of debate, the outcry came not from the anti-abortionists who would be cut off, but from the Pro Plan delegates. 'These people have a right to be heard,' Bella Abzug cried, leaving the platform and striding down the aisle to the microphone." Feminists believed that they had shown sensitivity to the conservatives' strong feelings on abortion in that their celebration after adoption of the reproductive rights plank "was quieter than the demonstration for ERA the night before." In addition, they remembered, the pro-choice delegates let "the songs and chants of the antichoice minority go unanswered" because they recognized "how deeply those opposing them felt about the resolution and respected their feelings."[73]

Most planks were passed by overwhelming margins, and one, on equal access to credit, was unanimously approved. LWV leader Ruth Clusen, then chairing the session, proclaimed with satisfaction, "The critics who said we could never all agree on anything—we have just proved them wrong."[74]

In the end, all twenty-six proposed planks were adopted except the last one—to establish a separate cabinet-level office for women's issues—but no one seemed to care; its defeat was interpreted as a sign that women wanted a full and equal role in national political life rather than anything that hinted of auxiliary status. Anna Quindlen, reporting for the *New York Times,* observed that some suspected this measure was "designed to provide a job for one of the commissioners." Betty Friedan was among them. The separate office, she said was a bad idea, "sort of a BIA [Bureau of Indian Affairs] for women," adding that some "opposed it fearing that Bella would end up as head of it."[75]

As time ran out at the final session, delegates adopted a new resolution presented by the IWY Commission—which meant they emerged from the conference with twenty-six planks after all. It called on the president to establish another women's commission that would promote and assess prog-ress on the Plan of Action and provide for a Second National Women's Conference as called for in Abzug's 1975 bill.[76]

Midge Costanza gave the last address. "We have spent four days together," she said, "and after twenty-five years of active political and public life, I can stand before you and I can say I am a woman and somehow it has a new meaning . . . It has a whole new identity and a hell of the lot of pride." Those four days, she proclaimed, had been "the most exhilarating four days of my life and the most meaningful." Costanza then asked the audience: "What now?" Would Houston "become just a great exhilarating memory . . . something you will always remember as a historical event and nothing more? It cannot be," she said. "You must go back to your community . . . and defeat those elected officials" not "sensitive" to their needs and demands. As the representative of the president, and knowing "the depth of Jimmy Carter's commitment to women," she assured them they could count on Carter to be sensitive as he responded to the messages that they sent out to the nation and the world.[77]

Then Margie Adam, a California songwriter, performed "We Shall Go Forth," a song she had composed for the occasion, with lyrics meant to send participants on their way on an inspirational note.[78]

All through the conference, planned and unplanned events produced emotional highlights for the feminist majority. The five plenary sessions—not just the opening ceremonies—were thrilling and inspiring according to many of the news outlets that carried them live on national television. Presidential daughter-in-law Judy Carter addressed the crowd, as did former Presiding Officer Jill Ruckelshaus and UN assistant secretary-general Helvi Sipilä. Former congresswoman and state department official Patsy Mink was a crowd favorite along with Congresswomen Margaret Heckler and Yvonne Brathwaite Burke. The audience surprised (and annoyed) the no-nonsense Margaret Mead by affectionately singing "Happy Birthday, Dear Margaret" when she wanted to get on with her speech urging them to save the world from war. According to the press, many conference speakers gave some of the best oratorical performances of their careers.[79]

Several unforeseen developments, including the adoption of the revised minority rights plank, turned out to be highlights of the conference. Few would ever forget when Coretta Scott King read its concluding section while surrounded by bodyguards and scores of photographers who recognized the tremendous historic significance of this occasion. Many listeners wept as she proclaimed that from Houston there should go forth "a new force, a new understanding, a new sisterhood against all injustice that has been born here. We will not be divided and defeated again." The New Jersey delegates began to sing "We Shall Overcome" and all joined in, deeply moved as they held hands with their neighbors.[80]

Afterward many testified to the powerful impact of the moment. Betty Friedan praised the minority women for replacing the "bland and general resolution" IWY planners had designed for them with the newly written comprehensive plank that addressed all their needs and promoted female solidarity. "This dignified, confident, brilliantly organized and executed presentation by the minority women was quite unlike the old defensive hostile railing that used to accuse the women's movement of being a white middle class affair." She found it profoundly moving, bringing her and all around her to tears. Noticing a middle-aged black woman and a "beautiful young Chinese-American women" crying, Friedan "realized that I, and the dignified white-haired woman next to me, and the blue-jeaned girl across the aisle were crying too." Even the "press box women stood and sang, clasping hands." It was "impossible to imagine a similar moment in a convention of men," she said. "But it was not a sentimental gesture. A real bridge had been crossed."[81]

Friedan's endorsement of the plank calling for lesbian rights was wildly applauded as a magnificent gesture of reconciliation, perhaps the chief example of feminists coming together, caught up in the spirit of Houston.[82] A few weeks later, in a column published in the *New Republic*, she stated: "Somehow, even I changed at Houston." Although she had objected strongly "to the confusion of feminism with lesbianism" in Houston, she realized she "objected even more strongly to the way the right wing was trying to fan a hysteria of hate and fear against homosexuals." It would have been wrong and immoral, she wrote, "to sacrifice the civil rights of lesbians to appease the right wing."[83]

Kate Millett, radical theoretician of the movement, who had been much maligned by the press after coming out as a lesbian, had come to Houston just to see if the delegates would actually pass the proposed sexual preference plank. She could not believe that the mainstream feminists who had refused to support the rights of lesbians in the past would do so now in this official, highly public setting. As the plank was presented, one reporter found her "huddled," listening in a dark corner near the speaker's platform wearing a phony press pass and fearful of being thrown off the convention floor. Hearing rumors that Friedan was going to speak for the plank, Millett murmured, "Yes, oh yes, let us heal all the wounds at once." When the plank passed, the reporter wrote, she was beyond joy, beaming with pride that these women "who were taught to laugh at faggots and dykes . . . had come to understand that this vote is morally important enough to get over that."[84]

The reporter Anne Taylor Fleming, in her *New York Times* story, "That Week in Houston," spoke of the huge sense of satisfaction she discerned in the delegates who were immensely proud of themselves for having adopted the lesbian rights plank in bold defiance of the political right. This, she wrote, seemed to confirm to the women delegates that they were, in fact, better than men. It was "impossible to imagine a comparable group of men conquering their sexual fear of each other and rising to embrace male homosexuals, and these women knew that."[85]

Being together with like-minded women was more than reassuring: it was thrilling. For ERA advocates caught up in a protracted struggle to ratify the ERA—a fight they had not expected and feared losing—being together with others who shared their passion and their pain was cathartic. At one point in the discussion, Jean Westwood, a former chair of the Democratic National Committee, rose and declared, "I am a Mormon woman speaking in favor of ERA," and the audience went crazy.[86] When the ERA amendment passed shortly thereafter, the audience simply could not be controlled. Its adoption by overwhelming margins unleashed powerful emotions, leading to singing and dancing in the aisles—forcing Abzug to adjourn for the rest of the day.[87]

IWY leaders were jubilant. The women's movement, they believed, had turned a corner. It had put aside differences, expanded networks, and developed the diverse grassroots support they had hoped for. In addition, in the National Plan of Action they had a clear agenda that they could now use their collective power to achieve.

Gloria Steinem saw in the Plan clear evidence that the women's movement and movements for minority rights, so often at odds in American history, had now come together. Reproductive rights, including the right to abortion, were fully a part of the feminist agenda—which now also included defense of the rights of lesbians. "Ironically," said Steinem, "the effort to frighten women off was exactly what caused many to vote for civil rights for lesbians, even though they might not have supported that issue before." The National Plan of Action symbolized an end to the breach between younger, more radical feminists and older, reform-minded, relatively conservative women who worked within "the system." Now they would be working together for common goals. All this, Steinem declared, was owed to Bella Abzug, the one person who could make that bonding possible, one of the few people who was trusted and respected by both sides.[88]

On the sexual preference plank, many women left Houston dreading the consequences of including it in their recommendations, and some later second-guessed the decision. But at the conference most women's rights advocates at least temporarily lent their support. A study by sociologist Alice Rossi, an eminent sociologist in the unique position of being a member of the IWY Commission while conducting research on the IWY and its participants, said the National Women's Conference was what social scientists call a "greedy event": it fully captured the attention of participants who were caught up in the moment. As a result, their past views and associations had a lessened effect on their thoughts and actions compared to what they were experiencing. In the case of the feminists, this made them even more expansive and tolerant.[89]

For many feminists who attended, particularly women new to the movement, the National Women's Conference was a defining, life-changing moment. The "spirit of Houston" would continue to thrill and inspire them for a long time to come. Houston broadened their horizons as they encountered people and ideas with which they might never have come into contact and made them feel empowered. Some were inspired to run for higher office, including Ann Richards, who became governor of Texas; Maxine Waters, who was elected to multiple terms as a congresswoman from California; and Jane Frank (later Harman), a staff member in the Carter administration who became a congresswoman from California and later director of the Woodrow Wilson International Center for Scholars.

Rossi's study showed that others, particularly those who played less active roles in the conference, were actually less inclined to seek prominence and power, having perhaps been awed and intimidated by the stellar performances of feminist luminaries that weekend, which made them feel less competent themselves. But even these women, particularly those from rural areas or small towns who had been the only feminists in their vicinity, came away from Houston feeling less isolated and better prepared to work for change in their communities.[90]

Some developed more faith in women's ability to work together. Even old political hands such as Elly Peterson were surprised—and extremely pleased—by the way women came together in Houston. Writing to her old friend Lenore Romney, she said, "It was my most exhilarating political experience since the first Romney campaign. I was just uplifted—as I saw those women begin to do what I have preached for lo these many years . . . come together—understand the essence of power in politics and finally once and for all believe that others are interested in their problems and are willing to help THEM if they but reach out their hand." The Houston conference, she concluded, was the culmination of a new era of political activism from which women had learned much. "If I had had that group 10 years ago organization would be a dream," she wrote. "But I think it has taken these 10 years to season them and make them understand politics."[91]

The bitter conflicts with conservatives during the summer only underscored the thrilling sense of solidarity and strength feminists felt as the national conference came to an end. One joked to columnist Ellen Goodman, "We have met the enemy, and for once, it isn't us!" Republican feminist Tanya Melich, a delegate from New York, recalled later the thrill of "sisters" "being together honorably for a great cause." She wrote: "Even now, nearly twenty years later, women who don't know each other will find themselves reminiscing about Houston in the same way war veterans, strangers on sight, quickly become close as they talk about Normandy, Inchon, or Hue."[92]

Press coverage of the National Women's Conference was largely positive though conservative pundits were critical and in somewhat predictable ways. George Will (who was in Houston) reflected pensively on the women's movement's "long, winding road" from Seneca Falls to Houston, sounding somewhat sympathetic to women for resenting the "unequal distribution of power over the arranging of the life they create." But he dismissed the National Women's Conference as a "poignant" exercise "in that touching earnestness that liberal reformers bring to the task of voting the dawn of the new world." He wrote: "Addressing one another as 'sister' and invoking the spirit of their 'foremothers,' they tried to wash from society the grime of irrationality with a cleansing rain of resolutions." But in the end they overreached. The affirmation of the rights of lesbians, he opined, led many delegates to leave Houston "weighted down by the fear that the conference was to make ratification of the ERA even more unlikely."[93]

Former Nixon speechwriter Pat Buchanan's reaction was also patronizing but much less generous—in fact, it was characteristically nasty: "What the Houston confab produced was a warmed-over hash of the radical liberalism that generally stunk up the '60s." The main point of his column, "Where Jimmy Should File the Houston Agenda," was that if Carter wanted a second term, he would thank the "grizzled, battle-weary vets of the National Women's Conference, promise to study the agenda, give the girls some milk and cookies, and send them on their way. Then, he will call in Hamilton Jordan and tell him to file that 25-point 'Womandate' on the same shelf where the Scranton Commission Report and the Kerner Commission Report are gathering dust." Why? "Because the National Plan of Action . . . points

Mr. Carter in precisely the opposite direction from where the national majority is headed."[94]

Covering the conference for the John Birch Society's publication, *American Opinion,* Susan L. M. Huck called it "a monstrosity whelped by the United Nations, out of the State Department, with Bella Abzug as midwife" and an "unprecedented example of how those supporting the New World Order operate." Focusing on the exhibit hall, she stated, "Perhaps because we have become so accustomed to treason, the heaviest odor remained that of militant lesbianism," and she condemned the State Department for allowing gays and prostitutes as well as the "old-line Stalinoids" and other "active enemies of United States" to participate. She charged that conservative women's views were barely tolerated and that when pro-life delegates tried to wave their signs on the convention floor, "female hoodlums led by Gloria Steinem physically assaulted them."[95]

This virulent denunciation of the conference to which feminists paid little attention contrasted sharply to coverage in the mainstream media. Like the *New York Times,* most media outlets seemed to accept the feminists' view that they, not the conservatives, represented the majority of American women. This of course led feminist leaders to wonder why the media gave so much attention to the conservative protesters, their rally, and the claim that it represented a vast grassroots movement. "If the American people saw George Wallace bus in 10,000 for a rally after Jimmy Carter won the nomination," Smeal asked, "who would believe for a moment that the Wallace people were representative?"[96]

Optimists among the feminists, however, hoped the media's extravagant coverage of the conservatives would work to their advantage. One wrote to Liz Carpenter, "It was gratifying to see the venom and hatred displayed so clearly on Phyllis Schlafly's face when she spoke to a national TV audience during the media coverage of the conference. I think that that revelation will do more to support the aims of the Women's movement as stated in Houston, than all the press releases that will follow, could accomplish."[97]

Many wished that Egyptian president Anwar Sadat had not chosen this particular weekend for traveling to Israel. Though contributing to world peace—a major goal of IWY—it nonetheless put news stories about the National Women's Conference beneath the fold in many newspapers. It also kept large numbers of Americans—most notably Jimmy Carter—captivated by events in Jerusalem instead of Houston.[98]

Otherwise, feminists were thrilled by the massive coverage the conferences received and happy that the press had effusively passed along to the world the messages they hoped to send. The once skeptical *Washington Post* declared that in Houston "women from all regions, backgrounds, and circumstances shared not only common concerns but an impressive amount of energy and organizing skill." *Time* magazine published a long and detailed account of the conference in its December 5, 1977, issue—with runner Peggy Kokernot and the Torch on the cover and a tiny image of Anwar Sadat added to the upper right hand corner at the last minute.[99]

Time proclaimed that in Houston, American women had reached "some kind of watershed in their own history and in that of the nation." For many women the National Women's Conference had brought about "an end to the psychological isolation that had constrained their activities and ambitions." They learned that "many other middle-of-the-road, American-as-Mom's-apple-pie women shared with them a sense of second-class citizenship and a craving for greater social and economic equality."[100]

An almost giddy feminist press celebrated the conference for the confidence it instilled. "Houston transformed us all," wrote Lindsy Van Gelder in *Ms.* magazine. "We learned that we could excel at serious parliamentary procedure, and still indulge in singing 'Happy Birthday' to speaker Margaret Mead; to knit and to nurse babies during debates; to laugh with Bella as she banged the gavel to adjourn and wished us 'Good night, my loves.' We were sensitized to minorities . . . formed and fortified dozens of networks that will live beyond Houston and help implement the Plan, from a new national coalition to help battered wives, to an organization of feminist elected officials, to a continuing caucus of American Indians and Alaskan Natives."[101]

Press coverage recognized that the Houston conference had not only brought more women into this movement, it had enhanced the movement's credibility and placed women's issues at the top of the national political agenda. To Megan Rosenfeld of the *Washington Post,* the National Women's Conference proved that "the woman's movement . . . is no longer a small group of intellectuals . . . It has developed into a force considered socially acceptable by presidents' wives and housewives from South Dakota, by the middle-aged and older women as well as the young."[102] Most media outlets agreed that, although the November weekend with its conference and counterconference demonstrated that American women were not all of one mind, the National Women's Conference made it clear that the women's movement was sufficiently united to remain a force in American politics and perhaps become increasingly powerful.

The mainstream media presented the women's movement not only as politically influential but as a progressive, comprehensive, and unified movement for change. *Newsday*'s David Behrens stated that the National Plan of Action proved the women's movement "is also an egalitarian movement, an umbrella for the civil rights movement and the movement for economic equality, for the environmental and consumer movements and the movement for participatory democracy." Positive press came even from abroad. The *London Evening Standard* pronounced: "Mainstream feminism has evolved into the most broadly based movement for egalitarianism that America possesses ... The women's movement is now a truly national, unified engine of change which could conceivably become the cutting edge of the most important human issues America faces in the next decade."

This was what the women who had envisioned and planned the IWY conferences had hoped for. As they left Houston, feminists were inspired, ready to go forth and use their newfound solidarity to implement the Plan and convinced that public opinion would be on their side.

Caught up in their own conference experience, however, even those who were aware of the protest rally across town had little sense of how the IWY effort had empowered conservative women. They had no idea just how hard feminists were going to have to fight in the future just to preserve what the women's rights movement had already achieved.

CHAPTER 11

Launching the Pro-Family Movement

> Meanwhile, across town at the Houston Astro Arena, a new and formidable women's movement became visible on the national scene for the first time. ERA opponent Phyllis Schlafly had organized a Pro-Family Coalition with a host of pro-life leaders. Together they planned and mobilized a massive "Pro-Life, Pro-Family" counter-rally that became a stunning success unlike anything seen before or since.
>
> —ELAINE DONNELLY, "WHAT WOMEN WANTED,"
> *NATIONAL REVIEW*, 2004

In the fall of 1977, as Bella Abzug and IWY Commission leaders prepared for Houston, Phyllis Schlafly and IWY Citizens' Review Committee (CRC) leaders planned their response to the IWY conference Schlafly ridiculed as the "Federally Funded Festival for Frustrated Feminists." Having tried and failed to stop it, they vowed to turn defeat into victory.

Like feminists, CRC leaders knew the media would descend like locusts on Houston. If they planned carefully, the feminists' big weekend could provide them a tremendous opportunity to publicize their own ideas and demonstrate their strength and unity.[1] They, too, wanted to send a message to the nation: this was not an ephemeral uprising against the IWY: it had become a "pro-family movement" intent on becoming more, not less, involved in politics.

Over the summer there had been considerable debate about strategy. At a late-summer gathering in Chicago, CRC leaders considered two plans. In the first, they would try to gain access to the IWY conference for large numbers of "observers" and seek to have an impact on the National Plan of Action beyond what could be accomplished by the small band of conservative delegates. This plan depended on whether or not IWY leaders decided to permit active participation from non-delegates, information they expected to glean from a mole on the IWY Commission. If observer participation was allowed, they would bring resolutions and "set in motion our own M.M.O.P.P. plan" (the "Monitoring and Mobile Operation Partnership Program" devised by feminists to maximize the effectiveness of their forces during a conference) to get them adopted. Schlafly would give directions using a bullhorn and they would get the "men delegates from Mississippi" to "help on mikes" along with their "gals who are astute parliamentarians." In short, this was a plan to circumvent the outcome of the summer elections and control the IWY conference in Houston from the galleries.[2]

The "Alternative Second Idea," the one chosen, was to "have our own conference in Houston at the same time of IWY," again with Schlafly as their leader. The chief advantage was that they would have full control. They could "pass our own recommendations," "certify our own votes by notaries," "set up our 'Rules & Regulations' to govern meeting," and "specify procedures for presentation of results to President Carter, Congress, state Legislatures, Press, etc." It would be confined to one day so that they could also monitor the IWY conference.[3]

For either plan, success would depend on "complete cooperation of our Texas Eagles, WWWW, churches, Pro-life, Pro-Family, etc." Their contact in South Carolina, Rene Welch, assured them of Mormon support, reminding them that the LDS "Prophet has sent out an edict or message to all members to do all they can." With twelve hours' notice, she boasted, her church could alert thousands. The plan also called for trying to "enlist aid of Private Enterprise" by showing them "how they are being 'ripped off' by Women's Lib and government control."[4] After agreeing on this plan, the organizers chose the time and date for the rally—1:00 to 3:00 p.m. on Saturday, November 19, 1977—to coincide with opening day of the National Women's Conference in Houston.

It is not clear whether Schlafly attended that planning meeting, but the rally was definitely not her idea. Although she has been hailed as a genius for organizing the protest rally in Houston that gave a tremendous boost to conservatives, the idea came from Lottie Beth Hobbs and Schlafly was initially opposed. Hobbs had been a vice president of Schlafly's Eagle Forum since it was founded in 1975. At the same time, she continued to lead

WWWW (Women Who Want to Be Women), the organization she had founded in 1975. By 1977 she at times referred to it as the "Pro-Family Forum." After attending the June 24–26 state IWY meeting in Texas, which had been dominated by feminists, she was determined that the National Women's Conference—which would also take place in her home state—would not proceed unchallenged. She envisioned a counter-rally that would compare in size, scale, and drama with the IWY conference, and grab the attention of the press.[5]

Schlafly later graciously praised Hobbs as the "indispensable leader" who "had the vision to see that the Pro-Family Rally could be accomplished despite almost insurmountable odds," but initially she thought Hobbs's proposal was far too great a risk. Schlafly acknowledged that during summer deliberations she "did not believe a Pro-Family Rally of any important size could ever take place." People would have to travel so far at their own expense, and IWY planners had already reserved nearly every hotel and public space in the city. She warned Hobbs that the burden would be on her and "her women" in Texas. But Hobbs agreed to shoulder the responsibility of securing a location, arranging the program, and supervising the myriad details that would be required to pull off such an undertaking.[6]

Rosemary Thomson was also skeptical. "Many of us were 'doubting Thomases,' to say the least," she wrote a year later in *The Price of LIBerty.* How could they get "Christian women" to travel "all the way to Texas," especially since the rally would be on the weekend before Thanksgiving when they "would want to be home preparing for the holiday?" But Hobbs, "a Bible teacher from Ft. Worth, put on the full armor of God (Ephesians 6:11–18) and met the challenge of Women's Lib head-on."[7]

Lottie Beth Hobbs's enthusiasm was contagious. "Hobbs had the determination to do the hard work and to motivate others to do likewise," Schlafly recalled, and everyone went into action.[8] Again Dianne Edmondson of Oklahoma stepped up, volunteering to "make another tape for the churches." The new tape, "Where Do We Go From Here," repeated accusations voiced in the Helms hearing about lurid lesbian activities, communist infiltration, and even witchcraft at the state IWY meetings, and urged churches to charter buses and get as many people as possible to Houston.[9]

Right away the conspirators reached out to their allies in the pro-life movement, with great results. IWY Citizens' Review Committee and March for Life leader Nellie Gray, also a native Texan, worked closely with Hobbs to plan the rally they dubbed the "Pro-Life, Pro-Family Rally." The National Right to Life organization, the largest pro-life organization, was quick to respond. Cincinnati Right to Life leader Stephanie Varga (elected as a delegate to Houston) agreed to help, saying, "If we can get thousands to march in Washington" to the annual March for Life protest on the anniversary of *Roe*, "we can get them to Houston, too."[10] Utah Right to Life leader Doris Wilson said she was sure her group could charter a plane to bring women from their state.[11] The *National Right to Life News* ardently promoted the rally, boasting that "the 'other show' would outdraw the main event" and that "Tennessee Volunteers for Life" alone planned to bring twenty busloads and a chartered airliner of participants to Houston.[12]

Hobbs's supporters in Texas also pitched in to help with the arrangements. In Houston, many organizations, including Eagle Forum, the WWWW, Right to Life, Life Advocates, and the Mormon women's organization, the Relief Society, offered assistance. Thomson was elated. It seemed that "a network of like-minded women was meshing from coast to coast."[13] More than ever, opponents of the ERA and abortion were joining forces, building on the spirit of collaboration forged during the summer IWY meetings.

Hobbs and Gray also worked together on another key part of the emerging plan, preparing a "Request to the President and Congress" that could be signed by people unable to get to Houston. The document, consisting of four resolutions, was distributed by the thousands throughout the nation.[14] According to press reports, the petitions demanded "that Congress mandate a 'right to life' amendment which would protect the life of all people, including children, and fetuses from the moment of conception." Another resolution opposed preschool child development financed by the federal government and favored private sector control of day care centers. A third resolution strongly opposed ratification of the ERA. The last opposed "homosexual/lesbian rights, including their right to adopt children and teach in schools."[15]

The goal was to have as many of the resolutions as possible signed and sent to the Pro-Family, Pro-Life Coalition at a Houston post office box. Those present at the rally would "vote" to affirm their support for the resolutions, and a chartered plane waiting at the airport would fly the documents to Washington immediately.[16]

In late September, Rosemary Thomson dispatched a "What to Do Between Now and Houston" letter to CRC coordinators in which she laid out Hobbs's plan for the rally and urged them to get as many people and signed resolutions as possible to Houston. Should they "need motivation for your members" or for themselves, they should order copies of Edmondson's new tape "designed especially for church women" and "available by mail for $2.00 each." She urged them to be on the alert "for TV and radio promotions of IWY" and "ask (under the 'fairness doctrine') to present your side," and "keep the letters-to-the-editor going."[17]

Thomson also announced plans devised by CRC coalition members and March for Life leaders during the Helms hearings in mid-August "to set every Monday through November 14, for prayer and fasting for the family and for the Pro-Family Rally." The idea was to use money saved on food to pay for printing, rent, and travel for speakers at the Houston rally. Many CRC affiliates were also planning Pro-Family Rallies at their state capitols. Thomson thanked them for all their "work and dedication on behalf of women of traditional values," and signed off with: "Ours is the *real* women's movement!"[18]

Kathryn Dunaway and her lieutenants in Georgia appealed to religious conservatives across their state, asking that they do everything in their power to get Christians to Houston for the November 19, 1977, rally and/or sign the resolutions. In an early November letter to Georgia "pastors," she explained that, since conservative delegates would be vastly outnumbered in Houston, the report adopted at the National Women's Conference would definitely "not reflect the thinking of most U.S. women and men." Thus it was imperative to have "a greater crowd at our meeting Nov 19th" to "convince the Lawmakers Bella's Bunch does not represent most people in the U.S." Dunaway reported that Georgia governor George Busbee was lending a hand. He had signed a Proclamation designating November 19 as "Family Day" and the week of November 20–26, 1977, as "Family Week."[19]

Regarding those who planned to travel to Houston, Dunaway explained that they would have to take the buses straight to their rally and back home, as there was little chance of finding hotel rooms at this late date. Nonetheless, "this can be a fun trip and an educational one also with talks about ERA, IWY etc. with materials available, singing, games Friday and Sun a.m. church Service and Christian songs. All on the Buses."[20] She enclosed a song sheet for the "fun" bus trips, with words to familiar songs repurposed for the occasion. There was "Bella's Bunch" sung to "Santa Claus Is Coming to Town" (warning, "You'd better look out" for the "bunch" coming from New York to "fuss and fume"). There was also "Hey, Look It Over" (about how the ERA would harm the family and "send our girls to war") and "Stop the ERA," to be sung to the tune of then-familiar jingle, "See the U.S.A. in Your Chevrolet":

Stop the E.R.A.
In the U.S.A.
Don't let them take our rights away.
Everywhere you go
Let the people know
We're women—that's what we want to stay.[21]

The response to Dianne Edmondson's tape "Where Do We Go from Here?" was, in Thomson's words, "beyond anyone's wildest imagination." While orders for the tape issued in midsummer had been impressive, there were twice as many requests for the new one.[22] According to Schlafly, "Edmondson's excellent cassette on Women's Lib and its attack on the family" persuaded "hundreds, perhaps thousands" of women "that they could do something constructive for God and Country" by attending the rally.[23]

Meanwhile, Lottie Beth Hobbs crisscrossed the nation, speaking in nearly every state—wherever a receptive audience beckoned. In mid-October she reported to Thomson that "the momentum building in various parts of the nation is incredible, encouraging and thrilling." Stop-ERA veterans Shirley Curry and Tottie Ellis and their "valiant workers in Tennessee" chartered fifty buses. Planes and buses were also scheduled to bring protesters from Alabama, Georgia, Louisiana, Kansas, Missouri, Utah, California, Mississippi, New York, and elsewhere. And resolutions poured in from every state. A CRC leader in New Mexico phoned Thomson saying she was circulating 10,000 resolutions in the southern half of her state alone, and lining up people for the rally.[24]

From Arizona, Donna Carlson reported, "Things are really popping!" Seventeen new Eagle Forum chapters had formed since the state IWY meeting and there were plans for a rally at the state capitol the day of the Houston rally.[25] In New York, conservatives made plans for a "Pro-Family Conference" in Albany to show that the Commission on International Women's Year did "not speak for American women" and certainly not for members of the Eagle Forum, Mormons, and pro-life groups. But there was also bad news. The key Eagle Forum organizer in Ohio, an elected delegate to IWY, had fallen asleep at the wheel while returning from a speaking engagement and was injured and unable to go to Houston. They were all running themselves ragged.[26]

Hobbs still faced one major problem: finding a site for the rally. IWY organizers, she believed, had "gotten wind of our plans" and were doing all they could to thwart them. But, she reported, God answered her prayers and "a Christian businessman" had secured the Astro Arena, a part of the Astrodome complex, which would seat 12,000. Enough contributions had come in with the resolutions to make the down payment, and Hobbs planned to pass the hat at the rally to pay the rest.[27]

Schlafly was now fully on board and, along with Hobbs, Edmondson, and others, speaking at rallies to build turnout for the Pro-Life, Pro-Family rally and for other simultaneous rallies planned for some state capitols. Her annual October training conference in St. Louis was devoted to preparing for Houston and drew new participants from people who had been elected during the summer as delegates. There was still much to do.[28]

Besides mobilizing rally participants, Schlafly and the IWY Citizens' Review Committee leaders had to figure out the best use of the conservative delegates inside the National Women's Conference, women and men who would have to get their message across while "enduring the hostility of the lib delegates." Schlafly and the delegates chose Indiana state senator Joan Gubbins, head of her state's delegation, to be the pro-family floor leader.[29] Gubbins would have help from several CRC leaders also elected as delegates, including Rosemary Thomson, Dianne Edmondson, and South Carolina state representative Norma C. Russell (who described herself as Gubbins's "first lieutenant"). Thomson and Edmondson drafted a "Minority Report" they would attempt to present at the Houston conference.[30]

Otherwise, the conservatives' pre-Houston efforts went into dealing with the press. In the weeks leading up to the conference, they jockeyed with feminists to gain the attention of the media and control the message. In numerous interviews—at which Schlafly complained of too little press attention and accused the media of favoring the feminists—and in the *Phyllis Schlafly Report*, Schlafly charged that the National Women's Conference was a "charade" put on to trick the nation into believing there was strong grassroots support for radical feminism. She predicted it would backfire and that Americans would be thoroughly alienated. Schlafly charged Abzug and others on the IWY Commission with putting out "phony tips to the media that pro-family persons and groups would cause a 'confrontation,' 'disruption,' and possibly 'physical violence'"—despite the fact that these predictions were completely baseless and "merely bait to get the press to travel to Houston." Gubbins repeatedly told reporters that her side had no intention of disrupting the proceedings and planned "to behave like ladies at all times."[31]

Schlafly and the CRC leaders expressed outrage that Abzug and other IWY leaders had accused them of collaborating with the Klan and the press was accepting it as fact. The media was full of stories on this subject. A Mississippi reporter noted that "the national press has seized upon the 'Klan connection'" in his state, pointing to a *Rolling Stone* story stating that Mississippi "with its traditional flair for overreaching" had elected "a group of alleged Nazis." Dallas Higgins, one of the Mississippi elected delegates, said she had been besieged by news reporters from all over the country ever since the first news articles connected her to the Klan.[32]

But CRC leaders never acknowledged that the press received information directly from the Klan. Higgins's husband George freely admitted being a KKK leader. During the Florida state meeting, he showed his calling card identifying him as "Grand Dragon of the Realm of Mississippi, United Klans of American, Inc." On the back was the slogan, "The only reason you are White today is because your ancestors practiced & believed in segregation Yesterday." He claimed to have controlled the IWY meetings in his state. Imperial Wizard Robert Shelton, a notorious Alabama Klan leader, also boasted that the Klan had "infiltrated" the state IWY meetings, and he made national news with his declaration that he and other Klansmen would be in Houston to protect "their women" from lesbian assault. Borrowing a page from its surveillance of civil rights workers, the KKK planned to attend to take photos and gather information on lesbians and feminists, the "misfits of society," to forward to Klan members in the women's home states.[33]

CRC leaders laid the blame for the allegations of Klan involvement squarely on the feminists, who certainly did all they could to publicize these reports once they appeared in the press. Abzug's late-September presentation to Congress had named the Klan and Robert Shelton in particular as part of the coalition seeking to "disrupt" IWY proceedings.[34] Later, Thomson and other elected delegates received a news release from Abzug repeating the charge. The CRC leader was furious that the press release, "datelined the U.S. State Department and mailed with the government's 'free' postage frank," had attacked "those who did not support the proposed National Plan of Action, equating us with the Ku Klux Klan."[35] How outrageous, she said, that Abzug should accuse the pro-family delegates, "Christians from many denominations who believe the Bible's moral principles," of being "extremists."[36]

It was especially galling, Thomson said, that "the particularly family-oriented Mormon Church was singled out for special vilification." Mormons were outraged that feminists named them, along with the Klan, as among the "disrupters." Conservative women in Utah founded a Utah Association of Women to show support for their delegation. Insisting they were "moderately conservative politically," but not "extremist," they held a rally on the capitol steps featuring Senator Orrin Hatch and intended to show "support for women's rights without the ERA, show respect for the unborn, and support the traditional family lifestyle."[37]

Joan Gubbins told reporters she'd like to find a way to sue Bella Abzug for accusing IWY opponents of Klan connections.[38] These charges, she insisted, not only defamed them but also put them in danger. After Missouri delegates identified as Klan members in a NOW newsletter and the media picked up the story, their chair, Ann O'Donnell, issued a press release charging that the false allegation threatened the safety of her delegation.[39]

Schlafly claimed the "IWYers" were making up charges "that the Ku Klux Klan is leading a giant conspiracy of Catholics, Mormons, Baptists, and Lutherans against ERA and IWY" out of "sheer desperation." In an *Eagle Forum Newsletter* she wrote, "This is not only false—it is ridiculous! Of course, all Eagles know that there has been NO contact between any of us and the KKK, and that the KKK has done NOTHING to defeat ERA." "When you hear charges of 'KKK,' 'conspiracy,' and other epithets and extremist charges," she wrote, "just remember: (1) This proves there are NO good arguments for ERA, and (2) it is a smokescreen to hide the radical/lesbian pressure groups spending our tax dollars through the IWY."[40]

The IWY Citizens' Review Committee leader in Mississippi, Eddie Myrtle Moore, elected leader of the state's IWY delegation, complained that there had been "a smear on the Mississippi delegates." Addressing a reporter for the Associated Press, she declared, "As chairman I can assure you that not one member is a Klansman. The Klan has nothing to do with this delegation."[41] Moore had the delegates sign affidavits to that effect, and even the Klansman's wife, Dallas Higgins, complied, but then undermined Moore's efforts by admitting to the press she had attended Klan rallies "as a concerned citizen."[42]

Moore and other CRC leaders were indignant that the IWY Commission chose to appoint at-large delegates to compensate for the lack of diversity in some delegations. The commission appointed nine at-large delegates from Mississippi, eight of them black women prominent in the civil rights movement. They were a sharp contrast to the staunchly conservative all-white elected delegation, which included six men. Returning from a meeting of IWY delegation heads in Washington, Moore held a press conference at the Mississippi Farm Bureau office in Jackson, where she accused IWY leaders of using the diversity issue to stack the deck in Houston even more surely in favor of the ERA.[43]

On October 28, three weeks before the conference and counterconference were to begin, CRC media chair Elaine Donnelly sent a substantial press package to all networks, print media, news services, and wire services. She included a thorough report presenting her version of IWY history, describing the background and purposes of the CRC. She repeated accusations that Abzug had promised Congress to make these meetings open to all but discriminated against women with conservative points of view—labeling it the "Abzugate Scandal." Donnelly handed out copies of the IWY Commission's proposed resolutions and the CRC's "translations."[44] She also provided contact information for conservative leaders and delegates, who were then deluged with requests for interviews. *U.S. News & World Report* delighted Rosemary Thomson by sending a photographer "to 'shoot' me in my kitchen for their National Women's Conference coverage." Even better, the story ran with the title "Why Women's Lib Is in Trouble."[45]

With two weeks to go before the fateful weekend, Citizens' Review Committee advisory board member Kathleen Teague, a professional in public relations, arranged a press breakfast in Washington, D.C., where Schlafly outlined the CRC's positions. Schlafly then flew to Houston to set up camp at the Ramada Inn. According to the *Wall Street Journal*, she shared the hotel with feminist delegates and a lesbian motorcycle club, and had around-the-clock guards. Donnelly, assisted by Missouri Eagle Forum leader Ann McGraw, worked with a dozen "Eagles" to set up operations at the Ramada Inn Civic Center, including an elaborate pressroom with typewriters and telephones for the journalists—arrangements that vastly outclassed accommodations for the press at the IWY conference. Donnelly announced plans to hold daily morning press conferences throughout the four-day weekend to comment on both the IWY conference and the protest rally.[46]

With just days before the opening of the National Women's Conference, the Pro-Family Coalition ran a paid advertisement in several Houston papers that drew many participants to the conservatives' rally. Covering nearly half of a page, the ad depicted an innocent little blond-haired girl wearing a First Communion dress and holding a bouquet of flowers, saying, "Mommy, when I grow up can I be a lesbian?" It added, "If you think this is shocking, read what the IWY is proposing for your children."[47]

Finally the countdown to Houston was over, and it was time for the showdown. IWY Citizens' Review Committee leaders assembled at the

Ramada Inn for a banquet for the pro-family delegates and Pro-Life, Pro-Family Rally leaders. Lottie Beth Hobbs, presiding, introduced the stars who were to speak at the rally: Mildred Jefferson of National Right to Life and Nellie Gray of March for Life; IWY Citizens' Review Committee officers Rosemary Thomson and Elaine Donnelly; and Joan Gubbins who would be the floor leader for the conservative delegates. Hobbs then read a passage from Gideon (Judges 7) in which three hundred men chosen by God routed hordes of Midianites—an inspirational message about the power of a few to overcome evil multitudes when chosen by the Lord.[48]

Then, as Thomson recalled, they stood together for a final prayer and to sing "God Bless America" as "TV cameras rolled and journalists' strobes flashed." It was "a spiritual encounter," she said. "With denominational ties stripped away, we were united in Christ. We had done all that was humanly possible without funds or formal organization. Now the 'battle was the Lord's'!"[49]

On Friday, November 19, 1977, the day before the conference and counter-rally began, Schlafly held a press conference timed to compete with Abzug's. Implementing their well-oiled plans to divert press attention from the feminists and get out their own message, Donnelly distributed media packages, offered briefings, and arranged interviews with conservative delegates. ABC's *Good Morning America* featured a "Face-off segment" in which Shirley Spellerberg debated First Daughter-in-law Judy Carter about the president's support of the ERA and extension of the deadline.[50] In the afternoon, as the Torch of Freedom was arriving and the ERA rally beginning, Congressman Robert Dornan presided over another "ad hoc hearing" featuring many of the same people who testified at the Helms hearings in September. They repeated their charges of fraud and outrageous behavior for the benefit of the press.[51]

On Saturday morning, as the National Women's Conference opened with great fanfare, Rosemary Thomson and the sorely outnumbered conservative delegates found it profoundly depressing. They were disgusted as the young runners delivered the torch to the First Ladies, considering the "big production" a cynical ploy to appear patriotic for the hordes of reporters. Still, Thomson complained, "Not even the media's watchful eye persuaded IWY officials to allow an invocation," and "all Chairperson Abzug permitted was a moment of silence!" When the "parade of celebrities and first ladies" praised the meeting and "plugged the Equal Rights Amendment," Thomson and her compatriots "wondered if they had read the National Plan of Action they were endorsing."[52]

The Saturday afternoon session offered more misery as the conference turned to the presentation of planks and voting. Conservative floor leader Joan Gubbins, Rosemary Thomson, and other pro-family delegates were vocal, demanding time at the microphones to modify proposals they had no hope of defeating. As one feminist described the situation, it quickly became clear that "a comfortable majority favored the Plan" and "reliance on procedural questions emerged as the tactic of anti-change forces."[53]

According to the conservatives, the IWY-appointed chairs rarely gave them the floor, although they managed to gain recognition long enough to inject a few brief statements and present motions to amend or substitute resolutions. Alice Ward, a pro-family delegate from Ohio, spoke against the plank on prevention of child abuse, pointing out that "spanking is now called child abuse" and insisting "there is big publicity to turn in child abusers." Another Ohio delegate, Mary Gigandet, moved to include the "pre-born" in the protections against child abuse, but the chair declared the motion to be out of order.[54] In the debate on federally sponsored child care, Gerri Madden of Hawaii charged that the "similarity between Hitler's camps and these youth camps might produce the same consequences." The pro-family contingent managed to introduce a substitute plank requiring preschool child programs be controlled solely by the private sector, but it was voted down and the original recommendation adopted.[55]

When the plank on education came up, Barbara Zapotocky of Nebraska proposed a substitution motion (also voted down) calling for teaching respect for the republican form of government, the free enterprise system, all authorities including parents, and absolute values of right and wrong.[56] The conservatives' attempt to modify a plank calling for more women in elected and appointed positions to insert the word "qualified" was also defeated.[57] Feminist accounts noted that one of the session chairs, Anne Saunier, rebuked a conservative woman who insisted on addressing her as "chairman."[58]

Dianne Edmondson's effort to amend the plank supporting ERA ratification to read "only if done within the original seven-year period"—with Betty Friedan's surprising support—was not the only attempt to modify that key plank. Evelyn Pitschke of Indiana, self-described "chairman" of the National Association of Lawyers Who Oppose the Equal Rights Amendment, spoke against it on the grounds that "Section 2" gave too much power to the federal government. Rosemary Thomson tried to introduce a substitute amendment opposing the ERA, but the chair ruled that it was incomplete and thus out of order. When the ERA plank passed and supporters went wild in celebration, conservative delegates sat silently.[59]

As time passed, the pro-family delegates grew more frustrated, complaining that their attempts to modify or amend planks were repeatedly defeated or ruled out of order and that, as in the summer state meetings, they were victims of discrimination and railroading. Susan Roylance, the Mormon woman who had emerged as floor leader of the conservative coalition at the Ellensburg, Washington, meeting, sought and gained an audience with Bella Abzug to demand that conservative voices be heard during the debates. According to Roylance, only then did Abzug intervene—and just in time. When it appeared that debate on the reproductive rights plank would be cut off without pro-life delegates being able to speak, Abzug left the podium and, according to *Time*, told several Pro-Plan floor leaders, "I won't stand for this. These people have got a right to speak against this."[60]

At that point Ann O'Donnell, head of Missouri's delegation and an NRLC national leader, stood and offered an eloquent plea to women not to tie their quest for liberty to "the destruction of babies." O'Donnell, who had told *Washington Post* reporters that she had "always been a feminist" and did not "plan on being driven out because I oppose abortion," pleaded with feminists not to degrade their movement by championing abortion.[61]

"It is the antithesis of the feminist women's movement to oppress the less powerful," she declared. "It is therefore absolutely ridiculous for people who call themselves feminists to suggest that they kill their unborn children to solve our social problems." Clearly differing with many conservatives on the issue of federally supported child care—and ignoring feminists' long record of advocating such programs—O'Donnell said women should demand that society "provide programs so that a woman can fulfill her personhood and her personhood includes nurturing and nursing of unborn and born children." The decision before the delegates was a critical one, she insisted. "If we do not drive this flaw from what is called the feminist movement, this flaw would be responsible for the death of the women's movement."

O'Donnell then ended her speech saying: "I appeal to this assembly, to think about what you are saying if you pass this resolution. You ask for reproductive freedom, but all freedom is based on recognition of the rights of those who are less powerful than you, and the unborn children are the least powerful and most helpless. You have more to offer this country, very positive things to offer, and the promise of the women's movement will be destroyed if you go on record in support of this unjust, destructive resolution."[62]

Footage of O'Donnell's speech appeared on the evening news. For conservatives, this brief speech was the highlight of the conference, coming just before one of the lowest points, the passage of the reproductive rights plank which included abortion. Press reports described pro-life delegates as visibly distressed when adoption of the plank was announced. According to *Time*, one of them, "shaking and weeping," cried, "I never thought they would come to this. It's murder!" Another said, "It will be old people next." Feminists claimed that they treated O'Donnell's statement respectfully and that, when the plank passed, the celebration was more restrained in respect for those who opposed it.[63]

On several occasions, feminists, especially nondelegates observing from the galleries, were anything but respectful, especially when conservatives made inflammatory statements in the debate over the lesbian rights plank. Rosemary Thomson recalled indignantly that, when a Florida delegate stated that granting equality to homosexuals would "destroy the family" and was "against the laws of God," "catcalls and jeers echoed around the hall." Feminists again reacted with hostility when Oklahoma delegate Winnie Matthews spoke against the plank, saying, "We would never advocate a stoning or a burning at the stake, or a throwing in the river of a homosexual. And as long as homosexuals keep their sexual preferences in private, the same as adulterers and adulteresses . . ." There was a huge reaction from the audience and the chair had to rap them back to order before she could continue: "As soon as they keep their standards in private, our nation does not discriminate against them."[64]

Although the conservative delegates were united on this particular issue, they did not always vote as a bloc. Feminists were pleased to see that, on some occasions, the "anti-change" delegates "broke ranks," voting with the majority on several planks including child care, child abuse, employment, and credit. One of the men from Mississippi said they often split on issues but voted as a bloc against the ERA, abortion, and homosexual rights. Another Mississippi delegate, Curtis Caine, told the press that his delegation had no trouble supporting sections of the Plan that were "reasonable" and "proper." He and his wife, Lynn, were John Birch Society members who said their main concern was placing so much power in the hands of the federal government.[65] Near the end of the conference, the Mississippi delegation issued a flyer protesting massive extension of federal power:

TO ALL THOSE HERE ASSEMBLED BE IT KNOWN AND
REMEMBERED, AS THE FEDERAL CHAIN FORGED AT THIS

TIME AND PLACE IN THE HISTORY OF OUR GREAT REPUBLIC
BINDS MORE TIGHTLY IN THE YEARS TO COME, THAT THE
GREAT, SOVEREIGN STATE OF MISSISSIPPI DID NOT FORGE ITS
LINKS.[66]

Joan Gubbins repeatedly tried to introduce the conservatives' "Minority Report" during the conference. Before offering alternatives to each plank in the proposed National Plan of Actions, it presented a general statement reflecting their inter-related goals of limiting federal power and government-funded social programs and protecting traditional gender roles and family structures. It opened with a general statement that all of their recommendations were based on "logical, progressive, Judeo-Christian principles which are in keeping with the principles upon which the United States of America was founded." Declaring that the free enterprise system was what had brought the nation its prosperity, it insisted that its continued existence depended on freedom from government controls and regulations. American women, it insisted, must "stop seeking federal solutions to personal problems." And rather than demand more freedoms, they should "call this Nation to its knees in repentance for its licentiousness committed in the name of freedom."[67]

Calling for limits on taxation and nonessential government spending, the report opposed any kind of national health program as expensive and likely to eliminate freedom of choice. It objected to a strong federal role in many areas of life, including caring for the needy and educating young children, which should be left to parents and families, the private sector, and to local governments, which were more reflective of community needs. It denounced the IWY and the World Plan of Action drafted by the Mexico City IWY conference and adopted by the UN, and insisted that the nation agree to no further UN treaties until it showed more concern to people living in totalitarian countries. Reflecting the conservatives' commitment to strengthening national security, the report opposed disarmament, reduction in military spending, and the "brainwashing of school children to pacifist goals." On the ERA and abortion, it declared, women should reject "the unisex 'equality' that the so-called Equal Rights Amendment would bring about if ratified" and demand "that the sanctity of innocent life be safeguarded from conception to natural death."[68]

However, the conservatives' recommendations indicated that they shared many of the feminists' concerns while disagreeing about solutions. For instance, the feminist-supported plank on the media suggested that it expand its portrait of women to a variety of roles; the Minority Report recognized the need to further explore the roles of women but not "at the expense of the traditional, family-centered women's life style." Feminists called for new federal programs to aid older women and opposed mandatory retirement; the Minority Report objected to development of federal programs but supported ones run by state and local government and private women's groups to "enable elderly women to live with dignity and security" and they too endorsed a ban on mandatory retirement. Regarding employment, the feminists' plank called for removal of barriers; the conservatives agreed that "qualified" women deserved equal opportunities but they objected to any new quotas favoring women.[69]

The Minority Report agreed with feminist demands that criminal codes dealing with rape provide for graduated degrees of the crime, that victims have to provide no more corroborating evidence than other victims of violent crimes, and that confidentiality of victims' records be guaranteed. It even supported the "concept of rape crisis centers" when established by local and service organizations and not the federal government. But it rejected the concept of marital rape.

Most interestingly, the report expressed no opposition to birth control or contraception. In fact, before calling for a human life amendment and promoting "conscience clauses" to protect individuals' or institutions' right to refuse to participate in abortion, the report declared that "with today's modern methods of contraception (even after rape), no woman today should ever become pregnant unless she chooses to do so."[70] Oklahoma delegate Phyllis Lauringer told the press that "women's rights just need to be kept within limits so they do not overstep the bounds of someone else's rights— like the life of an unborn child. Women's rights have a limit just like everyone else's rights." Another woman in their delegation, Winnie Matthews, added, "We are all concerned [about women's rights], but the difference is in our solutions."[71]

Attempts to present the Minority Report for consideration by the full conference produced the last and most dramatic display of conflict between feminists and conservatives. As the three-day conference was near an end, Joan Gubbins tried again to present the report, but the chair, Addie Wyatt, ruled her out of order. At that point Gubbins and Thomson alerted the other delegates, "We're walking. Let's go!"[72] Followed by about a hundred delegates, some carrying "Pro-Family" and "Republicans Against the ERA" signs and all chanting "Rubber Stamp! Rubber Stamp!" they marched out of the hall.

With reporters in hot pursuit, Gubbins staged an impromptu press conference, blasting the National Plan of Action as a costly scheme that would "increase the federal intervention into the lives of freedom-loving Americans," enable homosexuals "to marry, adopt children, and teach in schools," take away "the right to life of the unborn," create a "unisex society," and "mandate the Federal government as a cradle to grave 'sugar daddy.'" Declaring that "we have done what our constituents elected us to do—vote against this IWY farce," Gubbins told the crowd of reporters, "I'm going home to put a turkey in the oven for my family!"[73]

In the end, IWY leaders agreed to include the Minority Report and it was printed in full in their final report to the president and Congress.[74]

Much of the conservative protest at the National Women's Conference was visual, meant for the cameras. Pro-family delegates wore daisy-topped gold ribbons with "Majority" on them. During discussion of the reproductive rights plank, they held up a banner saying "Give Life a Chance." According to Thomson, "abortionists" in the crowd, "whipped to a frenzy by anti-life speakers . . . ripped down" the banner "featuring pictures of happy babies," and "in its place, these chanting, jeering women had hoisted a sign: 'If men could get pregnant, abortion would be sacred.'" After the vote on the plank including abortion, pro-family delegates staged a demonstration in which they held up giant color photographs of aborted fetuses. When the gay rights plank was adopted, conservative delegates rose and, at a signal from Joan Gubbins, turned their backs to the podium and bent their heads as if in prayer.[75]

The conservative delegates played to the press, and the press was eager to offer them a forum. But it was not always to their advantage, for it brought to light disturbing signs of bigotry. When asked about Klan intentions for Houston, Dallas Higgins, the Klan leader's wife, who had denied Klan membership, said, "If *we* were going to disrupt the convention *we* would have done it in Mississippi." She then complained that conference organizers were punishing her by denying her request for a private hotel room and believed they planned to make her room with a "black lesbian." Communists, she said, were attempting to "take over our country" through the women's movement and the IWY, having tried and failed to do so through the blacks. At her side, her Klan leader husband agreed, stating, "Women's rights and civil rights go hand in hand."[76]

When a reporter asked other Mississippi delegates about their all-white delegation with a Klan leader's wife, Billy Temple "hastened to deny that the women's rights movement had anything to do with civil rights or that the antis were segregationists." Few of the participants knew each other beforehand, he insisted, and they "had not found out until the voting was over that they had elected someone with Klan connections." But his wife, Norma, noted derisively that, while the conservative coalition was organized through churches, most of the blacks at the conference were invited by the pro-ERA people who were "promising the poor and underprivileged a gravy train."[77]

In some cases white racist and antifeminist sentiments blended with anti-Semitism. According to Andrea Dworkin, attending the conference as part of the press corps (with *Ms.* credentials) and gathering material ultimately used in her 1983 book *Right-wing Women*, some southern delegates charged that the feminist movement was part of a Jewish conspiracy to encourage women to work outside the home and to have abortions, both of which reduced the birth rate among "Aryan" women. One of the men from Mississippi (whom she assumed was a delegate, since he was sitting with the other delegates on the floor) acknowledged that he was in the Klan—indeed, a high-ranking officer. Additionally, she reported, he characterized homosexuality as "a Jew sickness" and "a lust that threatened to wipe out the family," adding that homosexual teachers should be found out and run out of any town they were in and up to "Jew New York."[78]

Of course, conservative leaders had no control over the many people—including white supremacists and religious bigots—who responded to their call to come to Houston and protest. Dworkin had a lengthy interview with a minister and would-be governor of Oklahoma, the bearer of a notorious sign that appeared everywhere in the press saying "Woman's Libbers, E.R.A. LESBIANS, REPENT. Read the BIBLE while YOUR [*sic*] ABLE." Dworkin wrote that the man was convinced the women's movement was a communist conspiracy, "an internal poison in America." He claimed that the Russians invented abortion and their agents insidiously implanted it in America, after which it was spread by liberals and Jews in an effort "to exterminate Americans and damn them in the eyes of God." Now the communists had new tools, lesbians in the women's movement who would turn the United States into Sodom and Gomorrah, leading God to hate the United States and destroy it and allow the Russians to win. Dworkin said that she was asked "a hundred times" if she was Jewish; then, "despite my clear presence as a lesbian-feminist with press credential plastered all over me from the notorious *Ms.* magazine, it was as a Jew that I was consistently challenged and, on several occasions, implicitly threatened. Conversation after conversation stopped when I answered that yes, I was a Jew."[79]

Other bigots who came to Houston gave the members of the press corps who hoped for violence exactly what they wanted, only outside the hall. On opening day of the conference, a group carrying signs that read "Who Needs Jews, Dikes, Abortian [*sic*] and Communism" and "L.A. White Women Oppose IWY Convention, Reds, Feds, Dykes and Kikes" got into a fight in front of the convention center. As they tried to enter the conference, a group of delegates returning from a joint minority rights/lesbian caucus off-site started chanting "Ku Klux Klan, Scum of the Land," then joined hands and surrounded the protesters.

One man punched the woman closest to him, knocking her to the ground, and a full-fledged brawl broke out. The press scrambled to cover it and then to interview the group afterward. One of the men told reporters that he and the others were members of the Klan, but another one hastened to correct him, saying they were members of the "Christian Defense League," not the Klan. Their leader, a minister in the New Testament Church of God and the New Christian Crusade Church, said the League had five hundred members and ten thousand supporters nationally. They believed that a group of Jewish bankers controlled governments around the world as well as the UN and that the U.S. government and the IWY were "lackeys" of the conspiracy. One of the women stated, "The biggest lie ever told is that the Jews are the chosen people." The League, she said, believed that "white Christians are the chosen people" and that mixing of races, "mongrelization," is the cause of the increasing immorality in the world.[80]

Such brazen expressions of bigotry were embarrassing to those conservatives who hoped to distance themselves from "extremists." The Utah delegation issued a press release denying any connection with the Klan. They claimed that IWY organizers "sought to destroy our credibility by name-calling and trying to link us with extremist groups like the Ku Klux Klan."[81] LDS members were especially sensitive to charges of racism because of recent attention to church policies that denied black Mormons any role in their clergy. (These would be officially revised in 1978 allowing black *men* to serve.) When the vote was taken on the minority rights plank, the Utah delegates rose in support. Many of them considered it the high point of their conference participation. Feminists were also thrilled. According to the *Salt Lake City Tribune*, "minority women and other delegates rushed to the Utah delegation." A tearful Coretta Scott King embraced State Representative Georgia Peterson, the Utah delegation leader.[82]

Moments like this encouraged many feminists to believe that conservative women were coming around to their views, but that was rarely the case. Alice Rossi, the sociologist and IWY commissioner conducting a study of IWY participants, applied the "colder instrument of a quantitative analysis" as a corrective to impressions that could be misleading. Her study showed that their experiences solidified the conservative delegates' antifeminist views, giving them a "sharpened sense of their differences" from their opponents. In addition, she found that the pro-family delegates emerged from the conference more united than those who had supported the plan. One of Rossi's most interesting findings was that qualitative comments the feminists made on their surveys indicated that "they admired and respected these [conservative] delegates for the strength of their convictions under the difficult circumstances of being a very small minority at an overwhelmingly Pro-Plan convention."[83]

Phyllis Schlafly also heaped praise on the pro-family delegates who "faithfully fulfilled their commitment to serve in the IWY conference. They sat like ladies in their seats through hour after hour of harassment, procedure instead of substance, pro-ERA propaganda speeches, and sheer boredom." Wrote Schlafly, of the women who had to give up their weekends to participate in the Houston protests, the delegates were making "the biggest sacrifice of all because they remained inside the IWY convention hall listening to offensive speeches or trivial procedures, and enduring the hostility of the lib delegates, while having to miss the fun and inspiration of the Pro-Family Rally." For that, Schlafly wrote, "they deserve our admiration and thanks."[84]

On Saturday November 19, 1977, the day of the Pro-Life, Pro-Family Rally, Rosemary Thomson, Dianne Edmondson, and other embattled conservative delegates at the IWY conference waited anxiously for news, eager to hear how their carefully laid plans turned out. Meanwhile, Elaine Donnelly and other CRC leaders ("fortunate" enough not to be elected as delegates) were busy with rally preparations.[85]

Donnelly later described her "strange fear of apprehension" as her cab approached the Astro Arena that morning. "It was such a tremendous risk, and I knew the national press would focus on empty seats as evidence that the Pro-Family Coalition couldn't compete with Women's Lib." She could see the stadium seats were almost deserted. But as the driver turned a corner into the parking lot, there were row after row after row of buses from dozens of states "neatly lined up" and a huge crowd "streaming toward the Arena from cars, campers, and vans."

As the opening ceremonies approached, the crowds kept pouring in. There were "entire families with homespun signs, fathers carrying children piggyback, waved and blew kisses to friends. The happiest thing I heard as I picked my way through the crowded aisles to reach the front was that there were no more seats! People were hugging each other, tears in their eyes," she said. "No one could believe the rally was such a thundering success."[86]

Donnelly recalled being "deeply moved by the spectacular panorama" before her. "Children's choirs, workingmen, mothers, and young people of all races, religions, occupations, and nationalities joined in spiritual and patriotic songs." For her, as media chairman, the biggest thrill was the huge turnout from the press. Disgusted by the way the press was "bedazzled" by the celebrities at the National Women's Conference and "heaped attention on the feminist stars and first ladies," she loved it that network correspondents and reporters "were everywhere with microphones, cameras and surprised expressions," adding, "Washington writer Barbara Howar—darling of the Jet Set—sat stiffly in the front row looking stunned!"[87]

Dianne Edmondson's sensational tape aimed at arousing Christian conservatives had served its purpose. By church buses and other means, they poured into Houston for the rally. One group traveled for twenty hours. Another took forty-four hours to get to Houston. There were fifty busloads from Tennessee alone, attributed to the work of Eagle Forum leaders Shirley Curry and Tottie Ellis, who had filled the buses with the aid of Baptist, Catholic, Church of Christ, as well as pro-life groups.[88] One fourteen-year-old Church of Christ member told reporters the trip took eighteen hours each way, but said that was OK: "I'm here to stand up for what's right." They planned to start the trip back right after the rally without even stopping for dinner.[89] A thirty-four-year-old mother of nine from Bismarck, North Dakota, said she felt she had to come, that her state "had to be represented at a pro-family rally," adding she strongly opposed the ERA because it would give so much power to the federal government. She had driven to the rally with six women in a yellow van and told an interviewer, "We felt we had the Lord knocking on the top of the van all the way down."[90]

From Utah came two chartered planes that flew in Saturday morning and returned home Saturday night; the 150 protesters were picked up by local LDS church members and shuttled to the hall. According to the *Salt Lake City Tribune*, "the parking lot was jammed with row after row of buses with signs reading, 'The ERA Is a Turkey,' 'God's Way,' and 'God Knew What He Was Doing—He Made Adam First.'"[91]

A constant theme was that this rally, unlike the IWY conference, was paid for by private citizens there on their own dime. These were simply individuals making sacrifices great and small for the cause. Myrna Tulloch of Bountiful, Utah, a Right to Life member, said, "People are caring enough and fear the IWY enough to give up Christmas and a few extra presents to be here." Another woman told reporters her neighbors took up a collection to cover her expenses.[92]

Elaine Donnelly described being touched by the presence of people of all races, but the press described the scene differently. Judy Klemesrud of the *New York Times* noted that the audience was almost all white. Sociologist Ruth Brown, attending the rally as part of her research, counted but three African Americans in the entire audience. Other reporters also noted that it contrasted sharply with the gathering it was protesting: whereas the IWY conference was historic in its diversity, the number of blacks at the Pro-Family rally could be counted on one hand.[93]

Donnelly's comment reflected the organizers' sensitivity on race. White racists were clearly part of their constituency, but this was not something they wanted on display at the rally. They denied the Christian Defense League, the white supremacist group that had gotten into a street brawl outside the National Women's Conference, permission to distribute its literature at the rally.[94] They included two African Americans among the speakers.

Rally organizers were proud to include a large contingent of men whose presence contributed to the pro-family, antifeminist vibe. There were several male speakers, including former Houston mayor Louie Welch, head of the city's chamber of commerce and most likely the unnamed "Christian businessman" who had helped Hobbs to secure the venue for the rally. The Astro Arena had been constructed while he was mayor. The current mayor, Fred Hofheinz, was very supportive of the National Women's Conference. He had hired the city's best-known feminist, Nikki Van Hightower, as the nation's first official women's advocate, and she had worked hard to bring the NWC to Houston. When the Houston City Council abolished her position earlier in the year, Mayor Hofheinz moved her to his office, where she continued the same duties. Hofheinz had appeared onstage at the opening plenary to give a welcome.

Welch was clearly on the side of the conservatives. In 1977 he presided over the Houston Chamber of Commerce, which refused to support the NWC. At the Pro-Family Rally, Welch gave the welcome, saying, "I believe that the future of this nation depends upon the maintenance of the family as the strongest single unit in our society."[95]

According to Judy Klemesrud of the *New York Times*, the speakers sat on a blue-carpeted platform in the front of the enormous arena, "underneath a large American flag and big red letters that spelled out the words, 'From Us to the President and Congress.'" The sign referred to the signed resolutions that had been pouring into the Pro-Life, Pro-Family headquarters for months, supplemented by thousands more brought to Houston to the rally. Boxes filled with the signed petitions were prominently displayed on the stage behind the podium. To the right of the podium the Oklahoma pastor's sign, "Woman's Libbers E.R.A. Lesbians REPENT Read the Bible While Your [sic] Able," was visible.[96]

Fort Worth businessman Lee Goodman, acting as master of ceremonies, started out the rally with: "This is the most significant day in the history of our country. This is the day that we saved life." Pastor Paige Patterson, president of Criswell College in Dallas, prominent and influential in the Southern Baptist Convention gave the opening prayer.[97] After that, there was a parade of flags and a roll call of the states. One woman described the sheer joy of being there with other conservative Christians, watching the presentations of the flags from the fifty states "with glistening eyes" as each state reported on the numbers of buses and rallies that indicated such tremendous support for the pro-life, pro-family message.[98]

The line-up of conservative stars then delivered speeches that, according to Schlafly, were "well worth the long, tiresome bus trip to Houston." In her speech, "Why a Pro-Family Rally," Lottie Beth Hobbs insisted that the "barriers" the feminists at the National Women's Conference were seeking to do away with were not "barriers" at all but "safeguards" that "wise men and women of the past have carefully built . . . into our system." Removal of these safeguards, she declared, would "plunge us into social and moral destruction."[99]

Nellie Gray, wet-eyed as she approached the podium, said, "I actually weep that we have to have a rally such as this in America," holding up a red rose representing an unborn child. "We have a mentality in America that is anti-life, anti-family, anti-God," one stemming from a "group of special interests who seem to think that it [abortion] is to their interest. But we know that it is not to the interest of America or the people or the preborn child."[100] The "women-libbers," she declared, "are trying to dress up abortion, but no matter how you dress it up, it comes down to killing a baby."[101]

Dr. Mildred Jefferson wowed the audience, especially those whose main concern was abortion and who were proud that she had come to Houston and put the full force of nation's largest and most influential pro-life organization into this fight against federally funded feminism. One self-described "rank and file" soldier in the pro-life movement was thrilled by Jefferson's presence and her words. "Suffice to say," Rita Burke reported later in the *National Right to Life News*, "the words of Dr. Mildred Jefferson, our own Massachusetts physician surgeon and President of National Right to Life, held all spellbound" when she declared, "Womanhood is on the move and we will not retreat until we push back every threat to womanhood, home and family. By denying the right to life of the unborn, women are denying themselves the right to be a woman."[102]

A famous missionary and writer, Elisabeth Elliott, gave an address called "Let Me Be a Woman" in which she emphasized that "the highest freedom is obedience to the divine designer of us all."[103] *Atlanta Constitution* reporter Carole Ashkinaze, in an article, "God Stronger Than Carter, Stop-ERA Leader Declares," wrote: "Over and over, speakers invoking the Scripture and the name of Jesus Christ attempted to assure the ERA opponents that they are not in the minority as they are at the National Women's Conference, where fewer than twenty-five percent of the elected delegates share their views." Repeatedly, she reported, speakers whipped the crowd "into a feverish state of excitement" as they spoke of "God's design" for society and the "holiness of their battle to preserve the sanctity of the family."[104]

Among the speakers were several who denounced homosexuality and the feminists' call for tolerance and protection against discrimination. One speaker, introduced as "a former homosexual," gave credit to God for his "change in life style" and drew loud cheers for declaring that homosexuality "is an abomination unto God." Many carried signs denouncing homosexuality. Anita Bryant's taped message, like Schlafly's address, reminded listeners at the rally that they had divine power on their side, saying, "If God be for us, who can be against us?"[105]

Clay Smothers, a Dallas newscaster and representative in the Texas state legislature, also blasted "sexual perversion" as well as abortion, which he denounced as murder. As a legislator he had introduced a bill to bar homosexuals from college campuses in the state.

Smothers was one of the two blacks chosen as speakers, but his performance at the rally did anything but dispel the appearance of racism. Instead he played heavily to white supremacist as well as homophobic sentiments.

Smothers, a recent convert to the Republican Party, had been a George Wallace delegate to the 1972 Democratic National Convention—although he ended up nominating himself for president.[106] He played to the audience with statements like "President Carter says the minority vote put him in office. Well, he's wrong. It was the Christian vote!"; "Don't dare stereotype me"; and "I don't like Andrew Young," the African American civil rights veteran appointed by Carter as the United States's representative at the UN. "I don't care how black he is . . . I'm tired of government welfare, all I want is opportunity." According to the *New York Times,* Smothers "repeatedly brought the crowd to its feet with such declarations as 'I have enough civil rights to choke a hungry goat' and 'Mr. Carter, I want the right to segregate my family from these misfits and perverts.'"[107]

"We are tired of Bella Bella," Smothers told the crowd. "I am sick of Presidents' wives backing this mess, especially Mrs. Ford's joyous reaction to the infamous Supreme Court Pro-Abortion decree! It is time men and women start obeying their God-given convictions of truth. Mr. Carter has to stand up and say, 'I don't want to be President if I have to support murder and sexual perversion.'"[108] When the crowd started interrupting almost every sentence he uttered with wild applause and amens, Smothers exulted, "I am overcome. I feel like I'm in a Black Baptist church!"[109]

In Schlafly's view, the "most exciting part of all" was when Lottie Beth Hobbs announced "that there were 300,000 pro-family petitions massed on the stage, and they are still coming in." The crowd adopted the four Pro-Family Resolutions in a single vote. These proposals, Schlafly declared, not the feminists' National Plan of Action, "speak for the majority of Americans."[110]

Of course, their whole purpose was to mobilize the majority of Americans to continue their crusade for righteousness into the future, to put their nation back on the right course, and to reassert its identity as a Christian nation. To do that, they must take back their country from the politicians who had been catering to the feminists. The rally was about religion, but it was also about politics. In fact, it was about the need to support politicians who had no qualms about combining religion and politics, but not in the manner of Jimmy Carter, who they believed had fully backed the IWY as well as the ERA. Schlafly blasted the government for having spent taxpayers' money to support sin and perversion, then played her trump card, reminding them that "we have someone on our side more powerful than the president of the United States."[111]

Congressman Robert Dornan was the last to address the crowd. He was the only national elected official on the stage, which underscored the point rally organizers wanted to make: the federal government was in the hands of officials who, as Dornan put it, approved of "sexual perversion" and the "murder of unborn babies in their mother's wombs." He, too, took aim at the president and at the First Lady, who played such a highly visible and supportive role at the National Women's Conference, and was loudly cheered as he declared his disgust at seeing Rosalynn Carter, Betty Ford, and Lady Bird Johnson on the stage with "Abzug."[112] The *National Right to Life News* likened his delivery to "the fire and passion of a fundamentalist preacher." In any case, Dornan insisted that "the real majority are those who love and respect their god." He declared to thunderous applause, "We will tell Jimmy Carter that the real rally for America was here."[113]

The main point of Dornan's address was reflected in its title, "Let Your Voice Be Heard in Washington." According to one report, he exhorted the crowd, "Go to your congressmen and senators. Tell them what you think of their voting record on IWY and how you expect them to vote in the future."[114] He then turned to the huge crowd of reporters crowded around the stage, urging them to tell the truth about what had happened that day at the rally and predicting that, if they did, it would change the course of history.[115]

The "truth" Dornan wanted to be told was that conservative women had created a new and enduring "pro-family" coalition, a force politicians would now have to reckon with. Some politicians, including Dornan and Senator Jesse Helms, were clearly already on board. The Pro-Family Rally signaled the advent of a unifying movement that joined single-issue conservative campaigns related to abortion, the ERA, child care, education, and gay rights into a common defense of the traditional family.

Organizers of the Pro-Life, Pro-Family Rally considered it to have been an enormous success. Recalling how they had persevered "in the fact of insurmountable odds," a jubilant Rosemary Thomson proclaimed, "The Lord had pulled off an undeniable miracle—with a little help from Christian women."[116]

In the December 1977 *Phyllis Schlafly Report*, Schlafly proclaimed it "one of the most amazing events that ever happened." Elaine Donnelly claimed that, in addition to the enormous crowd that filled the seats, aisles, and balconies of the Astro Arena, local safety officials had "kept another 2,000 listening outside." The *National Right to Life News* reported that rally leaders had chartered "a small plane to fly the petitions to Washington and place them at the feet of the President" but had to get another plane: "A small plane would not hold them all."[117]

Their impressive numbers, their successful petition campaign, and their unequivocal rejection of the IWY agenda commanded full coverage from the press. *Time* magazine's cover story stated, "Cheer for cheer, epithet for epithet, the 'pro-family' gathering easily matched the ardor of its counterpart in the Sam Houston Coliseum, and its rhetoric was substantially greater."[118] According to the decidedly non-neutral *National Right to Life News*—which relished the wide media coverage of the rally and emphasized the role played by its leader, Dr. Jefferson—"the pro-family, pro-life conclave . . . outdrew and outscored the official gathering" held across town.[119]

James Kilpatrick, who had months earlier declared joyfully that the IWY might be the rallying cry of a resurgent right, was at the rally and jubilant. Elaine Donnelly later recalled finding him "writing notes and looking out at the huge, enthusiastic crowd from his perch behind a stack of petition boxes." Kilpatrick, she said, "marveled at the resolve and energy of the women and families in the arena, and predicted that the impressive event was only the beginning of something really big."[120]

The IWY meetings in the states and the massive Houston rally had electrified conservative women. Those new to political activism vowed to remain involved. Dr. Mildred Jefferson proclaimed that the silent majority had found its voice: "They are grumbling and will be heard from shore to shore and city to city."[121]

Two Mississippi women, just home from the rally, expressed what many others were thinking and feeling when they wrote: "Leaving Houston's Astro Arena, we felt we had witnessed a great breakthrough, a turning point for our country." Quoting Dornan, they predicted that if the press would only be fair in reporting what had taken place that weekend in Houston, "our representatives will realize the great silent majority is on the move to take the nation under God's guidance."[122]

CHAPTER 12

We Shall Go Forth

We shall go forth from this place
Proud of the things we've done,
Sharing the things we've won . . .
Taking with us the pride of knowing we can decide
We shall not fail.

—MARGIE ADAM, SONG PERFORMED AT
THE CLOSE OF THE NATIONAL WOMEN'S
CONFERENCE, NOVEMBER 21, 1977

IWY leaders returned from the National Women's Conference upbeat. They began the New Year 1978 with high hopes and big plans. In a cheery version of its newsletter, *Update 9: After Houston,* sent out to conference participants in February, the IWY Commission proclaimed the Houston conference a great success. To the Smithsonian went the banners and buttons, the posters and funny hats, to take their place alongside the sashes of the suffragists—and Susan B. Anthony's gavel, loaned by the museum for use at the Houston conference. Now it was time "to build on the great spirit and unity that emerged from our historic meeting" and make sure it was followed with action.[1]

After Houston: Update 9 brought news of extensive follow-up activities in the states. Across the nation, supporters of the National Plan of Action were hard at work to promote its implementation, establishing speakers' bureaus and task forces, holding hearings and town meetings, and making sure IWY records were safely stashed in libraries and archives. In many places IWY state coordinating committees worked closely with state commissions on women, meeting with governors, legislators, and members of Congress and urging them to take action on the recommendations produced by state IWY meetings and the Houston conference.[2] Most delegates engaged in follow-up activities of some kind. Alice Rossi's survey of delegates after they returned home showed that 86 percent gave a talk about the National Women's Conference to at least one local group; 60 percent gave an interview to a local paper; and 52 percent appeared on a local television or radio program.[3]

The February *Update* also brought word that, in Washington, IWY Commission members and staff were already working with women in Congress on legislation related to the Plan. In January 1978 they met at the White House with Midge Costanza and "leading women in the Administration" to develop implementation plans. They began setting up the Continuing Committee of the Conference mandated in Houston that was to monitor progress on the Plan after the IWY Commission filed its report and disbanded. In addition, the newsletter described plans for the commission's "profusely-illustrated" 220-page final report entitled *The Spirit of Houston: The First National Women's Conference: An Official Report to the President, the Congress and the People of the United States.*[4]

After Houston: Update 9 ended with lyrics from the song performed at the end of the conference by California singer and songwriter Margie Adam, which captured their exuberance and confidence.[5]

On March 22, 1978, IWY Commission members presented *The Spirit of Houston* to President Carter at a highly publicized formal ceremony at the White House. Representatives of state IWY coordinating committees joined in the fanfare. Carter was effusive in his praise for their work, noting how delighted "Rosalynn, Judy, and Midge, three members of my family," had been with the conference and the "tremendous success that you ensured in bringing to the forefront of American consciousness the determination and competence, idealism, persistence, courage, sound judgment, of the women of our Nation." In his speech, probably drafted by Costanza, Carter noted that "it was a potentially explosive situation and one that could have brought a great deal of disharmony and discouragement to those who have been in the forefront of the fight for women's rights," but that, "under the superb leadership of Bella Abzug, and with your help, the conference was a complete success." The president then assured his listeners that he, his cabinet, and the "members of my official and personal family" would work to "keep the spirit of Houston alive."[6]

Midge Costanza had promised her audience at the closing session of the Houston conference that her boss would take the report seriously, and he did. As mandated in the original bill, the president was obligated to submit a formal response including his recommendations for action to Congress within 120 days of receiving the report. Even before the March presentation, Carter's domestic policy staff, headed by Stuart Eizenstat, was working to assess progress already made on the goals enunciated in the National Plan of Action and to determine what additional steps would be necessary to implement it.[7] But the president was not as sanguine about the Houston conference as his remarks at the ceremony suggested. Within the administration there were growing concerns about public perceptions of the IWY and its leadership.

Carter, having managed to garner support from social conservatives and liberal feminists in his 1976 election bid, never gave up on the idea that he could retain the support of both. As president he continued to meet with conservative religious leaders, hoping that their shared identity as born-again Christians would keep them in the fold and that they—like the feminists— would accept his moderate stances on social issues, including his compromise position on abortion. Yet the IWY had created a yawning chasm between these groups and Carter was about to fall into it.

First the president tried to step back from the abyss. Carter realized he had to deal with the controversial IWY program he had inherited but he wanted to contain the damage—an approach that would get him in trouble with both sides.

In part, Bella Abzug was the issue. The Houston conference had made its presiding officer an icon in the eyes of many women's rights supporters. On the other hand, conservatives already hostile to Abzug were further inflamed. In the December 1977 *National Right To Life News*, editor Bill Moloney roundly rejected a suggestion from the National Council of Christian and Jews that "Right to Life" and "Right to Choose" advocates find a way to reconcile, saying, "Try sitting down at breakfast some morning to dunk a bagle [*sic*] with Bella Abzug, who said as recently as Nov. 13 that 'anti-abortion forces are linked with such ultra right wing groups as the Ku Klux Klan.' Put yourself on a love-seat at Tiffany's with this broad-beamed belter who has so much guff that Howard Cosell in the next booth sounds like a Trappist."[8] Even among feminists there were many who feared repercussions based on controversial stances taken in Houston, and some blamed Abzug.

With the March presentation ceremony looming and the IWY Commission soon to disband, Midge Costanza had urged Carter to re-appoint the commission or establish a new presidential commission to carry out the Plan as called for in the final resolution adopted in Houston. Costanza pressed hard, declaring that failure to do so "would result in a historic and catastrophic discontinuity in Presidential commitment to the concerns of women. It would be the first time since 1961 that no commission or advisory council, directly accountable to the President, was operational. To the public this could be interpreted as a retreat at the highest level of government, from a commitment to equality for women."[9] Costanza was under considerable pressure from Bella Abzug and Gloria Steinem to get Carter to agree. Costanza joked with Carter about how dealing with Menachem Begin and Anwar Sadat had given him a far easier day than she had had with Steinem and Abzug, who kept calling to ask, "Has he made a decision yet?" Carter repeatedly delayed, saying, "Give me the report. Let's work with Congress and see what we can do."[10] Finally he agreed to appoint a new commission, the National Advisory Committee for Women (NACW), but defined it as a solely advisory body with no authority or budget.

Still, there was the question of who should lead it. Should he appoint Abzug? Once again Rosalynn Carter counseled him against it, but after Eizenstat and Carter's press secretary Jody Powell advised him to continue with Abzug, he gave in.[11] To offset Abzug's polarizing reputation, Carter sought a more moderate feminist to cochair the committee.

Carter's first choice was Cleta Deatherage, an Oklahoma Democrat and member of the state legislature who had supported the embattled ERA. She had also served on the Oklahoma IWY coordinating committee. But Deatherage, who hoped to continue her previously promising political career in the state where conservatives totally overran IWY supporters, publicly refused to serve with Abzug. Carter, Deatherage said, wanted someone to rein in Abzug, something no one could do. More importantly, she wanted "to try to forget that IWY happened," adding that like "a lot of people" she was tired of national women's movement leaders who were out of step with the majority of American women. Deatherage was angry that the IWY had saddled Democrats like her who supported women's rights with a divisive and politically ruinous agenda with the ERA deadline little more than a year away. She accused Abzug of having caved in to lesbian activists in the summer of 1977, influenced by her designs on the gay vote in her quest to become mayor of New York. It was an embarrassing episode and clear indication that not all feminists had come away from Houston happy.[12]

Carter then turned to Carmen Delgado Votaw of Maryland, a leader of the National Conference of Puerto Rican Women and one of his appointees on the IWY Commission. Votaw was actually suggested by Abzug and was known for her wisdom and calm demeanor. She accepted. This time Carter also appointed an honorary chair, his daughter-in-law Judy Carter, a staunch ERA advocate and IWY supporter who, like Rosalynn Carter, was committed to securing ratification and working hard to gain the support of more traditional women. Judy, described by the *New York Times* as having "a tough mind behind the magnolia-blossom exterior," could perhaps add a southern sensibility to the group and soften its radical image. On June 20, 1978, the president announced the members of the National Advisory Committee on Women. The forty appointees included many holdovers from the IWY Commission and represented a wide diversity of ethnic and political affiliations. But once again the appointees consisted solely of feminists.[13]

The holdovers included labor leader Addie Wyatt; Claire Randall, general secretary of the National Council of Churches of Christ in the U.S.A.; Mildred Jeffery, National Women's Political Caucus president; Koryne Horbal, a Democratic National Committee's women's caucus member and U.S. representative on the UN Commission on the Status of Women; Sey Chassler, editor of *Redbook*; and Eleanor Smeal of NOW. Significantly, National Gay Rights Task Force leader Jean O'Leary was again appointed.

Notable newcomers included Unita Blackwell, an African American woman from Mississippi, a former sharecropper, and one of the Mississippi Freedom Democratic Party members who had challenged the seating of the state's all-white delegation at the 1964 Democratic National Convention. In 1976 she had been elected mayor of Mayersville, Mississippi. As a member of her state's IWY coordinating committee in 1977, she denounced the takeover of the state meeting by white conservatives, telling the press, "Even if they say they are for God, country, and family, they're the same group of people that have always oppressed black people" in the state.[14] The NACW also included Billie Nave Masters, who had served in Houston on the Indian Women's Caucus; Tin Myaing Thein, who was cochair of the Asian and Pacific Women's Caucus; and Carolyn Reed, secretary-treasurer of Household Technicians of America and a member of the Commission on the Status of Women in New York City.

Carter appointed several celebrities, including Erma Bombeck, famous for her newspaper columns, and Marlo Thomas, actress and producer, well known for her *Free to Be . . . You and Me* record and television program advocating gender-neutral child-rearing and rejection of gender stereotypes. Lane Kirkland, secretary-treasurer of the AFL-CIO, was another new member. Esther Landa, national president of the National Council of Jewish Women, was appointed, as well as several other leaders of national women's organizations, including Piilani C. Desha of Hawaii, president of Business and Professional Women's Clubs, and Marjorie Bell Chambers, the president of the AAUW.

The president also chose two women who had distinguished themselves in Houston and were rising stars among the Democrats: Ann Richards, a county commissioner in Texas, and Maxine Waters, a member of the California legislature and the California Commission on the Status of Women. He also appointed Gretta DeWald, director of the Women's Division of the Democratic National Committee. Two prominent Republicans, Mary Crisp, the cochair of the RNC, and former IWY Commission Presiding Officer Jill Ruckelshaus, also came on board.

Relations between the new committee and President Carter, however, were less than ideal. Abzug and other commission members saw themselves as advocates for the National Plan of Action. Carter saw them as advisers on women's issues, who as his appointees, were expected to be supportive. The committee expected him to meet with them, at least in the beginning, as he often did with new presidential commissions, but Carter preferred that they be debriefed by his staff. And whereas the appointees had come to equate support for feminism with support for the agenda adopted in Houston, Carter did not see things that way. Moreover, he was a fiscal conservative seeking to limit government spending and more interested in downplaying the controversial conference rather than adopting new and expensive programs.

As a committee than a commission, the National Advisory Committee on Women had no investigative authority nor funding or office space other than what they could persuade various federal agencies to contribute. Alexis Herman, director of the Women's Bureau, allowed them to use three small offices in the Labor Department and Abzug spent weeks on the phone "cadging supplies, equipment, and staff workers from other government offices." The new cochairs set up task forces to monitor implementation of various aspects of the National Plan of Action until the committee's first meeting in early fall 1978.[15]

* * *

Meanwhile Midge Costanza, the IWY's crucial advocate for feminism within the White House, was losing influence. Ever since she was appointed to Carter's senior staff, there had been tension between her and male staffers who did not share their boss's interest in feminism and regarded her as an unwelcome token. In their eyes she was an interloper promoting her own concerns and not a team player. It made things worse that she was the first person within the administration to call for the resignation of Bert Lance, their Georgia buddy who was accused of financial improprieties. They complained about her openly to the press and leaked stories about her as a weak manager of an ineffective office.[16]

In April 1978, Carter replaced Costanza in the public liaison post with Anne Wexler, a deputy undersecretary of commerce who had impressed Hamilton Jordan as "the most competent woman in Democratic politics in this country." Wexler was a supporter of the women's movement, but she was also a political pragmatist who worked to persuade rather than to demand in order to get the interest groups she worked with behind the president, and not vice versa. Costanza was still on the White House staff, but her responsibilities narrowed to "women's issues."[17]

Costanza continued to believe that her friend Jimmy Carter was deeply committed to women's rights despite their difference of opinion on federal funding of abortion. As she represented the president at women's events, she continued to assure feminists that Carter was on their side. But to some it seemed that Carter relied on Midge Costanza, along with his wife and daughter-in-law, to represent him and his commitment to women's rights while he kept his distance.

Back in November 1977, just before the Houston conference, an article titled "The Trouble with Midge" appeared in *Newsweek* that was peppered with unfavorable comments from her coworkers. Costanza had met with Carter for reassurance. He described the meeting in his diary: "Met with Midge Costanza, who's been quite concerned about adverse publicity lately. She's been buffeted badly, and I reconfirmed my confidence in her and asked her to stay closer to me. I've been concerned about her involvement in the abortion and gay rights business, but she takes a tremendous burden off me from nut groups that would insist on seeing me if they couldn't see her."[18]

Costanza was despised by social conservatives, perhaps not as much as Bella Abzug, but close. An article in the January 1978 *NRL News* entitled "Skids Being Greased for Midge Costanza?" gleefully declared, "It seems certain that President Carter will have to make a choice before long: to jettison the 'loud mouth pushy broad' as she calls herself, or to put up with continuing nettlesome acts bordering on defiance from one of his own staff members." The author recounted an array of Costanza offenses, including her groundbreaking White House meeting with gay rights leaders and her criticism of Carter's position on denial of public funding of abortion.[19]

By the summer of 1978, Costanza critics outside and inside the administration were calling for her dismissal. But she continued to push hard to achieve feminist goals and to affirm the president's support even as other feminists became unhappy with Carter, dismayed by recent ERA defeats and his position on abortion, which was unchanged.

With the deadline for the ERA less than a year away, feminists began to focus on ERA extension. In January 1978, Costanza had met with Eleanor Smeal and Arlie Scott of NOW to discuss ERA strategy and the possibility of extending the deadline for ratification. In February she convened an expanded planning session that included representatives from ERAmerica, the National Women's Political Caucus, the Federation of Business and Professional Women, and the League of Women Voters, in addition to NOW.[20]

On July 9, 1978, on the one-year anniversary of the death of ERA champion Alice Paul, a massive march on Washington organized by NOW, the largest ERA march to date, was followed by a day of lobbying on Capitol Hill. Defying a heat wave, a crowd estimated at between forty and fifty-five thousand women and men—dressed in white like the suffragists in the massive parade Paul had organized in 1913—marched down Pennsylvania Avenue to demand ERA ratification and an extension of the deadline. A fund-raiser followed that night, featuring an auction (including one of Abzug's hats), and a concert by singer Margie Adam.[21]

There was also a rally where marchers heard speeches by dozens of celebrities and politicians, including Jean Stapleton, Marlo Thomas, Betty Friedan, and Eleanor Holmes Norton. All spoke of their frustrations but also of their determination to buckle down and get the ERA ratified. "Everybody's for it but we don't have it!" Bella Abzug told the crowd. "They have allowed a highly organized minority to stop the will of a majority. We assumed that we would have it without difficulty and that was a mistake." Congresswoman Barbara Mikulski told the audience to "be prepared for a very long haul. We will work this summer like we have never worked before . . . We will march into history . . . Mrs. Schlafly, wherever you are, eat your heart out!"[22]

Elizabeth Holtzman, leading the drive for ERA extension in the House of Representatives (with Birch Bayh taking the lead in the Senate), stated,

"We need an extension of time to fight the lies about the Equal Rights Amendment. It is a fulfillment of the American dream and not a threat to anyone . . . Time is on our side and we will win." Organizers urged the audience to besiege every member of Congress. Former congresswoman Patsy Mink declared, "We must not leave Washington . . . without having a firm commitment, yes or no, from every member of this body. And if they dare to turn us down . . . we will turn them out on the next election day!"[23]

Increasingly frustrated, feminist leaders like Steinem, who had softened her sometimes radical rhetoric in the past year in an effort to make the government-sponsored National Women's Conference a success, warned of growing impatience: she told the crowd, "The lawful and peaceful stage of our revolution may be over. It's up to the legislators. We can become radical, if they force us. If they continue to interfere with the ratification of the ERA, they will find every form of civil disobedience possible in every state of the country." According to the *Washington Post*, Steinem was loudly cheered as she cried, "We are the women our parents warned us about, and we're proud!"[24] Several speakers demanded more support from Carter. Reporters noted that many in the crowd "jumped up and cheered" as Abzug "urged President Carter to go on national television and make a major speech about 'the human rights of American women' as he has for human rights abroad."[25]

The *Washington Post* also reported that Midge Costanza "won an ovation with an attack on anti-ERA leader Phyllis Schlafly," who had earlier in the day on ABC-TV's "Issues and Answers" denounced the demonstrators as "the same crowd who went down to Houston last November . . . a combination of federal employees and radicals and lesbians who spent $5 million of our taxpayers' money." But Costanza's announcement that she had "brought a message of support from her boss" immediately prompted "a mixture of moderate applause and wide-spread boos and cries of 'Where is he?'"[26]

Neither the president nor any other members of the Carter family were present at the rally. Many demonstrators felt that they should have been, as they were vacationing at nearby Camp David. Still, in Costanza's speech, she loyally affirmed Carter's commitment to the cause, which other speakers questioned.

At the end of July 1978, President Carter presented his report to Congress regarding the administration's response to the National Plan of Action. Many feminists were disappointed, viewing it as primarily a statement about accomplishments already made, not promises of further action. By then Costanza's duties—with the exception of liaison for women's issues—had been reassigned, and her office was moved to the White House basement. She resigned on August 1, 1978.[27]

What a few feminists knew but kept to themselves, and what conservatives would have shouted from the rooftops had they known, was that Midge Costanza and Jean O'Leary had been involved in a romantic affair even before she became one of Carter's senior aides. When Costanza left Washington, she and O'Leary left together to live in California.[28]

Afterward, Carter increasingly relied on the more moderate women's rights advocates within his administration. Ironically, these included Sarah Weddington, a southerner far more like the Carters in temperament and style than Costanza, but famous—or infamous—as the lawyer who had argued *Roe v. Wade* before the Supreme Court. Carter chose Weddington as Costanza's replacement in an apparent attempt to appease feminists that further outraged conservatives. Pro-life groups protested, while many feminists criticized Weddington for "compromising herself" by working for Carter, who opposed federal funding for abortions. Weddington's offer to meet with the National Advisory Committee for Women at their next meeting was declined.[29]

After reviewing Carter's report to Congress (sent September 17, 1978), NACW cochairs Abzug and Votaw concluded that, in his effort to rein in federal spending, the president had ignored and would continue to ignore many of the proposals suggested in the National Plan of Action. They requested that Carter meet with the committee. The group was distressed that, while Carter praised the National Plan of Action in his message to Congress as a "national agenda to achieve women's full rights and equality" and said he was working to carry it out, he was nonetheless proposing a $15 billion cut in major domestic spending at the same time he was seeking significant increases in spending on the military. Abzug worried that the cuts would "seriously hurt jobs programs, welfare reform demonstration projects, preventive health services, vocational and sex equity education programs, family planning services, and other programs of importance to women." She concluded that, "Once again, women's needs were to be sacrificed to the bottomless pit of the Pentagon." In addition, Carter was also advocating guidelines that would lock women into discriminatory wage patterns that would keep them from closing the "notorious wage gender gap."[30]

After some delay, Carter agreed to see them. On short notice Weddington invited the committee to meet with him at the White House—after four o'clock in the afternoon on November 22, 1978, the day before Thanksgiving, and for a mere fifteen minutes. Nevertheless, committee members scrambled to book flights and on November 21 gathered in Washington, D.C.[31]

Abzug had not yet arrived and Votaw was presiding at the meeting to prepare what they would say to the president, when it soon became clear that many committee members were frustrated and angry. They believed they had serious and important issues to discuss concerning the programs being advocated—or not—by the man who had pledged to do for women what LBJ had done for blacks. Yet Carter seemed to have little time for them. Brownie Ledbetter of Arkansas recalled, "Most of us wanted to be home with our families at Thanksgiving" and "we were really pissed" that they had come all that way—some from as far as Hawaii, California, and Texas—for a fifteen-minute meeting. Ann Richards got up and said, "We need more than just a photo op!" Maxine Waters and Addie Wyatt introduced a resolution to call off the meeting and request a longer one with time to discuss the serious issues they wanted to take up with the president. A few minutes later they voted to cancel and went home. Ledbetter said, "I must say, everyone felt good about it."[32]

When Abzug arrived in D.C. and heard the news, she begged them to reconsider, aware that she would take the heat for it. Brownie Ledbetter recalled that she "hardly got home before Bella was on the phone saying, 'How could you let this happen, for God's sake? He is the president of the United States!' And she was just furious that we had made that strategic error." Waters also recalled that Abzug "felt that this was going to create a huge problem." She knew that they would be "coming after her."[33] Abzug and Votaw talked with Carter on the phone, trying to "soften the effect" and smooth things out—which Abzug thought had worked. "He apologized for the brevity of the scheduled meeting, sounded very friendly and understanding, and agreed to a longer session at a future date."[34]

When a meeting with the president finally took place on January 12, 1979, scheduled with only a week's notice, tensions were still running high. Again the committee met the day before to prepare for the meeting and review a statement they planned to present to the president. In it they expressed their concern for the fate of the ERA and urged Carter to make it a top priority. They also addressed the administration's budget recommendations and objected to the proposed cuts in domestic programs and increases in military spending. One of the few male members, Richard Rossie of Georgia, regarded by most members as "the president's man" on the committee, objected to the statement for touching on subjects outside the committee's jurisdiction and expertise. Others, including *Redbook* editor Sey Chassler, wanted it revised to be stronger and less supplicating in tone.[35]

Again, Abzug was not present for the preliminary meeting: she was on the West Coast, honoring a long-scheduled speaking engagement, and flew all night in order to make it back in time for the Friday meeting with Carter. But she agreed with the wording and content of the statement, and with a press release, "President Carter Challenged on Social Priorities by National Advisory Committee for Women." Votaw had sent it to the White House Press Office for distribution after the meeting.[36]

According to Votaw, in anticipation of the meeting, she and Abzug carefully laid out a plan. The cochairs were to make opening statements, and then nine committee members would discuss issues from the statement concerning the ERA, education, employment, health, the need to appoint more female judges, and the upcoming UN conference on women. If Bella talked too much, Votaw was supposed to signal her by tapping a pencil on the table.[37]

When Carter arrived, he had seen the press release that criticized his proposed budget, faulted him for failing to advance the National Plan of Action, and announced that the committee would discuss these matters at a press conference in the Rose Garden following their meeting. As the meeting began, Carter spoke first, visibly angry and red in the face. Abzug got riled and argued back at the president as Votaw's pencil tapped away in vain.[38]

Interestingly, people present at this highly consequential meeting remembered it in very different ways. As Abzug recalled, she opened the meeting by introducing members of the committee and Carter blew kisses to several he knew personally. He apologized for the brevity of the scheduled meeting back in November, then said he had become discouraged about his relationship with the committee, which he hoped would be better in the future. The cochairs and the nine committee members made their points as planned, and the meeting ended up lasting at least twice the half hour that had been scheduled.[39] Abzug recalled that she "spoke with feeling" but "at no time did I shout or get angry. I thought we had made our point and that our working relationship with the White House would be greatly improved . . . I never displayed my over-celebrated temper to him."[40]

Brownie Ledbetter recalled Carter was on the attack from the beginning, saying (in her paraphrased version): "I appointed you. You're my commission. How could you do this to me? I supported you on ERA. I didn't agree with you on abortion, but I let you do your thing. What do my inflation policy and my military policy have to do with women?" But

Ledbetter thought that Abzug handled it "brilliantly." "It was so totally respectful, without the slightest bit of rancor. With great care, she explained what those policies had to do with women. It was beautifully done." She, too, thought things would be all right.[41]

Eleanor Smeal remembered it differently. She recalled that, as they left the room, she was very worried, thinking, "'My God. We've just been bawled out by the president of the United States.' He was talking in a normal tone of voice but I felt we had been read the riot act."[42]

Abzug and Votaw went outside in the Rose Garden for the press conference. According to her supporters and the press, Abzug was gracious and conciliatory. Sey Chassler recalled her telling the press it had been a good meeting, stating, "We made some points with the president, and he has agreed to meet with us more frequently, and there will be a greater liaison with the White House with the commission and on the future of the platform of issues that the previous commission has produced."[43]

Then Abzug was tapped on the shoulder and given a note saying that Hamilton Jordan wanted to see her before she left. He also asked to see Votaw—first. Jordan told Votaw that the committee's criticism of the president was untenable. They were going to fire Bella but wanted Votaw to stay on and lead the committee. She protested, explaining that the decision to issue the press release was made by the committee without Bella even present.[44]

Then it was Abzug's turn. This time Jordan brought in the president's counsel, Robert Lipshutz. Jordan handed Abzug a letter of dismissal, saying that Carter had decided to replace her. Abzug was shocked and demanded an explanation. Jordan cited the decisions to cancel the November meeting and issue the critical press release. She explained that she had been present for neither decision and said she was being made a scapegoat. Lipshutz bristled, called her a liar, said he hated the word "scapegoat," and added "Next you'll be saying we fired you because you're Jewish."[45]

Abzug said that her being fired would hurt the president with women. But, realizing the decision had been made, she asked for time to talk with the committee about how it should be handled. She said she would like her departure to be handled quietly, to allow her to resign voluntarily and without a fuss, explaining that she was having personal problems: her beloved husband, Martin, had just had a heart attack. According to Abzug, Jordan snapped back at her, saying if she was having personal problems she should not be heading a committee.[46]

Abzug left, badly shaken, and headed back to the National Advisory Committee on Women office at the Labor Department. As she recalled, when she arrived she was "in tears at the shabby way she had been treated." But the office phone was ringing, with Hamilton Jordan on the line. He insisted that she resign immediately because the press already knew she was leaving and was demanding information, and he needed to know what to do. Abzug "told him to do whatever he pleased" and hung up.[47] Brownie Ledbetter arrived at the commission office and heard Bella on the phone with Jordan, asking for time to handle the crisis and sobbing. She was saying, "For God's sake, let me resign. Give me that bit of dignity." "It was a real screw job," Ledbetter said. And "the press knew the whole time."[48]

According to news reports, senior staffers Jordan, Powell, and Gerald Rafshoon had decided Abzug should be fired as soon as they had seen the advisory committee's press release. A *New York Times* story sympathetic to the White House reported that, after Jordan showed the draft press release to the president, Carter was irritated and made a tentative decision to fire. However, according to one presidential aide, "it was a decision that was reinforced by the meeting itself." Another staff member said, "She lit into him in front of nearly forty other people."[49]

The *New York Times* article stated that the president told this committee that was "formed in the wake of the stormy National Women's Conference in Houston" that he recognized the committee's importance and wanted to work more closely with them, but "that its confrontational politics sapped the strength of the Administration's efforts on behalf of women." Moreover, he was quoted as telling them, "there should be no need for the White House to 'cringe' in advance of a meeting with a committee set up to provide advice and assistance." The article also pointed out that, according to White House officials, at the end of the meeting "the other commission members rose and applauded Mr. Carter as he left the room." Then they "drew Mrs. Abzug aside and cautioned her to make a positive statement about the session to the reporters waiting outside the West Wing." One "White House official" informed the *New York Times*, "Bella was told that the relationship with the committee had been neither positive nor productive and that the President felt it required new leadership."[50]

According to the *Washington Post*, however, Carter knew going into the meeting that they would be firing Abzug afterward, but he and his staff chose not to do it beforehand and risk an angry confrontation with the committee. Carter's male senior staffers, who seemed quite pleased with themselves over Abzug's abrupt dismissal, readily leaked the story of Abzug's departure to the press, while Sarah Weddington refused to comment. Apparently, along with the president, the male advisers presumed that most women on the advisory committee and across the nation did not think Abzug represented their thinking, that Carter would take political heat only from the far left, and that the president would look strong and decisive. Steinem later stated, "We found out that Carter's staff were telling him that he was looking 'weak' and that he should do something to look strong and macho" and "Bella was sacrificed to that need."[51] No doubt it occurred to them that social conservatives would be especially pleased: the White House was now purged of the more radical feminists, with Costanza and then Abzug dismissed in humiliating fashion.

Gloria Steinem and other commission members immediately called upon the entire commission to resign in protest, and the majority, including cochair Votaw, did so. Steinem dubbed it the "Friday Night Massacre," and with it Bella Abzug became a feminist martyr.[52]

Afterward members of the National Advisory Committee for Women hit the telephones asking all the members to resign in protest. The majority did so, ranging from lesbian rights leader Jean O'Leary to Republican Party leader Mary Crisp. Jill Ruckelshaus also resigned. The White House had counted on Votaw to stay on but she also quit (though politely, even going by the White House to submit her resignation letter in person). The departing committee members held a press conference, which, according to the press "began with a wake-like solemnity but took on the atmosphere of a rally." They issued a statement saying, "The President's response was not to the issues we brought to him, but rather to use our co-chair, Bella Abzug, as a scapegoat in an effort to suppress our independence."[53]

Abzug's abrupt dismissal set off a media firestorm. Across the nation scores of editors and pundits weighed in on Abzug's personality and reflected on expectations of women in politics in comparison to what was expected of men. Some said Abzug's fall from political grace was a warning about what happens when a woman is seen as overly ambitious, aggressive, or outspoken. Some women candidates reported being advised not to wear a hat while campaigning lest they be associated with the belligerent Bella. Abzug believed that, had she been a man, the same qualities would have been seen as signs of strength. Her firing also produced a flood of mail, some of it from conservatives congratulating Carter for the decision. Schlafly sent a glowing telegram, her singular endorsement of a Carter decision.[54]

Much of the mail, however, came from people protesting the president's deliberate humiliation of a feminist icon. Even those who thought Bella was too radical or overly brusque believed that the former congresswoman, who had so effectively championed women's rights while in office, deserved better treatment. A Harris poll showed that Americans disapproved of the firing by almost two to one. After Abzug appeared on the popular *Phil Donahue Show,* she received a flood of mail from outraged women. One wrote, "When President Carter fired you, he fired me." Betty Friedan denounced the firing as an insult to the women's movement.[55]

The firing of Abzug also dealt a serious blow to the unity feminists achieved during I W Y 1977. The committee members who resigned told the press they believed "all women and men of like mind will refuse to participate in an advisory committee in which disagreement with the president and legitimate criticism are not acceptable." But many feminists who were moderates and pragmatists remained on the committee, believing it was essential that feminists continue to work with the president. They were also given assurances of more access to Carter.[56]

Some of those who remained, such as Ann Richards who had risen so rapidly from county commissioner to presidential adviser, no doubt hated to see it come to an early and abrupt ending. Civil rights movement leader Unita Blackwell, who had overcome poverty and racism to become mayor of Mayersville, Mississippi, in 1976, also continued on the committee despite that fact that she loved Bella and never forgot Abzug's death-defying trips to Mississippi in the 1950s to defend Willie McGee. She said Bella had urged her "to stay on and fight."[57] However, Carolyn Reed of the Household Technicians of America resigned, winning admiration from Steinem and others. Steinem said that, even though Sarah Weddington was "semi-threatening people who quit," Reed told the press, "As a household worker, I've learned never to confuse access with influence."[58]

The remnant of the committee and Carter's new appointees served on a reconstituted President's Advisory Committee on Women. It was led temporarily by Marjorie Bell Chambers, the AAUW president who had led the Women's Conference Network—the "Truth Squad" that had defended I W Y before Congress and the nation in the fall of 1977. Chambers praised Bella as "a prime leader of the women's movement" and publicly criticized the manner of her firing but thought feminists needed to hold on to their positions, noting that "the opposition is already attacking the membership of the committee."[59]

The *New York Times* commented that Marjorie Chambers, a Republican and "reputed to be milder and more low-key in her approach than Mrs. Abzug," had stepped "into the thunderous breach," adding that Chambers actively supported the E R A but had "avoided involvement in more controversial issues such as lesbian's rights and abortion." Shortly thereafter, with Weddington and Carter eager to smooth things over, the advisory committee was invited to have dinner with the Carters at the White House where he said he had no intention of limiting the range of their issue considerations, expected them to be independent, even at times critical, but hoped they could work closely together.[60] Later Carter appointed as permanent chair Lynda Bird Johnson Robb, daughter of President Lyndon Johnson and wife of Virginia lieutenant governor Charles Robb, and a moderate feminist who had appeared alongside her mother at the Houston IWY conference. According to Sarah Weddington, Robb accepted only after being assured by Carter that "the committee would be independent and that she could call him directly."[61]

All of these women were willing to work with Weddington, Midge Costanza's replacement as Carter's point person on women's issues. Catherine East apparently had confidence in her. East wrote to Rosalynn Carter urging her to get her husband "to consult with you, Judy [Carter] and Sarah Weddington on women issues rather than Jody Powell or Ham Jordan, who manage to hurt the ERA and the women's movement with every move." But Abzug and her supporters regarded Weddington as an apostate. Again the press was more than ready to highlight disagreement among women, in such articles as the February 1979 *Washington Post* article "The Weddington Way; Can a Soft-Spoken, Tough-Minded Southern Lawyer Prevail on Women's Issues in the White House Where Midge Costanza and Bella Abzug Struck Out?" Among other things, Weddington's critics complained that she got credit for securing ERA extension, a victory for which Costanza had fought so hard. The bill championed by Congresswoman Elizabeth Holtzman and Senator Birch Bayh was adopted in December 1978, but Costanza was not invited to the bill signing.[62] In a way the situation began to resemble the Ford years, when more radical, left-leaning feminists criticized the administration from outside while moderate feminists remained inside, though perhaps not as fully a part of "the establishment" as during the Ford presidency.

In the eyes of Abzug and her supporters, the mandate of the reconstituted President's Advisory Committee headed by Lynda Robb was too limited. This new committee, Abzug wrote later, was "even forbidden to lobby for women's programs on Capitol Hill," which left the National Plan of Action "without an official advocacy presence there." The Continuing Committee of the Conference (CCC), a large, diverse body set up by Abzug and Votaw as directed by the National Plan of Action, still existed, however, and over the years would work toward implementation of the Plan as best it they could from outside the government.[63]

Despite all the uproar over Abzug's dismissal, President Carter was still eager to be—and to be seen as—a supporter of the women's rights cause. He and Rosalynn took pride in what they saw as a strong record of support for women's issues, including the appointment of an unprecedented number of women.[64] Later, in an interview with the author, they said it was understood between them that, if the opportunity came up, he would appoint the first woman to the Supreme Court. He even had one in mind, Shirley Hufstedler, a distinguished judge serving on the U.S. Court of Appeals whom he appointed as secretary of education. And although many feminists said he did not do enough for the ERA, Carter believed he had done all that he could. Both the First Lady and daughter-in-law Judy Carter spent tremendous amounts of time promoting ratification. The three of them, plus Walter and Joan Mondale, working first with Costanza and then with Weddington, fought hard to line up the votes needed for ERA extension—despite cautioning from Stuart Eizenstat, who suggested there was little congressional support for it. Rosalynn Carter insisted that, for her, the failure to secure ERA ratification was one of the chief disappointments of their four years in the White House.[65]

Feminists were particularly upset with the president over his position on abortion, which had remained unchanged. Many had hoped they could convert him on this issue. But Carter held firm to his position of being personally opposed to abortion but unwilling to support a constitutional amendment to ban it. He accepted *Roe v. Wade* but was also willing to accept and enforce the ban on federal funding for abortions. This position many feminists could not stand.[66] They found Carter exasperating and he felt the same way toward them. After leaving office he remained angry at the feminist leaders he had dealt with as president, saying to the author—with fervor—that if you did not agree with them on everything, they did not give you credit for being with them on anything.[67]

Carter also acknowledged that his support among social conservatives had eroded steadily during his presidency but said, in comparison to the defection of many feminists, "*that* didn't hurt my feelings!"[68] Throughout his administration he continued to support the movement and to woo feminist voters. But he also tried to woo and repair relations with social conservatives furious about gay rights leaders being invited to the White House and the federal government aiding and abetting feminism, particularly through the IWY.[69]

*   *   *

After Houston, feminists found themselves on the defensive, trying to make further progress and avoid losing ground. Despite extension of the deadline of the ERA to 1982, they failed to win more states. Many politicians who had voted in Congress for the ERA opposed the extension. Some, including those seeking cover for a change of mind, insisted that they still supported ratification, but extension was of questionable legality. But the many votes against extension clearly reflected the power of the backlash.

The fight to gain the last three states continued until the bitter end in 1982. Much of the fighting took place in the South where most states had not ratified, including Carter's home state of Georgia. Some feminists seemed to be giving up, frustrated that the ratification battle was consuming so much time and money, resources that they could put to use on other issues. Mary Heriot, a NOW leader from South Carolina, recalled, "We believed in the ERA, but we did not anticipate that we would be working on it for such a long time." It meant that "all our other goals went on the back burner" and when it failed we had "absolutely nothing to show for it." Her colleague Tootsie Holland resented the fact that, even after it was clear there was little chance of ratification in her state, national NOW leaders insisted that the ERA be their top priority. "The reason we worked on the ERA [in its last years was] because we were in the capital city and we had to. They made us."[70]

ERAmerica had actually commissioned a study to assess the chances an extension of the ERA deadline would yield a victory—something to ponder, given that the right would most likely continue to benefit from the controversy. But the organization continued to fight—no longer under Elly Peterson and Liz Carpenter, who became honorary cochairs, but under new leaders from the next generation, Democrat Sharon Percy Rockefeller (Charles Percy's daughter married to West Virginia governor John D. "Jay" Rockefeller IV) and Republican Helen Milliken, (First Lady of Michigan from 1969 to 1983).[71]

Despite the lack of progress on the ERA, the movement continued to win victories in the courts. These included legal battles against economic discrimination and sexual harassment. According to a prominent legal scholar, federal courts seemed to be governed by a "de facto ERA" and to rule repeatedly in support of gender equality. During the battle over the ERA, as conservatives repeatedly insisted they had no quarrel with the basic concept of women's equality but considered a constitutional amendment unnecessary, they appeared to have conceded the basic issue of women's equality.[72] Yet the ERA was hugely important as a symbol as well as a means of furthering feminist goals. The inability to get the ERA ratified suggested to many Americans that the feminist movement was flagging and fading—which was very dispiriting to feminists.

From 1978 to 1982 there were feminists as well as politicians who gave the ERA only token support, but most refused to give up. It seemed unbelievable that after so much success the women's rights movement could not get the handful of additional legislators needed to get the last three states. In battleground states, ERA coalition leaders tried to learn from past mistakes, to elect more pro-ERA candidates in the off-season (at that time many legislatures met biennially), and to lobby more effectively during legislative sessions. There were tensions between national leaders of NOW and heads of ERA coalitions in unratified states. NOW leaders sent workers to bolster the efforts of locals, but their approaches—such as sending NOW "missionaries" to Utah to take the ERA message directly to the people, door-to-door in groups of two, in a not-too-subtle dig at Mormons—were not always well received. In Illinois, local leaders worried that the influx of demonstrators from across the country demanding that the legislature ratify the ERA only made it more unlikely. And to Schlafly's delight some ERA advocates brought bags of pigs' blood to the capitol and spelled out the names of the anti-ERA legislators on the marble walls—a tactic, she said, that lawmakers found "unpersuasive." In North Carolina, seasoned ERA leaders, aware of sensitivity about "outsiders" in state politics, sought NOW's cooperation in keeping out-of-state activity out of the public eye. NOW leaders felt they were not getting enough respect and recognition, given all the money their organization was pouring into the campaign.[73]

Hard-pressed feminists in the South resented suggestions that they were at fault for not getting their states to ratify. For example, South Carolina NOW leader Tootsie Holland was outraged that "a bunch of Yankee women blame us. They really do! They say 'You women just don't know how to do it.'" In Holland's view these women had no idea what southern feminists were up against. She wanted to say to them, "Come down here and see how fast they run *your* ass out of town."[74]

ERA supporters struggled against such division and self-doubt. Liz Carpenter understood their frustrations: they had done everything possible to get three more states, yet "not a governor, a lieutenant governor, or a speaker was able to rally enough votes to get it through." Meanwhile, their opponents had only to rally "behind one woman who was able to cast fear in so many hearts." Carpenter urged them not to blame themselves for the amendment's defeat or to turn on one another. "A few leading ERA supporters claim that if we hadn't had to stage marches with the always present lesbian contingent, it would have been easier," she noted. Granted, feminists sometimes "looked a lot scrubbier than the pink ladies in their hats and gloves." But it was important, she insisted, to recall such arguments had been used "back in the suffrage days when even white leaders like Carrie Chapman thought it was wiser if her black supporters avoided the public efforts." Yet, Carpenter asked, "how can you justify a battle for inclusion when you exclude some of your own?" And she declared emphatically: "The ERA movement was not just for neat, tidy suburban Junior Leaguers. It was for all women."[75]

Carpenter's sidekick Elly Peterson believed that, "in retrospect, our problems began to mount in Houston. Most of us thought that it would be a plus for the women's movement and, of course, in many ways it was. But in terms of the ERA, it gave new impetus to the anti group" led by Schlafly, Peterson's old antagonist whom she regarded as "an opportunist—a born loser until she could identify *against* her own sex." Peterson was especially critical of the press for giving equal coverage "to a jack leg religious rally which wouldn't have been covered with one inch of press any other time."[76]

Peterson was distressed by the actions of other Republicans. It was deeply disturbing and painful that George and Lenore Romney, for decades her closest friends and allies in furthering progressive ideas in the GOP, had begun publicly opposing the ERA. Devout Mormons, the Romneys took the position of their church, with George Romney denouncing ERA supporters for engaging in a "concerted attack on the family and on morality as taught by the prophets through the ages."[77]

After Senator Orrin Hatch wrote a blistering denunciation of the ERA in a fund-raising letter sent out by the Conservative Caucus, Peterson sent an equally emphatic letter to him expressing her "dismay and shock" that a fellow Republican would do such a thing.

> That you are against it, is of no concern to me – that is your privilege and I understand the belief of your church. That you would use U.S. Senate stationery and the tactics of falsehood and fear to try to do this is unbelievable and in my many, many years of working for the Rep party I have never read a more bigoted letter.
>
> In calling the amendment "evil" are you, in your lofty post saying that the many Republican and Democratic Senators, Congressmen and Governors who have backed this bill are evil?

Do you realize how many of them are classed as "respectable conservatives" in the sense they would never stoop to this kind of tactic?

And to tell many of these women that there are state laws guaranteeing their husband will support them – really! Have you, in your great wisdom, decided why this is to be? How you can become a U.S. Sen and not understand the diff between private lives and legislation is beyond me . . .

Your tactics only confirm the opinion held by a majority of people today that we cannot put our trust in our elected officials. How difficult you make it for those who are really trying to upgrade this image and work for America.

For shame, Senator!
A saddened Republican worker,
Elly M. Peterson[78]

That a growing number of right-wingers, backed by "well-financed organizations" like the Conservative Caucus, were working against the ERA meant that it was in real danger, she told fellow ERA supporters. Pulling it "out of the fire before 1982 will take a massive effort." It was "absolutely necessary that we wake up, become hard-nosed politicians—and fight this thing TO WIN."[79]

As the 1980 election approached, feminists in the Democratic Party were divided over whether or not to back Carter's bid for reelection. During the hotly contested primaries they split between Carter and Ted Kennedy. Abzug passionately supported Kennedy and pressed feminist friends to join her. Some, including Gloria Steinem, felt she could not support Carter but neither could she support Kennedy. She agreed with her friend Robin Morgan who said (in reference to the 1969 Chappaquiddick scandal and Mary Jo Kopechne, who had drowned in Kennedy's car), "This we cannot live with. A dead woman's body. At the very least, just don't endorse."[80]

Eleanor Smeal said later that she believed "Bella's firing was the beginning of the end of Jimmy Carter's reign." Carter and his advisers, she said, believed he "was too far exposed to the left" with this commission. "So he picked on the most vocal person, and he wanted to get big press doing it . . . Carter thought, what was he losing: a few people in New York? They didn't understand the spirit of Houston, which had gone throughout the country." Moreover, his policies, including cutting the kinds of social programs advocated in the National Plan of Action, positioned him "so far to the right that he helped bring on a challenge by Ted Kennedy" in the 1980 primary.[81]

At the Democratic National Convention, Carter won the nomination but lost the fight over the platform. Bella Abzug, who headed the Kennedy forces on the platform committee, insisted on planks she knew Carter opposed. Together with Midge Costanza and leaders of NOW and the National Women's Political Caucus, she created a Coalition for Women's Rights that challenged the Carter camp on two key elements of the party platform: strengthening the ERA plank to include "the Democratic Party shall offer no financial support and technical campaign assistance to candidates who do not support the ERA" and amending the pro-choice plank to call for government funding of abortions for poor women. They won on both issues.[82]

Sarah Weddington tried, without success, to negotiate with the coalition to soften the wording of the planks; as she told the *Washington Post*, "They were unwilling to accept anything but their own language." Kennedy recalled that Abzug was "indispensable on the platform" but was really tough on Carter. He seemed almost sympathetic. "As I remember," he said, "she gave the Carter people a fit . . . Even after I conceded, they insisted on a roll call over things, which was sort of humiliating to them—you know, to get beaten again."[83]

Carter was left with a platform that was problematic. This included support for gay rights, the first time that a major party had endorsed this issue in its platform. The requirement that any candidate who wished to receive funds from the national party must actively support ERA ratification was deeply resented by some Democrats in unratified states—especially in the South, where support for the amendment seemed a futile sacrifice.[84]

Some members of the press criticized feminists for their hardball politics. The *Washington Post* reported, "feminists, in effect, held a gun at Carter's head. Eleanor Smeal, president of the National Organization for Women, threatened that her group might throw support to Independent presidential hopeful John B. Anderson if the ERA plank failed." But liberal Democratic women believed, as Betty Friedan put it, "In order for us to swallow our bile and go for Carter, we have to have some response. Males here are still treating us with contempt." Midge Costanza, referring to the Democratic Party's "equal-division rule" which allotted 50 percent of the delegate seats to women, boasted that women had defeated "the Democratic power bosses who dared to give us equal presence but not equal power . . . We used that presence and turned it into power." And, echoing President Carter's remark in 1977 after the Supreme Court decision upholding the constitutionality of the congressional ban on federal funding of abortions, she exacted a complete measure of revenge served cold with the statement, "Today we told the Democrats that life is, indeed, unfair."[85]

As the convention ended, leaders of the Democratic Women's Task Force hailed what Abzug called "a historic victory, an enormous victory" regarding the platform. "The White House . . . has always failed to understand 'women's issues,' but they may understand them a bit better today." Friedan for once agreed with Abzug, stating, "This renews my faith in the democratic process and the Democratic Party." The strong feminist planks in the platform, she believed, "may very possibly make the difference in the election" between President Carter and Ronald Reagan.[86]

Meanwhile, feminists at the Republican National Convention were having quite a different experience as their party chose to side with the pro-family movement. After Houston, Republican women who identified with the women's rights movement, encouraged by RNC cochair Mary Crisp and the Republican Women's Task Force, and stimulated to political action by the ERA battles and the IWY state conferences, had run for office in greater numbers. When they managed to win their party's nomination, they did well: in 1978 most of the women elected as state legislators were Republicans. In addition, Nancy Landon Kassebaum was elected to the Senate from Kansas, and Olympia Snowe was elected to the House of Representatives from Maine. According to Tanya Melich, exit polls showed that the Republican rank and file was not part of Schlafly's constituency or supporters of the Religious Right. GOP feminists hoped that "once a moderate man was nominated in 1980"—someone like George H. W. Bush, progressive Illinois congressman John Anderson, or even Gerald Ford—"the bigots in the party would again be a vocal minority with minimal influence."[87]

Instead, GOP feminists had watched with horror and frustration as the women of the pro-family movement and the religious right it had helped to create were embraced by leaders of the New Right, while "relatively moderate" Republican leaders did nothing to stop it. Instead, Tanya Melich later recalled bitterly that, even though most of the New Right leaders who were behaving "like the arbiters of correctness" for the GOP were "renegades, outsiders, [and] sometimes former Democrats," the Republican establishment "let them get away with it." Increasingly they "went along with the bigoted messages of the New Right's Republican candidates." In the past, she stated, many GOP leaders had "turned a blind eye to the southern strategy, seldom protesting against the racism that spewed forth from these candidates as long as it was effective" and helped to break "the hold of the Democrats on the South." Now, as Schlafly demonstrated that "misogyny could also win elections," few objected.[88]

The year 1980 would mark a major turning point in the history of the Republican Party: feminism was no longer to be supported but attacked. The two front-runners for the party's nomination, Ronald Reagan and George H. W. Bush, began the race with different positions on women's rights issues, but emerged as running mates united in support of a platform composed largely by the increasingly powerful GOP right wing. Both men had earlier supported the ERA and legalization of abortion, although Reagan had long since changed his position on these issues. George Bush was a different story.[89]

While in Congress, George H. W. Bush (and his wife, Barbara) had been backers of Planned Parenthood; as a Ways and Means Committee member he had been so tenacious in arguing for family planning that the chair had nicknamed him "Rubbers." Conservatives, including Rosemary Thomson, complained that as a congressman he had headed the "Republican Task Force on Population and Earth Resources," and sought to "assess the resistance to family planning by certain groups," concluding, "so far, it looks like opposition from religious groups . . . isn't too serious." After he left Congress in 1970, Melich recalled, he did not help the family planning movement in any significant way, but neither did he do anything to "dispel the perception that he was strongly pro-choice."[90]

As chairman of the Republican National Committee in 1973 and 1974, George H. W. Bush had been an ally of Republican feminists, and during the primaries, members of the Republican Task Force backed him. Mary Louise Smith, who succeeded Bush as RNC chair, later recalled: "We saw him as a moderate. He seemed to be on our 'wavelength.'" Bobbie Kilberg, who worked with Bush during Nixon's presidency, felt the same way. During the 1980 primary, in response to a presidential questionnaire distributed by the task force, Bush stated that his "commitment to equal rights for women is unequivocal" and that he believed "the Equal Rights Amendment will assure the rights of both men and women to equal treatment under the law." He also stated that he opposed a constitutional amendment to override *Roe*—although he "could support a constitutional amendment to give the states authority to regulate abortion."

As Melich recalled, only later did the GOP feminists realize that the Bush campaign was cultivating the New Right while they "executed a clever dual-ideology stratagem" that camouflaged it. Even when Bush showed clear signs of a change of heart, Melich and her allies continued to endorse him, assuming from his record and years of working with him in the GOP that he didn't really believe in many of the positions he espoused in 1980. Not until the GOP gathered in Detroit for the Republican National Convention did they realize the extent to which Bush had changed his "convictions" in order to compete in the altered landscape of GOP politics.[91]

By May of 1980, George H. W. Bush had realized he would not be the nominee and endorsed Reagan. He then laid low while his New Right allies maneuvered to get Reagan to select Bush as nominee for vice president. Although Reagan believed he needed a moderate as his running mate, choosing Bush posed a challenge, given his positions on the ERA and abortion. As Reagan issued the invitation, he specifically asked Bush if he would be "uncomfortable down the road," mentioning abortion in particular. But Bush responded that he had "no serious problem" with Reagan's position on any issues and "that the important thing was that he win the election in November." Questioned by the press about how he could support a platform that did not endorse the ERA and called for a constitutional amendment on abortion when he had supported ratification and opposed such an amendment throughout his campaign, Bush answered, "My view is that the big issues, the major issues in the fall, will be the questions of unemployment and the economy and there are going to be the questions of foreign affairs . . ." He then added, "I'm not going to say I haven't had differences at some point with Governor Reagan . . . [but] I'm not going to get nickel-and-dimed to death with detail." *Ms.* magazine later called Bush's action "one of the most dramatic and cynical policy reversals in modern American politics."[92]

Staunch social conservatives such as Jesse Helms hoped to get one of their own on the ticket with Reagan; in fact, at the convention Helms was maneuvering to get *himself* chosen to run for vice president. Many New Right and pro-family leaders opposed Bush. Before they would accept him as Reagan's running mate, Bush had to meet with them to assure them that his conversion had been sincere.[93]

Though forced to accept Bush, the pro-family and New Right forces had dominated the platform committee, leading the GOP to drop the party's forty-year record of support for the ERA. It also took a strong pro-life stance, not only opposing federal financing of abortions but calling for a "human life amendment." Going even further, they supported a plank making a pro-life position a prerequisite for appointment to the Supreme Court—an idea Charles Percy, now wary of standing up for feminist positions, nonetheless denounced as the "most outrageous I have ever seen in a Republican platform. Its design is the worst sort of extremism of the 1964 convention reincarnated . . . If moderate Republicans go home and feel they have been totally rebuffed, I hate to think what's going to happen to the party."[94]

Mary Crisp of Arizona, a feminist Republican and IWY delegate who had served on Carter's advisory committee before Abzug's dismissal, had been a faithful Republican for many years. She rose from a young Goldwater precinct captain to cochair of the Republican National Committee. But during the 1980 primaries Crisp had been fired for praising John Anderson's support for the ERA. In Detroit she made a dramatic speech before the platform committee, pleading with the members not to adopt these antifeminist positions, stating: "We are about to bury the rights of over 100 million American women under a heap of platitudes." Later, from the convention floor, Reagan rebuked Crisp, saying she "should look to herself and see how loyal she's been to the Republican Party for quite some time."[95]

GOP feminists and their male allies fought as hard as they could to keep the platform committee from retreating from the ERA and endorsing a human life amendment. Even Reagan's daughter Maureen, a staunch ERA supporter, appealed to the platform committee. But New Right leaders on Reagan's team worked with Schlafly and her supporters and kept firm control over the proceedings, while GOP feminists, largely shut out of the platform committee and delegate positions generally, were powerless to stop it. Only one pro-ERA governor, William Milliken of Michigan—whose wife, Helen, had followed Elly Peterson as Republican cochair of ERAmerica—addressed the platform committee on their behalf. Melich conjectured that most of the pro-ERA governors were Bush supporters and did not want to jeopardize his chances for the vice presidential slot. As in 1976, Elly Peterson appealed to Gerald Ford for help. But the days when he could turn things around were gone.[96]

Five years earlier, Jill Ruckelshaus had told the press, "Don't look for us in the streets. We have gone to the statehouse." Now the Republican feminists were back in the streets. On Monday, July 14, 1980, around twelve thousand ERA supporters, dressed in white, paraded in protest past the hall where the platform committee had defied their pleas and redirected GOP identity and strategy. Ruckelshaus, speaking on their behalf, declared: "My party has endorsed the Equal Rights Amendment for 40 years . . . Dwight Eisenhower endorsed ERA. Richard Nixon endorsed ERA. Gerald Ford endorsed ERA. But something happened in Detroit last week." She then cried out, "Give me back my party!"[97]

GOP feminists' protest march, as well as their efforts to publicize their party's change of heart on women's issues, got the attention of Reagan campaign leaders fearful about the impact on the fall campaign. The day after the march, Reagan met privately in his suite with sixteen of them, including Helen Milliken; former Ford cabinet member Carla Hills; Senator Nancy Kassebaum; Republican Women's Task Force leaders Pamela Curtis and Alice Tetelman; and his daughter Maureen. Former RNC leader Mary Louise Smith and Congresswoman Margaret Heckler were the chief spokespersons. Melich recalled that Reagan tried to use his legendary charm to reassure them he was not against women, but it failed to pacify these women, dismayed that their heartfelt positions were being abandoned.[98]

Then they asked: Would he be willing to appoint women to his cabinet and a woman to the Supreme Court? The women present recalled he "seemed to light up and for the first time became fully engaged." And to their surprise he agreed to do both, clearly liking the idea of being the first president to appoint a woman to the highest court in the land. During the campaign he would make that promise publicly.[99]

Reagan favored what he viewed as a compromise position, what would become known as his "Fifty States" policy. He promised to appoint a White House liaison to review state laws that discriminated against women and to enforce federal laws banning sex discrimination. The women pressed him to make a strong statement on women's rights during the convention. In his acceptance speech, Reagan stated that while "we have had a quarrel or two" on women's rights, it was "only as to the method of attaining a goal." He also announced his intention of establishing an alliance of all fifty governors and encouraging them to weed out and eliminate sexist laws and to monitor federal laws to ensure implementation and add more statutes if needed.[100]

After the convention, some Republican feminists swallowed their disappointment and worked to elect the Reagan-Bush ticket. Mary Louise Smith and Bobbie Kilberg organized a "Reagan-Bush Women's Policy Board" with an impressive number of GOP feminists, including Audrey Rowe, former NWCP chair, and Major General Jeanne M. Holm, Ford's special assistant for women's affairs. Tanya Melich later observed that in 1980, these women "believed they would be the conscience for women within the party. They knew they were in the minority, but they hoped to turn things around."[101]

However, Mary Crisp and many other feminists chose to support the candidacy of Republican congressman John Anderson, who ran as an independent and was courting the women's vote; indeed she became his campaign manager. The venerable Catherine East joined the Anderson campaign staff, developing a women's issue statement so attractive than even some feminist Democrats came out in support of the "unabashed feminist" John Anderson.[102]

In one of Crisp's speeches promoting Anderson—written by Catherine East and entitled "This Year in Detroit"—she declared that positions espoused by the GOP clearly demonstrated what a disaster Reagan's election would be. "The patriarchal zealots of the radical right are clearly in control of the Republican party, with Governor Reagan enthusiastically supporting their reactionary views on the role of women." If he was elected, "Efforts to achieve full partnership for women in all our institutions would be set back many years." Worse still, "Phyllis Schlafly might be Secretary of Health and Human Services and Nellie Gray would no doubt be Assistant Attorney General in charge of enforcing anti-abortion legislation." Crisp (and East) denounced the platform plank written by Senator Helms, "the chief architect of the Republican platform" that "would not even permit abortion to save the life of the mother." They warned—citing an assistant attorney general in charge of the criminal division of the Justice Department—that such a policy "would *require* that abortion be classified as first degree murder."

In rejecting its advocacy of women's legal rights, Crisp's speech declared, the Republican Party was rejecting its traditional conservative principles. "The rejection of the Equal Rights Amendment was heartbreaking to many Republican women who believed in the great traditions of the Republican Party." In addition, this speech written and delivered by "establishment" feminists predicted that the rejection of the ERA would only "spur on the militant fringe of the women's movement, who do not believe that women can achieve equality through legal means in our society." To "top it off," the GOP and Reagan had "the effrontery to call this a pro-family program." But the Anderson agenda "is the only truly pro-family program for America."[103]

Over a three month period, Mary Crisp spoke on Anderson's behalf in over thirty states, later saying that she believed that her "involvement in John Anderson's campaign was the most honorable action that I have taken in American politics." East resigned before the election, however, concluding that Anderson, though not an opponent of women's rights, did little to promote them.[104]

As the election approached, women's rights supporters had to confront the reality that Reagan might win. At that point, as Betty Friedan recalled, "some of the fine feminists and shrewd female politicians in the Carter Administration—Eleanor Holmes Norton, Anne Wexler—enlisted the help of Eleanor Smeal and myself and other feminist leaders, making a commitment to mobilize the full machinery of the White House for ERA and child care, *next time*."[105]

Democratic feminists, including NOW leaders, Friedan said, ended up "swallow[ing] the bile over Carter's insults and ineffectiveness, and supported him in the end out of realistic fear of the political alternatives." Steinem and Abzug even came out in support of him—or, rather, in opposition to Reagan—joining other feminists in taking out a full-page ad in the *New York Times*. But even then they could not seem to bring themselves to actually say the words "support Carter," instead stating emphatically that Reagan's election would bring disaster.[106]

It did little to affect the outcome. Whatever difference they were going to make in the 1980 presidential election had already been made. After Carter lost, Hamilton Jordan said that feminists had gotten—in the antifeminist Ronald Reagan—what they "richly deserved."[107]

CHAPTER 13

Onward Christian Soldiers

The battle for high morals and godly patterns always will remain unfinished business. Like the striving for perfection, there is no place to quit. Once a warrior enters the troop, it is a lifetime commitment. Let us put on the full armor and go forth to attain our objective of keeping America great by keeping America good!

—SHIRLEY CURRY, EAGLE FORUM NATIONAL
BOARD MEMBER, 1978

Like feminists, conservative women left Houston excited and proud. Their massive Pro-Life, Pro-Family Rally, they believed, had exposed as myth the idea that American women were united behind the women's rights movement. Equally important, it galvanized opponents of federally funded feminism who vowed to remain active and reap the political benefits of their newfound solidarity. Between the November 1977 show-down over IWY and the November 1980 presidential election—years in which feminists sometimes divided as they struggled to cope with an increasingly hostile political climate—women of the pro-family movement stayed the course set in Houston, not only frustrating feminists' efforts but inspiring the rise of the "Religious Right" and the right turn in the Republican Party.

Rosemary Thomson and other leaders of the pro-family movement rejoiced that their battle against feminists for control of IWY "woke up" women of traditional moral values. She compared the 1977 uprising of Christian women to the antebellum Great Awakening that fueled the moral reform movements of that era. "Our Pro-Family women now know who we are and where we are," she wrote in her 1978 retrospective, *The Price of LIBerty.* Just as important, the IWY experience served as their "boot camp," preparing them "for the offensive in the battle for our families and our faith."[1]

In fiery rhetoric loaded with military and religious metaphors, Thomson and other leaders of the conservative women's movement urged their followers to take back their country. "The front lines have been drawn . . . The storm troops of Women's Lib are entrenched in governmental outposts, one hand reaching into the public purse, the other upstretched in a sisterly clenched fist salute," she declared. God had "appointed the place" where believers had to fight: their mission was to awaken other like-minded women and men and spur them to action. "On Sunday morning we sing 'Onward Christian soldiers, marching as to war,'" Thomson reminded them. The time had come to show that they meant it, to fight the evil forces "engulfing our families, our churches, and our nation."[2]

After IWY, conservative women were not only fired up but also more capable and better trained for battle. The opportunities to develop skills in coalition building, convention planning, and media relations had been crucial, not so much for the women who had already been politically active through Stop-ERA and Eagle Forum, but for the newcomers mobilized in 1977.

Across the nation, women of the pro-family movement put these skills to work to roll back feminist gains. Among their primary targets were the state commissions on the status of women they accused of promoting feminism at taxpayers' expense. Efforts to do away with the commissions began in South Carolina in 1973, but their experiences during IWY made conservative women go after them with renewed purpose and vigor. After the stormy Ellensburg, Washington, IWY meeting in July 1977, conservative leader Susan Roylance demanded a referendum on the state women's commission: in a November vote—just weeks before the Houston conference—voters did away with the commission by a two-to-one margin. Returning from Houston, South Carolina state legislator Norma Russell went after her state's commission on women using "sunset laws," a newly popular means of eliminating bureaucracies by setting expiration dates. In all, nine states put an end to their women's commissions between 1977 and 1980.[3]

When unable to abolish the commissions, pro-family women insisted on the addition of conservative appointees. In a few states, including Massachusetts and New Hampshire, governors appointed commissions dominated by conservatives. The New Hampshire commission then voted to oppose the ERA, abortion rights, and shelters for battered women. More typically, adding conservative members resulted in gridlock and rendered the commission useless. Arkansas feminists, including Diane Blair, a leader of her state's commission and active in the National Association of State Commissions on Women, reluctantly concluded that, in the changed political climate after Houston, these commissions would no longer be a viable mechanism for achieving feminist goals.[4]

As for the ERA, after IWY, conservative women in unratified states were not only better organized but more determined than ever to kill it. The IWY experience had made a big difference, especially in states that had approved the amendment with little or no debate—with the result that, before IWY, there had been no public hearings or close votes that inspired conservatives to organize. In states that had ratified, movements to rescind gained strength, benefiting from the coalescence of conservatives into the pro-family movement. Rescission efforts peaked in 1979 in response to Congress's late-1978 decision to extend the ERA ratification deadline while refusing to accept the legitimacy of rescission.[5] Studies showed that for the rest of the ERA battle, the opponents tended to be more knowledgeable than proponents about where their political representatives stood on the amendment, more passionate about the issue, and more likely to take political action. According to one study, despite the national polls, within the nonratifying states there was a precipitous decline in support for the ERA that dropped below 40 percent.[6]

While feminists worked hard to elect new legislators who would aid their cause, the ERA's base of support diminished as politicians sensed a changing tide. In January 1978, Georgia blocked the amendment by a unanimous vote of the senate judiciary and the Alabama senate voted it down by a vote of 24 to 8. The following month, the South Carolina senate voted 23 to 18 against the ERA, and Virginia opponents shut down the amendment in a house committee. Florida announced that the legislature would not be voting on the amendment in 1978 because the sponsor removed it from the agenda realizing there were not enough votes for it to pass.[7]

In the late December 1978 congressional vote over extension, some who had voted for the amendment in 1972 demurred, insisting along with ERA opponents that, whatever the merits of the amendment, allowing extension but not rescission was unfair. Moreover, critics claimed extension was unconstitutional, as Congress approved the additional time by a simple majority vote rather than the two-thirds majority required for constitutional amendments. To highlight their refusal to accept extension as legitimate, Stop-ERA and the Eagle Forum held a huge "gala" in a Washington, D.C., hotel on March 22, 1979, the original ERA deadline. Schlafly declared they were celebrating more than the defeat of the proposed amendment. They were celebrating "the end of an ERA"—an "era of conservative defeats."[8]

Schlafly and many other conservative women attributed the change to the IWY. In a *Phyllis Schlafly Report* article entitled "The Houston Debacle," she wrote: "At the IWY event in Houston, the ERAers, the abortionists, and the lesbians made the decision to march in unison for their common goals. The conference enthusiastically passed what the media called the 'hot button' issues: ERA, abortion and abortion funding, and lesbian and gay rights. The IWY Conference doomed ERA because it showed the television audience that ERA and the feminist movement were outside the mainstream of America. ERA never passed anywhere in the post-IWY period."[9]

Women of the pro-family movement seized every opportunity to stoke conservative rage by spreading the word about the National Women's Conference and what had happened there. For instance, Oklahoma Eagle Forum members prepared a "display" of literature they claimed was gathered at the Seneca Falls South exhibit hall. The display, consisting of lurid and emotionally charged materials, became famous nationwide. Promoted in the *Phyllis Schlafly Report* as evidence of horrific misuse of federal funds by "radical and lesbian forces that are waging war on the American family," it was shown by conservatives in thirty states.[10] In February 1978, conservative women sponsored a "pro-family luncheon" in the Rayburn House Office Building for members of Congress at which they exhibited the "offensive and pornographic" display of "I.W.Y. materials" from Houston. They also presented the signed copies of the resolutions endorsed at the Pro-Life, Pro-Family Rally—by then almost one million in number.[11]

Conservative women insisted that all they had to do was show people the National Plan of Action to move like-minded women to action. One Houston veteran stated that the Plan was "the best recruiting tool I've ever had . . . I just spend twenty minutes reading it to them. That's all I have to do."[12]

Waging an all-out war against feminist-backed proposals, pro-family women won battles on many fronts. After President Carter announced his support for registering women for the draft, the Eagle Forum created the "Coalition

Against Drafting Women" and gathered twenty thousand signatures in protest. Both houses of Congress then voted down the proposal. When the Supreme Court ruled against registering women soon thereafter, conservative women claimed another victory. They were intent on retaining "women's right" to exemption. Limiting women's participation in the military was a particular passion of Elaine Donnelly's, as she was convinced it weakened the armed forces.[13]

Pro-family leaders also claimed victory in the September 1980 defeat of the proposed "Act to Prevent Domestic Violence," a major disappointment to feminists in the Carter administration who had worked hard for its success. The conservatives charged that centers for battered women were encouraging women to leave their families and were used as feminist training grounds. Conservatives, notably Senator Jesse Helms, argued it would promote "the disintegration of the family," prompting feminist columnist Ellen Goodman to write that, to the Religious Right, it appeared that an "intact family" was more important than an "intact ex-wife."[14]

Schlafly, Thomson, and other pro-family leaders were also proud of their progress in limiting abortion and preventing federal funding of it. Continuing the alliance with pro-life organizations forged during the 1977 fight against IWY, they worked hard to build support for the Human Life Amendment introduced by their ally Senator Jesse Helms. The eagerness of pro-life advocates to gain political power, and the fact that New Right leaders were willing and financially able to give them badly-needed support, pushed the pro-life movement further to the right.[15]

Pro-family movement leaders also worked with Helms to stop the United States from signing the Convention on the Elimination of All Forms of Discrimination Against Women (CEDAW), adopted at the IWY Mexico City conference in 1975 and passed by the UN General Assembly in 1979. At the 1980 "Mid-Decade conference" (of the 1975–1985 Decade for Women) held in Copenhagen to assess progress in implementing the World Plan of Action, Sarah Weddington gave conditional approval to the document on behalf of the United States. From the conservative women's perspective, CEDAW was totally unacceptable. Some took their cue from the Vatican, which opposed CEDAW because it promoted women's control over reproduction, which the Catholic Church feared would foster abortion.[16]

As Thomson saw it, CEDAW "defined 'equality' in terms of family planning and abortion rights, public child care, flextime in employment, domestic violence legislation, revisions of school textbooks and establishment of a New International Economic Order based on interdependence." Furthermore, she insisted, if approved by the Senate, CEDAW would have the same effect as ratification of the ERA, "superseding our own Constitution!" Schlafly declared that, once again, "Unable to persuade Americans voluntarily to go along with their censorship attempts, the fems are trying to get the UN to do this job for them."[17]

The U.S. failure to sign CEDAW stood in sharp contrast to nearly all UN member states. Most signed it right away, and CEDAW began to have positive effects on government policies regarding women around the world. That the Carter administration could not prevail over Helms and his pro-family allies was a clear and dramatic reflection of how much American politics had changed since the days when the Ford administration and a supportive Congress were eager for the United States to be in the vanguard in international efforts on behalf of women's rights.[18]

These victories reflected conservative women's success in convincing politicians that they were important to please. Their well-demonstrated ability to mobilize social conservatives and unite previously hostile religious groups had made quite an impression. Increasingly politicians, particularly Republicans, had concluded that by championing family values they could avoid these women's fury and gain their staunch support. Although feminists continued to perceive conservative women, including Schlafly, as pawns of men eager to legitimize their own opposition to feminism, these conservative women had changed American politics by demanding successfully that politicians stop supporting feminists and indeed stand up to them without compromise.

After Houston pro-family leaders had been courted by male strategists for the New Right who were determined to build a successful conservative movement and could not help but notice their success in rallying conservatives, including Mormons, Catholics, and previously apolitical religious conservatives politicized by the fight against the ERA, abortion, and the IWY. Men such as Paul Weyrich, Richard Viguerie, and Howard Phillips did all they could to assure that religious conservatives remained on the warpath, recognizing antifeminism as a powerful wedge with which to unite conservatives across class lines and break up the New Deal coalition. These men have often been credited—and claimed credit—for persuading the Republican Party to emphasize "the social issues." Recruitment of social conservatives, Viguerie later boasted, was the key to the GOP's success; by adding this "third leg" to the Republican Party's "two-legged stool—national defense and economic conservatives"—they strengthened the conservative movement and made the GOP competitive.[19]

New Right leaders made deliberate and highly successful efforts to recruit conservative clergymen such as Reverend Jerry Falwell to help them woo the Religious Right. At their urging, Falwell, who had once criticized African American ministers for political activism, totally abandoned his opposition to mixing religion and politics. In 1979 he founded the Moral Majority, which grew rapidly and began to wield considerable political power. Weyrich, a devout Catholic, and Phillips, a recent Jewish convert to Christianity, reached out to Baptist evangelist James Robison, who soon became the primary spokesperson for a group called "the Religious Roundtable," devoted to mobilizing Southern Baptists and other evangelicals.[20] There was little if any protest from pro-family women who considered enlisting men in their battle to defeat feminism to be a main goal.

Tanya Melich, who as a Republican feminist was bitterly opposed to Schlafly and what she stood for, nonetheless felt that Schlafly and other conservative women got little credit for what they had accomplished. For instance, Paul Weyrich, boasting about the crucial role of the Religious Right in the conservative comeback in the late 1970s, admitted that for several years he had tried and failed to convince southern preachers of the importance of political action. But he insisted that "what galvanized the Christian community was not abortion, school prayer, or the ERA" but the 1978 efforts of the Carter administration to deny tax-exempt status to religious academies on the grounds that they maintained segregation. Weyrich claimed that Christians "felt able to deal with these other issues [including ERA and abortion] on a private basis without having to be concerned over public policy." But the IRS threat made them suddenly make a connection between "their opposition to government interference and the interests of the evangelical movement, which now saw itself on the defensive and under attack by the government. That was what brought those people into the political process. It was not the other things." Richard Viguerie likewise insisted the IRS controversy was what "kicked the sleeping dog. It galvanized the Religious Right. It was the spark that ignited the Religious Right's involvement in real politics."[21]

The IRS crisis was certainly one of the many developments that politicized the Religious Right, but it was definitely not the first. As Melich recognized, Schlafly had "built a Religious Right constituency of fundamentalist and evangelical women in the South" over several years and "introduced the ministers to the New Right politics of the Republican party." Schlafly believed that, in addition, she made a crucial contribution to the conservative movement by showing conservatives that they could win.[22]

The Moral Majority and the Religious Roundtable were but two of the many politically oriented organizations presenting themselves as Christian defenders of the family established between 1977 and the 1980 election. James Dobson, a psychologist, established "Focus on the Family" in 1977. The next year Terry Dolan, Howard Phillips, Paul Weyrich, and Richard Viguerie founded Christian Voice, dedicated to recruiting and training evangelical Christians to participate in elections. In 1979, Beverly LaHaye founded Concerned Women for America (CWA), an all-Protestant counterpart to Schlafly's Eagle Forum, but pursuing similar goals. LaHaye claimed she had suddenly been inspired to create the organization after watching TV with her minister husband, Moral Majority cofounder Tim LaHaye, and hearing Betty Friedan claim to represent American women.[23] No doubt years of watching Schlafly's success—together with encouragement from male conservatives, including her husband—also influenced her to take this step.

This expansion of pro-family organizations was clearly demonstrated in 1980 when the Carter administration sponsored the White House Conferences on the Family (WHCF). Critics said it was an attempt to bolster his image as a supporter of the family before the 1980 election. Carter declared it was an effort to "reach out to all Americans" and learn from them about how the government could best help families who were, more than ever before, being "pounded by successive waves of deep and often unpredictable change." There was trouble from the start, beginning with an early decision to change the word "Family" in the conference title to "Families," setting off a strong, negative reaction from the pro-family movement determined to limit the definition of "family" to persons related by blood, adoption, or marriage and to exclude unmarried partners, unwed mothers and their children, and especially homosexual relationships.[24]

In fairness, Carter was honoring a campaign pledge to hold such conferences, but it appeared that, in going forward with the conferences, the administration had learned little from the controversy surrounding IWY. As in 1977, plans called for open meetings in the states where participants could vote on recommendations and delegates to send to a culminating conference, although this time there would be three regional conferences held in Baltimore, Minneapolis, and Los Angeles in June and July 1980; their recommendations would then be combined into one final report.[25]

Again few conservatives were appointed to leadership positions. Schlafly was not only passed over as a commissioner, her efforts to have the Eagle Forum included in a coalition of non-governmental organization involved in the WHCF were rebuffed. Adding to the pro-family leaders' sense of alienation and anger, at the initial meeting of the NGOs, the Eagle Forum representative was asked to leave by officials claiming the organization's invitation had gone out by mistake. But, as in 1977, pro-family movement leaders again resolved to emerge victorious.[26]

Having mobilized for IWY and never demobilized, in 1980 they were ready for battle in what they regarded as "IWY revisited." Schlafly again tapped Rosemary Thomson to lead conservative efforts and devoted her annual Eagle Forum training weekend to preparing to challenge feminists at federally funded conferences. Assuring listeners that the IWY was "still alive and well," that the IWY Continuing Committee was working hard to implement the National Plan of Action, and that it planned to confront the pro-life, pro-family coalitions at the upcoming White House Conferences on the issue of separation of church and state, she urged them to gird their loins for this next skirmish. The response was tremendous: the Christian soldiers were ready to march. Thomson later recalled, "Anyone who ever doubted that the five million dollars squandered on IWY were unwittingly the best federal funds ever misspent should have tried to get into the overflowing WHCF caucus that evening!"[27]

At Rosemary Thomson's suggestion, leaders of several pro-family organizations created the National Pro-Family Coalition on the White House Conference on Families to try to win the majority of delegates elected at state WHCF meetings. Intent on sending President Carter and Congress a message "that citizens of traditional moral values, not feminists, gays and secular humanists, are still the majority in America," conservatives turned out en masse at the preliminary, open meetings that together attracted more than one hundred thousand people. They blasted Carter's policies and sought to elect conservatives as delegates to the three regional conferences. This time Connie Marshner, who headed the successful 1971 campaign to persuade Nixon to veto the child care bill and then became a key figure at the New Right think tank the Heritage Foundation, was a key ally in mobilizing and directing the pro-family forces.[28]

Their first effort, led by Marshner, was in Virginia, where according to one critical observer they "came by the busloads" wearing blue dots and voting as a bloc against such measures as "family planning" and "family-life education" in the schools. They managed to win most of the delegate slots in a few states, including Virginia, Michigan, Oklahoma, and some in Oregon, and gave feminists a real fight in many other states. Ultimately they won only 250 of 1,500 delegate positions in elections they claimed had been rigged. Thomson claimed that "in the name of strengthening families" the delegates had "approved the right to abortion, the Equal Rights Amendment, nondiscrimination against homosexuals, federally funded child care programs, national health insurance and a guaranteed annual income for poor families."[29]

Again pro-family forces tried to turn defeat into victory with the help of the media. They staged counter-conferences coinciding with the regional meetings in Baltimore and Los Angeles. And on the closing day of the last WHCF meeting held in July in Los Angeles, pro-family leaders held a massive gathering to protest and to adopt their own recommendations. This time the protest rally was organized by Beverly LaHaye, who assumed the leadership role played by Lottie Beth Hobbs in 1977. More than seven thousand men, women, and children turned out for what Thomson described as "a day-long extravaganza" featuring "a stunning array of pro-family leaders, pastors and entertainers."[30]

Speakers included Phyllis Schlafly and National Right to Life leader Dr. Mildred Jefferson, who had been on the speakers' platform in Houston. Joining them were representatives of the growing pro-family coalition, including ministers Jerry Falwell and Tim LaHaye, New Right leaders Howard Phillips of the Conservative Caucus and Senator Jesse Helms. A Nevada Eagle Forum leader, Janine Triggs, one of the conservative delegates to the WHCF, received a standing ovation when she reported to the crowd about what she had seen there: "We must go home and alert our friends and neighbors to the fact that the very existence of the American family is being threatened—not by a foreign enemy, but by our own government."[31]

Schlafly denounced the White House Conferences on the Family for passing resolutions favoring abortion, the ERA, and homosexuality, and charged that most voting delegates were women's lib leaders who "used the 'families' conference to promote their own hidden agenda to achieve 'liberation'"—putting women's rights ahead of family values. The proposals adopted, she charged, constituted "an attack on God's plan for the family and an attack on common sense" and would drive up federal spending. In a foreword to *Withstanding Humanism's Challenge to Families: Anatomy of a White House Conference*, Rosemary Thomson's account of the 1980 fight, Schlafly wrote: "[The WHCF] should encourage taxpayers of traditional moral values to run—not walk—to their precinct polling place and vote for candidates who will respect American families and defend them from attack."[32]

Conservatives had been so numerous, visible, and vocal at the meetings —and protested the results so strenuously—that the WHCF was largely interpreted as a conservative victory. Once more, with the help of the press, conservatives succeeded in making themselves seem more numerous than they were. The *Detroit Free Press*, for example, wrote: "The Baltimore conference ... revealed the true extent of a phenomenon observers had been following for some time: the rise of the Pro-Family Coalition." The Gannett News Service had the same reaction: "The Pro-Family Movement ... is rapidly becoming (if it isn't already) an important political force. Pro-Family leaders believe the movement will succeed in its self-described mission of restoring morality to America . . . It was the Pro-Family group that stole the headlines at . . . (WHCF) regional conference meetings." And the Associated Press broadcast across the nation Connie Marshner's declaration of war: "The battle lines are being drawn. There is forming a constituency in this nation for policies that will be based not on fulfilling the economic needs of people but on a return to traditional moral values."[33]

Paul Weyrich, calling himself the pro-family movement's "political mechanic," boasted, "Three years ago in Washington, D.C. we had three groups focusing on family matters. Now we have 23." Richard Viguerie pronounced the pro-family movement as perhaps the most potent political force in the nation: "No political movement in America has the potential to reach as vast a constituency as the pro-family movement. It is an incredibly dynamic coalition of groups—with the moral commitment which inspires its members."[34]

Rosemary Thomson was elated by the show of conservative strength. "Our pro-family ranks had grown dramatically since Houston," she wrote. "[Whereas] in 1977, opposition to the International Women's Year had been waged for the most part by Christian ladies," dismissed by some as "a fringe group of mostly ineffective, emotional women which did not deserve serious consideration," the White House Conferences "brought husbands, businessmen, laborers, and pastors into the fray."[35]

This impressive display of pro-family strength, Thomson wrote, was "not what Bella Abzug had had in mind in her closing remarks to the National Women's Conference—that neither 'women nor the country would ever be quite the same.'" Although the defenders of the traditional family had failed to win the most delegate seats or prevail in voting on resolutions, she wrote, "We win, nevertheless," as conservatives would "be ready to register to vote, work for, and elect pro-family candidates . . ."[36]

The rapid mobilization of impassioned conservatives determined to take back their country from feminists and the politicians who supported them had a major impact on elections. In 1978 and in 1980 they were increasingly well organized and well funded—the result of newly organized political action committees such as the National Conservative Political Action Committee (NCPAC) with coffers swelled by direct mail solicitations: Conservatives claimed this was their only way to get out their message as well as raise money given the "liberal bias" of the media. In 1978 the pro-family coalition targeted liberal members of Congress who had supported the women's rights movement. In an election in which the Republican Party made major gains, they knocked off about half of their list.[37]

In addition, thirty new GOP members were elected, many from the South—including Newt Gingrich, a young history professor from Georgia who was destined to play a key role in advancing the conservative agenda. A Gingrich campaign official described their strategy: "We went after every rural southern prejudice we could think of," including "appealing to the prejudice against working women, against their not being home." Jesse Helms was reelected by a 10 percent margin (53 percent to 43 percent) with the aid of the pro-family "army" and $6.7 million—a new record for spending in a senate campaign—raised by NCPAC. Tanya Melich, horrified by the new direction her party was taking in the South, called it "an impressive show of political power for the new partnership of racism and sexism in pursuit of Republican victory."[38]

In 1980 the pro-family movement helped defeat several powerful members of the Senate, including George McGovern and Frank Church. Thomson rejoiced that there was "a net gain of ten pro-lifers elected to the U.S. Senate." Schlafly was particularly delighted with the defeat of an old nemesis, Indiana's Birch Bayh, a key supporter of feminism, the main champion of the ERA in the Senate, and a former member of the IWY Commission, as well as Congresswoman Elizabeth Holtzman, who, along with Bayh, were the "two Congressional sponsors of the unfair, crooked ERA Time Extension passed in 1978." Things had changed drastically since Bayh's disparaging comment to the IWY Commission about wanting to commit mayhem when confronted with this housewife from Illinois presuming to tell the women of America what they wanted. That Bayh was replaced with a soon-prominent Republican and family values defender, Dan Quayle, was another sign of the changing times.[39]

Pro-family forces took satisfaction in seeing blue-collar workers deserting the Democratic Party in growing numbers. Thomson was especially pleased with a description of the pro-family movement published in the *Washingtonian*. Journalist Lewis Koch wrote that the movement consisted of people "frustrated and unhappy with much of what the federal government is doing or encouraging, or allowing. Inflation has often ripped apart their budgets, denied them mortgages, and pushed the American Dream beyond their grasp." At the same time these people were losing their children to forces they considered "unacceptable if not damnable." "Their church-going families are assaulted by films and TV programs that border on pornography. They feel surrounded by people who want to legalize marijuana, dispense birth-control pills like Slurpies [*sic*], and do not mind if unmarried men and women or, worse, homosexuals are living—and fornicating—next door . . . To them the enemy of the family is the federal government: controls, regulations, bureaucrats, often out of touch with local community standards and values."[40]

While liberals voiced a lament soon to be prominent in the national political discourse—that the voting habits of less affluent Americans were inconsistent with their economic interests—Thomson thought it a tremendous mark of success that people were increasingly putting moral concerns ahead of economic concerns. For the Republican Party, long seen as the party of big business rather than labor, embracing the pro-family movement's positions enabled it to claim to be the champion of the family without championing programs designed to protect jobs or wages or providing enhanced services to meet the needs of poorer members of society.[41]

In the South especially, the IWY provided a boost to the GOP, offering it a new southern strategy with which to realize long-standing ambitions in the region—a development with enormous consequences for national politics. IWY mobilized and politicized social conservatives while the conferences were going on, but afterward it provided the GOP with an effective means of appealing to regional prejudices. Between the November 1977 showdown in Houston and the November 1980 presidential election, pro-family forces and their GOP allies exploited the opportunity presented by the IWY to link radical, "un-Christian" feminism with the civil rights movement and tie them both to the Democratic Party.

During the Nixon era the Republican Party had pursued a southern strategy based on race. Nixon also made tentative efforts to reach out to northern "white ethnics," primarily Catholics, egged on by Patrick Buchanan who insisted, "Our future is in the Democratic working man, Southern Protestants and Northern Catholics."[42] But he had failed to recognize the potential of a gender-based strategy in the South.

Nixon's overtures to white southern conservatives had been constructed to appeal to white Democrats angry about federal support for the civil rights movement without alienating moderates in the South and elsewhere in the nation. By the late 1970s there was even more of a need for "coded language" to soften or disguise appeals to racism.[43] Ironically, just as it became unacceptable to be overtly racist, it was increasingly acceptable to be overtly antifeminist. IWY became a part of the coded language.

The consensus in support of the women's rights movement of the early 1970s had disappeared—if in fact it had ever really existed. With women actively opposing feminism, many politicians felt liberated from the earlier perception that they must cater to women's rights advocates. At the same time, denunciation of feminism and IWY enabled conservatives to safely employ familiar arguments about innate differences and natural or divinely created hierarchies, and cast the federal government as in thrall to radical reformers, the enemy of the American way of life, while placing the blame squarely on the Democrats.

The intense identification between the women's movement and the civil rights movement—intentionally and proudly cultivated by the National Commission on the Observance of International Women's Year—inspired black and white supporters of the two movements, but it inflamed many white women and men in the South. The prominence of African American women—including civil rights veterans—on state coordinating committees; the programs at state IWY meetings celebrating civil rights movement heroines such as Modjeska Simkins of South Carolina, who in Houston protested the seating of the all-white Mississippi delegation; and the fact that Coretta Scott King was not only appointed to the IWY Commission but in Houston was afforded almost as much honor and attention as Lady Bird Johnson, Betty Ford, and Rosalynn Carter—was galling to white racists.[44]

Efforts to encourage sisterhood between black and white feminists through the IWY worked. In its final report, members of the biracial state IWY coordinating committee that had been vanquished in the Mississippi takeover declared: "The State Meeting made clear to us that sexism and racism are the same. Those who are against equal rights for women are also opposed to equal rights for blacks. Therefore both black and white women have to fight both sexism and racism or whichever one they may choose, it really means the same thing." Similar comments came from Dr. Marianna Davis, head of the South Carolina delegation, who said that through IWY she came to believe for the first time that the women's movement was her movement, too—that the two causes were inseparable. Many delegates left Houston saying that the spontaneous joining of hands and singing of the civil rights anthem "We Shall Overcome" after the adoption of the minority rights plank—seen by many as the merger of the movements for women's rights and civil rights for African Americans—was the highlight of their conference experience. It was also one of the events most highlighted by the press.[45]

However, white supremacists were equally fired up by the idea that the women's movement was an extension of the civil rights movement, and they mobilized in part as an opportunity to strike back. As noted above, conservatives who had strongly opposed the civil rights movement were much in evidence during the IWY challenge. Women for Constitutional Government members who were members of the IWY Citizens' Review Committee testified at the Helms hearings. Members of the American Party, which nominated George Wallace in 1968, took an active part in opposing IWY, as did members of extremist, violent groups, including the White Nationalist Movement and the Ku Klux Klan.[46] Modjeska Simkins, who had spent her long life working for racial justice as a member of the NAACP, said she recognized old foes at the South Carolina state meeting, including John Birch Society and Klan members. When she was nominated for a slot on the state delegation to Houston, they put out what she called "a communist smear sheet" on her, a page from the records of the House Un-American Activities Committee (HUAC) of the McCarthy era. The notorious Klan leader Robert Shelton protested the use of taxpayers' money to organize the IWY state meetings, saying that if Congress should do that, "then it should give $5 million to the Klan to fight for segregation."[47]

Schlafly denied knowledge of any KKK involvement in IWY or anti-ERA activities or having ever met a member of the Klan. "We don't have people like that around where I live." In an interview she surmised that Klan boasts about influence during IWY may have been efforts to "mooch in and take credit for what we were doing." However, as she put it, "I have always said I am very tolerant, I let people be against ERA for the reason of their choice." And she said, "we had plenty of blacks" in the anti-ERA movement, mentioning the "lobby days" at the Illinois capitol in particular.[48]

Klan leader Robert Shelton also claimed to be tolerant. In Houston he stated to reporters, "While we are an independent organization, we work with any group with a Christian base; and, yes, we are working with some Christian groups—it's time they have come out and taken a stand against the women's movement and the IWY meetings in particular." Shelton was committed to supporting the movement of Christian conservatives to take back their country from liberals who allowed such an event as the IWY to take place and with federal support. Regrettably, he stated, "We [the KKK] got into this too late to be effective, but we'll keep working."[49]

To some analysts of southern politics it seemed that the IWY revived the fighting spirit of white civil rights opponents who saw in it a new opportunity to strike back at the federal government. After the Mississippi takeover, seasoned journalist Bill Minor, a leading analyst of Mississippi politics, observed in his column that the state had just gotten "a look-see" at "a new form of militant conservatism" that had "emerged to replace the old-time anti-black militancy of the White Citizens' Councils and the Ku Klux Klan."[50]

The new militant conservatism, Minor wrote, was "ostensibly not racist" but "comes out of a strong reactionary backlash led by religious fundamentalism, self-acclaimed patriotic organizations and some old-time staunchly conservative political groups." Minor stated, "Their overall enemy now is not the black man but 'liberalism' in any form, as they see it." In place of opposition to civil rights and voting rights bills, they were focused on "such issues as ERA, gay rights, and abortion."[51]

Invoking the IWY gave the GOP a means of appealing to angry white conservatives on these issues while also channeling their anger about the new state of affairs since the Civil Rights Act of 1964 and the Voting Rights Act of 1965 barely ten years earlier. In his 1982 autobiography, white nationalist leader Richard Barrett, one of the conservatives who took over the Mississippi IWY meeting, spelled that out, stating that IWY, "a government-backed, stacked deck, pro-lesbian menagerie," had "afforded the common people the first opportunity since the anti-integration protests to make known, in large turnouts, that they were neither colonial lackeys nor unthinking slaves of Washington."[52]

Barrett, a George Wallace admirer who hoped to see white Americans unite in a "Nationalist" movement, abhorred the "fact" that nonwhite immigration and the failure of white women to reproduce in large numbers was leading to racial suicide, and called on white Americans to rise up and save themselves and their nation. He praised women of "founding-American stock" who for years "had seen Negroes and hippies used in the name of 'civil rights,'" and "watched their husbands and sons abused in the name of 'voting rights,'" until finally these "wives and daughters quietly took the field against 'equal rights' and the tide began to turn" and "the real American woman conquered." Barrett admired Phyllis Schlafly and praised her profusely, calling her the "charming First Lady of Femininity" who was helping to ensure that a "Second American Revolution" ended in victory. He gave ERA opponents credit for setting "the clapper of nationalism in motion." After IWY, he added, "the moral, womanly woman became increasingly prominent in my speeches."[53]

The IWY also drew the wrath of southern conservatives opposed to recommendations in the National Plan of Action on religious grounds. Within the massive Southern Baptist Convention (SBC), resentment of the denomination's moderate support of the women's rights movement was exacerbated by the IWY. It contributed to the conservative "takeover" of the SBC in 1979 in which IWY critics—such as Reverend Charles Stanley of Atlanta's First Baptist Church and Dallas pastor Paige Patterson, who gave the invocation at the Pro-Life, Pro-Family Rally—were involved.[54]

After Houston, the women's movement was perceived as even more radical, and the idea that the federal government had supported the National Women's Conference—which endorsed not only the ERA but federally funded abortion and homosexuality—further inflamed conservatives. In 1979 the conservative insurgents in the SBC seized power from the moderates, and under new leadership the large and powerful denomination officially denounced the ERA, abortion, and gay rights and expelled the women newly admitted to its seminaries. Within a few years the Southern Baptist Convention would officially remind women of the biblical injunction to be subservient to their husbands. (Jimmy Carter ultimately left the denomination in protest.) The Southern Baptist Convention went from a denomination that eschewed political involvement to one of the strongest allies of the Republican Party—called by one pundit the GOP's "largest PAC."[55] The IWY gave Republicans a welcome opportunity to direct all of this outrage against Jimmy Carter and the Democrats.

As James Kilpatrick had predicted in 1977, pro-family and New Right forces did indeed use IWY as a rallying cry and with great effectiveness. In Richard Viguerie's *The New Right: We're Ready to Lead*, published in the fall of 1980 just in time for the presidential election, he boasted that the New Right was registering millions of new voters in preparation for the most important election of the twentieth century and attributed much of that success to the IWY. The new voters, he said, included many who "had turned out for the pro-family rally in Houston to counter Bella Abzug's 'women's lib conference.'" He quoted Paul Weyrich, who warned that "as pro-family groups become better educated in the political process," a lot of politicians "who today thumb their noses at the whole notion of a pro-family coalition are going to be humbled."[56]

That Carter had been elected in 1976 in part because of born-again Christians accounted for the viciousness of their attacks on him during the 1980 election. They were like lovers scorned. According to Rosemary Thomson, as minister's wife and Eagle Forum leader Shirley Curry campaigned for Reagan, invariably "a good Christian lady would furtively inquire, 'Mis' Curry, do you reckon Mr. Reagan's a born-again Christian?'" And "tongue in cheek" Curry would reply, "I don't care if he is or not. I'd rather vote for a crook who votes right than someone who claims to be born-again and votes like the devil!"[57]

Richard Viguerie argued that, as religious conservatives were "much more important" in Carter's election than even blacks, they found it "difficult to understand why for almost four years Carter had given the born-again Christian the back of his hand." Instead, Carter surrounded himself with "people who routinely reject Biblical principles regarding sexual behavior, family responsibility, abortion, and other key moral issues." Viguerie gloated about the rift that had opened between Carter and more liberal Democrats and that groups Carter thought were his base instead backed Kennedy. Moral Majority leader Reverend Jerry Falwell proclaimed that the newly mobilized "great Christian army" was about to show "the godless minority of treacherous individuals who have been permitted to formulate national policy . . . [that] they do not represent the majority" and that they will no longer "permit the destruction of their country by godless, liberal philosophies."[58]

Carter had indeed surrounded himself with women like Abzug, Costanza, Steinem, O'Leary, and then Weddington whom conservatives perceived as godless liberals. At the pro-family protest in Houston, "the President's wife" was denounced for attending "the wrong rally." Such was the outrage of the Religious Right that one minister called for the clothes she and the other First Ladies had worn at the National Women's Conference to be burned.[59]

That Carter inherited the IWY, took little interest in it, refused to attend the Houston conference, failed to fully support the National Plan of Action, fired Costanza, and publicly humiliated Abzug did not matter. New Right strategists recognized the value of the IWY to their cause and hung it—like an albatross—around his neck.

Meanwhile, women of the pro-family movement worked arduously to get Ronald Reagan nominated and elected. Many New Right leaders favored other candidates. Richard Viguerie first backed Illinois Congressman Phil Crane. Then he jumped ship and backed Texan John Connally, stating, "John Connally is a leader and that Ronald Reagan is not a leader but a spokesman" who had not built "a conservative power structure that would carry on his conservative principles." Even Senator Jesse Helms, who had helped Reagan immensely in 1976, did not unequivocally endorse his candidacy until well into the spring of 1980. That was not the case with the women leading the pro-family movement. Not only Schlafly—a long-time Reagan fan—but also Rosemary Thomson, Nellie Gray, Elaine Donnelly, Shirley Curry, Tottie Ellis, and other leaders who had worked together to oppose feminists over the ERA, IWY, and in 1980 the White House Conference on Families were behind him from the beginning to the end of the 1980 presidential campaign. They were immensely proud of the role their Christian army played in his victory.[60]

Elaine Donnelly boasted that, after the 1977 pro-family rally in Houston, attendees "went home to learn the basics of grassroots politics, which they saw as the key to stopping Bella Abzug and her radical agenda." After helping get Reagan nominated, they applied their skills and their fervor first during the primary and then during the general election. Shirley Curry and Tottie Ellis, another Eagle Forum leader and Church of Christ pastor's wife, who served as Tennessee state coordinator for Reagan, exemplified pro-family women's commitment to his candidacy: during the primary the two women traveled through the southern states in a self-financed voter registration drive to ensure there would be enough pro-family votes to carry the state for Reagan.[61]

Pro-family movement women also worked hard to gain influence at the 1980 Republican National Convention, becoming precinct delegates, county and state Republican Party officials, and voting delegates. Whereas only 29 percent of the delegates were women, many of them were from the pro-family movement. While media coverage of the 1980 Republican National Convention focused on the feminist Republicans, said Elaine Donnelly with satisfaction, she and other pro-family delegates "were quietly writing and counting the votes for platform language reflecting Reagan's views."[62]

As for his views, after Reagan's nomination pro-family movement women were thrilled to see their candidate, as Rosemary Thomson put it, "ignoring the warning of politicos to shun the growing religious coalition." Thomson described the thrilling moment when Reagan "unflinchingly joined leaders of the Pro-Family Movement" to address the National Affairs Briefing in Dallas, Texas, in September 1980. This event, sponsored by Ed McAteer's Religious Roundtable, drew more than seventeen thousand religious conservatives eager to hear speeches by Phyllis Schlafly, Carolyn Gerster of Right to Life, Connie Marshner and Paul Weyrich of the Heritage Foundation, Reverend Jerry Falwell of the Moral Majority, and the candidate, Ronald Reagan.[63]

To a worshipful audience, Reagan said in pitch-perfect tone exactly what they had longed to hear: "Religious America is awakening, perhaps just in time for our country's sake . . . You and I are meeting at a time when traditional Judeo-Christian values, based on the moral teachings of religion, are undergoing what is perhaps their most serious challenge in our nation's history." He denounced those who threatened "to remove from our public policy debate the voice of traditional morality." "We have all heard it charged that whenever those with traditional religious values seek to contribute to public policy, they are attempting to 'impose' their views on others." However, he declared, such criticism must stir them to action. The danger was real and they must act to save the nation and traditional values. "If we have come to a time in the United States when the attempt to see traditional moral values reflected in public policy leaves one open to irresponsible charges, then the structure of our free society is threatened . . . [T]he First Amendment was written to . . . protect those values from government tyranny."[64]

However, the GOP establishment moved to take charge of the general election campaign, as they tried to steer the party's nominee in a different direction. According to Thomson, the "grass-roots workers who had pulled Mr. Reagan through the primary" found themselves "ousted from the leadership positions and ignored by more prominent GOP elite." People who had done nothing to get Reagan to this point now "held a moist finger to the wind" and, fearful of losing their control of the party and their influence to the Reaganites, "scrambled to take credit" for the coming Reagan victory. This is how Rosemary Thomson viewed it when Republican feminists sought to deal with the disappointment of Reagan's appointment and the disturbing GOP platform by forming a group to "advise" the Reagan campaign.[65]

The conservatives were amazed at the feminists' audacity and dismayed at the reaction of the Reagan campaign. As Rosemary Thomson recalled,

"angry that the GOP Platform had rejected the feminist minority's demand
for ERA, a handful of former IWY commissioners organized a Women's
Policy Board as part of the Reagan Bush Committee to advise the campaign
'on issues of importance to women.'" Once again there were no pro-family or
pro-life women included. This would not be allowed to stand. Thomson
wrote, "The outcry from the ladies who had worked to nominate Mr. Reagan
in the first place reverberated across the country and through the halls of the
Committee's national headquarters."[66]

A contrite Reagan was soon phoning an irate Phyllis Schlafly, insisting
he "knew nothing about this until after the announcement was made."[67]
Schlafly accepted his explanation but informed him in no uncertain terms
that if he did not remedy the situation by appointing some sort of pro-family
advisory board, it was likely his most loyal supporters would sit out the rest
of the campaign.[68]

On October 1, 1980, the campaign responded by creating a Reagan
Campaign Family Policy Advisory Board with Rosemary Thomson, Tottie
Ellis, Lottie Beth Hobbs, Beverly LaHaye, Dr. Carolyn Gerster, and several
other conservative women leaders plus a rabbi, Seymour Siegel, and
Congressman Henry Hyde as members. Connie Marshner was the chair,
and Marilyn Thayer was hired as a "Special Family Adviser" on the campaign
staff. The official announcement stated that the committee's task was to "lay
the groundwork for a major Reagan Administration effort to promote a
national rededication to traditional American family values."[69] Schlafly was
not appointed; most likely the campaign managers considered it too risky.
The fact that Schlafly was so well-known and so reviled by those not sharing
her views led to her being passed over in favor of lesser-known pro-family
women.

The advisory board met weekly with Reagan campaign political coordinators, making suggestions for outreach to blue-collar, middle-class, pro-
family voters. Thomson recalled that, they took it upon themselves to point
out issues of concern that had not been considered important by professional
politicians who had lost touch with their constituencies. They also wrote
memos to Reagan's campaign staff to suggest policies in keeping with pro-
family values.[70]

When Election Day came, Thomson predicted a landslide for Reagan
but knew "the event was in the hand of God." "Before the night was over,"
she recalled, "we knew He had answered America's prayers." Not only did
Reagan carry forty-four states, including every southern state except Georgia,
he had a new Republican majority that "would generally share our views,"

also elected with the aid of pro-family women and men: "The majority of moral Americans had spoken." After the election, Thomson wrote, "In four short years, cooperation among pro-family, pro-life and religious leaders had made the Pro-Family Movement a force to be reckoned with."[71]

Elaine Donnelly would always insist that Reagan's nomination was made possible by "the powerful pro-family movement [that] worked tirelessly" to make it happen. In an article she entitled "What Women Wanted," she declared that his victory in November "would not have been possible without the army of conservative and pro-life women nationwide."[72]

Looking back years later, Schlafly, Hobbs, Thomson, Donnelly, Curry, Edmondson, and the others who had laid the foundation of the pro-family movement and the Religious Right were proud of what they had accomplished, and so quickly. "Feminists in 1977 thought that their historic IWY conferences would inspire women to take over the world," Donnelly wrote. "The irony is that the conference did have that effect, but those who were motivated the most were admirers of Ronald Reagan."[73]

A Nation Divided

The real significance of Houston was to bury the idea that so-called "women's issues" are a sideshow to the center-ring concerns of American politics.

—DAVID BRODER, *WASHINGTON POST*, 1977

What a difference a decade had made. In the early 1970s both Democrats and Republicans supported feminist goals, encouraged by the vociferousness of the women's rights movement and the quiescence of conservative women. By 1980 the two parties were lined up on opposite sides of a fierce battle between advocates of women's rights and family values, a battle that continues to divide the nation.

In the 1970s, from beachheads within Republican and Democratic administrations and in Congress, feminists urged politicians to revise laws and policies in keeping with changed circumstances and remove barriers to women's full and equal participation in American life. The strength of the antifeminist backlash that emerged by mid-decade was a testament to their success. The conservative women's movement was relatively small and composed largely of political novices. Yet it had an impact that belied its size, largely due to the experience and acumen of its leaders—most of them Republican activists who had been fighting, and losing, battles against moderates and liberals in their own party.

The 1977 International Women's Year conferences marked an important turning point in the history of these two women's movements and in the evolution of American political culture. IWY succeeded as feminists had hoped in diversifying and uniting the women's rights movement, ending historic conflicts that had divided white and minority women, straight women and lesbians. It also affirmed the primacy of reproductive freedom; demonstrated the widespread, bipartisan support for feminism; and inspired more women to become politically active.[1]

IWY also empowered the conservative women's movement as a rival for political power. The fight against feminists to control these federally-funded conferences allowed conservative women activists to expand their numbers and attract allies from a wide range of religious groups and political organizations angered by federal support for social change and eager to "take back their country." As advocates of women's rights, minority rights, gay rights, reproductive rights, and federal programs from child care to a national health system united behind the National Plan of Action, those who opposed them on any or all of these issues came together in an enduring pro-family coalition.[2]

After the National Women's Conference and the Pro-Family Rally in Houston, women's rights leaders and conservatives alike spoke of IWY as a watershed event and both claimed victory in the conflict. The IWY conferences were indeed transformative, but they produced no clear victory for either side. Instead, they ushered in a new era in American politics—the beginning rather than the end of a protracted struggle over women's rights and family values.

For the rest of the 1970s, feminists fought to realize the goals formulated in Houston. The public fallout between feminist leaders and President Jimmy Carter was a blow to the women's rights movement as well as to his candidacy for reelection. But the platform adopted at the 1980 Democratic National Convention—heavily influenced by Bella Abzug—demonstrated the party's continued support for the women's movement.

In sharp contrast, the platform adopted at the 1980 Republican National Convention—heavily influenced by Phyllis Schlafly—demonstrated the power of the rapidly expanding pro-family movement. The opposition of these social conservatives to federal programs to aid women and promote gender equality dovetailed with the desire of fiscal conservatives to curb government spending and regulation; all agreed that an overreaching federal government was the cause of the nation's problems. New Right strategists, intent on building a powerful conservative movement through the Republican Party, embraced as allies the pro-family activists and worked with them to mobilize Christian conservatives before the 1980 election.

Pro-family forces avidly supported Ronald Reagan, who claimed their values as his own. More surprising, the staunchly antifeminist platform they demanded as the price for their support was accepted by moderate party leaders such as George H. W. Bush, whom Republican feminists regarded as allies. Embracing the pro-family movement, with its strong support from Catholics, blue-collar workers, and white southerners—key elements of the Democrats' New Deal coalition—seemed to them to be a winning strategy.

The GOP's embrace of the pro-family movement was seen by many Republican feminists as a shocking betrayal. Tanya Melich called the alliance with the Religious Right a "Faustian bargain": in return for their support, Republicans would allow pro-family movement leaders to dictate party policy on social issues. Over the years, as it became clear this arrangement would continue, Melich became even more angry with the party she loved. In what she called "an insider's report from behind the lines," she charged that in 1980, the party betrayed its heritage as the party of liberty and, in a cynical attempt to become the majority party, launched "The Republican War Against Women."[3]

After 1980, women would remain highly politicized and deeply divided in their views on policy issues. The presidential election that year revealed two new trends that proved to be enduring. Women voted at a higher rate than men for the first time in American history, and there was a "gender gap" favoring the Democratic Party. Though women split their votes almost equally between Reagan (46 percent) and Carter (45 percent), exit polls showed that men gave 54 percent of their votes for Reagan, creating an eight-percentage-point difference between women's and men's choices.[4]

Analysts attributed the gender gap—which reflected women's stronger support for spending on domestic programs than on defense—to the women's movement, which had taught women to see their own values in political terms. Feminists, led by NOW's Eleanor Smeal, were quick to identify and publicize the gender gap in a last-ditch effort to ratify the ERA and generally enhance their political clout. In the early 1980s, both Smeal and Bella Abzug, who declared Carter's defeat a lesson for Democrats, published books predicting the gap would lead to major advances for women and feminist goals, and warned that politicians ignored it at their peril.[5]

The discovery of the gender gap put Republicans on the defensive. In 1982, Reagan advisor Lee Atwater warned of a potential "sex-based political realignment" that "could lock the GOP into permanent minority status" if Republicans did not take action. They needed to be very careful in their "public expressions" on economic issues, war and peace, and social issues, as well as show working women the party was not against them and was "sensitive to their needs." At the same time, he suggested—as have many political scientists—that the gender gap could be read as an indicator of men's declining support for Democrats, the result of men's preference for a "man's man" like Reagan. Some GOP strategists also took comfort in the idea that this was more of a "marriage gap" and a "racial gap," pointing out that most white married women tended to vote for Republicans. Thus, while GOP leaders understood the enhanced importance of women's votes, they would try to win them, not by changing their policy positions but through symbolic appointments and gestures and by embracing policies that appealed to their pro-family base.[6]

For the rest of the twentieth century, the Republican Party would continue to court these voters, becoming increasingly reliant upon them, and alienating many moderate voters in the process. As disaffected Democrats, especially white southerners, signed on with the GOP, the Republican Party became more uniformly conservative and the Democratic Party became more uniformly liberal.[7] Democrats continued to support women's rights, along with civil rights for African Americans and Hispanics, and to be increasingly supportive of what became known as the LGBT community. The Republican Party became more racially and ethnically homogeneous as well as more socially conservative as it doubled down in its defense of the traditional family.

The pro-family movement focused heavily on the abortion issue, and their efforts to restrict it met with considerable success despite the fact that the majority of Americans continued to support *Roe v. Wade*. Conservatives also succeeded in popularizing a negative image of feminism that led many to eschew the label, even as they supported its goals. But in other battles to roll back feminist gains, they faced disappointment. Just as advocates of a "Reagan Revolution" found it impossible to abolish popular social programs, such as Social Security or Medicare, that Americans had come to count on, there was no going back to the days before Title VII of the Civil Rights Act of 1964 banned gender discrimination in employment, and Title IX of the Education Acts of 1972 banned gender discrimination in education. When the women's movement broke down barriers to education and jobs, it created openings that women of all political persuasions poured through.

Years of passionate debates on gender-related issues proved to be transformative. As the personal became political and the political became personal, and issues laden with religious or moral significance remained in the forefront of national debates, politicians increasingly found that moderation was devalued, consensus was impossible, and compromise was no longer tolerated by constituents. With Democratic and Republican politicians lined up on either side of these volatile gender-related issues, they tended to demonize their opponents and define issues strictly in partisan terms, a situation that contributed to political gridlock and made it more difficult for lawmakers to address the pressing problems confronting the nation.

Since 1980, each side has made progress when "its party" was in power. As president, Ronald Reagan did much to advance the pro-family movement's agenda, though not nearly as much as its leaders wanted and expected.[8] Weeks after he was elected, Phyllis Schlafly boasted to her followers that it was "clear from our victories in the November election" that we "have become the most powerful and effective movement in America today." Rather than "let this mighty movement fade away as we congratulate ourselves," she declared, they must "use our movement and its weapons—sharpened and polished through eight and a half years of battles—to achieve other goals for God, Family, and Country."[9]

Schlafly counted on Reagan's support, but he and his staff were mindful of the gender gap, the widespread support for women's rights, and that Schlafly was anathema to many women, including many Republicans. Reagan appointed lesser-known Schlafly allies Elaine Donnelly, Rosemary Thomson, and Lottie Beth Hobbs to advisory boards, and named moderate Republicans Elizabeth Dole and former IWY Commissioner and Congresswoman Margaret Heckler to his cabinet.[10] However, he neither admitted Schlafly to his inner circle nor appointed her to a position within his administration. And in 1982, when Schlafly held her second "gala" to celebrate the demise of the ERA—a star-studded event full of leading conservative men including Senator Jesse Helms, Richard Viguerie, Jerry Falwell, and Congressman Robert Dornan who served as master of ceremonies—Reagan chose not to attend. Instead he sent Schlafly a handwritten note the afternoon of the banquet saying he and Nancy would not be coming.[11]

In his first year as president, Reagan shocked and angered his pro-family, pro-life supporters by appointing a moderate, Sandra Day O'Connor, to the Supreme Court, and they vigorously opposed her confirmation.[12] Still, Reagan's policies generally reflected the powerful influence of the conservatives who had helped put him in power. His administration slashed domestic programs and denounced welfare as encouraging dependency and the disintegration of the family. It also imposed gag orders on what medical professionals could tell women patients, ended research on contraception, and supported abstinence-based sex education. In what became known as the "Mexico City policy," the administration banned aid to agencies engaged in population control abroad if they directly or indirectly supported abortion, thus slashing hundreds of millions of dollars in aid for family planning in poor countries.[13]

During Reagan's campaign for reelection in 1984, Republicans reached out to women voters, encouraging women to run as delegates to the GOP convention and featuring many of Reagan's female appointees as speakers. But social conservatives continued to maintain firm control of the platform. The platform committee, which included Phyllis Schlafly and Elaine Donnelly, denounced welfare for shattering "family cohesion" by "providing economic incentives to set up maternal households and by usurping the breadwinner's economic role in intact families." It also reaffirmed support for a human life amendment, a ban on federal funding for abortion (the Hyde Amendment), and a pro-life litmus test for appointment of judges—all part of the 1980 GOP platform—and added a new clause calling for legislation to give "the unborn" the protections of the Fourteenth Amendment.[14]

Meanwhile, feminist Democrats worked hard to get Walter Mondale to choose New York Congresswoman Geraldine Ferraro for his running mate. In 1984, they were thrilled to see Ferraro on the ticket—breaking the second-highest barrier to women's progress in American politics. Though the Mondale-Ferraro ticket lost, her nomination further politicized women's rights advocates in both parties, leading large numbers of women to register to vote and furthering the trend begun in 1980 of more women than men turning out to vote.[15]

After being reelected, Reagan did much to reward his conservative constituency, including appointing the conservative Catholic, staunchly antifeminist Antonin Scalia to the Supreme Court. The administration also filed a brief with the Supreme Court to undo *Roe v. Wade* and an amicus brief in support of the plaintiffs in the *Grove City College v. Bell* case which weakened enforcement of Title IX. Reagan then vetoed a "Restoration of Civil Rights" bill passed by a defiant Democrat-controlled Congress that managed to overturn his veto.[16]

As the 1988 presidential election approached, women's rights supporters in the Republican Party placed their hopes on George H. W. Bush. Given his background as a moderate on social issues and his wife Barbara Bush's pro-choice views, they hoped to gain his support in getting the party to be at least neutral on women's abortion rights. As he campaigned, Bush, who favored a "kinder, gentler, nation," departed from the GOP's harsh line on abortion and supported allowing exemptions in cases involving rape or danger to the health of the mother. He also proposed a "toddler tax credit" for "families of modest means"—accepted by Schlafly as long as it did not discriminate against one-income families. However, faced with a strong challenge from televangelist Pat Robertson, George Bush doubled his efforts to gain the support of the Religious Right. Their backing—combined with the racist appeal of the infamous Willie Horton television ads damning opponent Michael Dukakis for a prisoner furlough program resulting in a black man raping a white woman—ensured his victory.[17]

As president, Bush—like Reagan—appointed moderate Republican women to his cabinet: he appointed first Elizabeth Dole and later Lynn Martin as secretary of labor, and named as secretary of commerce Barbara Franklin, who had led the effort to recruit women for federal appointments during the Nixon administration. Also like Reagan, Bush handed out a few minor appointments to conservative women but chose to appoint Rosemary Thomson and Elaine Donnelly, not Schlafly. But on the social issues, Bush did even more to cater to the Religious Right than Reagan, some women's rights advocates in his party concluded.[18]

George H. W. Bush vetoed four pro-choice bills in 1989 alone, including one that would have allowed federal funding of abortions for victims of rape and incest. In that case, eight pro-choice Republican congresswomen voted to override the veto. His first Supreme Court appointment, David Souter, who proved to be a moderate on abortion, infuriated the Religious Right. Thus, when Thurgood Marshall died in 1991, Bush appointed as his successor Clarence Thomas, an African American opposed to affirmative action and, like Scalia, a conservative Catholic hostile to feminism. Christian conservatives mobilized to assure Thomas's confirmation, and boasted that the "tens of thousands of phone calls" they made to wavering senators assured his success.[19]

In his 1992 bid for reelection, after Bush defeated a primary challenge from Patrick Buchanan who was backed by Phyllis Schlafly, he banked even more heavily on a pro-family message. Mary Crisp and other leaders of a newly-formed Republican National Coalition for Choice tried to get the party to remove anti-abortion language from the platform. They released a statement from conservative icon Barry Goldwater predicting dire results for the party if it did not soften its stand on abortion, but Schlafly and a newly-created RNC Coalition for Life organization beat back the challenge.[20]

The 1992 Republican National Convention featured a parade of anti-feminist, pro-life speakers. In the most famous speech of the convention, Patrick Buchanan, now backing Bush against Democratic nominee Bill Clinton, portrayed Bush as leading the forces of righteousness against their enemies: "There is a religious war going on in this country. It is a cultural war as critical to the kind of nation we shall be as the Cold War itself. This war is for the soul of America. And in that struggle for the soul of America, [Bill] Clinton and [Hillary] Clinton are on the other side, and George Bush is on our side."[21]

The contrast between the 1992 Republican and Democratic conventions was striking. Governor Ann Richards of Texas, the convention chair, opened her remarks with the words "I'm pro-choice and I vote" to thunderous applause. As the Democratic nominee, Bill Clinton made a strong and successful play for women's votes, proclaiming that as "the grandson of a working woman, the son of a single mother, the husband of a working wife," he had "learned that building up women does not diminish men." And though, according to Tanya Melich, the Bush campaign "tried to make Hillary Clinton the 'family values' equivalent of the Antichrist," Bill Clinton and the Democrats played up the fact that she was a lawyer as well as a mother, and spoke of the Clintons' feminist partnership as a major asset. The lineup of speakers at the Democratic convention included six pro-choice Republican women who endorsed Bill Clinton. Feminists and other liberal constituency groups including African Americans and gays seemed to have as much say in determining party positions on social issues as the Religious Right had in the GOP. In the ongoing contest between advocates of women's rights and family values, the battle lines were more fully and clearly drawn than ever before.[22]

In the 1992 election, women voted for Clinton over Bush 45 percent to 37 percent. African American women played an especially important part in Clinton's victory. While 41 percent of white women voters supported him, 86 percent of black women (and 77 percent of black men) gave Clinton their vote. Clinton fared the worst with white men, winning only 37 percent of their votes.[23]

Pro-family evangelicals turned out to vote in droves that year, more than ever before. They constituted 24 percent of the electorate, with 60 percent of them voting for Bush. However, Clinton's victory suggested that many Americans had found the Republicans' embrace of religious extremists alienating. Significantly, this presidential election was the first in which baby boomers and suburbanites were a majority of the voters. And with women now 54 percent of the electorate, the "women's vote" carried considerable weight.[24]

For women in politics, especially Democrats, 1992 proved to be a banner year. In 1991, the all-male Senate Judiciary Committee's grilling of law professor Anita Hill, after she accused Clarence Thomas of sexual harassment at his confirmation hearing, infuriated large numbers of women from both parties and inspired many to run for office. Twice as many women filed for office as had in 1990. Women's political fund-raising groups such as the National Women's Political Caucus (NWPC) and EMILY's List (acronym for Early Money is Like Yeast) reported that contributions had doubled since the hearings. The five women senators elected that year— including Dianne Feinstein, Barbara Boxer, and the first African American woman senator, Carol Moseley Braun—were all Democrats, as were twenty of the twenty-three women elected to the House, where the number of women swelled from twenty-eight to forty-seven. The press called 1992 "the Year of the Woman" but "the Year of the Democratic Woman" would have been more accurate. A trend of more women running as Democrats than Republicans was established that would continue well into the next century.[25]

Many in the Religious Right were angered and distressed by Clinton's election, but its leaders saw long-term advantages. Ralph Reed, head of the Christian Coalition, the organization Pat Robertson had founded in 1989 after his failed presidential bid, stated: Democrats "elected an openly pro-abortion, pro-gay rights liberal to the presidency for the first time in the history of this country. Now you are going to have a face on modern liberalism, and everybody is going to be able to see it in a way they haven't seen it before." Membership in the Christian Coalition more than doubled in 1993.[26]

America during Bill Clinton's two terms was a virtual war zone between the president and an embattled GOP. He acted quickly to remove the gag rule regarding information on reproductive rights and to rescind the Mexico City policy—policies put in place by Reagan that Bush had continued. Clinton supported women's reproductive rights, launching a campaign to cut the rate of teen pregnancy, and he defended women's right to choose abortion, though he emphasized that the goal was for it to be "safe, legal, and rare." Conservatives derided Clinton's advocacy of family planning and defense of abortion rights, and during his administration, campaigns of intimidation and violence against abortion clinics increased.[27]

Clinton's "Don't Ask, Don't Tell" policy on gays in the military was regarded as too weak by gay rights advocates, but it outraged conservatives.

With Schlafly's assistance, Elaine Donnelly, avid opponent of women being drafted or serving in combat, established in 1993 a Center for Military Readiness dedicated to preserving the strength of America's armed forces by restricting the participation of women and gays.[28]

In the 1994 midterm elections, a high turnout by conservatives gave Republicans control of the House of Representatives for the first time in forty years and Newt Gingrich was elected Speaker of the House. The press explained this as the result of the growing wrath of the "Angry White Male (AWM)," opposed to feminism, racial quotas, gay rights, and liberal social programs. Fifty-four percent of male voters cast their votes for Republicans compared to forty-six for Democrats, while among women the number was reversed.[29] The ensuing battle between Clinton and Congress led to a government shutdown that in the court of public opinion worked in the president's favor. And in 1996 Clinton defeated the Republican challenger, Senator Bob Dole, in an election featuring the largest gender gap since exit polls began, with women favoring Clinton by 54 percent to 37 percent.[30]

However, when Clinton's personal misconduct gave them an opportunity, Gingrich and other defenders of family values, expressing outrage at his behavior, moved to impeach him. Ultimately they were unsuccessful, and Gingrich and several other Clinton accusers were revealed to be engaged in personal misconduct of their own. Clinton survived, with a flourishing economy boosting his approval ratings to impressive levels.[31]

While conservatives despised Clinton and all he stood for, seeming to hate "Slick Willie" in a visceral, personal way, women's rights advocates supported him. Clinton appointed a record number of women to his cabinet and to other positions in the administration, including America's first female attorney general, Janet Reno, and first woman secretary of state, Madeleine Albright. When given the opportunity to make an appointment to the Supreme Court, Clinton chose Ruth Bader Ginsburg, who had played a central role in the expansion of women's legal rights since the early 1970s. Feminists generally applauded Clinton's record, which included promoting and signing a Violence Against Women Act that quadrupled funding for battered women's shelters, a Family and Medical Leave Act that allowed workers—male or female—to take up to twelve weeks of unpaid work leave to care for a sick family member or a new child, the first increase in the minimum wage in over six years, and expansion of the Head Start program— though many believed aspects of the welfare reform program harmed women and children.[32]

Hillary Clinton also attracted scorn from conservatives and admiration from feminists. Many Americans found it inappropriate for Bill Clinton to treat his wife almost like a co-president, and resented this First Lady who incarnated what they found disconcerting about the changing roles of men and women. In an interview with journalist Gail Sheehy, Hillary Clinton said she believed that for many "wounded men" she represented the "boss they never wanted to have" or "the wife who went back to school and got an extra degree and a job as good as theirs . . . It's not me, personally, they hate—it's the changes I represent." On the other hand, women's rights supporters were delighted to have a First Lady who was even more strongly identified with feminism than Betty Ford and the most activist First Lady since her idol, Eleanor Roosevelt. Hillary Clinton famously headed the administration's effort to create a national health program, which failed after encountering massive Republican resistance. To an extent, she then turned to pursuits more typical for a First Lady. However, she took a leading role in establishing a children's health insurance program, the greatest expansion in children's health care since 1965 when Medicaid was first enacted.[33]

In the eyes of women's rights advocates in the United States and throughout the world, Hillary Clinton's finest moment as First Lady came when she addressed the 1995 Fourth World Conference on Women held in Beijing, China. There were calls from Republicans to boycott the conference to protest Chinese human rights violations, and around the world Catholic groups were denouncing the upcoming conference as an "antifamily" rally. There were also concerns from the State Department, fearful of offending a Chinese government defensive about its one-child policy. However, the First Lady chose to go to China and declare: "It is a violation of human rights when babies are denied food or drowned simply because they were born female." Offering a twelve-part plan to advance the status of women worldwide, Clinton also called for equal educational and economic opportunity for girls and women around the world, criticized genital mutilation in Africa and elsewhere, and denounced the trafficking of girls and women as prostitutes.[34]

Hillary Clinton's powerful statement that "Human rights are women's rights, and women's rights are human rights" instantly made her an international celebrity. Few realized that Clinton's speech was associated with a campaign involving Bella Abzug, Charlotte Bunch, and other American feminists who, since the 1975 Mexico City International Women's Year Conference twenty-five years earlier, had devoted themselves to advancing women's rights worldwide. They played a major role both in getting the UN to sponsor the conference and getting Hillary Clinton to attend. Abzug, leading the United States's NGO delegation from a wheelchair, cheered Clinton on, declaring that the Beijing meeting, highlighted by this staunchly feminist speech by the First Lady, was a "jump start" for the new century.[35]

As America moved into the twenty-first century, the nation continued to see a struggle between advocates of women's rights and family values. And many of the veterans of the battles of the 1970s fought on.

Betty Friedan remained active as a writer and as a professor at several universities, including the Institute for Women and Work at Cornell. Until her death in 2006, she served both as a promoter and an analyst of the women's rights movement she helped to start.[36] Gloria Steinem remained one of the most visible and active of American feminists, traveling and speaking widely to promote women's rights in the United States and abroad, and publishing books and articles that introduced new generations to feminist ideas.[37] Charlotte Bunch founded and directed a Center for Women's Global Leadership at Rutgers University, an academic center and NGO that works with the UN on policy and advocacy.[38]

Mary Crisp finally gave up on her campaign to rescue her beloved GOP from the pro-family forces, concluding "it was like a cry in the wilderness," but continued to serve on the boards of the National Women's Political Caucus, Planned Parenthood, the ACLU, and the National Abortion Rights Action League. She died in 2007.[39] Tanya Melich continued to lament the rightward shift in her party. In her 1996 book *The Republican War Against Women* she had urged Republican moderates and independents to form a new Republican Party both fiscally conservative and socially progressive. Afterward she continued to write for magazines and newspapers, authoring such articles as "Why the GOP Should Have Listened to Mary Crisp" in which she argued that alienated Republican women voting for Democrats was one of the reasons Democratic candidates had such an edge with women voters.[40] As president of the Feminist Majority Foundation (FMF) and publisher of *Ms.* magazine, Eleanor Smeal actively promoted women's rights and defended previous gains, pointing to polls that showed most women voters and large numbers of men supported feminist goals.[41]

Bella Abzug died in 1998, her dream of returning to Congress unfulfilled. But there were many women's rights supporters among the growing number of women in the House and the Senate. Americans sent a record number of women to Congress in 2000, including Hillary Clinton; while still serving as First Lady, she was elected senator from New York—with overwhelming support from women voters. After the election, the Senate had thirteen women (ten Democrats and three Republicans), and the House had fifty-nine women (forty-one Democrats and eighteen Republicans).[42] Many of the Democrats were ardent champions of women's rights. When Bella Abzug died, New York Congresswoman Carolyn Maloney had eulogized her on the House floor, saying, "Make no mistake, there is not an American woman alive who does not have more rights, commands more respect, or enjoys more opportunity as a result of Bella's work." She praised Abzug for reaching out to younger women and inspiring "the women's movement well into the next millennium," and declared, "It is my responsibility, the responsibility of other women in Congress, and the women of this Nation to keep that spirit alive."[43]

As for the conservatives, Lottie Beth Hobbs largely remained out of politics but continued to promote "Biblically-based ideas" through a journal, *The Family Educator*, and through speeches and numerous books that appealed strongly to conservative Christian women. Some of her books had more than twenty-five printings in English and were translated into several foreign languages. She died in 2016.[44] Susan Roylance, a Mormon leader in the fight against feminists at the 1977 IWY conferences, continued the fight through a LDS-affiliated organization she founded in 1978 called Families United. Following the defeat of the ERA, the organization worked to "protect American families" from "the homosexual and radical feminist movements," and to fight the spread of feminist ideas abroad. After encountering Bella Abzug and other American feminists at a UN meeting, Roylance expanded the organization's operations under a new name, United Families International, to combat the influence of her old adversaries who, she said, were trying "to rewrite the world family culture" through UN programs.[45] Elaine Donnelly continued to oppose the full integration of women and gays into the armed forces through her Center for Military Readiness, often testifying before Congress and speaking at conservative gatherings.[46]

Phyllis Schlafly continued to promote her pro-family agenda through numerous books and the *Phyllis Schlafly Report*, weekly syndicated columns, radio commentaries heard on six hundred stations, and a weekly radio talk show called "Eagle Forum Live" on Saturdays broadcast by over a hundred stations. She still conducted annual Eagle Council training sessions to prepare political activists, including young women, to carry on the fight. While some of the early pro-family organizations, including Jerry Falwell's Moral Majority, had ceased to operate, Schlafly presided over an expanded, technologically savvy Eagle Forum, in which Shirley Curry, Shirley

Spellerberg, Dianne Edmondson, and Elaine Donnelly remained active. Lionized as the heroine of the conservative movement within the GOP, she remained influential in Republican politics, mobilizing her followers through the Internet for rapid response on pending state and national legislation. She never missed a GOP national convention, often accompanied by Donnelly, and carefully monitored the production of the platform that remained steadfast in support of pro-family positions. In her eighties, Schlafly spoke of Republican national conventions as "one of my hobbies," and boasted of the "big role" she played in "beefing up" the pro-life plank in 1984 and then "keeping the same language ever since."[47]

As the 2000 presidential election approached, candidates were highly conscious of the trend that first surfaced in 1980 toward women voting in larger numbers than men and of the gender gap favoring Democrats.[48] As a candidate, George W. Bush tried to win over conservatives and moderate women by promising to "restore civility" in the wake of the Bill Clinton and Monica Lewinsky scandal, and using a "W Stands for Women" slogan. And while promoting a larger "reverence for life" agenda that included adoption and tougher drunk driving laws, he avoided talk of ending the right to abortion. According to the *New York Times*, "voters were encouraged to believe that while Mr. Bush was anti-choice, he was not out to reverse *Roe v. Wade*."[49] Bush still lost the women's vote to Al Gore by 11 percent (Bush 43 percent and Gore 54 percent), though a Republican-dominated Supreme Court settled the contested election in his favor.

Once in office, like Ronald Reagan and George H. W. Bush, George W. Bush appointed women to several high-visibility positions. Over his presidency he would name six women to positions in his cabinet, including Condoleezza Rice, the first African American national security advisor, and Elaine Chao, the first Asian American woman cabinet member. In his first term the White House hosted a reception welcoming back the women whose careers in government had begun with Barbara Franklin's recruitment campaign during the Nixon administration. Given that the reception fell on the day the Iraq war began, however, this celebration of the GOP's contribution to women's progress in the early 1970s received little attention.[50]

As for policy related to women, Bush sponsored two programs he hoped would appeal to them, including a "Family Time Flexibility Act" and the "No Child Left Behind" program intended to raise standards in public schools. After the terrorist attacks on September 11, 2001, Bush justified the bombing of Afghanistan in part as protecting women and girls from the vicious misogyny of the Taliban, and First Lady Laura Bush became a strong advocate for programs to aid Afghan women.[51]

George W. Bush understood he was likely to be most successful with white women voters who shared the values of the pro-family movement and he was eager to cultivate their support. Throughout his presidency, he aimed to please Christian conservatives who expected much of this president who, unlike his father, was a "born again" evangelical. Bush took the extraordinary step of establishing a White House Office of Faith-Based and Community Initiatives through which religious groups could apply to provide federally funded social services. Billions of dollars were awarded. The American Civil Liberties Union and Americans United for Separation of Church and State criticized this program as an unconstitutional electoral strategy enacted in order to bolster support for Bush and the GOP.[52]

Bush went to great lengths to promote a pro-life agenda. On his first day in office in 2001, he reinstated the Mexico City policy Clinton had lifted: more than any other single issue, the changing fate of this policy under successive administrations exemplified the push and pull between the pro-life GOP and the pro-choice Democratic Party.[53] Bush also promoted abstinence-only sex education programs, prohibited use of federal funds to distribute contraceptives, and opposed human cloning and funding for embryonic stem cell research—key issues for Christian conservatives. In addition, he supported a ban on late term called "partial birth" abortions by the pro-life movement.

As Bush began his third year in office, the *New York Times* editorialized that "the lengthening string of anti-choice executive orders, regulations, legal briefs, legislative maneuvers and key appointments emanating from his administration suggests that undermining the reproductive freedom essential to women's health, privacy and equality is a major preoccupation of his administration—second only, perhaps, to the war on terrorism." In Bush's second term he appointed two pro-life Supreme Court justices, John Roberts and Samuel Alito. Both were Catholics, giving the court a Catholic majority for the first time in history. Pro-life leaders praised him for doing more "to build a culture of life than any president."[54]

First Lady Laura Bush privately disagreed with her husband about ending *Roe v. Wade* and on gay rights, later telling an interviewer these issues were points of contention between her and her husband throughout his presidency. On both issues the president played to the religious right. In 2004 he risked alienating his base by endorsing civil unions for same-sex couples and a state-based approach to determining the issue. However, as he campaigned for reelection, Bush threw his support behind a proposed constitutional amendment to forbid same-sex marriage.[55]

In the hard-fought race with John Kerry in 2004, Bush benefited from vigorous state campaigns to turn out evangelical voters when gay rights issues were on the ballot. Ironically, the continuing controversy over gay rights—rather than its resolution—benefitted Republicans, and in tight races, helped tip the scale in their favor.[56]

Without question, women's fear of terrorism also helped Bush win reelection. Support for Bush from what pundits called "security moms" led to a dramatic decline in the gender gap, which shrunk to only 3 percent in favor of Democrats, the smallest in recent years and a major factor in John Kerry's loss.[57]

Owing to the disastrous war in Iraq and an economy in free fall, Bush ended his presidency with one of the lowest approval ratings in American history. Within his own party, conservatives criticized him for expanding rather than shrinking the federal government; isolationists denounced the war in Iraq as "unnecessary and unwise"; and nativists—including Phyllis Schlafly—opposed his efforts to reform immigration policy. But as Bush left office, many advocates of family values still admired him. One leader of Concerned Women for America insisted that Bush set the standard that all presidents should follow.[58]

In the 2008 election, with Hillary Clinton seeking her party's nomination, women and women's issues played a more significant role in American politics than ever before. The Democratic primary was an extraordinary and historic contest in which the leading contenders were a white woman and a black man. They endured numerous crude expressions of racism and misogyny, displayed sometimes in surprisingly open settings. Airport gift shops across the nation sold nutcrackers made to look like Hillary Clinton, with her legs as the handles. She faced negative comments about her hair, her clothes, her cleavage, and speculation that the nation would not want to watch a woman president aging in office. Women reporters at CNN said they had been cautioned not to wear pantsuits on camera lest they look too much like Hillary Clinton.[59]

Though the early favorite to become the Democratic Party nominee, Clinton lost to Barack Obama in a lengthy and bruising primary that forced advocates of both racial and gender equality to make a tough choice. Gloria Steinem, who like many feminists admired both candidates, chose to back

Clinton because of her greater experience, and was attacked for ranking sex over race. She found such comments surprising, owing to her "lifetime of arguing that sexism and racism were linked, not ranked," and very painful.[60] Hillary Clinton put "eighteen million cracks" in the political glass ceiling, but as she conceded to Obama, that seemed small comfort to the millions of American women who had supported her and hoped to elect the first woman president.

Emerging from the primaries as the Republican nominee, John McCain quickly restored the gender issue to the forefront of debate by selecting Alaska Governor Sarah Palin, until then virtually unknown on the national stage, as his running mate. In assuming that selecting Palin would lead disappointed Hillary voters to embrace his candidacy, McCain revealed himself to be woefully ignorant of the intra-gender war among American women that had been going on for decades. Feminists mocked his assumption in a widely circulated, doctored photograph of suffragists demonstrating in front of the White House in 1918 holding a banner stating: "Mr. McCain, America's Women Have Not Waited Two-hundred and Thirty-two Years for Sarah Palin."[61]

In the general election, Barack Obama defeated John McCain with the aid of a massive twelve-point advantage with women voters. In addition, in 2008 millions of young voters, more liberal and progressive on social issues than most of their elders, also strongly backed the Democratic nominee. Analysts noted that a generation of young voters who had come of age during the Bush presidency was giving the Democrats a major advantage, just as the previous generation who grew up in the Reagan years had fueled the GOP surge of the mid-1990s. While the gap was particularly striking among young women (twice as many identified with Democrats as with Republicans), even young men favored the Democrats, which made the under-thirty age group the only one in the electorate in which more men were inclined to identify with the Democratic Party.[62]

America had elected its first African American president, a major step forward and a sign of a changing electorate. Barack Obama proved to be an ardent feminist, and married to one—Michelle Obama, who prior to becoming First Lady worked as a lawyer, a Chicago city administrator, and a community outreach worker. At one point during his presidency Barack Obama published an article about himself in *Glamour* magazine, entitled "This is What a Feminist Looks Like." He demonstrated his commitment to promoting and defending women's rights from his first day in office. The first legislation Obama signed into law was the Lilly Ledbetter Fair Pay Act, erasing the statute of limitations on filing a pay discrimination suit. He also hastened to rescind the Mexico City policy, lift the ban on embryonic stem cell research, and eliminate federal funding for abstinence-only education. His presidency would prove to be as significant for its promotion of women's rights as Bush's was for its fealty to pro-family positions.[63]

Obama appointed a record number of women to positions in his administration, including Hillary Clinton as secretary of state. In addition, he created the most demographically diverse administration in history. He named two more women, Sonia Sotomayor and Elena Kagan, to the Supreme Court. Obama became a champion of the LGBTQ community, not only lifting the ban on gays and lesbians in the military but appointing an openly gay man to head one branch of the military.[64]

Early in Obama's presidency, he established a White House Council on Women and Girls with Valerie Jarrett, assistant to the president and a senior advisor, as chair and Christina "Tina" Tchen, assistant to the president and chief of staff to the First Lady, as executive director. Somewhat similar to the programs directed by "establishment feminists" in the White House in the 1970s, the council's stated purpose was to promote fair treatment of women within the federal government, in the United States, and around the world.

As he signed the executive order creating the council, President Obama's comments made it clear that in his view, there was no contradiction between promoting women's rights and family values. Moreover he stressed that the issues facing women "are not just women's issues. When women make less than men for the same work, it hurts families who find themselves with less income, and have to work harder just to get by. When a job doesn't offer family leave," he said, "that also hurts men who want to help care for a new baby or an ailing parent. When there's no affordable child care, that hurts children who wind up in second-rate care, or spending afternoons alone in front of the television set."[65]

In March 2011 the White House Council on Women and Girls issued an eighty-five-page report reminiscent of the June 1976 report of the Ford-appointed National Commission on the Observance of International Women's Year, which began by describing "Today's Realities" on which its recommendations were based. The new report, *Women in America: Indicators of Social and Economic Well-Being*, offered a picture of American women in the areas of demographic and family changes, education, employment, health, and crime and violence, meant to "enhance our understanding both of how far American women have come and the areas where there is still work to be done."[66]

Conservatives were outraged that the president's signature achievement, the Affordable Care Act, not only required insurance companies to cease charging women more than men and to cover maternity and newborn care, it required company supported insurance policies to cover all FDA-approved methods of contraception. The pro-life movement promptly challenged this provision, insisting that requiring Catholic and other institutions opposed to contraception to include it in health care coverage of their employees was a violation of religious freedom. The issue of federal support for Planned Parenthood, a major provider of health services to low-income women, also incited a ferocious battle between the president and women's rights advocates on one hand, and the pro-life movement and many Republican congressmen on the other. More than once, Republicans in Congress threatened to shut down the federal government over the issue, with Senator Ted Cruz, a presidential hopeful who found this to be a winning issue with evangelicals, in the lead.[67]

With an African American in the White House, using his power to advance the rights of women, minorities, and the LGBTQ community, American politics had never been so polarized or bitterly partisan, nor political gridlock more intense. More than a few members of Congress, including moderate Republican senator from Maine, Olympia Snowe, left in disgust. Early in his presidency, Obama had made overtures to Republicans, offering concessions for their support that angered some in his own party, but he was rebuffed by Republicans intent on downsizing the government and determined to make him a one-term president.[68] Obama's election had enraged elements within the GOP base. When expressions of racism considered politically unacceptable since the 1970s resurfaced, Republican leaders did little to discourage it. Instead, many of them played to their base, themselves vilifying the president to the extent that compromise with him became almost impossible.

As the 2012 presidential election got under way, Republicans fully expected to emerge victorious and many sought the nomination. The field included eleven men and one woman, arch-conservative, born-again Christian and Schlafly admirer Michele Bachmann, congresswoman from Minnestoa. Women voters reacted strongly against the Republicans' efforts to outdo one another in attacks on abortion and even family planning. Pundits referred to a "Republican War on Women" as if it were something new, as Republicans denied any such war existed. Yet gaffes by Republican men, mostly notably one from Todd Akin, a congressman who opposed allowing abortions for rape victims, created major problems for the GOP. His statement, "If it's a legitimate rape, the female body has ways to shut the whole thing down," led many women to recoil in horror. Establishment Republicans called for him to drop out of the election, but Phyllis Schlafly, an influential backer, insisted he stay in. Romney made gaffes of his own, roundly ridiculed for his boast that he had "binders full of women" he could appoint, as well as his denunciation of the "forty-seven percent" of Americans dependent on federal largesse and his calls for illegal immigrants to "self-deport."[69]

On Election Day the race appeared to be dead even but Republicans expected to win. Barack Obama won handily, largely due to strong support from women voters. Obama won the two-party vote among women voters by twelve points (56 to 44 percent) while Romney won among men by an eight-point margin (54 to 46 percent). The Gallup agency reported that the gender gap was the largest in its history, that the "preferences of men and women have never differed more than in the 2012 election." Gallup suggested that Romney appealed more strongly to men because of his business background, while "Obama's campaign stressed maintaining the social safety net, raising taxes on the wealthy, maintaining abortion rights, and requiring healthcare coverage for contraception."[70] Pundits failed to mention that women's rights supporters who recalled the Mormons' crucial role in the fight against feminism in the 1970s would have been at least as concerned about Mitt Romney's religion as evangelicals, whom some predicted would shun Romney, but in the end put aside doctrinal differences and supported him.

Afterward, in order to diagnose what went wrong and strategize for the future, the Republican National Committee conducted what it called the "most comprehensive post-election review" ever made of an electoral loss— soon known as "the Autopsy." Unveiling the results, RNC leaders emphasized the need to expand the party's base and reach out to African American, Latino, Asian, women, and gay voters. Except for the part about gays, this sounded much like the recommendations proffered by Elly Peterson, George Romney, and Gerald Ford in the mid-1970s, just before the Republican Party made its sharp turn to the right. GOP leaders also noted that to avoid alienating women and younger Americans who held more liberal views on social issues, the party needed to show more tolerance of ideological diversity. True to form, however, in the report GOP leaders emphasized that their policies were generally sound; they just needed to be communicated more effectively.[71]

For the rest of Obama's presidency, the Republican base became more angry and vocal about the need to "take back their country." Rather than reach out to African Americans and Hispanics, many in the GOP worked to repress the black vote and curtail immigration. Rather than reach out to women and to gays, they fought harder against abortion and gay marriage. New developments in Obama's second term, including executive orders benefitting children of illegal immigrants as well as key Supreme Court decisions legalizing gay marriage and limiting the restrictions states could place on abortion, infuriated many Christian conservatives, who called for defiance of federal actions that violated their religious freedom. Ted Cruz declared these were "among the darkest hours of our nation."[72]

Meanwhile, women's rights supporters had much to celebrate in a president who, in his second inaugural address, declared that belief in the shared equality of Americans had guided the United States "through Seneca Falls and Selma and Stonewall," iconic moments in the history of the women's movement, the civil rights movement, and the fight for LGBT rights. "It is now our generation's task to carry on what those pioneers began," he concluded, and promised to continue to fight for equal rights for all Americans.[73]

Later in 2013, at a White House ceremony, President Obama presented Gloria Steinem with the Presidential Medal of Freedom. Obama praised her as "a trailblazing writer and feminist organizer . . . at the forefront of the fight for equality and social justice for more than four decades," and through her reporting and speaking, shaping "debates on the intersection of sex and race," and bringing "critical problems to national attention." Steinem's selection for this prestigious award unleashed a flood of commentary as people from many perspectives interpreted it as a sign of the times. Pro-life leaders insisted that the selection of this "unworthy recipient" by "the most pro-abortion president in this nation's history" tarnished the medal and the honor of the nation, and demonstrated how deeply institutionalized the "unspeakable crime" of abortion had become. Supporters of the women's rights movement were delighted to see the president honoring one of their own.[74]

The 2016 presidential election cycle placed the passionate disagreements over women's and gender issues in high relief. In contrast to her first bid for the Democratic nomination, Hillary Clinton emphasized more strongly the historic nature of her campaign and the need to defend as well as expand women's rights which were under fire from the right. Older women who had been part of the women's rights movement or saw themselves as its beneficiaries were strongly supportive, seeing the election of a woman president as long overdue. They had been "Ready for Hillary" for years. Clinton made a strong play to working mothers, especially single mothers, promising enhanced opportunities and more support. "We speak of a glass ceiling," she said, when these women did not "even have a secure floor under them."[75] African American women, responding to Clinton's promises to strengthen the safety net as well as her long record of support for minority and women's rights, turned out to vote in the primaries in high numbers and proved to be among the strongest Hillary supporters. Young, white, unmarried women, another key segment of the Democratic base, tended to support her opponent, Vermont senator Bernie Sanders, whose campaign focused on the issue of income inequality. Many young women saw it as a greater problem for their generation than sex discrimination. However, when Hillary Clinton won the nomination, and Sanders endorsed her, most supported her.

As the Republican primary got under way, many leaders of the GOP establishment backed Jeb Bush and funded his campaign lavishly. But far right Republicans were determined to nominate one of their own. In 2014 Phyllis Schlafly had published a fiftieth anniversary edition of her *A Choice Not an Echo*, in which she castigated establishment Republicans for refusing to nominate the most conservative candidate in every presidential election from 1964 to the present, except in 1980. It was high time, she insisted, for this to stop.[76]

As Donald Trump, a billionaire businessman from New York who had never held office, emerged as the leading contender for the Republican nomination, the GOP establishment seemed to have lost control of the party. At the same time, the party's right wing was torn between supporters of Ted Cruz and Donald Trump, the last candidates standing.

Trump, a thrice-married former Democrat with a long history of scandalous behavior with women who had once declared himself pro-choice, seemed an unlikely candidate to attract Christian conservatives. He was awkward around them, unfamiliar with their ideas and expressions, and even the Bible itself. After his invocation of "Two Corinthians" while addressing students at Liberty University, many scoffed, but the university's president, Jerry Falwell Jr., endorsed him. Trump also seemed to know little regarding the major tenets of the pro-life movement. When newscaster Chris Matthews pressed him to say whether or not women who had abortions should be punished, Trump said yes—despite the fact that for almost four decades, the pro-life movement had gained ground in part by insisting these women were victims rather than villains, and abortion providers were the ones deserving punishment.[77]

Donald Trump also had a long history of making sexist remarks and continued to do so as a candidate. Several times during the primaries his shocking statements led the press to predict his candidacy was finished— including when he said that journalist Megyn Kelly of Fox News had "blood coming out of her eyes, blood coming out of her wherever," when she questioned him about terms he had used for women, from "fat pigs" to "dogs, slobs and disgusting animals." But Trump's deliberate defiance of the norms of political correctness seemed to be the key to his popularity. At his rallies, some of his supporters engaged in misogynous rants against Hillary Clinton, shouting "Trump that bitch" and even "Kill her."[78]

Polls showed that Trump's strongest support came from white men without college degrees, men who responded to his charges that the establishment had sold them out in international trade agreements and subjected them to unfair competition from hordes of illegal immigrants. But racism and antifeminism as well as economic populism led many of them to support him. The fact that Trump had been the nation's "birther in chief" only enhanced his appeal among those who had questioned Barack Obama's legitimacy as president. And men with qualms about electing a woman president were especially hostile to the idea of electing Hillary Clinton, long hated by conservatives as a symbol of feminism. Trump's most avid supporters appeared to resent the gains of women and minorities, believing their progress had come at the expense of white men. They responded with special enthusiasm to his nostalgic slogan, "Make America Great Again," one also used during the Reagan-Bush campaign in 1980 as conservatives rallied to "take back their country."

Among those most attracted to Trump's message was Phyllis Schlafly, who would play a surprisingly important role in the 2016 election—her final battle against feminists and the political establishment. As the primaries began, she gave an hour-long interview to the archconservative *Breitbart News* in which she insisted that Donald Trump "is the only hope to defeat the Kingmakers" (her term for the GOP establishment). Her statement that Trump "represents everything the grassroots wants," said Julia Hahn, the reporter for *Breitbart*, "is certain to reverberate across the 2016 electorate."[79]

Not long thereafter, Trump met privately with Schlafly in St. Louis and, according to Schlafly, declared his complete fealty to her pro-family positions and promised to support them in the platform. He also pledged to support a major goal of the Religious Right: repeal of the "Johnson amendment," the IRS ruling from the 1960s prohibiting nonprofit charitable organizations, including churches, from direct involvement in electoral politics. Schlafly then went on television with Trump, and formally announced her endorsement. This astonished many conservatives because of their lingering questions about Trump's background as "an admitted pro-choice Democrat" and Ted Cruz's consistent support for conservative policies and avid courtship of Schlafly's endorsement.[80]

Schlafly was fully in support of Trump's defiant, anti-immigrant positions, which were her own. Though Trump has often been saluted, even by critics, for accurately assessing the mood of the electorate and framing the issues accordingly, his positions closely resembled those promoted by Schlafly and those who supported her America First as well as pro-family views. For years Schlafly had denounced immigration as a major threat to the survival of the kind of America that she loved and accused Democrats of "recruiting" illegals, intending to enfranchise them in order to expand their base of support. As passionate about national security as she was hostile to immigrants, since the terrorist attacks of September 11, 2001, Schlafly had demanded a well-guarded "fence" to secure the nation's southern border. In 2016 she applauded Trump's call for a wall between the United States and Mexico as well as his demand that Muslims be banned from entering the country. Schlafly compared Trump to her heroes: Barry Goldwater, who in 1964 had offered "a choice not an echo," and Ronald Reagan, who in the 1960s and most of the 1970s had been scorned but not intimidated by the establishment.[81]

Phyllis Schlafly's endorsement of Donald Trump led to the first major challenge to her leadership of the Eagle Forum since it was established in 1975—an attempted palace coup backed by Eagle Forum co-founder Shirley Curry and even Schlafly's daughter, Anne Cori. Both supported Ted Cruz. The two women and their co-conspirators were disturbed that Schlafly had chosen former Missouri GOP chair Ed Martin to succeed her as president of the Eagle Forum—passing over Curry, Cori, and Michele Bachmann—and they blamed Martin for "misleading" their aging idol. Schlafly acted quickly to assert her authority over her Eagle Forum empire. Wheelchair bound, she headed early to Cleveland for the Republican National Convention, determined to quell any attempts to deny Trump the nomination or efforts to soften the staunchly pro-family language in the platform.[82]

The 2016 Republican and Democratic conventions were studies in contrast—red, white, and blue pageants that put on full display the polarization afflicting American political culture as well as the distinctive differences between the parties. Reporters noted that there appeared to be as many minorities speaking on the platform at the Democratic convention as there were minority delegates at the GOP gathering. Leading Republicans, including George H. W. Bush, George W. Bush, John McCain, and Mitt Romney, declined to appear in Cleveland, and Ted Cruz appeared, only to be booed off the stage for refusing to endorse Trump, whereas a star lineup of enthusiastic Democrats competed for the privilege of addressing the convention in Philadelphia. Newspaper headlines screamed that the GOP platform was the most conservative in history, and that the Democratic platform was the most progressive ever.[83]

In mood and message the conventions could not have been more different. The message of the Republican convention seemed to be that the nation was in decline, with rising rates of crime and unemployment (which fact checkers in the press immediately challenged), its borders overrun by immigrants who, once in America, were committing vicious crimes; that Hillary Clinton was a power-hungry but weak leader whose policies had led to the rise of "Islamic terrorism,"; and that the nation was destined to have a grim future unless it elected Trump, who claimed that he could turn it all around and restore the nation to greatness. Trump strongly endorsed the pro-life and pro-family values of the platform, departing from it only on the issue of gay rights, a rather astonishing development never before seen at a GOP convention. The main message of the Democrats was that under Obama's leadership the nation had recovered from problems inherited from the Bush years, more Americans had access to health care, and the nation was becoming far more progressive— as demonstrated by the party's nomination of a woman as its candidate for president, a historic first celebrated as a major point of pride.

Clinton vowed to defend women's reproductive rights: Cecile Richards, president of Planned Parenthood, was invited to sit conspicuously with Bill Clinton in the Clinton family box. Yes, she acknowledged, there were problems to be solved, but the main message was that Americans were "Stronger Together," and working with one another under Clinton's leadership would address those problems—building on the legacy of President Obama who declared that Clinton was the most qualified person to ever run for president, even in comparison to Bill Clinton and himself.

Donald Trump's domination of the Republican primaries and emergence as the party's nominee sent shockwaves through the nation and shook up the GOP. For weeks after the convention, polls showed Hillary Clinton amassing a substantial lead as Trump made one gaffe after another, defying his campaign staff's efforts to rein him in and creating despair among GOP leaders. As they had many times in the past forty years, some pundits began to predict the downfall of the Republican Party and the end of its alliance with the Religious Right. Some speculated that the role of religion in American politics was waning, and the ability of the GOP to build majorities for their free trade, anti-tax policies by appealing to working-class voters' pro-family values might be declining.[84] Some Republican leaders were in despair about the likely impact of Trump's anti-immigrant, racist statements on the party's future as America approached the point where nonwhite voters would be the majority. Some Democrats joyfully concluded that, in Trump's success, the GOP establishment was paying the price of its cultivation of right-wing extremists and its failure to denounce bigotry.

For the rest of the summer Clinton enjoyed a sizable lead, with strong support from Democratic women and minority voters, and, after receiving Bernie Sanders's endorsement, began doing well among young voters. She had considerable support from white, married women, a group that usually voted Republican. Most surprising was the level of support for Clinton from white men, although there was a striking difference between college-educated white men who supported Clinton and white men without college educations who constituted Trump's core constituency.

In September, however, polls began to show an improvement in Trump's position after Clinton faced renewed criticism for indiscreet use of a private server while secretary of state and Trump made major changes in his campaign staff. There was outrage when Trump chose the head of the arch-conservative website *Breitbart News*, Steve Bannon, a bitter enemy of establishment Republicans, as CEO of his campaign staff—a choice celebrated by white nationalists such as KKK leader David Duke who saw Trump's nomination as vindication of his long-scorned views. But Trump drew praise for selecting a savvy conservative strategist and pollster Kellyanne Conway as his campaign manager, making her the first woman to ever manage a Republican presidential campaign. Conway, a former lawyer, described by Elaine Donnelly as one of the "brainy blonde barristers" inspired by Reagan to defend the cause of conservatism, had in speeches to conservative women bemoaned feminism as "gloom and doom" and the province of man-haters. She urged women wanting success in the workplace to "look feminine," and argued that "femininity is replacing feminism as a leading attribute for American women." In the past, Conway, a consultant billed as an expert on the gender gap, had frequently been hired to advise male clients on how to appeal to women or to repair the reputations of those who had erred, most notably Todd Akin, famous for his "legitimate rape" comment. Described by people close to Trump as a genius at diplomacy and "the kind of woman he likes around . . . to guide him but not criticize him," Conway was much more successful than the two men who preceded her in the post in gaining Trump's cooperation.[85]

Conway set out to repair relations with a constituency that contrasted sharply from Bannon's *Breitbart* readers: moderate white Republicans, especially women. Under her guidance Trump began to reach out to minorities—which critics denounced as a ploy to appease white Republicans alienated by Trump's racism. With the aid of Trumps daughter Ivanka, the Trump campaign also began to promote a child-care plan and maternity leave, a more obvious attempt to woo women voters. At the same time, Trump sought to bolster his candidacy by making a powerful appeal to pro-family movement supporters. Speaking to the Values Voters Summit, he promised that under "a Trump administration, our Christian heritage will be cherished, protected, defended, like you've never seen before." He vowed to keep the Supreme Court from falling into the hands of liberals, a disaster that would result in "a country that is no longer your country."[86]

On Labor Day—just as the campaign entered its final stretch—Phyllis Schlafly died of cancer, a big surprise to most of the nation. The press coverage was voluminous and varied as commentators assessed the life and legacy of this woman who all agreed was one of the most polarizing figures in American history. Her biographer, historian Donald Critchlow, emphasized that Schlafly, "the symbol of right-wing extremism to feminists and a hero to the Religious Right," had changed the course of history. Not only did she defeat feminists in the battle over the ERA, in the late 1970s, "she gave Republicans and conservatives a sorely needed victory at a time when many predicted the demise of the party itself and with it conservatism." In 2016, he wrote, Schlafly had once again "caught the winds of political change as she endorsed Donald Trump," who "tapped into her old base through his call for 'Making America Great Again' and securing the nation's borders. Trump's nomination as the Republican Party's candidate for president," Critchlow declared, "marked Schlafly's final victory."[87]

Even from the grave, Phyllis Schlafly and others evoking her memory rallied conservatives to her cause, now championed by Donald Trump. In a posthumously published book released just days after her death, *The Conservative Case for Trump*, she laid out what was at stake in the election. As described by *Breitbart News*, the book capped "Schlafly's last great political battle," pushing for the election of Donald Trump, "whom she saw as America's last hope."[88]

At Schlafly's funeral, held in the massive Cathedral Basilica of Saint Louis, Trump received a standing ovation as he repaid his debt to the leader of the family values crusade and seized the opportunity to present himself as its new champion. "A movement has lost its hero," he said in his eulogy. "And believe me, Phyllis was there for me when it was not at all fashionable." She was "looking down on us right now," he declared, "and I'm sure she's telling us to keep up the fight." Looking skyward, he added, "We will never, ever let you down."[89]

Trump backers continued to evoke Schlafly's memory to rally her supporters as they pointed out the high stakes in this presidential election. In coverage of her funeral, a *Breitbart News* reporter lamented that Clinton was leading among women and college-educated whites. She insisted that, if these elite groups "who have the financial means to remove themselves from the effects of mass migration and trade globalization . . . were to install Hillary Clinton in the White House . . . it could forever extinguish Schlafly's dream of preserving the nation she loved."[90]

Meanwhile women's rights organizations, including the Feminist Majority Foundation led by Eleanor Smeal, and Planned Parenthood led by Cecile Richards, sought to rally women's rights supporters, emphasizing to them that Hillary Clinton had "stood up for women's health and rights time and again." Richards reminded her supporters of Trump's statements such as calling "pregnancy an 'inconvenience' for employers and stating that pumping breast milk at work was "disgusting.'" She insisted that "the choice in this election couldn't be more clear. Donald Trump has made a long career out of disrespecting and demeaning women. He wants to punish women who have abortions, and put out-of-touch extremists on the Supreme Court." Calling the troops to action, Richards insisted that "women would be the reason Trump loses this election."[91]

As polls tightened going into the fall, it was anyone's guess which candidate, and which vision for America, would emerge victorious. Hillary Clinton's domination of the presidential debates, and the discovery of a taped episode in which Trump boasted about groping women—saying "when you're a star they let you do it"—led her to surge in the polls once again with just weeks to go before the election. Many pundits predicted not just a Clinton victory, but a "wave election" in which Democrats not only retained the presidency but took control of the Senate. Then, with eleven days to go, the election was rocked by an "October surprise," in which FBI Director James Comey—defying the bureau's policy against actions that might impact an election—announced the discovery of additional e-mails potentially relevant to the investigation of Clinton's use of e-mail, although the FBI had not yet read the e-mails. Trump insisted that the FBI would "never re-open" this investigation without strong evidence of grave criminal wrongdoing. Clinton's surge collapsed. Between this "evidence" against Hillary Clinton, and Kellyanne Conway's successful portrayal of Trump as a good family man, sensitive to women's needs, many women considering Clinton who normally voted Republican returned to the fold. Two days before the election, Comey released another statement asserting that the new e-mails revealed nothing of significance.[92]

On the eve of the election, in an extraordinary scene outside Philadelphia's Independence Hall, Hillary and Bill Clinton took the stage along with Michelle and Barack Obama before a crowd of over thirty thousand people. As one reporter noted, the Clintons and Obamas—the only Democratic occupants of the White House since 1980—were going for broke, audaciously presenting themselves as "united in a mission to broaden America's notions of what leadership could look like" and pleading for the opportunity to continue and expand upon the gains of the Obama administration.[93]

Meanwhile, Trump crisscrossed the nation, holding rallies even in states long considered Democratic strongholds, including in the so-called "Rust Belt" with high unemployment rates. Trump promised to restore lost jobs, but in addition wooed voters with attacks on racial, ethnic, and religious "others" and appeals based on stereotypical masculinity—focusing on Clinton's alleged corruption and criminality but also her lack of "stamina." Again, he held up the specter of a liberal-dominated Supreme Court, and warned in Schlafly-like rhetoric that this was the last chance to save the nation, indeed to restore an America that once was. Both sides proclaimed that this was one of the most important elections in American history.

On election day, polls were virtually unanimous that Clinton would emerge victorious. Across the nation, Clinton supporters—including countless starry-eyed little girls and elderly women hoping to see a woman president in their lifetime—prepared to celebrate a great victory, the final shattering of the glass ceiling. Instead, their hopes were shattered as state after state that had been expected to go for Clinton was called for Trump. The fact that Hillary Clinton won the popular vote by over two million votes, but failed to gain enough Electoral College votes to become president, made the defeat even more of a blow.

Trump supporters, however, were jubilant. This included not just angry white men, his chief constituency, but angry white women—the women of the pro-family movement and their political descendants. While Clinton had performed much better with white women than any Democratic presidential candidate in decades, winning 51 percent of white women with college degrees and married women by 2 points—62 percent of non-college women voted for Trump, proving fatal to Clinton's candidacy. The conservative, anti-establishment movement that had been building since the 1970s had taken back their country, not only from the liberal Democrats but from the GOP establishment, which Schlafly's son John called "the corrupt bipartisan cartel that has run our national government since Ronald Reagan left office." It was one of the most stunning upsets in American political history.[94]

It was clear that the polarization of American politics had reached a new and ominous level and that the nation was more divided than ever. Women's and gender issues remained at the forefront of American politics, as they had been since 1977 when David Broder declared that Houston had buried the idea "that so-called 'women's issues' are a sideshow to the center-ring concerns of American politics."

After 2016, the battle over women's rights and family values that polarized American politics would continue. Women's rights supporters, however shocked and angry, made it clear they were determined to fight on. This was hardly their first setback. And like conservative women, they often responded to setbacks with new determination to succeed. Looking back over the history of the American women's movement—including the battle for political equality—provides many lessons, one of which is that progress is not linear, but continues as long as women remain determined to bring about change.[95]

For women's rights advocates who took part in the International Women's Year conferences of 1977 and the National Women's Conference in Houston, that year was a major milestone. 2017 is an important anniversary, a time to contemplate the significance of these events, to reflect upon past gains and losses, and to plan for the future. In November 2007, Gloria Steinem, Eleanor Smeal, Charlotte Bunch, and many other IWY veterans participated in a thirtieth-anniversary symposium sponsored by Hunter College, home of the Bella Abzug Leadership Institute, a center devoted to mentoring young women for future leadership roles. In a keynote address, Steinem declared that "the Houston conference turned feminism from a small grassroots effort into a national movement," and empowered "a generation that would not have heard of [feminism] without the conference." The celebration featured speeches by many participants in the National Women's Conference, presentations by scholars who studied it, and workshops in which young women developed a National Plan of Action of their own, appropriate for the twenty-first century.[96]

Writing about the event in her *Newsweek* column, Anna Quindlen recounted her own experience as a young reporter covering the Houston conference for the *New York Times* in 1977. Reading over her columns, she wrote, she was "chagrined at how bloodless I made an event that was the human equivalent of a four-day fireworks show." Most newspapers had sent female reporters to Houston, she said, and "some of us were afraid of being in the tank for freedom." She had "bent over backward to be a dispassionate observer." Yet watching the proceedings, Quindlen realized "the demands—child care, an end to job discrimination, the Equal Rights Amendment—were all things I wanted myself." Today she sees the National Women's Conference as "a proud moment, not just for women, but for America."[97]

In her recent book, *My Life on the Road*, Gloria Steinem emphasized that her experiences in Houston were personally transformative, and that her "life was changed by a new sense of connection—with issues, possibilities." But she was "not alone in being a different person after Houston." In the years since, she writes, "I've met diverse women who were there, and every one has told me of some way in which she, too, was transformed: her hopes and ideas of what was possible—for the world, for women in general, and for herself."[98]

They were inspired to try to change the world. And they did. If in the immediate aftermath of the 1977 conference, or during the backlash of the 1980s, some feminists feared that they overstepped—or had contributed in any way to the conservative uprising that swept through national politics and captured the GOP—today they take great pride in the decisions made in Houston that they view as bold, brave, and prescient.

At the end of the earth-shaking National Women's Conference, Steinem had wondered, "Would anybody in the future know or care what had happened here?" In 2017, it seems that the answer is yes. There is increased interest among scholars and analysts who recognize the National Women's Conference as a transformative event in U.S. history.[99]

Forty years after the Houston conference, the nation is more racially and ethnically diverse, and most Americans hold progressive views on women's and gender issues. The fact that so many Americans, particularly young Americans, now embrace ideas that had been considered so controversial back in 1977 suggests that in time, the nation may look back upon the National Women's Conference as a historic milestone as inspirational and iconic as the Seneca Falls Convention.

Acknowledgments

This book has been long in the making and I have many debts that I grate-fully acknowledge.

First I would like to thank several key participants in the events described in the book who were willing to talk with me about their experi-ences and impressions. I am grateful to First Lady Rosalynn Carter and President Jimmy Carter, Midge Costanza, Gloria Steinem, Charlotte Bunch, Carmen Delgado Votaw, Phyllis Schlafly, Ann Mulloy Ashmore, Pam Elam, Sally Lunt, Cora Norman, Keller Barron, Eunice "Tootsie" Holland, Mary Heriot, Malissa Burnette, Pat Callair, Nancy Moore, Victoria Eslinger, and Candy Waites for interviews that were crucial to this project. Two key members of the staff of the National Commission on the Observance of International Women's Year, Shelah Leader and Patricia Hyatt, generously allowed me to see the manuscript of their book, which provided valuable insight into the inner workings of the IWY Secretariat, *American Women on the Move: The Inside Story of the National Women's Conference, 1977,* and offered helpful comments as I was completing my own manuscript. Jo Freeman, who participated in the New York IWY meeting and the Houston conference—a wonder who has long been an activist, analyst, archivist, and photographer of the women's movement—generously shared insights as well as materials from her personal IWY collection. I also appreciate the work and assistance of Diana Mara Henry, the official photographer of IWY.

I profited from hundreds of interviews conducted in 1977 at the IWY conferences by the oral history team led by Constance Ashton Myers of the University of South Carolina. With grants from USC, I am working with Andrea L'Hommedieu, oral historian at the South Caroliniana Library, to digitize these interviews and make them available online—hoping to encourage further scholarship on IWY. In addition, interviews that my former student Sheryl Hansen Smith conducted with women and men on both sides of the bitter battle over IWY in Mississippi were extremely valuable. Material on feminists and conservatives in South Carolina—gathered by my students in several classes dedicated to preserving the history of the women's movement and now housed at the university library's South Carolina Political Collections—has also been very helpful.

I was fortunate to receive tremendous support for this project, which I believe was due to widespread recognition of the troubled state of our political culture and my insistence that this book would help readers understand how we got here. It was a great pleasure to be the Hrdy Fellow at the Radcliffe Institute for Advanced Study at Harvard University. With the Arthur and Elizabeth Schlesinger Library on the History of Women in America—one of my favorite places on earth—next door, the year at the RIAS provided an incredible opportunity to conduct research, as well as to discuss my findings with others. In addition, a year in Washington, D.C., as a fellow at the Woodrow Wilson International Center for Scholars which is designed to bring scholars and policy makers together, was a joy and a privilege. I also received generous funding from the National Endowment for the Humanities. This included both a summer research grant in the early stages of my research, and later, a year-long fellowship while I was working on the book at the National Humanities Center in North Carolina, generously welcomed into their community of scholars as a visiting fellow. The Gerald R. Ford Presidential Foundation provided a travel award that enabled me to conduct crucial research at the Ford Presidential Library in Ann Arbor, Michigan. My home institution, the University of South Carolina, particularly the Office of the Provost and the Women's and Gender Studies Program, has been generous with research awards at several stages of the project, and allowed me time for research and writing, that most valuable asset of any scholar.

There are many individuals at each of these places to whom I am eternally grateful. These include, at the Radcliffe Institute, the director, Judith Vichniac; fellows' advisor Lindy Hess; the dean, Drew Gilpin Faust, who during the year became Harvard University president; and her successor, Barbara Grosz, who gave me, Nancy Cott, and Jane Mansbridge the incomparable opportunity to discuss women's history and politics with Phyllis Schlafly over dinner following her lecture. At the Schlesinger Library, I benefited from the work of Nancy Cott, the director, and Kathryn Jacob, the curator of manuscripts, who built the library's vast collection of material on the women's movement, and from the expertise of Ellen Shea, the head of research services, who was so helpful with my research and patient with my requests, as were Sarah Hutcheon, Laurie Ellis, Anne Engelhart, and Diana Carey. At the Wilson Center, Sonya Michel, then director of United States Studies, and Janet Spikes, the librarian, helped make my time there very rewarding. I also thank the remarkable staff of the National Humanities Center, particularly Kent Mullikin, Geoff Harpham, Eliza Robertson, Brooke Andrade, Joel Elliott, and Don Soloman.

William McNitt, director of the Ford Presidential Library, was tremendously helpful, as was Donna Lehman, archivist, who was generous with her expertise and her insights. Special thanks are due to Steve Hochman, director of research for the Carter Center, and to the staff of the Jimmy Carter Presidential Library, a great place to work. I also appreciate the assistance provided by Kelly Wooten of Duke University Libraries; Rachel Dreyer of the Eberly Family Special Collections Library at Penn State University; Danielle Kovacs of the University of Massachusetts, Amherst Library; Emily Swenson of the Bentley Historical Library at the University of Michigan; Jeffrey M. Flannery of the Library of Congress; Jenny Sternaman of the Ronald Reagan Library; and Deborah Pentecost and Rebekah Gantner of the Eagle Forum Archives. Closer to home, I appreciate the aid provided by Herb Hartsook, Andrea L'Hommedieu, Kathy Snediker of the USC Libraries, and the ever helpful Lori Vann of the History Department.

I am also indebted to other scholars. I profited greatly from the tremendous body of scholarship on the women's rights movement and on the political transformation of the 1970s. This book is intended to expand our knowledge on both of these topics and bridge the gap between them by focusing on the feminists working within the political establishment and the conservative women with whom they competed for political influence. I was pleased to be a part of a group of scholars led by Bruce Schulman and Julian Zelizer who together demonstrated the transformational role of the 1970s in American politics and benefitted from their research and insights. I gained much from collaboration with a group of historians and political scientists assembled by Angie Maxwell and Todd Shields at the University of Arkansas, all seeking to shed light on the legacy of 1970s feminism for current politics. Angie Maxwell, Sara Evans, and Jane De Hart read drafts of my manuscript and offered valuable suggestions. I am grateful to Sara Evans and Jane De Hart for this assistance and even more for their example as historians who write with scholarly perspective about events in which they were involved. Together with Donald Mathews, Jane De Hart also demonstrated through a pioneering study of the Equal Rights Amendment the great value of examining both sides of the battle. Daniel K. Williams, an authority on politics and religion, also read the manuscript carefully and saved me from some errors. He and Jennifer Donnally both offered important suggestions on the pro-life movement. I'll always remember my birthday lunch with Jennifer Donnally in Chapel Hill when we exchanged information and compared ideas for six hours straight.

I appreciate Nancy Baker's willingness to educate me about the rescission issue and allow me to profit from her exhaustive research, Carole Bucy's assistance regarding the Ronald Reagan administration and women, Doreen Mattingly's work on Midge Costanza, Robin Morris's work on conservative leader Kathryn Dunaway, my former student Laura Foxworth's work on women's issues and the Southern Baptist Convention, Yale law professor Reva Siegel's research on the ERA, and Catherine Rymph's work on Republican women. I also thank Kathryn Kish Sklar and Thomas Dublin for the service they provided to scholars through their incomparable online database *Woman and Social Movements*, which includes extensive documents section relating to the National Women's Conference and IWY.

Along the way I have enjoyed working with a large, energetic group of research assistants at USC whose work was essential, especially graduate students Jennifer Gunter, Michele Coffey, Laura Foxworth, Caroline Peyton, Kyna Herzinger, Caitlyn Mans, Jillian Hinderliter, Micki Blakely, Aaron Haberman, Annie Boiter-Jolley, and Chris Sixta Rinehart, and also Stephen Miller, my research assistant at Vanderbilt, who was with me at the very beginning as we learned together about the rise of the New Right. I also thank undergraduate students Alexandra Chapman, Bella Wenum, Elizabeth Layne, Kate Shropshire and Skylar McClain at USC; Katia Johnstone, Keisha Lai, and Jennifer McAmis at the Wilson Center; Alex Snell and Beverly Washington at Harvard; and Sara Farnsworth and Audra Odom at the University of Southern Mississippi, who were all tremendously helpful and fun to work with.

I am especially grateful to my editor at Bloomsbury, Jacqueline Johnson, for her skill, patience, and encouragement. Working with her has been a real pleasure. Nancy Miller, editorial director, has taken a great interest in the book and been very supportive. In addition, as the project comes to a close, managing editor Sara Kitchen and publicist Sarah New have been a great help. I also thank my agent, Lisa Adams, of the Garamond Agency, who has been with me in this journey from start to finish.

My sons, Scott Wheeler and Jesse Wheeler, both talented writers, helped at times with edits and transcriptions, as well as lots of encouragement. My sister, Carol Spruill, a former dean at Duke Law School whose special area of interest is poverty law, has always shared my passion for issues related to women's rights and politics and has taught me so much over the years. My late mother, Edna Whitley Spruill, an ardent supporter of women's rights and the Equal Rights Amendment, read everything I ever wrote with such pleasure and was always encouraging and inspiring. I could not ask for a more loving or supportive family. I am very grateful to all of them.

I am extremely fortunate to have as my husband Don H. Doyle, also a historian, who loves history, research, writing, and keeping up with current politics as much as I do. We talk about these things nonstop. Don understands the thrills as well as the frustrations of writing, and is a great listener, critic, and editor. I love him dearly and much appreciate all of his support and encouragement. This book is dedicated to him.

Notes

CHAPTER I: FOUR DAYS THAT CHANGED THE WORLD

1   Jane Kramer, "Road Warrior: After Fifty Years, Gloria Steinem Is Still at the Forefront of the Feminist Cause," *New Yorker*, October 19, 2015, 53. Gloria Steinem, *My Life on the Road* (New York: Random House, 2015), 53–67.

2   NCOIWY, *National Women's Conference Official Briefing Book: Houston, Texas, November 18 to 21, 1977* (U.S. Government Printing Office, Washington, D.C., 1977), 1–18; NCOIWY, *American Women on the Move: National Women's Conference Program* (Washington, D.C., 1977); Judith P. Zinsser, "From Mexico to Copenhagen to Nairobi: The United Nations Decade for Women, 1975–1985," *Journal of World History* 13 (2002): 139–67.

3   Lindsy Van Gelder, "Four Days That Changed the World: Behind the Scenes in Houston," *Ms.*, March 1978.

4   Tom Brokaw, "Opening of the Largest Gathering of American Women Ever Held," November 18, 1977, and Carole Simpson, *Opposing Voices Heard at Women's Conference*, November 21, 1977 (New York: NBC), NBC Learn; NCOIWY, *The Spirit of Houston: The First National Women's Conference: An Official Report to the President, the Congress and the People of the United States* (Washington, D.C.: U.S. Government Printing Office, 1978), 125, 173, 205–6; Anna Quindlen, "Women's Parley Begins Action over a Rights Agenda for Nation: No Confrontations Materialized," *New York Times*, November 20, 1977; George F. Will, "Earnest 'Sisters' Voting for a New World," *Washington Post*, November 24, 1977; Sally Quinn, "The Pedestal Has Crashed: Pride and Paranoia in Houston," *Washington Post*, November 23, 1977; Rosemary Thomson, *The Price of LIBerty* (Carol Stream, IL: Creation House, 1978); Megan Rosenfeld and Bill Curry, "Women's Conference Passes Abortion, Gay Rights Measures," *Washington Post*, November 21, 1977. On Sadat, see *Time*, December 5, 1977 (with tiny corner photo of Sadat on a page featuring the IWY conference).

5   Mildred Hamilton, "Conference That's Like a Convention," *San Francisco Examiner & Chronicle*, November 20, 1977; NCOIWY, *The Spirit of Houston*, 136, 172; Judy Klemesrud, "At Houston Meeting, 'A Kaleidoscope of American Womanhood,'" *New York Times*, November 19, 1977; Judy Klemesrud, "A Reporter's Notebook: Symbolic Attire," *New York Times*, November 21, 1977; Bruce J. Schulman, *The Seventies: The*

Great Shift in American Culture, Society, and Politics (Cambridge, MA: Da Capo Press, 2001), 186.

6   NCOIWY, *Spirit of Houston*, 119–26.

7   Ibid. For names and biographical sketches of all commission members, see 243–49.

8   Caroline Bird, *What Women Want: From the Official Report to the President, the Congress, and the People of the United States* (New York: Simon and Schuster, 1979), 62–65; Anna Quindlen, "Women Relay the Movement's Torch from Seneca Falls to Houston," *New York Times*, October 7, 1977; Susan Ware, *Game, Set, Match: Billie Jean King and the Revolution in Women's Sports* (Chapel Hill, University of North Carolina Press, 2011).

9   Bird, *What Women Want*, 34–35; NCOIWY, *Spirit of Houston*, 123–125, 130, 142, 154, 157, text of Angelou poem 195; Carole Ashkinaze, "National Women's Conference to Begin Friday in Houston," *Atlanta Journal-Constitution*, November 19, 1977, section A.

10 Bella S. Abzug, *Bella: Ms. Abzug Goes to Washington* (New York: Saturday Review Press, 1972), 3–7, 37–38, 126–27; Suzanne Braun Levine and Mary Thom, *Bella Abzug: How One Tough Broad from the Bronx Fought Jim Crow and Joe McCarthy, Pissed Off Jimmy Carter, Battled for the Rights of Women and Workers, Rallied Against War and for the Planet, and Shook up Politics Along the Way; An Oral History* (New York: Farrar, Straus and Giroux, 2007), 48–55, 149–66; Quinn, "The Pedestal Has Crashed."

11 Abzug, *Bella*, 3–7, 37–38, 126–27; Levine and Thom, *Bella Abzug*, 44–56, 49–66.

12 NCOIWY, *Spirit of Houston*, 243–49; Bird, *What Women Want*, 62, 63.

13 NCOIWY, *Spirit of Houston*, 175–76, 290; NCOIWY, "American Women on the Move: Houston National Women's Conference Program," November 1977.

14 NCOIWY, *Spirit of Houston*, 9, 119–70; Quinn, "The Pedestal Has Crashed."

15 NCOIWY, "American Women on the Move," 175–84; Alice S. Rossi, *Feminists in Politics: A Panel Analysis of the First National Women's Conference* (New York: Academic Press, 1982), 324.

16 For the National Plan of Action, see NCOIWY, *Spirit of Houston*, 13–97 or Bird, *What Women Want*, 83–178.

17 NCOIWY, *Spirit of Houston*, 13–97; Bird, *What Women Want*, 83–178.

18 Loretta Ross, "Loretta Ross on the Origins of 'Women of Color,'" n.d., http://www.racialicious.com/2011/03/03/for-your-womens-history-month-loretta-ross-on-the-origin-of-women-of-color/ (accessed May 17, 2012); Steinem, *My Life on the Road*, 61–65.

19 NCOIWY, *Spirit of Houston*, 70–75, 155–157, quotation 157.

20 Plank 21, NCOIWY, *Spirit of Houston*, 83–86.

21 Dudley Clendinen and Adam Nagourney, *Out for Good: The Struggle to Build a Gay Rights Movement in America* (New York: Simon and Schuster, 1999), 291–309; Robert O. Self, *All in the Family: The Realignment of American Democracy Since the 1960s* (New York: Hill and Wang, 2012); Sara M. Evans, *Tidal Wave: How Women Changed America at Century's End* (New York: Free Press, 2003), 49–53; Judy Klemesrud, "Women's Movement at Age 11: Larger, More Diffuse, Still Battling," *New York Times*, November 15, 1977.

22 On Friedan's disagreement with many other feminists about lesbianism as a goal of the movement, see Daniel Horowitz, *Betty Friedan and the Making of the Feminine Mystique: The American Left, the Cold War, and Modern Feminism* (Amherst: University of Massachusetts Press, 1998), 231–36; Quinn, "The Pedestal Has Crashed."

23 NCOIWY, *Spirit of Houston*, 148–49, 152.

24 Mead quoted in Quinn, "The Pedestal Has Crashed"; Stapleton quoted in Bird, *What Women Want*, 35; Tanya Melich, *The Republican War Against Women: An Insider's Report from Behind the Lines* (New York: Bantam Books, 1998), 100.

25 Kathryn Kish Sklar, "How Did the National Women's Conference in Houston in 1977 Shape a Feminist Agenda for the Future?," *Women and Social Movements (WASM)*, Kathryn Sklar and Thomas Dublin, eds. (Alexandria, VA: Alexander Street Press). http://womhist.alexanderstreet.com.

26 NCOIWY, *Spirit of Houston*; Thomson, *Price of LIBerty*; Phyllis Schlafly, "Pro-Family Rally Attracts 20,000," *Phyllis Schlafly Report* 11, no. 5, section 2 (December 1977).

27 Peggy Simpson, "Feminists, Conservatives Face Houston Standoff," *Commercial Appeal*, September 11, 1977, Martha Swain clippings collection in possession of the author; Kay Mills, "Those Aren't Prayer Meetings," *Daily Breakthrough*, September 14, 1977; Phyllis Schlafly, "IWY: A Front for Radicals and Lesbians," *Phyllis Schlafly Report* 11, no. 1, section 2 (August 1977); Thomson, *Price of LIBerty*.

28 Jane J. Mansbridge, *Why We Lost the ERA* (Chicago: University of Chicago Press, 1986), 110; Carol Felsenthal, *The Sweetheart of the Silent Majority: The Biography of Phyllis Schlafly* (Garden City, NY: Doubleday, 1981), 259–61, 264.

29 Phyllis Schlafly, "Federal Financing of a Foolish Festival for Frustrated Feminists," *Phyllis Schlafly Report* 10, no. 10, section 2 (May 1977).

30 Thomson, *Price of LIBerty*; Schlafly, "IWY: A Front for Radicals and Lesbians"; Phyllis Schlafly, "What Really Happened in Houston," *Phyllis Schlafly Report* 11, no. 5, section 2 (December 1977).

31 Thomson, *Price of LIBerty*, 92–102; Ruth Murray Brown, *For a "Christian America": A History of the Religious Right* (Amherst, NY: Prometheus, 2002); Neil J. Young, "The ERA Is a Moral Issue: The Mormon Church, LDS Women, and the Defeat of the Equal Rights Amendment," *American Quarterly* 59, no. 3 (September 2007): 623–44.

32 Marjorie J. Spruill, "The Mississippi 'Takeover': Feminists, Antifeminists, and the International Women's Year Conference of 1977," in *Mississippi Women: Their Histories, Their Lives*, vol. 2, Martha H. Swain, Elizabeth Anne Payne, and Marjorie Julian Spruill, eds. (Athens: University of Georgia Press, 2010), 287–313; Erin M. Kempker, "Battling 'Big Sister' Government: Hoosier Women and the Politics of International Women's Year," *Journal of Women's History* 24 (Summer 2012): 144–70; Bob Schwartzman, "Klan Cardholder Wanted to Help," *Today*, July 18, 1977; Betty J. Blair, "Klan's Spies' Plan to Disrupt Feminist Party," *Detroit News*, September 1, 1977.

33 Jennifer Donnally, "The Politics of Abortion and the Rise of the New Right" (Ph.D. diss., University of North Carolina at Chapel Hill, 2013). See also coverage in *National Right to Life News* from September 1977 through January 1978.

34 The Schlesinger Library at Harvard University contains National Commission for the Observance of International Women's Year Records including the reports sent to the NCOIWY from each state, which often included clippings. Many state archives also have material on the state meetings. For a prime example of the press enjoying the conflict among women at a state IWY meeting, see "Editorial: In Perfumed Combat," *Montgomery Independent*, July 15, 1977, NCOIWY Records, Schlesinger Library, Radcliffe Institute, Harvard University, hereafter NCOIWY Records, SL.

35 Spruill, "Mississippi Takeover," 51–52; Bird, *What Women Want*, 51–52; Simpson, "Feminists, Conservatives Face Houston Standoff."

36 Judy Klemesrud, "10,000 Foes of Equal Rights Plan in 'Pro-Family Rally' in Houston," *New York Times*, November 20, 1977; Anne Taylor Fleming, "That Week in Houston: It Was Said That the Women's Movement Was in a State of Disarray; the National Women's Conference Proved Otherwise," *New York Times*, December 25, 1977; Pat Reed, "Pro-Family Groups Ink Proposals," *Daily Breakthrough*, November 20, 1977; Brown, *For a "Christian America*," 112.

37   Klcmesrud, "10,000 Foes"; Thomson, *Price of LIBerty*, 144–45.

38   Judy Klemesrud, "Equal Rights Plan and Abortion Are Opposed by 15,000 at Rally: Like
     a Black Baptist Church," *New York Times*, November 20, 1977; Reed, "Pro-Family Groups
     Ink Proposals"; "IWY Folds Tent; 300,000 Protest Signatures Flown to White House,"
     National Right to Life News, January 1978; Carole Ashkinaze, "God Stronger Than Carter,
     Stop-ERA Leader Declares," *Atlanta Journal-Constitution*, November 20, 1977.

39   Quinn, "The Pedestal Has Crashed"; "IWY Folds Tent."

40   Quinn, "The Pedestal Has Crashed."

41   Ibid.

42   Thomson, *Price of LIBerty*, 138–50.

43   Ibid.; Rosemary Thomson, *Withstanding Humanism's Challenge for Families: Anatomy of
     a White House Conference* (Morton, IL: Traditional Publications, 1981), 22; Schlafly,
     "What Really Happened in Houston."

44   For examples see NCOIWY, *Spirit of Houston*, 205–6; "What Next for U.S. Women:
     Houston Produces New Alliances and a Drive for Grass-Roots Power," *Time*, December
     5, 1977; "IWY Folds Tent"; Susan L. Huck, "Five Million Dollar Misunderstanding,"
     American Opinion, January 1978, 1–4, 75–91.

CHAPTER 2: THE RISE OF THE FEMINIST ESTABLISHMENT

1   Ellen Goodman, "Women's Movement Comes Full Circle: Ellen at Large," *Mercury*,
     November 7, 1977, box 220, folder "November 1977, Houston Conference," National
     Organization for Women (NOW) Records (MC 496), Schlesinger Library, Radcliffe
     Institute, Harvard University, Cambridge, MA, hereafter, NOW Records, SL.

2   "Women March on Houston: Feminists and Their Foes Square Off Around the Big
     National Meeting," *Time*, November 28, 1977. In early 1976, the magazine had reported
     the women were 53 percent of registered voters in the United States but held only 5
     percent of the elective offices, but the total, 7,000, was twice what it had been five years
     earlier.

3   Dan T. Carter, *The Politics of Rage: George Wallace, the Origins of the New Conservatism,
     and the Transformation of American Politics* (Baton Rouge: LSU Press, 1995); Dan T.
     Carter, *From George Wallace to Newt Gingrich: Race in the Conservative Counterrevolution,
     1963–1994* (Baton Rouge: LSU Press, 1996); William C. Berman, *America's Right
     Turn from Nixon to Clinton* (Baltimore: Johns Hopkins University Press, 2001).

4   Telegram, George C. Wallace to Miss Alice Paul, National Women's Party, July 20,
     1968, folder 26, box 23, Catherine Shipe East Papers (MC 477), Schlesinger Library,
     Radcliffe Institute, Harvard University, hereafter East Papers, SL.

5   Janet K. Boles, *The Politics of the Equal Rights Amendment: Conflict and the Decision
     Process* (New York: Longman, 1979), 51–56.

6   "Women of the Year: Great Changes, New Chances, Tough Choices," *Time*, January 5,
     1976.

7   Susanna Downie and National Women's Conference Committee, "Part I: How the
     National Plan of Action for Women Came Into Being," in *Decade of Achievement:
     1977–1987: A Report on a Survey Based on the National Plan of Action for Women*
     (Washington, D.C: National Women's Conference Committee, 1988), 5–7. Downie
     noted that the report, including this history of IWY, was written "with substantial help
     from Sarah Harder, Catherine East, Kay Clarenbach, and Mim Kelber." Kelber was a
     key aide to Bella Abzug and her speechwriter while Azbug served in Congress and as
     IWY presiding officer.

8   Kathleen A. Laughlin, "Introduction: President's Commission on the Status of Women" n.d., Women and Social Movements, ASM; Dorothy Sue Cobble et al., *Feminism Unfinished: A Short, Surprising History of American Women's Movements* (New York: Liveright Publishing Corporation, 2015), 47–50; PCSW, *American Women: Report of the President's Commission on the Status of Women* (Washington, DC: U.S. Government Printing Office, 1963).

9   Laughlin, "Introduction: President's Commission"; Cobble et al., *Feminism Unfinished*, 47–50; PCSW, *American Women*.

10   NCOIWY, ". . . To Form a More Perfect Union . . ." *Justice for American Women; Report of the National Commission on the Observance of International Women's Year* (Washington, D.C.: U.S. Government Printing Office, 1976), 3–9; PCSW, *American Women*; Jo Freeman, "How 'Sex' Got Into Title VII: Persistent Opportunism as a Maker of Public Policy," http://www.jofreeman.com/lawandpolicy/titlevii.htm (accessed April 4, 2015).

11   Downie and National Women's Conference Committee, "Decade of Achievement"; Laughlin, "Introduction: President's Commission"; NCOIWY, ". . . To Form a More Perfect Union . . ." 3–9; PCSW, *American Women*; Cobble et al., *Feminism Unfinished*, 50–51; Robert O. Self, *All in the Family: The Realignment of American Democracy Since the 1960s* (New York: Hill and Wang, 2012), See especially part 1, "This is a Man's World," which describes the "breadwinner liberalism" behind Great Society programs.

12   Downie and National Women's Conference Committee, "Decade of Achievement"; Elizabeth Singer More, "Report of the President's Commission on the Status of Women: Background, Content, Significance," n.d., Schlesinger Library, Radcliffe Institute, Harvard University, https://www.radcliffe.harvard.edu/sites/radcliffe.harvard.edu/files/documents/report_of_the_presidents_commission_on_the_status_of_women_background_content_significance.pdf.

13   Kathleen A. Laughlin, "Introduction to the Women and Social Movements State Commissions Database," *Women and Social Movements of the United States [WASM], 1600–2000, Scholars' Edition,* Kathryn Kish Sklar and Thomas Dublin, eds, (Alexandria, VA: Alexander Street Press, 2009); Anita Miller, "The Uncertain Future of Women's Commissions," *Graduate Woman* 74 (June 1980): 10–15; Mildred Norris, "Status of Women in Mississippi, Report of the Governor's Commission on the Status of Women," June 2, 1967, McCain Library, University of Southern Mississippi; Kathleen A. Laughlin, "Kathryn (Kay) Frederick Clarenbach," *Notable American Women: Race in the Conservative Counterrevolution, 1963–1994* (Baton Rouge: LSU Press, 1996).

14   Downie and National Women's Conference Committee, "Decade of Achievement"; Betty Friedan, *The Feminine Mystique* (New York: W. W. Norton, 1963).

15   Flora Davis, *Moving the Mountain: The Women's Movement in America Since 1960* (Champaign: University of Illinois Press, 1999), 38–43. The Virginia senator Howard Smith, who introduced Title VII, acted in part at the urging of friends in the National Women's Party; Carl M. Brauer, "Women Activists, Southern Conservatives, and the Prohibition of Sex Discrimination in Title VII of the 1964 Civil Rights Act," *Journal of Southern History* 49, no. 1 (1983): 37–56; Cobble et al., *Feminism Unfinished*, 55–59.

16   Davis, *Moving the Mountain*, 1999, 45–47, 52–55; Hernandez resigned from the EEOC. Graham was not reappointed despite feminists' urging. Both of them were elected vice presidents of NOW at its inaugural conference. Cynthia Harrison, *On Account of Sex: The Politics of Women's Issues, 1945–1968* (Berkeley: University of California Press, 1988), 192–209; "Aileen Hernandez, Former President National Organization for Women," *Makers*, http://www.makers.com/aileen-hernandez (accessed April 14, 2016).

17 Barry Friedman, *The Will of the People: How Public Opinion Has Influenced the Supreme Court and Shaped the Meaning of the Constitution* (New York: Farrar, Straus and Giroux, 2009), 290.

18 Gail Collins, *When Everything Changed: The Amazing Journey of American Women from 1960 to the Present* (New York: Little, Brown, 2009), 82–83.

19 Betty Friedan, *"It Changed My Life:" Writings on the Women's Movement, with a New Introduction* (Cambridge: Harvard University Press, 1976), 93–108, quotation 95; Harrison, *On Account of Sex*, 192–306; Biography and Chronology, Finding Aid, Catherine Shipe East Papers, 1941–1995, MC 477, Schlesinger Library, Radcliffe Institute, Harvard University, Cambridge, MA.

20 NOW, "Founding: National Organization for Women," accessed October 16, 2015, http://now.org/about/history/founding-2/; Graham told Friedan he had suggested creation of such a group to mainstream women's organizations such as the American Association of University Women and the League of Women Voters, but they had declined. Harrison, *On Account of Sex*, 193; Betty Friedan, "Statement of Purpose: National Organization for Women," 1966, NOW Website, http://now.org/about/history/statement-of-purpose/; Davis, *Moving the Mountain*, 1999, 53.

21 Friedan, "NOW Statement of Purpose."

22 Downie and National Women's Conference Committee, "Decade of Achievement."

23 Susan M. Hartmann, *From Margin to Mainstream: American Women and Politics Since 1960* (New York: Knopf, 1989), 20–21, 50–52.

24 Collins, *When Everything Changed*, 70–71; Kathleen A. Laughlin, "How Did State Commissions on the Status of Women Overcome Historic Antagonisms Between Equal Rights and Labor Feminists to Create a New Feminist Mainstream, 1963–1973?," *Women and Social Movements of the United States [WASM], 1600–2000, Scholars' Edition*, Kathryn Kish Sklar and Thomas Dublin, eds, (Alexandria, VA: Alexander Street Press, 2009); Cobble et al., *Feminism Unfinished*, quotation 63.

25 Davis, *Moving the Mountain*, 1999, 66–68.

26 Ibid.

27 NOW, "Honoring Our Founders & Pioneers," http://now.org/about/history/honoring-our-founders-pioneers/(accessed October 16, 2015); Davis, *Moving the Mountain*, 1999, 49–68. After NOW organized in South Carolina in 1970, Columbia feminists confronted one of the editors of the local newspaper, insisting it stop carrying separate "female" and "male" want ads. After he "more or less threw them out of his office," they met every Sunday night for two months to clip such ads out of the newspapers and mail them to the EEOC office in Atlanta. The paper changed its policy. Marjorie J. Spruill, "Victoria Eslinger, Keller Bumgardner Barron, Mary Heriot, Tootsie Holland, and Pat Callair: Champions of Women's Rights in South Carolina," in *South Carolina Women: Their Lives and Times*, vol. 3 (Athens: University of Georgia Press, 2012): 373–408, 395; Friedan, *It Changed My Life*, 116–44.

28 Sara Evans, *Tidal Wave: How Women Changed America at Century's End* (New York: Simon and Schuster, 2010); Ruth Rosen, *The World Split Open: How the Modern Women's Movement Changed America* (New York: Penguin, 2001).

29 Sara Evans, *Personal Politics: The Roots of Women's Liberation in the Civil Rights Movement and the New Left* (New York: Vintage Books, 1979); Evans, *Tidal Wave*; Rosen, *The World Split Open*; "'Our Bodies, Ourselves': A Brief History and Reflection, by OBOS Founders Judy Norsigian, Vilunya Diskin, Paula Doress-Worters, Jane Pincus, Wendy Sanford, and Norma Swenson," *Our Bodies, Ourselves*, accessed April 14, 2016, http://www.ourbodiesourselves.org/history/impact-and-influence/bwhbc-and-our-bodies-ourselves-a-brief-history-and-reflection/.

30 Davis, *Moving the Mountain*, 1999, 66–93; Evans, *Personal Politics*; Evans, *Tidal Wave*, especially 49–52; Friedan, *It Changed My Life*, quotations 199–202.

31 Collins, *When Everything Changed*, 199–203; Carolyn G. Heilbrun, *The Education of a Woman: The Life of Gloria Steinem* (New York: Ballantine, 1995).

32 Friedan, *It Changed My Life*, 199–202; National Organization for Women, "Highlights from NOW's Forty Fearless Years," 2010, http://www.now.org/history/timeline.html.

33 *Revolution: Tomorrow Is NOW* (New York: NOW, 1973); Daniel Horowitz, *Betty Friedan and the Making of the Feminine Mystique: The American Left, the Cold War, and Modern Feminism* (Amherst: University of Massachusetts Press, 1998), 231–32.

34 Evans, *Tidal Wave*.

35 Rachel Blau and Ann Snitow Duplessis, *The Feminist Memoir Project: Voices from Women's Liberation* (New York: Three Rivers Press, 1998), 10–11; Carol Hanisch, "The 1968 Miss America Project: The Origins of the 'Bra-Burner' Moniker," in *The Feminist Memoir Project: Voices from Women's Liberation* (New York: Three Rivers Press, 1998), 197–202.

36 Patricia Bradley, *Mass Media and the Shaping of American Feminism, 1963–1975* (Jackson: University of Mississippi Press, 2004), 63–64, 68–70; Jean Hunter, "A Daring New Concept: 'The Ladies' Home Journal' and Modern Feminism," *NWSA Journal* 2, no. 4 (Autumn 1990): 583–602.

37 The account of the strike below is based largely on the description in Friedan, *It Changed My Life*, 184–92; Rosen, *The World Split Open*, 92–93.

38 "Nation: Women on the March," *Time*, September 7, 1970; "Leading Feminist Puts Hairdo Before Strike," *New York Times*, August 27, 1970; Deborah Siegel, *Sisterhood Interrupted: From Radical Women to Grrls Gone Wild* (New York: Palgrave Macmillan, 2007); Davis, *Moving the Mountain*, 1999, 114–16; Friedan, *It Changed My Life*, 184–92.

39 "Woman's Rights Advocates Chart Legislative Support: Recommendations Itemized Hearings Criticized," *Christian Science Monitor*, April 27, 1970, http://proquest.umi .com/pqdweb?did=264404812&sid=3&Fmt=10&clientId=73174&RQT=309&VName= HNP.

40 Davis, *Moving the Mountain*, 1999, 147. Historians generally refer to them as "liberal feminists," moderate and pragmatic, working to gain for women rights and privileges men enjoyed in America, economic independence, equal access to jobs and education, and full participation in politics and government.

41 Catherine East, "Chronology of the Women's Movement in the U.S.: 1961–1975," in *National Women's Conference Official Briefing Book: Houston, Texas, November 18 to 21, 1977* (Washington, D.C.: U.S. Government Printing Office, 1977), 33; Evans, *Tidal Wave*, 61–63; Davis, *Moving the Mountain*, 1999, 147–49, 186–87. See, for example, the Center for American Women and Politics at Rutgers University, founded by Ruth Mandel in 1971, http://www.cawp.rutgers.edu/, and the Center for Women Policy Studies in Washington, D.C., founded by Jane Roberts Chapman and Margaret Gates in 1972, http://www.centerwomenpolicy.org/default.asp.

42 Tanya Melich, *The Republican War Against Women: An Insider's Report from Behind the Lines* (New York: Bantam, 1998), 18.

43 Liz Carpenter, *Getting Better All the Time* (New York: Simon & Schuster, 1987), 121, 124.

44 Ibid., 120–25.

45 Ibid., 124–25.

46 Ibid., 127–28; Evans, *Tidal Wave*, 72.

47 "Early History NWPC," *National Women's Political Caucus*, http://www.nwpc.org/history (accessed June 20, 2014); Carpenter, *Getting Better All the Time*, 131.

48 Friedan, *It Changed My Life*, 211–13; Evans, *Tidal Wave*, 71–72.

49 "Early History NWPC"; Sara Fitzgerald, *Elly Peterson: "Mother" of the Moderates* (Ann Arbor: University of Michigan Press, 2014), 179–83; Horowitz, *Betty Friedan and the Making of the Feminine Mystique*, 70–76; Evans, *Tidal Wave*, 70–76; John Gizzi, "When Will McCain Be Cushioned by Conservatives?," *Human Events*, March 28, 2008. See http://humanevents.com/2008/03/28/when-will-mccain-be-cushioned-by-conservatives/; Melich, *Republican War Against Women*, 33, 18–19, 217–18.

50 Catherine E. Rymph, *Republican Women: Feminism and Conservatism from Suffrage Through the Rise of the New Right* (Chapel Hill: University of North Carolina Press, 2006), 217–19; Melich, *Republican War Against Women*, 19, 47–48; "Early History NWPC."

51 "Early History NWPC." For Republicans, the number rose from 17 percent in 1968 to 30 percent in 1972. For Democrats, it rose from 13 percent to 40 percent.

52 Spruill, "Champions of Women's Rights," 379–80. The challenge, led by Victoria Eslinger, Janet Wedlock, and Margaret Young, failed when McGovern forces, despite his promise of support, undermined it in a parliamentary maneuver they believed necessary to prevent Stop McGovern forces from blocking his nomination; Bruce Miroff, *The Liberal's Moment: The McGovern Insurgency and the Identity Crisis of the Democratic Party* (Lawrence: University of Kansas Press, 2007), 77–81; Davis, *Moving the Mountain*, 1999, 188.

53 Ibid., 188–92.

54 Charlotte Curtis, "Modest Gains Please Republican Feminists," *New York Times*, August 21, 1972.

55 "Early History NWPC"; Davis, *Moving the Mountain*, 1999, 188–92; Miroff, *The Liberal's Moment*; Spruill, "Champions of Women's Rights." Schlafly was one of the conservatives opposed to "Rockefeller Republicans" trying to "McGovernize" the GOP. Phyllis Schlafly, "Conservatives Win Rules Fight in Miami," *Phyllis Schlafly Report* 6, no. 2 (September 1972); Melich, *Republican War Against Women*, 28–31.

56 Davis, *Moving the Mountain*, 1999, quotation 127, 186–87.

57 Ibid., 211–20; Evans, *Tidal Wave*, 134–35; "Comes the Revolution: Joining the Game at Last, Women Are Transforming American Athletics," *Time*, June 26, 1978.

58 Davis, *Moving the Mountain*, 1999, 148–52; Dean J. Kotlowski, "Stops and Starts: Women's Rights," in *Nixon's Civil Rights: Politics, Principle, and Policy* (Cambridge, MA: Harvard University Press, 2001), 255–56.

59 "International Women's Year Activities: United States of America," n.d., folder "National Commission Meeting July 1, 1976," box 29, National Commission on IWY, meeting July 1, 1976, Patricia Lindh and Jeanne Holm Files, 1974–1977, Gerald R. Ford Presidential Library, University of Michigan, Ann Arbor, hereafter Lindh and Holm Files, Ford Library.

60 Davis, *Moving the Mountain*, 1999, 282–83; Melich, *Republican War Against Women*, 31–33.

61 Jane J. Mansbridge, *Why We Lost the ERA* (Chicago: University of Chicago Press, 1986), 8–10.

62 Davis, *Moving the Mountain*, 1999, 121–36; Emily Badger, "That One Time America Almost Got Universal Child Care," *Washington Post*, June 23, 2014; Nancy L. Cohen, "Why America Never Had Universal Child Care," *New Republic*, April 24, 2013.

63 Carol Felsenthal, *The Sweetheart of the Silent Majority: The Biography of Phyllis Schlafly* (Garden City, NY: Doubleday, 1981), 234; Strom Thurmond, "Equal Rights for Women" (press release, April 10, 1972), SCERA box 1, folder 2, South Carolina Political Collections.

64 Fitzgerald, *Elly Peterson*, 157; AP, "Women's Equality Amendment Clear: Allows Requirement of Combat Service," *Clarion-Ledger*, March 23, 1972.

65 Donald G. Mathews and Jane Sherron De Hart, *Sex, Gender, and the Politics of ERA: A State and the Nation* (New York: Oxford University Press, 1990), 35–50; UPI, "Clipping on ERA Fight in Senate," *Delta Democrat-Times*, March 3, 1972.

66 Davis, *Moving the Mountain*, 1999, 33; Mathews and De Hart, *Sex, Gender, and the Politics of ERA*, 53.

67 Felsenthal, *Sweetheart of the Silent Majority*, 234–35; Winifred D. Wandersee, *On the Move: American Women in the 1970s* (Boston: G. K. Hall, 1988), 177–78.

68 *Reed v. Reed*, 1971; Irin Carmon and Shana Knizhnik, *Notorious RBG: The Life and Times of Ruth Bader Ginsburg*, 2015; "Tribute: The Legacy of Ruth Bader Ginsburg and WRP Staff," American Civil Liberties Union, https://www.aclu.org/tribute-legacy-ruth-bader-ginsburg-and-wrp-staff (accessed July 11, 2016). Some ERA opponents said *Reed* made the amendment unnecessary. Feminists replied that *Reed* came only after the House had approved the ERA and the Senate was clearly about to follow suit, and that in *Reed* the Court had still not applied the same critical standard or review as it applied in cases where legal distinctions were made on the basis of race or ethnic origin. Ginsburg supported—and still supports—adding an Equal Rights Amendment to the Constitution. NCOIWY, "*. . . To Form a More Perfect Union . . .*" 373.

69 Davis, *Moving the Mountain*, 1999, 175–76.

70 Ibid., 175–80; David J. Garrow, *Liberty and Sexuality: The Right to Privacy and the Making of Roe v. Wade* (New York: Macmillan, 1994), 335–88. Sixteen states and the District of Columbia liberalized abortion laws by 1973; "A Stunning Approval for Abortion," *Time*, February 5, 1973.

71 "A Stunning Approval for Abortion."

72 Sandra Stencel, "Abortion Politics," in *Editorial Research Reports 1976*, vol. 2 (Washington, D.C.: CQ Press, 1976), 765–84, http://library.cqpress.com/cqresearcher/document.php?id=cqresrre1976102200#REF[6].

73 A 1975 Gallup Poll showed that three out of four Americans believed that abortion should be legal in some circumstances; A 1975 Harris Survey revealed that a 54–36 percent majority supported *Roe v. Wade*; Louis Harris, "The Harris Poll: Pro-Abortion Stand Seen Not Harmful to Candidates," *Herald-Tribune*, April 12, 1976. Lydia Saad, "Majority of Americans Still Support *Roe v. Wade* Decision," *Gallup*, January 22, 2013. A 1975 poll commissioned by the National Conference of Catholic Bishops showed that slightly more than 44 percent of the 4,067 persons polled said the abortion issue was not sufficiently important to them to be the sole issue on which they would base their vote. A 1976 *New York Times* and CBS News poll showed that 67 percent agreed that "the right of a woman to have an abortion should be left entirely up to the woman and her doctor." Robert Reinhold and New York Times News Service, "Poll: Voters Fail to Weigh Issues," *Dispatch*, February 19, 1976.

74 Dean J. Kotlowski, "Deeds Versus Words: Richard Nixon and Civil Rights Policy," *New England Journal of History* 56, no. 2 (January 1999): 135; Kotlowski, "Stops and Starts," 224–26, 234.

75   Kotlowski, "Stops and Starts," 224–27, 234, 237–38. After a trip to South Carolina during which he met several strikingly attractive women legislators who were Republicans, he phoned RNC chair George H. W. Bush, suggesting that the party seek out more women candidates like these. *Harper's* magazine later called this Nixon's "Southern Belle Strategy." "Southern Belle Strategy," *Harper's*, September 2009.

76   Laura Joy Foxworth, "The Spiritual Is Political: The Modern Women's Movement and the Transformation of the Southern Baptist Convention" (Ph.D. diss., University of South Carolina, 2014); Daniel K. Williams, *God's Own Party: The Making of the Christian Right* (New York: Oxford University Press, 2012), 94–99.

77   Kotlowski, "Stops and Starts," 250–52; Melich, *Republican War Against Women*, 31–33; Janet M. Martin, *The Presidency and Women: Promise Performance and Illusion* (College Station: Texas A&M University Press, 2003), 145; Timothy Stanley, *The Crusader: the Life and Tumultuous Times of Pat Buchanan* (New York: Thomas Dunne Books, 2012), 55–69.

78   Lee Stout, *A Matter of Simple Justice: The Untold Story of Barbara Hackman Franklin and a Few Good Women* (University Park: Pennsylvania State University Libraries, 2012), xxi.

79   Ibid., 16; Biography and Chronology, Finding Aid, Catherine Shipe East Papers, 1941–1995, MC 477, Schlesinger Library, Radcliffe Institute, Harvard University, Cambridge, MA.

80   Stout, *A Matter of Simple Justice*, 16–17.

81   Ibid., 18, 78–80; Kotlowski, "Deeds Versus Words: Richard Nixon and Civil Rights Policy," 135; Kotlowski, "Stops and Starts," 224–27, 237–38; Stephen E. Ambrose, *Nixon: The Triumph of a Politician, 1962–1972*, Vol. 2. (New York: Simon and Schuster, 1989), 468–69; Julie Nixon Eisenhower, *Pat Nixon: The Untold Story* (New York: Simon and Schuster, 1986), 321–22.

82   Stout, *A Matter of Simple Justice*, 19–20.

83   Ibid., 21–23.

84   Ibid.

85   Kotlowski, "Stops and Starts," 230–31; Stout, *A Matter of Simple Justice*, 26.

86   Ibid., 31–32.

87   Martin, *The Presidency and Women*, 133–36; Kimberly Voss, "Vera Glaser: A Journalist's Ode to Offbeat Washingtonian Politics," *Hall Institute of Public Policy*, May 5, 2009.

88   Kotlowski, "Stops and Starts," 231; Martin, *The Presidency and Women*, 132.

89   Kotlowski, "Stops and Starts," 242–44.

90   Stout, *A Matter of Simple Justice*, 57–76.

91   Ibid., 32–34, 57–59, 68–91, 191; Martin, *The Presidency and Women*, 132, 140, 144, 151–53.

92   Stout, *A Matter of Simple Justice*, 103–58.

93   Ibid., 91, 192, 84–85, 147–148. In 2003, There was a White House reception to honor these women at the completion of "A Few Good Women," their collective oral history conducted by Penn State University archivist Lee Stout.

94   Kotlowski, "Stops and Starts," 242–44; Martin, *The Presidency and Women*, 154.

95   Melich, *Republican War Against Women*, 31; Stout, *A Matter of Simple Justice*, 91, 92; "The Administration: Help Wanted (Female)," *Newsweek*, August 21, 1972.

96   Stout, *A Matter of Simple Justice*, 84; Rymph, *Republican Women*, 216; Kotlowski, "Stops and Starts," 235; Eisenhower, *Pat Nixon*, 321–22; "ERA Brochure," n.d., Nancy Moore Papers, South Carolina Political Collections, University of South Carolina, hereafter Moore Papers, SCPC.

97 Melich, *Republican War Against Women*, 35.

98 Ibid., 33–37.

99 Stout, *A Matter of Simple Justice*, 96–98; Clare Crawford, "From Watergate to Womankind, Bill and Jill Ruckelshaus Fight for Their Ideas," *People Magazine*, April 12, 1976; James F. Clarity, "Women's Aide Joins Nixon Staff," *New York Times*, March 2, 1973.

100 Kotlowski, "Stops and Starts," 239.

101 Melich, *Republican War Against Women*, 33–39.

102 Laura Mansnerus, "Obituary Bella Abzug, 77, Congresswoman and a Founding Feminist, Is Dead," *New York Times*, April 1, 1998; "Flashback: Elizabeth Holtzman on Nixon's Legacy," *New York Daily News*, April 22, 2015.

CHAPTER 3: TO FORM A MORE PERFECT UNION

1   On Ford merely tolerating his wife's feminist views, Ellen Goodman, "The Patrons of Betty Ford," *Washington Post*, October 4, 1976; "Betty Ford: No Separate Bedroom for Her," *Detroit Free Press*, August 21, 1975; Betty Ford, *The Times of My Life* (New York: Ballantine, 1979), 219; Elizabeth Peer, "Woman of the Year," *Newsweek*, December 29, 1975; "Talking Points, Swearing-in of Rod Hills, 10/28/75," n.d., folder "10/20/75 Swearing-in Ceremony of Roderick Hills," box 18, Presidential Speeches and Statements: Reading Copies; Leesa E. Tobin, "Betty Ford as a First Lady: A Woman for a Women," *Presidential Studies Quarterly* 20, no. 4 (1990): 761–67.

2   Jeanne M. Holm, "Ford's Record on Women's Rights," *Washington Post*, October 19, 1976; "Minutes, Women Appointees and Anne Armstrong and Betty Ford," September 4, 1974, folder "Women Appointees—Sept. 4, 1974," Lindh and Holm Files, Office of Public Liaison, box 1, Gerald R. Ford Presidential Library, Ann Arbor, Michigan, hereafter Lindh and Holm Files, Ford Library.

3   Janet M. Martin, *The Presidency and Women: Promise, Performance, and Illusion* (College Station: Texas A&M University Press, 2003), 168–82.

4   "President Ford '76 Fact Book: President Ford Issues—Women," 1976, Gerald R. Ford Presidential Library, Ann Arbor, Michigan; Tanya Melich, *The Republican War Against Women: An Insider's Report from Behind the Lines* (New York: Bantam, 1998), 43–48, 50; Myra MacPherson, "The Blooming of Betty Ford," *McCall's*, September 1975.

5   Peer, "Woman of the Year"; Tobin, "Betty Ford as a First Lady: A Woman for Women," *Presidential Studies Quarterly* 20, no. 4 (1990): 361–62; John Robert Greene, *Betty Ford: Candor and Courage in the White House* (Lawrence: University Press of Kansas, 2004); Barbara Howard, "Spotlight on Betty Ford: A New Breed of Wife in the Nation's Capital," *Family Circle*, November 1974. The insight that Betty Ford "lived the 'feminine mystique'" comes from Donna Lehman at the Ford Presidential Library.

6   "Betty Ford: No Separate Bedroom for Her"; Donnie Radcliffe, "A First Lady's Plan to Meet the Press," August 24, 1974, General Subject File, "President—Personal: Family—Betty Ford (1)," box 49 Philip Buchen Files, 1974–77, Gerald R. Ford Presidential Library, Ann Arbor, Michigan; Peer, "Woman of the Year"; "Meeting Notes—Liz Carpenter" October 1974, box 51, Sheila Weidenfeld Files, Gerald R. Ford Library, University of Michigan, Ann Arbor.

7   Marlene Cimons, "First Lady Sticks to Her Guns on ERA," *Los Angeles Times*, February 18, 1975, sec. 4:6.

8   Ford, *The Times of My Life*, 212, 219, 221–24; Greene, *Betty Ford: Candor and Courage in the White House*, 63–65; "A Fighting First Lady," *Time*, March 3, 1975.

9   Greene, *Betty Ford*, 66–68; "A Fighting First Lady"; Nancy Gibbs, "In Memory: Betty Ford, Former First Lady, Clinic Founder," *Time*, July 8, 2011.

10   "Informal Typed Note, Author Not Identified" February 8, 1975, General Subject File, "President—Personal: Family—Betty Ford (1)," box 49; Philip Buchen to: Nancy Howe, Marba Perrott, Nancy Rowe, Sheila Weidenfeld, cc. to Don Rumsfeld and Jerry Jones, n.d., General Subject File, "President—Personal: Family—Betty Ford (1)," box 49, all in Buchen Files, Ford Library; Greene, *Betty Ford*, 2004, 66–68.

11   Betty Ford, *The Times of My Life*, 221; Greene, *Betty Ford*, 66–68; Carol Felsenthal, *The Sweetheart of the Silent Majority: The Biography of Phyllis Schlafly* (Garden City, N.Y.: Doubleday and Company, Inc., 1981), 253; Susan M. Hartmann, *From Margin to Mainstream: American Women and Politics Since 1960* (New York: Knopf, 1989), 137–38.

12   Peer, "Woman of the Year"; Nellie Gray quoted in Daniel K. Williams, *Defenders of the Unborn: The Pro-Life Movement Before Roe v. Wade* (New York: Oxford University Press, 2016), 230.

13   "Timeline of Elizabeth (Betty) Bloomer Ford's Life and Career," Gerald R. Ford Presidential Library and Museum. The Ford Library contains around sixty linear feet of material pro and con sent in response to this interview; Greene, *Betty Ford*, 67; Peter Kumpa, "A Free Spirit in the White House," *Sun*, August 17, 1975, section K1; Gerald Ford, *A Time to Heal: The Autobiography of Gerald Ford* (New York: Harper and Row, 1979), 306, 307; Louis Harris, "Betty Ford a Strong Asset," *Detroit Free Press*, August 9, 1976; Tobin, "Betty Ford as a First Lady," 1990; Peer, "Woman of the Year."

14   Laura Kalman, *Right Star Rising: A New Politics, 1974–1980* (New York: W. W. Norton, 2010), xix–7.

15   Ibid.

16   Holm, "Ford's Record on Women's Rights"; Megan Kolodgy, "Fair Play," *Michigan Daily*, October 26, 2005. According to Donna Lehman of the Ford Presidential Library, Ford stood up to intense pressure from friends in the world of college football to sign Title IX. Aide Patricia Lindh, who was an athlete herself, wanted Ford to sign the Title IX implementation document in a highly public, celebratory way, but he would not, instead signing it alone and at night.

17   Phyllis Schlafly, "Father-Son, Mother-Daughter Flap," *Eagle Forum Newsletter*, August 1976.

18   Richard A. Viguerie, *The New Right: We're Ready to Lead* (Falls Church, VA: The Viguerie Company, 1980), 51–52; Kalman, *Right Star Rising*, 162–65; Ford, *A Time to Heal*, 295.

19   Donald T. Critchlow, *Phyllis Schlafly and Grassroots Conservatism: A Woman's Crusade* (Princeton, NJ: Princeton University Press, 2005), 142–145, quotation 145; Sara Fitzgerald, *Elly Peterson: "Mother" of the Moderates* (Ann Arbor: University of Michigan Press, 2014), 109–15; Catherine E. Rymph, *Republican Women: Feminism and Conservatism from Suffrage Through the Rise of the New Right* (Chapel Hill: University of North Carolina Press, 2006), 177–187.

20   Rymph, *Republican Women*, 204–6.

21   "President Ford Tells Republicans the GOP Must Be More Inclusive," *NBC Nightly News* (New York: NBC, March 8, 1975), https://archives.nbclearn.com/portal/site/k-12/browse/?cuecard=2977.

22   Melich, *Republican War Against Women*, 45–47; Timothy Stanley, *The Crusader: The Life and Tumultuous Times of Pat Buchanan* (New York: Thomas Dunne, 2012), 82.

23 Ruth Murray Brown, *For a "Christian America": A History of the Religious Right* (Amherst, NY: Prometheus, 2002), 136.

24 Gerald R. Ford, "Address to a Joint Session of the Congress," Online by Gerhard Peters and John T. Woolley, American Presidency Project, August 12, 1974, http://www. presidency.ucsb.edu/ws/index.php?pid=4694; NCOIWY, ". . . *To Form a More Perfect Union . . .*" ii.

25 Anne Armstrong, "Women's Programs: Briefing Book Revisions, August 19, 1974," folder "Ford, Betty—Briefings," box 21, Lindh and Holm Files, Ford Library; "Correspondence," folder "WE 3 9/1/74—1/29/75," box 6 WHCF Subject File "WE3 Family Planning 1/31/76 (Exec)," Gerald R. Ford Presidential Library, Ann Arbor, Michigan.

26 Daniel K. Williams, *God's Own Party: The Making of the Christian Right* (New York: Oxford University Press, 2012), 130.

27 Williams, *Defenders of the Unborn*, 230; Donald T. Critchlow, "Mobilizing Women: The 'Social Issues,'" *The Reagan Presidency: Pragmatic Conservatism and Its Legacies*, ed. W. Elliott Brownlee and Hugh Davis Graham (Lawrence: University Press of Kansas, 2004), 298.

28 Neil J. Young, "We Gather Together: Catholics, Mormons, Southern Baptists and the Question of Interfaith Politics, 1972–1984" (Dissertation, Columbia University, 2008), 204; Louis Harris, "The Harris Poll: Pro-Abortion Stand Seen Not Harmful to Candidates," *Herald-Tribune*, April 12, 1976.

29 United Nations, *Meeting in Mexico: The Story of the World Conference of the International Women's Year (Mexico City, 19 June–2 July 1975)* (New York, 1975); Olcott, *"The Greatest Consciousness -Raising Event in History": The 1975 International Women's Year Conference and the Challenges of Transnational Feminism* (New York: Oxford University Press, forthcoming).

30 Karen Peterson, "Women's Year Whimpers In," *Chicago Tribune*, January 1, 1975; Mildred Marcy, "Document 188—Foreign Relations of the United States, 1969–1976, Volume E–14, Part 1, Documents on the United Nations, 1973–1976—Historical Documents—Office of the Historian," *U.S. Department of State*, June 1, 1976, https:// history.state.gov/historicaldocuments/frus1969-76ve14p1/d188.

31 Susanna Downie and National Women's Conference Committee, "Part I: How the National Plan of Action for Women Came Into Being," in *Decade of Achievement: 1977–1987: A Report on a Survey Based on the National Plan of Action for Women* (Washington, D.C: National Women's Conference Committee, 1988), 5–7; "Memo, Robert S. Ingersoll, Deputy Secretary of State, to President Ford, Dec.18, 1974," folder Executive Order (1), box 26, National Commission on IWY Annual Report, Patricia Lindh and Jeanne Holm Files 1974–1977, Gerald R. Ford Library.

32 Betty Ford, *The Times of My Life*, 220.

33 Ruth Bacon, "Ruth Bacon to Friends Everywhere" (Newsletter No. 7-75, U.S. Center for IWY, December 1975), box 29, folder "U.S. Center for IWY 1975," Lindh and Holm Files, Ford Library.

34 Betty Ford, "Betty Ford's Speech to International Women's Year Conference 1975" (Cleveland, Ohio, October 25, 1975), Frances Kaye Pullen Files, Gerald R. Ford Presidential Library, Ann Arbor, Michigan.

35 Jocelyn Olcott, "Empires of Information: Media Strategies for the 1975 International Women's Year," *Journal of Women's History* 24, No. 4 (Winter 2012): quotations 31.

36 Ibid., 241–66; Jocelyn Olcott, "Transnational Feminism: Event, Temporality, and Performance at the 1975 International Women's Year Conference," in *Cultures in*

Motion, ed. Daniel T. Rodgers, Bhavani Raman, and Helmut Reimitz (Princeton University Press, 2013), 241–66; Nima Naghib, *Rethinking Global Sisterhood: Western Feminism and Iran* (Minneapolis: University of Minnesota Press, 2007), 60, n.11; Shah Mohammad Reza and Gerard De Villiers, *The Imperial Shah: An Informal Biography* (Boston: n.p., 1976).

37 "Jeanne Davis to Gen Scowcroft, June 9, 1975, Sub Mrs. Ford's Attendance at IWY Con in Mex City," folder "Cheney-Rumsfeldgrams (2)," Gerald R. Ford Presidential Library. In Mexico City, Leah Rabin encountered difficulties from proponents of a recommendation against Zionism who tried to prevent her from speaking.

38 NCOIWY, *". . . To Form a More Perfect Union . . ."* 8, 365–67.

39 Olcott, "Transnational Feminism"; Jocelyn H. Olcott, "'A Happier Marriage?' Feminist History Takes the Transnational Turn," in *Making Women's Histories: Beyond National Perspectives,* ed. Pamela Nadell and Katherine Haulman (New York University Press, 2013); Olcott, *The Greatest Consciousness-Raising Event in History*; American journalists sympathetic to the women's movement complained about this tendency and did their best to provide accurate coverage. Peggy Simpson, "1979: Covering the Women's Movement," *Nieman Reports,* accessed April 16, 2016, http://niemanreports. org/articles/1979-covering-the-womens-movement/; Peggy Simpson, "Mexico City Remembered," *Daily Breakthrough,* November 18, 1977, WASM; Judy Klemesrud, *New York Times,* June 29, 1975.

40 Jill Ruckelshaus, "Who Shall Speak For Our Nation's Women? An American Dialogue," *". . . To Form a More Perfect Union . . ."* 365–67; Letter and Report from Ruth Bacon, Director of the United States Center for the International Women's Year to Secretary of State Kissinger, July 24, 1975, Foreign Relations of the United States, 1969–1976, Volume E–14, Part 1, Documents on the United Nations, 1973–1976—Office of the Historian, Department of State.

41 Judith P. Zinsser, "From Mexico to Copenhagen to Nairobi: The United Nations Decade for Women, 1975–1985," *Journal of World History* 13 (2002): 139–67.

42 Other American women who would remain active in the international women's movement included Mildred Persinger, Arvonne Fraser, and Charlotte Bunch who founded a Center for Women's Global Leadership at Rutgers University. Biographical Sketches of Activists at UN World Women's Conferences, WASM; Click—Global Feminism—United Nations Conference on Women, CLIO Visualizing History, https://www .cliohistory.org/click/politics-social/global/?video=1509; NCOIWY, *". . . To Form a More Perfect Union . . ."* 8, 365.

43 Gerald R. Ford, "Executive Order Establishing a National Commission on the Observance of International Women's Year, 1975," in *". . . To Form a More Perfect Union . . ."* 117–20; Gerald R. Ford, "Remarks Upon Receiving the Report of the National Commission on the Observance of International Women's Year, 1976. July 1, 1976."

44 NCOIWY, *". . . To Form a More Perfect Union . . ."* 381. See for information about the IWY Secretariat, which was housed in the State Department, and a list of persons on the Secretariat. Virginia Allan, Deputy Assistant Secretary of State for Public Affairs and Chair of the 1969 President's Task Force on Women's Rights and Responsibilities, and Deputy Secretary Robert S. Ingersoll, were very supportive. Mildred Marcy of the U.S. Information Agency served as Coordinator of the Secretariat, with Catherine East of the Labor Department as Deputy Coordinator. Most of the staff were consultants serving on a short-term or part-time basis, many of them loaned by other federal agencies.

45 "Remarks of the Vice President Opening Session of the National Commission on the Observance of International Women's Year, 1975, DRAFT" April 3, 1975, folder: National Commission Meeting April 15, 1975, box 28, National Commission on IWY, Meeting—April 15, 1975, Lindh and Holm Files, Ford Library.

46 Frederic A. Birmingham, "Jill Ruckelshaus: Lady of Liberty," *Saturday Evening Post*, April 1973; Clare Crawford, "From Watergate to Womankind, Bill and Jill Ruckelshaus Fight for Their Ideas," *People Magazine*, April 12, 1976; Lois Romano, "Jill Ruckelshaus: Back in the Fishbowl," *Washington Post*, May 18, 1983.

47 Birmingham, "Jill Ruckelshaus"; Romano, "Jill Ruckelshaus"; Phyllis Schlafly, *The Power of the Positive Woman* (New Rochelle, N.Y.: Arlington House, 1977), 172–73.

48 NCOIWY, ". . . *To Form a More Perfect Union* . . ." 81, 123–36.

49 Ibid. For list and biographical sketches of Commission Members, see 123–136.

50 NCOIWY, ". . . *To Form a More Perfect Union* . . ." 381.

51 Ibid., A list of individuals serving on the Secretariat and their agencies is on 381.

52 Schlafly, *Power of the Positive Woman*, 172–73, 290 n. 66.

53 Cynthia Harrison, "Creating a National Feminist Agenda: Coalition Building in the 1970s," in *Feminist Coalitions: Historical Perspectives on Second-Wave Feminism in the United States*, Stephanie Gilmore, ed. (Urbana: University of Illinois Press, 2008); "Coalition Opens Drive for a 'Women's Agenda,'" *New York Times*, December 3, 1975.

54 Harrison, "Creating a National Feminist Agenda"; Shelah G. Leader and Patricia R. Hyatt, *American Women on the Move: The Inside Story of the National Women's Conference, 1977,* (Lanham, MD: Lexington Books, 2016).

55 NCOIWY, ". . . *To Form a More Perfect Union* . . ." 9.

56 "Clipping, Congresswoman Margaret Heckler of Massachusetts Speech on Floor of Congress, Congressional Record—House H12275" October 1, 1976, folder: National Commission Meeting July 1, 1976, box 29, National Commission on IWY, Meeting—July 1, 1976, Lindh and Holm Files, Ford Library.

57 "Margaret Heckler and Alan Alda, Co-Chairs, ERA Committee of the NCOIWY, to Jill Ruckelshaus, Report of ERA Committee" January 15, 1976, folder "National Commission Meeting January 15, 1976 (1)," box 28, National Commission on IWY, Meeting—April 15, 1975, Lindh and Holm Files, Ford Library; NCOIWY, ". . . To Form a More Perfect Union . . ." 219–220. The pro–ERA organizations, not the federal government, supplied the staff, office space, and funds for ERAmerica.

58 Ibid., 121–22.

59 "The U.S Interdepartmental Task Force for IWY 1975: Report and Recommendations," n.d., folder "Jill Ruckelshaus," box K30, Arthur F. Burns Papers, Gerald R. Presidential Library, Ann Arbor, Michigan.

60 NCOIWY, ". . . *To Form a More Perfect Union* . . ." ii, iv–v.

61 Ibid., quotation vi, 13–99. The commission selected journalist Dorothy Jurney of the *Miami Herald* to write and edit the report.

62 Ibid., v, 13, 99; NCOIWY, "DRAFT: Manual for State and Territorial IWY Coordinating Committees for Planning and Conducting the Meetings for Women" February 1977, 96.

63 NCOIWY, ". . . *To Form a More Perfect Union* . . ." 64–67.

64 Ibid., quotations 30.

65 Ibid., 32–33, 139–40.

66 Leader and Hyatt, *American Women on the Move*, Chapter Four. The first state report was written by attorney Sylvia Roberts who had won the *Weeks v. Southern Bell* case on appeal while vice president of NOW's Legal Defense and Education Fund.

67   NCOIWY, "... *To Form a More Perfect Union* ..." 13–17, 224–35.

68   Ibid., 13–17, 224–35.

69   Ibid., 26–31; "'Congresswoman Margaret Heckler of Massachusetts,' Speech on Floor of Congress, Oct. 1, 1976, *Congressional Record*—House H12275," n.d., folder "National Commission Meeting July 1, 1976," box 29, "National Commission on IWY, Meeting—July 1, 1976," Lindh and Holm Files, Ford Library.

70   NCOIWY, "... *To Form a More Perfect Union* ..." 84–89, 148–60.

71   Ibid., 78–83, 267–80.

72   Ibid., 26–31.

73   Ibid., 26–31, 218–20, 373–77.

74   "... *To Form a More Perfect Union* ..." 236–46.

75   Eileen Shanahan, "Ford Orders Review of All U.S. Laws to Find and Halt Unjustified Sex Bias," *New York Times*, July 2, 1976, http://query.nytimes.com/gst/abstract.html?res=9406E2D9143FE334BC4A53DFB166838D669EDE.

76   Ford, *A Time to Heal*, 327–29.

77   Jean Christensen, "Feminist Pushes Local Action: Working for ERA" (Clipping, *Kansas City Star*, September 26, 1976), folder, "National Commission Meeting July 1, 1976," box 29, "National Commission on IWY, Meeting—July 1, 1976," Lindh and Holm Files, Ford Library.

78   Fitzgerald, *Elly Peterson*, 201; Phyllis Schlafly, "ERA and the Republican Platform," *Phyllis Schlafly Report* 10; No. 2, Section 2 (September 1976).

79   Fitzgerald, *Elly Peterson*, 201–2; "Statement of Elly M. Peterson before Republican Platform Committee, August 9, 1976," box 25, Speeches Folder, Elly M. Peterson Papers, Bentley Historical Library, University of Michigan, Ann Arbor, hereafter Peterson Papers, Bentley Library.

80   Williams, *God's Own Party*, 131; Williams, *Defenders of the Unborn*, 230–33. Dole, seeking to become Ford's running mate, met with Reagan delegates to learn what kind of statement on abortion they would accept, then asked Senator Jesse Helms, staunch Reagan supporter and perhaps the GOP's strongest proponent of a human life amendment, to draft the platform plank.

81   Melich, *Republican War Against Women*, 80–81; Williams, *God's Own Party*, 131–32.

82   Melich, *Republican War Against Women*, 80–81; H. Harrison Jenkins, "Women Will Win With Republicans or Democrats," *Columbia Record*, October 12, 1976, Irene Neuffer Papers, South Caroliniana Library, University of South Carolina, Columbia; "Campaign of 1976—Republican Platform Re: Women's Concerns," folder, Lindh and Holm Files, Ford Library.

83   Shanahan, "Ford Orders Review of All U.S. Laws to Find and Halt Unjustified Sex Bias."

84   "News Release" September 9, 1976, folder "Campaign of 1976—President Ford Committee (2)," box 7, Lindh and Holm Papers, Ford Library; Peterson Papers,, Bentley Library.

85   In October, Peterson wrote to Ford senior staffers in jest, stating that, in return for their work, "Feminists for Ford" expected "Five cabinet posts, Four assistant secretaries, Three general counsels, Two heads of bureaus, AND ONE SUPREME COURT JUSTICE!" Fitzgerald, *Elly Peterson*, 203–13.

86   "President Ford '76 Fact Book. President Ford Issues—Women."

87   Harrison, "Creating a National Feminist Agenda."

88   Ibid.

89 Jules Witcover, *Marathon: The Pursuit of the Presidency, 1972–1976* (New York: Viking Press, 1977), 541; Fitzgerald, *Elly Peterson*, 203–9; Melich, *Republican War Against Women*, 81.

90 Ibid.; Williams, *God's Own Party*, 132; Fitzgerald, *Elly Peterson*, 203–7.

91 Melich, *Republican War Against Women*, 81–82.

92 Ibid., 82.

93 R. W. Apple, Jr., "Ford Gains Edge Over Reagan," *New York Times*, August 18, 1976; Melich, *Republican War Against Women*, 50, 63–64.

94 Leader and Hyatt, *American Women on the Move*. Leader and Hyatt served on the IWY staff from 1975 until it disbanded in 1978 and offer insights and information from their perspective as insiders.

95 Vera Glaser, "Bella's Bellows Fan the Flames," n.d., folder 29, box 18, East Papers #477, SL; Correspondence between Shelah Leader and the Author, November 21, 2015.

96 Glaser, "Bella's Bellows Fan the Flames."

97 Harrison, "Creating a National Feminist Agenda: Coalition Building in the 1970s," 20; NCOIWY, *Spirit of Houston*, 10.

98 Leader and Hyatt, *American Women on the Move*.

99 Ibid.; Congresswoman Millicent Fenwick reported that RNC chair Mary Louise Smith worried that having these conferences in 1976 would take too much attention away from the elections. "Providing for a National Women's Conference," *Congressional Record—House*, December 10, 1975, H 12195. Lindh noted in the memo that the president had supported the proposal for the conferences but insisted on a change of date to avoid having them in 1976. Pat Lindh, "Schedule Proposal for the President," December 11, 1975, folder "National Women's Conference (International Women's Year—1976) 2," box 11, Lindh and Holm Files, Ford Library; East's comments on Schlafly come from an interview with Catherine East in the Women in the Federal Government Oral History Project at the Schlesinger Library, Radcliffe Institute, Harvard University and cited in Leader and Hyatt, *American Women on the Move*.

100 "Providing for a National Women's Conference"; Leader and Hyatt, *American Women on the Move*.

CHAPTER 4: WHAT'S WRONG WITH "EQUAL RIGHTS" FOR WOMEN?

1 "Today's Realities" references Part II of the report of the Ford-appointed National Commission on the Observation of International Women's Year in which they explained how women's lives changed in ways that required the government to revise laws written in an earlier era. NCOIWY, "*. . . To Form a More Perfect Union . . .*" *Justice for American Women: Report of the National Commission on the Observance of International Women's Year* (Washington, D.C.: U.S. Government Printing Office, 1976), 13–99.

2 William Chafe, *The Paradox of Change: American Women in the 20th Century* (New York: Oxford University Press, 1991).

3 Rosemary Thomson, *The Price of LIBerty* (Carol Stream, IL: Creation House, 1978), quotation (my emphasis), 17.

4 Brochure for the "Women's Forum," a New Organization Created by Phyllis Schlafly as an "Alternative to 'Women's Lib,'" and the predecessor to the Eagle Forum which continued to use that phrase on its newsletters," 1975, Nancy Moore Papers, South Carolina Political Collections, University of South Carolina, hereafter Moore Papers, SCPC.

5   Thomson, *Price of LIBerty*, 12–14.

6   Ibid.,12–13; For details of Thomson's life, see this obituary published by the Iowa state legislature. "State Representative Rosemary Thomson," https://www.legis.iowa.gov/legislators/legislator?ga=77&personID=1185 (accessed February 27, 2016).

7   Thomson, *Price of LIBerty*, 13.

8   Ibid., 14.

9   Ibid., 14–15; Tanya Melich, *The Republican War Against Women: An Insider's Report from Behind the Lines* (New York: Bantam, 1998), 31–32; Emily Badger, "That One Time America Almost Got Universal Child Care," *Washington Post*, June 23, 2014; Gail Collins, *When Everything Changed: The Amazing Journey of American Women from 1960 to the Present* (New York: Little, Brown and Company, 2009), 288; Nancy L. Cohen, "Why America Never Had Universal Child Care," *New Republic*, April 24, 2013.

10 Joseph A D'Agostino, "Connie Marshner," *Human Events* 57, no. 37 (2001): 12; Susan Faludi, *Backlash: The Undeclared War Against American Women* (New York: Crown, 1991), 242–42; "Christian Right Roots: Marshner and McGraw," http://www.publiceye.org/christian_right/values-voters/Values%20Voters-09-19.html (accessed May 1, 2015); Dan Nowicki, "Direct Mail Another Legacy of '64 Goldwater Campaign," *AZ Central The Arizona Republic*, April 12, 2014, http://www.azcentral.com/story/azdc/2014/04/13/direct-mail-goldwater-legacy/7622041/# (accessed May 1, 2015).

11 William Martin, *With God on Our Side: The Rise of the Religious Right in America* (New York: Broadway, 1996), 174–75.

12 Thomson, *Price of LIBerty*, 51.

13 Ibid.

14 Ibid., 45–51, quotation 51.

15 Janet K. Boles, *The Politics of the Equal Rights Amendment: Conflict and the Decision Process* (New York: Longman, 1979). For lists of organizations supporting or opposing the ERA in 1972, see 196–202.

16 Ann Wood, "They Want to Start New Era with ERA" (clipping from *Daily News*, April 22, 1975), folder "National Commission Principals," box 29, National Commission on IWY, Meeting—July 1, 1976, Patricia Lindh and Jeanne Holm Files, 1974–1977, Gerald R. Ford Presidential Library, Ann Arbor, Michigan, hereafter Lindh and Holm Files, Ford Library.

17 Donald T. Critchlow, *Phyllis Schlafly and Grassroots Conservatism: A Woman's Crusade* (Princeton: Princeton University Press, 2005); Ruth Murray Brown, *For a "Christian America": A History of the Religious Right* (Amherst, NY: Prometheus, 2002), 53–54; Carol Felsenthal, *The Sweetheart of the Silent Majority: The Biography of Phyllis Schlafly* (Garden City, NY: Doubleday, 1981).

18 Critchlow, *Phyllis Schlafly*, 47–49; Brown, *For a "Christian America"*; Felsenthal, *Sweetheart of the Silent Majority*.

19 Ibid., 103–150.

20 Brown, *For a "Christian America,"* 47–49; Critchlow, *Phyllis Schlafly*, 97–98; Felsenthal, *Sweetheart of the Silent Majority*, xviii.

21 Brown, *For a "Christian America,"* 48; Felsenthal, *Sweetheart of the Silent Majority*, 198–214.

22 Ibid., 3–6.

23 Critchlow, *Phyllis Schlafly*, 48; On right-wing Republican women's view of themselves as moral crusaders, selflessly protecting their families and their nation, see Catherine E.

Rymph, *Republican Women: Feminism and Conservatism from Suffrage through the Rise of the New Right,* (Chapel Hill: University of North Carolina Press, 2006), 126–30; Jayne Schindler, "Phyllis Schlafly's Example," Phyllis Schlafly Institute, December 25, 2013, http://phyllisschlaflyinstitute.com/index.php?title=Jayne_Schindler; Thomson, *Price of LIBerty*, 7.

24 Critchlow, *Phyllis Schlafly*, 4, 33, 61, 71–72.

25 Phyllis Schlafly, *A Choice Not an Echo* (Alton, IL: Pere Marquette Press, 1964). For an analysis of the book's contents and its role in GOP history, see Rymph, *Republican Women*, 174–76; Brown, *For a "Christian America,"* 47–50, 53–54; In an interview with the author, Schlafly brought up Ruth Brown's book, noting that, according to Schlafly's friends in Oklahoma, Brown "showed up at everything," was "polite," but "never gave a clue" as to what side she was on. That made them suspicious, but when she examined the book, Schlafly found it to be "reasonably accurate." Marjorie J. Spruill Interview with Phyllis Schlafly, February 22, 2005, in the possession of the author.

26 Rymph, *Republican Women*, 176–87; Critchlow, *Phyllis Schlafly*, 137–62; "'Some People Must Think Republican Women Are Easily Fooled': A Federation State President Protests the Unfair and Divisive Tactics Being Employed by the Nominating Committee's Candidate for President of the National Federation of Republican Women," 1968, folder on the 1968 NFRW Battle, box 7, Kathryn Fink Dunaway Papers, Manuscripts, Archives and Rare Book Library, Emory University, Atlanta, GA, hereafter Dunaway Papers, Emory; Felsenthal, *Sweetheart of the Silent Majority*, 179–97.

27 Ibid., 194–96; Critchlow, *Phyllis Schlafly*, 155–62.

28 Ibid., 160–62; Brown, *For a "Christian America,"* 48.

29 Lyndon Johnson, said Schlafly, was "advancing communism while getting American boys killed in the guise of fighting it" and doing nothing about communists ninety miles away in Cuba. Felsenthal, *Sweetheart of the Silent Majority*, 209, 239–41, quotation 240–41.

30 Critchlow, *Phyllis Schlafly*, 217.

31 Thomson, *Price of LIBerty*, 47.

32 Felsenthal, *Sweetheart of the Silent Majority*, 240; "Shirley Spellerberg | TexasGOPVote," *TEXASGOPVOTE*, http://www.texasgopvote.com/users/shirley-spellerberg (accessed April 17, 2016).

33 Phyllis Schlafly, "What's Wrong with 'Equal Rights' for Women?," *Phyllis Schlafly Report* 5, no. 7 (February 1972).

34 Ibid.; On O'Donnell's ERA advocacy, see Rymph, *Republican Women*. 216–17.

35 Schlafly, "What's Wrong with 'Equal Rights' for Women?"

36 The seven states, in order, were: Hawaii, New Hampshire, Delaware, Iowa, Idaho, Kansas, and Nebraska. Eileen Shanahan, "Equal Rights Amendment Is Approved by Congress," *New York Times*, March 22, 1972; Brown, *For a "Christian America,"* 29.

37 Ibid., 29; Felsenthal, *Sweetheart of the Silent Majority*, 269; Nancy Elizabeth Baker, "'Too Much to Lose, Too Little to Gain': The Role of Rescission Movements in the Equal Rights Amendment Battle, 1972–1982" (diss., Harvard University, 2003), 103–6.

38 Brown, *For a "Christian America,"* 30.

39 Critchlow, *Phyllis Schlafly*, 218–24.

40 Felsenthal, *Sweetheart of the Silent Majority*, 266–67.

41 Critchlow, *Phyllis Schlafly*. Note: The ACU is the sponsor of the annual Conservative Political Action Conference (C-PAC). Though women's and family issues loom large

at C-PAC conferences today, the account of the ACU's early history on its Web site indicates no interest in these subjects at the time.

42 Critchlow, *Phyllis Schlafly*, 219.

43 Ibid.; Donald G. Mathews and Jane Sherron De Hart, *Sex, Gender, and the Politics of ERA: A State and the Nation* (New York: Oxford University Press, 1990), 59–60.

44 Critchlow, *Phyllis Schlafly*, 218–21; Brown, *For a "Christian America,"* 52.

45 Critchlow, *Phyllis Schlafly*; Felsenthal, *Sweetheart of the Silent Majority*, 261–63; Brown, *For a "Christian America."* On Dunaway, see Robin Marie Morris, "Organizing Breadmakers: Kathryn Dunaway and the Georgia STOP ERA Campaign," in *Entering the Fray: Gender, Politics, and Culture in the New South*, Jonathan Daniel Wells and Sheila R Phipps, eds. (Columbia: University of Missouri Press, 2008), 164; "Kathleen Teague Rothschild," *SourceWatch*, http://www.sourcewatch.org/index.php/Kathleen_Teague_Rothschild (accessed March 6, 2016); Mathews and De Hart, *Sex, Gender, and the Politics of ERA*, 59.

46 Ruth Murray Brown, *For a "Christian America,"* 51; Janet K. Boles, *The Politics of the Equal Rights Amendment: Conflict and the Decision Process* (New York: Longman, 1979), Boles's study of the ERA battle found considerable JBS involvement. See 4–5, 67, 70, 79–82, 86, 94, 153, and 182.

47 Mathews and De Hart, *Sex, Gender, and the Politics of ERA*, 59–60, 62, 217.

48 Brown, *For a "Christian America,"* 36–37, 94.

49 Boles, *The Politics of the Equal Rights Amendment*, 5, 68–69.

50 Brown, *For a "Christian America,"* 45; Samuel R. Berger, *Dollar Harvest: The Story of the Farm Bureau* (Lexington, MA: Heath Lexington Books, 1971), chapter 10.

51 Phyllis Schlafly, "Are You Paying for Women's Lib and the ERA? The Taxpayer Is Footing Much of the Bill, but There Are Ways to Stop It," *Human Events*, February 23, 1974.

52 Vera Glaser, "Women's Year: Peril on the Right," *Philadelphia Inquirer*, August 23, 1977.

53 Elizabeth Gillespie McRae, "White Womanhood, White Supremacy, and the Rise of Massive Resistance," in *Massive Resistance: Southern Opposition to the Second Reconstruction*, Clive Webb, ed. (New York: Oxford University Press, 2005).

54 On Texas, see Boles, *The Politics of the Equal Rights Amendment*, 79–80; See stationery listing WCG officers on Mrs. Elizabeth S. Dowles, National President, WCG, to Ms. Patricia Lindh, January 14, 1976, folder "Women for Constitutional Government," box 38, "Women's Organizations File," Lindh and Holm Files, Ford Library; "George Ann Pennebaker Obituary," Thomas McAfee Funeral Homes, October 24, 2004, http://www.thomasmcafee.com/obituaries/George-Pennebaker/#!/Obituary; Nancy Weaver, "Delegates Brace for IWY Storm: State Again Fuels U.S. Controversy. Delegates-Elect: 20 Whites, 6 Men, All Conservative," *Clarion-Ledger*, November 17, 1977; Mary Cain's Column, *The Summit Sun*, February 15, 1973, and Linda Sanders, "One-Woman Newspaper Fights Feds, Feminists, *Clarion-Ledger*, January 25, 1976, Subject Files, Mississippi Department of Archives and History, Jackson, MS; Theresa M. Hicks Papers, South Caroliniana Library, University of South Carolina, Columbia, hereafter Hicks Papers, SCL.

55 Schlafly biographer Donald Critchlow wrote, "While many of the anti-ERA activists held conservative beliefs that were anti-big government, anti-egalitarian, and fearful about moral disorder in society, they never had contact with the segregationist Right— the Ku Klux Klan, the Minutemen, or white separatist groups." See Critchlow, *Phyllis Schlafly*, 222, 223, 230, 252.

56 Correspondence between Phyllis Schlafly and Jean Robinson, Confidential Secretary to Governor George Wallace, April 9, 1973, April 17, 1973, folder "Mrs. Phyllis Schlafly," Governor Wallace, Administrative Files (SG22715), Alabama Department of Archives and History.

57 Boles, *The Politics of the Equal Rights Amendment*, 4.

58 About the history of evangelicals and increased political activism in the 1970s, see Paul Boyer, "The Evangelical Resurgence in 1970s American Protestantism," in *Rightward Bound: Making America Conservative in the 1970s*, Bruce J. Schulman and Julian E. Zelizer, eds., (Cambridge, MA: Harvard University Press, 2008): 29–51.

59 Curry worked with Schlafly to create the Eagle Forum in 1975 and Ellis and Hobbs became members of its board of directors. Brown, *For a "Christian America,"* 65–66, 75–78.

60 Ibid., 65–66; Nancy E. Baker, "'No Women's Libber': Texas Feminist Hermine Tobolowsky and the Fight over Equal Rights," in *Texas Women: Their Histories, Their Lives*, Stephanie Cole, Rebecca Sharpless, and Elizabeth Turner, eds. (Athens: University of Georgia Press, 2015).

61 Brown, *For a "Christian America,"* 65–66; for a list of her publications, see About the Author: Lottie Beth Hobbs, Harvest Publications, http://www.harvestpublications .com/ (accessed August 10, 2016).

62 Ibid., 57, 65–66.

63 Laura Joy Foxworth, "The Spiritual Is Political: The Modern Women's Movement and the Transformation of the Southern Baptist Convention" (Ph.D. diss, University of South Carolina, 2014); Marjorie J. Spruill, "Victoria Eslinger, Keller Bumgardner Barron, Mary Heriot, Tootsie Holland, and Pat Callair: Champions of Women's Rights in South Carolina," in *South Carolina Women: Their Lives and Times*, Marjorie Spruill, Joan Marie Johnson, and Valinda Littlefield, eds., (Athens: University of Georgia Press, 2012), 373–408; "Churches" (WWWW flyer, n.d.), Nancy Moore Papers, SCPC; Daniel K. Williams, *God's Own Party: The Making of the Christian Right* (New York: Oxford University Press, 2012); Brown, *For a "Christian America,"* 65–75.

64 Foxworth, "The Spiritual Is Political"; Williams, *God's Own Party*, 65–75.

65 Neil J. Young, "We Gather Together: Catholics, Mormons, Southern Baptists and the Question of Interfaith Politics, 1972–1984" (Ph.D. diss., Columbia University, 2008); Neil J. Young, *We Gather Together: The Religious Right and the Problem of Interfaith Politics* (New York: Oxford University Press, 2016), 157–58; Brown, *For a "Christian America";* Schlafly quotation, Spruill Interview with Schlafly.

66 For a full treatment of the relationship between the LDS and the women's rights movement from a historian who is a Mormon and attended the IWY meeting in Utah, see Martha Sonntag Bradley, *Pedestals and Podiums: Utah Women, Religious Authority, and Equal Rights* (Salt Lake City: Signature, 2005); The LDS insists that opposition to the ERA did not mean the church opposed equal rights. See "Mormonism and Politics/Equal Rights Amendment: Why Did Church Leaders Oppose the Equal Rights Amendment (ERA) in the United States?" FairMormon http://en.fairmormon .org/Mormonism_and_politics/Equal_Rights_Amendment (accessed September 2, 2016).

67 Ibid.; Neil J. Young, "The ERA Is a Moral Issue: The Mormon Church, LDS Women, and the Defeat of the Equal Rights Amendment," *American Quarterly* 59, no. 3 (September 2007): 623–44.

68 Author's conversation with Phyllis Schlafly, Radcliffe Institute for Advanced Study, Harvard, October 2008.

69   Bradley, *Pedestals & Podiums*; Phyllis Schlafly, "The First Ladies of the Legislatures," *Phyllis Schlafly Report* 9, no. 8, section 2 (March 1976); Young, "The ERA Is a Moral Issue."

70   Kay Mills, "'Those Aren't Prayer Meetings They Hold on Sunday, Those Are Precinct Meetings,' Says Joe Neal, the Only Black in the Nevada Senate," reprint in the *Daily Breakthrough*, September 14, 1977; Lee Davidson, "FBI Files Shed Light on Ezra Taft Benson, Ike and the Birch Society," *Salt Lake Tribune*, November 16, 2010, http://archive.sltrib.com/story.php?ref=/sltrib/news/50349153-78/benson-hoover-fbi-society.html.csp (accessed March 14, 2016).

71   O. Kendall White, "Mormonism and the Equal Rights Amendment," *Journal of Church and State* 31 (Spring 1989): 249–67; Bradley, *Pedestals & Podiums*.

72   "First Presidency Issues Statement Opposing Equal Rights Amendment," *Ensign* 6 (December 1976): 79.

73   Young, "The ERA Is a Moral Issue"; White, "Mormonism and the Equal Rights Amendment"; Bradley, *Pedestals & Podiums*, 159–60.

74   Boles, *The Politics of the Equal Rights Amendment*, 71; Felsenthal, *Sweetheart of the Silent Majority*, 279.

75   Critchlow, *Phyllis Schlafly*, 220; Felsenthal, *Sweetheart of the Silent Majority*, 277–81.

76   Val Burris, "Who Opposed the ERA? An Analysis of the Social Bases of Antifeminism," *Social Science Quarterly* 64, no. 2 (1983): 12; Kent L. Tedin et al., "Social Background and Political Differences Between Pro- and Anti-ERA Activists," *American Politics Quarterly* 5, no. 3 (July 1977): 395–404; Carol Mueller and Thomas Dimieri, "The Structure of Belief Systems Among Contending ERA Activists," *Social Forces* 60, no. 3 (March 1982): 657–76; Critchlow, *Phyllis Schlafly*, 221; For analysis of pro- and anti-ERA activists' motives based on extensive interviews, see Donald G. Mathews and Jane Sherron De Hart, *Sex, Gender, and the Politics of ERA: A State and the Nation* (New York: Oxford University Press, 1990).

77   Jerome L. Himmelstein, "The Social Basis of Antifeminism: Religious Networks and Culture," *Journal for the Scientific Study of Religion*, 25, no. 1 (March 1986): 1–15; Boyer, "The Evangelical Resurgence in 1970s American Protestantism"; Young, *We Gather Together*, 2016, 138–41.

78   Brown, *For a "Christian America*,*"* 37, 38.

79   Thomson, *Price of LIBerty*, 62–64.

80   Neil Young explains that the highest of the heavenly realms, "Exaltation," could not be reached alone but only by temple-married couples who were eternally paired, "sealed," to one another in a temple ceremony. See Young, "The ERA Is a Moral Issue." 631.

81   Brown, *For a "Christian America*.*"*

82   Ibid., 74–78; Young, *We Gather Together*, 2016, especially 154–60.

83   Ibid., 155–58; Brown, *For a "Christian America"* (Schlafly quoted on 78); Second quotation from Spruill Interview with Schlafly.

84   Ibid., 155–58; Williams, *God's Own Party*.

CHAPTER 5: AN ALTERNATIVE TO "WOMEN'S LIB"

1   Rosemary Thomson, *The Price of LIBerty* (Carol Stream, IL: Creation House, 1978), 47–48.

2   Janet K. Boles, *The Politics of the Equal Rights Amendment: Conflict and the Decision Process* (New York: Longman, 1979), 67–68; Carol Felsenthal, *The Sweetheart of the*

Silent Majority: The Biography of Phyllis Schlafly (Garden City, NY: Doubleday, 1981), 270–72.

3   Boles, *The Politics of the Equal Rights Amendment*, 68.

4   Ibid.; Neil J. Young, *We Gather Together: The Religious Right and the Problem of Interfaith Politics* (New York: Oxford University Press, 2016), 160. Young stated that the Mormon Church instructed LDS volunteers "to never mention their religious faith when working against the amendment but instead to describe themselves as 'concerned citizens.'"

5   Rosemary Thomson, *The Price of LIBerty* (Carol Stream, IL: Creation House, 1978), 64; "How Nine Convinced 22,680—or—God Uses Small and Broken Things," n.d., Kathryn Fink Dunaway Papers, Manuscripts, Archives and Rare Book Library, Emory University, Atlanta, GA, hereafter Dunaway Papers, Emory.

6   Felsenthal, *Sweetheart of the Silent Majority*, 244–45; Thomson, *Price of LIBerty*, 47; Schlafly described their victory as the result of a "ten-year David-and-Goliath struggle waged across America" by "a little band of women, headquartered in the kitchen of my home on the bluffs of the Mississippi." Phyllis Schlafly, "Eyewitness: Beating the Bra Burners," *George*, June 1977.

7   Donald G. Mathews and Jane Sherron De Hart, *Sex, Gender, and the Politics of ERA: A State and the Nation* (New York: Oxford University Press, 1990), 50–53.

8   For Schlafly's own account of their victory, see video *Phyllis Schlafly Speech on Doing the Impossible—Defeating the ERA* (Ft. Lauderdale, FL, 2007), https://www.youtube.com/watch?v=VLMICpeZBXg.

9   Phyllis Schlafly, "Women's Lib Suppresses Freedom of Press," *Phyllis Schlafly Report* 7, no. 3, section 2 (October 1973); Felsenthal, *Sweetheart of the Silent Majority*, 311–14; Phyllis Schlafly, "The Right to Be a Woman," *Phyllis Schlafly Report* 6, no. 4 (November 1972).

10 Felsenthal, *Sweetheart of the Silent Majority*, 269, 303–4, 313–14.

11 Ibid., 313, 314.

12 Donald T. Critchlow, *Phyllis Schlafly and Grassroots Conservatism: A Woman's Crusade* (Princeton, NJ: Princeton University Press, 2005), 226–27; Felsenthal, 4, 160–61; Phyllis Schlafly, "Big Money and Tough Tactics to Ratify E.R.A.," *Phyllis Schlafly Report* 8, no. 11, section 2 (June 1975). In the *PSR*, Schlafly detailed for readers this and other "personal attacks," including this incident and "activist black lawyer" Florynce Kennedy, who, Schlafly said, "repeatedly appeared on radio programs and encouraged her listeners to 'hit Phyllis Schlafly in the mouth. Instead of so much argument, people should slap.'"

13 Felsenthal, *Sweetheart of the Silent Majority*, 303.

14 Ibid., 304.

15 Ann McGraw, "Tribute to Phyllis Schlafly," Phyllis Schlafly Institute, June 4, 2014, http://phyllisschlaflyinstitute.com/index.php?title=Ann_McGraw (accessed February 28, 2016).

16 Dianne Edmondson, "Tribute to Phyllis Schlafly," Phyllis Schlafly Institute, December 25, 2013, http://phyllisschlaflyinstitute.com/index.php?title=Dianne_Edmondson (accessed February 28, 2016).

17 Elaine Donnelly, "One Side Versus the Other Side: A Primer on Access to the Media" (Eagle Forum Education and Legal Defense Fund, 1981), box 1, Elaine Chenevert Donnelly Collection 357M, Bentley Historical Library, University of Michigan, Ann Arbor, hereafter Donnelly Collection, Bentley Library.

18 Schlafly quotions from Marjorie J. Spruill Interview with Phyllis Schlafly, February 22, 2005, in possession of the author.

19 "The Equal Rights Amendment Falters, and Phyllis Schlafly is the Velvet Fist Behind the Slowdown, *People Magazine*, Vol. 3, no. 16 (April 28, 1975); Thomson, *Price of LIBerty*, 48; AP, "ERA Foes Let Them Eat Cake," *The State*, April 17, 1975; Thank you note to Mom's Bakery, Dunaway Papers, Emory.

20 A John Birch Society–affiliated group in South Carolina, the Committee to Protect Women's Rights, sent its own state legislators a copy of this packet of information that had been used in Texas. It is in the papers of the state Stop-ERA leader. Irene Neuffer Papers, South Caroliniana Library, University of South Carolina Libraries, Columbia, hereafter Neuffer Papers, SCL.

21 Boles, *The Politics of the Equal Rights Amendment*, 79–80; Jane J. Mansbridge, *Why We Lost the ERA* (Chicago: University of Chicago Press, 1986), 72–82.

22 Critchlow, *Phyllis Schlafly*, 223.

23 Phyllis Schlafly, "The First Ladies of the Legislatures," *Phyllis Schlafly Report* 9, no. 8, section 2 (March 1976).

24 McGraw, "Tribute to Phyllis Schlafly."

25 Edmondson, "Tribute to Phyllis Schlafly"; Barbara Dolan Atherton, "Phyllis Schlafly," June 13, 2014, http://phyllisschlaflyinstitute.com/index.php?title=Barbara_Dolan_Atherton (accessed March 9, 2016).

26 Thomson, *Price of LIBerty*, 47; Rosemary Thomson, "A Christian View of ERA" (pamphlet reprinted from *Moody Monthly*, Moody Bible Institute, Chicago, 1974), box 3, Dunaway Papers, Emory.

27 Thomson, *Price of LIBerty*, 49.

28 Lottie Beth Hobbs, "Ladies, Have You Heard?" box 3, Dunaway Papers, Emory.

29 Thomson, "A Christian View of ERA."

30 Phyllis Schlafly, "What's Wrong With 'Equal Rights' for Women?," *Phyllis Schlafly Report* 5, no. 7, February 1972.

31 Hobbs, "Ladies, Have You Heard?"

32 Thomson, "A Christian View of ERA."

33 Felsenthal, *Sweetheart of the Silent Majority*, 236, 237.

34 Hobbs, "Ladies, Have You Heard?"

35 Ibid.

36 Felsenthal, *Sweetheart of the Silent Majority*, 238; Critchlow, *Phyllis Schlafly*, 300.

37 Hobbs, "Ladies, Have You Heard?"

38 Spruill Interview with Schlafly; Schlafly, "What's Wrong With 'Equal Rights' for Women?"

39 Hobbs, "Ladies, Have You Heard?"

40 Thomson, *Price of LIBerty*, 52.

41 Felsenthal, *Sweetheart of the Silent Majority*, 279–80; Phyllis Schlafly, "How E.R.A. Will Affect Churches and Private Schools," *Phyllis Schlafly Report* 8, no. 8, section 2 (March 1975); Materials distributed by anti-ERA organization, Operation Wake-Up, in New York, "ERA Poses Danger of Women's Draft," and editorial, "Equal Rights Will Do Wrong!" *Jewish Press*, March 25, 1977, Midge Costanza Online Archive, http://www.midgecostanzainstitute.com/pdfs/scripter/anti_era/Jewish_Press_and_Operation_Wake_up_on_drafting.pdf.

42 Schlafly, "What's Wrong With 'Equal Rights' for Women?"

43 Critchlow, *Phyllis Schlafly*, 229; Phyllis Schlafly, *The Power of the Positive Woman* (New Rochelle, NY: Arlington House, 1977), 229–71; *Phyllis Schlafly Speech on Doing the Impossible—Defeating the ERA*.

44 Schlafly, "The Right to Be a Woman."

45 Phyllis Schlafly, "Women in Industry Oppose Equal Rights Amendment, *Phyllis Schlafly Report* 6, no. 12, section 2 (July 1973).

46 Thomson, *Price of LIBerty*, 64.

47 Ibid., 51.

48 Phyllis Schlafly, "Section 2 of the Equal Rights Amendment," *Phyllis Schlafly Report* 6, no. 10, section 2 (May 1973); Felsenthal, *Sweetheart of the Silent Majority*, quotation 281.

49 Andrew H. Merton, *Enemies of Choice: The Right-to-Life Movement and Its Threat to Abortion* (Boston: Beacon Press, 1981), 90–116, 126–33.

50 Thomson, "A Christian View of ERA," 24.

51 Schlafly, "Women in Industry Oppose Equal Rights Amendment; Phyllis Schlafly, "E.R.A. Means Abortion and Population Shrinkage," *Phyllis Schlafly Report* 8, no. 5, section 2 (December 1974).

52 Thomson, *Price of LIBerty*, chapters 3, 4, and 12, quotation 30.

53 Ibid., chapters 3, 4, and 12.

54 Ruth Murray Brown, *For a "Christian America": A History of the Religious Right* (Amherst, NY: Prometheus, 2002), 42–45; Boles, *The Politics of the Equal Rights Amendment*, 80–82, quotation 80.

55 Ibid., 70–71.

56 Felsenthal, *Sweetheart of the Silent Majority*, 270–71; Phyllis Schlafly, *Eagle Forum Newsletter*, December 1975.

57 South Carolina Anti-ERA Flyer, n.d., Nancy Moore Papers, South Carolina Political Collections, University of South Carolina, hereafter Moore Papers, SCPC; Boles, *The Politics of the Equal Rights Amendment*, 70–71.

58 Sara Fitzgerald, *Elly Peterson: "Mother" of the Moderates* (Ann Arbor: University of Michigan Press, 2014), 110; Felsenthal, *Sweetheart of the Silent Majority*, xvii–xviii.

59 Marjorie J. Spruill, "The Conservative Challenge to Feminist Influence on State Commissions on the Status of Women," *Women and Social Movements of the United States, 1600–2000, (WASM), Scholars' Edition,* eds. Kathryn Kish Sklar and Thomas Dublin (Alexandria, VA: Alexander Street Press, 2009), http://asp6new.alexanderstreet.com.pallas2.tcl.sc.edu/was2/was2.object.details.aspx?dorpid=1002104578&fulltext=spruill; Schlafly, "Section 2 of the Equal Rights Amendment."

60 Ibid.

61 State of South Carolina, County of Richland, Court of Common Pleas, *Theresa Hicks in Behalf of Herself and Others Too Numerous to Mention as a Class v. The Commission on the Status of Women* . . . February 2, 1973, Columbia, South Carolina. Jack F. McGuinn, Attorney for Petitioners. In *Phyllis Schlafly Report*, 6, no. 10, section 2, May 1973, 3–4, quotation on 4, Theresa M. Hicks Papers, South Caroliniana Library, University of South Carolina, Columbia, SC, hereafter Hicks Papers, SCL.

62 Phyllis Schlafly, "Are You Financing Women's Lib and ERA?," *Phyllis Schlafly Report*, 7, no. 7, section 2 (February 1974); Janine A. Parry, "'What Women Wanted': Arkansas Women's Commission and the ERA," *Arkansas Historical Quarterly*, Vol. LIX, No. 3, Autumn 2000, 265–98.

63 Schlafly, "Are You Financing Women's Lib and ERA?"; Phyllis Schlafly, "Playboy and Rockefeller Foundations Finance ERA," *Phyllis Schlafly Report* 7, no. 9, section 2 (April 1974).

64 "Phyllis Appointed to Commission," *Phyllis Schlafly Report* 9, no. 2, section 2 (September 1975).

65 Hartmann, *From Margin to Mainstream*, 135–41.

66 Schlafly, *Eagle Forum Newsletter*, December 1975.

67 Ellen Goodman, "Fear of the ERA," *Washington Post*, November 18, 1975.

68 "Telegram, Mrs. Tobin Armstrong, Counsellor to the President, to Mrs. Phyllis Schlafly," September 26, 1974, folder "Schlafly Phyllis and Fred and Anne," box 2810 WHLF Name Files, Gerald R. Ford Presidential Library, Ann Arbor, Michigan, hereafter Name Files, Ford Library.

69 Schlafly, *Power of the Positive Woman*, 171–73.

70 Ibid., Schlafly, "Big Money and Tough Tactics to Ratify E.R.A."

71 NCOIWY, ". . . *To Form a More Perfect Union* . . ." *Justice for American Women: Report of the National Commission on the Observance of International Women's Year* (Washington, D.C.: U.S. Government Printing Office, 1976), 219; "Clipping, Congresswoman Margaret Heckler of Massachusetts Speech on Floor of Congress, *Congressional Record*—House H12275," October 1, 1976, folder: National Commission Meeting July 1, 1976, box 29, National Commission on IWY, Meeting—July 1, 1976, Patricia Lindh and Jeanne Holm Files 1974–1977, Gerald R. Ford Presidential Library, Ann Arbor, Michigan, hereafter Lindh and Holm Files, Ford Library.

72 "Women's Forum" (brochure, August 1975), folder 34, "Other Organizations, 1974–75," carton 30, National Organization for Women (NOW) Records (MC 496), Schlesinger Library, Radcliffe Institute, Harvard University, Cambridge, MA, hereafter NOW Records, SL.; "Eagle Forum: The Alternative to Women's Lib" (brochure, 1975), hereafter Moore Papers, SCPC.

73 *Eagle Forum Newsletter*, January 1976.

74 Phyllis Schlafly, "The Ripoff of the Taxpayers Known As: The Commission on International Women's Year, or, Bella Abzug's Boondoggle," *Phyllis Schlafly Report* 9, no. 6, section 2 (December 1976); "Copy of Page S6924 from the *Congressional Record* Senate, May 11, 1976," *Phyllis Schlafly Report* 9, no. 6, section 2 (January 1976).

75 "Margaret Heckler and Alan Alda, Co-Chairs, ERA Committee of the NCOIWY, to Jill Ruckelshaus, Report of ERA Committee," January 15, 1976, and Jill Ruckelshaus to Mr. President, February 5, 1976, folder "National Commission Meeting January 15, 1976 (1)," box 28, National Commission on IWY, Meeting—April 15, 1975, Lindh and Holm Files, Ford Library.

76 "Elaine Donnelly's Letters to President Ford" n.d., folder "Elaine Donnelly," WHSF Name Files, Ford Library.

77 Donald T. Critchlow, "Mobilizing Women: The 'Social Issues,'" in *The Reagan Presidency: Pragmatic Conservatism and Its Legacies*, W. Elliott Brownlee and Hugh Davis Graham, eds. (Lawrence: University Press of Kansas, 2004): 293–326, 300.

CHAPTER 6: THE GATHERING STORM

1 Jo Freeman, "Something Did Happen at the Democratic Convention," *Ms.*, October 1976, 113–115 and http://www.jofreeman.com/conventions/DemCon1976.htm.; Kandy Stroud, *How Jimmy Won: The Victory Campaign From Plains to the White House* (New York: William Morrow, 1977), 326.

2 Ibid.; For example, see ERA pamphlet targeting African Americans developed by SC NOW members, Nancy Moore Papers, South Carolina Political Collections, University of South Carolina, hereafter Moore Papers, SCPC; Freeman, "Something Did Happen at the Democratic Convention"; Jura Koncius, "Byline," *Washington Post*, December 20, 1979, section Style C.

3 Freeman, "Something Did Happen at the Democratic Convention"; Stroud, *How Jimmy Won*, 326–27.

4   Janet M. Martin, *The Presidency and Women: Promise, Performance, and Illusion* (College Station: Texas A&M University Press, 2003), 212–15; Doreen Mattingly, "The (Limited) Power of Female Appointments: Abortion and Domestic Violence Policy in the Carter Administration," *Feminist Studies* 41, no. 3 (2015): 538–65.

5   Marjorie J. Spruill Interview with President Jimmy Carter and First Lady Rosalynn Carter, Atlanta, GA, May 14, 2009, in the possession of the author.

6   Scott Kaufman, *Rosalynn Carter: Equal Partner in the White House* (Lawrence: University Press of Kansas, 2007), 29–30; Gail Sheehy, "Ladies and Gentlemen, The Second President—Sister Rosalynn," *New York* magazine, November 22, 1976.

7   Winifred D Wandersee, *On the Move: American Women in the 1970s* (Boston: G. K. Hall, 1988), 159–62; Stroud, *How Jimmy Won*, quotations 114–15; Kaufman, *Rosalynn Carter*, 2007, especially 10–33.

8   Kaufman, *Rosalynn Carter*, 55.

9   Ibid., 55–57; Winifred D. Wandersee, *On the Move*, 159–62.

10   Spruill Interview with President Jimmy Carter and First Lady Rosalynn Carter.

11   "Hilda G. Moe to Sheila Greenwald," March 18, 1977, General Correspondence, folder 2, ERAmerica Records (MSS60475), Library of Congress, hereafter ERAmerica Records, LC.

12   Martin Schram, *Running for President, 1976: The Carter Campaign* (New York: Stein and Day, 1977), 304–307.

13   Elizabeth Athanasakos, "Memorandum from the IWY Presiding Officer, No. 1" November 17, 1976, folder "National Commission Meeting, July 1, 1976," box 29, National Commission on IWY, Meeting—July 1, 1976, Patricia Lindh and Jeanne Holm Files, Gerald R. Ford Presidential Library, University of Michigan, Ann Arbor, hereafter Lindh and Holm Files, Ford Library.

14   "Temporary Convenors Named by the National Commission," folder 22, box 21, Catherine Shipe East Papers (MC 477) Schlesinger Library, Radcliffe Institute, Harvard University, hereafter East Papers, SL; "Memorandum from the IWY Presiding Officer, No. 1, Nov. 17, 1976," November 17, 1976, folder "National Commission Meeting, July 1, 1976," box 29, National Commission on IWY, Meeting—July 1, 1976, Lindh and Holm Files, Ford Library; Shelah G. Leader and Patricia R. Hyatt, *American Women on the Move: The Inside Story of the National Women's Conference, 1977* (Lanham, MD: Lexington Books, 2016).

15   Marjorie J. Spruill Interview with Midge Costanza, San Diego, California, December 21, 2007, in the possession of the author; William Grimes, "Midge Costanza, a Top Assistant to Carter, Dies at 77," *New York Times*, March 24, 2010; "The Midge Costanza Institute—the Study of Politics and Public Policy," http://www.midgecostanzainstitute.com/ (accessed August 12, 2014).

16   Laura Kalman, *Right Star Rising: A New Politics, 1974–1980* (New York: W. W. Norton, 2010), 260; Stroud, *How Jimmy Won*, 179–80; Garrett Epps, "The Myth of Hamilton Jordan," *Washington Post*, December 17, 1978. Historian Susan Hartmann wrote, "Among the 'good old boys' that Carter brought with him from Georgia, his key assistant, Hamilton Jordan, in particular did not appreciate powerful women and appeared particularly contemptuous of feminists. Susan M. Hartmann, "Feminism, Public Policy, and the Carter Administration," in *The Carter Presidency: Policy Choices in the Post-New Deal ERA* (Lawrence: University Press of Kansas, 1998): 224–43, quotation 227.

17   Spruill Interview with Costanza; Spruill Interview with President Jimmy Carter and First Lady Rosalynn. In the interview he said he just "fell for" Midge from the beginning of their campaigning together.

18 "Memo, Midge Costanza to the President, 'IWY Commission Nominees,'" March 16, 1977, folder "International Women's Year 3/77–3/78," box 132, Margaret McKenna Files, Jimmy Carter Presidential Library, Atlanta, GA, hereafter McKenna Files, Carter Library. For more information on the Carter appointees, see "Jimmy Carter: National Commission on the Observance of International Women's Year, 1975 Appointment of Members and Presiding Officer of the Commission," http://www.presidency.ucsb.edu/ws/?pid=7247 (accessed August 24, 2014); NCOIWY, *The Spirit of Houston: The First National Women's Conference: An Official Report to the President, the Congress and the People of the United States.* (Washington, D.C.: U.S. Government Printing Office, 1978), 243–49.

19 NCOIWY, *Spirit of Houston*, 243–249.

20 Spruill Interview with Midge Costanza; On the Carter White House and gay rights, see William B. Turner, "Mirror Images: Lesbian/Gay Civil Rights in the Carter and Reagan Administrations," in *Creating Change: Sexuality, Public Policy, and Civil Rights*, John D'Emilio, William B. Turner, and Urvashi Vaid, eds. (New York: St. Martin's, 2000), 3–28.

21 NCOIWY, *Spirit of Houston*, 243–49; Cynthia Harrison, "Creating a National Feminist Agenda: Coalition Building in the 1970s," Stephanie Gilmore, ed. (Urbana: University of Illinois Press, 2008); Leader and Hyatt, *American Women on the Move*.

22 Leader and Hyatt, *American Women on the Move*.

23 NCOIWY, *Spirit of Houston*, 251.

24 Marjorie J. Spruill, "The Mississippi 'Takeover': Feminists, Antifeminists, and the International Women's Year Conference of 1977," in *Mississippi Women: Their Histories, Their Lives*, vol. 2, Martha H. Swain, Elizabeth Anne Payne, and Marjorie Julian Spruill, eds. (Athens: University of Georgia Press, 2010), 287, 313; Mildred Norris, "Status of Women in Mississippi, Report of the Governor's Commission on the Status of Women," June 2, 1967. Mississippi is the prime example of the contrast in appointments to the state women's commission in the 1960s and IWY coordinating committees in 1977, McCain Library, University of Southern Mississippi, Hattiesburg, MS.

25 Spruill Interview with Costanza; Robert D. McFadden, "Mrs. Abzug Rejects Administration Job: Ex-Representative Appears Closer to Running for Democratic Mayoral Nomination," *New York Times*, February 20, 1977.

26 Suzanne Braun Levine and Mary Thom, *Bella Abzug: How One Tough Broad from the Bronx Fought Jim Crow and Joe McCarthy, Pissed Off Jimmy Carter, Battled for the Rights of Women and Workers, Rallied Against War and for the Planet, and Shook up Politics Along the Way; An Oral History* (New York: Farrar, Straus and Giroux, 2007), 44–54; The exact words of *Jackson Daily News* editor Frederick Sullens were: "If Mrs. Abzug ever again appears in Mississippi, either as a lawyer or as an individual, it will be one time too often. She's the sort of person for whose company we care less than nothing at all . . . Too bad the courts don't have authority to send some lawyers to the electric chair along with their clients." Abzug nonetheless went to Jackson the next day, March 8, 1951. She was eight months pregnant, later losing the baby. She and Martin were always convinced that the stress of that visit to the state—one particularly difficult because every hotel refused her a room and she had to spend the night in the women's bathroom of the Jackson bus station as they paged her all night to let her know her adversaries knew where she was—led to the miscarriage. Leandra Zarnow, "The Legal Origins of 'The Personal Is Political': Bella Abzug and Sexual Politics in Cold War America," in

Breaking the Wave: Women, Their Organizations and Feminism, 1945–1985, Kathleen A. Laughlin and Jacqueline L. Castledine, eds. (New York: Routledge, 2011), quotation 37. Zarnow is also the author of a biography of Bella Abzug to be published by Harvard University Press.

27 Amy Swerdlow, *Women Strike for Peace: Traditional Motherhood and Radical Politics in the 1960s* (Chicago: University of Chicago Press, 1993).

28 "Bella Abzug: The Trail and the Tears," *Washington Post*, October 28, 1986.

29 Marjorie J. Spruill Interview with Gloria Steinem at the Thirtieth Anniversary of the National Women's Conference, Hunter College, New York, NY, November 10, 2007, in the possession of the author.

30 Levine and Thom, *Bella Abzug*, 37, 41.

31 Bella S. Abzug, *Bella: Ms. Abzug Goes to Washington* (New York: Saturday Review Press, 1972), especially 3–7, 37–38, 126–27, quotation 3; Leader and Hyatt, *American Women on the Move*; Levine and Thom, *Bella Abzug*, 48–55, 149–166.

32 Bella Abzug/Andy Warhol Cover, *Rolling Stone*, October 6, 1977.

33 Laura Mansnerus, "Obituary: Bella Abzug, 77, Congresswoman and a Founding Feminist, Is Dead," *New York Times*, April 1, 1998.

34 Abzug, *Bella*, 3.

35 Levine and Thom, *Bella Abzug*.

36 Spruill Interview with Costanza; Spruill Interview with President Carter and First Lady Rosalynn Carter.

37 "Elly Peterson to Sheila Greenwald," March 27, 1977, container #1, folder "General Correspondence #2," ERAmerica Records, LC.

38 Levine and Thom, *Bella Abzug*; Spruill Interview with Costanza.

39 Leader and Hyatt, *American Women on the Move*.

40 NCOIWY, "Manual Revisions, Agenda Letter No. 17 Subject: Consideration of Commission Recommendations," March 17, 1977, box 3, Kathryn Fink Dunaway Papers, Manuscripts, Archives and Rare Book Library, Emory University, Atlanta, GA, hereafter Dunaway Papers, Emory.

41 Ibid.; Paula Bernstein, "Fems' Frazzle-Dazzle and Lotsa Lib Service Wins for ERA, Abort," July 11, 1977, clipping, *New York Daily News*, New York folder 2, National Commission on the Observance of International Women's Year Records, Schlesinger Library, Radcliffe Institute, Harvard University, hereafter NCOIWY Records, SL.

42 Feminist Majority Foundation, "The Feminist Chronicles, 1953–1993, 1977," http://www.feminist.org/research/chronicles/fc1977.html (accessed August 17, 2014).

43 Ibid.; Lisa Cronin Wahl, "'A Mormon Connection?' The Defeat of the ERA in Nevada," *Ms.*, July 1977, 68.

44 "John Birch Society Claims Credit for ERA Defeats" (flyer distributed by South Carolina Coalition for the ERA, n.d.), cites as source *American Opinion*, April 1977, Moore Papers, SCPC; Donald G. Mathews and Jane Sherron De Hart, *Sex, Gender, and the Politics of ERA: A State and the Nation* (New York: Oxford University Press, 1990), 50–53, 79–80.

45 Mathews and De Hart, *Sex, Gender, and the Politics of ERA*, 79–90.

46 "Gwendolyn Sawyer Cherry, Esq.," *Gwen S. Cherry Black Women Lawyers Association*; "State Sen. Lori Wilson—Were Her Faults Ignored Because She's Married to a Powerful Newspaper Executive?" *Lakeland Ledger*, March 14, 1978; Kimberly Voss, "The Florida Fight for Equality: The Equal Rights Amendment, Senator Lori Wilson and Mediated Catfights in the 1970s," *Florida Historical Quarterly* 88, no. 2 (Fall 2009): 36.

47 Feminist Majority Foundation, "The Feminist Chronicles;" Voss, "The Florida Fight for Equality, 202–4. ERAmerica published Wilson's speech in a widely distributed brochure, "Why ERA Is in Trouble in the South," ERAmerica Records, LC; AP, "ERA Defeat Appears Certain In Senate Vote Today," *Herald-Tribune*, April 13, 1977; There was a strong correlation between the response of the South to the Nineteenth Amendment and the proposed ERA. Nine of the ten states that refused to ratify the woman suffrage amendment were south of the Mason-Dixon line. Southern states, joined by Illinois and Missouri, Schlafly's two "home states" where she directed the opposition, and the heavily Mormon states of Utah, Nevada, and Arizona defeated the ERA. Marjorie J. Spruill, *New Women of the New South: The Leaders of the Woman Suffrage Movement in the Southern States* (New York: Oxford University Press, 1993).

48 *New York Times*, April 1, 1977; on Mississippi, see the chapter "Murder in Mississippi," in *The South in the History of the Nation: A Reader*, vol. 2, eds. William A. Link and Marjorie J. Spruill (Boston: Bedford/St. Martin's, 1999); Phyllis Schlafly, "Congratulations and Appreciation," *Eagle Forum Newsletter*, May 1977.

49 Robert Shepard, "ERA Boycott Muscles 15 States," *Pittsburgh Press*, April 2, 1978, section F; Voss, "The Florida Fight for Equality"; Phyllis Schlafly, *Eagle Forum Newsletter*, December 1975, May, 1977.

50 Susan M. Hartmann, *From Margin to Mainstream: American Women and Politics Since 1960* (New York: Knopf, 1989), 144–45; Kalman, *Right Star Rising*, 259–61.

51 Ibid.

52 Mattingly, "The (Limited) Power of Female Appointments."

53 Ibid., 11–12; Myra MacPherson, "Bella's Battle Lost; After the Ax, The Bravado Remains," *Washington Post*, January 16, 1979, section Style B.

54 Patricia Parish Williams, "Right to Life: The Southern Strategy," *Southern Exposure* 4, no. 4, *Generations Women in the South* (Winter 1977): 82–85.

55 Dudley Clendinen and Adam Nagourney, *Out for Good: The Struggle to Build a Gay Rights Movement in America* (New York: Simon and Schuster, 1999), 291–309; William A. Link, *Righteous Warrior: Jesse Helms and the Rise of Modern Conservatism* (New York: St. Martin's, 2008), 181.

56 Marjorie J. Spruill Interview with Charlotte Bunch at the Thirtieth Anniversary of the National Women's Conference, Hunter College, New York, NY, November 10, 2007, in the possession of the author; "NOW Task Force on Sexuality and Lesbianism Testimony Before the 1976 Democratic Convention Platform Committee," n.d., folder 41, "Task Force on Sexuality and Lesbianism," carton 38, National Organization for Women (NOW) Records (MC 496), Schlesinger Library, Radcliffe Institute, Harvard University, Cambridge, MA, hereafter NOW Records, SL; Jean O'Leary, "'From Agitator to Insider': Fighting for Inclusion in the Democratic Party," in *Creating Change: Sexuality, Public Policy, and Civil Rights*, 87–92.

57 Ibid., 91; Spruill Interview with Costanza; Doreen J. Mattingly, "'Rainbow of Women': Diversity and Unity at the U.S. 1977 International Women's Year Conference," *Journal of Women's History*, 26, no. 2 (Summer 2014): 88–112; Clendinen and Nagourney, *Out for Good*, 287–90; "Carter Names Lesbian in Political Payoff," *The Spotlight*, September 27, 1976, Theresa M. Hicks Papers, South Caroliniana Library, Columbia, SC, hereafter Hicks Papers, SCL.

58 Spruill Interview with Bunch; O'Leary, "From Agitator to Insider," 2000, 91; Spruill Interview with Costanza.

59 Chai R. Feldblum, "The Federal Gay Rights Bill: From Bella to ENDA," in *Creating Change: Sexuality, Public Policy, and Civil Rights*, 149–53; O'Leary, "From Agitator to Insider," 2000, 89; Spruill Interview with Costanza.

60   Charlotte Bunch, "A Brief History of Lesbian Organizing for IWY, or How Lesbian Rights Made It onto the Agenda for Houston" (typed manuscript for presentation to Houston delegates, 1977), folder 94, box 3, Charlotte Bunch Papers (85-M30–85-M66; T-170), Schlesinger Library, Radcliffe Institute, Harvard University, hereafter Bunch Papers, SL; Deborah Diamond Hicks, "Lesbians Map Conference Strategy," *Daily Breakthrough*, November 19, 1977; NCOIWY, "Sexual Preference: Why Is Lesbianism a Woman's Issue? From International Women's Year Workshop Guidelines," 1977. According to Charlotte Bunch, the booklet was prepared by Jean O'Leary, assisted by Jean Crosby, Pokey Anderson, and Bunch, all members of the National Gay Task Force Women's Caucus.

61   "Memo from Martha Griffiths, IWY Commissioner, to Presiding Officer and Members of National Commission on the Observance of IWY," April 14, 1977, box 1, Shelah Leader Collection, SL. IWY National Commission staff members Shelah Leader and Patricia Hyatt speculate that Catherine East telephoned Griffiths after the meeting and probably drafted the letter for Griffiths's approval. They state that East strongly agreed that there should be no discrimination against lesbians and gays but believed that tactically including it was a grave strategic error. Leader and Hyatt, *American Women on the Move*; Rosemary Thomson, *The Price of LIBerty* (Carol Stream, IL: Creation House, 1978), 95, 121–22.

62   O'Leary, "From Agitator to Insider."

63   Bunch, "A Brief History of Lesbian Organizing for IWY"; Spruill Interview with Bunch; O'Leary, "From Agitator to Insider."

64   Martha Andrews, "International Women's Year $5 Million Fraud," *The Voice of Liberty*, Fall 1977, box 3, L. Marion Gressette Papers, South Carolina Political Collections, University of South Carolina.

65   "Abzug File" Name Files, Jimmy Carter Presidential Library, Atlanta, GA, hereafter Name Files, Carter Library.

66   Elaine Woo, "James J. Kilpatrick Dies at 89," *Los Angeles Times*, August 17, 2010; James J. Kilpatrick, "Carter Hands $5 Million Kitty over to Bella," *Human Events*, April 16, 1977.

67   Ibid.

68   Phyllis Schlafly, "Federal Financing of a Foolish Festival for Frustrated Feminists," *Phyllis Schlafly Report* 10, no. 10, section 2 (May 1977); "Clipping, Congresswoman Margaret Heckler of Massachusetts Speech on Floor of Congress, Congressional Record—House H12275" October 1, 1976, folder: National Commission Meeting, July 1, 1976, box 29, National Commission on IWY, Meeting—July 1, 1976, Lindh and Holm Files, Ford Library.

69   Phyllis Schlafly, "IWY $5 Million Appropriation," *Eagle Forum Newsletter*, April 1976; Phyllis Schlafly, *Eagle Forum Newsletter*, June 1976.

70   Schlafly, "Federal Financing."

71   Thomson enclosed an Eagle Forum brochure and an updated 1977 version of her 1975 pamphlet "A Christian View of the Equal Rights Amendment." "Rosemary Thomson to President Jimmy Carter," March 30, 1977, "Rosemary Thomson," Name Files, Jimmy Carter Presidential Library.

72   "Mildred Marcy to William Drummond," n.d., "International Women's Year 1977," McKenna Files, Carter Library; "Phyllis Schlafly to Stop ERA Members," January 1977, folder "IWY," box 3, L. Marion Gressette Papers, South Carolina Political Collections, University of South Carolina, Columbia, SC, hereafter Gressette Papers, SCPC.

73 Thomson, *Price of LIBerty*, 92; Denise Grady, "Nellie Gray, Anti-Abortion Activist, Dies at 88," *New York Times*, August 15, 2012, section U.S., http://www.nytimes.com/2012/08/16/us/nellie-gray-anti-abortion-activist-dies-at-88.html.

74 Thomson, *Price of LIBerty*, 93.

75 Ibid.

76 Ibid., 93–94.

77 Ibid., 92–94. The quotation is from Thomson, paraphrasing Gray.

78 Ibid., 96–97; See IWY Citizens' Review Committee materials in these collections: Dunaway Papers, Emory; Elaine Chenevert Donnelly Papers, Bentley Historical Library, University of Michigan, Ann Arbor, hereafter Donnelly Papers, Bentley Library; folder "International Women's Year 1977," box 3, Gressette Papers, SCPC.

79 Ruth Murray Brown, *For a "Christian America": A History of the Religious Right* (Amherst, NY: Prometheus, 2002), 65–67.

80 "Thomson to IWY Citizens' Review Chairman," May 1, 1977, box 1, Dunaway Papers, Emory.

81 Ibid.

82 "Review Board Formed to Monitor IWY Committee," *Columbia Record*, May 27, 1977, IWY Citizens' Review Committee materials, folder "International Women's Year 1977," box 3, L. Marion Gressette Papers, South SCPC.

83 Schlafly, "Federal Financing," 2–4.

84 "IWY Conferences," *Eagle Forum Newsletter*, May 1977.

85 Thomson, *Price of LIBerty*, 94.

86 Nancy Elizabeth Baker, "'Too Much to Lose, Too Little to Gain': The Role of Rescission Movements in the Equal Rights Amendment Battle, 1972–1982" (diss., Harvard University, 2003).

87 Martha Andrews, "International Women's Year $5 Million Fraud," *The Voice of Liberty*, Fall 1977, Gressette Papers, SCPC.

88 Thomson, *Price of LIBerty*, 85.

89 "Documentation of IWY Citizen's Review Committee/Eagle Forum Involvement," n.d., folder "Oklahoma," box TY07240, NCOIWY Records, SL; Marjorie J. Spruill Interview with Ann Mulloy Ashmore, Hattiesburg, MS, May 3, 2003, in possession of the author.

90 Linda Owens, "ERA Foes Accused of Interfering With Women's Meeting," *State*, June 9, 1977, section C.

CHAPTER 7: ARMAGEDDON STATE BY STATE

1 NCOIWY, *The Spirit of Houston: The First National Women's Conference: An Official Report to the President, the Congress and the People of the United States* (Washington, D.C.: U.S. Government Printing Office, 1978), 99–117; Rosemary Thomson, *The Price of LIBerty* (Carol Stream, IL: Creation House, 1978), 92–102.

2 Though most IWY state coordinating committee members were chosen by the Ford-appointed IWY Commission and the IWY staff, some were chosen by the Carter appointees. Dr. Marianna Davis, a busy English professor at Benedict College in Columbia, SC said no repeatedly when asked to serve—until she found that it was Maya Angelou who instructed the IWY staff to keep calling Davis until she said yes. Kate Shropshire Interview with Marianna Davis, March 24, 2010, International Women's Year Conference Oral History Collection, South Caroliniana Library, University of South Carolina, Columbia, SC, hereafter IWY Conference Oral History Collection, SCL.

3 NCOIWY, *Spirit of Houston*, 251; Janice Moor, *Mississippi IWY Coordinating Committee Final Report, July 8–9, 1997*. National Commission on the Observance of

International Women's Year Records, Schlesinger Library, Radcliffe Institute, Harvard University, hereafter NCOIWY Records, SL; NCOIWY.

4 NCOIWY, *Manual for State and Territorial IWY Coordinating Committees for Planning and Conducting the Meetings for Women* (United States: The Commission, 1976); NCOIWY, *Spirit of Houston*, 99.

5 Ibid.; NCOIWY, *Manual for State and Territorial IWY Coordinating Committees.*

6 NCOIWY, "Manual Revisions, Agenda Letter No. 17, Subject: Consideration of Commission Recommendations," March 17, 1977, box 3, Kathryn Fink Dunaway Papers, Manuscripts, Archives and Rare Book Library, Emory University, hereafter Dunaway Papers, Emory; Charlotte Bunch, "A Brief History of Lesbian Organizing for IWY, or How Lesbian Rights Made It onto the Agenda for Houston" (typed manuscript for presentation to Houston delegates, 1977), box 3, folder 94, Charlotte Bunch Papers (85-M30—85-M66; T-170), Schlesinger Library, Radcliffe Institute, Harvard University, hereafter Bunch Papers, SL; NCOIWY, *Spirit of Houston*, 99; NCOIWY, *Sexual Preference: Why Is Lesbianism a Woman's Issue? from International Women's Year Workshop Guidelines* (Washington, D.C.: U.S. Government Printing Office, 1977).

7 Carole Askinaze, "ERA Opponents Rail Against Women's Meeting," *Atlanta Journal-Constitution*, May 14, 1977.

8 Cora Norman, program chair for the Mississippi IWY meeting, recalled inviting Dr. Shelton Hand, Mississippi College law professor and expert on family law, to be on a panel. He declined, saying he had other commitments, then appeared at the meeting as part of the group of conservative challengers. Sheryl Hansen (Smith) interview with Cora Norman, April 7, 1992, vol. 432, Mississippi Oral History Collection, McCain Library, University of Southern Mississippi, Hattiesburg, MS. In 1992 and 1993, Sheryl Hansen (now Smith), conducted numerous interviews with feminist and conservative participants in the Mississippi IWY meeting that are part of this collection.

9 "A Capsulized Look at the State Meetings," July 8, 1977, folder "July 13–15, 1977," box 1, Shelah Leader Collection, Schlesinger Library, Radcliffe Institute, Harvard University, hereafter Leader Collection, SL; Caroline Bird, "State Meetings: Every Woman Her Say," in *The Spirit of Houston*, 99–113, especially 104. See also the final reports housed in state libraries and archives or collected in the National Archives or the Schlesinger Library, Radcliffe Institute, Harvard University.

10 "Planners Hope for 1,000 at Weekend IWY Meet," *Clarion-Ledger*, July 3, 1977; South Carolina IWY Committee, "The South Carolina Woman: Heritage to Horizons," June 1977, box 3, folder "South Carolina," NCOIWY Records, SL; NCOIWY, *Spirit of Houston.*

11 NY State Women's Meeting, "Calling All Women" (promotional flyer), http://www.dianamarahenry.com/wotm/NYState_Women_s_Meeting.html (accessed June 5, 2016).

12 NCOIWY, *Spirit of Houston*, 99–108.

13 Marjorie J. Spruill, "The Mississippi 'Takeover': Feminists, Antifeminists, and the International Women's Year Conference of 1977," in *Mississippi Women: Their Histories, Their Lives*, vol. 2, Martha H. Swain, Elizabeth Anne Payne, and Marjorie Julian Spruill, eds. (Athens: University of Georgia Press, 2010), 287–313; Suzanne Braun Levine and Mary Thom, *Bella Abzug: How One Tough Broad from the Bronx Fought Jim Crow and Joe McCarthy, Pissed Off Jimmy Carter, Battled for the Rights of Women and Workers, Rallied Against War and for the Planet, and Shook up Politics Along the Way; An Oral History* (New York: Farrar, Straus and Giroux, 2007), 197.

14   Flyer, Dunaway Papers, Emory. This account of the Georgia IWY meeting is drawn
     primarily from the Dunaway Papers and these sources: Robin Marie Morris, "Organizing
     Breadmakers: Kathryn Dunaway and the Georgia STOP ERA Campaign," in *Entering
     the Fray: Gender, Politics, and Culture in the New South*, Jonathan Daniel Wells and
     Sheila R. Phipps, eds. (Columbia: University of Missouri Press, 2008); Thomson, *Price
     of LIBerty*; Bird, "State Meetings," in *Spirit of Houston*, 99–113, especially 104; news-
     paper clippings included in the report of the Georgia Coordinating Committee,
     NCOIWY Records, SL; Georgia Coordinating Committee on the Observance of
     International Women's Year Records, 1975–1978, Georgia Department of Archives and
     History Library.

15   Phyllis Schlafly, "Federal Financing of a Foolish Festival for Frustrated Feminists,"
     Phyllis Schlafly Report 10, no. 10, section 2 (May 1977).

16   Thomson, *Price of LIBerty*, 93; On Dunaway seeing herself as a token, see Carole
     Ashkinaze, "Are Federal Funds Used to Lobby for the ERA?," *Atlanta Journal-
     Constitution*, February 26, 1977, box 3, Dunaway Papers, Emory.

17   STOP ERA of Georgia and Eagle Forum of Georgia, "Dear Friends," April 7, 1977,
     box 1, Dunaway Papers, Emory; Thomson, *Price of LIBerty*, 94.

18   The pastor of Atlanta's First Baptist Church was Charles Stanley, a fervent critic of the
     ERA and feminism, later involved in the conservative takeover of the Southern Baptist
     Convention. Kathryn Dunaway to Charles Stanley, January 17, 1977, box 2, Dunaway
     Papers, Emory; Morris, "Organizing Breadmakers," 173.

19   Rosemary Thomson, "To CRC Chairmen and Eagle Forum Chapter Presidents," July
     5, 1977, box 1, Dunaway Papers, Emory.

20   Morris, "Organizing Breadmakers," 173.

21   NCOIWY, *Spirit of Houston*, 104; Carole Ashkinaze, "ERA Opponents Rail Against
     Women's Meeting," *Atlanta Journal-Constitution*, May 14, 1977.

22   Thomson, *Price of LIBerty*, 96.

23   Ashkinaze, "ERA Opponents Rail Against Women's Meeting."

24   Ibid.

25   Ibid.

26   Schlafly, "Federal Financing."

27   Kathryn Dunaway, "Memo to IWY Citizens' Review State Chairman," May 10, 1977,
     box 2, 34, Dunaway Papers, Emory.

28   Clipping, Carol Richards, "Women's Movement Faceoff Brewing," Gannett News
     Service, folder "Georgia 1977," box 1, NCOIWY Records, SL.

29   NCOIWY, *Update 5* (U.S. Dept. of State, May 31, 1977).

30   Ibid.

31   Ibid.; Bird, "State Meetings," *Spirit of Houston*, 105.

32   Steve Ahrens, "Hansen, ERA for Fight Women's Year Meet," *Idaho Statesman*, July 14,
     1977, in clippings prepared for White House Briefing on IWY, September 20, 1977,
     folder "International Women's Year 3/77–3/78," Margaret McKenna Files, Jimmy
     Carter Presidential Library, Atlanta, GA, hereafter McKenna Files, Carter Library.

33   NCOIWY, *Update 5*.

34   Ibid.; Correspondence, Patricia Hyatt, IWY Public Information Office, 1975–1978,
     with the author, November 11, 2015.

35   NCOIWY, *Spirit of Houston*, 104.

36   Ibid., 99–108; "A Capsulized Look at the State Meetings."

37   Phyllis Schlafly, "IWY: A Front for Radicals and Lesbians," *Phyllis Schlafly Report* 11,
     no. 1, section 2 (August 1977).

38 "A Capsulized Look at the State Meetings."

39 NCOIWY, *Spirit of Houston*, 113.

40 NCOIWY, *Update 5.*

41 NCOIWY, *Spirit of Houston*, 204–105; "International Women's Year, 1977 Collection, 1975—1978," *State Historical Society of Missouri*, n.d. See extensive primary sources in this collection, http://shs.umsystem.edu/stlouis/manuscripts/s0228.pdf.; Mary Berkery, "The New Suffragists of 1977 and the Challenge of Coalition Building at Missouri's International Women's Year State Meeting," *Missouri Historical Review* 107, no. 1, (October 2012).

42 Jennifer Donnally, "The Politics of Abortion and the Rise of the New Right" (Ph.D. diss., University of North Carolina at Chapel Hill, 2013); Bill Curry and Megan Rosenfeld, "Crucial Test for Women's Conference," *Washington Post*, November 18, 1977; Mary Ziegler, *After Roe: The Lost History of the Abortion Debate* (Cambridge, MA, Harvard University Press, 2015), 201–202.

43 Ibid.; Donnally, "The Politics of Abortion and the Rise of the New Right."

44 NCOIWY, *Spirit of Houston*, 104–105; Berkery, "The New Suffragists of 1977."

45 Ibid.

46 "A Capsulized Look at the State Meetings."

47 Jesse Helms, "What Happened to Congressional Intent?," *Congressional Record*, July 1, 1977, S11474–75; William A. Link, *Righteous Warrior: Jesse Helms and the Rise of Modern Conservatism* (New York: St. Martin's, 2008), 181–85; Dick Behn, "Antifeminism: New Conservative Force," *Ripon Forum*, September 1, 1977.

48 Letter from NWPC Leader Gael Muramoto to State Chairs with Upcoming IWY Conferences, June 16, 1977, Re: Organizing Feminists to Prevent Anti-ERA, Anti-Abortion Take-Over at IWY Conferences; Mary Peace Douglas to Ms. Audrey Rowe Colom, NWPC President, June 10, 1977; and Report from MMOPP Organizer Elly Anderson, Entered into the CR by Sen. Jesse Helms, in *Congressional Record*, 1977, S 11474, S 11475.

49 Thomson, "To CRC Chairmen and Eagle Forum Chapter Presidents," July 5, 1077, Dunaway Papers, Emory.

50 Ibid.; Kathryn Dunaway, "Suggestions for Houston Texas" (handwritten notes, Chicago, IL, August 3, 1977), box 2, Dunaway Papers, Emory.

51 Thomson, "To CRC Chairmen and Eagle Forum Chapter Presidents."

52 Ibid.

53 AP, "Normal Turns Bananas for Women's Year Talk," *Register-Republic*, June 7, 1977, and Sharen Johnson, "Women's Conference Split by ERA," *Morning Star*, June 11, 1977, box 3, Dunaway Papers, Emory; Richards, "Women's Movement Faceoff Brewing."

54 Sharen Johnson, "Abzug Visit Conference: Travel-Worn, Sleepless," *Morning Star*, June 13, 1977.

55 Thomson, "To CRC Chairmen and Eagle Forum Chapter Presidents" Thomson, *Price of LIBerty*, on Percy, 91–92, 114, 122, 123.

56 AP, "Normal Turns Bananas for Women's Year Talk," and Johnson, "Womens' Conference Split by ERA," Johnson, "Abzug Visits Conference: Travel-Worn, Sleepless."

57 Ibid.; Schlafly, "IWY: A Front for Radicals and Lesbians"; Betty J. Blair, "Klan's Spies' Plan to Disrupt Feminist Party," *Detroit News*, September 1, 1977.

58 Ibid.

59 Elaine Donnelly, "Instructions for IWY Conference in Michigan," and Trudy Westfall, "Rival Coalitions Seek Control," *State Journal* (Lansing, MI), June 11, 1977, both in box 3, Dunaway Papers, Emory.

60 Ibid.

61 Ibid.

62 Behn, "Antifeminism: New Conservative Force."

63 Caitlin Mans, "'Heritage to Horizons': The History of the 1977 International Women's Year Conference in South Carolina" (master's thesis, University of South Carolina, 2013).

64 Blair, "Klan's Spies' Plan to Disrupt"; Collection of anti-IWY materials sent to Gressette by Oliver Willis, folder "International Women's Year 1977," box 3, L. Marion Gressette Papers, South Carolina Political Collections, University of South Carolina Library, Columbia, SC, hereafter Gressette Papers, SCPC; Mans, "Heritage to Horizons."

65 Julie Gregory (Greenville, SC), state president of Women for Constitutional Government, to Theresa Hicks, November 8, 1973, folder 8, Theresa M. Hicks Papers, South Caroliniana Library, University of South Carolina, Columbia, SC, hereafter Hicks Papers, SCL; South Carolina International Women's Year Committee, "The South Carolina Woman: Heritage to Horizons," NCOIWY Records, SL; Kate Salley Palmer, "I Enjoy Being a Girl," Cartoon. *The State*, August 6, 1982, Kate Salley Palmer Papers, South Carolina Political Collections, University of South Carolina.

66 Constance Ashton Myers Interview with Modjeska Simkins, June 1977, IWY Conference Oral History Collection, SCL.

67 The South Carolina International Women's Year Committee, "The South Carolina Woman: Heritage to Horizons"; Myers Interview with Modjeska Simkins, SCL; Cherisse Jones-Branch, "Modjeska Monteith Simkins: I Cannot Be Bought and Will Not Be Sold," in *South Carolina Women: Their Lives and Times*, vol. 3, Marjorie J. Spruill, Valinda W. Littlefield, and Joan Marie Johnson, eds. (Athens: University of Georgia Press, 2012), 221–39.

68 "Press Release by Norma C. Russell," June 17, 1977, folder "International Women's Year, 1977," box 3, Gressette Papers, SCPC.

69 Marjorie Lipsyte, "IWY: Houston Nov. 19 ERA, Abortion Key Issues," *New Directions for Women* 6, no. 3, (Autumn 1977). Copy received by Imogene Borganelli, Greenville, MS, folder 4, box 57, AAUW Collection, Williams Library, University of Mississippi.

70 Ibid.; Statement by Shelah Leader, Carton 1, Shelah Leader Collection 97-M10, Schlesinger Library, Radcliffe Institute, Harvard University, hereafter Leader Collection, SL.

71 Lipsyte, "IWY: Houston Nov. 19 ERA, Abortion Key Issues."

72 Doreen J. Mattingly, "'Rainbow of Women': Diversity and Unity at the U.S. 1977 International Women's Year Conference," *Journal of Women's History*, 26, no. 2, Rainbow of Women (Summer 2014): 88–112.

73 Faith Middleton and Candace Page, "Clippings from the *Providence Journal*, June 13, 1977, in the report of the Massachusetts Coordinating Committee, box TY07564, NCOIWY Records, SL.

74 Ibid.

75 Ibid.

76 Ibid.

77 Puerto Rico took no action, since it was not a state; For a table with information on the state meetings, including location, date, number attending, number of elected delegates, and whether the meeting "defeated all," "adopted all," or took "no action" on the "core," see NCOIWY, *Spirit of Houston*, 114–15.

78 UPI, "Va. Women's Conference Ends: Controversial Resolutions Passed," *Daily Progress*, June 13, 1977; Levine and Thom, *Bella Abzug*, 198.

79   Carol Lacey, "Ex-St. Paulite Will Be in Center of Parley," *St. Paul Dispatch*, November 18, 1977, folder "November 1977—Houston II," carton 220; Carol Lacey, "Delegates Forming Caucus to Back Meeting's Action Plan," *St. Paul Dispatch*, November 18, 1977, folder "November 1977—Houston II," carton 220, National Organization for Women (NOW) Records (MC 496), Schlesinger Library, Radcliffe Institute, Harvard University, Cambridge, MA, hereafter NOW Records, SL; Mattingly, "'Rainbow of Women': Diversity and Unity at the U.S. 1977 International Women's Year Conference"; Cynthia Harrison, "Creating a National Feminist Agenda: Coalition Building in the 1970s," Stephanie Gilmore, ed. (Urbana: University of Illinois Press, 2008).

80   "NWPC, June 16, 1977, To State Chairs with Upcoming IWY Conferences, from Gael Muramoto, Membership Director, Re: Organizing Feminists to Prevent Anti-ERA, Anti-Abortion Take-Over at IWY Conferences; Mary Peace Douglas to Ms. Audrey Rowe Colom, NWPC, K St, Washington, DC, June 10, 1977," in *Congressional Record*, 1977, S 11474, S 11475.

81   Levine and Thom, *Bella Abzug*, Smeal quoted, 199; Mans, "Heritage to Horizons."

82   Marjorie J. Spruill Interview with Charlotte Bunch, Hunter College, New York, NY, November 10, 2007, in the possession of the author.

83   Ibid.

84   Ibid.

85   Ibid.

86   Ellen Cohn, "'Mama Said There'd Be Days Like This,'" *Village Voice*, July 11, 1977.

87   NCOIWY, *Spirit of Houston*, 107–8. Mayor Thomas Bradley Notes: California State Meeting, June 16–19, UCLA, "Final Report to the National Commission on the Observance of International Women's Year, 1977," California file, box TYO7194, NCOIWY Records, SL.

88   Schlafly, "IWY: A Front for Radicals and Lesbians"; NCOIWY, *Spirit of Houston*, 108.

89   Irene Wolt, "California Feminists Beat Back Right Wing," *In These Times*, July 6–12, 1977, California Report to IWY National Commission, National Commission Papers, SL).

90   Ibid.

91   Schlafly, "IWY: A Front for Radicals and Lesbians."

92   "A Capsulized Look at the State Meetings."

CHAPTER 8: OUT OF THE KITCHEN AND INTO THE COUNTERREVOLUTION

1   Rosemary Thomson, *The Price of LIBerty* (Carol Stream, IL: Creation House, 1978), 130.

2   Afterwards, Ann Ashmore wrote, "That the Conference would be taken over by extremist, ultra-conservative groups could not have been foreseen. Even in our wildest speculations no one inside or outside the Committee ever dreamed that what did happen was going to happen." Ann Mulloy Ashmore, Chair, to Dorothy Spinks, Southwestern Regional Coordinator, July 15, 1977, folder "Oklahoma 1," box TY07240, National Commission on the Observance of International Women's Year Records, Schlesinger Library, Radcliffe Institute, Harvard University, hereafter NCOIWY Records, SL.

3   Marjorie J. Spruill Interview with Ann Mulloy Ashmore, Hattiesburg, MS, May 3, 2003, in possession of the author.

4   Thomson, *Price of LIBerty*, 129–131; Newspaper reports, Oklahoma IWY Coordinating
    Committee Final Report, 1977, folder "Oklahoma 1977," box 3; Preface to the coordi-
    nating committee's report, folder "Oklahoma 1," NCOIWY Records, SL.

5   Betty J. Blair, "Klan's Spies' Plan to Disrupt Feminist Party," *Detroit News*, September
    1, 1977.

6   On Edmondson's background, see her Web site https://www.blogger.com/profile/
    18019399026774105673 (accessed April 26, 2015). She continued to be very active in
    the pro-life, pro-family movement and was a leader in GOP politics in Texas. Ruth
    Murray Brown, *For a "Christian America": A History of the Religious Right* (Amherst,
    NY: Prometheus, 2002), 99; Thomson, *Price of LIBerty*, 129–131.

7   Mrs. Bob Johnson, "Dear Friend" (Letter, Broken Arrow, OK, June 1977), Kathryn
    Fink Dunaway Papers, Manuscripts, Archives and Rare Book Library, Emory
    University, Atlanta, GA, hereafter Dunaway Papers, Emory; Thomson, *Price of LIBerty*,
    130–31; Brown, *For a "Christian America,"* 107–8; Phyllis Schlafly described the tapes
    as playing a key role in building the audience for the Pro-Family, Pro-Life Rally in
    Houston in 1977. Marjorie J. Spruill Interview with Phyllis Schlafly, February 22,
    2005, in possession of the author.

8   Brown, *For a "Christian America,"* 107–8; Thomson, *Price of LIBerty*, 130–31.

9   James J. Kilpatrick, "Christians 1,000; Lions 200," *Ledger*, July 9, 1977; Dick Behn,
    "Antifeminism: New Conservative Force," *Ripon Forum*, September 1, 1977.

10 Materials in the Oklahoma IWY coordinating committee's report indicate that the
    organizers were angry and frustrated that IWY lawyer Linda Dorian agreed to
    Edmondson's request without knowing she was the CRC chair and "not a friend of the
    conference." See "Evaluation of the Oklahoma Coordinating Committee, Jan Dreiling,
    Program Chair," folder "Oklahoma 1977," box 3, NCOIWY Records.

11 Kilpatrick, "Christians 1,000; Lions 200"; Thomson, *Price of LIBerty*, 130.

12 William P. Hustwit, *James J. Kilpatrick: Salesman for Segregation*, (Chapel Hill: UNC
    Press, 2013).

13 Kay Mills, "'Those Aren't Prayer Meetings They Hold on Sunday, Those Are Precinct
    Meetings,' Says Joe Neal, the Only Black in the Nevada Senate," September 14, 1977,
    reprint in the *Daily Breakthrough*; Ellen Cohn, "'Mama Said There'd Be Days Like
    This,'" *Village Voice*, July 11, 1977; Dixie Snow Huefner, "Church and Politics at Utah
    IWY Conference," *Dialogue: A Journal of Mormon Thought* 11, no. 1 (1978): 62; Neil J.
    Young, "The ERA Is a Moral Issue: The Mormon Church, LDS Women, and the Defeat
    of the Equal Rights Amendment," *American Quarterly* 59, no. 3 (September 2007): 635.

14 John M. Crewdson, "Mormon Turnout Overwhelms Women's Conference in Utah,"
    New York Times, July 25, 1977.

15 "JoAnn Freed, Staff Coordinator, Utah IWY Coordinating Committee, to Rosalynn
    Carter," April 25, 1977, "International Women's Year," Name Files, Jimmy Carter
    Presidential Library, Atlanta, GA, hereafter Name Files, Carter Library.

16 "For Immediate Release," January 2, 1977, "Clipping from the *Deseret News*," n.d., and
    "Today, the Prelude for Tomorrow," speech by Belle Spafford, folder "Utah," National
    Commission on the Observance of International Women's Year Records, Schlesinger
    Library, Radcliffe Institute, Harvard University, hereafter NCOIWY Records, SL.

17 John M. Crewdson, "Mormon Women Dictate Convention to Libbers," *Morning News*,
    August 5, 1977, Martha Swain clippings collection in possession of the author.

18 Ibid.

19 Phyllis Schlafly, "The First Ladies of the Legislatures," *Phyllis Schlafly Report* 9, no. 8,
    section 2 (March 1976); Angelyn Nelson, "Utah IWY Delegates to Examine Issues," *Salt*

Lake City Tribune, July 19, 1977, folder "Utah," box T707240, IWY National Commission Papers, SL; Huefner, "Church and Politics at Utah IWY Conference," 60, 66.

20 Mills, "'Those Aren't Prayer Meetings They Hold on Sunday, Those Are Precinct Meetings,' Says Joe Neal, the Only Black in the Nevada Senate."

21 Crewdson, "Mormons Turnout Overwhelms," 235.

22 Crewdson, "Mormon Women Dictate Convention to Libbers."

23 Ibid.

24 "Homemakers Take Over" (clipping from unidentified Nebraska newspaper, July 1977), Martha Swain clippings collection in possession of the author

25 Ibid.

26 Ibid.

27 Vera Glaser, "Women's Year: Peril on the Right," *Philadelphia Inquirer,* August 23, 1977.

28 "Homemakers Take Over."

29 Rosemary Thomson, "To CRC Chairmen and Eagle Forum Chapter Presidents," July 5, 1977, Dunaway Papers, Emory.

30 Ibid.

31 Ibid.

32 Ibid.

33 Ibid.

34 Cassandra Tate, "Washington State Conference for Women Opens in Ellensburg on July 8, 1977," HistoryLink.org, http://www.historylink.org/File/10259 (accessed September 4, 2016).

35 Jean Withers, Lynn Morrison, Ruth Jones, Fredericka Foster, *The Women of Ellensburg: Report of the Washington State International Women's Year Conference 1977,* featured on the website of the Washington State Historical Society, http://digitum.washingtonhistory.org/cdm/compoundobject/collection/digipubs/id/542/rec/1; The story of the Washington IWY meeting is very well documented and accessible. For the report of the state coordinating committee, news clippings, and interviews with feminist and conservative leaders conducted in 2007, see "International Women's Year Oral History Project," *Washington State Historical Society,* http://www.washingtonhistory.org/research/whc/oralhistory/IWYOralHistory/ (accessed July 12, 2016).

36 Ibid.; for this section on the Washington IWY meeting.

37 Ibid.; AP story, clipping from unidentified newspaper, "Women's Meets End as Battles," ca. July 11, 1977, NCOIWY Records, SL.

38 Ibid.

39 Behn, "Antifeminism: New Conservative Force," 243.

40 NCOIWY, *Spirit of Houston,* 214.

41 Mink served for twelve terms, part before and part after 1977 (1965–1976, 1990–2002).

42 Phyllis Schlafly, "IWY: A Front for Radicals and Lesbians," *Phyllis Schlafly Report* 11, no. 1, section 2 (August 1977); Jesse Helms, "Statement," *Congressional Record,* July 21, 1977, S 12500-10.

43 NCOIWY, *Spirit of Houston;* Beverly Creamer, "Untitled Article," *Honolulu Advertiser,* July 1977.

44 Creamer, "Untitled Article"; University YWCA, "Special Post-IWY Issue," *Woman Alive,* August 1977.

45 Erin M. Kempker, "Battling 'Big Sister' Government: Hoosier Women and the Politics of International Women's Year,'" *Journal of Women's History* 24, no. 2 (Summer 2012): 144–70.

46   Cohn, "Mama Said"; Behn, "Antifeminism: New Conservative Force."

47   Cohn, "Mama Said."

48   Suzanne C. Brickman, "Women's Meeting Gears Up in Albany," *Schenectady Gazette*, July 9, 1977, folder "New York," box 2, NCOIWY Records.

49   Suzanne Braun Levine and Mary Thom, *Bella Abzug: How One Tough Broad from the Bronx Fought Jim Crow and Joe McCarthy, Pissed Off Jimmy Carter, Battled for the Rights of Women and Workers, Rallied Against War and for the Planet, and Shook up Politics Along the Way; An Oral History* (New York: Farrar, Straus and Giroux, 2007).

50   Associated Press, "Women's Meets End as Battles."

51   Erin M. Kempker, "Women at the Crossroads: Feminists, Conservatives, and Gender Politics in Indiana, 1950–1980" (Ph.D. diss., Purdue University, 2008), 246.

52   Ibid., 214, 236.

53   Ibid., 145–46, 153–54.

54   Ibid., 153.

55   Blair, "Klan's Spies' Plan to Disrupt."

56   "Opinion: Extremists Are Taking over Women's Struggle for Equality," *Courier-Journal*, July 21, 1977. The editorial was not signed, but Carol Sutton had become the editor in 1974, making her the first woman managing editor of a major U.S. daily newspaper, box 1, Shelah Leader Collection, Schlesinger Library, Radcliffe Institute, Harvard University, hereafter Leader Collection, SL.

57   Kempker, "Battling 'Big Sister' Government," 152.

58   "Opinion: Extremists Are Taking Over Women's Struggle for Equality"; Catherine East, "Chronology of the Women's Movement in the U.S., 1961–1975," in NCOIWY, *National Women's Conference Official Briefing Book: Houston*, 231.

59   Schlafly, "IWY: A Front for Radicals and Lesbians"; Carolyn Kortge, "Schlafly Says Women's Movement Is Dying in an Anti-Feminist Surge," *Eagle & Beacon*, August 3, 1977.

60   AP, "Women's Rights Backlash Troubles Carter Aide," *Gadsden Times*, July 10, 1977, NCOIWY Records, SL.

61   AP, "Women's Rights Backlash Troubles Carter Aide."

62   Peggy Simpson, "Feminists, Conservatives Face Houston Standoff," *Commercial Appeal*, September 11, 1977, Martha Swain Papers; Cornelia McDuffy Turner, "IWY Meet Turns into Battle over ERA," *Mobile Press-Register*, July 10, 1977.

63   Bessie Ford, "Anti-Feminist Group Scores Victory in Montgomery," *Athens News Courier*, July 10, 1977.

64   Diane J. McEwen and Linda Hays, *The Alabama Celebration of International Women's Year: Report of the State Conference Held Saturday, July 9, 1977, Montgomery Civic Center, Montgomery, Ala.*, 1977. Alabama report. NCOIWY Records, SL.

65   AP, "Women's Rights Backlash," July 10, 1977.

66   Ibid.

67   "Editorial: In Perfumed Combat," *Montgomery Independent*, July 15, 1977, NCOIWY Records, SL.

68   Ray Jenkins, "Editorial," *Montgomery Advertiser*, July 12, 1977.

69   Sara Schwieder, "Disputes over ERA, Abortion Mar IWY Conference," *Tampa Times*, July 18, 1977; Dianne Selditch, "Both Sides Claim Win in ERA Split," *Sentinel Star*, July 18, 1977. Both in box 3, Dunaway Papers, Emory.

70   James Walker, "ERA Battle Disrupts Women's Convention," *Tampa Tribune*, July 17, 1977; Sybil? To Kathryn Dunaway (Letter, July 19, 1977); Dianne Selditch, "ERA

Forces Split on Delegation Nominations," *Sentinel Star*, July 16, 1977; and James Walker, "Stop-ERA Forces Hit Women's Meet," *Tampa Tribune*, July 18, 1977, all in box 3, Dunaway Papers, Emory.

71 AP, "Confrontation Expected at Women's Conference in Orlando," *Daily News-Chief*, July 15, 1977, box 3, Dunaway Papers, Emory; Walker, "ERA Battle Disrupts Women's Convention."

72 Walker, "ERA Battle Disrupts Women's Convention."

73 Beth Dunlop, "Anti-ERA Forces Thwart Meeting," *Miami Herald*, July 18, 1977; and AP, "Stormy Conference Ends, No Agreement on Issues" (clipping, n.d.), both in box 3, Dunaway Papers, Emory.

74 Levine and Thom, *Bella Abzug*, 198, 199; Carmen Delgado Votaw, "Thirty Years of Struggle and Triumph for the Women's Movement," address to the Veteran Feminists of America conference, Harvard University, March 24, 2007, copy in possession of the author.

75 Bob Schwartzman, "Klan Cardholder Wanted to Help," *Today*, July 18, 1977.

76 Walker, "ERA Battle Disrupts Women's Convention."

77 AP, "Stormy Conference Ends, No Agreement on Issues."

78 Marjorie J. Spruill, "The Mississippi 'Takeover': Feminists, Antifeminists, and the International Women's Year Conference of 1977," in *Mississippi Women: Their Histories, Their Lives*, vol. 2, Martha H. Swain, Elizabeth Anne Payne, and Marjorie Julian Spruill, eds. (Athens: University of Georgia Press, 2010), 287–313, 299; Nancy Weaver, "Delegates Brace for IWY Storm: State Again Fuels U.S. Controversy. Delegates-Elect: 20 Whites, 6 Men, All Conservative," *Clarion-Ledger*, November 17, 1977.

79 Sheryl Hansen (Smith) Interview with Cora Norman, April 7, 1992, vol. 432, and Interview with Alison Steiner, September 28, 1992, vol. 416, Mississippi Oral History Collection, McCain Library, University of Southern Mississippi; "To Bella Abzug, Chair, National Commission on Women. From: Kathie Gilbert, a Citizen of the State of Mississippi and Vice-Chair Mississippi IWY Coordinating Committee" (Minority Report, July 1977), Cora Norman Papers; Weaver, "Delegates Brace for IWY Storm"; Linda Williams, "Feminists, Antifeminists See IWY Meeting as Grassroots Test," *South Mississippi Sun*, November 15, 1977, vertical file, "National Women's Conference," Mississippi State Archives, Jackson, MS.

80 Williams, "Feminists, Antifeminists"; Jean Town, "Jackson Attorney Gives ERA Con Point of View," *Daily Herald*, July 12, 1977, and David Crary (AP), "Conservative Lawyer Helped Engineer Anti-ERA Victories," *Commercial Dispatch*, July 12, 1977, both in folder "Mississippi," box TY071996, NCOIWY Records, SL; Peggy Simpson, "Feminists, Conservatives Face Houston Standoff"; "Get Mixed Reaction," *Clarion-Ledger*, July 9, 1977.

81 David Bates, "ERA Opponents Dominate Women's Gathering," *Clarion-Ledger*, July 10, 1977, section A; L. C. Dorsey, "International Women's Year Meeting" (clipping from unidentified newsletter, n.d.), Martha Swain clippings collection in possession of the author; Sheryl Hansen (Smith) Interview with Cora Norman.

82 Janice Moor, *Mississippi IWY Coordinating Committee Final Report, July 8–9, 1977*, 1977; Marjorie J. Spruill and Sara Farnsworth Interview with Cora Norman, Jackson, MS, 2000, in the possession of the author.

83 Nancy Weaver, "Klansman's Wife Equates Women's Rights with Communism," *Clarion-Ledger*, November 17, 1977; Weaver, "Delegates Brace for IWY Storm"; AP, "IWY 'Alerted' About Voting," *Daily News*, September 28, 1977, vertical file, "National Women's Conference," Mississippi State Archives.

84   Spruill, "Mississippi Takeover," 299–301; Diane Gaus, "Women's Year Confab Called," *Daily News*, July 9, 1977, Dunaway Papers, Emory.

CHAPTER 9: MAMA SAID THERE'D BE DAYS LIKE THIS

1   Marjorie J. Spruill, "The Mississippi 'Takeover': Feminists, Antifeminists, and the International Women's Year Conference of 1977," in *Mississippi Women: Their Histories, Their Lives*, vol. 2, Martha H. Swain, Elizabeth Anne Payne, and Marjorie Julian Spruill, eds. (Athens: University of Georgia Press, 2010), 287–313, 301.
2   Ellen Cohn, "Mama Said There'd Be Days Like This," *Village Voice*, July 11, 1977.
3   Marjorie Lipsyte, "IWY: Houston Nov. 19 ERA, Abortion Key Issues," *New Directions for Women* 6, no. 3, (Autumn 1977). Copy received by Imogene Borganelli, Greenville, MS, folder 4, box 57, AAUW Collection, Williams Library, University of Mississippi.
4   Spruill, "Mississippi Takeover."
5   Peggy Simpson, "Feminists, Conservatives Face Houston Standoff," *Commercial Appeal*, September 11, 1977, Martha Swain clippings collection in possession of the author; David Bates, "ERA Opponents Dominate Women's Gathering," *Clarion-Ledger*, July 10, 1977, section A.
6   "Boost for Pro-Life Seen in Responses to IWY Meetings: Helms Plans Special Hearings," *NRL News*, September 1977; "Predict 'Counter Convention' to Outpull IWY in Houston," *NRL News*, December 1977.
7   Carolyn Kortge, "Schlafly Says Women's Movement Is Dying in an Anti-Feminist Surge," *Eagle & Beacon*, August 3, 1977.
8   Emphasis hers. Phyllis Schlafly, "IWY: A Front for Radicals and Lesbians," *Phyllis Schlafly Report* 11, no. 1, section 2 (August 1977).
9   Ibid.
10   Kay Mills, "Those Aren't Prayer Meetings," *Daily Breakthrough*, September 14, 1977.
11   Ibid.
12   John M. Crewdson, "Mormon Turnout Overwhelms Women's Conference in Utah," *New York Times*, July 25, 1977.
13   Dick Behn, "Antifeminism: New Conservative Force," *Ripon Forum*, September 1, 1977.
14   Ibid.
15   "Memo: Beth Abramowitz to Stu Eizenstat. Subject IWY" (July 22, 1977). The memo from Abramowitz gives background and discusses problems with the IWY, including lawsuits filed by critics and issues about whether or not elected delegates are representative, since some groups bused in people and controlled meetings. Note: at the top, in handwriting, it reads, "xc: Beth: This is an excellent report. Please see my comments." On a circulation list, there are checks next to the names "Bert" and David." Handwritten marginal comments seem to have come from David R. The comment that the IWY program appeared to be "going sour" and that the president should keep a "low profile" appears to have been written by Bert Lance. folder "Women's Issues," DPS [Stuart] Eizenstat files 323, Jimmy Carter Library, Atlanta, GA. Beth Abramowitz, Assistant Director of the Domestic Council Policy Staff, had attended the National Women's Conference and made a presentation in the "Briefings from Women at the Top" series.
16   "Summary of Executive Committee Meeting," August 10, 1977, carton 1, National Commission on the Observance of International Women's Year Records, Schlesinger Library, Radcliffe Institute, Harvard University, hereafter NCOIWY Records, SL; NCOIWY staff members Leader and Hyatt recall that Liz Carpenter dashed off the letter and that after she left Steinem and Chassler revised it. Shelah G. Leader and Patricia R. Hyatt, *American Women on the Move: The Inside Story of the National Women's*

Conference, 1977 (Lanham, MD: Lexington Books, 2016); "Bella Abzug to President Jimmy Carter," July 11, 1977, "Bella Abzug," Name Files, Carter Library; "Lee Novick, Conference Coordinator, IWY Secretariat to Midge Costanza," July 27, 1977, and "Bella Abzug to Hon. Jimmy Carter (Signed by National Commission Members)," August 12, 1977, folder "NACW Items Pre 1/12/79," box 13, Sarah Weddington Files, Jimmy Carter Presidential Library, Atlanta, GA, hereafter Weddington Files, Carter Library.

17   Ibid.

18   Ibid.

19   "Memo: Beth Abramowitz to Stu Eizenstat. Subject IWY" (July 22, 1977).

20   Ibid.

21   Marjorie J. Spruill Interview with Charlotte Bunch at the Thirtieth Anniversary of the National Women's Conference, Hunter College, New York, November 10, 2007, in the possession of the author.

22   Ibid.; Jean O'Leary, "'From Agitator to Insider': Fighting for Inclusion in the Democratic Party," in *Creating Change: Sexuality, Public Policy, and Civil Rights*, John D'Emilio, William B. Turner, and Urvashi Vaid, eds. (New York: St. Martin's, 2000), 89–91.

23   Dudley Clendinen and Adam Nagourney, *Out for Good: The Struggle to Build a Gay Rights Movement in America* (New York: Simon and Schuster, 1999), 310.

24   Jana S. Vogt, "Oklahoma and the ERA: Rousing a Red State, 1972–1982" (Ph.D. diss., University of Oklahoma, 2010), 117–19.

25   "Biography of Catherine East, 1916–1996." Finding Aid, Catherine Shipe East Papers (MC 477), Schlesinger Library, Radcliffe Institute, Harvard University, hereafter East Papers, SL; NCOIWY, *The Spirit of Houston: The First National Women's Conference: An Official Report to the President, the Congress and the People of the United States* (Washington, D.C.: U.S. Government Printing Office, 1978), 166; IWY Commission staff members Shelah Leader and Patricia Hyatt state that in addition to East's concern about including an antidiscrimination plank, she was exasperated with Abzug's administrative style and found working with her extremely stressful to the point it was physically debilitating. This led East to take early retirement, although she felt guilty about leaving her old friend Kay Clarenbach to deal with Bella without her help. Leader and Hyatt, *American Women on the Move.*

26   Memo: Beth Abramowitz to Stu Eizenstat. Subject IWY, July 22, 1977, Eizenstat Files, Carter Library.

27   "Kathryn Dunaway to President Carter," July 27, 1977, "Kathryn Dunaway," Name Files, Carter Library.

28   Ibid.

29   Jimmy Carter: "Women's Equality Day, 1977 Remarks on Signing Proclamation 4515," August 26, 1977. Online by Gerhard Peters and John T. Woolley, The American Presidency Project. http://www.presidency.ucsb.edu/ws/?pid=7996 (accessed December 22, 2015); "Summary of Executive Committee Meeting," August 10, 1977, carton 1, NCOIWY Records, SL.

30   Tanya Melich, *The Republican War Against Women: An Insider's Report from Behind the Lines* (New York: Bantam, 1998), 95.

31   Ibid.

32   Ibid.; In December 1977, Schlafly announced she had decided not to run, in part because she "was afraid Fred would think I didn't need him anymore. A man needs to feel psychologically needed as well as financially needed, and it causes problems if the wife is financially and emotionally so self-sufficient that he feels unnecessary." Carol

Felsenthal, *The Sweetheart of the Silent Majority: The Biography of Phyllis Schlafly* (Garden City, NY: Doubleday, 1981), 113.

33   "Summary of Executive Committee Meeting," NCOIWY Records, SL.

34   Ibid.; Jesse Helms, "Dear Colleagues" (Letter, Washington, D.C., September 7, 1977), Kathryn Fink Dunaway Papers, Manuscripts, Archives, and Rare Book Library, Emory University, hereafter Dunaway Papers, Emory; Link, *Righteous Warrior: Jesse Helms and the Rise of Modern Conservatism* (New York: St. Martin's, 2008), 183–85.

35   "Sarah Simms to Kathryn Dunaway" (Letter, June 28, 1977), box 3, Dunaway Papers, Emory.

36   Rosemary Thomson, "To CRC Chairmen and Eagle Forum Chapter Presidents," July 5, 1977, box 1, Dunaway Papers, Emory.

37   For examples of these testimonials being collected, see folder "International Women's Year 1977," box 3, L. Marion Gressette Papers, South Carolina Political Collections, University of South Carolina; Kathryn Fink Dunaway Papers, Emory. Rosemary Thomson, *The Price of LIBerty* (Carol Stream, IL: Creation House, 1978), 99–101.

38   In the 1980s, McDonald would replace JBS Founder Robert Welch as national chairman, serving until 1983, when his plane was shot down by the USSR when it veered into Soviet airspace on its way to Korea. McDonald was going to a world anti-communist meeting to promote the Western Goals Foundation, an organization he cofounded with Ohio Republican John Ashbrook to strengthen western civilization and prevent "any merger with totalitarians." The JBS honors him as "the only U.S. Congressman lost to the communists during the Cold War." "Rep. Larry McDonald," John Birch Society, http://www.jbs.org/about-jbs/larry-mcdonald (accessed December 23, 2015). Senator Helms was also en route to the meeting and considered switching to KAL 007 but was talked out of it by Senator Steve Symms, who was also part of the group. "Remembering Korean Air Lines Flight 007 / The Jesse Helms Center," Jesse Helms Center, http://www.jessehelmscenter.org/archives-and-museum/online-exhibits/remembering-korean-air-lines-flight-007/ (accessed April 11, 2016).

39   Elizabeth Moore, "Witnesses Say Feminist Faction Suppressed Others," *NRTL News*, October 1977; "Boost for Pro-Life Seen in Responses to IWY Meetings: Helms Plans Special Hearings," *NRTL News*, September 1977; *Phyllis Schlafly Speech on Doing the Impossible—Defeating the ERA* (Ft. Lauderdale, FL, 2007), https://www.youtube.com/watch?v=VLMICpeZBXg; Thomson, *Price of LIBerty*, 99–104.

40   Ibid.; "International Women's Year: Is $5 Million of the Taxpayers' Money Being Misspent?," *Congressional Record—Senate*, October 3, 1977, 31977–83.

41   "International Women's Year: Is $5 Million of the Taxpayers' Money Being Misspent?"

42   Ibid.

43   Schlafly, "IWY: A Front for Radicals and Lesbians."

44   "International Women's Year: Is $5 Million of the Taxpayers' Money Being Misspent?"

45   Ibid.

46   Moore, "Witnesses Say"; "Boost for Pro-Life Seen"; "News Release: Statement of Senator Jesse Helms Opening Second Day of Hearings on International Women's Year," September 15, 1977, and "McDonald Opposes IWY Tactics" (press release, September 19, 1977), box 3, Dunaway Papers, Emory.

47   Rosemary Thomson, "Dear Citizens' Review Coordinator," September 26, 1977, box 3, Dunaway Papers, Emory.

48   Ibid.

49   Bella Abzug, "To Fellow Commissioners," September 2, 1977, folder "Sept. 15, 16, 1977," carton 1, Shelah Leader Collection, Schlesinger Library Institute, Harvard University, hereafter Leader Collection, SL.

50   "New Coalition Braces for Attacks Against IWY," *Women Today* 7, no. 19 (September 19, 1977).

51   Bella Abzug, "International Women's Year Observation," *Congressional Record* 123, part 24 (September 22, 1977).

52   Ibid.

53   Patricia Schroeder, "Widespread Support for IWY Conference," *Congressional Record* 123, part 24 (September 21, 1977). The groups involved included: American Association of University Women, American Jewish Committee, Americans for Democratic Action, B'nai B'rith Women, Black Women Lawyer's Association, ERAmerica, Girl Scouts of the U.S.A., League of United Latin American Citizens, Mexican American Women's National Association, National Abortion Rights Action League, National Conference of Puerto Rican Women, National Council of Jewish Women, National Education Association, National Federation of Business and Professional Women's Clubs, Inc., National Gay Rights Task Force, National Women's Democratic Club–Political Action Committee, National Women's Political Caucus, National Women's Party, NETWORK (religious lobby), Project on the Status and Education of Women, Association of American Colleges, Religious Coalition for Abortion Rights, Wider Opportunity for Women, Women's Equity Action League, http://asp6new.alexanderstreet.com.pallas2.tcl.sc.edu/was2/was2.object.details.aspx?dorpid=1001257060.

CHAPTER 10: CREST OF THE SECOND WAVE

1   Charles B. Gordon, "Even Validity of Feminism Under Attack at This Stage," *Jackson Daily News*, November 16, 1977.

2   Linda Williams, "Feminists, Antifeminists See IWY Meeting as Grassroots Test," *South Mississippi Sun*, November 15, 1977, vertical file, "National Women's Conference," Mississippi State Archives, Jackson, MS.

3   Bill Curry and Megan Rosenfeld, "Crucial Test for Women's Conference," *Washington Post*, November 18, 1977, section A.

4   Caroline Bird and NCOIWY, *What Women Want: From the Official Report to the President, the Congress, and the People of the United States* (New York: Simon and Schuster, 1979), 53; Kay Mills, "Women's Movement at the Crossroads: Edith to Be in Houston? Stapleton Will, For Sure," *Detroit Free Press*, November 11, 1977, folder "November 1977, Houston Conference," box 220, National Organization for Women (NOW) Records (MC 496), Schlesinger Library, Radcliffe Institute, Harvard University, Cambridge, MA, hereafter NOW Records, SL.

5   NCOIWY, *The Spirit of Houston: The First National Women's Conference: An Official Report to the President, the Congress and the People of the United States.* (Washington, D.C.: U.S. Government Printing Office, 1978), 193.

6   Ibid., 193–202.

7   Ibid.; Karey Bresenhan and Beverly Hebert, "Seneca Falls Torch Relay," *Daily Breakthrough*, November 1977; Anna Quindlen, "Women Relay the Movement's Torch from Seneca Falls to Houston," *New York Times*, October 7, 1977.

8   "Minutes, Executive Committee Meeting 12/13/77," folder "Jan. 19, 1978," Shelah Leader Collection 97-M10, Schlesinger Library, Radcliffe Institute, Harvard University, hereafter Leader Collection, SL. Bird and NCOIWY, *What Women Want*, 53; Jack

Anderson and Les Whitten, "Sometimes Battling Bella More Harmful Than Good," *El Paso Times*, December 28, 1977; "Mormon Media Image," *Sunstone*, January 1978; Frank Hewlett, "Utah Senators, Church Ask Apologies," *Salt Lake Tribune*, November 22, 1977, Jo Freeman Papers.

9 Betty J. Blair, "Klan's Spies' Plan to Disrupt Feminist Party," *Detroit News*, September 1, 1977; Peggy Simpson, "Feminists, Conservatives Face Houston Standoff," *Commercial Appeal*, September 11, 1977, Martha Swain clippings collection in posses-sion of the author; "White House Briefing on International Women's Year Materials" September 20, 1977, folder "IWY 3/77–3/78," Margaret McKenna Files, Jimmy Carter Presidential Library, Atlanta, GA, hereafter McKenna Files, Carter Library.

10 Gannett News Service, "Gloves Are Off," *Courier-Post*, November 18, 1977, folder "November 1977—Houston II," carton 220, NOW Records, SL; NCOIWY, *National Women's Conference Official Briefing Book: Houston, Texas, November 18 to 21, 1977* (Washington, D.C., U.S. Government Printing Office, 1977). This material had also been distributed at a briefing IWY leaders held for White House staffers earlier in the fall.

11 Sara Fritz, "Women Gird for Houston Fight," *Tribune*, November 17, 1977; "Conservative Women Duel with Feminists: Historic Houston Conference," *Evening Tribune*, November 18, 1977; UPI, "$40,000 to Keep Women in Order," *Nevada State Journal*, November 18, 1977, all in folder "November 1977—Houston II," carton 220, NOW Records, SL.

12 Bird and NCOIWY, *What Women Want*, 28–29, 55–58; Mildred Hamilton, "A Hard Look/Battle of the Sexes—with Women on Both Sides," San Francisco *Examiner and Chronicle*, November 18, 1977, folder "November 1977—Houston II," carton 220, NOW Records, SL.

13 NCOIWY, *Update 7* (U.S. Dept. of State, September 1977), folder "Sept. 1977," Carter Presidential Library; "To Bella Abzug, Chair, National Commission on Women. From: Kathie Gilbert, a Citizen of the State of Mississippi and Vice-Chair Mississippi IWY Coordinating Committee" (Minority Report, July 1977), NCOIWY Records, Schlesinger Library, Radcliffe Institute, Harvard University, hereafter NCOIWY Records, SL.

14 NCOIWY Office of Public Information, U.S. Department of State, "Summary Sheet of Press Reports on the Tactics of Radical Right Wing Groups" (Washington, D.C., November 1977), box 18, folder 30, Catherine East Records #477, SL; Nancy Weaver, "Women's Group Shocked at Delegation," *Clarion-Ledger*, September 9, 1977; "IWY Selects Nine Delegates from State," *South Mississippi Sun*, September 29, 1997; Nancy Weaver, "Nine at-Large Members Must Carry Rights Banner," *Clarion-Ledger*, November 17, 1977.

15 Pat Nixon (who was ailing) and Jacqueline Kennedy Onassis were the only living First Ladies who did not attend. After the conference, Gloria Steinem wrote to Onassis, a good friend, saying, that before the Houston conference, "I think I not only believed the press about [the conference's likely] failure and the strength of the ultra right forces, but also thought somewhere inside that women couldn't pull off such a big, populist event. If I had known how very wrong I was, I would have urged you to go. Now I'm sorry that I didn't." Carolyn G. Heilbrun, *The Education of a Woman: The Life of Gloria Steinem* (New York: Ballantine, 1995), 320.

16 "Memorandum for: Midge Costanza, Margaret McKenna, Jane Frank, From: Hugh Carter, Subject: IWY Conference," November 3, 1977. In same folder, Memorandum to: Jane Wales, Jane Frank, Bunny Mitchell, Kathy Cade, Midge Costanza, Esther Peterson, Margaret McKenna, Stu Eizenstat, David Rubenstein, Joanne Hurley, from

Beth Abramowitz, November 17, 1977, summarizing the Carter administration's accomplishments on women's issues, presumably for use at the Houston conference. Folder "International Women's Year," 3/77–3/78, box 132, McKenna Files, Carter Library; NCOIWY, *Spirit of Houston*. Names of the presenters appear on 290–91.

17 AP, "IWY 'Alerted' About Voting," *Daily News*, September 28, 1977, 130, vertical file, "National Women's Conference," Mississippi State Archives, Jackson, MS; NCOIWY, *Spirit of Houston*, 130.

18 Ibid., 111, 165.

19 Jean O'Leary, "'From Agitator to Insider': Fighting for Inclusion in the Democratic Party," in *Creating Change: Sexuality, Public Policy, and Civil Rights*, John D'Emilio, William B. Turner, and Urvashi Vaid, eds. (New York: St. Martin's, 2000), 91–92; Charlotte Bunch, "A Brief History of Lesbian Organizing for IWY, or How Lesbian Rights Made It onto the Agenda for Houston" (typed manuscript for presentation to Houston delegates, 1977), 1, box 3, folder 94, Charlotte Bunch Papers (85-M30—85-M66; T-170), Schlesinger Library, Radcliffe Institute, Harvard University, hereafter Bunch Papers, SL; NCOIWY, *Spirit of Houston*, 165.

20 "Jean O'Leary to Dear Delegate," November 11, 1977, folder "International Women's Year 1977," box 3, L. Marion Gressette Papers, South Carolina Political Collections; on the 1848 controversy over endorsing woman suffrage, see Sally Gregory McMillen, *Seneca Falls and the Origins of the Women's Rights Movement* (New York: Oxford University Press, 2008).

21 Georgie Anne Geyer, "Politics Threaten Future of Women's Movement, by Georgie Anne Geyer, Washington—from Portland, Oregon *Oregonian*, Nov. 1, 1977," *Oregonian*, November 1, 1977, clipping, Sept.–Nov. 1977, folder "Nov. 1977 Houston Conference," carton 120, NOW Records, SL.

22 O'Leary, "From Agitator to Insider," 91–92; Deborah Diamond Hicks, "Lesbians Map Conference Strategy," *Daily Breakthrough*, November 19, 1977; Carol R. Richards, "Carrying the Torch for U.S. Womanhood," Gannett News Service, *Courier-Post*, November 18, 1977, folder "November 1977–Houston II," carton 220, NOW Records, SL.

23 Bird and NCOIWY, *What Women Want*, 60–61; "Editorial," *Washington Post*, November 18, 1977.

24 Judy Klemesrud, "Women's Movement at Age 11: Larger, More Diffuse, Still Battling," *New York Times*, November 15, 1977.

25 Simpson, "Feminists, Conservatives Face Houston Standoff."

26 Ellen Goodman, "Women's Movement Comes Full Circle: Ellen at Large," *Boston Globe*, November 7, 1977.

27 Marlene Cimons, "Women's Peace Parley Shunned by Feminists," *Daily News*, November 6, 1977, box 220, folder "November 1977, Houston Conference," NOW Records, SL; "Phyllis Schlafly Press Conference, Friday a.m., November 18" (Houston, TX), folder 10 "NOW Officers Komisar," box 4, NOW Records, SL.

28 Lori Rodriguez, "Kum Baya Room to Offer Listeners at Women's Parley," *Chronicle*, November 17, 1977, folder "November 1977–Houston II," carton 220, NOW Records, SL; Beverly Hebert, "Kum Baya," *Daily Breakthrough*, November 19, 1977.

29 NCOIWY, *Spirit of Houston*, 126; "Conservative Women Duel with Feminists: Historic Houston Conference," *Evening Tribune*, November 18, 1944.

30 Gloria Steinem, "An Introductory Statement," in Bird, *What Women Want*, 17; Heilbrun, *The Education of a Woman*, 320.

31 NCOIWY, *Spirit of Houston*, 141, 142, 152, 160, 161, 162.

32 Ibid., 172–73.

33 Ibid., 173. A list of the oral historians appears on 297; Myers placed the tapes in the National Archives, and later donated her copies to the South Caroliniana Library which is preparing an online database on IWY. International Women's Year Conference Oral History Collection, South Caroliniana Library, University of South Carolina, Columbia, SC, hereafter IWY Conference Oral History Collection, SCL; Rosemary Thomson, "Dear Citizens' Review Coordinator" September 26, 1977, box 3, Kathryn Fink Dunaway Papers, Manuscripts, Archives, and Rare Book Library, Emory University.

34 NCOIWY, *Spirit of Houston*, 123, 172, 177–78. For list of official international visitors, see 291–93.

35 "COYOTE (Organization). Records, 1962–1989: A Finding Aid, Schlesinger Library," Harvard University Library, http://oasis.lib.harvard.edu/oasis/deliver/⊠sch00278 (accessed December 17, 2015); NCOIWY, *Spirit of Houston*, 1978, 172–73, 175–84.

36 NCOIWY, *Spirit of Houston*, 173; for copies of the *Daily Breakthrough*, folders 1–5, box 5, Series 9 (Publications), Houston Area NOW and Other Feminist Activities Collection, 1970–1996, University of Houston Libraries.

37 Ellen Pratt Fout, "'We Shall Go Forth': The Significance of the National Women's Conference, November 18–21, 1977" (master's thesis, University of Houston, 2000), 91; Ellen Pratt Fout, "'A Miracle Occurred!': The Houston Committee of International Women's Year, Houston, 1977," *Houston Review* 1, no. 1 (2003): 8; Prudence Mackintosh, "The Good Old Girls," *Texas Monthly*, January 1978; NCOIWY, *Spirit of Houston*, 169. Members are listed on 260.

38 On Sadat, see *Time,* December 5, 1977 (with tiny corner photo of Sadat on a page featuring the IWY conference); *New York Times*, November 20, 1977.

39 Carol Bartholdi, "Visitors Have Reservations about Houston Hotel," *Daily Breakthrough*, November 19, 1977.

40 Sally Quinn, "The Pedestal Has Crashed: Pride and Paranoia in Houston," *Washington Post*, November 23, 1977.

41 Lindsy Van Gelder, "Four Days That Changed the World: Behind the Scenes in Houston," *Ms.*, March 1978; Judy Klemesrud, "A Reporter's Notebook: Symbolic Attire," *New York Times*, November 21, 1977; NCOIWY, *Spirit of Houston*, 173.

42 Ibid., 129.

43 Ibid., 126, 129; Sally Quinn, "The Pedestal Has Crashed: Pride and Paranoia in Houston," *Washington Post*, November 23, 1977.

44 Tom Brokaw, "Opening of the Largest Gathering of American Women Ever Held," *NBC Today Show* (New York: NBC, November 18, 1977), NBC Learn; NCOIWY, *Spirit of Houston*, 93–203; Karey Bresenhan and Beverly Hebert, "Seneca Falls Torch Relay," *Daily Breakthrough*, November 18, 1977.

45 Bird, *What Women Want*, 64–65, quotation 65; NCOIWY, *Spirit of Houston*, 128–29; Judy Anderson, "Excitement in Houston: Women's Big Rights Gathering," *Examiner and Chronicle*, n.d., Jo Freeman Papers.

46 Quinn, "The Pedestal Has Crashed: Pride and Paranoia in Houston."

47 NCOIWY, *Spirit of Houston*, 128–29, 193, see full text of the poem, 195.

48 Sara Fitzgerald, *Elly Peterson: "Mother" of the Moderates* (Ann Arbor: University of Michigan Press, 2014), 232; NCOIWY, *Spirit of Houston*, 130.

49 Bird, *What Women Want*, 65, 67–69; Karen Malnory, "Women on the Move," *Daily Breakthrough*, November 19, 1977; NCOIWY, *Spirit of Houston*, 195.

50 Ibid., 138.

51   Quinn, "The Pedestal Has Crashed: Pride and Paranoia in Houston."

52   NCOIWY, *Spirit of Houston*, 138, 219–20.

53   Ibid., For full text of Abzug's address, see 217–19. Note: Throughout her career, Abzug benefitted from collaboration with Mim Kelber, her speechwriter as well as co-author and fellow activist.

54   Tanya Melich, *The Republican War Against Women: An Insider's Report from Behind the Lines* (New York: Bantam, 1998), 97–98.

55   Ibid., 98. Carpenter's speech, 221–222.

56   Ibid., 41. Jordan's speech, 223.

57   Carol Lacey, "Ex-St. Paulite Will Be in Center of Parley," *St. Paul Dispatch*, November 18, 1977; Carol Lacey, "Delegates Forming Caucus to Back Meeting's Action Plan," *St. Paul Dispatch*, November 18, 1977, folder "November 1977—Houston II," carton 220, NOW Records, SL; NCOIWY, *Spirit of Houston*, 130–34.

58   Ibid., 155–59; Carmen Delgado Votaw, "Thirty Years of Struggle and Triumph for the Women's Movement" (speech delivered at the Veteran Feminists of America conference, Harvard University, March 24, 2007), 4, copy in possession of the author; Suzanne Braun Levine and Mary Thom, *Bella Abzug: How One Tough Broad from the Bronx Fought Jim Crow and Joe McCarthy, Pissed Off Jimmy Carter, Battled for the Rights of Women and Workers, Rallied Against War and for the Planet, and Shook up Politics Along the Way; An Oral History* (New York: Farrar, Straus and Giroux, 2007), 211; for Steinem's recollections about that night and its significance, see Gloria Steinem, *My Life on the Road* (New York: Random House, 2015), 61–64.

59   Jacqueline St. John Interview with Anonymous, November 20, 1977, IWY Conference Oral History Collection, SCL.

60   Jean O'Leary, "'From Agitator to Insider': Fighting for Inclusion in the Democratic Party," in *Creating Change: Sexuality, Public Policy, and Civil Rights*, 92; Carole Ashkinaze, "Women Approve a Gay Rights Resolution," *Atlanta Journal-Constitution*, November 21, 1977; Rachelle DeLaney, "'Gay' Issue Splits Georgia, Florida Units," Jacksonville, FL *Times-Union*, November 22, 1977, folder "Nov 1977 GAY/LESBIAN RIGHTS," carton 120, NOW Records, SL; "What Next for U.S. Women: Houston Produces New Alliances and a Drive for Grass-Roots Power," *Time*, December 5, 1977.

61   Alferdteen Harris, Interview with Cora Norman, November 1977, IWY Conference Oral History Collection, SCL; O'Leary, "From Agitator to Insider," 2000, 91, 92; "What Next for U.S. Women: Houston Produces New Alliances and a Drive for Grass-Roots Power," *Time*, December 5, 1977, 22.

62   Anna Quindlen, "Women's Conference: The Follow-up Is Next," *New York Times*, November 23, 1977; Jay Kleinberg Interview with Eleanor Haney, November 1977, IWY Conference Oral History Collection, SCL.

63   Marjorie Abrams Interview with Jan Glover, November 1977. The quotation is from Abrams. IWY Conference Oral History Collection, SCL.

64   Constance Ashton Myers Interview with Betty Friedan, November 1977, IWY Conference Oral History Collection, SCL.

65   In a pre-conference interview Friedan said she was "coming out of her quiet time" and preparing to launch a new effort to get the ERA ratified by the 1979 deadline. Mary Lu Abbott, "Betty Friedan to Make Comeback," *Chronicle*, November 17, 1977, folder "November 1977—Houston II," carton 220, NOW Records, SL; NCOIWY, *Spirit of Houston*, 148.

66   Ibid., 166; "What Next for U.S. Women."; Betty Friedan, "The Women at Houston," *New Republic*, December 10, 1977, folder 226, carton 7, 215–59, Betty Friedan Papers

(MC 575), Schlesinger Library, Radcliffe Institute, Harvard University, hereafter Friedan Papers, SL; Marjorie J. Spruill Interview with Charlotte Bunch, Hunter College, New York, NY, November 10, 2007, in the possession of the author; O'Leary, "From Agitator to Insider," 91–92.

67 Betty Friedan, "Feminism's Next Step: Betty Friedan Declares That the Women's Movement Requires New Directions That Transcend Sexual Politics, Feminism," *New York Times*, July 5, 1981, section *New York Times Magazine*.

68 Quinn, "The Pedestal Has Crashed."

69 "What Next for U.S. Women," 21; James J. Kilpatrick, column, *Right to Life News*, January 28, 1978; NCOIWY, "What the Press Said," *Spirit of Houston*, 173.

70 Ibid., 162.

71 Ibid., 154.

72 Ibid., 148; Levine and Thom, *Bella Abzug*, 208–9.

73 NCOIWY, *Spirit of Houston*, 163.

74 Ibid., 145.

75 "What Next for U.S. Women"; Quindlen, "Women's Conference"; Friedan, "The Women at Houston."

76 NCOIWY, *Spirit of Houston*, 170.

77 Ibid., 168, Costanza speech appears in full on 232.

78 Ibid., 170. Music and lyrics appear on 171.

79 Ibid., passim. Other featured speakers included IWY Commission and union leader Addie Wyatt; Commissioner Cecilia Preciado-Burciaga and Commissioner Carmen Delgado Votaw (in Spanish); American Indian and Alaskan Native Billie Masters; and Brenda Parker, a high school student who was president of the Future Homemakers of America.

80 Ibid., 158–60.

81 Friedan, "The Women at Houston."

82 Anne Taylor Fleming, "That Week in Houston: It Was Said That the Women's Movement Was in a State of Disarray; the National Women's Conference Proved Otherwise. Women," *New York Times*, December 25, 1977, 138.

83 Friedan, "The Women at Houston."

84 Fleming, "That Week in Houston."

85 Ibid.

86 NCOIWY, *Spirit of Houston*, 149.

87 Ibid., 151, 152.

88 Gloria Steinem, "An Introductory Statement," in Bird, *What Women Want*, 16–17.

89 Alice S. Rossi, *Feminists in Politics: A Panel Analysis of the First National Women's Conference* (New York: Academic Press, 1982), 323–25.

90 Ibid.

91 Fitzgerald, *Elly Peterson*, 232, 233.

92 Goodman, "Women's Movement Comes Full Circle"; Melich, *Republican War Against Women*, 100.

93 George F. Will, "Earnest 'Sisters' Voting for a New World," *Washington Post*, November 24, 1977, section A.

94 Patrick Buchanan, "Where Jimmy Should File the Houston Agenda," *Washington Weekly*, December 8, 1977, clippings, folder "1977—Houston Conference," carton 220, NOW Records, SL.

95 Susan L. Huck, "Five Million Dollar Misunderstanding," *American Opinion*, January 1978, 1–4, 75–91; "Susan Huck Obituary—Washington, D.C./*Washington Times*," January 25, 2007. See excerpts from right-wing media coverage in the January 1978

issue of the *Phyllis Schlafly Report*. Huck wrote for many archconservative publications and served as a ghostwriter for several members of Congress, including Representative Larry McDonald (D-GA).

96 Jane Daugherty, "Stage Set for Action on Eve of Women's Conference," *American-Statesman*, November 18, 1977, folder "November 1977—Houston II," carton 220, NOW Records, SL.

97 Jacquelyn Ronan to Liz Carpenter, November 23, 1977, folder "General Correspondence #2," ERAmerica Records, Library of Congress.

98 Jimmy Carter, *White House Diary* (New York: Farrar, Straus and Giroux, 2010), 138–141. Carter's diary on November 18–21 contained nothing about the Houston conference despite his wife's participation. He notes that on Sunday, November 20, they moved up a special prayer service for Middle East peace to 8:15 a.m. so that he could "come home and watch the speeches by Sadat and Begin."

99 "What Next for U.S. Women."

100 Ibid.

101 Megan Rosenfeld, "Multitude of Voices on Women's Issues," *Washington Post*, November 20, 1977.

102 Melich, *Republican War Against Women*, 94.

CHAPTER 11: LAUNCHING THE PRO-FAMILY MOVEMENT

1 Rosemary Thomson, "Dear Citizens' Review Coordinator," September 26, 1977, box 3, Kathryn Fink Dunaway Papers, Manuscripts, Archives and Rare Book Library, Emory University, hereafter Dunaway Papers, Emory.

2 Kathryn Dunaway, "Suggestions for Houston Texas" (handwritten notes, Chicago, IL, August 3, 1977). One sentence in the notes reads: "Get 'Secret' information from our I.W.Y. National member—such as what new rules have been set up for observers," box 2, Dunaway Papers, Emory University Library.

3 Dunaway, "Suggestions for Houston Texas."

4 Ibid.

5 William Martin, *With God on Our Side: The Rise of the Religious Right in America* (New York: Broadway Books, 1996), 165; Ruth Murray Brown, *For a "Christian America": A History of the Religious Right* (Amherst, NY: Prometheus, 2002), 111.

6 Phyllis Schlafly, "Pro-Family Rally Attracts 20,000," *Phyllis Schlafly Report* 11, no. 5, section 2 (December 1977); Rosemary Thomson, *The Price of LIBerty* (Carol Stream, IL: Creation House, 1978), 138–39.

7 Ibid., 138; Martin, *With God on Our Side*, 165.

8 Schlafly, "Pro-Family Rally Attracts 20,000."

9 Brown, *For a Christian America*, 111–12, 117; Thomson, *Price of LIBerty*, 139.

10 Nellie Gray, "Action Memo No. 77-7 to ProLife, Profamily, StopERA, and Allied Participants at State IWY Meetings" (Washington, D.C., August 10, 1977), folder "International Women's Year 1977," L. Marion Gressette Papers, South Carolina Political Collections, University of South Carolina Library.

11 Thomson, *Price of LIBerty*, 139.

12 "Predict 'Counter Convention' to Outpull IWY in Houston," *National Right to Life News*, December 1977, hereafter *NRL News*.

13 Thomson, *Price of LIBerty*, 139.

14 Ibid., 139–41.

15 Pat Reed, "Pro-Family Groups Ink Proposals," *Daily Breakthrough*, November 20, 1977.

16   Ibid.; "IWY Folds Tent—300,000 Protest Signatures Flown to White House," *NRL News*, January 1978.

17   Thomson, "Dear Citizens' Review Coordinator."

18   Ibid.

19   Kathryn Dunaway, "Dear Pastor" (letter, Atlanta, GA, November 11, 1977), box 3, Dunaway Papers, Emory.

20   Ibid.

21   Ibid.

22   Thomson, *Price of LIBerty*, 139.

23   Phyllis Schlafly, "What Really Happened in Houston," *Phyllis Schlafly Report* 11, No. 5, section 2 (December 1977).

24   Thomson, *Price of LIBerty*, 141–42; Brown, *For a "Christian America,"* 111.

25   "Donna Carlson to Kathryn Dunaway," September 20, 1977, Dunaway Papers, Emory.

26   "Rally Protests 'Lib,'" *Times-Record*, November 18, 1977, folder "November 1977—Houston II," carton 220, National Organization for Women (NOW) Records (MC 496), Schlesinger Library, Radcliffe Institute, Harvard University, Cambridge, MA, hereafter NOW Records, SL; Thomson, *Price of LIBerty*, 142–43.

27   Ibid., 141–43; Martin, *With God on Our Side*, 165; Schlafly, "Pro-Family Rally Attracts 20,000."

28   Rosemary Thomson, "To CRC Chairmen and Eagle Forum Chapter Presidents," July 5, 1977, box 1, Dunaway Papers, Emory; Nancy Weaver, "Delegates Brace for IWY Storm: State Again Fuels U.S. Controversy. Delegates-Elect: 20 Whites, 6 Men, All Conservative," *Clarion-Ledger*, November 17, 1977.

29   Clipping from *Democrat*, n.d., folder "Clippings, Sept.–Nov 1977, Houston Conference," carton 120, NOW Records, SL; Phyllis Schlafly, "Houston Proves Radicals and Lesbians Run IWY," *Phyllis Schlafly Report* (December 1977).

30   Clipping from *Democrat*; Schlafly, "Houston Proves Radicals and Lesbians Run IWY"; Gay Gellhorn Sa'adah, "The National Women's Conference," Columbia, SC, *Black News*, December 17, 1977, South Carolina Women's Rights Collection, South Carolina Political Collections, University of South Carolina.

31   Schlafly, "What Really Happened in Houston"; Gubbins quoted, "Woman's Place Is in Houston," *Daily News*, November 18, 1977, folder "November 1977—Houston II," Carton 220, NOW Records, SL.

32   Linda Williams, "Feminists, Antifeminists See IWY Meeting as Grassroots Test," *South Mississippi Sun*, November 15, 1977, vertical file, "National Women's Conference," Mississippi State Archives, Jackson, MS; Nancy Weaver, "Klansman's Wife Equates Women's Rights with Communism," *Clarion-Ledger*, November 17, 1977.

33   Bob Schwartzman, "Klan Cardholder Wanted to Help," *Today*, July 18, 1977; Betty J. Blair, "Klan's Spies' Plan to Disrupt Feminist Party," *Detroit News*, September 1, 1977; Nancy Weaver, "Klan 'Security' Group Keeps Eye on Feminists," *Clarion-Ledger*, 1977.

34   Bella Abzug, "International Women's Year Observation," *Congressional Record* 123, part 24 (September 22, 1977): 30449–51.

35   Thomson, *Price of LIBerty*, 29.

36   Ibid.

37   "Group Plans Rally for IWY Delegation," Salt Lake City, *Deseret News*, Nov. 7, 1977, folder "1977—HOUSTON CONFERENCE," carton 220, NOW Records, SL.

38   Joe Ward, clipping, *Courier-Journal*, November 17, 1977, folder "November 1977—Houston II," Carton 220, NOW Records, SL.

39   Sa'adah, "The National Women's Conference."

40 Phyllis Schlafly, "ERAers and IWYers Get Desperate," *Eagle Forum Newsletter*, September 1977.

41 Candace Lee, "2 Groups to Attend IWY Confab," *Daily News*, November 15, 1977, vertical file, "National Women's Conference," Mississippi State Archives, Jackson, MS.

42 Weaver, "Klansman's Wife."

43 "State Women's Year Group Not Going 'Liberal,'" *Clarion-Ledger*, September 28, 1977; AP, "IWY 'Alerted' About Voting," *Daily News*, September 28, 1977, vertical file, "National Women's Conference," Mississippi State Archives, Jackson, MS; Weaver, "Delegates Brace for IWY Storm"; Williams, "Feminists, Antifeminists."

44 CRC press materials in Elaine Chenevert Donnelly Papers, Bentley Historical Library, University of Michigan, Ann Arbor; CRC press materials in folder "International Women's Year 1977," box 3, Gressette Papers, SCPC.

45 "Why Women's Lib Is in Trouble," *U.S. News & World Report*, November 28, 1977.

46 Thomson, *Price of LIBerty*, 142; Judy Klemesrud, "Equal Rights Plan and Abortion Are Opposed by 15,000 at Rally: Like a Black Baptist Church," *New York Times*, November 20, 1977; June Kronholz, "Women Take Over Houston for 3 Lively Days," *Wall Street Journal*, November 24, 1977; Phyllis Schlafly, "Eagle Media Coverage," *Phyllis Schlafly Report* (December 1977).

47 David Behrens, clipping, *Newsday*, November 18, 1977; Hamilton, "A Hard Look."

48 Thomson, *Price of LIBerty*, 143, 144.

49 Ibid.

50 Sherry Woods, *Miami News* TV/Radio Editor. "2 Local Stations to Relay Reports on Women's Conference in Houston," folder "November 1977—Houston II," box 220, NOW Records, SL.

51 Phyllis Schlafly, "IWY Citizens Review," *Phyllis Schlafly Report* 11, no. 5, section 2 (December 1977).

52 Thomson, *Price of LIBerty*, 144.

53 NCOIWY, *The Spirit of Houston: The First National Women's Conference: An Official Report to the President, the Congress and the People of the United States* (Washington, D.C.: U.S. Government Printing Office, 1978), 143.

54 Ibid., 144.

55 Ibid., 145.

56 Ibid., 146.

57 Ibid., 146–47.

58 Ibid., 154.

59 Ibid., 148–49, 152.

60 Mildred Andrews Interview with Susan Roylance, May 3, 2007 Washington Women's History Consortium Oral History Project, http://www.washingtonhistory.org/research/whc/oralhistory/IWYOralHistory/; "What Next for U.S. Women: Houston Produces New Alliances and a Drive for Grass-Roots Power," *Time*, December 5, 1977.

61 Bill Curry and Megan Rosenfeld, "Crucial Test for Women's Conference," *Washington Post*, November 18, 1977.

62 "Ann O'Donnell's Statement Opposing Abortion Plank," *NRL News*, January 1978.

63 Quotations, "What Next for U.S. Women"; "Opposing Voices Heard at Women's Conference," *NBC Today Show* (New York: NBC, November 21, 1977), NBC Learn https://archives.nbclearn.com/portal/site/k-12/flatview–cuecard=5835 (accessed September 5, 2012).

64 Thomson, *Price of LIBerty*, 11; "Opposing Voices Heard at Women's Conference."

65　Judy Klemesrud, "Men at the Women's Conference: Few in Number, but Hard to Miss," *New York Times*, November 22, 1977; Sheryl Hansen (Smith) Interview with Dr. Curtis Caine and Lynne Caine, February 28, 1993, Mississippi Oral History Program, vol. 438, McCain Library, University of Southern Mississippi; "John Birch Leader from Miss. to Speak," *Times-Picayune*, April 21, 1988; NCOIWY, *Spirit of Houston*, 145, 166.

66　Flyer Issued by the Mississippi Delegation to the National Women's Conference, Houston, Texas, given by Mississippi delegate Curtis Caine to Interviewer Sheryl Hansen (Smith), November 1977, flyer in possession of the author; Klemesrud, "Men at the Women's Conference."

67　NCOIWY, *Spirit of Houston*. For full text of the report, see 265–72. It was signed by State Senator Joan Gubbins, Indiana; Ann Patterson, Oklahoma; Frances Weidman, Alabama; State Senator Georgia Peterson, Utah; Carmie Richeson, Hawaii; Ruth Waite, Florida; Laurentia Allen, Massachusetts; Kay Regan, Washington; Betty Hanicke, Kansas; Vivian Adams, Illinois; State Representative Norma Russell, South Carolina; Eddie Myrtle Moore, Mississippi; Betty Babcock, Montana; and Beverly Adams, Georgia. All were elected delegates.

68　Ibid., 265–72.

69　Ibid.

70　Ibid.; Angelyn Nelson, "Utah IWY Unit Will Object To First Lady," *Salt Lake City Tribune*, November 22, 1977, Jo Freeman Papers.

71　Susan Witt, "Battle Lines Drawn for Women's Meeting," *Tribune*, clipping, n.d., folder "November 1977—Houston Conf. III," box 220, NOW Records, SL.

72　Thomson, *Price of LIBerty*, 148.

73　Carole Ashkinaze, "Women's Meeting Ends in Wrangling," *Atlanta Constitution*, November 22, 1977; NCOIWY, *Spirit of Houston*, 265; Thomson, *Price of LIBerty*, 148–50.

74　Ibid.

75　NCOIWY, *Spirit of Houston*, 136–37, 166; "What Next for U.S. Women."

76　Weaver, "Klansman's Wife," emphasis mine.

77　"Meet the Delegates: Mississippi Style," *Daily Breakthrough*, November 19, 1977.

78　Andrea Dworkin, *Right-wing Women* (New York: Perigee, 1983), 114–15.

79　Ibid., 33, 111.

80　UPI, "Men Punch Women Leaving Rally," *Atlanta Journal-Constitution*, November 20, 1977; Carol Bartholdi and Marilyn Mock, "Right Wing Extremists in Houston Cause Havoc: Far Right Street Fight," *Daily Breakthrough*, November 20, 1977; NCOIWY, *Spirit of Houston*, 166.

81　Dworkin, *Right-wing Women*, 112.

82　"Utah IWY Delegate Plans Minorities Organization," *Salt Lake City Tribune*, November 22, 1977, section A; NCOIWY, *Spirit of Houston*, 157.

83　Alice S. Rossi, *Feminists in Politics: A Panel Analysis of the First National Women's Conference* (New York: Academic Press, 1982), 102, 232.

84　Schlafly, "Houston Proves Radicals and Lesbians Run IWY."

85　Schlafly, "What Really Happened in Houston"; Thomson, *Price of LIBerty*, 144.

86　Thomson, *Price of LIBerty*, 145.

87　Ibid., 146.

88　Schlafly, "What Really Happened in Houston."

89　Angelyn Nelson, "150 Utahns Join Protest to IWY Meeting," *Salt Lake City Tribune*, November 20, 1977, section A.

90 Klemesrud, "Equal Rights Plan"; Carole Ashkinaze, "God Stronger Than Carter, Stop-ERA Leader Declares," *Atlanta Journal-Constitution*, November 20, 1977.

91 Schlafly, "What Really Happened in Houston"; Nelson, "150 Utahns Join Protest to IWY Meeting."

92 Ibid.; Schlafly, "What Really Happened in Houston."

93 Judy Klemesrud, "10,000 Foes of Equal Rights Plan in 'Pro-Family Rally' in Houston," *New York Times*, November 20, 1977; Brown, *For a "Christian America,"* 112–13.

94 Bartholdi and Mock, "Right Wing Extremists in Houston Cause Havoc."

95 Klemesrud, "10,000 Foes"; Judy Klemesrud, "Houston Hosts, If Not Toasts, Feminists," *New York Times*, November 18, 1977; "Remembering LGBT History: 'Shoot the Queers': Houston's 1985 Anti-Gay Referendum and Backlash," *Daily Kos*, May 20, 2012.

96 Klemesrud, "10,000 Foes."

97 Schlafly, "Pro-Family Rally Attracts 20,000"; Laura Joy Foxworth, "The Spiritual Is Political: The Modern Women's Movement and the Transformation of the Southern Baptist Convention" (Ph.D. diss., University of South Carolina, 2014).

98 Rita Burke, "International Women's Year Conference as Observed by Two South Shore Residents: a Virtuous Woman Is Worth More Than Rubies," (clipping from *NRL News*, n.d.), Massachusetts Report, NCOIWY Records box TW07564, SL.

99 Schlafly, "What Really Happened in Houston."

100 Reed, "Pro-Family Groups Ink Proposals."

101 Klemesrud, "Equal Rights Plan."

102 Burke, "International Women's Year Conference as Observed by Two South Shore Residents."

103 Ibid.

104 Ashkinaze, "God Stronger Than Carter."

105 Ibid.; Thomson, *Price of LIBerty*, 146.

106 Jonathan Levin, "42 Delegations Assist Frances in Balloting for V.P. Choice," *Globe-Times*, July 14, 1972; Hunter S. Thompson, *Fear and Loathing at Rolling Stone: The Essential Writing of Hunter S. Thompson*, Jann Wenner, ed. (New York: Simon & Schuster, 2012), 232.

107 Thomson, *Price of LIBerty*, 146; "IWY Folds Tent"; Klemesrud, "10,000 Foes."

108 Burke, "International Women's Year Conference as Observed by Two South Shore Residents."

109 Klemesrud, "10,000 Foes"; Brown, *For a "Christian America,"* 113.

110 Schlafly, "Pro-Family Rally Attracts 20,000."

111 Thomson, *Price of LIBerty*, 146.

112 Ibid., 147.

113 "IWY Folds Tent"; Senator Jesse Helms did not attend but was represented by his legislative assistant, Carl Anderson.

114 Ibid.; Ashkinaze, "God Stronger Than Carter."

115 "Rep. Dornan Blasts 'First Ladies' at IWY," *NRL News*, January 1978.

116 Thomson, *Price of LIBerty*, 144–45.

117 "IWY Folds Tent."

118 "What Next for U.S. Women," 22.

119 "IWY Folds Tent."

120 Elaine Donnelly, "What Women Wanted—Reagan Appealed to and Developed a Generation of Female Conservatives," *National Review Online*, June 7, 2004.

121 "IWY Folds Tent."

122　Mrs. Paul Hogue and Mrs. Houston Howie to Dear Friend (Jackson, MS, November 23, 1977), folder "International Women's Year 1977," box 3, Gressette Papers, SCPC.

CHAPTER 12: WE SHALL GO FORTH

1　NCOIWY, *Update 9: After Houston* (U.S. Dept. of State, February 1978).

2　Ibid.

3　Alice S. Rossi, *Feminists in Politics: A Panel Analysis of the First National Women's Conference* (New York: Academic Press, 1982), 105.

4　*Update 9*; On follow-up activities involving Abzug, the IWY Commission, and officials within the Carter administration in response to the IWY conference, see folder "International Women's Year, 3/77–3/78," box 132, Margaret McKenna Files, Jimmy Carter Presidential Library, Atlanta, GA, hereafter McKenna Files, Carter Library. Among them is a memo from Barbara Blum, deputy administrator to McKenna who was associate counsel to the president, "Subject: Follow-up to the IWY and Meeting with the President," December 14, 1977. cc to Midge Costanza, Jane Frank, Esther Peterson. Suggests "it could be practically and politically productive for the President to request an analysis of each IWY resolution by the appropriate Federal agencies." Such an analysis could give the President an opportunity to take a positive follow-up action which will be well received by both IWY supporters and IWY antagonists (for their different reasons). A letter from Bella Abzug to McKenna and other IWY supporters within the administration dated February 13, 1978, invited the recipients to a "briefing meeting" on February 27, 1978, enclosed the National Plan of Action, and stated: "Our most imp task—now that we have this document—is to ensure that there is a serious response from the President with clear directives to his Administration and the Congress that require prompt action on the proposals. We know that you share our commitment to implementing the NPA, and many of you have already taken the initiative through your own offices to follow through on the Houston recommendations"; NCOIWY, *The Spirit of Houston: The First National Women's Conference: An Official Report to the President, the Congress, and the People of the United States* (Washington, D.C.: GPO, 1978). Mim Kelber, Bella Abzug's aide and speechwriter, was Chief Editor/Writer. Caroline Bird, a consultant to the IWY National Commission, was the Chief Writer of the report. She later produced an abridged version of it for the public, published in 1979 by Simon and Schuster under the title *What Women Want*.

5　*Update 9*; NCOIWY, *Spirit of Houston*, 170, music and lyrics, 171.

6　Jimmy Carter, "The White House Remarks of the President at a Reception for International Women's Year, The East Room" (press release, March 22, 1978), folder "International Women's Year, 3/77–3/78," box 132, McKenna Files, Carter Library.

7　Section 7, P.L. 94–167. "An Act to Direct the National Commission on the Observance of International Women's Year 1975, to Organize and Convene a National Women's Conference and for Other Purposes," legislink.org/us/p1-94-167; Elizabeth A. Abramovitz, Assistant Director for Education and Women's Issues, Domestic Policy Staff to Margaret A. McKenna, Deputy Counsel, March 14, 1978, folder "International Women's Year, 3/77–3/78," box 132, McKenna Files, Carter Library.

8　Bill Moloney, "Breakfast with Bella," *NRL News*, December 1977, 6.

9　Memorandum for: The President, From Margaret Costanza, Subject: Establishing a National Commission for Women and an Interdepartmental Task Force by Executive Order, folder "International Women's Year, 3/77–3/78, box 132, McKenna Files, Carter Library.

10   Suzanne Braun Levine and Mary Thom, *Bella Abzug: How One Tough Broad from the Bronx Fought Jim Crow and Joe McCarthy, Pissed Off Jimmy Carter, Battled for the Rights of Women and Workers, Rallied Against War and for the Planet, and Shook up Politics Along the Way; An Oral History* (New York: Farrar, Straus and Giroux, 2007), 214–15.

11   Martin Schram, "The Story Behind Bella's Departure: It Was a Matter of Minutes To Decide Bella Had to Go," *Washington Post*, January 17, 1979.

12   Vivian Vahlbert, "Thanks, but No Thanks, Cleta Tells White House," *Daily Oklahoman*, May 19, 1978; Jana S. Vogt, "Oklahoma and the ERA: Rousing a Red State, 1972–1982" (Ph.D. diss., University of Oklahoma, 2010), 108.

13   Judy Klemesrud, "Judy Carter: Trouble-Shooter for the Equal Rights Amendment," *New York Times*, November 8, 1977; Jimmy Carter, "National Advisory Committee for Women Appointment of 40 Members," Online by Gerhard Peters and John T. Woolley, The American Presidency Project, June 20, 1978, http://www.presidency.ucsb.edu/ws/?pid=30974.

14   Marjorie J. Spruill, "The Mississippi 'Takeover': Feminists, Antifeminists, and the International Women's Year Conference of 1977," in *Mississippi Women: Their Histories, Their Lives*, vol. 2, Martha H. Swain, Elizabeth Anne Payne, and Marjorie Julian Spruill, eds. (Athens: University of Georgia Press, 2010), 287–313, 300; Nancy Weaver, "Nine at-Large Members Must Carry Rights Banner," *Clarion-Ledger*, November 17, 1977; Unita Blackwell and JoAnne Prichard Morris, *Barefootin': Life Lessons from the Road to Freedom* (New York: Crown, 2006).

15   Bella S. Abzug, *Gender Gap: Bella Abzug's Guide to Political Power for American Women* (Boston: Houghton Mifflin, 1984), 65, 66.

16   Tom Mathews with Eleanor Clift and Thomas M. De Frank, "The Trouble with Midge," *Newsweek*, November 7, 1977, 9.

17   "Anne Wexler, 79; Power Broker Founded 1st Big D.C. Lobbying Firm Led by a Woman," *Washington Post*, August 9, 2009; Martin Weil, "Anne Wexler, Political Adviser and Lobbyist, Dies at 79," *Washington Post*, August 8, 2009; Richard Moe and Michael Berman, Carter Presidency Project Interview, Miller Center, University of Virginia, Charlottesville, January 15, 1982, http://web1.millercenter.org/poh/transcripts/ohp_1982_0115_moe.pdf.

18   "The Trouble With Midge"; Jimmy Carter, *White House Diary* (New York: Farrar, Straus and Giroux, 2010), 127.

19   Abzug, *Gender Gap*, 64–65; "Skids Being Greased for Midge Costanza?," *NRL News*, January 1978.

20   Midge Costanza to James Fallows, Subject State of the Union Address (memo, December 6, 1977); Jane Wales to Margaret Costanza, Subject Meeting with NOW Representatives (memo, White House, January 31, 1978); Jane Wales/Shelly Weinstein to Margaret Costanza (memo, White House, February 11, 1978); Jane Wales to Margaret Costanza, Subject ERA Planning Meeting—February 13, 1978 (memo, White House, February 13, 1978), Archives Project, Midge Costanza Institute, http://www.midgecostanzainstitute.com/#.

21   Joseph Dalton, "Winding Down a Day for the ERA," *Washington Post*, July 10, 1978; James Lardner and Neil Henry, "Over 40,000 ERA Backers March on Hill," *Washington Post*, July 10, 1978; "Demonstrators Vow to Besiege Offices on Hill," *Washington Post*, July 10, 1978; Judy Luce Mann, "1919 Suffragettes Join in ERA March," *Washington Post*, July 10, 1978; Archives Project, Midge Costanza Institute. http://www.midgecostanzainstitute.com/#.

22 Lardner and Henry, "Over 40,000 ERA Backers March"; David M. Dismore, "July 9, 1978: Feminists Make History with Biggest-Ever March for the Equal Rights Amendment | Feminist Majority Foundation Blog," *Feminist Majority Foundation*, July 9, 2014, https://feminist.org/blog/index.php/2014/07/09/july-9-1978-feminists-make-history-with-biggest-ever-march-for-the-equal-rights-amendment/.

23 "Demonstrators Vow to Beseige Offices on Hill"; Lardner and Henry, "Over 40,000 ERA Backers March."

24 "Demonstrators Vow to Besiege Offices on Hill."

25 "Clipping, After ERA March, Sober Spirits," n.d., Archives Project, Midge Costanza Institute.

26 Lardner and Henry, "Over 40,000 ERA Backers March"; Costanza urged Rosalynn Carter to attend the rally and make brief remarks. Memorandum for the First Lady from Margaret (Midge) Costanza, July 5, 1978; Statement by the President of the United States to be Delivered by Margaret "Midge" Costanza, Assistant to the President, ERA March and Rally, July 9, 1978. Archives Project, Midge Costanza Institute.

27 Abzug, *Gender Gap*, 65; Karen De Witt, "Miss Costanza Resigns as Assistant to Carter, Citing Problems of Style," *New York Times*, August 2, 1978. In her resignation letter Costanza stated: "In recent months I have had to deal increasingly with the subject of approach rather than that of substance, spending valuable time and energy on discussions of whether I have spoken out too much, what my relations are to your other senior staff, or where my office is located"; "Costanza Treated 'Miserably,' Say Feminist Leaders," clipping n.d., folder 43, box 27, Catherine East Papers, Schlesinger Library, Radcliffe Institute, Harvard University, hereafter East Papers, SL.

28 Doreen J. Mattingly, *A Feminist in the White House: Midge Costanza, the Carter Years and America's Culture Wars* (New York: Oxford University Press, 2016). They parted ways in 1980 but remained close friends and political allies.

29 "The Weddington Way: Can a Soft-Spoken, Tough-Minded Southern Lawyer Prevail on Women's Issues in the White House Where Midge Costanza and Bella Abzug Struck Out?," *Washington Post*, February 11, 1979; Doreen Mattingly, "The (Limited) Power of Female Appointments: Abortion and Domestic Violence Policy in the Carter Administration," *Feminist Studies*, n.d., 41, no. 3. (2015): 538–65; Schram, "The Story Behind Bella's Departure: It Was a Matter of Minutes to Decide Bella Had to Go," *Washington Post*, January 17, 1979.

30 Abzug, *Gender Gap*, 67.

31 Ibid.

32 Levine and Thom, *Bella Abzug*, 217; According to Abzug, they became even angrier later when they learned "that the President was taking the time to fly to Utah the following week to receive an award from the Mormon Church." Abzug, *Gender Gap*, 68.

33 Levine and Thom, *Bella Abzug*, quotations 215–18; Abzug, *Gender Gap*, 67–69.

34 Ibid.

35 Ibid.

36 Myra MacPherson, "Bella's Battle Lost: After the Ax, The Bravado Remains," *Washington Post*, January 16, 1979; Abzug, *Gender Gap*, 69; Bella S. Abzug and Carmen Delgado Votaw, Co-Chairs, National Advisory Committee for Women, Statement to President Carter, January 12, 1979, box 14, Sarah Weddington Files, Jimmy Carter Presidential Library, Atlanta, GA, hereafter Weddington Files, Carter Library.

37 Ibid., 69; Marjorie J. Spruill Interview with Carmen Delgado Votaw at Veteran Feminists of America Conference, Harvard University, March 24, 2007.

38 Levine and Thom, *Bella Abzug*, 218–21; Spruill Interview with Votaw.

39 Abzug, *Gender Gap*, 70–72.

40 Ibid., 66, 72.

41 Levine and Thom, *Bella Abzug*, 218–19.

42 Ibid., 219.

43 Ibid., 220.

44 Ibid.; Abzug, *Gender Gap*, 72.

45 MacPherson, "Bella's Battle Lost"; Abzug, *Gender Gap*, 72–73; Hamilton Jordan, Assistant to the President, to Bella Abzug, Co-Chairperson, National Advisory Committee for Women, January 12, 1979, folder "Abzug, Bella (1/79–6/80)," Name Files, Jimmy Carter Presidential Library, Atlanta, GA, hereafter Name Files, Carter Library.

46 Abzug, *Gender Gap*, 73.

47 Ibid.

48 Levine and Thom, *Bella Abzug*, 220–21.

49 Terence Smith, "Carter, in Angry Exchange, Ousts Bella Abzug from Women's Unit," *New York Times*, January 13, 1979, 1, 7.

50 Ibid.

51 MacPherson, "Bella's Battle Lost"; Levine and Thom, *Bella Abzug*, 221; Steinem is probably referring to developments the previous summer. A memo in Jordan's files labeled "personal and confidential" contains documents related to an "informal group of advisers" Carter selected to advise him frankly and bluntly and in strictest confidence about how the administration could be more successful: Clark Clifford, Sol Linowitz, Lloyd Hackler, and Irving Shapiro. "Memo, Hamilton Jordan to Jimmy Carter, June 28, 1978. Labeled Personal and Confidential; Memo to Hamilton Jordan from Lloyd Hackler, July 7, 1978, folder "Informal Advisors' Group," box 47, Chief of Staff Hamilton Jordan Files, Carter Presidential Library; Hackler's memo to Jordan dated July 7, 1978 (after the meeting), gave his blunt critical advice as follow-up, urging that Carter "MUST be perceived as more in charge and not allowing [sic] people who are appointed . . . to continue to act disloyally and urging that to demonstrate this new firmness and lack of vacillation, that Carter fire some high level people, clearly indicating he won't put up with that."

52 Levine and Thom, *Bella Abzug*, 219–26.

53 Gloria Steinem, *Moving Beyond Words: Age, Rage, Sex, Power, Money, Muscles: Breaking Boundaries of Gender* (New York: Simon and Schuster, 1994), 203.

54 Abzug, *Gender Gap*, 75; Flora Davis, *Moving the Mountain: The Women's Movement in America Since 1960* (Champaign: University of Illinois Press, 1999), 196–97; Letters from the Public Regarding the Firing of Bella Abzug, n.d.; folder "Bella Abzug, (1/79–6/80)," Name Files, Carter Library. Joan Gubbins and Donna Carlson were among those congratulating Carter on Abzug's firing. Sarah Weddington to Senator Joan Gubbins, March 13, 1979, folder "Joan Gubbins," Name Files, Jimmy Carter Library.

55 Steinem, *Moving Beyond Words*, 203; Abzug, *Gender Gap*, 75; Betty Friedan, *The Second Stage*, 2nd ed. (Cambridge: Harvard University Press, 1998), 203; Percy, trying to placate the conservatives, wrote Carter recommending that he appoint Rosemary Thomson to the NACW. He enclosed an article on the reaction to the Houston conference, and identified six leaders in the battle, including Thomson. Senator Charles H. Percy to the President, January 4, 1979, folder "Rosemary Thomson," Name Files, Carter Library.

56 Steinem, *Moving Beyond Words*, 203; "Abzug Colleagues Resign to Protest Ouster by Carter," *Washington Post*, January 14, 1979.

57 Blackwell and Morris, *Barefootin'*, 214–15, 259.

58   Steinem, *Moving Beyond Words*, 203; Levine and Thom, *Bella Abzug*, 223.

59   Georgia Dullea, "White House Fails to Mend Fences with Key Women's Groups," *New York Times*, January 20, 1979.

60   "Headliners: A President's Choice," *New York Times*, January 21, 1979, section E; Sarah Weddington to Hon. Gretchen Kafoury, congresswoman from Oregon, March 14, 1979, "Abzug, Bella (1/79–6/80)," Name Files, Carter Library.

61   Karen De Witt, "New Head of Carter's Advisory Panel on Women," *New York Times*, May 10, 1979.

62   Catherine East to Rosalynn Carter, January 29, 1979, box 13, Weddington Files, Carter Library; *A Feminist in the White House*; AP, "Women's Panel Pick Said to Be Mrs. Robb: White House Aide Reports Choice for Post Mrs. Abzug Had Held," *New York Times*, May 9, 1979, section A; "The Weddington Way."

63   Abzug, *Gender Gap*, 74. The Continuing Committee changed its name to "The National Women's Conference Committee" in 1981. In 1986 the NWCC released an update on implementation of the National Plan of Action. Susanna Downie and National Women's Conference Committee, "Part I: How the National Plan of Action for Women Came into Being," in *Decade of Achievement: 1977–1987: A Report on a Survey Based on the National Plan of Action for Women* (Washington, D.C.: National Women's Conference Committee, 1988), 5–7.

64   Historian Susan Hartmann praised the numbers and the talents of the feminists Carter empowered during his presidency, concluding "Carter's appointments may well have constituted his greatest contribution to the considerable range of feminist policy that ensued during his administration." Hartmann, "Feminism, Public Policy, and the Carter Administration," in *The Carter Presidency: Policy Choices in the Post-New Deal Era*, Gary M. Fink and Hugh Davis Graham, eds., (Lawrence: University Press of Kansas, 1998): 224–43.

65   Marjorie J. Spruill Interview with President Jimmy Carter and First Lady Rosalynn Carter, Atlanta, GA, May 14, 2009, in the possession of the author; Klemesrud, "Judy Carter"; Dumbrell praises Carter's efforts to advance women and women's rights, especially his and Rosalynn's and Judy's work for the ERA. He states that Carter's "record in this area runs counter to any view of the Carter Presidency as standing aloof from legislative arm-twisting and as innocent of the ways of Washington. For example, Carter engaged in such arm-twisting and bargaining to gain votes for ERA extension, and North Carolina Congressman Lamar Gudger's switch was followed by the release of $1.6 million in federal funds for Asheville Airport." John Dumbrell, *The Carter Presidency: A Re-Evaluation* (Manchester: Manchester University Press, 1995), 75.

66   Mattingly, "The (Limited) Power of Female Appointments."

67   Spruill Interview with the President Carter and First Lady Rosalynn Carter.

68   Ibid.

69   Meeting with his cabinet, Carter discussed Abzug's dismissal and assured them (quoting the minutes) that "his decision was in no way related to a change in Administration policy or in his personal view regarding the vital importance of women's issues to the country. The president asked for the continuing active support of the Cabinet in pursuing such goals as the passage of the Equal Rights Amendment and increased employment opportunities for women." Confidential Memorandum for the Vice President and Members of the Cabinet, from Jack Watson, Subject Cabinet Minutes for Last Meeting (January 15th, 1979), January 17, 1979, folder "Staff Offices, Office of Staff Secretary, Handwriting File 1/12/79–1/18/79," box 115, Carter

Presidential Library. Letters in Falwell's file mention that Carter had a breakfast meeting on January 22, 1980, with Falwell, Dr. Oral Roberts, Reverend Jim Bakker, and eleven other evangelical leaders, folder "Dr. Jerry Falwell," Name Files, Jimmy Carter Presidential Library, Atlanta, GA.

70 Marjorie J. Spruill, "Victoria Eslinger, Keller Bumgardner Barron, Mary Heriot, Tootsie Holland, and Pat Callair: Champions of Women's Rights in South Carolina," in *South Carolina Women: Their Lives and Times*, vol. 3, Marjorie Julian Spruill, Joan Marie Johnson, and Valinda W. Littlefield, eds. (Athens: University of Georgia Press, 2012): 373–408, 394.

71 Sara Fitzgerald, *Elly Peterson: "Mother" of the Moderates* (Ann Arbor: University of Michigan Press, 2014), 234–35.

72 Reva B. Siegel, "Constitutional Culture, Social Movement Conflict and Constitutional Change: The Case of the De Facto ERA," 2005–06 Brennan Center Symposium Lecture, *California Law Review* 94, no. 5 (2006): 1323–1486.

73 Deborah Churchman, "NOW Recruits Volunteers to Work for ERA Passage," *Christian Science Monitor*, December 24, 1981; Phyllis Schlafly, "Eyewitness: Beating the Bra Burners," *George* magazine, June 1997; Donald G. Mathews and Jane Sherron De Hart, *Sex, Gender, and the Politics of ERA: A State and the Nation* (New York: Oxford University Press, 1990), 107–23.

74 Eunice ("Tootsie") Holland visit to history professor Marjorie Spruill's senior seminar, March 26, 2008, South Carolina Women's Rights Collection (SCWRC), South Carolina Political Collection, University of South Carolina. The collection contains material on the women's movement in the state collected by the students in this and similar classes. These include transcripts of talks by visitors to the class.

75 Liz Carpenter, *Getting Better All the Time* (New York: Simon & Schuster, 1987), 141–42.

76 Fitzgerald, *Elly Peterson*, 236. On Schlafly, 243.

77 Ibid., 236–40.

78 Elly M. Peterson to Senator Orrin G. Hatch, March 27, 1977, folder "General Correspondence #2," container 1, ERAmerica Records, Library of Congress.

79 Fitzgerald, *Elly Peterson*, 236–40.

80 Levine and Thom, *Bella Abzug*, 227.

81 Ibid., 225–26.

82 Jo Freeman, "Feminist Coalition Faces Down Carter Campaign," *In These Times* 4, no. 33 (August 27, 1980), 2; Mattingly, *A Feminist in the White House*.

83 Karlyn Barker and Bill Peterson, "The Democrats in New York: The Women Delegates: Some Victories But a Sense of Frustration, Division," *Washington Post*, August 13, 1980, section A; Levine and Thom, *Bella Abzug*, 227.

84 Barker and Peterson, "The Democrats in New York."

85 Ibid.

86 Ibid.

87 Tanya Melich, *The Republican War Against Women: An Insider's Report from Behind the Lines* (New York: Bantam Books, 1998), 113, 115.

88 Ibid., 106.

89 Jon Meacham, *Destiny and Power: The American Odyssey of George Herbert Walker Bush* (Random House, 2015), 209–56; Melich, *Republican War Against Women*.

90 Quotation from Bush is from Thomson, *The Price of LIBerty* (Carol Stream, IL: Creation Horse, 1978), 126. She gave the source as *U.S. News & World Report*, May 7, 1976: 46–49; Melich, *Republican War Against Women*, 119.

91 Ibid., 119–21.

92   Meacham, *Destiny and Power*, 253, 255; Ellen Chesler, "The Long History of the War on Contraception," *Ms.* blog, February 12, 2012, http://msmagazine.com/blog/2012/02/14/conservative-war-on-contraception-is-nothing-new/.

93   Meacham, *Destiny and Power*, 245; Sara Diamond, *Roads to Dominion: Right-Wing Political Movements and Political Power in the United States* (New York: Guilford Press, 1995), 208–9; Paul Weyrich, "George Bush Choice Raises Troublesome Questions," *Conservative Digest*, August 1980; "Bush Meets with Right-to-Lifers; Abortion Question Important," *Conservative Digest*, September 1980.

94   Melich, *Republican War Against Women*, 158.

95   Mary Dent Crisp, "My Journey to Feminism," in Nancy M. Neuman, *True to Ourselves: A Celebration of Women Making a Difference* (San Francisco: Jossey-Bass Publishers, 1998); Tanya Melich, "Why the GOP Should Have Listened to Mary Crisp," Women's Media Center, May 7, 2007, http://www.womensmediacenter.com/feature/entry/why-the-gop-should-have-listened-to-mary-crisp; Douglas Martin, "Mary D. Crisp, 83, Feminist G.O.P. Leader, Dies," *New York Times*, April 17, 2007.

96   Fitzgerald, *Elly Peterson*, 239–40; Crisp, "My Journey to Feminism."

97   First Ruckelshaus quotation in "Women of the Year: Great Changes, New Chances, Tough Choices," *Time*, January 5, 1976; Second Ruckelshaus quotation, Melich, *Republican War Against Women*, 157; Fitzgerald, *Elly Peterson*, 240.

98   Melich, *Republican War Against Women*, 158–60. Tanya Melich, "O'Connor's Tenure Began One Hot Summer," We.News, July 18, 2005, http://womensenews.org/story/our-daily-lives/050718/oconnors-tenure-began-one-hot-summer#.VCmSdxbOv7Q.

99   Ibid.; Maureen Reagan described the feminists' getting this promise that day as no less than a "major political coup." Rymph, *Republican Women*, 229.

100 Ibid., Melich, *Republican War Against Women*, 158–60.

101 Melich, *Republican War Against Women*, 167–68.

102 Ibid., 168–69; Mary Dent Crisp, "My Journey to Feminism."

103 Catherine East, "A Vote for Anderson/Lucey Is a Vote for Women's Rights," n.d., folder 64, box 25, East Papers, SL.

104 Crisp, "My Journey to Feminism."

105 Emphasis added. Friedan, *The Second Stage*, 193, 203.

106 Ibid.

107 Hamilton Jordan quotation cited in Hartmann, "Feminism and Public Policy," 240 n.9.

CHAPTER 13: ONWARD CHRISTIAN SOLDIERS

1   Rosemary Thomson, *The Price of LIBerty* (Carol Stream, IL: Creation House, 1978), 7; Rosemary Thomson, *Withstanding Humanism's Challenge for Families: Anatomy of a White House Conference* (Morton, IL: Braun Press, 1981), 146; Alice S. Rossi, *Feminists in Politics: A Panel Analysis of the First National Women's Conference* (New York: Academic Press, 1982), 233. Rossi's study showed that the conservatives left Houston with "not only a keen commitment to future political action but [relative to the feminists] a more unified sense of shared beliefs."

2   Thomson, *Price of LIBerty*, 153–54.

3   "History of Referendum Measures—Elections & Voting—WA Secretary of State," accessed June 23, 2016, https://www.sos.wa.gov/elections/initiatives/statistics_referendummeasures.aspx; Marjorie Spruill, "The Conservative Challenge to Feminist Influence on State Commissions on the Status of Women," *Women and Social*

Movements in the United States: Scholar's Edition, Kathryn Kish Sklar and Thomas Dublin, (Alexandria, VA: Alexander Street Press, 2009) http://womhist.alexander-street.com/scholars/mainscholars.html; Susan M. Hartmann, *From Margin to Mainstream: American Women and Politics Since 1960* (New York: Knopf, 1989), 147.

4   Hartmann, *From Margin to Mainstream*, 147; Anita Miller, "The Uncertain Future of Women's Commissions," *Graduate Woman* 74 (June 1980): 10–15; Janine A. Parry, "'What Women Wanted': Arkansas Women's Commissions and the ERA," *Arkansas Historical Quarterly* 59, no. 3 (2000): 265–98; Janine A. Parry, "Putting Feminism to a Vote: The Washington State Women's Council (1963–1978)," *Pacific Northwest Quarterly* 91, no. 4 (2000): 171–82; for extensive materials on Blair's work with the state commission and national association, see Diane Blair Papers, Special Collections Department, University of Arkansas Library, Fayetteville, AR.

5   Mississippi was a prime example of states where there had been no major public skirmish over ERA—only there it was not because the state ratified right away but because conservatives kept it bottled up in committee and it never reached the floor of the legislature for consideration. Marjorie J. Spruill, "The Mississippi 'Takeover': Feminists, Antifeminists, and the International Women's Year Conference of 1977," in *Mississippi Women: Their Histories, Their Lives*, vol. 2, Martha H. Swain, Elizabeth Anne Payne, and Marjorie Julian Spruill, eds. (Athens: University of Georgia Press, 2010), 287–313; Nancy Elizabeth Baker, "Too Much to Lose, Too Little to Gain: The Role of Rescission Movements in the Equal Rights Amendment Battle, 1972–1982" (Ph.D. diss.: Harvard University, 2003), 15–16.

6   Donald T. Critchlow and Cynthia L. Stachecki, "The Equal Rights Amendment Reconsidered: Politics, Policy, and Social Mobilization in a Democracy, *Journal of Policy History* 20, no. 1, 2008, 163–65.

7   Phyllis Schlafly, "ERA Suffers 1978 Defeats," *Phyllis Schlafly Report* 11, no. 8, section 2 (March 1978).

8   Phyllis Schlafly, "A Short History of E.R.A.," *Phyllis Schlafly Report*, 20, no. 2, section 1 (September 1986); In the midst of the program "ERA Follies," parodies starring Stop-ERA members impersonating Gloria Steinem and Bella Abzug, the ceremony was interrupted when emcee Orrin Hatch announced the room would have to be evacuated immediately. A caller had said two bombs have been placed "under Phyllis's chair." Carol Felsenthal, *The Sweetheart of the Silent Majority: The Biography of Phyllis Schlafly* (Garden City, NY: Doubleday, 1981), 7–8.

9   Schlafly, "A Short History of E.R.A."

10   Ruth Murray Brown, *For a "Christian America": A History of the Religious Right* (Amherst, NY: Prometheus, 2002), 118. Organizers of the Seneca Falls South exhibits accepted any group that applied and paid the $50 fee; Phyllis Schlafly, "Houston Proves Radicals and Lesbians Run IWY," *Phyllis Schlafly Report*, (December 1977).

11   Kathryn Dunaway and Betty Benning, "Dear Congressman" (Atlanta, GA, April 17, 1978), folder "International Women's Year 1977," box 3, L. Marion Gressette Papers, South Carolina Political Collections, University of South Carolina.

12   Brown, *For a "Christian America,"* 117.

13   "About Elaine Donnelly," *Center for Military Readiness*, http://www.cmrlink.org/about-elaine-donnelly (accessed April 28, 2016).

14   Doreen Mattingly, "The (Limited) Power of Female Appointments: Abortion and Domestic Violence Policy in the Carter Administration," *Feminist Studies* 41, no. 3 (2015): 538–65; Hartmann, *From Margin to Mainstream*, 147–48; Ellen Goodman, "Wife-Beating Bill in Serious Trouble," *Reading Eagle*, September 30, 1980.

15 Mary Ziegler, *After* Roe: *The Lost History of the Abortion Debate* (Cambridge, MA: Harvard University Press, 2015), 201–205.

16 Estelle B. Freedman, *No Turning Back: The History of Feminism and the Future of Women* (New York: Random House, 2002), 107–12; Thomson, *Withstanding Humanism's Challenge*, 146.

17 Ibid., 146; Phyllis Schlafly, "ERA Enforced by the United Nations?," *Phyllis Schlafly Report* 40, no. 8 (March 2007).

18 Freedman, *No Turning Back*, 107–12; Judith P. Zinsser, "From Mexico to Copenhagen to Nairobi: The United Nations Decade for Women, 1975–1985," *Journal of World History* 13 (2002): 139–67; *Report of the World Conference of the International Women's Year, Mexico City, 19 June–2 July 1975* [Document]—United Nations E/CONF.66/34 (New York: United Nations, 1976).

19 Brown, *For a "Christian America,"* 132–36; Richard Meagher, "Remembering the New Right Political Strategy and the Building of the GOP Coalition," *Public Eye* 24, no. 2, Summer (2009); Richard A. Viguerie, *The Establishment vs. the People: Is a New Populist Revolt on the Way?* (Chicago: Regnery Gateway, 1983), 64.

20 Meagher, "Remembering the New Right"; William Martin, *With God on Our Side: The Rise of the Religious Right in America* (New York: Broadway Books, 1996), 174–76, 197–203; Connie Paige, *The Right to Lifers, Who They Are, How They Operate, and Where They Get Their Money* (Summit Books: 1983), 155; Sara Diamond, *Roads to Dominion: Right-Wing Political Movements and Political Power in the United States* (New York: Guilford Press, 1995), 166–72.

21 Martin, *With God on Our Side*, 173; Meagher, "Remembering the New Right"; Viguerie is quoted in an essay that explains why this controversy was so important. Joseph Crespino, "Civil Rights and the Religious Right," in *Rightward Bound: Making American Conservative in the 1970s* (Cambridge, MA: Harvard University Press, 2008), 90–105, quotation page 91.

22 Tanya Melich, *The Republican War Against Women: An Insider's Report from Behind the Lines* (New York: Bantam Books, 1998), 104; For another Schlafly critic who sees her as "developing and delivering" social conservatives and antifeminist arguments to the emerging New Right without being appreciated for it by Republicans, see Jean Hardisty, *Mobilizing Resentment: Conservative Resurgence from the John Birch Society to the Promise Keepers* (Boston: Beacon Press, 1999), 75–76; Donald T. Critchlow, "Mobilizing Women: The 'Social Issues,'" in *The Reagan Presidency: Pragmatic Conservatism and Its Legacies*, W. Elliott Brownlee and Hugh Davis Graham, eds. (Lawrence, KS: University Press of Kansas, 2004): 293–326 111, 112.

23 Brown, *For a "Christian America,"* 167–70; Susan Faludi, *Backlash: The Undeclared War, Against American Women* (New York: Crown Publishers, 1991), 247–48.

24 "White House Conferences on Families: Listening to America's Families" (pamphlet prepared for elected delegates, June 1980), 6, http://files.eric.ed.gov/fulltext/ED198914.pdf; Martin, *With God on Our Side*, 177–78.

25 "White House Conferences on Families: Listening to America's Families."

26 Thomson, *Withstanding Humanism's Challenge*, 112; Nadine Brozan, "White House Conference on the Family: A Schism Develops: The 'Moderate' Grouping 'Advocacy' Is Disavowed," *New York Times*, January 7, 1980.

27 Thomson, *Withstanding Humanism's Challenge*, 21–22.

28 Ibid., 3–4, 9, 11–12; Martin, *With God on Our Side*, 174–77, 180–81.

29 Martin, *With God on Our Side*, 176–77; Annelise Orleck, *Rethinking American Women's Activism* (New York: Routledge, 2014), 203; Nadine Brozan, "2d Day of Family

Conference: Workshops and a Walkout: 'I Am a Christian' Broad Range of Issues," *New York Times*, June 7, 1980; Thomson, *Withstanding Humanism's Challenge*, 87–89.

30 Brown, *For a "Christian America,"* 150–51; Thomson, *Withstanding Humanism's Challenge*, 127.

31 Ibid., 127.

32 Ibid., v.

33 Ibid., 124–25.

34 Ibid., 125, 128.

35 Ibid., 124.

36 Ibid., 9, 124–25.

37 Meagher, "Remembering the New Right"; Richard A. Viguerie, *The New Right: We're Ready to Lead* (Falls Church, VA: Viguerie Company, 1980), 95–100.

38 Meagher, "Remembering the New Right"; Viguerie, *The New Right*, 95–100; In 1978, Gingrich ran against a woman, State Senator Virginia Shapard, denouncing her for supporting the ERA and using the slogan: "Newt will take his family to Washington and keep them together; Virginia will go to Washington and leave her husband and children in the care of a nanny." Melich, *Republican War Against Women*, 108.

39 Diamond, *Road to Dominion*, 209; Laura Kalman, *Right Star Rising: A New Politics, 1974–1980* (New York: W. W. Norton, 2010), 354–55; Thomson, *Withstanding Humanism's Challenge*, 155; Viguerie, *The New Right*, 61; Phyllis Schlafly, "Stop ERA Victories in 1980," *Phyllis Schlafly Report* 14, no. 5, section 1 (December 1980).

40 Thomson, *Withstanding Humanism's Challenge*, 125–26, 155.

41 Ibid.

42 Thomas J. Sugrue and John D. Skrentny, "The White Ethnic Strategy," in *Rightward Bound: Making America Conservative in the 1970s*, Bruce J. Schulman and Julian E. Zelizer, eds., (Cambridge, MA: Harvard University Press, 2008): 171–92; Timothy Stanley, *The Crusader: The Life and Tumultuous Times of Pat Buchanan* (New York: St. Martin's, 2012), 70–71, 83.

43 Dan T. Carter, *The Politics of Rage: George Wallace, the Origins of the New Conservatism, and the Transformation of American Politics* (Baton Rouge: LSU Press, 1995); Dan T. Carter, *From George Wallace to Newt Gingrich: Race in the Conservative Counterrevolution, 1963–1994* (Baton Rouge: LSU Press, 1996); Earl Black and Merle Black, *The Rise of Southern Republicans* (Cambridge, MA: Harvard University Press, 2002).

44 Lessie M. Reynolds, ed., *Final Report of the State Meeting: "The South Carolina Woman: Heritage to Horizons"* (Columbia, SC: South Carolina International Women's Year, 1977); "Women for Racial and Economic Equality" (flyer, National Women's Conference, Houston, Texas, 1977), copy in possession of the author; NCOIWY, *The Spirit of Houston: The First National Women's Conference: An Official Report to the President, the Congress and the People of the United States* (Washington, D.C.: U.S. Government Printing Office, 1978), 142; Spruill, "The Mississippi 'Takeover'"; Unita Blackwell and JoAnne Prichard Morris, *Barefootin': Life Lessons from the Road to Freedom* (New York: Crown, 2006). Blackwell, who served on Carter's National Advisory Committee on Women, later won a McArthur Fellowship (the "genius award").

45 Janice Moor, *Mississippi IWY Coordinating Committee Final Report, July 8–9, 1977*, 1977; Interview with Dr. Marianna Davis, November 20, 1977, International Women's Year Conference Oral History Collection, South Caroliniana Library, University of South Carolina, Columbia, SC, hereafter IWY Conference Oral History Collection, SCL; Caroline Bird, *What Women Want: From the Official Report to the President, the*

Congress, and the People of the United States (New York: Simon and Schuster, 1979), 35; Lyle Denniston, "A Song Helped Unite Women at Houston," *Washington Star*, November 21, 1977, Jo Freeman Papers.

46 Brown, *For a "Christian America"*; Caitlin Mans, "'Heritage to Horizons': The History of the 1977 International Women's Year Conference in South Carolina" (University of South Carolina, 2013); Nancy Weaver, "Delegates Brace for IWY Storm: State Again Fuels U.S. Controversy. Delegates-Elect: 20 Whites, 6 Men, All Conservative," *Clarion-Ledger*, November 17, 1977; Spruill, "Mississippi Takeover"; Vera Glaser, "Anti-Feminists Target Women's Year Meeting: Klan, Birchers, Aid Schlafly," *Detroit Free Press*, August 25, 1977; Vera Glaser, "Women's Year: Peril on the Right," *Philadelphia Inquirer*, August 23, 1977.

47 Constance Ashton Myers Interview with Modjeska Simkins, June 1977, IWY Conference Oral History Collection, SCL; Betty J. Blair, "Klan's Spies' Plan to Disrupt Feminist Party," *Detroit News*, September 1, 1977.

48 Marjorie J. Spruill Interview with Phyllis Schlafly, February 22, 2005, in possession of the author.

49 Blair, "Klan's Spies' Plan to Disrupt."

50 Bill Minor, "Militant Conservatives Form New Coalition," *Delta Democrat-Times*, July 14, 1977.

51 Ibid.

52 Richard Barrett, *The Commission* (Jackson, MS: Barrett, 1982), 133, 149. Barrett, a Jackson, Mississippi lawyer, was a native of New Jersey who moved to Mississippi for its more compatible political climate. In the book he described having served as legal counsel for a New Jersey Stop-ERA group that sought to overturn a ruling allowing "women's libbers and lesbians" to set up teaching centers in public schools. He claimed that the momentum and publicity from the successful lawsuit turned the tide against the ERA, leading to the defeat of the state ERA referendum in 1975.

53 In his autobiography Barrett included photos of himself posing with George Wallace and with Phyllis Schlafly. The Schlafly photo was taken at the 1977 American Bar Association Convention in Chicago. Ibid., 293–301, 352; Sonia Scherr, "White Supremacist Richard Barrett Murdered in Mississippi Home," Southern Poverty Law Center, April 22, 2010, https://www.splcenter.org/hatewatch/2010/04/22/white-supremacist-richard-barrett-murdered-mississippi-home. In *The Commission*, Barrett also called for resettling nonwhite Americans abroad, saying that "the Negro race . . . possess[es] no creativity of its own." He launched campaigns on behalf of several 1960s-era murderers of African Americans, including Byron de la Beckwith, who assassinated Medgar Evers, and Edgar Ray Killen, who was convicted of manslaughter in connection with the deaths of three civil rights workers in Mississippi in 1964. He ran for governor of Mississippi multiple times; Sheryl Hansen (Smith) interviewed Barrett about his role in IWY, however, he refused to sign the agreement donating it to the University of Southern Mississippi oral history program because it had recently named a building in honor of two African Americans. Richard Barrett to Amendia Netto, USM Oral History Program, March 5, 1993.

54 Laura Joy Foxworth, "The Spiritual Is Political: The Modern Women's Movement and the Transformation of the Southern Baptist Convention" (Ph.D. diss., University of South Carolina, 2014), especially page 137.

55 Foxworth, "The Spiritual Is Political"; "President Jimmy Carter Leaves Southern Baptist Convention," http://www.adherents.com/largecom/baptist_SBC_Carter.html (accessed July 10, 2016).

56   Viguerie, *The New Right*, 165, 197. The IWY was used as a rallying cry, but Viguerie also discusses other key issues that exercised conservative voters, such as the Panama Canal issue.

57   Thomson, *Withstanding Humanism's Challenge*, 147.

58   Viguerie, *The New Right*, 156–58. The Falwell quotation appears in the introduction.

59   Rev. Frank Rottier, "Repent, You Filthy Women, or Face God's Holocaust!" (from *LaSalle News-Tribune*, LaSalle, IL, n.d.). The minister, Reverend Frank Rottier, stated: "The three presidents' wives who boldly gave their support and encouragement to this abominable infestation of our society ought to take all the clothes they wore at that conference and publicly burn them, and bathe in disinfecting waters (baptized anew) and appear before their respective churches and confess their sins of public support for such abominable propaganda and thus help save our country from the destructions that are otherwise sure to come," box 18, folder 30, Catherine East Papers, Schlesinger Library, Radcliffe Institute, Harvard University, hereafter East Papers, SL.

60   Kalman, *Right Star Rising*, 347–49; William A. Link, *Righteous Warrior: Jesse Helms and the Rise of Modern Conservatism* (New York: St. Martin's, 2008), 210; Thomson, *Withstanding Humanism's Challenge*, 138–41.

61   Elaine Donnelly, "What Women Wanted: Reagan Appealed to and Developed a Generation of Female Conservatives," *National Review Online*, June 7, 2004, http://www.freerepublic.com/focus/news/1151429/posts; Thomson, *Withstanding Humanism's Challenge*, 147.

62   Donnelly, "What Women Wanted."

63   Thomson, *Withstanding Humanism's Challenge*, 148.

64   Ibid., 148–50.

65   Ibid.

66   Ibid.

67   Ibid.

68   Ibid., 150–51.

69   Ibid.

70   Ibid.

71   Ibid., 152, 154.

72   Donnelly, "What Women Wanted."

73   Ibid.

EPILOGUE: A NATION DIVIDED

1   Gloria Steinem, "An Introductory Statement," in *What Women Want: From the Official Report to the President, the Congress and the People of the United States*, by Caroline Bird (New York: Simon & Schuster, 1978), 16–17; Gloria Steinem, "Houston and History," in *Outrageous Acts and Everyday Rebellions*, 2nd ed. (New York: Henry Holt and Company, 1995), 303–16.

2   Elaine Donnelly, "What Women Wanted: Reagan Appealed to and Developed a Generation of Female Conservatives," *National Review Online*, June 7, 2004, http://www.freerepublic.com/focus/news/1151429/posts.

3   Tanya Melich, *The Republican War Against Women: An Insider's Report from Behind the Lines* (New York: Bantam Books, 1998), 117–135. On page 303 Melich called the 1992 Houston convention "the denouement of the Faustian bargain that Bush had struck in 1980. He'd willingly let the right take over his party to win himself the White House . . . He'd let them institute policies that sought to relegate women to their

pre-Enlightenment status. He'd let them set his domestic social agenda and bully him on economic policy so he could play the great statesman on the post–cold war stage. There was a price to pay, and in 1992 George Bush paid it: The price was the White House."

4 Susan J. Carroll, "The Gender Gap as a Tool for Women's Political Empowerment: The Formative Years, 1980–84," in *Eighteen Million Cracks: The Legacy of Second Wave Feminism in American Politics,* Angie Maxwell and Todd Shields, eds., in progress; "The Gender Gap in Presidential Elections: Fact Sheet," Center for American Women and Politics (CAWP), Eagleton Institute of Politics, Rutgers University, December 2012; The CAWP offers these definitions: "The 'gender gap' in voting is the difference in the percentage of women and men who support a given candidate, generally the leading or winning candidate. It is the gap between the genders, not within a gender. Even if women and men favor the same candidate, they may do so by different margins, resulting in a gender gap. The 'women's vote' describes the behavior of women as a voting bloc, or the divisions among women voters for or against a given issue or candidate." "Gender Gap and Women's Vote—Gender Gap Advisory," *Center for American Women and Politics,* October 28, 2004.

5 Susan J. Carroll and Richard L. Fox, *Gender and Elections: Shaping the Future of American Politics* (Cambridge: Cambridge University Press, 2010); Eleanor Smeal, *Why and How Women Will Elect the Next President* (New York: Harper and Row, 1984); "The Gender Gap, Then and Now: A *Ms.* Conversation with Eleanor Smeal," *Ms.,* Summer 2016; Bella S. Abzug with Mim Kelber, *Gender Gap: Bella Abzug's Guide to Political Power for American Women* (Boston: Houghton Mifflin, 1984).

6 Carroll, "The Gender Gap as a Tool for Women's Political Empowerment"; After the gender gap hurt Republican candidates in the 1982 off-year elections, and in anticipation of the 1984 presidential race, Atwater, a Reagan strategist, wrote a fascinating internal memo on the gender gap, its possible causes, the threat to the GOP, and possible ways to deal with it. Lee Atwater, Memo to James A. Baker III, through Edward J. Rollins, November 23, 1982, folder "Women—Gender Gap" (1 of 2), box 35, Elizabeth Dole Files, Ronald Reagan Presidential Library, hereafter Dole Files, Reagan Library.

7 Peter Applebone, *Dixie Rising: How the South Is Shaping American Values, Politics, and Culture* (New York: Harcourt, Brace, and Co., 1996); Dan T. Carter, *From George Wallace to Newt Gingrich: Race in the Conservative Counterrevolution, 1963–1994* (LSU Press, 1996).

8 Early in Reagan's presidency, Richard Viguerie attacked him in print for backing away from conservative principles. But Schlafly and most leaders of the Religious Right remained avid Reagan supporters, even as they criticized him for focusing on economic and foreign policy issues at the expense of social issues. Donald Critchlow, "Mobilizing Women: The 'Social Issues,'" in W. Elliott Brownlee and Hugh Davis Graham, *The Reagan Presidency: Pragmatic Conservatism and Its Legacies* (Lawrence: University Press of Kansas, 2003): 293–326, 212; As columnist E. J. Dionne pointed out, it was "striking how much loyalty Ronald Reagan won from this constituency without delivering much to them at all . . . There was no school-prayer amendment, no anti-abortion amendment, no school-choice program." William Martin, *With God on Our Side: The Rise of the Religious Right in America* (New York: Broadway Books, 1996), 309–10.

9 Phyllis Schlafly, "Does Reagan Know Who Elected Him?" *Phyllis Schlafly Report* 14, no. 5, section 1 (December 1980).

10 Reagan appointed Donnelly to the Defense Advisory Committee on Women in the Armed Services and Thomson to the National Advisory Council on Women's Educational Programs; Reagan appointed Heckler as Secretary of Health and Human Services, but, according to Melich, surrounded her with New Right and pro-family "protectors" on her staff, making her a "prisoner in her own agency." Melich, *Republican War Against Women*, 188–189; Memo to James Baker III from Wendy Borcherdt, May 21, 1982, indicates concern that Reagan was "very vulnerable" with women voters and discusses steps to remedy that. There were only tepid efforts to carry out the 50 States plan of identifying discriminatory laws and revising them state by state. File "Women's Constituency/50 States Project," box 6411 Dole Files, Reagan Library.

11 Elizabeth Bumiller, "Schlafly's Gala Goodbye To ERA: 1,000 Celebrate the Death of the Amendment," *Washington Post*, July 1, 1982; For Schlafly's descriptions of the 1979 and 1982 celebrations, see *Phyllis Schlafly Report*, 21, no. 1 (August 1987); Copy of note from Ronald Reagan to Phyllis Schlafly, June 30, 1982, delivered to her at the Shoreham Hotel, folder "Conservatives—General–1982 [4 of 6]," Dole Files, Reagan Library.

12 Elizabeth Dole to Morton Blackwell, RE: Conservative Organization Reaction to Sandra O'Connor Nomination. (Memorandum, July 8, 1981), OA 6386 Dole Files, Reagan Library; Martin, *With God on Our Side*, 227–30; New Right leader Morton Blackwell served as the administration's liaison with the conservative movement, expected to keep them pacified and mobilized at the same time. Neil J. Young, *We Gather Together: The Religious Right and the Problem of Interfaith Politics* (New York: Oxford University Press, 2016), 209–11.

13 Melich, *Republican War Against Women*, 214–15; Donald T. Critchlow, *Phyllis Schlafly and Grassroots Conservatism: A Woman's Crusade* (Princeton: Princeton University Press, 2005), 281–83.

14 Jo Freeman, "The Search for a Radical Flank: The Women's Movement and the 1984 Democratic & Republican Conventions," 1984, http://www.jofreeman.com/conventions/1984-conventions-and-women.htm; Jo Freeman, "The 1984 Republican Convention," accessed August 6, 2016, http://www.jofreeman.com/photos/repub1984/repub1984-01.htm; Melich, *Republican War Against Women*, 202–3.

15 Carroll, "The Gender Gap as a Tool for Women's Political Empowerment"; Melich, *Republican War Against Women*, 209.

16 Ibid., 190–91, 221–24.

17 Martin, *With God on Our Side*, 264–95; Melich, *Republican War Against Women*; 231–34, 246; Morgan Whitaker, "The Legacy of the Willie Horton Ad Lives On, 25 Years Later | MSNBC," *MSNBC*, October 21, 2013, http://www.msnbc.com/msnbc/the-legacy-the-willie-horton-ad-lives; "Willie Horton—Top 10 Campaign Ads—TIME," *Time*, accessed July 30, 2016, http://content.time.com/time/specials/packages/article/0,28804,1842516_1842514_1842557,00.html.

18 See the thorough and impressive oral history project and the book that tells this history and features transcripts from the interviews. Lee Stout, *A Matter of Simple Justice: The Untold Story of Barbara Hackman Franklin and A Few Good Women* (University Park: Pennsylvania State University Libraries, 2012), 185; Bush appointed Donnelly to the Presidential Commission on the Assignment of Women in the Armed Forces and Thomson to the National Commission on Drug-Free Schools; Melich; *Republican War Against Women*, 224, 270–71, 287–96, 303.

19 Ibid., Martin, *With God on Our Side*, 317.

20 Jon Meacham, *Destiny and Power: The American Odyssey of George Herbert Walker Bush*, 495–502; Elaine Woo, "Mary Crisp, 83; Quit GOP Post in Clash with Reagan Over Abortion Rights, ERA," *Los Angeles Times*, April 24, 2007; Colleen Parro, "How the Republican National Platform Has Remained Pro-Life—Fall 2004," *RNC for Life Report*, Fall 2004, http://www.rnclife.org/reports/2004/fall2004/; As Melich describes, my aunt, Vivian Spruill Petura, strongly urged the committee to drop the anti-abortion plank which, she insisted, was alienating many Republicans. Melich, *Republican War Against Women*, 216, 312–15.

21 Martin, *With God on Our Side*, 262–98, 309–17, 325–28, Buchanan quotation 325; Witt, *Running as a Woman: Gender and Power in American Politics*, 17–18.

22 Jo Freeman, *We Will Be Heard: Women's Struggles for Political Power in the United States* (Lanham, MD: Rowman & Littlefield, 2008), Chapter 10; Melich, *Republican War Against Women*, 316.

23 Jo Freeman, "Feminism vs. Family Values: Women at the 1992 Democratic and Republican Conventions," jofreeman.com, 1992, http://www.jofreeman.com/conventions/1992conven.htm; Nancy Woloch, *Women and the American Experience* (New York: McGraw-Hill, 2011), 564; "The Gender Gap: Three Decades Old, as Wide as Ever," *Pew Research Center*, March 29, 2012, http://www.people-press.org/2012/03/29/the-gender-gap-three-decades-old-as-wide-as-ever/.

24 Martin, *With God on Our Side*, 328; Woloch, *Women and the American Experience*, 564–65.

25 Witt, *Running as a Woman*; Woloch, *Women and the American Experience*, 564–65; Sarah Kliff and Soo Oh, "Why Aren't There More Women in Congress?," *Vox*, August 16, 2016, http://www.vox.com/a/women-in-congress.

26 Martin, *With God on Our Side*, 329; Freeman, "Feminism vs. Family Values."

27 Ellen Chesler, "The Long History of the War on Contraception," *Ms. Blog*, February 12, 2012, http://msmagazine.com/blog/2012/02/14/conservative-war-on-contraception-is-nothing-new/; William H. Chafe, *Hillary and Bill: The Clintons and the Politics of the Personal* (Durham, NC: Duke University Press, 2016), 167, 257–61, quotation 258.

28 Elaine Donnelly, "Gays in the Military: A Losing Cause," *National Review*, November 4, 2010, http://www.nationalreview.com/corner/252507/gays-military-losing-cause-elaine-donnelly; Josh Israel, "The Woman Who Has Never Stopped Fighting To Keep LGBT Americans Out Of The Military," *Think Progress*, May 23, 2014, http://thinkprogress.org/lgbt/2014/05/23/3439070/elaine-donnelly-center-for-military-readiness/.

29 Richard Morin and Barbara Vobejda, "'94 May Be the Year of the Man," *Washington Post*, November 10, 1994; "The Gender Gap: Huge Myth, Important Reality," https://roper-center.cornell.edu/public-perspective/ppscan/75/75001.pdf (accessed August 21, 2016); Charles Krauthammer, "Myth of the Angry White Male," *Washington Post*, May 26, 1995.

30 "Clinton Benefits From Gender Gap, Exit Polls Show," AP, November 6, 1996, http://www.cnn.com/ALLPOLITICS/1996/news/9611/06/exit.poll.update/; Chafe, *Hillary and Bill*, 249–51.

31 Ibid.

32 Ibid., 172–75, 265; "The Clinton Presidency: Timeline of Major Actions," https://clinton5.nara.gov/WH/Accomplishments/eightyears-02.html (accessed August 21, 2016).

33 Chafe, *Hillary and Bill*, 223–33, 240–41, quotation 230.

34 Ibid., 241; Amy Chozick, "Hillary Clinton's Beijing Speech on Women Resonates 20 Years Later," *New York Times*, September 5, 2015, http://www.nytimes.com/politics/

first-draft/2015/09/05/20-years-later-hillary-clintons-beijing-speech-on-women-resonates/.

35   Chafe, *Hillary and Bill*, 241; "USA: Hillary Clinton Asked to Boycott UN Women's Conference," *AP Archive*, August 21, 1993; Jo Freeman, "Beijing Report: The Fourth World Conference on Women," 1996, http://www.jofreeman.com/womenyear/beijingreport.htm; Suzanne Braun Levine and Mary Thom, *Bella Abzug: How One Tough Broad from the Bronx Fought Jim Crow and Joe McCarthy, Pissed Off Jimmy Carter, Battled for the Rights of Women and Workers, Rallied Against War and for the Planet, and Shook up Politics Along the Way: An Oral History* (New York: Farrar, Straus and Giroux, 2007), 261–77; Alan H. Levy, *The Political Life of Bella Abzug, 1976–1998: Electoral Failures and the Vagaries of Identity Politics* (Lanham, MD: Lexington Books, 2013), 267–312, quotation 300.

36   Margalit Fox, "Betty Friedan, Who Ignited Cause in 'Feminine Mystique,' Dies at 85," *New York Times*, February 5, 2006; Friedan's memoir entitled *Life So Far* was published in 2000.

37   Samiha Shafy, "Within Reach: Gloria Steinem's Life-Long Fight for Women's Rights," *Der Spiegel*, July 6, 2016, http://www.spiegel.de/international/world/gloria-steinem-and-the-possibility-of-a-clinton-presidency-a-1101464-2.html; Gloria Steinem, *My Life on the Road* (New York: Random House, 2015).

38   President Bill Clinton awarded Bunch the Eleanor Roosevelt Award for Human Rights in 1999. For a film about the campaign to "bring an understanding that 'women's rights are human rights,'" see http://www.makers.com/charlotte-bunch.

39   Julie Berebitsky, "Crisp, Mary Dent," American National Biography Online, accessed August 13, 2016; Jefferson Morley, "Mary Dent Crisp: Can She Sell Pro-Choice to the Republican Party?," *Los Angeles Times*, August 16, 1992, http://articles.latimes.com/1992-08-16/opinion/op-6680_1_republican-party.

40   Melich, *Republican War Against Women*; Tanya Melich, "Why the GOP Should Have Listened to Mary Crisp," *Women's Media Center*, May 7, 2007, http://www.womensmediacenter.com/feature/entry/why-the-gop-should-have-listened-to-mary-crisp.

41   "The Gender Gap, Then and Now: A *Ms.* Conversation with Eleanor Smeal," and Katherine Spillar, "Betting on the Gender Gap: The Women's Vote in the High-Stakes Elections of 2016," both articles in *Ms.*, Summer 2016.

42   "The Gender Gap: Party Identification and Presidential Performance Ratings," *Center for American Women and Politics*, accessed August 22, 2016, http://www.cawp.rutgers.edu/sites/default/files/resources/ggprtyid.pdf; "Gender Gap in the 2000 Elections," *Center for American Women and Politics*, December 2000, http://cawp.rutgers.edu/sites/default/files/resources/pressrelease_12-00_gg2000.pdf.

43   Carolyn B. Maloney, "The World Lost A Great Leader On The Passing Of Bella Abzug," *Capitolwords*, April 1, 1998.

44   "About the Author: Lottie Beth Hobbs," *Harvest Publications* http://www.harvestpublications.com/ (accessed April 17, 2016).

45   In 2002 UFI published what it describes as "the highly-acclaimed 'United Nations Pro-Family Negotiating Guide' now known as the 'Bible' of Pro-family work at the UN." "UFI Overview," *United Families International* http://unitedfamilies.org/ (accessed January 19, 2016).

46   Dana Milbank, "Sorry We Asked, Sorry You Told," *Washington Post*, July 24, 2008.

47   Eagle Forum operations have expanded dramatically: it operates an Eagle Forum Education Center in St. Louis issuing publications, running leadership training

programs, holding conferences and—through the Eagle Forum University run by Schlafly's son Andrew—posts free courses on topics in U.S. history and government. Andy Schlafly also edits an alternative to *Wikipedia* (which he sees as too liberal) called *Conservapedia*. "Eagle Forum Education Center," *Eagle Forum* http://www.eagleforum. org/center/ (accessed August 8, 2016); Phyllis Schlafly obituary on Eagle Forum website September 9, 2016; *Conservapedia* http://www.conservapedia.com/Main_Page (accessed August 8, 2016; Jo Freeman, "The Feminist Ghost at the Conservative Political Action Conference," jofreeman.com, February 2003, http://www.jofreeman. com/rightreport/cpac03.html; Marjorie J. Spruill Interview with Phyllis Schlafly, February 22, 2005.

48   "The Gender Gap: Party Identification and Presidential Performance Ratings"; "Gender Gap in the 2000 Elections."

49   Editorial, "The War Against Women, *New York Times*, January 12, 2003.

50   Stout, *A Matter of Simple Justice,* 185–86, 190–93.

51   "The Gender Gap in Presidential Elections"; Laura Flanders, "What Has George W Ever Done for Women?," *The Guardian*, March 26, 2004, https://www.theguardian. com/world/2004/mar/26/gender.uk; Kathleen Parker, "Laura Bush's Fight for Women," *Washington Post*, June 19, 2012.

52   Steve Benen, "Leap of Faith: Bush 'Faith-Based' Initiative Violates Constitution, Subsidizes Religious Discrimination, Critics Charge," Americans United for Separation of Church and State, March 2001 https://www.au.org/church-state/march-2001-church-state/featured/leap-of-faith (accessed September 13, 2016).

53   Steven Ertelt, "President Bush Will Leave Strong Pro-Life Legacy on Abortion, Bioethics Issues," *LifeNews.com*, January 16, 2009, http://www.lifenews.com/2009/ 01/16/nat-4750/; Molly Redden, "The Unauthorized History of the GOP's 30-Year War on Planned Parenthood," *Mother Jones*, August 21, 2015, http://www.motherjones. com/politics/2015/08/30-year-history-gop-attacks-defund-planned-parenthood.

54   Ertelt, "President Bush Will Leave Strong Pro-Life Legacy"; Editorial, "The War Against Women," *New York Times*, January 12, 2003.

55   Russell Goldman, "Laura Bush Supports Gay Marriage, Abortion," *ABC News*, May 10, 2010.

56   Garance Franke-Ruta, "George W. Bush's Forgotten Gay-Rights History," *Atlantic*, July 8, 2013, http://www.theatlantic.com/politics/archive/2013/07/george-w-bushs-forgotten-gay-rights-history/277567/.

57   Flanders, "What Has George W Ever Done for Women?"; Guido H. Stempel and Thomas K. Hargrove, *The 21st-Century Voter: Who Votes, How They Vote, and Why They Vote* (Santa Barbara, CA: ABC-CLIO, 2016), 389.

58   Richard A. Viguerie, *The Establishment vs. the People: Is a New Populist Revolt on the Way?* (Chicago: Regnery Gateway, 1983); Ertelt, "President Bush Will Leave Strong Pro-Life Legacy."

59   Gloria Steinem, *My Life on the Road* (New York: Random House, 2015), 165–66.

60   Ibid., 166–69.

61   Linda Beail and Rhonda Kinney Longworth, *Framing Sarah Palin: Pitbulls, Puritans, and Politics* (New York: Routledge, 2013), 119.

62   Jeffrey Jones, "Gender Gap in 2012 Vote Is Largest in Gallup's History," *Gallup*, November 9, 2012, http://www.gallup.com/poll/158588/gender-gap-2012-vote-largest-gallup-history.aspx; Scott Keeter, "Gen Dems: The Party's Advantage Among Young Voters Widens," *Pew Research Center*, April 28, 2008, http://www.pewresearch. org/2008/04/28/gen-dems-the-partys-advantage-among-young-voters-widens/.

63 Maya Rhodan, "President Obama at Women's Summit: This Is What a Feminist Looks Like," *Time*, June 14, 2016, http://time.com/4369002/barack-obama-united-state-of-women-summit/; "*Glamour* Exclusive: President Barack Obama Says, 'This is What a Feminist Looks Like,'" *Glamour*, September 2016.

64 According to the *Post*, Obama placed women and minorities in 53.5 percent of those posts compared to George W. Bush who installed women and minorities in 25.6 percent and Bill Clinton whose number was 37.5 percent. Juliet Eilperin, "Obama Has Vastly Changed the Face of the Federal Bureaucracy," *Washington Post*, September 20, 2015, https://www.washingtonpost.com/politics/obama-has-vastly-changed-the-face-of-the-federal-bureaucracy/2015/09/20/73ef803a-5631-11e5-abe9-27d53f250b11_story.html; Elisabeth Bumiller, "Obama Ends 'Don't Ask, Don't Tell' Policy," *New York Times*, July 22, 2011, http://www.nytimes.com/2011/07/23/us/23military.html?_r=0; Steven Ertelt, "President Barack Obama's Pro-Abortion Record: A Pro-Life Compilation," *LifeNews.com*, March 7, 2010, http://www.issues4life.org/pdfs/news_20100307a.pdf; Ertelt, "President Bush Will Leave Strong Pro-Life Legacy."

65 "President Obama's Record on Empowering Women and Girls," *The White House*, accessed July 31, 2016, https://www.whitehouse.gov/women.

66 United States and White House Council on Women and Girls, *Women in America: Indicators of Social and Economic Well-Being.* (Washington, D.C.: U.S. Dept. of Commerce, Economics and Statistics Administration, 2011), http://purl.fdlp.gov/GPO/gpo5928.

67 Chesler, "The Long History of the War on Contraception"; Steven Ertelt, "Barack Obama Forces Taxpayers to Fund, Promote Worldwide Abortions," LifeNews.com, January 1, 2009, http://www.lifenews.com/2009/01/01/nat-4781/; Burgess Everett and Katie Glueck, "Ted Cruz's Big Moment," *Politico*, September 28, 2015, http://www.politico.com/story/2015/09/ted-cruz-planned-parenthood-2016-government-shutdown-214098.

68 "Olympia Snowe: Why I'm Leaving the Senate," *Washington Post*, March 2, 2012; Azmat Khan, "The Republicans' Plan for the New President," PBS *Frontline*, January 15, 2013, http://www.pbs.org/wgbh/frontline/article/the-republicans-plan-for-the-new-president/; Robert Draper, *Do Not Ask What Good We Do: Inside the U.S. House of Representatives* (Free Press, 2012).

69 Paul Kane and Nia-Malika Henderson, "Todd Akin Rape Comments Prompt GOP to Pull Campaign Funding, Calls to Exit Race," *Washington Post*, August 20, 2012, https://www.washingtonpost.com/politics/with-todd-akins-rape-comments-abortion-is-back-in-the-campaign-spotlight/2012/08/20/c497bae4-eac7-11e1-a80b-9f898562d010_story.html; Rachel Weiner, "Mitt Romney Stumbles Over 'War on Women,'" *Washington Post*, April 11, 2012, https://www.washingtonpost.com/blogs/the-fix/post/a-war-on-women-trap-for-mitt-romney/2012/04/11/gIQAtym2AT_blog.html; Paige Bradley Frost, "The Real Problem with Romney's 'Binders' Blunder," *Huffington Post*, October 18, 2012, http://www.huffingtonpost.com/paige-bradley-frost/mitt-romney_b_1977970.html.

70 While Obama's twelve-percentage point lead among women was less than his fourteen-point advantage over McCain in 2008, Romney did better than McCain among men by eight points. Jones, "Gender Gap in 2012 Vote Is Largest in Gallup's History."

71 Shushannah Walshe, "RNC Completes 'Autopsy' on 2012 Loss, Calls for Inclusion but No Policy Change," *ABC News*, March 18, 2013, http://abcnews.go.com/Politics/OTUS/rnc-completes-autopsy-2012-loss-calls-inclusion-policy/story?id=18755809; Jennifer Rubin, "GOP Autopsy Report Goes Bold," *Washington Post*, March 18, 2013.

72   Trevor LaFauci, "Dead and Loving It: How the GOP Learned Nothing from Its 2012 Autopsy Report," ThePeoplesView, April 28, 2016, http://www.thepeoplesview.net/main/2016/4/27/dead-and-loving-it-how-the-gop-learned-nothing-from-its-2012-autopsy-report.

73   "Inaugural Address by President Barack Obama," Whitehouse.gov, January 21, 2013, https://www.whitehouse.gov/the-press-office/2013/01/21/inaugural-address-president-barack-obama.

74   Michelle Kort, "Gloria Steinem Receives Top National Honor," *Ms.* blog, November 20, 2013; Andrew M. Greenwell, "Honor Among Killers: President Obama Awards Gloria Steinem Medal of Freedom," *Catholic Online*, August 14, 2013, http://www.catholic.org/news/politics/story.php?id=52020.

75   Matthew Yglesias, "Hillary Clinton's Plan to Use Feminism to Sell Big Government," *Vox*, September 19, 2014, http://www.vox.com/2014/9/19/6405561/hillary-clintons-secure-floor.

76   Phyllis Schlafly, *A Choice Not an Echo, Fifty Years Later* (New York: Perseus, 2014); Richard A. Viguerie, *Takeover: The 100-Year War for the Soul of the GOP and How Conservatives Can Finally Win It* (Washington, D.C.: WND Books, 2014).

77   Brandon Ambrosino, "A Tale of Two Falwell Brothers," *Politico*, July 21, 2016, http://www.politico.com/magazine/story/2016/07/jerry-falwell-jonathan-gop-convention-trump-evangelical-conservative-christians-214082.

78   Ashley Parker, Nick Corasaniti, and Berenstein, "Voices From Donald Trump's Rallies, Uncensored," *New York Times*, August 3, 2016.

79   Julia Hahn, "Phyllis Schlafly Makes the Case for President Trump," *Breitbart News*, January 10, 2016, http://www.breitbart.com/big-government/2016/01/10/phyllis-schlafly-makes-the-case-for-president-trump/ (accessed September 14, 2016).

80   Ibid.; "Trump's Values Voter Summit Remarks," *Politico*, September 9, 2016; Jo Mannies, "Phyllis Schlafly Praises Trump as the Change GOP Needs," *St. Louis Public Radio*, July 20, 2016, http://news.stlpublicradio.org/post/phyllis-schlafly-praises-trump-change-gop-needsream/0; Ruth Conniff, "RNC 2016: White Rage in Cleveland," *The Progressive*, July 22, 2016, http://www.progressive.org/news/2016/07/188874/rnc-2016-white-rage-cleveland.

81   Center for Individual Freedom Vice President Renee Giachino, "Interview with Phyllis Schlafly on Immigration Reform," CFIF website: http://www.cfif.org/htdocs/legislative_issues/federal_issues/hot_issues_in_congress/immigration/Phyllis-Schlafly-Immigration-Reform.htm (accessed September 14, 2016); Phyllis Schlafly, "Trump and Reagan: Similarities and Differences," *Phyllis Schlafly Report*, Eagle Forum, May 2016, http://www.eagleforum.org/publications/psr/may16.html.

82   "Phyllis Schlafly's Last Stand: The Inside Story of the Conservative Icon's Internal Battle for Survival," *Breitbart*, accessed August 19, 2016, http://www.breitbart.com/2016-presidential-race/2016/04/25/phyllis-schlaflys-last-stand-inside-story-conservative-icons-internal-battle-survival/; Mannies, "Phyllis Schlafly Praises Trump as the Change GOP Needs"; Joseph Weber, "Turmoil Grips Conservative Schlafly Organization, amid Trump-Cruz Tensions," Fox News, April 20, 2016, http://www.foxnews.com/politics/2016/04/20/turmoil-grips-conservative-schlafly-organization-amid-trump-cruz-tensions.html.; Leigh Ann Caldwell, "GOP Activists Work to Prevent Fight with Trump Over Party Platform," *NBC News*, March 28, 2016.

83   "Editorial: The Most Extreme Republican Platform in Memory," *New York Times*, July 18, 2016, http://www.nytimes.com/2016/07/19/opinion/the-most-extreme-republican-platform-in-memory.html?_r=0; Katrina Vanden Heuvel, "The Most Progressive

Democratic Platform Ever," *Washington Post*, July 12, 2016, https://www.washington-post.com/opinions/the-most-progressive-democratic-platform-ever/2016/07/12/82525ab0-479b-11e6-bdb9-701687974517_story.html.

84 For example, see Eduardo Porter, "Donald Trump's Rise Shows Religion Is Losing Its Political Power," *New York Times*, April 5, 2016; Ambrosino, "A Tale of Two Falwell Brothers."

85 Jonathan Martin, Jim Rutenberg, and Maggie Haberman, "Donald Trump Appoints Media Firebrand to Run Campaign," *New York Times*, August 17, 2016, http://www.nytimes.com/2016/08/18/us/politics/donald-trump-stephen-bannon-paul-manafort.html?_r=0; Tommy Christopher, "David Duke Show Celebrates Trump's Breitbart Hire: We've 'Taken Over the Republican Party!,'" *Mediaite*, August 21, 2016, http://www.mediaite.com/online/david-duke-show-celebrates-trumps-breitbart-hire-weve-taken-over-the-republican-party/; Stassa Edwards, "Trump Campaign Hires 'Gender Gap' Expert Kellyanne Conway, Who Touts 'Femininity, Not Feminism," *The Slot* http://theslot.jezebel.com/trump-campaign-hires-gender-gap-expert-kellyanne-conway-1782959310; Christina Wilkie, Elise Foley, and Ryan Grim, "Donald Trump's Campaign Manager Rose Quickly By Playing To His Ego," *Huffington Post*, August 20, 2016, http://www.huffingtonpost.com/entry/donald-trump-campaign-manager-kellyanne-conway_us_57b75ad1e4b0b51733a372bc.

86 Danielle Paquette, "Inside Donald Trump's Strategy to Win Back Women," July 20, 2016, *Washington Post*; "Trump Values Voter Summit Remarks," *Politico*, September 9, 2016, http://www.politico.com/story/2016/09/full-text-trump-values-voter-summit-remarks-227977.

87 Donald T. Critchlow, "How Phyllis Schlafly Led America to Donald Trump," *Marketwatch*, September 8, 2016, http://www.marketwatch.com/story/how-phyllis-schlafly-led-america-to-donald-trump-2016-09-08 (accessed September 10, 2016).

88 Julia Hahn, "Conservative Legend Phyllis Schlafly Dies at 92," *Breitbart News*, September 5, 2016, http://www.breitbart.com/2016-presidential-race/2016/09/05/conservative-legend-phyllis-schlafly-dies-92/ (accessed September 14, 2016).

89 Thomas Kaplan, "Donald Trump Praises Phyllis Schlafly as a Conservative 'Hero' at Her Funeral," *New York Times*, September 10, 2016.

90 Hahn, "Conservative Legend Phyllis Schlafly Dies at 92."

91 Cecile Richards to Planned Parenthood email list, September 9, 2016.

92 David Cole, "What James Comey Did," *New York Review of Books* LXIII, no. 19 (December 8, 2016): 4.

93 Rebecca Traister, "Shattered," *New York* magazine, November 12, 2016.

94 Gail Collins, "The Glass Ceiling Holds," *New York Times*, November 11, 2016; Katie Rogers, "White Women Helped Elect Donald Trump," *New York Times*, November 9, 2016; John Schlafly, "The Choice, Not an Echo," November 8, 2016, www.eagleforum.org/publications/column/choice-not-echo.html.

95 Collins, "The Glass Ceiling Holds."

96 The conference was organized by Pam Elam who had been a delegate in Houston, and Liz Abzug, Bella's daughter, who founded the institute along with her sister Eve and Erica Forman. Melissa Silverstein, "A Report from Freedom on Our Own Terms," *Women's Media Center*, November 15, 2007, http://www.womensmediacenter.com/feature/entry/wmc-exclusive-a-report-from-freedom-on-our-own-terms.

97 Anna Quindlen, "Quindlen: Out Of The Skyboxes," *Newsweek*, October 9, 2007, http://www.newsweek.com/quindlen-out-skyboxes-103507.

98 Steinem, *My Life on the Road*, 53–54.

99 Ibid., 66.

Index

A Note on the Author

Marjorie J. Spruill is a professor of history at the University of South Carolina. A native of Washington, North Carolina, she received her B.A. at the University of North Carolina at Chapel Hill, a master's degree from Duke University, and a Ph.D. from the University of Virginia. She previously taught at the University of Southern Mississippi and Vanderbilt University where she was associate provost. A specialist in U.S. women's history, political history, and southern history, she has published extensively on the history of the woman suffrage movement as well as more modern women's movements. Spruill has been active in the history profession, serving as adviser to several museums and films and on the editorial boards of several journals. She is currently a member of the editorial board of the *Journal of American Studies* published by the British Association for American Studies. She spent a year at the National Humanities Center in the Research Triangle Park in North Carolina, supported by a Fellowship from the National Endowment for the Humanities (NEH). She has been a fellow at the Radcliffe Institute for Advanced Study at Harvard University and the Woodrow Wilson International Center for Scholars in Washington, D.C. Spruill lives in Folly Beach, South Carolina.